Marian Barry

SUCCESS

International English Skills

for Cambridge IGCSE®

Student's Book

Fourth edition

CAMBRIDGE
UNIVERSITY PRESS

CAMBRIDGE
UNIVERSITY PRESS

University Printing House, Cambridge CB2 8BS, United Kingdom

One Liberty Plaza, 20th Floor, New York, NY 10006, USA

477 Williamstown Road, Port Melbourne, VIC 3207, Australia

4843/24, 2nd Floor, Ansari Road, Daryaganj, Delhi – 110002, India

79 Anson Road, #06–04/06, Singapore 079906

Cambridge University Press is part of the University of Cambridge.

It furthers the University's mission by disseminating knowledge in the pursuit of education, learning and research at the highest international levels of excellence.

www.cambridge.org

Information on this title: education.cambridge.org

© Marian Barry 2017

First published by Georgian Press (Jersey) Limited 1998
Second edition 2005
Reprinted and published by Cambridge University Press, Cambridge 2010
Third edition 2015
Fourth edition 2017

20 19 18 17 16 15 14 13 12 11 10 9 8 7 6 5 4 3 2 1

Printed in the United Kingdom by Latimer Trend

A catalogue record for this publication is available from the British Library

ISBN 978-1-316-63705-0 Paperback

....

....

Contents

Contents chart

SPEAKING / PRONUNCIATION	LANGUAGE STUDY / GRAMMAR SPOTLIGHT	VOCABULARY AND SPELLING	EXAM-STYLE QUESTIONS	ASSESMENT OBJECTIVE FOCUS
Expressing fears and giving someone confidence	Figurative meanings Apostrophes Present simple and continuous	Spelling patterns: *qu* and *ph* Why are words misspelt? Homophones Adjectives to describe people Colour images	Writing: Exercise 5 Exercise 6 Speaking Listening: Exercise 4 (Multiple-choice questions)	R1, W3, S4, S5
Interview: neighbourhood and home life Showing enthusiasm Persuading Role play: Spend, spend, spend	Order of adjectives Borrowed words Gerund or infinitive	Describing a place and its atmosphere Doubling consonants Suffixes: multi-syllable words	Writing: Exercise 5 Exercise 6 Speaking Listening Exercise 2 (Note-making) Reading Exercise 2 (Multiple matching)	R2, W3, W5, L1, S1
Stressing key words Expressing warnings	Headlines Redundant words Passives Verbs with two objects	Compound nouns *A five-kilometre walk*, etc. Suffixes: words with a final -e	Speaking Reading/Writing: Exercise 4 (Note-making) Reading: Exercise 3 (Summary) Listening: Exercise 6 (Multiple matching)	R3, L1, L3, S4, S5
The letter *g* Asking for a favour	Connectors Words often confused The future with *will* and *going to*	The letter g Euphemisms Ways of walking	Speaking Listening: Exercise 1 (Short extracts) Reading: Exercise 2 (Multiple matching) Writing: Exercise 6	R1, R2, W2, L1, L2, S5
Asking for information Describing films The letters *c* and *ch* Strategies for interrupting	*So … that* and *such … that* *Will* for prediction The superlative + present perfect	Adjectives to describe films Film vocabulary The letters *c* and *ch*	Speaking Writing: Exercise 5 Exercise 6 Reading: Exercise 2 (Multiple matching) Listening: Exercise 3 (Multiple matching)	R1, R2, W3, L1, L2, S4, S5
Shifting stress Expressing blame and guilt	*Quite* Punctuating direct speech Adverbs of frequency	Adjective collocations Adjective suffixes Adverbs as intensifiers Homophones The weather	Writing: Exercise 5 Exercise 6 Speaking Listening: Exercise 5 (Completing notes)	R1, R2, W3, S1
Interactive skills Silent letters	Problems and advice *Should / ought / need / must / had better* Punctuation 'Text speak'	The suffixes -*ment* and -*al* Silent letters Idioms	Reading: Exercise 1 (Reading) Writing: Exercise 5 Exercise 6 Speaking	R3, R4, W5, S4
Expressing surprise Consoling and commiserating The suffix -*tion/-ion*	Narrative tenses Reported speech Relative clauses Formation of adverbs The interrupted past continuous	The sea Onomatopoeic words The prefixes *mal-* and *counter-* Homonyms The suffix -*tion/-ion*	Reading: Exercise 2 (Multiple matching) Writing: Exercise 5 Exercise 6 Speaking	R2, W2, W3, S5
Expressing disappointment Regular and irregular plurals	Adding extra emphasis Rhetorical questions The past perfect passive Passives with two objects – revision	Regular and irregular plurals Animal vocabulary Adjectives describing feelings	Reading: Exercise 2 (Multiple matching) Writing: Exercise 5 Exercise 6 Speaking Listening: Exercise 3 (Multiple matching)	R1, W1, W2, W3, L4, S1, S4
Product development meeting and role play Linking sounds	Understanding visual data Amounts and approximations Questioning and criticising statistics Superlatives of long and short adjectives Adverbs of degree	Work-related expressions Similes Suffixes: -*able* or -*ible*? 'Eye' idioms	Writing: Exercise 5 Exercise 6 Speaking	R3, R4, W5, L1, L2, S4, S5

v

Overview of Cambridge IGCSE English as a Second Language

Reading and Writing

Students will take either:

Paper 1 (Core) – 1 hour 30 minutes – 60 marks in total – Grades C–G

or **Paper 2 (Extended)** – 2 hours – 80 marks in total – Grades A*–E

Exercise number	Type of exercise	Description	Total marks Core	Extended
Exercise 1	Reading	Students read a text and answer a series of questions which require single word/phrase answers.	9	13
Exercise 2	Multiple matching	Students read a text and answer a series of questions testing more detailed comprehension. Students match the correct answer to the question.	8	10
Exercise 3	Note-making	Students make brief notes on a text under a supplied heading or headings.	7	9
Exercise 4	Summary	Students write a summary of 80 words (Core) or 100 (Extended) about an aspect or aspects of a text. The text will be a different text from Exercise 3, for both Core and Extended.	12	16
Exercise 5	Writing	Students write 100–150 words (Core) or 150–200 words (Extended) of continuous prose in response to a short stimulus and/or short prompts. The purpose, format and audience are specified.	12	16
Exercise 6	Writing	Students write a report, review or article of 100–150 words (Core) or 150–200 words (Extended) in response to a short stimulus. The purpose, format and audience are specified and will be different to Exercise 5.	12	16

Listening

Students will take either:

Paper 3 (Core) – Approximately 40 minutes – 30 marks in total – Grades C–G

or **Paper 4 (Extended)** – Approximately 50 minutes – 40 marks in total – Grades A*–E

Exercise number	Type of exercise	Description	Total marks Core	Extended
Exercise 1	Short extracts	Students listen to four short extracts of dialogue or phone messages and answer questions on each. Questions require short answers, no longer than three words each.	8	8
Exercise 2	Note-making	Students listen to a formal talk and complete gaps in notes/sentences.	8	8
Exercise 3	Multiple matching	Students listen to six short, informal monologues and match each speaker to appropriate content.	6	6
Exercise 4	Multiple-choice questions	Students listen to an informal discussion between two speakers and answer 3-option multiple-choice questions.	8	8
Exercise 5 (Extended only)	Completing notes	Students listen to a talk and complete gaps in notes/sentences. Then they listen to a short discussion based on this talk, and complete sentences using no more than three words.	-	10

Speaking

Approximately 10–15 minutes – 30 marks in total (syllabus 0511) or grades 1–5 (syllabus 0510)

Students take part in a discussion with the teacher on a set topic. After a short warm-up which is not assessed, students are allowed 2–3 minutes to read the speaking test card which has been selected from a range of cards. The cards include prompts to guide the discussion. Students are not allowed to make written notes. The conversation itself should last 6–9 minutes. In syllabus 0510 marks for the Speaking component do not contribute to the overall grade. Instead, students will be marked from 1 (high) to 5 (low).

Weighting for qualification		
Assessment objective	0511	0510
AO1: Reading	30%	35%
AO2: Writing	30%	35%
AO3: Listening	20%	30%
AO4: Speaking	20%	Separately endorsed

Skill	Assessment objectives	
AO1: Reading	R1	identify and select relevant information
	R2	understand ideas, opinions and attitudes
	R3	show understanding of the connections between ideas, opinions and attitudes
	R4	understand what is implied but not directly stated, e.g. gist, writer's purpose, intention and feelings
AO2: Writing	W1	communicate information/ideas/opinions clearly, accurately and effectively
	W2	organise ideas into coherent paragraphs using a range of appropriate linking devices
	W3	use a range of grammatical structures and vocabulary accurately and effectively
	W4	show control of punctuation and spelling
	W5	use appropriate register and style/format for the given purpose and audience
AO3: Listening	L1	identify and select relevant information
	L2	understand ideas, opinions and attitudes
	L3	show understanding of the connections between ideas, opinions and attitudes
	L4	understand what is implied but not directly stated, e.g. gist, speaker's purpose, intention and feelings
AO4: Speaking	S1	communicate ideas/opinions clearly, accurately and effectively
	S2	develop responses and link ideas using a range of appropriate linking devices
	S3	use a range of grammatical structures and vocabulary accurately and effectively
	S4	show control of pronunciation and intonation patterns
	S5	engage in a conversation and contribute effectively to help move the conversation forward

The information in this section is taken from the Cambridge syllabus document. Teachers should refer to the appropriate syllabus document for the year that their students are entering for examination to confirm the details. More detailed information about the Cambridge IGCSE English as a Second Language examination, including support available for teachers and students, can be obtained from Cambridge International Examinations, 1 Hills Road, Cambridge CB1 2EU, United Kingdom, and online at www.cie.org.uk

Cambridge University Press and Marian Barry would like to thank Garan Holcombe for his advice and input into the material for this fourth edition.

Introduction

Dear Student,

In this book you will find all the support and information you need to help you prepare for the Cambridge IGCSE English as a Second Language syllabus.

This *Success International English Skills Student's Book* helps you to develop each skill you will need for success in your course – whether it is note-making, summary writing, reading comprehension, composition writing, listening or speaking. You will learn to communicate effectively and make good sense.

The Cambridge syllabus has two levels, known as Core and Extended. This book covers both levels, but aims to stretch and challenge you to reach a higher level than you perhaps thought possible.

As you use the book, what is expected of you is made very clear. You will always understand what you are doing and why you are doing it. It is a good idea to check the **Contents Chart** each time you start a new unit. Here, you will see all your learning objectives for the unit. You will also see how what you are going to study relates to what you have already done.

The units are structured to build up the skills gradually, starting with the easier aspects of learning, such as recognising and understanding information. For example, you might have to write an article for a website for teenagers. Before you start, you will be given lots of help with vocabulary and the style to use, so when it is your turn to write independently you'll be able to do so confidently and easily. The **Exam focus** at the end of each unit explains the **skills** you have practised. *Success International* is **topic-based**, and you will be practising your language skills while deepening your understanding of a range of contemporary issues.

Exams can include questions on topics of international relevance. Students often feel unable to talk or write knowledgeably about such topics, but there is no need to feel like this. The book provides the factual information and ideas you might need, as well as helping you to think about them in a straightforward way. As your thinking skills develop, your ability to analyse new ideas naturally increases, so you will feel ready to face the topics you might meet in an exam.

As you progress through each unit of the book, you will enjoy having interesting themes to explore at the same time as improving your language techniques. You will pick up new vocabulary and structures quite painlessly.

Students sometimes have lots of good ideas but struggle to get them down on paper. The exercises in the *Success International English Skills Student's Book* will help you overcome that kind of frustration because each topic is broken down into small bits. This means you can get each part of an exercise clear in your mind before moving on to the next part. In the end, you'll have an overview of a whole topic, and will find you can produce an excellent email or article, or present an impressive talk to your group.

On the subject of talking, this book provides many opportunities for you to share your ideas in English with your group. Discussion is a great way to share ideas with other people, take a concept further or get ready for an interesting listening or reading exercise. Don't forget to use the photographs in the book to stimulate ideas.

Developing students' ability to express themselves in writing is an important goal of the course. There are several exercises that show the difference between a simple, basic way of writing and a more developed style, which is appropriate for a young adult. Improving your writing style means learning various language and personal skills, but the results are well worth the effort.

During the course, you will be helped to evaluate your progress so you can see what you need to do next to keep extending and developing yourself. I hope you will use the **Advice for Success** at the end of each unit, as this will help you **reflect** on what you have achieved in the unit. Everyone is different, so mark the Advice for Success according to whether the suggestions are a top priority for you, or interesting but not a top priority. Write down your personal priorities and make sure you follow them through. The Advice for Success also gives ideas for further progress, as well as advice on exam techniques. At the end of each unit there are **Exam-Style Questions** for you to practise.

I have enjoyed writing these books for you.

Kindest regards,

Marian Barry

Unit 1
Happiness and success

In this unit you will:

- read about work-life balance and adult literacy
- write a description of someone's character and appearance
- listen to an interview about achievement
- practise showing control of intonation while expressing fears and giving someone confidence
- focus on the following assessment objectives: R1, W3, S4, S5

A What is happiness?

1 Quiz

Complete this online quiz in pairs to find out how happy you are. Don't worry about individual words – just try to understand the main ideas.

1   Which statement best describes your feelings about your education?
    a   My talent is not recognised.
    b   I'm very clear about how I like to work.
    c   Other people's approval is very important.

2   How do you feel about relationships?
    a   I think people should accept me for who I am.
    b   I know what I have to give, but sometimes I fail.
    c   I try hard to be an ideal son/daughter/friend.

3   Which statement best describes your relationship with your closest friend?
    a   Our relationship is so good we never argue.
    b   We do argue, but we make up afterwards.
    c   We like to get every little problem off our chests.

4   Which statement best describes your feelings about your home?
    a   It's a place to rest my head.
    b   My heart lifts when I come home.
    c   I feel proud when I tell someone my address.

5   You've got a chance to redecorate your bedroom. Do you:
    a   let your parents choose the colour scheme and carpet?
    b   go for whatever makes you feel good?
    c   select something stylish you saw on a website or in a magazine?

6   What are your feelings about other people?
    a   I believe people sometimes have a hidden motive.
    b   I give individuals the benefit of the doubt.
    c   I trust people and then feel let down.

7   You've been invited to a big party. All your friends will be there. You hate parties. Do you:
    a   tell everyone you're going but don't turn up?
    b   explain your feelings in a light-hearted way?
    c   go anyway and feel miserable?

8   You're feeling proud of a new outfit. A 'friend' makes a hurtful remark. Do you:
    a   give a sharp reply/say something nasty back?
    b   ignore it?
    c   promise yourself never to wear it again?

9   How do you choose your clothes?
    a   I go for classics.
    b   For comfort and personal taste – favourite colours, cuts and fabrics.
    c   I like to be fashionable.

10 What are your feelings about family and personal relationships?
    a   I believe that I have a duty to others.
    b   I'll make sacrifices, but I know my limits.
    c   I believe I must be happy in whatever I do.

11 What is the most important part of your home?
    a   Main reception room
    b   Bathroom, kitchen, bedroom or 'den'
    c   Front entrance

12 How do you deal with difficult situations?
    a   I avoid situations that might hurt me.
    b   I remove myself from any situation that keeps causing me pain.
    c   I keep going even if a situation is difficult for me.

13 How would you describe your life?
    a   I've no time to pursue personal goals.
    b   I've a clear sense of meaning and purpose.
    c   I have too much to do and I feel all over the place.

14 Which best describes your friendships?
    a   I'd like to have more.
    b   I choose my friends.
    c   My friends choose me – I'm liked and accepted.

15 You're relaxing at home after a hard day when a friend phones. Do you:
    a   get someone to tell her you're out?
    b   get someone to tell her you'll call back?
    c   take the call?

See the end of Unit 1 for quiz scores.

2 Discussion

A Do you think the happiest people are those who live their life in their own way? Why/Why not? Do we all have a right to happiness?

Explain your ideas to your group.

B What makes you happy? Read some comments made by students about what makes them happy:

'Finding a $10 note in the pocket of my jeans when I thought I didn't have any money.'

'Going to a football match and seeing my side win.'

'A surprise long-distance call from a really close friend.'

Now add your own ideas. Be specific!

C Share your ideas around your group.

D What can you do when you feel unhappy?

Study these comments:

'I go to my room and listen to music. Music is an escape for me.'

'I talk to my dad and he tells me how he coped in a similar situation.'

Discuss your ideas with your partner.

3 Formal and informal styles

Here is some informal or colloquial language from the quiz and the scores. Match it to the more formal equivalents.

1 I feel all over the place.

2 We like to get every little problem off our chests.

3 You're waiting for life to come and bring you happiness.

A I lack a clear sense of my goals in life.

B You aren't taking responsibility for making yourself happy.

C We always tell each other what we are feeling bad about, even if it's something unimportant.

4 Spelling patterns and speech sounds

You've just completed a quiz. In English spelling, *q* is always followed by *u*. *Qu* is a spelling pattern. The speech sound is /kw/.

Can you guess the following words, each containing the pattern *qu*? Use your dictionary to check that your spelling is correct.

1 The king is married to her.

2 He started the essay with words from his favourite poem.

3 This is the sound a duck makes.

4 A celebration meal which a very large number of people attend.

Ph is another spelling pattern, and sounds like /f/. It's in *ph*one, *ph*otograph and *ph*rase.

What other sounds and spelling patterns do you know?

4

5 Approaches to spelling

Select the strategies you use to help you spell.

- ☐ I remember how the word looks on the page (visual recall).
- ☐ I use spelling rules.
- ☐ I link spelling patterns with speech sounds (e.g. *q+u* is a pattern and sounds like /kw/).

Everyone makes spelling mistakes! You can improve your spelling by using a combination of all these approaches. One useful method, described below, is called 'Look, say, cover, check'.

6 Look, say, cover, write, check

This method focuses on each letter group in a word so you won't miss any letters out. It also stops you putting letters into a word that don't belong there – even if they sound as if they do! It can be used with other strategies, such as spelling rules and linking speech sounds to spelling patterns.

Break into syllables

To help you remember how a word looks, break it into syllables. For example, *quality* has three syllables: qua/li/ty.

Qualification has five syllables: qua/li/fi/ca/tion.

Break these words into syllables:

question
automatic
quarrel

Take a mental photograph

Cover the word with a piece of paper. Then move the paper so that you can see the first syllable only. Study the syllable carefully, 'photographing' it in your mind and saying the syllable to yourself. Then move the paper along so that you can see the next syllable. Repeat the process, until you have mentally 'photographed' the complete word.

Test yourself

Cover up the whole word. Write it from memory. Then check your spelling with the original. If your spelling was correct, write out the word three times from memory to reinforce the visual recall. If you didn't get it right, repeat the whole process until you are sure you can spell the word accurately.

7 Tricky words

Here are some words students find hard to spell correctly. Make sure you understand the meaning of each one, using a dictionary if necessary. Can you pronounce it properly? Say it aloud to your partner to check.

VOCABULARY		
cupboard	responsible	wrist
committee	embarrassment	calm
activities		

How well can you spell these tricky words? Use the 'look, say, cover, write, check' method. Remember to break each word into syllables first. When you have mastered the spelling of each word, move on to the next. Finally, use each word in a sentence to show its meaning.

8 Why are words misspelt?

A Try this exercise in a pair or group of three.

Study each tricky word in exercise 7 again. Do you notice anything about the word that makes it extra hard to spell? Think about these questions.

Is the problem the fact that we do not pronounce some of the letters in the word? These are called **silent letters**.

Is the problem the **ending** of the word? Do we make mistakes because the sound of the ending is different from the correct spelling?

Is the problem the fact that the word is a **plural**? What happens to the word when it changes from singular to plural?

Is the problem the fact that there are **double letters** in the word? Do we make mistakes because we are not sure whether to use a double or single letter?

B When you have decided why each word is tricky, make a note.

Examples: Cupboard is tricky because you can't hear the *p*, so you might forget to put it in.
Activities is a tricky word because the singular is *activity*. You might forget to change the ending to *-ies* when you write the plural form.

5

C Write down examples of other words which have silent letters and -*ies* plurals.

Examples: p is not only silent in *cupboard*. You can't hear it in *receipt, raspberry* or *psychology*.

Dictionary, story and *memory* are other words which have -*ies* plurals. But words like *boy* and *railway* just add *s* to make the plural.

D When you have written as much as you feel you can, discuss your results with other pairs or groups.

9 How helpful is your dictionary?

Dictionaries give you the meaning of words and help you to spell. Does your dictionary also:

- tell you how to pronounce the word?
- tell you the grammatical class (verb, noun, adverb)?
- tell you if the word belongs to more than one grammatical class (e.g. nouns that can be used as verbs)?
- tell you if a noun is countable or uncountable?
- give you example sentences?
- give you any idiomatic expressions using the word(s)?

If the answer to most of these questions is no, you need a new dictionary! Before you spend a lot of money on a digital or print version, ask your teacher or your classmates for their ideas.

10 Getting organised

Have you got a spelling and vocabulary book? If not, start one now. Plan the layout carefully. Use columns, notes on pronunciation, space for translations and example sentences. You'll find it a great aid to memory. It will be an enormous help in understanding the patterns of English.

B Happy not to be a high-flyer

1 Before you read

A Compare this description with the photograph.

Tina's short brown hair is cut in a boyish style. She looks alert, confident and ready for anything.

Do you agree with the description? Would you change anything?

B You are going to read about Tina's way of being happy. Before you read, try to answer these questions.

Where do you think the text comes from?

What do you think the style is going to be – chatty and informal, or formal and serious?

Who do you think the article is written for?

Vocabulary check

Make sure you know the meaning of these words from the text.

VOCABULARY		
priority	insignificant	trivial

2 Comprehension check

Now read the article. Then answer the questions that follow.

1 Why do Tina's friends think her job isn't good enough for her?

2 What does Tina think is the most important part of her life?

3 Why is Tina not ambitious?

4 Describe Tina's attitude to life.

3 Principles of a happy life

Psychologists, analysing the ingredients for living a happy life, have come up with the following dos and don'ts. Unfortunately, the words *do* and *don't* are missing.

Working with a partner, **skim read** the list quickly to get the main ideas. Write *Do* or *Don't* next to each point.

_____ regret decisions you made in the past.

_____ be angry with your parents.

_____ value status and material possessions more than people.

_____ spend a lot of time envying other people.

_____ be realistic about how much you can achieve.

_____ choose a job that gives you real satisfaction.

Now discuss your opinions in groups.

Tina Barry, production assistant at a TV company, is happy standing still on her career ladder

My mum always wanted me to do well at school and to have a high-status job, but that sort of thing isn't a big priority for me. I did have the potential to do well and go to university, but I was just too busy
5   having a good time. My relationships have always been far more important to me than academic or career success.

'My present job basically involves working as an assistant, and friends still insist I could have
10   achieved more in my working life. When I was younger, I did feel I had to set myself goals and attain them within a certain period. I successfully ran my own business for a while, but having kids put life back into perspective.

15   'There have been times when I could have taken on a lot more responsibility at work, but I imagine that if I had a more senior role at work, another part of my life would have to give, and I'm not prepared to risk that. I'm just not the sort of person who
20   can trample on others to get to the top. I find it satisfying to do a productive job because I like to feel I'm doing something useful, but I'm not into climbing the career ladder now.

'The biggest priorities in my life are my husband, David, and our young children – son Greg and   25
daughter Fleur. If I'm ever fed up after a day at work, I just spend some time playing with the children, and the enjoyment I get from them makes me realise how insignificant and trivial my worries at work can be.

'Occasionally, I'm reminded of how tied down   30
I am – if a friend goes off travelling, for example. But I suppose an important part of happiness is to accept life's limitations, and to learn to enjoy the things that you *can* do.'

7

4 Finding examples

Work in groups of two or three. **Scan** the text to find examples of how Tina follows the 'principles of a happy life' referred to in exercise 3. (Scanning means looking to 'spot' answers or evidence.)

Example:
Tina says she had the potential to go to university but it wasn't a priority. She was too busy having a good time. This shows she doesn't regret decisions made in the past.

5 Sharing ideas

A   When your group has finished, check your examples with those of another group. Are there any differences? Make any corrections you need to. Include new, interesting ideas on your own list.

B   Suggest some 'happiness principles' to share with your group. Try to base them on your own experience.

Examples:
Do try to be tolerant of other people.
Don't be too self-critical.

6 Discussion

Although Tina says she's happy not to be a high-flyer, some people say they get fulfillment from being promoted to highly demanding jobs. Would you be prepared to make any sacrifices in your personal life in order to have a high-flying career? Why/Why not?

7 Goal setting

A Tina says that, when she was younger, she set herself goals. Is goal setting a good idea? Does it help you achieve things, or should you take each day as it comes? Should you ever change your goals?

B Have you any goals of your own? Take a few minutes to think and then write them down. Divide them into daily, medium-term and long-term goals. Share them with others or keep them private if you prefer.

Examples:
A goal for today is to tidy my bedroom.
A medium-term goal is to improve my fitness by swimming twice a week.
A long-term goal is to travel the world.

Daily goal _____

Medium-term goal _____

Long-term goal _____

8 Figurative meanings

Tina says, 'I'm just not the sort of person who can *trample* on others to get to the top.'

The literal meaning of *trample* is to tread heavily on something in a way that damages it.

Example: *They trampled over the garden, ruining the new plants.*

Tina uses *trample* figuratively, meaning that she would not behave in a way that would hurt the feelings of others.

In each of the following sentences, one word is used figuratively. Underline the word, and then discuss its meaning with your partner. Finally, write sentences of your own to illustrate the meanings. Don't forget to use a dictionary when you need to.

1 I spent the day wrestling with our financial problems.

2 My heart lifts when I come home.

3 We're fighting the authorities who want to close our village school.

4 His face broke into a smile when he heard the news.

5 I'm tired of battling with staff who refuse to accept different working conditions.

6 After his wife's death, he buried himself in his work.

7 She's crippled by shyness.

The English language is full of figurative uses of words. Reading and listening to authentic English will develop your awareness. Work towards including examples in your own vocabulary.

9 Homophones

Tina says that she doesn't want a more senior role at work. *Role* here means job.

Role has the same sound as *roll*, but each word has a different spelling and meaning. *Roll* can refer to a bread roll, or be used as a verb, meaning movement, e.g. *roll the ball along the ground*. Words with the same sound but different spellings are called **homophones**.

The following sentences are based on students' writing. Choose the correct homophone in each case. Can you explain the meaning of the incorrect one?

1 There's no plaice / place like home.

2 I was in terrible pane / pain when I broke my arm.

3 You need peace / piece and quiet for your work.

4 I read the hole / whole book in one evening.

5 We're not aloud / allowed to stay out late.

6 We have a pear / pair tree in the garden.

7 The wind farms will be a horrible site / sight.

8 Their / There are six people in my family.

9 I answered four / for questions.

10 He's got a saw / sore throat.

10 More homophones

Work in small groups to try to find a homophone for each of these words.

1	steal	**6**	bear
2	male	**7**	tail
3	your	**8**	sale
4	week	**9**	poor
5	hour	**10**	wail

Now put each word into a sentence to show its meaning.

C The price of greatness

1 Before you listen

Name someone who you think deserves to go down in history for their work or achievements. Why do you think this person should be admired? Try to be specific.

Example: Marie Curie – because her discoveries led to the development of X-rays and successful treatments for cancer.

Make a few notes.

What do you know of their background and personal life? If you don't know very much, what picture do you have in your mind of them? Do you imagine a happy home life or one dominated by struggle and conflict? Why/Why not? Write down your ideas.

Share your ideas with the rest of the group.

2 Vocabulary check

Match the words which you are going to hear with their definitions. You will hear the first six in an interview.

1	genius	A	something that makes it difficult for you to do what you want
2	inner drive	B	very interested
3	genetic	C	reach an extremely high standard
4	setback	D	unhappy feelings, anxiety, depression
5	excel	E	(a person of) exceptional ability
6	psychological unease	F	a permanent feeling that life has been unfair to you, personally
7	embittered	G	inherited through your parents
8	intrigued	H	a strong determination to achieve

3 Listening: Radio interview 🔊 CD 1, Track 2

Listen to this radio interview and choose the best answer for each question.

1 According to Steve, the disadvantages suffered by great achievers when they were children:
   a made it more difficult for them to reach their potential.
   b drove them to excel.
   c made the public more sympathetic to their achievements.
   d embittered them for life.

2 The interviewer's attitude to the information that suffering is a significant factor in great achievement is
   a doubtful. c horrified.
   b amused. d intrigued.

3 What, according to Steve, did great achievers need when they were children?
   a understanding
   b companionship
   c solitude
   d training

4 Steve's message to ordinary children who are hoping to fulfil their potential is:
   a discouraging – you'll probably never make it as a real superstar.
   b supportive – everyone should develop his/her abilities.
   c cautious – try to achieve but take care not to get depressed.
   d excited – there's a wonderful future ahead of you.

9

4 Post-listening discussion

A According to the speaker, the greatest thinkers had unhappy lives. Does this surprise you at all? Why/Why not?

B Do you agree that being very successful is '5% talent and the rest hard work'? Explain your views.

5 Apostrophes (1)

These sentences come from the script of the radio interview. Why are the apostrophes used, do you think? Discuss your ideas with your partner.

1 Steve's been reading an absolutely wonderful book.
2 You can't just pick out one or two factors.
3 It's a very complex web.
4 They've probably suffered from depression.
5 I wouldn't say you ought to stop trying to achieve your potential.
6 You mightn't be the next superstar.

Pronunciation

Practise saying the contracted forms to your partner. Try to make the contraction smooth and natural-sounding.

6 Apostrophes (2)

With a partner, study the exact position of the apostrophes in these sentences.

1 Someone's stolen the doctor's bag.
2 He got a parents' guide to zoos.
3 All the passengers' luggage goes in the hold.
4 There are no men's toilets on this floor.
5 Give me Brendan's shoes.
6 I spoke to the children's favourite teacher.
7 Can I introduce Maria's husband?

What conclusions can you come to about using apostrophes? Write down your ideas.

7 Correcting sentences

Now correct the following sentences by adding apostrophes where they are necessary.

1 The teachers listened to Carols views.
2 Theyve bought a new car.
3 I went to my mothers office.
4 Please dont touch the babies clothes.
5 Its hard to explain the programmes success.
6 She works in the womens ward of the hospital.
7 Hes training to be a ladies hairdresser.
8 Youll find her in the teachers workroom – all the staff go there.
9 He mightve become the next Einstein.
10 She couldnt understand why her cat had lost its appetite.

Practise saying the sentences aloud to your partner.

8 Speculating about a photograph

Study this photograph with a partner. Read how three students have described the person in it. Which comments do you most agree with? Try to explain why.

A *He looks big and heavy-set. He's got a warm, humorous expression. He could be a farmer or a sailor.*

B *He has a pleasant expression and friendly smile. He looks confident and also trustworthy. He could be a lawyer or a businessman.*

C *He's fair-skinned with swept-back hair. He's rather sensitive-looking. He could be an artist or a ballet dancer.*

The photograph is of Alexander Garcia, a high-flying entrepreneur who started his own business selling mobile phones at 17, and became a multimillionaire at the age of 21. He has decided to share his business skills and help others start small businesses. He particularly supports applications from people who want to start a business in an area of high unemployment.

9 Describing personal qualities

Here are some comments about Alex that internet users have posted on a website about entrepreneurs.

Study them with a partner. Make sure you understand each one.

When he's deciding whether to invest in a business idea he gets negative comments, such as 'It's not worth it, Alex, that project is a waste of money. The applicant is too uneducated to do well.' But he doesn't think like that. He believes everyone deserves a chance to succeed.

He has invested in small businesses with no guarantee of success, but he says that it was worth it because now, all over the world, people are running a business they are proud of.

He thinks there are still huge economic problems and lots of poverty. But he reminds us that if we make the world a fairer place, everyone will benefit.

When he hears about an exciting project he's filled with enthusiasm. He relies on friends saying 'Wait a minute Alex, you've got to do this or do that to avoid disaster.'

He believes that encouraging people to believe in their future is vital. Even if others think he is too optimistic, he just has to do what he thinks is right.

His work involves constant travel, which can be exhausting, and his work does not always go well. What has kept him going is having good friends who share his values.

After reading people's comments about Alex's life, do you think it is right to draw the following conclusions about him? Scan the text again if you need to. Answer yes or no.

He has:

1 the courage to take risks.
2 benefited from positive advice.
3 bad memories he cannot forget.
4 accepted stress as part of his life.
5 support from people around him.
6 trouble trusting others.
7 self-belief.
8 a positive outlook.
9 determination.
10 difficulty adjusting to change.

10 Discussion

1 Alex might be successful, but is he happy? What are your views?
2 Is there anything about Alex's approach to life you would choose for yourself? Try to explain why.
3 Do you think Alex is a good example to younger people? Could he be a role model (a person who inspires others to copy them)? Why/Why not?
4 Does Alex share any qualities with your own personal heroes or heroines?

11 Drafting a paragraph

Write a paragraph of about 75 words describing the kind of person you think Alex is. Try to give reasons for your opinions.

When you've finished writing, show your paragraph to a partner. Does he/she think you should change anything? Do you agree? Make a second draft, putting in the changes you both agreed on.

D Obstacles and challenges

1 Expressing fears and giving someone confidence

In pairs, read the following dialogue.

A: I've got to recite a poem in front of the whole school.

B: How do you feel about it?

A: To tell you the truth, I'm a bit worried about it.

B: Don't worry. You'll be fine. Everyone thinks you're great!

When people want to express fears, they use these expressions. Select the one(s) that sound most fearful.

- I feel sick every time I think about it.
- To tell you the truth, I'm a bit scared about it.
- I'm not really sure I can cope.
- To be honest, I'm not sure I'll be able to do it.
- The thought of it bothers me.
- I'm terrified!

Here are some expressions you can use to give someone confidence. Which do you prefer?

There's nothing to worry about. You'll do a wonderful job.
You'll be fine. Nothing can go wrong.
Things will be all right. We're all supporting you.
Don't get too upset. It'll all go well.

Practice

Practise expressing fears and giving someone confidence in pairs. A should explain what he/she has to do. B should give reassurance. Then swap over. Base your dialogues on these situations:

- a fear of taking an exam
- a fear of competing in a race
- a fear of giving a talk in front of the school
- a fear of going to the dentist.

2 Pre-reading discussion

You are going to read about Monica, a woman who didn't learn to read until she was an adult. Discuss the following questions.

1 What everyday problems do you think not being able to read would present?

2 Why might someone who was unable to read not try to get help to learn?

3 What effect do you think not being able to read might have on him/her?

3 Vocabulary check

Make sure you know the meaning of these words from the text. Use a dictionary if necessary.

VOCABULARY		
bullied	illiterate	volunteer

4 Reading: Textual organisation

Read the text carefully and match each paragraph with one of these headings.

A Effects on Sally's education

B Hiding the problem

C Unhappy school days

D Qualifying as a parent-educator

E Sally's birth

F Monica's work today

G Learning to read

Facing Fears

Monica Chand's childhood memories are of crippling stomach aches each morning before school, of missing lessons through illness and falling so far behind that she understood little but did not dare to
5 ask for help, and of silent misery as children bullied her. She says, 'I spent all those years feeling I had failed at school, but now I think school failed me, and when I had Sally, 17 years ago, I was determined it would not be the same for her.' She is sitting in
10 her tidy flat in south London. Sally, her teenage daughter, joins us. She is shy at first, but soon begins to exchange memories with her mother.

Monica is describing how it feels to be unable to read and write, to be illiterate in a world where just
15 about everything we do, and how we are judged, depends on our literacy skills. Few people, she says, realise what it means to be unable to read a road sign, safety instructions or the contents of a food packet, when every form you have to fill in, every note you need to write, is an impossible task. 20 Monica remembers it very clearly: 'I felt so conscious of not being able to join in the life other people were living.' Few understand what people do to disguise their inability to read and write. Monica explains, 'I would have the names of places 25 I wanted to go to written down, and then I'd show this and ask someone to help, explaining that I'd left my glasses at home or some such story. I'd carry a book or newspaper around and pretend to read it. You get good at fooling other people, but 30 you can't fool yourself. It makes the world a scary place.'

35 Her husband, Ravi, who died earlier this year, was unaware of her secret. She says, 'I'd just ask him to do the things I couldn't cope with and he accepted that. But it really came home to me when Sally was born. I felt very insecure as a mother, and as she grew up everyone around me was saying, 'You must read to her.' I felt so stupid because I couldn't.' Even 40 then she did not tell Ravi, although she smiles now and says, 'I think he must have known in his heart of hearts, but he was such a sweet man he never let on. I made sure he did the reading with Sally – I'd say I had to cook dinner and that it was a good way 45 for them to be close.' Sally remembers, 'Sometimes Mum would sit with us and seem to join in. I never realised she wasn't actually reading.'

Things changed when Sally went to primary school and Monica became a volunteer, working in the 50 school helping children without being paid. One morning the headteacher said they wanted to offer her a paid job as a helper. 'I just froze. I knew that would involve reading and writing – the things I'd avoided so far. But the headteacher had recognised 55 my problem. She took me under her wing and did reading with me every day so that I could take the job. As I learnt, she put me in with older children and I realised I could read and write. It was like a miracle.'

That was the beginning. When the present headteacher 60 took over he set up a parents' group and Monica was part of it. He asked them to write a book for parents teaching their children. Monica says, 'My first reaction was, "Ooh, I can't do that," but then I realised I could

contribute. And I wanted to because I realised there were other parents like me.' By now she was doing a 65 training course to become a parent-educator. 'The day I got my certificate – the first in my life – Sally and I went out for a really nice meal to celebrate.'

These struggles are in the past. Monica works in several schools and has just returned from a 70 conference in Cyprus where she gave a presentation on involving parents in reading. She also has a highly successful blog, which gets thousands of hits from users who post comments about her inspirational ideas. She says, 'Learning to read has 75 made the world a different place. Suddenly I feel there are so many things I can do. But the most important thing is that Sally hasn't been held back.'

Sally pulls a face. 'Mum was very pushy about studying and homework. She'd find fault with 75 everything because she was so keen I should do well.' But Monica is unapologetic. 'Perhaps I pushed harder than other parents because I knew what failing feels like, and I suppose I was living my life through her. But we were both bursting with pride 85 the day she did really well in her GCSEs. I was in tears in front of everyone at school because I was so proud.' Sally is no less proud. She is sitting on the arm of the sofa near her mother, listening, and her smile is warm. She says, 'I think it was brave of 90 Mum. She's also shown me how important it is to take opportunities when they come. If she hadn't done that, she wouldn't have become the person she is now, with a great future.'

5 Comprehension check

1 Why did Monica dislike school? Give **two** reasons.

2 How did she hide from other people the fact that she couldn't read? Give **two** examples.

3 **i** Explain how Monica felt when she was offered paid work by the headteacher.

  ii Why do you think the headteacher wanted to employ Monica, despite her problems with reading?

4 Is the writer's attitude to Monica positive or negative? Give **two** details from the text to support your views.

5 Select the correct statements about Sally.
   - Her mother put pressure on her to achieve at school.
   - She is proud of her mother.
   - Sally noticed her mother's problems during bedtime stories.
   - Sally is confident about meeting challenges.

Look at the chart which shows the enrolments on an adult literacy programme.

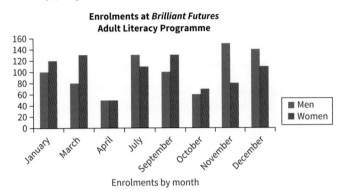

Enrolments at *Brilliant Futures* Adult Literacy Programme

Enrolments by month

a How many women were enrolled in January?

b How many men were enrolled in July?

c In which month were the numbers of enrolments for men and women equal?

d In which months did the enrolment for women exceed* that of men?

e Which was the best month for enrolments for men?

* exceed = be more than

6 Vocabulary: Odd one out

The following groups of adjectives each contain a word that doesn't describe Monica. Cross it out.

1 Monica as a child:

anxious   confident   tense   sensitive

2 Monica as a young mother:

private   insecure   angry   gentle

3 Monica now:

fulfilled   shy   understanding   honest

7 Post-reading discussion

A Monica accepted the challenge of learning to read as an adult. Why are challenges important? What challenges do you have in your own life?

B Monica says '*I suppose I was living my life through her*' (paragraph 7). What bad effects might living your life through another person have?

C Some people feel they will be happy if they have success, achievement, material things. Other people claim happiness comes from inside you. Where does Monica's happiness come from? Try to explain your views.

Read the information in the International Overview and look at the pie chart.

1 What percentage of the world population are unable to read and write?

2 What are the possible consequences of being illiterate, in UNESCO's view?

3 How far do you think literacy is important to the progress of a country?

4 Do you have any idea of the literacy rates in your own country? If you don't know, how could you find out?

8 Describing people

'He was such a sweet man' (paragraph 3). Monica only uses one adjective to describe her husband, Ravi. Do you think

INTERNATIONAL OVERVIEW

Nearly 17% of the world's population is illiterate. Two-thirds of illiterate adults are women.

Globally, 122 million young people are illiterate.

UNESCO believes education is the best means of breaking the connection between illiteracy and poverty, unemployment and ill-health. Currently, UNESCO is operating global literacy programmes specifically targeting the education of young people and girls.

World literacy

17%

83%

■ Literate
■ Illiterate

this is enough? Does she manage to give us a sense of what he was like from just that one word?

The writer tells us that as Sally listens to her mother, 'her smile is *warm*' (paragraph 7). What does that adjective suggest about the nature of Sally's relationship with her mother? What kind of person does Sally seem to be be?

9 Using a wide range of adjectives

When you are trying to describe the impression a person makes, you can refer to their appearance and their character.

You can use:

- specific single adjectives: *sensitive, charming*
- adjective compounds (adjective + noun + *-ed*): *broad-shouldered, fair-skinned, good-natured*
- compounds with *-looking: serious-looking* (instead of saying 'He looked as if he were a serious person.')

Compounds with *-looking* usually refer to a person's inner qualities: *capable-looking, studious-looking, miserable-looking. Good-looking* is an exception.

10 Adjective collocations

Study the adjectives in the box. Divide them into four groups, under the four headings. Work with a partner and use a dictionary to help you. Find translations if you need to.

Appearance   Hair   Voice   Character

VOCABULARY		
deep	husky	tolerant
wavy	shy	absent-minded
mean	placid	quiet
grating	ambitious	self-centred
straight	slim	dreamy

VOCABULARY		
quiet	well-dressed	overweight
self-centred	considerate	curly
dreamy	outgoing	skinny
plump	gentle	bad-tempered
altruistic	elegant	domineering
high-pitched	scruffy	frizzy
generous	argumentative	humorous

11 Positive and negative

You might not mind being called *slim*, but you probably wouldn't like to be called *skinny*! *Slim* has a positive connotation, whereas *skinny* is negative.

Study your word groups in exercise 11 again. Tick (✓) the words you think are definitely positive, and mark with a cross (✗) the ones you think are definitely negative.

12 Negative prefixes

Make the character traits below into their opposites by adding one of these prefixes:

dis-   im-   in-   ir-   un-

VOCABULARY		
responsible	secure	efficient
loyal	trustworthy	happy
mature	reliable	honest

Now put the words into sentences to show their meanings.

13 Colour

Colour is a big part of people's appearance. You could write '*He had black hair and blue eyes*'. However, your writing will get a better response if you say what shade of blue and what kind of black you mean.

15

Using an image from the natural world helps identify an exact shade of colour and produces more vivid writing.

Examples:
Her eyes were sapphire-blue.
His hair was jet-black.
She was wearing a raspberry-pink fleece.

Write sentences about people's appearance using these colour images.

VOCABULARY	
chestnut-brown	emerald-green
chocolate-brown	lime-green
cherry-red	jet-black
rose-pink	sky-blue
strawberry-blonde	lemon-yellow

Being creative

Make up some other associations of your own by linking colours to natural objects. Think about the people and colours around you.

Examples:
He's wearing a leaf-green jacket.
She was carrying a banana-yellow shopping bag.

14 Developing your writing style

Look at this description: *He was a responsible, loyal, outgoing, deep-voiced man.* How could we improve the style of this sentence?

One way of doing it is to use phrases beginning *with ...* and clauses beginning with *which/that ...* : *He was a responsible, loyal man, with a deep voice that his many friends loved.*

Underline the use of *with ...* and *which/that ...* in the following descriptions.

He had straight, dark-yellow hair and milky blue eyes that made him seem dreamy and peaceful. (Anne Tyler, *The Ladder of Years*)

She was a tall, fragile-looking woman in a pretty blue hat that matched her eyes. (Barbara Pym, *An Unsuitable Attachment*)

He was a tall, melancholy man with curly hair, rather romantic-looking in his long, sewer-man's boots. (George Orwell, *Down and Out in Paris and London*)

Conjunctions such as *but* introduce a contrast:

He had grown to be a large-boned man, but his face was still childishly rounded, with the wide eyes, the

downy cheeks, the delicate lips of a schoolboy.
(Anne Tyler, *Dinner at the Homesick Restaurant*)

15 Conveying character traits

Study this example again:

He had straight, dark-yellow hair and milky blue eyes that made him seem dreamy and peaceful.

Now look at this explanation of the way the writer achieves her effect. Do you agree with it?

We get a clear picture of the impression this man makes because of the writer's carefully chosen adjectives. She describes his eyes vividly as 'milky blue'. Milk is associated with innocence and childhood. Using an unusual expression like 'milky blue' emphasises the gentle, trusting qualities of the man. Choosing adjectives such as 'dreamy' and 'peaceful' strengthens the impression the man gives of being accepting and placid.

Choose one of the other examples from section 15 and try to write about it in the same way.

16 Writing your own description

Choose a friend to describe. Don't try to describe everything about him/her. Concentrate on a few special characteristics that convey your friend's uniqueness. For example, he/she may have sparkling eyes. Try to link physical characteristics to character traits.

Remember, use adjectives and colour images selectively. Don't overdo them. Make sure to use clauses.

Write about 75 words.

Feedback

Read your description aloud to your group. Listen carefully to the feedback. (Criticisms should be positive!) Are there any changes you would like to make after hearing the comments?

E Someone I admire

1 Example description

Read this article, which was sent to a teenage magazine that had a feature called 'Special Friends'.

How did the writer meet Simon? As you read, underline any words you don't understand.

My special friend

I'd like to describe my friend Simon. Simon is a mix of honesty and reserve. He's slight and studious-looking, and his dark-brown eyes are hidden behind a large pair of black-framed glasses. Simon is neat and particular - he even organises his downloads alphabetically!

One thing Simon isn't particular about is the way he dresses. He buys his clothes from second-hand shops, and for this reason the other students used to say he was scruffy. I knew Simon didn't like that but he didn't say anything about it. He used to be painfully shy and found it embarrassing to say what he thought about things. But one day he decided he wasn't going to let his shyness get the better of him any more. He decided to open up and speak his mind. I really admire Simon for doing that.

Simon is trustworthy and straightforward. When I was worried about an operation I was going to have, he talked with me about my fears. This helped me find the confidence to ask the doctors for a proper explanation of what was going to happen. I learnt from Simon that it is better to face what is scaring you than hide from it.

I know I'm a lucky person because in Simon I have a good friend I can always rely on.

Comprehension check

1 What impression does Simon make?

2 Why was he unhappy at school?

3 How do you know Simon is a determined person?

4 Why does the writer value Simon's friendship?

Format

A good description shows what the person is like by giving:

- key details about appearance
- examples of behaviour
- reasons why this person is unusual or valued.

Underline the key phrases that provide insight into Simon as a person and as a friend.

What comments can you make about the structure of the sentences? Think about clauses, descriptive vocabulary and reasons.

Beginnings and endings

What sentence is used to begin the article?

How is the article brought to a conclusion?

2 Comparing two styles

The following description was written by a student, Manos, as a first draft. What would you like to change to improve the style?

I am 16-years-old and I would like to describe my father. My father is a nice man. You can talk to him. He will not get angry. My friends like him. He's tall and big and not very fat. He is about normal size. He's got brown eyes, black hair and a nice face. His black hair has some white hairs in it. He makes a lot of things at home. He made a cabinet for me. It is for my DVDs. The cabinet is made from pine. I like my cabinet very much. It is very nice. I look after it all the time. He has made me a good desk. The desk is for my computer. He always wears a grey suit to work. He doesn't like his suit. It is not comfortable for him. He always likes jeans. He wears jeans a lot.

Manos showed his work to his partner. They discussed how he could improve his style. Are the changes an improvement, do you think? Why/Why not?

> My father's a friendly, approachable person who is popular with all my friends. He's a genial-looking, tall man of medium build with dark brown eyes and coal-black hair, streaked with grey. He's very practical and confident with his hands. He made me a pine cabinet for my DVDs, which I treasure, and an attractive computer desk. He has to dress formally for work in a smart suit, but he prefers casual dress and feels most comfortable in jeans.

3 Rewriting to improve style

Try to improve the style of the following text:

> My friend is a good person. Her eyes are big. They are green. They are nice eyes. She has short hair. It is very, very short. The colour is blonde. She smiles a lot. She has a nice smile. She shows her white teeth. Her clothes are nice. Her style of her clothes is different from other people. She looks at other people's clothes. She can see their character from their clothes. She is a very good student. Her work is always good. She gets high marks. She is kind. She helps me do my work too.

When you have finished, compare your draft with someone else's. What differences can you find, and what similarities?

4 Writing from notes

A Have you heard of Joseph Lister? Write down any facts you know about him.

B Now try to write the following description of Joseph Lister in full. You will need to change some words and add others.

I want / describe Joseph Lister. He be / surgeon who / be born / 1827. In those days / many patients die / after operations because their wounds / become / badly infect. Lister wonder if / bacteria / air / which make / meat decay / also make / wounds septic.

Lister decide / clean / everything which touch / patient's wounds / carbolic acid. Carbolic acid / destroy / all germs. As a result / these precautions / patients recover quickly / operations. The rate / infection / fall dramatically.

Lister develop / safe, antiseptic operations / which be / major medical advance. He receive / many awards / his work. I admire him because / he be dedicated / unselfish. He take / great personal risks / make this discovery. Surgery / use to be / highly dangerous. People be / terrify / surgeon's knife. Lister change / all that. Modern surgery be / lifesaver.

VOCABULARY

bacteria: **organisms that cause disease**
septic: **badly infected**
decay: **go bad, rot**
precautions: **actions taken to avoid danger**

GRAMMAR SPOTLIGHT

Present simple and continuous

One of the uses of the **present simple** is to describe facts that are usually or always true:

> *I **avoid** situations that might hurt me.*
> *I **choose** my friends.*

Look at the quiz in **section A1** and underline five more examples of the present simple.

The present continuous is used to talk about things that are happening at this moment:

> *Monica **is describing how** it feels to be unable to read and write.*
> *She **is sitting** in her flat in south London.*

Look at the final paragraph of the text in **section D4** and underline three more examples of the present continuous.

Some verbs do not usually take the continuous form:

> *I **don't understand**. Can you explain that again?*

Verbs like this include: *believe, belong, contain, know, like, love, mean, own, prefer, seem, suppose, understand, want, wish.*

Complete these sentences using the correct present tense of the verb in brackets.

1 That's strange – Josh _____ with his friend Ken. He never normally _____ with anyone. (*argue*)

2 You _____ very quiet this morning. Are you OK? (*seem*)

3 Tanya is very generous. Helping other people _____ her happy. (*make*)

Exam-style questions

Writing

Reading & Writing, Exercise 5

1   A famous person who was born and grew up in your town has died recently. The local council wants to erect a memorial to him or her, and has asked people to suggest suitable memorials. Write an email to the newspaper in which you:

- say why the town should remember this person and feel proud
- describe the kind of memorial you would like to see erected
- make suggestions for other ways to celebrate the life of this person.

Write about 100–150 words

Core [12 marks]

Reading and Writing, Exercise 5

2   A website for teenagers has asked its users to write an article describing someone they are close to. In your article, you should:

- describe the person's special qualities
- give examples of his/her behaviour
- explain why the relationship is important to you.

Write about 150–200 words.

Extended [16 marks]

Reading & Writing, Exercise 5

3   You have joined a penfriend organisation. You receive this email from your new penfriend.

Re: [subject]

Hi …

Thanks for your email. It was great to hear about your home, family and school. But I was a little bit disappointed that you didn't tell me what I really wanted to know … and that's what you're really interested in! What do you want to do with your life? What goals have you got?

Email soon! I can't wait to read your answers to my questions.

Best wishes,

Kim

Write an email in reply to Kim, describing your approach to life and your personal goals. Write about 100–150 words.

Core [12 marks]

Speaking

1 Becoming happier

Many young people say they are unhappy and feel negative about their lives. Why do you think this is? How could they develop a more positive approach? Try to explain your views.

You might consider such things as:

- the opportunity to enrich your life by doing more things that bring pleasure
- the advantages (or disadvantages) of planning your life and setting goals
- the value of role models in inspiring young people
- the idea that voluntary work with disadvantaged people makes us feel grateful for what we have.

You are free to consider any other related ideas of your own. You are not allowed to make any written notes.

2 The importance of people's names

Our first or given name is often very important to people. Discuss this topic with the assessor. You could use the following ideas to help develop the conversation:

- Why your parents gave you your name
- Names that are popular in your culture and any special meanings they have
- Whether the name people have affects their personality and the way people treat them
- The advantages and disadvantages of nicknames
- The idea that calling everyone by their first name is a good thing.

You are free to consider any other related ideas of your own.

Listening CD 1, Track 3

Listening, Exercise 4

You will hear Victor, a radio presenter, asking Carlos Gomez, a teenage blogger, some questions about his hobby as part of a radio feature on developing potential in young people. Listen to their conversation and choose the correct answer for each question. You will hear the interview twice.

Core [8 marks], Extended [8 marks]

1   The main reason Carlos started his blog was because:

    a   teenage blogs are very interesting to read

    b   he thought he had the skills to write a blog

    c   other blogs mainly reflected the interests of teenage boys.

2   When choosing to write about inventors, Carlos concentrates on:

    a   teenage boy inventors

    b   little-known inventors

    c   famous inventors.

3   One of the boys reading his blog changed from:

    a   playing computer games to reading

    b   watching action movies to reading

    c   posting comments on social media to reading.

4 His book review section is popular with:

    a people of all ages

    b booksellers

    c shopkeepers.

5 Carlos's attitude to the artwork in the *Wonderworld* series is:

    a admiring

    b strange

    c unimpressed.

6 We know the *Wonderworld* series is very popular at his school because:

    a students have bought the original artwork

    b many students are waiting for a copy

    c students want to buy sets of the *Wonderworld* series.

7 Carlos updates his blog on a regular basis because:

    a he does not want to disappoint his regular readers

    b he has free time in the evening and at lunchtime

    c he always has fresh news to share with users.

8 His advice for those who want to write a blog is to:

    a have an attractive visual presentation

    b make it enjoyable for readers

    c have good grammar and spelling.

ADVICE FOR SUCCESS

The Advice for Success section is for **you** to **help yourself**. Mark the Advice for Success according to whether the suggestions are a top priority for you, or interesting but not a top priority. You can adapt an idea in Advice for Success to make it fun for you. Keeping track with a notebook is a good idea as seen in the table below.

See point **6** for an example of how to improve your English outside the classroom.

1 Use a special combination of visual recall (look, say, cover, write, check method), speech sounds, spelling patterns and spelling rules to **learn new spellings**.

2 When you learn a language, it helps to have a good memory. **Improve your memory** by:

- highlighting key ideas.
- studying new vocabulary regularly and memorising it.
- reading through your class notes frequently.
- drawing pictures to illustrate words or concepts
- linking new words to words you already know.
- using new words and phrases in your speech and writing.
- learning something by heart because it means something special to you (e.g. a poem or pop song).

3 Find time each week to **organise your course notes**, to make it easy to find work from previous lessons. The work you do builds on what you have done before. This means you'll often have to look back at notes you made earlier.

4 **Draft your written work** two or three times. If you can't think of what to write, get something down on paper anyway. Show your written work to a friend. Listen to advice about improvements you could make.

5 Be prepared to work in groups and to be an active participant, but take responsibility for working alone at times too.

6 Practising your English outside class will help your progress. Here are some ways to do this:

- Get an English-speaking penfriend.
- Watch or listen to English programmes, films, videos, pop songs, video-sharing sites, etc.
- Make an arrangement with a friend who also wants to learn English, and practise speaking together once or twice a week.
- Read widely in English: books, magazines, newspapers, websites, blogs etc.

Exam techniques

7 When you **describe a person**, remember that a physical description is not usually enough to fully answer the question. You may also have to describe character and give reasons, examples and evidence to support your views.

Fun things to do	Method	Dates I did this
Practise English outside class.	Find a song on a video-sharing site with lyrics (song words) turned on. Listen to it lots!	22 Sept 24 Sept
Practise English outside class– higher level.	Listen to a song with friend again. Try to sing along with lyrics turned off! Turn the lyrics back on.	7 Jan 14 Jan
Watch an English film.	Find my favourite film on the internet. Watch it with a friend this weekend.	10 Nov 1 Dec 15 Jan
Watch an English film– higher level	Ask a friend to watch a film with me. Freeze a frame. Try to speak the words as if we were the characters in film!	2 March 12 March 5 April 3 May

Exam focus

This unit has helped to prepare you for exams which text your reading, writing, listening and speaking skills. The unit has helped to develop those skills in the following ways:

- You have produced **answers** on **detailed reading texts**, **made notes** and used them to write **connected paragraphs**.
- You have **listened** to two **radio interviews** and answered **multiple-choice questions**.

- You have learnt skills and language structures for **writing emails** and **articles in which you describe a person's appearance and qualities**.
- You have developed skills for **informal conversations** and more **formal discussions**.

Quiz scores

Unit 1, exercise 1: Are you living the life you want?

Mostly As

To be happy you've first got to do something! You can't just sit there and wait for happiness to come to you. You're spending too much time trying to stop anything from going wrong. Take a few risks, try some new things and see what happens.

Mostly Bs

Congratulations! You're probably as happy as a person can be. You've a strong sense of what you want, and you're prepared to live in a way that suits you, even though it may be unfashionable or present the wrong image. You try to strike a fair balance between your needs and those of others. You're at home with yourself, know your strengths and limitations and don't allow your failures or the failures of others to get you down.

Mostly Cs

You are trying hard to achieve happiness. What you don't realise is that happiness isn't an achievement but an attitude. You're trying to do what you think will make you happy but you may be disappointed because you're taking your values from outside. You often feel guilty about what you think you have done wrong. Try being more tolerant of yourself and of others.

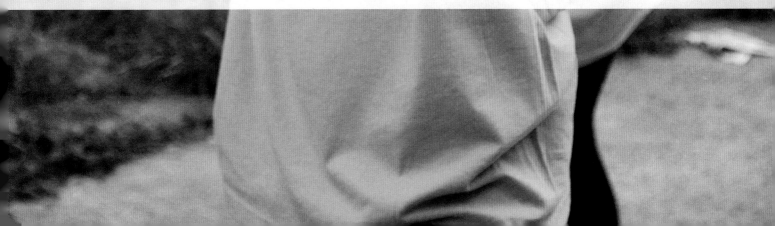

Unit 2
You and your community

In this unit you will:

- read about a scientist's new life in the US and a woman who started a charity
- understand the main ideas, opinions and attitudes in a text
- write an email welcoming an overseas guest
- listen to a discussion about helping local teenagers
- practise communicating effectively while persuading someone and showing enthusiasm
- focus on the following assessment objectives: R2, W3, W5, L1, S1

A Home town

1 Interview: introduction

The 'Home Town' website celebrates where we come from and where we live. It was set up to find out what home means to people.

Imagine that you write for or are being interviewed by the site. You will need to divide into two groups: Group A (Journalists) and Group B (Interviewees).

2 Group A: journalists

You are going to interview one of your classmates about their home town and family life.

Ask your interviewee for personal anecdotes, their opinions and attitudes.

Select any points you would like to raise in the interview.

Neighbourhood and home life

- [ ] some good points about the neighbourhood and its atmosphere
- [ ] a favourite family activity
- [ ] a happy family memory
- [ ] a special quality of his/her parents
- [ ] a value he/she has learnt from his/her family.

Personal information

- [ ] his/her pet hates
- [ ] a challenge or problem he/she is proud of overcoming
- [ ] the strangest experience he/she has ever had
- [ ] his/her personal goals.

What else would you like to find out? Add any other points to the lists.

Being flexible

Have alternative questions prepared in case your interviewee doesn't answer the first questions you ask him/her.

Examples:
How does your family usually celebrate holidays / religious festivals / other special occasions?
What are your brothers and sisters like? What do you quarrel about?
Tell me about your own bad habits (!)

If your interviewee has left home, change your questions to the past tense. Or your interviewee may prefer to talk about his/her life now. Let him/her decide.

Getting good descriptions

Remember to use open questions.

Examples:
What is/are your … like?
What do you … about …?
How do/does …?
Tell me about …
Tell me more about …

Explore the answers you get by asking (e.g. *Why, In what way?*)

3 Group B: interviewees

Before being interviewed, spend a few quiet minutes thinking about your home life. Visualise the street you live in, your house, your family; things you enjoy doing at home, what you like about where you live. If you have moved away from your home town, you can talk about the way you live now. You decide.

Dealing with personal questions

You have the right to avoid answering a question if you prefer. You can say things like:

That's personal. I'd rather not say, if you don't mind.

or

I can't answer that.

Being flexible

If you are flexible when answering questions, it will help the interviewer. For example, you can say: *I'd rather not answer that but I can tell you about my ….*

You can adapt a question by saying:

I'm afraid I don't know much about that, but I can tell you about my ….

Getting more time

If you need more time to think, you can say:

Let me think about that for a moment.

or

Well, let me see.

4 Honest feedback

Did you both feel the interview was successful? Why/Why not?

Remember, interviewing and being interviewed are real skills which even professionals have to develop. Don't be afraid to say what you would change next time round.

After the feedback, it is useful to record your decisions like this:

Next time I take part in an interview, I'll …

5 Reading

You are going to read about Chris Brown, a biochemist from England, who now lives in Seattle on America's Pacific coast.

As you read, number the following events in the order in which they happened.

a He went cycling around Leyland.

b He studied at university.

c He worked at a cancer research centre.

d He learnt more about fishing from his uncle.

e He got a job with a pharmaceuticals company.

f He went to live in the United States.

●●●

Home town

What does home mean for you?

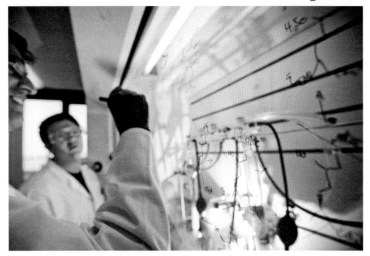

British research scientist Dr Chris Brown on his new life in America and what he misses about home.

Chris lives a long way away from the small terraced house in Leyland, in the north-west of England, where he grew up – thousands of miles away, in fact. He now lives in the vibrant city of Seattle, where he works as a biochemist in a pharmaceuticals company. Like many newcomers, Chris still misses his home town.

Chris says, 'Even though there is so much I love about America, I still miss seeing my family and friends back home. I Skype my parents every weekend – it's a good way to keep in touch. My parents are very sociable. When I Skype Mum and Dad, I'll often have a word with a friend who has just dropped in for a bite to eat.'

Happy memories

In his mind, Leyland stands for the carefree days of his childhood. He remembers playing with his sister and other children in the street after school. And he recalls sunny afternoons in the local park, building dens in the woods or fishing with a child's fishing rod in a muddy river:

'I was quite adventurous from a young age. I loved exploring the surrounding countryside on my bike. I was never really sporty, though, and didn't mind being alone sometimes, which is maybe why I've always liked fishing. One summer, when I was 16, I was allowed to travel to Ireland on the ferry on my own, to stay with my Uncle Pete. He

25

Home town

lived near a lake and took me out fishing in a rowing boat. It was magical to be on water that was like polished glass. The only sounds to be heard were the birds calling to one another. He taught me a lot too – you have to be patient, for example, to be a good angler, and have the right equipment as well.'

Starting a new life

'After I finished my postgraduate studies, I applied for a job at a cutting-edge cancer research centre here in Seattle, which has an international reputation for finding fantastic new treatments for cancer. Amazingly, I got it! But it was hard at first to get used to a new culture. Life in America was more different from England than I'd expected. People found my British accent amusing, which was a surprise. I'm always being asked to repeat things I've said, but it isn't rudeness – they're just being curious. My work here has worked out well, but I still feel homesick at times for the little things, like my mum's home-made Irish stew.

'When I was feeling low, my parents always encouraged me to give it time, not to give up. My mum left Ireland when she was a teenager to train as a nurse, and my dad left school at 14 to work in a factory, although he got more qualifications later. They persevered to achieve what they wanted, but they really love having fun and enjoying themselves, too.

'Gradually, I've made good friends here in Seattle. I have inspiring work colleagues who have mentored me. In my neighborhood*, the warmth of the people reminds me of home. They invite me round for barbecues or on hiking trips – they've been really kind.'

It's not all work

'I've lived in Seattle for nearly two years now and I've recently moved to a new job with even better career prospects and research opportunities. Seattle is also a great city for the arts, which I love, and for the outdoors. There are fascinating exhibitions and concerts right on my doorstep. If I want fresh air, I can be out of the city in no time, doing my favorite* hobby – hiking in the foothills of Mount Rainier!

'Will I live permanently in Seattle? Well, I'm considering it, but it's still early days. I'm not absolutely sure yet.'

* US spelling

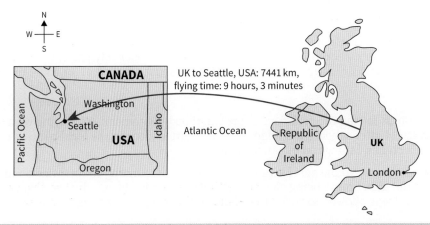

6 Discussion

In general, what do you think of the journalist's interview skills? Have you gained insight into what influenced Chris and the decisions he has made in his life? Why/Why not?

7 Detailed comprehension

Use skimming, scanning and detailed reading techniques to answer these questions.

1 What evidence is there that Chris enjoyed being independent when he was younger? Give **two** details.

2 People in Seattle find Chris's accent strange, but he does not mind having to repeat himself. What does this tell us about his personality? Give **two** details.

3 Choose the best summary of Chris's current relationship with his parents:

   a He is close to them but is able to live his own life.

   b He relies heavily on them for emotional support.

   c He feels contacting them is a duty, not a pleasure.

4 Which statement best expresses Chris's view of his leisure opportunities?

   a He has no time to get outside the city to enjoy nature.

   b The mix of indoor and outdoor activities suits him well.

   c Hiking in the mountains is his preferred way to relax.

5 How would you describe the tone of Chris's response to the interviewer?

   a He sounds enthusiastic and positive – he is enjoying his new experiences.

   b He sounds neutral – he does not mind where he lives or works.

   c He sounds disappointed – America has not met his expectations.

   Give **one** or **two** details from the text to support your choice.

6 How far, according to the map, did Chris travel when he came to the USA?

   a In which direction did he travel, east or west?

   b Over which ocean did his route take him?

   c What are the major cities near Seattle?

   d Where is Ireland in relation to England?

7 What were the benefits to Chris's career of his move to Seattle?

   A Make at least four brief points.

   B Now write a paragraph of about 40 words based on your points. Write in full sentences. Try to use logical connectors to make your paragraph flow.

Vocabulary

Find words in the text that mean the same as:

a drugs, medicines

b without worries

c small shelters made of branches and leaves

d a boat that takes passengers across a river, lake or sea

e a person who fishes for a hobby

f very modern

g unhappy because you are living away from home

h didn't give up

i advised, guided

j the countryside and nature.

8 Describing Chris

From what Chris says, what kind of person do you think he is? Choose the appropriate adjectives, checking in a dictionary if necessary.

VOCABULARY		
thoughtful	courageous	adventurous
academic	sociable	curious
lazy	sporty	impatient
open-minded		

9 Describing Chris's friends and family

Look at the adjectives in the box. Can you match the adjectives that have a similar meaning? Use a dictionary to check the meaning of any unfamiliar words. When you have matched the words, decide why they can all be used to describe Chris's family and friends. Look for clues in the text.

lively	down-to-Earth	supportive
close-knit	ordinary	dynamic
active	welcoming	fun-loving
hospitable		

10 Colloquial words and phrases

Chris uses some colloquialisms (informal words and expressions). You can often guess their meaning by analysing the context in which they are used. For example, he says that 'I'll often *have a word* with a friend who has just *dropped in for a bite to eat*.'

Do you think *have a word* is likely to mean a formal conversation or a friendly chat? Has someone who has *dropped in* arranged the visit in advance? Would you expect *a bite to eat* to be a large meal or a snack?

Match these colloquialisms from the text with the more formal expressions.

1	the little things	**A**	too soon to know
2	on my doorstep	**B**	very quickly
3	in no time	**C**	matters that are small but significant
4	early days	**D**	very near to where I live

11 Translation

What colloquialisms do you use in your own language? Can you think of any direct equivalents in your language for the colloquial expressions in the text in exercise 10?

12 Discussion

A Chris describes his parents in this way: '*They persevered to achieve what they wanted, but they really love having fun and enjoying themselves too.*' Could Chris himself be described like this? Why/Why not? How far do you think children acquire their parents' characteristics?

B Chris attributes a lot of his present success to his close-knit family. How far do you think early family life influences your chances of success later on? Apart from your family, where else can you find support and encouragement to help you achieve your goals?

C What do you think of Chris? Do you admire him? Why/Why not? In your own culture, can you think of someone you find inspiring? Share your ideas with your partner.

13 Idioms

Can you work out the meaning of the following common sayings about family life from their context?

1 I gave the job to my nephew rather than my neighbour's boy. After all, *blood is thicker than water*.

2 She gave the police evidence against him, even though he was *her own flesh and blood*.

3 When we lost all our money in business, we felt lucky that we had still got *a roof over our heads*.

B Favourite places

1 Discussion

Most of us have places that we especially like to visit. When you want relaxation and pleasure, where do you go? Do you head for wide, open spaces? Or, do you prefer urban environments?

2 Reading and vocabulary

Readers of a student website were asked to write about their favourite places.

Read about the way one student likes to spend her time. What does she do? Does the place sound inviting? Would you like to go there? Why/Why not?

When I've got some free time, I love visiting our local market. It's a large, outdoor market by the seafront. It's always busy. Even if I'm not going to buy anything, I really like the atmosphere, people of all ages and the cheerful sounds of stallholders calling to each other.

I'm usually tempted by the brightly coloured fruit, displayed so carefully, and impressed by the gorgeous cloth on sale. As the market is quite near the seafront, you can't escape the strong, fishy odours that mix with the smells of herbs, plants and vegetables. There's a secondhand stall I browse through, too, unable to resist the chance of finding something valuable. I once bought a wonderful old Chinese candlestick for just 50 cents! When I'm at the market I forget all about my everyday problems. I just relax, unwind and enjoy the sights and scenes around me.

Read the text again and underline the descriptive phrases. Then group them according to:

- Size and location.
- Atmosphere.
- Smells.
- Sounds.
- Colours.
- Emotions.
- Opinions.

3 Writing

Now close your eyes and imagine yourself in a favourite place of your own. Are you alone, or with family or friends? What are you doing? Take in all the sights, colours, sounds and smells of the place. Think about the way you feel when you go there.

When you're ready, try to write down your ideas on paper. Be prepared to make one or two drafts before you get the description just right. Use a dictionary to help. Don't forget to explain why this is one of your favourite places.

Descriptive phrases

To help complete your writing, choose from the descriptive words and phrases here. Check with a dictionary that the words you have chosen are appropriate for what you are describing.

Smells
sweet   fresh   smoky

Sounds
*cheerful sound of talk and laughter   peaceful
not a sound   noisy   silent   sound of birds calling*

Colours
colourful   bright   shining   rich   gorgeous   soft

Atmosphere
*tranquil   safe   warm and friendly   lively   cosy
comfortable   appealing   relaxing   brightly lit
mysterious*

Where is it?
*off the beaten track   right in the centre of town
only five minutes away   isolated
hard to get to but worth the effort*

Expressing feelings
When I'm there I …

*… feel close to my family or friends / like the solitude /
enjoy my own company.
… relax and unwind / forget my everyday problems.
… feel excited/happy/secure.
… experience the beauty of nature / enjoy the wonderful
things people have created.*

4 Reading aloud

Without writing your name on the paper, drop what you have written into a box. The papers can then be shuffled and you can take turns in selecting one and reading it aloud to your group.

5 Showing enthusiasm 🔊 CD 1, Track 4

Listen to the following descriptions of places. Notice how the most important words that show strong, definite feelings are stressed.

1 What an **amazing** place! It would make a **great** change from life in the city.

2 What a **lovely** place! I'm sure I'd appreciate the special **atmosphere**.

3 What **fun**! It would be a **superb** place to relax on holiday.

29

4 How **fascinating**! My friends and I **love** wildlife. We **must** go there.

5 How **interesting**! Now I'll see it through **new eyes**!

Practise saying the sentences to your partner. Make sure you sound enthusiastic. Stress the important words that show your attitude.

6 Order of adjectives

When adjectives are put before a noun, they follow a particular order:

opinion, size, age, colour, origin, material, purpose

Look at this sentence from the text in exercise 2:

*I once bought a **wonderful old Chinese** candlestick for just 50 cents!*

Opinion goes before age and age goes before origin.

Put the following adjectives into the correct order. Use the information above to help you.

1 I've lost a bag. *(sports canvas red)*

2 We stayed in a house. *(three-bedroomed Swedish beautiful)*

3 The new boss is a woman. *(friendly Egyptian middle-aged)*

4 I want to buy a jacket. *(leather good-quality black)*

5 I've bought a coat. *(warm winter woollen)*

6 Thieves stole a teapot. *(oriental silver priceless)*

7 Kieran got a case for her new tablet. *(inexpensive grey smart)*

7 Developing your writing style

Using too many adjectives before a noun is confusing. Three is usually enough. You can 'break up' a long description by adding a clause instead.

Examples:

1 Adjectives + noun + **with** (extra details):

*He decided to wear a cool white cotton shirt **with short sleeves**.*

2 Adjectives + noun + **made of** (material):

*He was wearing an amazing, long, purple cloak **made of velvet and silk**.*

(Note that commas are sometimes used between adjectives in longer sequences.)

3 Adjective + noun + **which** (a variety of information):

*She was wearing an Italian gold watch, **which looked very expensive**.*

*He has a reliable old scooter, **which he doesn't mind lending to people**.*

Practice

Combine each group of sentences into one longer sentence. Use the correct adjective order and a clause where appropriate. When you've finished, compare your answers with a partner's.

1 He gave her a box. The box was made of wood. It had a picture of a famous story on the lid. It was Russian. It was an unusual box.

2 She was wearing a brown suit. It was wool. It looked too warm for the weather.

3 The television is portable. It's white. It's Japanese. It has 100 channels.

4 It's a frying pan. It's copper. It's heavy. It's French. It has a lid.

5 Someone's taken my mug. It has my name on it. It's blue. It's a ceramic mug. It's used for coffee.

6 He has lost a coat. It's polyester. It's a school coat. It has his name on the inside.

7 Rosanna decided to wear a long dress. It was green and white. It was made of silk. She had bought it in America.

C Improving your neighbourhood
1 Discussion

A Have you ever campaigned to make your neighbourhood a better place to live in? What did you do? Were you successful? How proud do you feel of your achievement?

B How would you like to improve your neighbourhood for teenagers? Discuss your ideas in your groups.

2 Before you listen: Vocabulary check

You are going to listen to a discussion between two officials, John and Pamela, about the best way to convert a disused warehouse for the benefit of local teenagers.

Before you listen, make sure you know the meaning of these words and phrases:

VOCABULARY		
maintenance	voluntary	drain on resources
budget	wear and tear	premises
facilities		

3 Listening for gist 🔊 CD 1, Track 5

Listen to the conversation for general meaning first, and find answers to the three questions.

1 What facility does the woman want?
2 What facility does the man want?
3 What does Pamela say that shows she is changing her mind?

4 Detailed listening 🔊 CD 1, Track 5

Now listen for detail and choose the correct ending for each statement.

1 Pamela has already:
 a thrown away inappropriate applications
 b decided which applications are worth considering
 c contacted people whose ideas she preferred.

2 Pamela feels a study centre would:
 a be inexpensive to operate
 b be cheap to run but unpopular
 c only be used at weekends.

3 John thinks the public library is:
 a very popular with students
 b very busy but well-staffed
 c well-resourced and efficient.

4 Pamela believes leaving school with good qualifications is:
 a more important for teenagers than good social facilities
 b a guarantee of entry to a good job or further study
 c less relevant for modern teenagers than it was in the past.

5 John thinks a youth club would be:
 a a place where all students could make friends
 b fair to both academic and less academic students
 c a way to help teenagers prepare well for the future.

6 John mentions the way teenagers raised money for charity in order to show:
 a that they are capable of good behaviour and self-discipline
 b that they are capable of understanding the needs of disabled people
 c that they are capable of obeying the instructions given by a supervisor.

7 John thinks it would be possible to pay a supervisor a salary for:
 a more than one year
 b six or seven months
 c up to one year.

8 Pamela agrees to the youth club because:
 a so many local people want one
 b she knows a capable supervisor will be in charge
 c there have been so many teenage tragedies.

5 Follow-up

In general, whose views do you sympathise with – John's or Pamela's? Why?

Inference

When we use inference, we draw a conclusion based on the information we have, even if the information is incomplete or not directly stated.

Look back at question 3 in the previous exercise. You had to use **inference** to answer it correctly. Why? Try to explain your thinking.

More about inference

We are told that Pamela and John are 'officials' but do not know any more than that. We could infer more information from how they talk to each other.

31

Which statement do you think best expresses their working relationship?

a   John is Pamela's boss.

b   Pamela is John's boss.

c   They are both on equal terms.

Try to explain your choice, by referring to details you heard.

Idioms

People sometimes say: *I'm digging my heels in* or *I'm sticking to my guns* when they refuse to change their minds, despite pressure. Could these idioms be applied to John or Pamela? Why?/Why not?

6 Persuading: Stress and intonation 🔊 CD 1, Track 5

In their discussion, John and Pamela use the following polite phrases to persuade each other to listen to their point-of-view. Listen again and make a note of each one as you hear it. Notice how the words in **bold** letters are stressed. Do the phrases generally have a rising or a falling pattern?

☐ Do you **really** think it's a good idea …?

☐ (That) sounds all right in **theory**, but in **practice** …

☐ I take your **point**, **but** …

☐ (That's) all very well, **but** …

☐ That's true, **but** …

☐ Look at it **this** way …

Practise saying these phrases aloud to each other. How could you complete each one?

7 Role play: Spend, spend, spend

Your family has won $20 000 in a competition. You all took part in the competition, so you're having a family conference to discuss how to spend the money.

In groups of three or four, choose from the roles below. Your aim is to persuade the family that your ideas for spending the money are best. Use the phrases from exercise 6 to show you're listening to what they have to say, but that you want to express a different opinion.

Mum

You think it is important to spend the money on something sensible and practical, which will bring lasting benefits.

You want to spend it on new furniture, curtains, carpets and a new washing machine.

Dad

You want to save the money for the future. Eventually, the family will need money to move house, for the children's education or for retirement. It is silly to rush into spending the money without being sure of the best way to use it. A good investment account will earn high interest on the savings, so the money will be worth more in the future.

Daughter

You want the family to build a swimming pool in the garden. There is no swimming pool near your home and you are a keen swimmer. It would be a good way for the whole family to get exercise and to cool off after school/work in the summer.

Son

You think the money should be used for an exciting holiday of a lifetime that would be impossible to afford otherwise. You want the family to have a safari holiday in Kenya. You've always wanted to see wildlife in its own habitat, and everyone would learn so much from it.

D Making a difference

1 Pre-reading discussion

Some people can't stand the idea of going into hospital, even if they need treatment. Why do you think this might be?

Have you ever visited a friend in hospital? Did you bring a gift? What was it?

How did your friend feel about being in hospital?

What did you notice about the hospital atmosphere? Did the patients seem relaxed and comforted? Share your ideas with your group.

2 Reading for gist

You are going to read about Dolores who has worked to improve the experience of teenagers and children having treatment at her local hospital.

Read the article for general meaning. Has Dolores been successful?

The woman who put comfort into caring

Discovering a need

Dolores Albertino is proof that sometimes finding yourself in the wrong job can have wonderful consequences. Several years ago, the former
5 nurse and mother of two teenage sons returned to work at her local community hospital, but this time as a receptionist. 'The trouble is I was absolutely rubbish at the job,' says Dolores with a smile. Phones went unanswered, and she never
10 did master the computer, but that was because she spent time away from her desk chatting to and comforting the parents of sick children and the children themselves. 'I found it very frustrating that a child would ask for a simple thing, such as
15 ice cream, but because it was not meal time, they could not have it. I also knew that the families could benefit from meeting each other but, because of confidentiality, I could not pass on anyone's details.'

20 ### Making it happen

Dolores had never imagined starting a charity, but when she spoke to one of the doctors about these problems, he offered to help. He suggested putting together a plan and said he would support her. She
25 got the help of two families whose children were ill and they spent hours sitting around her kitchen table filling in charity forms. 'It was incredibly hard work, but I've never regretted it,' she says. To date, Dolores, the 'hopeless' receptionist, has
30 raised millions of dollars. 'I am very practical,' she says. 'I rolled up my sleeves and made it happen.' She believes the key reason the charity has been successful is that 'Everyone knows where every penny is going. The money does not disappear into one big pot.' 35

A nice place to be

Since the project began, the atmosphere of the children's unit has changed beyond recognition. Children asked for a place to play outdoors so Dolores developed a neglected area in the hospital grounds 40 and transformed it into a beautiful garden and play space. After children said that they didn't like walking down the sterile corridor to the ward, the corridor was given a makeover, too, with magical mosaics designed by the patients. There is now a common room for 45 teenagers, equipped with trendy furniture, internet access and a fridge full of snacks and fresh juices.

Parents, who are often very apprehensive when their children develop a health problem, were not forgotten either. The formerly drab ward 50

kitchen has been spruced up and parents can help themselves to coffee, tea, chocolate biscuits and crisps. Dolores also organises family liaison groups so parents can give each other mutual support. 'The
55 children need their parents or grandparents to be rocks – you see them looking into their eyes for help and support.' The whole community has worked to make the dream come true. Getting local schools to raise funds has been surprisingly easy. The
60 community has also pulled together by organising street parties, sponsored walks, sky dives, car washes, picnics and concerts. Joanna, the mother of 16-year-old Antoine, who is receiving treatment

at the hospital, says, 'Dolores is not working to a template. You see her listening, talking to the 65 medics and getting on with it. The charity brings comfort and much-needed fun to the children's unit. Everyone benefits.'

It's all worthwhile
Seeing her work spread nationwide is Dolores's dream. 'People everywhere will donate when 70 they can see good results. Coping with illness is a challenge, but children should not feel as if they are being punished because a doctor is sending them to hospital.'

3 Vocabulary

Match these words from the text with their definitions.

1	confidentiality	A	managing to deal with a difficult situation
2	neglected	B	treated harshly for doing something wrong
3	sterile	C	clinical, not homely
4	apprehensive	D	dull, lacking colour
5	drab	E	nervous, worried
6	template	F	not passing on private information
7	coping	G	ignored, lacking necessary attention
8	punished	H	a pattern to follow
9	spruced up	I	to make a place clean and fresh

Can you guess the meaning of the words *ward* (line 47) and *liaison* (line 50) from the contexts?

4 Post-reading discussion

Share your views on the following questions in your groups.

Tone

How do you think people reading the magazine article would feel at the end? Would they feel:

a saddened (It is depressing to think of children having health problems.)

or

b positive? (The story is an example of human kindness and strength of purpose.)

Author's main aim

Do you think the MAIN aim of the article is to:

a explain how to develop medical techniques for treating children?

b tell the reader what caring for sick children is like from a nurse's viewpoint?

c explain why sick children and their families need comfort, and how to achieve this?

d convey the viewpoints of everyone involved in caring for sick children?

Structure

Which is the best description of the structure of the article?

a It is a mixture of long and short sentences. There are several short paragraphs as well as long ones.

b The sentences are mainly long and complex. The article is composed of a few long paragraphs.

Style

Is the style chatty, technical, formal or neutral?

5 Comprehension check

1 What evidence is there that Dolores was not effective as a receptionist? Give **two** examples.

2 Why did Dolores want to make changes at the children's unit? Give **two** details.

3 How has she helped the children and teenagers? Give **two** details.

4 How has she helped parents? Give **two** examples.

5 What have schools and the local community done to help? Give **two** examples.

6 In about 70 words, describe Dolores's attitude and say why she has been successful at fundraising.

6 Further discussion

A Dolores says children and teenagers need the support of their families when they are ill. Do you think support from their friends is just as important as family support?

B Dolores has raised money to make a stay in hospital more comforting for patients and their families. Some people might say the money would be better spent on the latest medical technology, not a play space or furniture. What are your views?

C Have you ever taken part in fundraising for charity? Explain what you did and why. If you have not taken part in fundraising, would you consider doing so? What sort of charity would you choose to support? Discuss your ideas in your groups.

D Some people claim that money for health care should be provided by the government and not by charities. What are the advantages and disadvantages of using charities to support health care?

7 Colloquial language in context

With a partner, study these colloquial expressions from the text. Try to work out their meaning from the context.

1 I was *absolutely rubbish* at the job.

2 I *rolled up my sleeves* and made it happen.

3 The money does not disappear into *one big pot*.

4 The corridor has been given *a makeover*.

5 The children need their parents, or grandparents, to be *rocks*.

Try to find another colloquialism in the text and decide on its meaning.

8 Spelling: Doubling consonants when adding suffixes

Suffixes are word endings, such as:

-ed   -ing   -er   -est   -ish   -y   -able

Adding a suffix can change a verb tense, make a comparative or superlative form and change nouns into adjectives.

Look at these verbs from the magazine article with their endings:

*sit**ting**   chat**ting**   meet**ing**   work**ed**   send**ing***

Notice how the final consonant of *sit* and *chat* has been doubled, but not those in the other verbs. Can you say why?

The rule for adding suffixes to one-syllable words is:

double the final consonant if the word ends in one vowel + one consonant.

Examples:

cut	cutting
sun	sunny
spot	spotty
red	reddish
big	bigger
wet	wetter

Exceptions are one-syllable words which end with **w**, **x** or **y**.

Examples:

buy	buying
few	fewer
box	boxing

We do NOT double the consonant if a one-syllable word ends in either two vowels + one consonant, or one vowel + two consonants.

Examples:

n**ee**d	needing	needed	
w**ai**t	waiting	waited	
ada**pt**	adapting	adapted	adaptable
dou**bt**	doubting	doubted	
ta**lk**	talking	talked	

Practice

Look carefully at the one-syllable words in the sentences below. Check the pattern of the ending (one vowel + one consonant, one vowel + two consonants, or two vowels + one consonant). Add suitable suffixes to complete the words, doubling the final consonant where necessary.

1 When I arrived home I could hear the phone ring _____.

2 Yesterday was the hot _____ day of the year.

35

3 Ibrahim has stop _____ smoking.

4 We really enjoy _____ our day out yesterday.

5 That's the sad _____ news I have ever heard.

6 Let's visit the new shop _____ centre.

7 Stop chat _____ and do some work!

8 The baby is already walk _____.

9 We are send _____ our son to boarding school.

10 I bought these apples because they were much cheap _____ than the other ones.

11 Zena got tired of wait _____ and left.

12 He is always ask _____ for money.

13 Don't go look _____ for trouble.

14 Our school has a new swim _____ pool.

9 Adding suffixes to multi-syllable words

There are some longer words in the article, which double the final consonant when adding a suffix:

*Forgot**ten***   *regret**ted***

Others do not: *offer**ed***   *listen**ing***

Do you know why?

The rule for adding suffixes to words of two or more syllables is:

double the final consonant if the last syllable is stressed and it ends in one vowel and one consonant.

Examples:

*for**get***	*for**getting***	*for**gotten***
*pre**fer***	*pre**ferring***	*pre**ferred***

So, we do NOT double the final consonant if the stress is on the first syllable:

***off**er*	***off**ering*	***off**ered*
***list**en*	***list**ening*	***list**ened*

Or if the last syllable contains TWO vowels before the consonant, or one vowel and two consonants:

*expl**ai**n*	*expl**ai**ned*
*retu**r**n*	*retu**r**ned*

Practice

Add suitable suffixes to complete the words in these sentences, doubling the final consonant if necessary.

1 Theo regret _____ leaving his job, but it was too late.

2 Smoking is not permit _____.

3 The accident occur _____ last night in thick fog.

4 I reason _____ with him about his aggressive behaviour.

5 He has commit _____ a serious crime.

6 The earthquake happen _____ in the evening.

7 She explain _____ the begin _____ of the story to them.

8 I've always prefer _____ travelling by train.

10 Look, say, cover, write, check

Understanding how grammar and pronunciation work helps you understand English spelling. Learn these commonly misspelt words through the 'look, say, cover, write, check' method. Ask a friend to test you when you are confident you have learnt them correctly.

VOCABULARY		
beginning	swimming	travelled
preferred	shopping	dropped
occurred	happening	development
occurrence	happened	permitted

11 Words from different languages

Liaison is a French word that has come into English. English has a fascinating history of borrowing words from a vast number of languages. Many words came from invaders, colonisers, migrants and international trade.

With your partner, try to match the common 'loan' words in the box below with their language of origin. Use a dictionary to check the meaning of unfamiliar words.

VOCABULARY

athlete	bungalow	patio
tea	caravan	villa
cuisine	chocolate	ski
sofa	opera	karate

- Arabic
- Aztec
- Chinese
- French
- Greek
- Hindi
- Italian
- Japanese
- Latin
- Norwegian
- Persian
- Spanish

Can you guess why the word might have come from that language? Think about the climate, way of life, food, etc.

Check your pronunciation of the words with your partner. Finally, use each word in a sentence of your own.

Comparing languages

What English words do you use in your own language? What words in your language come from other languages? Share your knowledge with your group.

E Welcoming an exchange visitor

1 Reassuring your guest

In order to learn more about other cultures, many young people take part in exchange visits with students of their own age. They take turns going overseas to stay with each other's families. By doing so, they improve their understanding of another culture and way of life, improve their skills in another language and have a pleasant holiday at the same time.

Imagine that your family is going to take part in an exchange visit. Your guest, who you have not met before, and who is about your age, is coming from overseas to stay with you for three weeks. How do you think he/she might be feeling? Nervous, excited, worried?

In an email, how could you put your guest at ease and make your home and your local area sound inviting? Make a few notes under the following headings.

- Positive things about my home and family
- Enjoyable things to do together
- Exciting places to visit

What aspects of your home life or area would you NOT want to draw attention to (if any)? Why?

Beginnings and endings

Below are some common phrases used to begin an end an email. Complete them using the words from the box.

it   from   forward   to   forget   for

Beginnings

a   It was great _____ get your last email.

b   Thanks _____ your email.

c   Just a quick email _____ let you know ...

Endings

d   That's _____ for now.

e   Looking _____ to hearing from you.

f   Don't _____ to email soon.

2 Example email

Now read this example email. Underline the phrases used to welcome the visitor.

New Message

To: From:

Hi Jacob,

I'm really pleased you're coming to stay with us soon. My family consists of my mum, dad and my younger sister Betty and my pet cat Rufus. We're an easy-going, ordinary family and my parents are very approachable. They let us do more or less what we like as long as we tell them about it first.

We live in a three-bedroomed house with a small front and back garden. It's about ten minutes' walk away from the town centre, which has modern shops, three cinemas, clubs and a weekly market. We also have a great new swimming pool in town, so bring your swimming things! If you enjoy history, I'll show you our museum. It has some fascinating information about the history of my town.

I've made a list of the most interesting things to do and see in the area. I heard you are keen on watching football so I've booked two tickets to see a big match while you're here. I got my driving licence last month and dad has promised to let me use the car. We can explore the countryside and perhaps even camp for a night or two. The wildlife and countryside won't be as spectacular as Kenya but it's very peaceful and we might even see some wild ponies.

I can't wait to meet you, Jacob! Have a safe journey here.

Best wishes,
William

Comprehension

1. What is William's family like?
2. What kind of environment does he live in?
3. What has he planned for Jacob's visit?

Format

1. Do you think the email sounds welcoming? Why/why not? Underline the phrases that show the writer has considered the feelings of his guest. Does he give reasons for the plans he is making? What are they?
2. Does William mention the exchange visit straight away or does he begin his email in a more indirect way? Do you think his approach is a good one? Why/Why not?
3. The email has three main paragraphs. Do the paragraphs flow into each other?
4. Underline the opening and closing sentences of the email. Are they appropriate? Why/Why not?
5. Overall, the email is fairly short. Do you get a good enough picture of what the holiday is going to be like for Jacob? Why/Why not?

3 Finding a suitable tone

In pairs, read the following sentences taken from students' emails. If you were the recipient, which would make you feel at ease? Which might worry you? Put a tick against the sentences you like and a cross against the others.

As you work, discuss how any inappropriate expressions could be made more suitable. Correct any structural errors.

1. It'll be lovely to see you.
2. We're all looking forward to meeting you.
3. The food here will be rather distasteful for you.
4. At least when you are in the house try to behave with respect to my parents.
5. You'll be very welcome.
6. My friend, you can come and enjoy it but my family is very strict.
7. You'll soon feel at home.
8. The place itself is safety, you do not need to be afraid when walking, in case of thieves.

9   I would like to tell you that my parents are very good and they don't like people who drink too much.

10 Mostly, we will visit our countryside every day because here that is the only worth visiting place.

11 Mum and Dad always listen to our problems before giving their own point-of-view.

12 My family are selfishness and want someone to do things for them but I know such a thing will not inconvenient your visit to me.

13 We're going to have a wonderful time together.

14 We can go cycling through our beautiful countryside and have great parties on the beach.

15 As I already told you, this is a very small place, so don't think about hotels, theatres, cinemas and so on.

16 We can promise you the best time of your life.

Rewriting

Choose three of the sentences above that don't sound right, and rewrite them to make a more appropriate impression. Try them out on a partner. Does he/she agree that they sound more inviting?

4 Correcting mistakes

This email is from Jacob, who is writing to thank William for his holiday. Can you find the mistakes and correct them? The mistakes are to do with:

- prepositions
- missing words
- tenses
- punctuation
- spelling
- paragraphing
- vocabulary
- articles
- grammar.

There are also two sentences in the letter that are inappropriate in tone. You'll need to rewrite them.

Finally, rewrite the whole email correctly.

Hi William,

I'm back! I am writing to you to offer you my sincere thank you. I've had a great time staying with you and you're family last week. You were all so kind to me. I've got so many good memories of the trip. Everyone were so friendly – your family, the nieghbours, all the students at the college. Tell you're mum she is the best cooker in the world! Can she came and live with us hear? I really liked your town, by the way. I think you are lucky to live there. I had such a good time – we done so many interesting things! I send you some photos of our camping trip in my noxt email? You must come and stay with us soon! Do you remember I told you that our house is near a lake? Well, Dad's just fixed the boat, witch means we can go out on the lake on it, if you like! The beaches here are great and now the summer is in the way we'll able go swimming all the time. I know how much you love that. Whenever the weather is not so good, we can go to some of the malls in a centre of town - tourists love all the shops! What do you think? Will you come and stay to us? I look forward to receiving an email from you as soon as you are able to send one.

Write soon, William!

Love,

Jacob

5 Sentence completion

Nobody has a perfect home life. But we don't want to sound too negative when talking about it. When giving someone an impression of life at home, try balancing any negative ideas with more positive ones.

Try to complete these sentences positively:

1   Even though he is a nuisance at times, my little brother …

2   Despite being too dangerous for swimming, our local river …

3   Although we're a long way from the bright lights of the city, …

4   My parents are a tiny bit strict yet …

5   You'll probably find our way of life just a little strange at first, but …

6   We don't have a perfect house, but …

Reassurance

When British people are trying to reassure someone about something, they sometimes use expressions like '*a tiny bit awkward*', '*just a little bit* difficult'. What do you say in your language?

6 Surprise party: Tone and register

You recently arranged a surprise party for your parents' wedding anniversary. You went to a lot of trouble to make the party a success. Unfortunately, your cousin was ill and unable to attend.

Which of the following would you say to your cousin? Why?

1   Where were you? Everyone expected you to come.

2   Why didn't you arrive? You should have been there.

3   It was such a shame you couldn't make it.

4   You disappointed us very much.

7 Writing

Your cousin went to live abroad with her family when she was only two or three years old. Her parents have asked if she can stay with your family for a holiday. You have never actually met before. Write an email to your cousin in which you:

- introduce yourself
- describe your family and background
- tell her about enjoyable things to do together
- describe interesting places to visit.

Write about 150 words.

8 Reordering

The following email describes a surprise party. It is written to a relative who missed the celebration. First, reorder the sentences and put them into paragraphs and then decide on the correct sequence of paragraphs. What overall impression do you think the email will make on the recipient?

○ ○ ○   New Message

To : [   ]   From: [   ]

Dear Ella,

a   As you know, Mum and Dad didn't know anything about it.

b   Just before the end, Uncle Steve let off lots of fireworks in the garden.

c   She had decorated th e house beautifully.

d   Perhaps the DVD I'm sending you of the occasion will be a little compensation.

e   However, everyone understood that you were still feeling weak after the operation.

f   So you can imagine their surprise when, instead of going to the Blue Fountain, we arrived at Auntie Susan's house.

g   Hope you feel better soon.

h   No one looked tired or seemed inclined to go early.

i   It was a great shame you couldn't come.

j   Although most of the guests must have been over 50, the party went on until the early hours.

k   Despite the fact that we all missed you, we had a lovely day.

l   This was a wonderful way to round off the occasion.

m   Once again, I know how disappointed you were not to be there.

n   Just a short email to let you know about Mum and Dad's anniversary party.

o   They assumed I was taking them to a restaurant to celebrate.

Lots of love,
Krystyna

The world's most widely spoken languages, by numbers of native speakers and as a second language, are Mandarin Chinese, English, Spanish, Hindi and Arabic.

Linguists say that more than 6000 languages exist, though some are spoken by relatively few people. Sadly, hundreds of minority languages throughout the world are dying from lack of use. In Europe, for example, Breton, Scottish Gaelic and Romani are examples of languages in danger, while Karaim, a Turkic language of Lithuania, has fewer than 50 speakers left.

Experts predict this decline will continue and that, by the year 2030, there will be fewer than 3000 languages spoken in the world.

What do you think might cause people to stop speaking a particular language?

The chart shows the numbers of languages spoken in selected African countries.

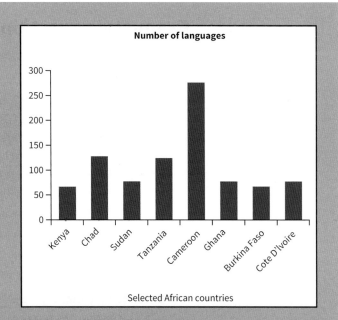

1 In which of these African countries are more than 100 languages spoken?

2 Does the information in the chart surprise you? Why/ Why not?

3 What could help preserve endangered languages?

41

GRAMMAR SPOTLIGHT

Gerund or infinitive?

A Certain verbs are followed by an **infinitive**:
*I was allowed **to travel** to Ireland.*
*I'm always being asked **to repeat** things.*
Can you find another example in paragraph 6 of the text in **section A5?**
Verbs like these include: *allow, ask, want, would like, promise, warn, remind, expect, decide, make, agree, refuse, offer, help, encourage, tend.*

B Certain verbs are followed by a **gerund** (-*ing* form):
*I didn't **mind being** alone.*
Can you find another example in paragraph 4 of the text in **section A5?**
Verbs like these include: *finish, hate, avoid, like, dislike, love, risk, imagine, deny, postpone, recall, enjoy, imagine, mind, miss, suggest.*

C There are a few verbs that can take **either** the gerund **or** the infinitive, depending on the meaning:
*He **remembers playing** with his sister.*
BUT
***Remember to take** your dictionary with you.*
Verbs like these include: *remember, forget, need, try, stop, go on.*
Discuss the difference in meaning between:
Her neighbour was in a hurry and didn't stop to talk.
Her neighbour didn't stop talking.

D The gerund is used after certain expressions, such as *can't stand, spend/waste time*:
*Some people **can't stand going** into hospital.*
*She **spent time chatting** to the parents of sick children.*

E The gerund, because it is like a noun, can be used as the subject of a sentence:
***Getting** local schools to raise funds has been easy.*
Can you find two more examples like this in the last paragraph of the text in **section D2?**

Exam-style questions

Writing

Reading & Writing, Exercise 5

1   The following note from your headteacher appears in your student e-newsletter: *Some new students will be joining us next term. They and their families are new to this area and I have decided to put together a 'Welcome pack' telling them about the school and neighbourhood. I would like to include articles about local places which you enjoy visiting. Please submit your articles by 10th December.*

Write an article aimed at the new students. In the article you should:

- describe one local place of interest
- say why you enjoy visiting it (e.g. the atmosphere, scenery.)
- explain why you think the new students will enjoy it, too.

Write about 150–200 words.

Extended [16 marks]

Reading and Writing, Exercise 5

2   You recently took part in a project to clean up your neighbourhood and improve your local park. Write an email to your friend saying what you achieved. In your email you should

- say what you enjoyed about the project
- describe how the improvements will benefit local people
- encourage your friend to get involved in a similar project.

Write about 100–150 words.

Core [12 marks]

Reading & Writing, Exercise 5

3   You recently took part in a fundraising activity in your community to raise money for charity. Write an email to a friend in which you:

- describe the aims of the charity
- explain how you raised funds for the charity
- encourage them to take part in a fundraising activity.

Write about 150–200 words.

Extended [16 marks]

Reading & Writing, Exercise 5

4   Your school recently held a Community Day, aimed at elderly people who wanted to improve their skills with computers and the internet. Write an article for your school newsletter in which you:

- describe how you helped
- explain how you think elderly people benefited from the day
- explain what you think you learnt from helping.

Write about 100–150 words.

Core [12 marks]

Speaking

1 Building a community

A community can be defined as a group of people that shares similar values and common interests. Some people say the happiest societies are built on a solid community foundation. Discuss this topic with the assessor.

You may wish to use the following ideas to help develop the conversation:

- how you feel about the community you belong to
- whether a strong community really makes people happier, more neighbourly and reduces crime
- the advantages and disadvantages of belonging to online communities
- whether some communities are restrictive and limit personal freedom
- whether globalisation has a positive or negative impact on community life.

You are free to consider any other related ideas of your own. You are not allowed to make any written notes.

2 Improving neighbourhoods

Neighbourhoods can be very diverse. While some are comfortable for residents of all ages, others lack basic amenities. There are a number of things that can be done to improve such neighbourhoods. Discuss this topic with the assessor.

You may wish to use the following ideas to help develop the conversation:

- how noise, litter or pollution could be reduced
- how places of entertainment could be developed
- whether wireless internet access in cafés and similar places would be helpful
- the value of parks and pleasant, open spaces for everyone to enjoy
- the importance of public transport facilities.

You are free to consider any other related ideas of your own. You are not allowed to make any written notes.

Listening 🔊 CD 1, Track 6

Listening, Exercise 2

You will hear a talk given by a student on a local radio programme. She is telling listeners about Riverside, the community where she lives.

Listen to the talk and complete the details below. Write **one** or **two** words only in each gap.

You will hear the interview twice.

Core [8 marks], Extended [8 marks]

Name: Neeta

Occupation: Student

(a) Family origins: ancestors came to Australia from .... in the early 20th century

Community: Riverside

Why Neeta likes living in Riverside: It has a strong sense of community.

People are friendly. When she goes shopping, even for small items **(b)** such as a .... or a loaf of bread, she always has to stop and talk with people she meets. The residents are caring. When her younger brother had an accident, **(c)** a neighbour comforted him and .... his knee.

How her family participates in community life:

Neeta belongs to an art club. **(d)** Her brother enjoys the .... and is a member of a hiking group. Her father is in an angling club. Her mother is a member of a community choir which raises money **(e)** for .... at the local hospital by giving fundraising concerts. Her grandmother keeps fit by attending a Tai Chi class and then has **(f)** tea with friends. She has known ....

Economic changes in the community

Newcomers have injected new life into Riverside, and started businesses, including a dressmaking service.

For the wedding anniversary of her parents, the dressmaker made:

(g) a .... dress for her mother and a silk shirt for her father.

Neeta believes Riverside provides:

(h) the sense of belonging that people require to feel .... and able to put down permanent roots.

Reading

Reading & Writing, Exercise 2

You are going to read a magazine article about four people sharing their ideas about a place which is special to them. For questions 1–10, tick the people A–D. The people may be chosen more than once.

Extended [10 marks].

Which person:

1   occasionally buys things?

	Person A	☐	Person B	☐
	Person C	☐	Person D	☐

2   enjoys hospitality?

	Person A	☐	Person B	☐
	Person C	☐	Person D	☐

3   has a persuasive manner?

Person A ☐   Person B ☐
Person C ☐   Person D ☐

4   likes the community associations?

Person A ☐   Person B ☐
Person C ☐   Person D ☐

5   is optimistic about the future?

Person A ☐   Person B ☐
Person C ☐   Person D ☐

6   is reluctant to leave?

Person A ☐   Person B ☐
Person C ☐   Person D ☐

7   enjoys relaxing close to nature?

Person A ☐   Person B ☐
Person C ☐   Person D ☐

8   enjoys the lack of a pressurised schedule?

Person A ☐   Person B ☐
Person C ☐   Person D ☐

9   feels guilty sometimes?

Person A ☐   Person B ☐
Person C ☐   Person D ☐

10   wears a uniform?

Person A ☐   Person B ☐
Person C ☐   Person D ☐

A   Anh

When I turn the key in the door of my shoe shop, I am in my favourite place. I stand in the middle of the shop floor for a few seconds, marvelling at the rows of stylish shoes in gorgeous colours. I used to sell my shoes in the market and I enjoyed the cheerful community atmosphere, but when I began to make a decent profit, I moved to this modern mall out of town. The mall is so good for my business. It compensates for the fact that I have to spend a long time getting there. I think some of the customers are put off by the price of the shoes, but I tell them that, though the shoes might be expensive, they cost nothing to try on! That bit of encouragement works very well and business is good! When the last customer leaves, it's time for me to go home, too, but I like to linger for a while, enjoying the tranquility that comes at the end of a good day's business.

B Roberto

My sister, Elsie, and I love going to our uncle's farm in the school holidays. We live in a small city flat so we particularly love the space and freedom on the farm. When we are there, we relax, unwind and forget all about schoolwork, busy timetables and exams. It's lovely waking up to the sound of the cows and sheep on the farm and feeling the whole day is ahead of me. I can't wait to get out of bed and get going. Even though the farm is isolated and there isn't any internet access, we find so many things to do, like riding on the quad bikes, swimming in the river or having a picnic in the woods. Sometimes we help my uncle with the farm work. Elsie loves looking after the cows, and I help with the sheep. We have delicious food, too. My aunt is a fabulous cook and fills the fridge with snacks and fresh juices and encourages us to help ourselves.

C Hayley

My favourite place is a cosy café with a roof-top terrace – not everyone knows about it. I go there at weekends and sit outside, surrounded by plants and sweet-smelling flowers, throwing a few crumbs from my cake to the birds, and enjoying the fresh air. At the café, I feel part of a simpler, more natural world. The owner is an artist and helps other local artists make a living by letting them display their paintings for sale. The pictures are of the most unspoilt places in our community, like the beaches and woods. They remind me of happy times spent collecting shells or splashing in the sea, but the pictures are too expensive for me to buy. There are some artistic cards on sale, though, and I can afford one of them from time to time. I know my friends would like the café, too, but I usually go alone and enjoy my own company for a change. I do sometimes feel it is maybe a little selfish of me not to share such an appealing place with them.

D Xing

I got my job in the Science Research Institute only a few months ago, just after leaving college, and I love it. People think a laboratory is a dull, sterile environment but to me it is a magical place, full of possibilities. As soon as I arrive, I put on my lab coat and feel very purposeful. I spend a lot of time doing experiments to develop a new kind of treatment for sick children. We have made good progress and the outcome is hopeful. If we actually developed a complete cure, it would be a dream come true. The working atmosphere in the team is warm and friendly. Some team members are much more experienced than me, but they never mind answering my questions or considering my suggestions for different ways to do things. We're not serious or working hard all the time, of course. We often stop to laugh, especially when my colleague Tim tells one of his jokes!

ADVICE FOR SUCCESS

The Advice for Success is for **you** to **help yourself**. Decide which suggestions you like best and mark them. You can adapt an idea in Advice for Success to make it fun for you. Keeping track with a notebook is a good idea.

1 Listen to people speaking English as often as you can. Notice the words they use to express their feelings in different situations (breaking bad news, making a complaint, expressing pleasure or annoyance). Also pay attention to the intonation patterns people use to show feelings. Try to imitate these patterns. By listening to radio plays and watching films and TV programmes, you will improve your ability to understand tone, register and intonation.

2 **Spelling and the grammatical system** go hand-in-hand. Understanding how words are spelt will help you understand more about grammar and vice versa. Knowledge of grammar will expand your range of strategies for word building (turning nouns into adjectives and so on) and for identifying the logic of irregular-looking spellings.

3 **Proofread** your work for mistakes. You can do this during the writing process, when you feel like a break from composing, and at the end. Use a spell-checker when proofreading. Use a dictionary, too – it is your friend. The more you use it, the quicker and more efficient with it you will become.

4 Download language-learning apps onto your smartphone. There are lots to choose from.

5 Some kinds of dictionary are a brilliant source of information about the history of the English language. Have fun browsing through a good dictionary, investigating 'borrowings' from other languages.

Exam techniques

6 Reading comprehension questions don't always have to be answered in your own words. You can answer some questions by **using words from the text**.

Exam focus

This unit has helped to prepare you for exams which test your reading, writing, listening and speaking skills. The unit has helped to develop those skills in the following ways:

- You have produced **answers** on **detailed reading** texts and **written** short **summaries**.
- You have **listened** to two **radio interviews** and **answered questions**.
- You have learnt skills and language structures for **writing detailed articles** and **emails in which you describe people's appearance and qualities**.
- You have participated in **a role play** and a variety of **discussions**.

Unit 3
Sport, fitness and health

In this unit you will:

- read about a project to help disadvantaged young people and a digital artist who changed her lifestyle
- practise writing summaries and making notes
- listen to recorded information at a sports centre
- practise stressing key words and expressing warnings directly in conversation
- focus on the following assessment objectives: R3, L1, L3, S4, S5

A Is sport always fun?

1 Note-making and summaries: Sharing ideas

In this unit you will be learning how to make notes and write summaries. To help you, the skills will be broken into small stages.

In some exercises, you will be asked to read a text, make notes on it, and then join your notes into a connected summary. Note-making practice is treated as one of the stages in learning to write a summary.

Making notes

With a partner, select the aspects of note-making you find most challenging:

- reading quickly and absorbing a lot of information
- deciding what to select from the text
- finding some words and phrases of similar meaning, where possible
- presenting notes clearly so they can be followed by someone who has not seen the original text.

In an exam, your notes don't have to be in your own words. However, it's a good idea to try to find some words and phrases of similar meaning rather than copying out chunks of texts.

Summarising

Unlike notes, summaries must be written in full sentences. In exam situations, you may have to write a summary based on the notes you completed and must use your own words wherever possible.

How difficult do you find:

- connecting ideas grammatically and in your own words?
- keeping to a strict word limit?

2 Discussion

Which sports on your school curriculum do you particularly like? Why?

3 Quiz

Work with a partner to complete the quiz about what you have learnt from doing sport at school or college. (If you've left school, look back at your experiences.)

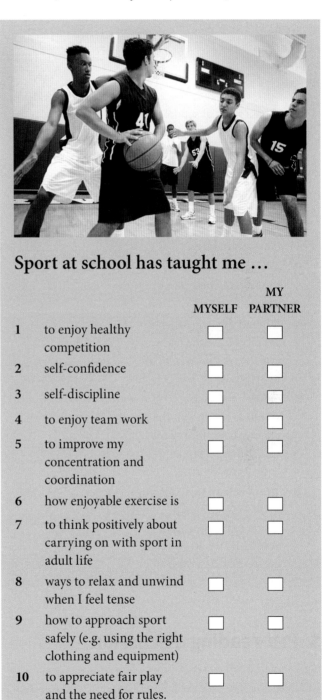

Sport at school has taught me ...

		MYSELF	MY PARTNER
1	to enjoy healthy competition	☐	☐
2	self-confidence	☐	☐
3	self-discipline	☐	☐
4	to enjoy team work	☐	☐
5	to improve my concentration and coordination	☐	☐
6	how enjoyable exercise is	☐	☐
7	to think positively about carrying on with sport in adult life	☐	☐
8	ways to relax and unwind when I feel tense	☐	☐
9	how to approach sport safely (e.g. using the right clothing and equipment)	☐	☐
10	to appreciate fair play and the need for rules.	☐	☐

4 Is sport always fun?

These comments were posted by students on a school chatroom. How far do you agree with the students' views about sport at school? Work with your partner and rank them from **0** (disagree totally) to **3** (agree completely).

		MYSELF	MY PARTNER
1	'I hate sport at school. It's so competitive and only fit children can do well.'	☐	☐
2	'I don't mind things we can do at our own pace like swimming or gymnastics, but I hate being forced to take part in races.'	☐	☐
3	'It's usually too hot or too cold to enjoy being outside.'	☐	☐
4	'I dread the time when we get picked for the team. I'm always the last one to be selected.'	☐	☐
5	'There's so much standing around on the playing field waiting for something to happen. Sport is just boring!'	☐	☐
6	'At my school we're forced to do the traditional sports our parents did. Why can't we do more up-to-date activities?	☐	☐

5 Pre-reading discussion

'Sports day' in many schools is a competitive event in which all children take part. Parents may attend to watch their children perform. Do you have a similar event in your school? Do you enjoy it? Why/Why not?

6 Predicting content

You are going to read an article in which the writer criticises the sports day at her son's primary school (a school for children aged 5–11). Pick the points you expect the writer to criticise:

- the value of the prizes
- the competitive aspect of the day
- the bad effect competitive sport has on some children
- the skills of the teachers
- her child's poor performance
- the time of year 'sports day' is held
- the fact that 'sports day' takes time away from academic subjects
- the young age of the children taking part.

7 Developing reading skills

Now read the article as fast as possible. When you read, try to absorb as much information as you can. Read easy sentences quickly and the more difficult sentences slowly. When reading, make a mental note of the key ideas in each part of the text. Think, 'How would I summarise this text in one or two sentences?'. When you read a word you don't know, either work out its meaning from context or use a dictionary. **You don't need to understand every word to understand the general meaning a text**.

8 Comprehension check

Try to answer these questions without looking at the text:

1. What symptoms do children who are afraid of sports day show?
2. Where was the 'sports day' held?
3. Why do some of the children who like running still find 'sports day' traumatic?

4 What does the writer feel for young children who are upset by 'sports day'?

5 How did the children feel about the team games played after the races?

6 What alternative to 'sports day' does the writer suggest?

One afternoon in the last week of term, I saw three children from my son's school in tears being comforted by teachers. That morning, my 11-year-old had stomach pains and had been retching into a bowl. Talking to other mothers, I heard about 5 other children with stomach ache or difficulty sleeping the night before.

What caused so much distress? Sports day – not sports day at a highly competitive independent school, but at a large village primary. For the 10 children who can fly like the wind, it causes no problem. For those who are poorly coordinated, overweight or just not good at sport, it is a nightmare. Even for those who enjoy running, but who fall halfway down the track in front of the entire 15 school and their parents, it can prove a disaster.

Why do we put our children through this annual torment? Some may say competition is character-building; or it's taking part that's important, not winning; or that it's a tradition of school life. 20 I just felt immense pity for those children in tears or in pain.

Team games at the end of the 'sports' produced some close races, enormous enthusiasm, lots of shouting – and were fun to watch. More 25 importantly, the children who were not so fast, nimble on their feet or skillful with the ball were hidden a little from everyone's gaze. Some of them also had the thrill of being on the winning side.

I wish that sports day could be abandoned and 30 replaced with some other summer event. Perhaps an afternoon of team games, with a few races for those who want them, would be less stressful for the children and a lot more fun to watch.

Finding the main ideas

Match the following main ideas to the relevant paragraphs (1–5) of the article:

A How team games produced a positive atmosphere on 'sports day'

B The reasons why sports days are still a part of school life

C An alternative to the traditional 'sports day'

D The explanation for the children's illnesses and fears

E The physical symptoms that fear of 'sports day' produces.

9 Checking predictions

How many of the points you selected in exercise 6 were mentioned in the article?

What did the writer say that you did not predict?

10 Choosing a headline

The title or headline of a text gives an idea of what the text is going to be about.

Which of these headlines do you prefer for the article you have just read? Explain your choice.

It is time that sports were banned from the school curriculum

Sports day torment

It is essential that protests are made about the unfair ways young children are treated on their school sports day

Mum *slams sports day

Sports day: How one school has upset many of its pupils

*slam = criticise severely

11 Note-making practice

Here is an exam-style note-making question, based on the article about 'sports day':

Read the newspaper article about a school sports day. Then write a set of notes based on the article, using the headings below.

- Reasons for having a sports day
- The negative effects of 'sports day'
- 'Sports day': possible improvements

Underlining relevant parts of the text

Re-read the article and underline the parts which are relevant to the question. Compare your underlined sections with your partner's. Do you both agree on what is relevant?

Making notes and checking your work

Make notes under the headings given. Use or adapt words and phrases from the text, but don't just copy out large parts of the original. You do not need to write complete sentences.

In pairs or threes, compare your notes.

1 Check the **content**:

Do you need to add anything or leave anything out? Is there any repetition?

2 Check the **language**:

Have you managed to avoid copying out large chunks of the text? Are your notes clear and concise?

3 Check the **presentation**:

Have you written the correct points under the correct headings?

12 Comparing two summaries

Summarising requires you to write in full sentences. The following two summaries, based on the article, were written by students. Analyse them by answering these questions:

1 Which summary copies directly from the text?

2 Which summary uses the student's own words as far as possible?

3 Which summary uses two linking words incorrectly?

4 The summaries have one mistake in common. What is it?

5 Which summary seems to show the best overall understanding of the text? Why?

Summary 1

Many reasons are given for having a sports day, such as the competition is character-building, or it's the taking part that is important, not the winning, or that it's a tradition of school life. Moreover, sports days can be a nightmare for those who are poorly coordinated, overweight or just not good at sport. Despite for those children who enjoy running but fall down on the track in front of the entire school it can prove a disaster. It is said that 'sports day'

should be abandoned and replaced by an afternoon of team games with a few races for those who want them but I think that would spoil a nice summer event.

Summary 2

Sports days at school are said to be valuable because they're a school custom, the competition is healthy, it develops character and the main point of the event is the enjoyment of playing. However, sports days can be traumatic, especially if the pupils are not slim, agile or capable at sport. Even the confident, athletic ones can be very upset if they fall over before a large audience. An afternoon of team games, with a few races for those who are interested, should be offered in the summer instead of 'sports day'. I believe most parents would prefer this to a competitive sports day.

B Enjoying sport safely

1 Compound nouns

Like *sports day*, many compound nouns are a combination of two nouns (or a gerund plus a noun, e.g. *running shoes*). By avoiding the need for a preposition, as in 'a day of sports' or 'shoes for running', compound nouns can help you write more concisely.

Some of these words can follow the word *sports* to make common compound nouns.

Write **sports** in the spaces as appropriate:

_____ bag		_____ equipment
_____ car		_____ hobby
_____ child		_____ instructor
_____ centre		_____ man
_____ club		_____ person
_____ drink		_____ time
_____ enjoyment	_____ woman.

Practice

Form compound nouns by writing suitable words from the box alongside these words. In each case more than one combination is possible.

swimming _____   skating _____

football _____   leisure _____

hockey _____   cricket _____

fitness _____

What other compound nouns do you know? Make a list with a partner.

VOCABULARY

match	programme	stick
bat	centre	field
costume	rink	pool
shorts	boots	shirt
players	hat	
team	trunks	

2 Pre-listening discussion

Do you ever go to a sports centre? What facilities do you use? Do you enjoy it? Why/Why not?

If you don't go to a sports centre, would you like to visit one? Why/Why not? What facilities do you think you would see there?

3 Listening to a recorded announcement 🔊 CD 1, Track 7

You are going to hear some recorded information about facilities available at a sports centre. Listen first for general meaning and try to complete the list of compound nouns, putting one word in each space:

1 open-air swimming _____
2 coin- _____ locker system
3 _____ rooms
4 _____ court
5 _____ tennis
6 cheap-rate _____
7 sports centre _____
8 application _____
9 reception _____
10 keep-fit _____ .

Now listen again and complete the diary. How much does membership of the sports centre cost?

Sports Centre Diary

Monday
A.M.   9–11 Swimming in the open-air pool
        (i)   Need _____
P.M.   (ii)   Sports centre _____

Tuesday
A.M.   10–11.30 Badminton court open
        (iii)   Bring _____
P.M.   Open for schools only

Wednesday
A.M.   9–11.30 Table tennis
        (iv)   Ask supervisor for _____
P.M.   (v)   Gym _____
        (vi)   Must wear _____

Thursday
A.M.   (vii)   Collect application form from _____
P.M.   (vii)   Senior citizens' _____

4 Marking the main stress 🔊 CD 1, Track 8

John and Ella are watching Poland and Finland play football. Ella is unsure about some things. Listen to the dialogue while you read. Why is the main stress marked in this way?

Ella: Is Poland playing in the **blue** and **green**?

John: No, Poland's playing in the **yell**ow and green.

Ella: Did you say **Fin**land was in the yellow and green?

John: No, I said **Po**land was in the yellow and green.

Ella: Is Poland playing **France** this season?

John: Poland plays France **eve**ry season.

Ella: Did Poland win a **few** of their matches last season?

John: They won **all** their matches last season!

Now practise reading the dialogue in pairs, marking the main stress as indicated. Why is a different word stressed in each answer?

Practice

With a partner, decide where the main stress falls in the following dialogue and mark it. Then practise the dialogue together.

A: Were you surprised about Kelly's behaviour on the field last night?

B: I'm never surprised about Kelly's behaviour!

A: Did you think the referee acted fairly?

B: No one thought the referee acted fairly.

A: Is anybody from your family going to see the game tomorrow?

B: Everybody's going to see the game tomorrow.

A: Do you think the match will be as exciting?

B: I don't think any match could be as exciting.

5 Analysing headlines

To save space in headlines, and to be dramatic, newspapers invent unusual word combinations, like **TRAGEDY BOAT**. Such 'compound nouns', although very creative, can be difficult to understand, especially when several nouns are strung together:

BOMB HOTEL HORROR PROBE

Underline the key words in the following newspaper report. Make sure you understand the meaning of *collision* and *compensation*.

> ### Crash woman rejects deal
> A female student, who was seriously injured when she was involved in a collision with a Kuranda bus in October, today rejected the compensation offered by Kuranda Bus Company.

How does the headline convey the key elements of the story? What compound noun is used? Do you think this is an invented compound or one in normal use?

Verb tenses

As in many headlines, the present simple tense is used. Why is this, when the report describes the rejection in the past tense?

Vocabulary

Why do you think the headline refers to *crash* and *deal*, when the report uses *collision* and *compensation*?

Articles

The report refers to **a** *collision* and **the** *compensation*. Why does the headline not use the articles?

6 Expanding headlines

Read the following headlines and answer the questions.

> ## COMA BABY HOPE: US SURGEON TO OPERATE

1   Read *coma baby hope* backwards. Does this provide clues to understanding?

2   How is the future expressed? Why?

3   Why is the colon used?

4   Try to rewrite the headline as a complete sentence.

> ## TRAIN BLAZE: CHILD FOUND 'UNHURT'

5   Why is the compound *train blaze* used rather than 'big fire on train'?

6   How is the passive voice of the present perfect tense conveyed in the headline?

7   Why is 'unhurt' in inverted commas, do you think?

8   Rewrite the headline as a complete sentence.

7 Noun or verb?

The following short words are common in newspaper headlines. Sometimes they are used as nouns, and sometimes as verbs. Choose one word from the box to complete each pair of headlines:

VOCABULARY		
aid	cut	jail
arm	head	vow

1 **a** REFUGEES TO GET FRESH _____
   b CHARITY SHOPS _____ HOMELESS

2 **a** JUDGE TO _____ MURDER INQUIRY
   b CRASH VICTIM DIES OF _____ INJURIES

3 **a** BABY'S _____ SAVED IN MIRACLE OP
   b POLICE CHIEF _____S CITY POLICE

4 **a** FATHER _____S REVENGE ON KILLER
   b PRESIDENT BREAKS ELECTION _____

5 **a** GOVERNMENT TO _____ WORKING HOURS
   b MORE EDUCATION _____S ON WAY

6 **a** JUDGE _____S TRAIN ROBBER
   b CONDITIONS IN WOMEN'S _____S 'SHOCKING'

8 Comparing languages

How does newspaper language in your country compare with English? What are the similarities and differences?

9 Discussion

What do you think has happened to the footballer in the picture?

How can you get hurt when you play sport? If you are hurt, what should you do?

Have you ever suffered an injury whilst taking part in sport? How did it happen? What helped you recover?

10 Rewording

When you write summaries, you need to use your own words without altering the meaning. For example:

If you carry out weight training, you would be well-advised to do this in a gym under expert supervision.

could become:

You should do weight training in a gym under the care of a qualified supervisor.

In groups of two or three, try to rewrite the following sentences about sports injuries, using your own words where you can. Can you also make the sentences more concise?

1 Many severe injuries to the body give rise to bleeding, swelling and pain.

2 In the first 24 hours, ice (or, alternatively, a packet of frozen peas) should only be used for short periods of no more than ten minutes at a time.

3 Ice should never, whatever the reason, be applied directly to the skin because there is a real danger of burns.

4 In the early stages, when there is a great deal of uncomfortable swelling and pain, you would be well-advised to rest the injured area.

5 Nevertheless, you must begin gentle movement and careful exercise of the injured part as soon as it is possible for you to do so.

6 Where possible, it is important that any exercise of the injured area is carried out under the careful supervision of a professional physiotherapist, and you can ask such a person to supervise any exercise.

7 Your doctor may prescribe painkillers or anti-inflammatory tablets or another kind of suitable medication to reduce the swelling and pain when your injury is painful for you, or it is noticed that the swelling is marked.

11 Writing a short summary

Read the introduction to a leaflet entitled 'Avoiding Sports Injuries'. In your own words, write a paragraph of about 45 words explaining how you can avoid getting injured when you play sport. Approach the task in a methodical way, as you did earlier in the unit.

When you have finished, ask a partner to check that you have:

- kept to the question set
- used your own words where possible
- left out unnecessary words and details
- left out opinions of your own
- connected the summary grammatically
- kept to the word limit.

55

Avoiding sports injuries

Active sports are becoming ever more popular. Whether for relaxation and as a way of reducing stress, for weight control, or to improve health and fitness, greater numbers of people of all 5 ages are taking part in various active sporting pursuits.

However, as more people take part, sports injuries are becoming more common. Fortunately, these injuries are seldom too serious, and if treated 10 properly and promptly, get better quickly – never to return. Nevertheless, if you are planning to start a fitness programme, you need to be aware of the ways injuries can be prevented in the first place.

You need systematic and sensible physical preparation to get fit for sport. Besides training for 15 strength and stamina, you should ensure that you get proper rest. It is essential never to try to train when you are tired, as tiredness itself can cause injury. It is also vital to use an appropriate technique when doing sport. Not only is it obviously very helpful in 20 achieving success in your chosen sport, but it can also greatly reduce the chance of sustaining an injury.

Protective equipment, such as helmets, gum shields, shin pads and other items, including comfortable and supportive footwear, will improve your 25 performance and help prevent unnecessary injury.

12 Expressing warnings

Warnings in spoken language are expressed more directly than in written language.

In pairs, read the following mini-conversations giving warnings about the possible dangers of sport and physical exercise:

1 A: I've just started to play cricket.

   B: Take care to use protective shin pads. They can stop you getting a nasty injury.

   A: Thanks. I'll remember that.

2 A: My brother is only three but he wants to learn to swim.

   B: Make sure he wears armbands, even in shallow water.

   A: You're right. I'm glad you told me.

3 A: We're going sailing in Hinton Bay on Saturday.

   B: Watch out for rocks in that area. You can easily run aground.

   A: That's true. I'll tell the others too.

Warnings

Take care to / Be careful to (take precautions)

Make sure you (take precautions)

Watch out for / Look out for (unseen danger)

Responses

Thanks. I'll remember that/I'll do that.

That's true. I'm glad you told me.

You're right. I will.

Practice

Create mini-conversations with a partner around the situations below, using the following pattern.

Student A: Talk about plans.

Student B: Give a warning.

Student A: Show you've understood the warning.

1 start jogging / need good running shoes to protect feet

2 lift weights at the gym for first time / proper supervision from instructor

3 hill walking alone / tell someone where you are going

4 swimming in sea on holiday / jellyfish sting you

5 mountain biking in a new area / lots of rain recently, ground muddy and slippery

C Motivation through sport

1 Pre-reading discussion

Would you enjoy teaching other young people how to play your favourite sport? Would you be good at it? What do you think are the qualities of a good sports coach?

2 Predicting content

You are going to read an article on the 'Second Chance' website about a sports project that brings together young people from different countries who have dropped out of school. The project teaches them about sports and communication skills. What information might you expect the article to include? Complete the list.

- Why communication skills are linked with sports
- _____
- _____
- _____
- _____ .

3 Vocabulary check

Before you read the article, try to match these words with their meanings.

1	truancy	A	face-to-face argument
2	top	B	non-attendance at school without permission
3	confrontation	C	people of the same age as each other.
4	context	D	piece of clothing worn on the upper part of the body
5	peers	E	conditions and circumstances

4 Developing reading skills

Read the article as quickly as possible. Concentrate on the general meaning rather than trying to understand every word. Remember to read more complex passages slowly.

5 True/false comprehension

Scan the text and decide if the following statements are true or false.

1 The minimum age for joining the project is 17.
2 Young people from any country can participate.
3 The main aim of the project is to teach young people new sports.
4 Participants have all had personal problems.

Second Chance

All 70 participants at the four-day course run by the European Association of Second Chance Schools (E2C) are 16- to 25-year-olds from disadvantaged backgrounds. They have no qualifications and all have had a mixture of difficulties – family problems, truancy and crime.

The participants are from Italy, France, Sweden, Germany, England and Ireland, and they have gathered at the South Leeds Sports Stadium in England to learn organisational and communication skills. The focus of the project is to help the young people acquire these skills through sport: first by learning how to play a variety of games, and then by learning how to coach each other in racket skills, athletics, netball, cricket or football.

The sessions are run by professional coaches who show the groups the basic skills of each sport and then demonstrate how to teach others the same skills.

Hands-on experience

Seventeen-year-old Nadia is a typical participant. She won't talk about her past except to say she had 'the usual' problems. Nevertheless, professional coach Riley says she has done particularly well at teaching football, learning to project her voice and taking command of the group with firm and clear requests. Nadia says, 'I'm enjoying the project as I'm learning new skills. When I go home, I'm going to get qualifications so I can get a job working with children.'

On the badminton courts, a group of youngsters from Spoleto, in northern Italy, is shown how to grip the rackets and practise with easy-to-control balls. The tutor accompanying them, Stefania Rosati, watches carefully to see how her students cope. 'They are enjoying the experience of being here as most of them haven't been abroad before. One of the most useful things for them is learning more self-discipline.' In the Italians' second session, pairs of them are asked to coach the rest of their group. Badminton coach Brian Harrison is impressed. 'Some are well-coordinated and find it easy, while others are finding it hard, but no one is getting impatient – they are working together,' he says.

Time to get tough

But it isn't all so positive. During the next session, one of the boys loses interest in being coached by his peers and wanders off. The participants leading the session ignore his behaviour in order to avoid a confrontation. Afterwards, though, they discuss it and suggest ways it could have been tackled sensitively and effectively. They also discuss other difficult situations, such as what to say to a participant who turns up in a fashionable top instead of the correct sportswear.

Barriers begin to disappear

Meeting other nationalities at the events is an important element of the programme that the participants enjoy. Although nationalities are not mixed for the coaching sessions, the sporting context gives the youngsters an opportunity to see how other cultures differ. Phillipe Marco, a tutor from Marseille, whose group are all originally from North African countries, says, 'They love discussing ideas with young people from other countries. It is opening their minds, and they are able to explain their beliefs to others. The sport and social events are helping to break down barriers.'

Confiding in a diary

The youngsters are given diaries to record their thoughts and experiences every day. Their comments reveal their enjoyment of meeting people from different backgrounds but with similar problems. 'All of us had challenges and barriers. I think we worked well as a team to overcome them,' and 'I have learnt there is more to sport than the obvious activities,' are typical of the responses.

One Swedish tutor sums up the experience of many of his colleagues with a report on a girl who attended the project: 'Before, she had been quite self-centred. During the course she has stopped focusing on herself and has really enjoyed everything.'

5   Participants learn how to coach each other in the skills.

6   The project gives people an opportunity to compare cultures.

7   There is an emphasis on competition and trying to win.

8   Nationalities are kept separate for coaching.

9   The participants write their thoughts in a daily journal.

6 Checking predictions

How much of what you expected to read about was actually mentioned in the article?

7 Writing a headline

With a partner, write a headline for the article. Look back at the guidelines earlier in the unit to help you.

8 Post-reading discussion

1   The participants are given diaries to record their thoughts and feelings. Why do you think they were asked to do this?

2   What are your feelings about this kind of social project? Do you think the positive effects it has on young people will make a permanent difference to them? Or, do you think the benefits will be forgotten when they return to their normal lives?

9 Making notes

Write a set of notes based on the article about the sports project, using the headings below. (Look back at exercise 11 Note-making practice if you need to.)

- Aims of the project
- What participants learn
- Reasons the project is popular

When you've finished, ask your partner to check the following:

Content: Is it all relevant? Should anything be left out?

Language: Is your language clear and precise?

Presentation: Have you put the right points under the right headings?

10 Correcting a connected summary

Study this exam-style question:

Read the article about the European Association of Second Chance Schools and then write a summary describing the aims of the project, what the participants learn to do and the reasons why they enjoy taking part. Write about 100 words, and use your own words as far as possible.

Here is one student's attempt to answer the question. Some of the information in the answer is unnecessary, making the answer too long. Cross out the unnecessary information.

The aim of the European Association of Second Chance Schools project is to encourage young people from European countries, who have not succeeded at school, to improve their ability to communicate and organise themselves. Sport is used as the medium for this. I think this is a very unusual idea and we should start a project like this in my country. Participants are taught a range of skills needed for a variety of sports and then they are expected to coach each other. Phillipe Marco came from Marseille in France with his students and he explained that his group liked telling the others about their views and beliefs, which might be the first time they have had the chance to talk to people who listen properly to them. Participants also have to learn self-discipline, to take trouble doing things, even if they don't feel like it, and to cope with troublesome behaviour from some of the others. They enjoy learning new skills, teamwork, sharing cultures, and discovering that they are not alone with their problems. One 17-year-old girl whose name is Nadia explained, 'I'm enjoying the project …. When I go home, I'm going to get qualifications so I can get a job working with children.'

11 Rewriting a summary

Now rewrite the summary. Make sure you use a range of linking words to connect the text. Keep within the approximate word limit.

12 Expressions of measurement

The article says that participants go on *a four-day course*. This is a concise way of saying that the course lasts for four days. One of the participants is described as *17-year-old Nadia*, which is a more concise way of saying Nadia is 17 years old. Similarly, we can say that a hotel that has been awarded three stars for quality is *a three-star hotel*, or a walk that is five kilometres long is *a five-kilometre walk*. Notice how the plural *s* is not used in the hyphenated words.

Practice

Rewrite each of these sentences using a number + noun form:

1   She uses a fitness video that lasts for fifty minutes.

2   He made a cut that was six inches long.

3   Ali got a contract worth a thousand dollars.

4   They ordered a meal that consisted of six courses.

5   I need a coin worth one pound for the locker.

6   The drive to work takes ten minutes.

7   Tanya gave birth to a baby weighing seven pounds.

8   I'd like a bag of sugar weighing two kilograms.

13 Vocabulary: Using fewer words

In the article, the word used for 'people taking part in the course' is *participants*.

The following words are also taken from the article. With a partner, choose the correct one to replace the words in italics in the sentences:

VOCABULARY		
obvious	abroad	overcome
challenge	ignore	

1   Learning to paddle the canoe was a *difficult and testing task* for Mario.

2   If you can *manage to control* your fear, bungee jumping is a thrilling experience.

3   If they behave like that again, you should *take no notice of* them.

4   The answer to the problem is *easy to see*.

5   Natasha's ambition is to go *to another country* to study.

Now put each word into a sentence of your own.

14 Redundant words

In the sentence, *The children stood patiently in a round circle and listened to the coach*, **round** is unnecessary because a circle is always round. It is common for people to repeat themselves in conversation, but when we write we should aim to be concise and avoid 'redundant' words.

With a partner, decide which words are redundant in the following sentences and cross them out:

1   When did you first begin to learn basketball?

2   Aysha bought new summer sandals for the children's feet.

3   He has some priceless old antiques in his house which are so valuable that it is impossible to say how much they are worth.

4   We received an unexpected shock on our return from holiday.

5   She was upset that the vase was broken as it was very unique.

6   Rosalie wasn't very helpful when I asked for some scissors to cut with.

7   He had to repeat himself many times, saying the words over and over again, before he was understood.

8   Since starting to play squash, Jeff has been unhealthily obsessed with winning every game.

INTERNATIONAL OVERVIEW

Work with a partner to test your knowledge of approaches to sport, health and fitness across the world.

1   The global 'rule' for the number of hours of sports practice required to reach world class standard is:

    1000   3000   10 000   15 000   20 000

2   In Ireland, pupils aged 5–12 can expect to do 37 hours per year of PE (physical education). How many hours can a pupil in the same age group expect to do in France?

    35   60   88   108   135

3   In which country can you expect to have the longest lifespan in good health?

    Switzerland   Argentina   Japan   Sweden

4   In which country can every child receive a nutritionally balanced free school lunch providing a third of the daily calories needed?

    India   Australia   Finland   Spain

D Health, diet and fitness

1 Pre-reading discussion

Sport itself cannot make you fit. You have to get fit for sport. A healthy diet is an important part of getting and staying fit.

Discuss with your partner what, if anything, you do to make sure you eat a balanced, healthy diet.

60

2 Predicting content

You are going to read a magazine article about Shalimar, a digital artist, who changed her lifestyle habits. Use the title, picture and introductory paragraph to help you predict the particular things she might mention in the article.

Write four points.

Audience awareness

Who do you think this article is **mainly** aimed at – the medical profession, children, professional sports players, general public, digital artists or elderly people?

What kind of language and style do you expect the writer to use? Do you expect to find a chatty style with lots of phrasal verbs? Or will the article be formal and use many specialised terms?

Writer's intention

What do you think the writer's intention is?

- [ ] to make people identify with Shalimar and change unhealthy habits
- [ ] to make people try harder to keep to fitness programmes
- [ ] to promote a particular diet and fitness programme.

3 Vocabulary check

The following words connected with food and fitness are used in the article. Can you explain their meaning?

VOCABULARY		
nibble	**snack on**	**packed lunches**
sluggish		

4 Reading

As you read, tick off these points:

- [ ] what makes Shalimar accept she is unfit
- [ ] unhealthy work patterns
- [ ] after-work habits

- [ ] success on the programme
- [ ] new routines
- [ ] Shalimar today.

Now Feeling on Top of the World

Digital artist Shalimar was so busy building her own online gaming company she never noticed she was getting unfit – until the day she couldn't run for a bus.

Shalimar Lee was late for work one morning and,   5
as her usual number 14 bus came around the corner, she sped up. As she climbed aboard, her heart was beating so fast she could hardly speak to the driver. She thought she might be going to collapse. This finally made her face the fact that   10
she was seriously unfit and she did not like it.

'I used to be very fit and played tennis and basketball at school. But when I went to university I gave up sport completely. Don't ask me why! After completing my degree, I got a great opportunity as a digital   15
artist. Within a few years I had started my own computer games company. I gave everything to my job, but I paid a price and that was my health. The bus incident proved my problems had got out of hand   20
and suddenly I couldn't stand it.'

61

For Shalimar, however, the idea of going on a fitness regime was inconceivable. 'I simply didn't think I had the time. Even when I wasn't at work, I was thinking of new story lines for my games,
25 researching, or updating my blog.' Her online games, which are internationally known, centre around a family of penguins, and Shalimar has already achieved the status of a minor celebrity in the blogosphere.

30 'I got so immersed in work, I never took a meal break and worked ridiculously long hours. I would sip high-energy drinks all day long and nibble biscuits. When I got home, I'd slump in front of the TV, and, rather than cook a proper meal, I
35 snacked on toast and chocolate spread. There was never anything much in the fridge anyway.' Not surprisingly, she didn't sleep well and would wake up feeling as if she needed another eight hours: 'I felt sluggish all the time, but I couldn't imagine how
40 to change things.'

No one ever mentioned that Shalimar seemed exhausted. No one, that is, until her mum decided to pluck up the courage. 'I was visiting my family one weekend. Mum waited until I was relaxed after
45 lunch and then plunged in. She had read that a new gym in the neighbourhood was starting up a fitness programme which not only included exercise, but offered information on developing a healthy lifestyle. Mum persuaded me that we should both
50 give the programme a try.' Shalimar wasn't exactly thrilled but felt she ought to go. After the very first class, she was hooked.

'I got fitter immediately. The exercises were good fun. Gabrielle, our instructor, was so motivational and gave us loads of encouragement. 55 She also told us about easy ways to replace bad habits with healthy ones, such as getting off the bus a stop earlier, and making time to shop for fresh ingredients. I used to leave feeling on top of the world.' 60

Shalimar explains that the programme focuses on making small changes that you can fit into your lifestyle. This, she feels, is the key to its success: 'I'm strict with myself now. However busy I am, I make up my packed lunch every day and leave the office 65 to eat it in a park down the road.' Her office is on the fourth floor and she now uses the stairs as much as possible instead of the lift. She also avoids fizzy drinks and drinks tea or water instead. 'I didn't need to go crazy to get healthy. Just a few simple, 70 sensible changes have made all the difference.'

It's hard to believe Shalimar was ever so unfit she couldn't run for a bus. 'I'm still busy but I don't feel exhausted anymore. I'm sure eating properly has also given my brain a boost because I find it so 75 much easier to conjure up new ideas for my games. I've got rid of my old habits for good and they are never coming back!'

Shalimar's business is also going from strength to strength. Her new computer game about a cute baby 80 giraffe is about to be launched onto the market. 'The team and I are so excited. I think this is going to be our most successful product yet.'

5 Post-reading discussion

A In your culture, how do you define a healthy lifestyle?

B We know Shalimar's mum needed to *pluck up the courage* in order to persuade her daughter to change her habits and join the fitness programme. Why did she need courage to raise this topic with her own daughter?

C Shalimar explains that the programme succeeds because it helps you make small changes that you can fit into your lifestyle. Do you agree that this approach would really work, or do you think bigger changes are necessary for people who are unfit because of unhealthy habits? What motivates **you** to have a healthy lifestyle?

D Shalimar feels a healthy diet has given her brain a boost. What evidence does she have? Do you feel nutritious food can make such a big difference to brain functioning?

Discuss your ideas in your group.

6 Writing a summary

Write a summary, based on the article, contrasting Shalimar's lifestyle before she began the fitness programme with her lifestyle now. Explain why she feels the fitness programme was particularly suitable for her. Try to use your own words as far as possible. Write about 100 words and not more than 120 words.

Approach

Approach your summary methodically: check key words in the question, underline relevant parts of the text, write notes in your own words and then connect them into a summary. You may need to make a few drafts before your summary is 'polished'.

When you have finished, compare your version with your partner's, and check that you have:

- included the relevant points
- put the points in the correct order
- left out unnecessary details
- left out your own personal opinions and ideas
- used suitable connectors/linking devices
- written grammatically correct English
- used the appropriate number of words.

7 Vocabulary: Phrasal verbs

The following phrasal verbs were used in the article. Can you use them in an appropriate form in these sentences

VOCABULARY		
give up	start up	plunge in
pluck up	conjure up	make up

1 He's trying to _____ an after-school judo club for children in the village.

2 She knew mentioning the topic would be unpopular but she decided to _____ anyway.

3 Antonio decided to _____ doing overtime and see more of his family.

4 He _____ the courage and asked Jane to marry him.

5 Although she didn't have much food in the fridge, Sally was able to _____ a delicious meal.

6 They _____ food parcels for people whose homes had been damaged in the flood.

8 Spelling: Adding suffixes to words with a final -e

In the text about Shalimar you saw these words with suffixes:

completing (complete + -ing)

encouragement (encourage + -ment)

Notice how the final -e of *complete* is dropped before the suffix, but the -e is kept in the word *encourag**e**ment*.

Can you explain why?

A final -e in a word is usually dropped when adding a suffix beginning with a *vowel*.

Examples:

dance	danc**ing**
educate	educat**ion**

The -e is usually kept when the suffix begins with a consonant.

Examples:

hope	hope**ful**
care	care**less**
improve	improve**ment**

There are some **important exceptions** to the above rule.

The -e is usually kept before the suffix -**able**.

Examples:

notice	notice**able**

The -e is usually kept when it ends with two vowels before the suffix.

Examples:

see	see**ing**
canoe	canoe**ist**

Practice

Read this newspaper report about the teaching of traditional dance in schools. Applying the rules for adding suffixes to words with a final -e, add the correct suffixes to the words in brackets.

Choose from the following suffixes:

VOCABULARY			
-ative	-ing	-ion	-ish
-ment	-tion	-ity	-ivity

More and more pupils are learning dance as part of their physical (educate) programme. It is a wonderful way of (have) fun and an (excite) way of keeping fit. Dance allows all pupils a chance to express their (create). Even the youngest pupils can learn simple (move) to music which act as an (introduce) to more complex traditional dance. Older pupils who lack (motivate) when it comes to competitive sport find traditional dance very (stimulate). Secondary school teachers say (participate) in such an enjoyable activity needs no (encourage).

Schools (achieve) a high standard may be selected for the Schools Dance Festival held each year. The Festival is a wonderful (celebrate) of traditional dance. Last year, the (style) costumes, great (diverse) of dances, (imagine) approaches and wonderful music made the evening particularly special.

Discussion

Do you (or would you) enjoy watching or taking part in traditional dances? Explain your views.

9 Word building

Working with a partner, choose a suitable suffix from the box to add to each of the ten words below. Sometimes more than one is possible.

VOCABULARY

-ing	-ly	-ness
-ion	-ment	

1 time
2 concentrate
3 refine
4 exercise
5 welcome
6 involve
7 ache
8 state
9 unique
10 aware.

Make sure your spelling is correct by checking with the rules for keeping or dropping the final -e.

Give each new word a grammar label (*noun*, *verb*, *adjective*, etc.). Refer to a dictionary if necessary.

Now use each word you have made in a sentence of your own.

10 Look, say, cover, write, check

Use the 'look, say, cover, write, check' method to learn these words, which are among those most frequently misspelt:

amaze	amazing	amazement	
argue	arguing	argument	
become	becoming		
excite	exciting	excitable	excitement
welcome	welcoming		
shine	shining		
invite	inviting	invitation	
surprise	surprising		
imagine	imaginary	imaginative	imagining
immediate	immediately		

GRAMMAR SPOTLIGHT

Passives

A   **Passives** are often used when we are reporting news, or explaining how something works:

A female student was seriously injured. (**section B5**)

The sessions are run by professional coaches. (**section C4**)

Find three examples of passives in the text in **section C10**.

B   Verbs like *give, offer, lend* and *send* can have **two objects**, a person and a thing:

We sent Julio a birthday card.

When we use these verbs in the passive, we usually start with the person:

Marianne was offered a place at Oxford University.

NOT *A place at Oxford University was offered to Marianne.*

There is an example of this in paragraph 8 of the article in **section D4**. Can you find it?

Exam-style questions

Speaking

1   Fitness and exercise

In some countries many people suffer from a lack of exercise. Why is this happening, do you think? What can be done to raise people's awareness of the importance of staying fit? Discuss this topic with the assessor.

You may wish to use the following ideas to help develop the conversation:

- ways to develop a more energetic lifestyle in general, such as walking or cycling rather than using buses or cars
- the increased consumption of snack foods, such as crisps and chocolate bars which are eaten quickly and do not satisfy hunger for long
- the fact that playing computer games, surfing the internet or watching TV can result in a lack of exercise
- the fact that in some countries children have less freedom to play outside than in the past
- the fact that increased use of washing machines and vacuum cleaners is reducing effort spent on keeping houses clean and comfortable.

You are free to consider any other related ideas of your own. You are not allowed to make any written notes.

2   Professional sport

Sport is popular all over the world and it is also big business. Top sports players are paid very large sums of money and are heavily in demand. Discuss this topic with the assessor.

You may wish to consider points such as:

- whether you personally enjoy watching professional sports games and matches
- the skills and abilities professional sports players require to become the best in their sport
- whether there should be stricter penalties for sports people who take drugs or cheat at sport
- the idea that international sports competitions create unpleasant rivalries that divide countries, rather than bring people of different nationalities together
- the view that professional sports people should not get involved in advertising commercial products.

You are free to consider any other related ideas of your own. You are not allowed to make any written notes.

Notes and summary writing

Reading & Writing, Exercise 4

1   Read the information from a health webpage about sleep and young people. Write a summary outlining why young people need more sleep than adults and the negative effects of lack of sleep on teenagers.

Your summary should be about 100 words long. You should use your own words as far as possible.

Extended [16 marks]

Healthy Living UK

Sleep – are you getting enough?

According to recent studies, children and teenagers get less sleep than they need. Lifestyle changes may be to blame, including staying up late to play online games or use social media.

Clinical studies showed that many modern teenagers are getting just over six hours' sleep, rather than the nine hours they need. Using technological tools, scientists have measured the impact loss of sleep has on young people. Their findings suggest a lack of sleep can cause worrying changes in a teenager's brain structure.

Throughout the night, everyone enters different stages of sleep. There are stages of light sleep, stages of dreaming sleep, called 'REM', and stages of deep or 'slow wave' sleep. The sleep researchers discovered that young people's sleep is different in quality from adult sleep because they need to spend 40% of their time asleep in slow wave sleep. The slow wave stage is the time when the brain carries out its development and healing functions which are essential for health. Teenagers' brains are not fully formed and they need to be asleep for long enough to get enough slow wave sleep. In contrast, adults spend only 4% of their time in slow wave sleep and more time in the lighter stages.

Dr Avi Salem, a sleep researcher whose work has been published internationally, has spent many years studying the effects of lack of sleep on teenagers and has come to some very significant conclusions. For example, using performance tests, Dr Salem and his team of researchers found that the 15-year-old volunteers who had insufficient sleep definitely performed less well on tests of mental ability, often only reaching the standard of a 13-year-old.

MRI brain scans show that sleep loss decreases the body's ability to extract sugar efficiently from the bloodstream, which makes the brain less active. The brain is therefore less able to learn because it cannot take in and understand information properly. One result of inadequate amounts of sleep on teenagers is that they find it more difficult to concentrate on and fulfil a goal that has been set for them. They also find it harder to imagine the possible consequences and negative effects of behaving in silly, destructive or impulsive ways.

Dr Salem explains the role of sleep in helping language learning. If a teenager is studying a foreign language during the daytime, his or her brain needs sufficient slow wave sleep to encode new words that were studied earlier into the long-term memory. This process is required for the retention and recall of new language. Without enough slow wave sleep new words are forgotten.

Sleep has always been important and there are many references in literature that praise the unique qualities of sleep. However, there is now more scientific evidence to support this and to prove just how much sleep matters.

Many adults manage on too little sleep and seem to find ways to cope, but when it comes to young people whose brains are still developing, can we afford to take the risk?

Reading & Writing, Exercise 3

2   Read the following article about people's fear of swimming and then complete the notes.

Healthy Living UK: Fear of Swimming

To what extent can you force children to cope with situations they find scary?

A concerned parent writes:

How seriously should you take a child's fear of the water? My son has a weekly swimming lesson at school which, for us, has become a nightmare scenario. His initial reluctance to swim has developed into a fear that seems little short of a phobia. We feel very strongly that it is important that he learns to swim, but each week, as the day of the lesson dawns, our son gets into a real state, which is emotionally exhausting for all of us. Should we give in to his extreme unwillingness to swim or, as we have been doing, force him to go ahead with his lessons?

A professor of child psychiatry replies:

This little boy's fear of water is a very natural and healthy response, but on the other hand, children are much safer if they are able to swim.

A lot of children find group swimming lessons difficult to cope with for various reasons. School pools can be cold and noisy, with lots of people shouting and splashing, which is very off-putting for someone who doesn't feel in control of the situation. So it is easy to see why this could be a nasty experience.

Fear or dislike of group lessons is understandable, given the situation, so these parents first need to teach their son to like water, probably in a pool that is warm rather than cold (presumably he doesn't have a problem in the bath, so the fear is probably not of water itself).

Choose a smallish, quiet pool, where the water is warm. Take it slowly and base it around having fun rather than focusing on getting on with swimming. He should get used to going underwater – it is much easier to start swimming while submerged.

His parents should not continue exposing him to repeated traumatic experiences, which are clearly so frightening for him, so they should speak to the teachers and see if they can take him out of his lessons until he feels that he is ready to rejoin the class. It really is not helpful to force him: his parents should work on

his unwillingness to swim outside the context of school and build up his confidence and skills.

A tutor at a swimming school replies:

I would suggest that this little boy would benefit from one-to-one tuition.

Obviously something is happening in school – maybe someone has ducked him or splashed him in the pool and he doesn't like it. His parents should try to find out if something specific has happened to cause this problem.

In a situation like this, pushing him won't help at all, but they mustn't give up on him either. Solo lessons should help. Perhaps the parents should take him swimming at the weekend and make sure it is fun, or get a teacher just for him.

It might be a good idea to leave the school lessons for a while. At the pool, they should forget the swimming aspect and just encourage him to enjoy the water.

At the swimming school we get a lot of adults who have been put off at a young age by being ducked or splashed, being taught to swim with a rope tied around the waist or a pole pushing them, and so, perhaps unsurprisingly, they have given up. Of course, there are people with a real fear of water, but they are more unusual.

We find that the main thing is helping individuals to become accustomed to getting their face wet. Bearing this in mind, perhaps bathtime would be a good time for the boy's parents to try this. They should also get him to put his mouth in the water and blow bubbles, and pour water over his head, starting at the back so that it is not too startling. A lot of people really hate getting their heads wet, but if he can overcome the problem in a non-threatening environment such as the bath, he will be off to a good start.

At the pool, wearing good goggles might make a difference to him. It really is worth investing in a decent pair.

At our children's weeks, I advise parents of children who are petrified of water not to put the pressure on and to be happy with whatever their children can actually achieve in the water.

You are going to give a talk to your school sports club about the fear of swimming. Prepare some notes to use as the basis for your talk, using these headings:

a Why some children fear learning to swim:

- *Fear of water is a natural response*
- _____
- _____

b Ways of overcoming a fear of swimming:

- _____
- _____
- _____
- _____

c How some adults were put off learning to swim:

- _____
- _____
- _____

Extended [9 marks].

Reading & Writing, Exercise 4

3 Read the following magazine article about raw food diets:

Write a summary outlining the advantages and disadvantages of a raw food diet. Your summary should be about 80 words long. Use your own words as far as possible.

Core [12 marks]

Healthy Living UK
Does a raw food diet make us healthier

When 17-year-old Ali told his friends he was giving up eating cooked food, they were stunned. Ali, a keen Kung Fu fighter, who is hoping to turn professional, is convinced that following a raw food diet, based on vegetables and fruit, is the key that will unlock sporting success.

Ali's sports coach is enthusiastic about the raw food diet. 'Raw food contains enzymes,' explains Mario Pina, who has written the successful book 'How to Achieve the Body of a Top Athlete.' 'If enzymes are preserved, we improve strength and stamina.' Ali is thrilled with his new eating habits: 'I find my recovery rate after training is shorter now,' he insists.

What do the experts think? Is a raw food diet really the way forward? I decided to contact Professor Benos, an international expert on nutrition. 'There is no scientific evidence that eliminating cooked food from the diet is beneficial,' said the professor. Enzymes are produced by the body to aid digestion, whether the food is cooked or raw.' However, Professor Benos acknowledges that eating a raw food diet may have some positive effects: 'A raw food diet is high in fresh food, which is richer in nutrients than some kinds of processed food. The diet also encourages more chewing and takes longer to digest so it is more satisfying. As a result we do not eat more than we need.'

On the other hand, Professor Benos has serious concerns about only eating raw foods: 'We may consume too much

fruit. Fruit contains a lot of natural sugars that cause dental erosion. Milk is eliminated (pasteurised milk is heated to high temperatures) so our intake of calcium is less, and we may fail to get enough iron and zinc.'

On balance, Professor Benos believes a raw food diet should be avoided. He says, 'The strongest evidence is that the healthiest diet has a wide range of both cooked and raw food, from all the food groups. A raw food diet may do no real harm over the short term, but I believe you should return to normal eating after a few weeks.'

Listening 🔊 CD 1, Track 9

Listening, Exercise 3

You will hear six people talking about sport. For each of the speakers 1–6, choose from the list, A–G, which opinion each speaker expresses. Write the letter in the box. Use each letter only once. There is one extra letter, which you do not need to use.

Core [6 marks], Extended [6 marks].

You will hear the full recording twice.

☐ Speaker 1   ☐ Speaker 2

☐ Speaker 3   ☐ Speaker 4

☐ Speaker 5   ☐ Speaker 6

A   Sport can prepare you for adult life.

B   Young people's experience of sport should be light-hearted.

C   The essence of sport is competition.

D   To be successful in sport, you need to start young.

E   Competitive sport should be introduced by the age of ten.

F   Sport should be a bigger part of the school curriculum.

G   Sportspeople make good role models.

ADVICE FOR SUCCESS

The Advice for Success is for **you** to **help yourself**. Decide which suggestions you like best and mark them. You can adapt an idea in Advice for Success to make it fun for you. Keeping track with a notebook is a good idea.

1 Before you start to read

Many students say they find it hard to 'get into' reading at length. These strategies will help you get into reading more easily:

Ask yourself:

- What is this text likely to be about?
- What do I already know about the topic?
- Who is this written for? (young people, the general public, children, specialists in a profession, people with a particular hobby?)

This will orientate you with regard to the likely style (technical, formal, chatty) and structure (long sentences and paragraphs, or short, simpler sentences and paragraphs) involved.

Think about the author's main aim (to advise, warn, give technical information, entertain and give opinions). This will help you see the difference between the main points and background information.

Skimming headlines, subheadings and photos, diagrams or charts will also help to give you a quick idea of what the text is about.

2   Most students would like to read faster but still absorb what they read. **Adjust your reading speed to your reading needs**. You can skim-read sentences that are easy to understand, or less relevant. Slow down (as much as you need to) over the parts that are more complex, or which contain key points.

Highlight important parts of the text (onscreen or with a highlighter pen).

After you have finished reading, ask yourself:

   • What were the main points of this text?

Make a short list. Check your list against the original text.

3   **Summarising** is a practical skill that you can make use of in all parts of the curriculum. Remember— when you summarise plots of films, sporting events and social occasions, you are practising this skill. As you become better at it, feel proud of the progress you make. Summarising is challenging, but don't be afraid of it.

Exam techniques

4   Exam **summary questions** are usually 'guided'. You are asked, for example, to outline the advantages

and disadvantages / trace the history of / explain the importance of something. You should:

a   underline key words in the question

b   look carefully at any headline, pictures, charts or subheadings to get a general idea of what the text is about before you start to read

c   read quickly, focusing on the hardest parts of the text

d   underline or highlight key words and phrases

e   make a rough draft of the key words and phrases in connected prose. Use your own words as far as possible

f   count the words. Make corrections to the grammar and spelling as required

g   write a final draft using the word limit in the question as a guide

h   proofread your summary for mistakes.

5   For **note-making questions,** in examination, use the above method as far as **d**.

Present your notes clearly, under the headings and bullet points provided. Write one point for each bullet. Full sentences are not needed.

Although a word limit is not given, your notes must be concise.

6   Where the note-making and summary exercises are based on the same text, you should write your notes using this strategy.

The summary you write will be based on the notes you have already made. The summary should be in full sentences, using your own words as far as possible, to show that you have a good range of vocabulary.

Exam focus

This unit has helped to prepare you for exams which test your reading, writing, listening and speaking skills. The unit has helped to develop those skills in the following ways:

▪   You have practised **reading** and **making notes** from a range of texts.

▪   You have **read** and **summarised** a variety of texts.

▪   You have **listened** to an **announcement** and **made notes**. You have also **listened** to different speakers and

selected the correct answer to multiple-matching questions.

▪   You have practised the correct **stress and intonation** for an **informal conversation**.

▪   **You have** taken part in **more formal discussions**.

Unit 4
Our impact on the planet

In this unit you will:

- read about the first railways and a sponsored cycle ride
- write a 'for' and 'against' argument
- listen to a discussion about car use
- practise asking someone for a favour
- explore climate change
- focus on the following assessment objectives: R1, R2, W2, L1, L2, S5

A Transport then and now

1 Pre-reading discussion

A Apart from the car, what is the preferred mode of transport in your country? Do you feel it is a safe and comfortable form of transport? Give reasons for your views.

B What do you like and dislike about travelling by train? If you have never been on a train journey, would you like to go on one? Why/Why not?

Brainstorming

You are going to read about how the arrival of the railways in the 19th century changed people's lives. How do you think people at that time might have felt about the idea of such a different, and strange, form of transport? What would they have wanted to know? What do you think they worried about? Brainstorm your ideas, and then share them in your group.

2 Vocabulary check

Before you read, check the meaning of these words.

VOCABULARY		
passenger	rigorously	novelty
suspicions	immobilised	

Early train travel

Trains and railway stations are such a common sight now, it is hard to believe that at one time they did not exist. Before the passenger train was developed, the only ways to travel – if people
5 travelled at all – were on foot, by boat, on horseback or camel, or by horse-drawn carriages or carts.

The earliest railways consisted of wagons pulled along rails by horses and were used for transporting raw materials and goods. The invention of the steam
10 engine changed things dramatically, and, in 1830, the Liverpool and Manchester Railway was opened in the north of England, the world's first passenger railway as we know it. The Railway Age had begun.

People's objections
15 The first railways were fiercely opposed by many people who feared that train travel was harmful to health. Some members of the medical profession, in particular, believed passengers might die from heart attacks caused by the extreme speed. There
20 were also widespread fears that noisy trains would destroy the beauty and gentle pace of life in the countryside. Furthermore, farmers opposed the idea of railways cutting through their farmland, as they believed that the smoke and steam would
25 destroy crops and scare their animals.

Safety concerns
There were many accidents on the first railways, which further increased people's distrust. When an accident happened, it made front-page news because people were eager to have their suspicions
30 confirmed. As a result, people's fears of travelling by train grew even more intense. Those who were brave enough to travel on trains registered numerous complaints about lost luggage, delays and breakdowns. A letter of complaint written
35 to a national newspaper and signed by many well-known and respected public figures, led to the government agreeing to improve standards.

When there was evidence that safety concerns
40 were being addressed, train travel became increasingly popular. A standardised clock giving the same time across the country was introduced to coordinate timetables and to avoid near misses

73

45 on the tracks. Regulations controlling the building of the tracks, bridges and tunnels were improved, and trains were rigorously checked by specially trained railway engineers. If a problem was found, then the train was immobilised until it was judged
50 to be safe.

Although the travelling public could never be given a guarantee of total safety, the accident rate declined. Moreover, people gradually became reassured that train travel was not likely to
55 cause health problems. People of all ages and across all sections of society slowly began to experience the excitement and novelty of travelling by train.

Wider horizons

Before the Industrial Revolution, villages and towns 60 were much smaller, and most people worked in the village or town where they were born. Train travel increased opportunities because local people could travel easily to take up a wider variety of jobs in different parts of the country. This also gave them 65 a chance to learn new skills and find out about a different way of life.

Finally, railway construction itself generated many new kinds of employment. Although the workers who maintained the tracks were on low wages, 70 getting a job as a skilled railway engineer was highly prized as it meant a good salary and prospects.

3 Reading

a Read the article about early train travel. Does it include any of the ideas you thought of and shared in your group?

b Scan the text to find the answer to these questions.

Which group of people:

1 feared that train travel could cause deaths in passengers?

2 worried that the trains would affect the way they earned a living?

3 put pressure on the government to make changes?

4 had the power to stop a train from operating?

5 found that a wider range of jobs and lifestyles were available?

6 carried out underpaid but essential building and maintenance work?

4 Making notes

Make brief notes on the text using the headings and bullet points below.

Fears of effects on rural life:

- _____
- _____
- _____
- _____

Safety improvements:

- _____
- _____
- _____

Impact on employment:

- _____
- _____
- _____

5 Post-reading task

1 What was the **main** benefit of the train to people in the 19th century? What was the **main** disadvantage?

2 Imagine that you are living about 150 years ago. What facts could you tell someone who is afraid of travelling by train to reassure them that train travel is safe?

Example: There is no evidence that travelling by train causes heart attacks.

3 Some people today are afraid of flying. Do you think it would help them to know how people used to feel about train travel?

6 Language study: Logical reasoning

A Study these sentences from the article with a partner. Underline the words you think are used to express reasoning.

When an accident happened, it made front-page news because people were eager to have their suspicions confirmed. As a result, people's fears of travelling by train grew even more intense.

The writer uses *because* to express reason and *as a result* to express consequence. Can you replace *because* and *as a result* with words of similar meaning? Use commas if necessary.

B   Here is another sentence from the text. Study it carefully and underline the words that express a logical connection. Notice where commas are used.

If a problem was found, (then) the train was immobilised until it was judged to be safe.

C   Which word in the following sentence is an alternative to *In addition*?

Furthermore, farmers opposed the idea of railways cutting through their farmland, as they believed that the smoke and steam would destroy crops and scare their animals.

7 Completing a text

Read this extract from a newspaper published in 1865 about the problems experienced by train passengers. With a partner, try to fill the gaps with words expressing reasoning and logical connection.

> Many of our readers are increasingly concerned about those passengers who, with no apology, bring live chickens, ducks and even lambs with them on train journeys, _____ these animals seriously disturb the comfort of others on the journey. _____, there have been reports of animals escaping from the compartment and getting out onto the track, which compromises everyone's safety.
>
> Due to the disruption caused by the selfishness of others, the number of passenger complaints has risen and the number of train tickets sold has fallen significantly, especially on market days.
>
> _____, train travel is likely to become even more expensive in future _____ the train companies cannot afford to operate trains at low capacity.

8 Spelling and pronunciation: The letter *g*

The letter **g** is a hard sound in words like *glass*, *great* and *peg*. The phonetic symbol is /g/.

gu in words like *guard* and *guest* is also pronounced /g/. (In a few words, like *extinguish*, **gu** is pronounced /gw/.)

Notice how **g** is pronounced in *Egypt*, *giant* and *generous*. This is sometimes called 'soft g' and the phonetic symbol is /dʒ/. What other words do you know that have this sound?

Recognition 🔊 CD 1, Track 10

Many of the words in the following list are taken from the information you have read. Listen to the words on the recording. Mark them **g** if you think the *g* sound is hard, pronounced /g/. Mark them **s** if the *g* sound is soft, pronounced /dʒ/.

1	engineer	**5**	passengers	**9**	regulations
2	rigorously	**6**	guarantee	**10**	registered
3	challenge	**7**	oxygen	**11**	significant
4	figure	**8**	apology	**12**	ageing

Practice

/g/ and /dʒ/ are voiced sounds. If you place your fingers on the spot where your vocal cords are and say the sounds, you will feel your vocal cords vibrate. Practise saying the words in the list clearly to your partner. Does he/she think you are pronouncing the words correctly?

9 Spelling patterns

Did you notice how all the /dʒ/ sounds in exercise 8 were followed by the letters *e*, *i* or *y*? Look back at the word list and circle this spelling pattern for each soft-**g** word.

But hard-**g** sounds are also sometimes followed by *e* or *i*, as in the words *get*, *tiger* and *girl*.

10 Vocabulary

Choose a word from the list in exercise 8 to match each of the following sentences:

1   She should offer one for breaking your vase.

2   We breathe in this gas.

3   He or she is trained to repair machines.

4   The people who pay to travel on a plane, train or boat.

5   It's worthwhile but sometimes difficult too.

6   To promise that something will happen.

7   A word with a similar meaning to 'rules'.

8   Another word for 'number'.

9   The aircraft should be checked in this way if a fault is suspected.

What do you notice about the sounds of the words in 1–5 and 6–9?

11 Odd word out

Circle the odd word out in each list. Can you say why it is different?

A   hygienic general vegetable gymnasium surgeon privilege changeable regard manager encourage

B   grateful vague magazine guard Portuguese pigeon dialogue angry catalogue guilt guess

12 Look, say, cover, write, check

The following words can be problematic to spell. Read them first and check that you understand the meaning of each one. Then use the 'look, say, cover, write, check' method to learn to spell them correctly. (See 1.1 What is happiness? exercise 6)

When you feel you have learnt them properly, ask your partner to test you. All the words are taken from previous exercises.

VOCABULARY		
changeable	luggage	rigorously
passenger	vegetables	catalogue
Portuguese	encourage	guard
privilege	apology	manager

Choose six of the words and put each one into a sentence to show its meaning.

13 Before you listen

What form of transport, if any, do you use to:

- get to school or college?
- go shopping?
- visit friends?
- go to places of entertainment?

How satisfied do you feel with the forms of transport you use? Is there any form of transport you would prefer? Try to explain your views.

Vocabulary check

Before you listen, make sure you know the meaning of these words and expressions.

VOCABULARY		
get a lift from someone	acid rain	asthma

14 Listening for gist 🔊 CD 1, Track 11

You are going to listen to a discussion between two friends, Paolo and Linda, on the results of a survey. The survey was carried out to determine patterns of car usage by pupils in their school. Listen to the discussion first for general meaning.

15 Listening and note taking 🔊 CD 1, Track 11

Now listen again and try to complete these notes:

1 Average weekly number of car journeys:
   _____ .

2 5% make more than
   _____ .

3 _____ admitted using
   a car when it was not necessary.

4 The school:
   a _____ .
   b has a train station only 5 minutes away.

5 Coming to school by train or bus is:
   a too expensive.
   b _____ (homes
      aren't near a bus stop or train station).

6 Parents' opinions of roads for walking or cycling:
   _____ .

7 Reasons for not wanting own car in future:
   a effect on the environment.
   b _____ .

8 When _____ they try
   to persuade them to get a small, fuel-efficient type.

16 Post-listening discussion

How do the results of the survey compare with your personal usage of the car?

Do you agree with Paolo and Linda that we should encourage people to use other forms of transport rather than the car? How feasible would that be for you and your family? Share your ideas with your group.

17 Euphemisms

Paolo says pupils prefer to get lifts instead of walking. He comments that the reason is 'just laziness'. This is a very direct statement. If he were telling the school the results of the survey, he would probably avoid this remark because he could cause offence. He might prefer to use a euphemism like 'pupils prefer to take a relaxed approach to getting where they want to go'.

Matching

Match the common euphemisms in italics with their meanings:

1 Her cardigan *had seen better days*.
2 I need the *bathroom*.
3 Discounts for *senior citizens*.
4 When is *the happy event*?
5 He's *careful with his money*.
6 The house *is in need of some modernisation*.
7 She's *looking the worse for wear*.
8 My grandfather has *passed away*.

A requires repairs and decoration
B toilet
C died
D very tired, dishevelled
E old people
F the birth
G mean, not generous
H was shabby, perhaps had holes in it

18 Asking for a favour

Study this dialogue:

Joe: Dad, could you do me a favour? Would you mind giving me a lift to the sports hall? I've got a basketball game.

Dad: When do you want to go?

Joe: In about half an hour.

Dad: Oh, all right.

Joe: Thanks, Dad. Are you sure it's not too much trouble?

Dad: No, I need to go out anyway.

Joe: Well, thanks a lot. That's nice of you.

Asking for a favour

Could you do me a favour?
Can I ask you something?
Would you mind giving me a lift?
Could you please …?

Checking

Are you sure it's not too much trouble?
Are you sure it's all right with you?
Are you sure it's not too inconvenient?
Are you certain it's not too much bother?
I hope it doesn't put you out.
Are you sure it's OK? I don't want to be a nuisance.

Expressing thanks

Thanks, that's nice of you.
Thanks a lot. That really helps me out.
Thanks very much. I really appreciate it.

Practice

Take turns asking for a favour in the following situations. Work in pairs. Try to sound a little tentative.

1   You need a lift to the cinema.
2   You need to be picked up from a party.
3   You need someone to post a letter for you.
4   You need someone to take a parcel round to a friend's house.
5   You need to borrow a tennis racket.
6   You need someone to pick up your jacket from the dry cleaner's.

B   Nature under threat

1   Pre-reading discussion

Do you own a bicycle? How often do you cycle and where do you usually go to? If you do not own a bicycle, would you like one?

In pairs, work out the advantages and disadvantages of cycling as a form of transport. When you have finished, compare your ideas with those of other pairs and add any new points to your list.

Advantages
It doesn't pollute the environment.

Disadvantages
You can get knocked off and hurt.

2   Predicting content

You are going to read a leaflet asking people to join a sponsored cycle ride. ('Sponsored' means that the people taking part will have asked 'sponsors' to donate money to charity.)

Look at the title of the leaflet and the pictures. What kind of people do you think will join the ride? What do you think the cycle route will be like?

3   Reading for gist

Skim-read the leaflet quickly to get a general idea of the content. There are three reasons the cycle ride is being held. What are they?

Bike to the future

Registration is now open for *Bike to the future* – Friends of the Earth's (FoE) annual sponsored cycle ride. So get off the sofa and sign up early for what promises to be another great May day out in the countryside!

5

Bike to the future is the most popular event in Friends of the Earth's calendar. Year after year, people have written in to tell us how much they've enjoyed the route, the warm and friendly atmosphere, and the high spirits of their fellow cyclists!

10

This year, *Bike to the future* will start near Hampton Court and take its riders through beautiful countryside to Eton. As ever, its gentle and undemanding 30 miles will be lined with refreshment stops, entertainment and lots of surprises. *Bike to*

15 *the future* is first and foremost a fun day out, but there's a serious message, too. The route will highlight the threats to the surrounding area from new road schemes – passing through Chobham Common, which is affected by plans to widen the M3, and areas

20 close to where sections of the M25 and M4 are also currently marked out for widening.

These are just a few reminders of the continuing threats to our health and environment from increased traffic and pollution due to unnecessary road

25 schemes. The funds raised from *Bike to the future* will help sustain our campaign to halt unnecessary road schemes in favour of transport options which encourage less, rather than more, travel by road.

So help us get there! Register now for *Bike to the*

30 *future* to give yourself time to sign up as many sponsors as you can.

All you need is a bike

The route and all the practical details are taken care of by experts. It will be easy to get to the start 35 and home again – South West Trains are is laying on special trains to take you and your bike to the start, and get you back to London from the finish. Marshals will guide you on the route, and first aid will be available for you and your bike if needed. 40

Good reasons to get sponsored

Once you've sent us your entry form and fee, we'll send you an official sponsorship form so you can start signing up your friends and workmates. Whether you cycle on your own or in a team, there 45 are loads of prizes for reaching fundraising targets, including *Bike to the future* badges and T-shirts, cycle accessories and even mountain bikes!

There are also prizes for your sponsors. Anyone who sponsors you for £5.00 or more will 50 automatically be entered in a prize draw.

The more the merrier

You're welcome to register on your own. However, it can be more fun in a group – and if you get together a team of ten or more, we'll give you a free *Bike to* 55 *the future* T-shirt. Your team-mates will also be able to order T-shirts at half price.

The ride ends within sight of Windsor Castle in the village of Eton.

4 True/false comprehension: skim reading

Are these statements about the cycle ride true or false? Skim read the text to spot the correct answers.

1   This is the first time the sponsored cycle ride has been held.
2   The day is primarily for enjoyment.
3   The cycle ride celebrates the victory over plans to develop Chobham Common.
4   Participants will help plan the route.
5   Extra trains to and from London will be provided.
6   Medical help will be available.
7   Prizes are only available to the teams.
8   Participants in teams of ten or more get a discount on the T-shirts.
9   The ride finishes at Chobham Common.

5 Post-reading discussion

Have you ever taken part in a sponsored charity event, e.g. a swim, a dance or a walk? Tell your partner what it was like.

6 Reordering an article

The following text, taken from an article on a school website, puts forward the pros and cons of cycling.

Try to reorder it so that it is in a logical sequence. The first and final sentences are provided. Finally, decide where the new paragraphs should start.

The pros and cons of cycling

a   Cycling at night is *particularly dangerous*, especially along dark country roads, as a motorist may not see you until it is too late.

b   *In addition*, owning a bike frees you from dependence on your parents to take you to places.

c   However, some of these problems *can be eliminated* if you take sensible precautions, such as using lights at night and wearing reflector strips.

d   *In conclusion, although there are certainly some drawbacks,* I feel that the personal enjoyment and freedom you get from cycling outweigh the disadvantages.

e   Cycling can be *dangerous* on busy roads and you can be seriously hurt if you are knocked off your bike by a motorist.

f   Cycling is an enjoyable, efficient and liberating mode of transport that has many benefits.

g   In the first place, cycling is cheap because second-hand bikes are *not expensive*.

h   *Attending* a cycling training scheme also enables you to cycle more safely and may help you identify the less polluted routes.

i   *Although* cycling has many advantages, there are some *drawbacks too.*

j   *Moreover,* many roads are polluted by traffic fumes which makes cycling unpleasant and unhealthy.

k   You can also save money by carrying out simple repairs yourself.

l   It also removes the frustrations of waiting around for a bus to turn up.

First sentence:

f   Cycling is an enjoyable, efficient and liberating mode of transport which has many benefits.

Last sentence:

d   *In conclusion, although there are some drawbacks,* I feel that the personal enjoyment and freedom you get from cycling outweigh the disadvantages.

7 What makes a good argument?

A   When you have reordered the article correctly, read it through or write it out in full to get a feeling of how the text flows.

B   The text above could be described as 'balanced'. Why, do you think?

C   The last paragraph shows the writer's point of view. Is this a good way of concluding an argument? Why/Why not?

D   A convincing article should help the reader understand the issues. Do you think the article 'The pros and cons of cycling' achieves this? Try to explain how you feel to your group.

8 Presenting contrasting ideas in the same paragraph

'The pros and cons of cycling' devotes separate paragraphs to the advantages and disadvantages of cycling. It then sums up at the end. An alternative to this approach is to consider contrasting ideas in the same paragraph.

The following extract comes from an article about whether cycle helmets should be made compulsory. Circle the word that contrasts one idea with its opposite:

I recognise that a feeling of freedom is part of the pleasure of cycling. Nevertheless, in my opinion, it is essential that cyclists are made aware of the dangers of not wearing a helmet.

Now rewrite the extract using a different linking word or phrase. Choose from: *although, however, but, yet, in spite of*. Make changes to the extract if you think it is necessary.

9 Presenting more contrasting ideas

Study these incomplete sentences. Notice the use of a contrast word in each one. Then try to complete each sentence in an appropriate way.

1 Car accidents continue to increase *despite*

2 The government has launched a big safety campaign to encourage cyclists to take a cycling test. *Nevertheless,*

3 A new airport is planned for our area *in spite of*

4 I have always been a keen supporter of the private car. *However,*

5 It seems unfair to stop cars going into the town centre, *yet*

6 A good train service would help to reduce our carbon footprint. *On the other hand,*

7 Cycling is not encouraged in the town, *although*

8 People are frightened of travelling by plane *even though*

9 The railway companies tell us train journeys are quick and comfortable, *but*

10 I would always travel by sea rather than by air *despite*

10 Language study: Linking words

Linking words have a variety of functions in constructing an argument. They can be used to express opinion, show contrast, express consequence and give reasons.

Working in pairs, try to add words or expressions under each of the following headings. Then compare your ideas with the rest of the group.

Listing	**Addition**
First of all	*also*
_____	_____
_____	_____

Contrast	**Reasoning**
but	*because*
_____	_____
_____	_____

Opinion	**Emphasis**
We think	*Above all*
_____	_____
_____	_____

Consequence	**Summing up**
so	*On balance*
_____	_____
_____	_____

11 Brainstorming

Brainstorming is a group work activity you'll be using regularly to help you come up with ideas on a topic. It's important because you can't write a convincing argument unless you have strong ideas to work with. Work in small groups to brainstorm ideas about the topic:

Should Eaves Wood be cut down to provide a car park for shoppers?

Imagine that the local council is considering cutting down a small wood near a shopping centre to make a car park for the convenience of shoppers. Write down points for and against the idea. Take five minutes to do this.

POINTS FOR	POINTS AGAINST
_____	_____
_____	_____

12 Text completion

A local student, Roland Chang, heard about the proposal to cut down the wood. He felt very strongly about it so he wrote to his local newspaper. Study his email carefully with a partner. Then try to complete each gap with appropriate linking words from the choices given.

1 However / On the other hand / Although / Because

2 In addition / In the first place / Nevertheless / But

3 to sum up / also / in my view / nevertheless

4 On the other hand / At the beginning / Furthermore / Finally

5 secondly / not at all / because / such as

6 for example / yet / thirdly / so

7 In addition / Therefore / Consequently / However

8 also / but / thirdly / last but not least

9 In the end / In my opinion / On the contrary / For instance

10 For example / After all / In fact / On the other hand

```
  ● ● ●                New Message
  ┌──────────────────────────────────────────┐
  To :  [                ]  From:  [                ]
  ├──────────────────────────────────────────┤
```

Dear Editor,

I was disappointed when I heard of the proposals to cut down Eaves Wood to make a car park for shoppers.

(1) _____ I agree that the town is short of car parks, this solution would be insensitive and wrong. **(2)** _____, the wood is an area of natural beauty. There are many ancient trees of an unusual kind. I often go there for a picnic or just to relax at weekends. The wood is **(3)** _____ a vital habitat for birds, animals and insects. If the trees were cut down, many species would be lost. **(4)** _____, the wood is right in the centre of a heavily polluted part of town. The trees help to make the air cleaner **(5)** _____ they trap dust, smoke and fume particles in their branches and leaves. The council says it is worried about global warming, **(6)** _____ trees help reduce the build-up of gases that contribute to global warming because they feed on carbon dioxide emissions. **(7)** _____, that area **(8)** _____ suffers from high noise levels from passing lorries and the railway line. The trees help reduce the noise levels and have a beneficial effect on the whole environment. **(9)** _____, cutting down the wood would be stupid, greedy and pointless. A car park may well attract shoppers to the town and increase the shopkeepers' trade. **(10)** _____, a unique and beautiful place would be destroyed. I would be very interested in hearing what your other readers think.

Yours faithfully,
Roland Chang

13 Discussion

Do you think the email is too formal, too informal or about right? Try to explain why.

How does Roland show an awareness of his audience in the letter?

Obviously, Roland is opposed to the council's plans. How convincing do you think his argument is? Try to mention particular examples to justify your opinion.

14 Words often confused

These words, some of which are taken from Roland's letter, are often confused. Complete each sentence with the correct alternative.

1 council/counsel

  a The _____ meets once a month.

  b The doctor may also _____ you about your personal problems.

2 affect/effect

  a The medicine didn't have any _____ on my cold.

  b The new rules _____ all aircraft over 30 years old.

3 there/they're/their

  a _____ are plenty of pegs for the children's coats and lockers for _____ shoes.

  b They said if _____ going to be late, they will let us know.

4 lose/loose

  a You must be careful not to _____ your passport.

  b Since I lost weight, my trousers have been too _____.

5 alternate/alternative

  a I have to work on _____ weekends.

  b The last bus had gone so walking home was the only _____.

6 lightning/lightening

  a The house was struck by _____.

  b The sun came up, gradually _____ the sky.

7 practice/practise

  a He tries to _____ the guitar once a day.

  b We have music _____ on Tuesdays.

8 past/passed

  a Have you seen Henry in the _____ few days? Yes, I _____ him in the street on Saturday.

  b Luckily, we all _____ our maths test.

C A new motorway for Rosville?

1 Pre-reading discussion

Study the photographs and try to describe them. How do you think the people in the cars are feeling? What causes traffic jams to build up on main roads and motorways? Is there any way of preventing them?

Brainstorming

Divide into two groups. Group A should try to list all the advantages of motorways. Group B should aim to list all the disadvantages.

When you have finished, compare your ideas. Can you add any new ideas between you?

Motorways – for and against

Advantages	Disadvantages
_____	_____
_____	_____
_____	_____

2 Reading an example email

Rosville's council is supporting government plans to build a new motorway. This will link Rosville to the capital and to some other large cities. Do you think this will be a good development for Rosville? Who is likely to benefit? Who might be against the idea? Try to think of reasons for your opinions.

Now scan the email quickly. Are any of the points you thought of in the discussion noted here?

> **New Message**
>
> To: _____ From: _____
>
> Dear Editor,
>
> We are delighted that a new motorway is being planned for Rosville because it will bring so many benefits to the town.
>
> In the first place, Rosville has suffered from the recession — many young people are unemployed after leaving school. The motorway will bring a much-needed boost to business, as communications will be faster, cheaper and more efficient. Consequently, businesses will find life easier, new companies will be attracted to Rosville and there will be more jobs for everyone.
>
> Furthermore, the new motorway will not only reduce commuting time for the large number of people who travel to the city daily, but will also provide them with a safer and more relaxing journey to work.
>
> Many readers might be worried about pollution from increased traffic. On the contrary, pollution will actually decrease as so many new trees, especially chosen for their ability to absorb car fumes, will be planted.
>
> Finally, the new motorway will also serve as a bypass for the large lorries that now go through Rosville town centre.
>
> There is no doubt that the motorway will really put Rosville on the map. If we want a bright future for ourselves and our children, we should all support it.
>
> Yours faithfully,
> The Rosville Business Group

3 Comprehension check

1 Where will the text in exercise 2 appear?

2 What are the writer's main points in favour of a new motorway?

3 How convincing do you find the argument? Give some reasons.

Vocabulary

Here are some definitions of words in the email. Try to find the words and underline them.

a a bad period in the country's economy

b something that helps and encourages

c routes linking one place to another

d to travel between home and work every day

e a main road built to avoid a town.

4 Analysing the email

Work in pairs to answer these questions on the email in exercise **2 Reading an example email**. They will help you analyse the way the model argument is structured.

1 Underline the word in the opening paragraph that expresses emotion. Which word introduces a reason for the feeling? Underline it. An opening paragraph should grab the reader's attention. Does this paragraph do that?

2 Which words are used in paragraph 3 for emphasis?

3 Paragraph 4 considers an opposing point of view. What is it? Which phrase is used to introduce a contrasting opinion?

4 *Finally* is used at the start of paragraph 5. Why?

5 The last paragraph should not leave the reader in any doubt as to what the writer thinks. It should have a confident tone. What do you think of the final paragraph of the email in exercise **2 Reading an example email?**

5 Putting forward an opposing viewpoint

The Rosville Nature Society held a meeting to discuss the email from the Rosville Business Group that appeared in the local newspaper. Look at the draft email they wrote in reply. Read the points carefully and make sure you understand each one.

Are any of the points similar to the list of disadvantages of motorways you made earlier?

DRAFT EMAIL

Dear Editor,

We were horrified to hear of the plans for a new motorway for Rosville and we are sure our feelings are shared by many of your readers. We believe the scheme would destroy the environment and damage wildlife. The motorway itself will cost a great deal of money to build. It would be better to use this money to help local businesses by improving the rail network. Commuters to the city would benefit from a better train service. The idea that the motorway will be more efficient is completely unfounded. The new road will soon attract

extra traffic. The suggestion that planting trees alongside the motorway will eliminate pollution is ludicrous. Trees can help. They cannot make up for the destruction of wildflowers and wildlife. Many of us cycle or walk across the present road to get to school or work. The new motorway that replaces the old road will split the area into two, making it impossible to get to the other side on foot or by bicycle. Please, people of Rosville, don't stand by and watch your environment being destroyed. We urge you to support the Rosville Nature Society campaign by writing to your local councillor.

Yours faithfully,
The Rosville Nature Society

6 Redrafting

Redraft the email so that it flows more smoothly. Remember, you will need linking words to show connection or contrast between ideas. Add words to express personal opinion or emphasis where you think it is appropriate. Finally, make sure you use paragraphs.

When you have finished, show your work to a partner. Does he/she agree that your email now flows more smoothly, has an appropriate tone and sounds more persuasive?

7 Relating to your target audience

Your email or article should reflect the interest of those who are going to read it. These people are called your 'target audience'.

Study the extracts A–E. Decide with a partner whether each extract comes from:

- a school magazine
- a letter to a local newspaper
- an e-newsletter for elderly people
- a music and video sharing website
- a report.

Decide whether the target audience in each case is:

- school pupils
- elderly people
- the general public
- the headteacher
- internet users.

A *I don't agree with the last post. I absolutely love the words to this song. It really captures the idea of fighting to save a troubled world. The images that go with the music really work for me as well.*

B *Most of us already have problems getting to school on time. The proposed cuts to the bus service will make things even worse. I suggest we have an urgent meeting to discuss a plan of action in the Common Room next Wednesday lunchtime.*

C *I am writing to express my concern about your suggestion printed in yesterday's Evening News that the greenhouse effect has no scientific basis. Like*

many of the readers of this newspaper, I have no doubt that the greenhouse effect is a reality that is becoming steadily worse.

D *Like most people of my age, I welcome the news that Redline buses are offering senior citizens free bus passes at weekends. Go to www.redlineseniorpass.com for further information.*

E *To sum up, our visit to the environmental centre to see bicycles being made from recycled metal and rubber was so worthwhile. If we could have permission for another visit later this term, our class would love to go again.*

8 Writing a report for the headteacher on a new facility

Students at your school have recently been provided with an outdoor covered seating area. Students can sit under the covered area at breaktimes, if they wish. The covered area is situated on the far side of the grounds away from the main school buildings. Your headteacher wants to find out what students think of their new facility. He would also like to know if it would be a good idea to construct a similar covered area for the younger students (8–12 years).

Write a report for the headteacher giving your views. You should be calm and objective about the new facility. Your report represents the views of the students, so your personal feelings should not dominate. A report should not be emotional in any way. In the final paragraph you can say clearly whether you think the new facility is a success. You should also say whether a similar facility would be good for the younger children. You can use these ideas and structure to help you.

Introduction

1   My reasons for writing this report: asked for by headteacher.

Main Paragraphs

Positive points about the facility:

1   protection from hot sun / some students concerned about sun damage

2   very useful in recent stormy weather / heavy rain / thankful we can go under cover

3 small tables are useful for packed lunches / writing

4 new friendships made as students from wider range of classes and different ages mix

5 peaceful in this part of the school grounds / can hear the birdsong / enjoy nature / relax properly

6 return to school refreshed / right mood to study.

Negative Points about the facility:

1 some distance from main buildings / quite a long walk (but students now getting more used to it)

2 fixed seats – inconvenient for friendship groups / chatting

3 not enough recycling bins–litter / insects / smells

Conclusion

Successful facility. Popularity gradually increasing. Consider adding seats not fixed to ground.

Should younger children have similar facility – yes! Possibly situate it near the water fountain / they get thirsty running around.

9 Writing a report on a proposal for the benefit of elderly people

In your neighbourhood, there is a very large open area called *Antalya Place*, which young people use for ball games. The town council is proposing to dig up the area and plant a flower garden with benches for elderly people. Trees will be planted, too. No ball games will be allowed. Your local council has asked for a report which represents the views of the people who will be affected.

Write a report for the council. You should try to be fair and objective about the development, as both groups have a right to enjoy the area in different ways. The final paragraph should show clearly whether or not you would recommend the proposal. Use the following outline to guide you.

Paragraph one: introduction
Points in favour

1 flower garden attractive / would brighten up area / flowers and plants provide a habitat for a wide variety of insect life

2 some old people lonely / have no meeting place / garden would provide focal point for meeting each other

3 trees welcome / provide shade / reduce pollution and noise levels / provide protection against wind.

Points against

1 young people need opportunity to practise ball games / most live in flats – no gardens or other space nearby

2 local football and netball teams are winning matches / will be less successful if cannot practise / morale and team confidence will sink

3 young people meet friends, have picnics, watch matches, enjoy themselves here / without this area, boredom and resentment might set in / vandalism might be a problem.

Final paragraph

Area is very large. Council could dig up one part on far side for small flower garden for the elderly / will still be enough space in main area for games – essential for teenagers.

10 Understanding a typical exam-style stimulus

An exam question will often provide a stimulus in the form of comments. Study this example. What does the question ask you to do?

There are proposals to develop a river near your home. A marina would be built, and tourists would be encouraged to come and use the river for boating and fishing. The council has asked you to write a report saying: *What you think of this idea?*

Here are some comments from local people. You can use these for ideas, or use ideas of your own.

'The development will create jobs, which we need.'

'Engine oil and litter from boats will pollute the water.'

'The plants that grow in the water will help to absorb pollution. Many of them will die if the river becomes developed.'

'The river is in a beautiful, relaxing setting. It's only right to encourage more people to benefit from the tranquility of the area.'

'Local people use the plants in the river as raw material for making things, such as reeds for making baskets. We will lose a valuable source of raw material if the river is developed.'

'If too much fishing goes on, the river will become over-fished and many species will die out, disrupting the sensitive ecology of the river.'

'Our area needs to become more modern and to progress. Developing the river will help us achieve this aim.'

11 Redrafting an exam-style answer

With a partner, study the answer below to the exam-style question in exercise 10. What do you think are the strengths of the answer? What do you feel are the weaknesses? Write them down.

I think it is a good idea to develop the river because it will create jobs, which we need in our area. The river is set in a beautiful, relaxing part of the countryside. It is only right to encourage more people to benefit from the tranquility of the area. Our area needs to become more modern and to progress. Developing the river will help us achieve this aim. The engine oil and litter from boats will pollute the water. The plants that grow in the water help to absorb pollution. Many of them will die if the river becomes developed. Local people use the plants in the river for raw material. We will lose a source of raw material if the river is developed. It will be bad for business. If too much fishing goes on, the river will become over-fished and many species will die out, disrupting the ecological cycle. I would recommend the river should be developed because there are more advantages than disadvantages in doing so. But sometimes I am not sure if it is the right thing to do. Thank you for asking me to write this report and I have done my best.

Strengths

_____

_____

_____

Weaknesses

_____

_____

_____

Try to redraft the report. Remember to set out your writing clearly with paragraphing and logical connectors. The target audience is the council who wants to consider both the advantages and the disadvantages, so aim to be objective and fair. However, the final paragraph should make it clear what you think is the right thing to do.

When you've finished, compare your version with a partner's. What are the main differences? Does he/she feel you have improved the original draft? How convincing is your argument and how well does it relate to the target audience?

D Global warming

1 Vocabulary check

Complete the gaps in the paragraph with the following expressions. There is one more than you need. Do not use any expression more than once.

VOCABULARY	
climate change	**greenhouse gases**
carbon emissions	**environmental pollution**
global warming	**carbon footprint**

_____ means a continuing rise in the Earth's average temperature. Many scientists think that this is the result of our production of _____, such as carbon dioxide, which become trapped and warm the Earth's atmosphere.

A _____ measures the total greenhouse gas emissions caused by the activities of a person, group or country. Richer countries have a bigger carbon footprint per person.

There are fears that global warming is causing _____ and so many governments are aiming to reduce their _____.

The pie chart shows the carbon footprint of a typical individual living in a More Economically Developed Country (MEDC).

1   Which sector has the greatest carbon footprint and which has the smallest?

2   Which of the following statements about the chart are true?

  a   Activities at home which use electricity contribute almost one-eighth to the carbon footprint.

  b   Private transport contributes 7% more than public transport to the carbon footprint.

  c   Recreation and leisure activities contribute less to the carbon footprint than holiday flights.

  d   House furnishings and buildings contribute just under 10% to the carbon footprint.

As a country develops, its carbon footprint increases. Can you find out the size of the carbon footprint of your country?

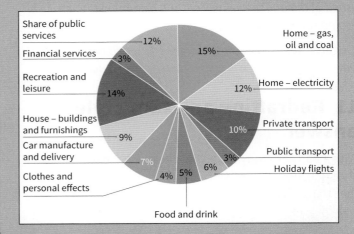

Share of public services — 12%
Financial services — 3%
Recreation and leisure — 14%
House – buildings and furnishings — 9%
Car manufacture and delivery — 7%
Clothes and personal effects — 4%
5%
6%
3%
Food and drink
Holiday flights
Public transport
Private transport — 10%
Home – electricity — 12%
Home – gas, oil and coal — 15%

2   Pre-reading discussion

A   Read the following statements about climate change. One of them is incorrect. Discuss the ideas with a partner and cross out the incorrect statement.

  1   Burning fossil fuels, such as oil, coal and gas, produces greenhouse gases, which may contribute to climate change.

  2   Wind, waves and sunlight are all renewable sources of energy. These can help reduce climate change.

  3   Nuclear energy is radioactive and produces greenhouse gases, which cause climate change.

  4   Climate change has caused unpredictable global weather patterns including floods, severe winters, drought and desertification.

B   How might the way of life in your country change if the climate became much warmer and drier, or much wetter and colder? Discuss the possible benefits and disadvantages.

C   Here are some things students are doing to help reduce climate change. Which one idea is not sensible? Cross it out.

  1   If it is cold, I put on a jumper rather than turn up the heating.

  2   We insulate our hot water pipes to keep them warm and more efficient.

3 We're installing air conditioning in more rooms in our house, to keep it at an even temperature.

4 We changed our light bulbs to the energy-efficient type.

5 We are going to put solar panels on our roof so we can use the sun's energy for light and heating.

Have you or your family made any similar changes to help the environment? Share your ideas in your groups.

3 Reading for gist

Deepak has written an article for his school magazine on climate change. Before you read, make sure you know the meaning of these words.

VOCABULARY		
intrigued	resourceful	ingenuity

89

Now read the article for general understanding.

4 Comprehension check

1 What has Deepak learnt about his lifestyle choices?

2 How have farmers in the Andes survived, despite more severe winters? Give **two** details.

3 Why are Bangladeshi farmers using wooden rafts?

4 Why is the future of the rice growers more secure?

5 What have the club members decided to do to help the environment?

6 What does Deepak invite the magazine readers to do?

5 Tone and register

The tone and register of this article are more informal than in the texts about the new motorway for Rosville (exercises 2 and 5). Underline any aspects of Deepak's writing that help create this impression. Do you think the tone and register he uses are appropriate for his audience? Why/Why not?

Friends of the Planet

Although I don't usually write to the school magazine, I have recently joined a school club, 'Friends of the Planet'. I thought you might be intrigued to know more about what we do.

The club members have been researching facts on global warming and putting them in our school blog. Do you know that by flying in a plane for an hour we produce the same carbon emissions as a Bangladeshi citizen produces in a whole year? Earlier this year, my whole family flew to America for a wedding so we definitely increased our carbon footprint. Being in the club has made me think more about the environmental impact of our lifestyle choices.

We have found out lots of other important things at the club, too, such as ways people in different parts of the world are coping with climate change.

In the Andes in Peru, for example, farmers have had to cope with much more severe winters. The bitterly cold weather had been killing the alpaca, a domesticated animal that provides milk, cheese, meat and wool. The farmers could have given up, but they learnt how to build strong shelters for the animals and developed veterinary skills. As a result, the communities are surviving and are even more resourceful than before.

In another part of the world, Bangladeshi farmers have found their own ways to overcome a problem of a different sort: widespread flooding. Using wooden rafts, the farmers developed vegetable gardens that float on water. Isn't that an amazing idea? And it works!

Finally, I want to tell you about Sri Lanka. Sea levels around the Sri Lankan coast were rising due to climate change and, consequently, the rice paddies were being contaminated by salt. It was extremely worrying because rice is the farmers' main crop. However, they experimented with different types of rice and found a strain of rice that can flourish in salty water! How is that for ingenuity!

In the club, we decided that, if other people can make changes, so can we. Therefore, we are going to make one small change every day to our carbon footprint. We will be doing things like using our bikes, recycling rubbish and turning off electrical appliances when we leave the room. It might not sound like much, but we think it will eventually make a real difference.

Would you like to reduce your carbon footprint? Then join us at the club to find out how! We meet at lunchtime on Thursday in Room 12. See you there!

GRAMMAR SPOTLIGHT

The future

A   We use *will* + the infinitive of a verb (without 'to') to talk about events in the future:

'*Bike to the Future*, **will start** near Hampton Court.

The route **will highlight** the threats to the surrounding area.

Can you find another example of *will* + verb in the fourth paragraph of the text in **section B3**?

B   We use *will* + *be* in passive future sentences:

Anyone who sponsors you for $5.00 or more **will** automatically **be entered** in a prize draw.

C   The short forms **I'll** and **we'll** are common in informal English:

We'll send you an official sponsorship form.

Can you find another example in the penultimate paragraph of the text in **section B3**?

D   We use *going to* + verb to talk about things we intend to do:

We are **going to put** solar panels on our roof.

Can you find another example of *going to* + verb in paragraph 7 of the article in **section D5**.

Exam-style questions

Speaking

1 Climate change

Many experts believe climate change may cause serious problems, such as unpredictable weather patterns leading to storms, drought or flooding. Discuss this topic with the assessor.

You may wish to use the following ideas to help develop the conversation:

- what you like or dislike about the climate where you live
- the challenges and problems your country might face if the climate became much hotter, colder or wetter
- what people themselves can do to reduce climate change
- what governments can do to reduce problems, such as drought or flooding
- whether there may be political conflicts in future over access to fresh water, rather than resources such as oil.

You are free to consider any other related ideas of your own. You are not allowed to make any written notes.

2 City living

We now know more about how carbon dioxide emissions can damage our planet. This has an implication for the way we live in cities. Discuss this topic with the assessor.

You may wish to use the following ideas to help develop the conversation:

- the idea that cities should be planned so that people can avoid motor transport and cycle or walk to most places
- whether electric cars, water taxis and free cycle hire should be encouraged
- the suggestion that car drivers should be banned from cities on certain days or pay a charge for entering the city
- the idea that one day each week people should not attend school or work, but use modern technology to work or study from home
- the view that large numbers of people moving to live in cities leads to more problems than benefits.

Listening 🔊 CD 1, Track 12

Listening, Exercise 1

You will hear four short recordings. Answer each question on the line provided. Write no more than three words for each detail. You will hear each recording twice.

Core [8 marks], Extended [8 marks].

1 a Where does this conversation take place?

_____

b What two things can you bring on the trip?

_____

2 a Which room has the student already been to?

_____

b Where exactly should the student go to find the room she needs? Give **two** details.

_____

3 **a** What is the title of the play?

_____

    b What can you do if you want to support the work of the theatre group?

_____

4 **a** Apart from visiting the gift shop, what else does the speaker suggest the visitors to the environmental centre will enjoy?

_____

    b How long do they need for the practical activity?

_____

Reading

Reading & Writing, Exercise 2

You are going to read an extract from a magazine article, in which four young people share their thoughts on caring for the environment. For questions a–j, choose from the people A–D. The people may be chosen more than once.

Core [8 marks], Extended [10 marks]

Which person:

a says nature can be harmed but never destroyed?

b believes if people destroy the planet, we will have nowhere else to live?

c felt self-conscious when caring for the environment?

d says everyone can help reduce their carbon footprint?

e feels gratitude for the way the planet supports life?

f claims humans are capable of benefiting from the environment as well as damaging it?

g envies the freedom animals have to decide on the habitat they prefer?

h sees nature flourishing even in an urban environment?

i believes we should take care of nature because nature takes care of us? [Extended]

j feels a deep sense of belonging in the natural world? [Extended]

A **Elizabeth**

I used to take the wonderful planet we live on for granted but I don't now. I recently read a powerful novel called 'Oxygen', about life in the future where the air is so contaminated with carbon dioxide and other greenhouse gases you can't go outside. When I finished this disturbing book, I stepped out onto my balcony with my mind full of horrible images and a feeling that a natural catastrophe could occur any second. Then I felt the air on my skin and it was as if I had never felt air before. I could not stop breathing in pure oxygen and feeling so thankful. We can't see the air we breathe, yet we can't survive without it. In a million, billion invisible ways, nature is looking after each one of us. When I went back inside, I felt calmer. If you think your carbon footprint does not matter, you should read 'Oxygen'. It will change your life, like it did mine. I never drop litter now, always recycle all my family's rubbish, cycle rather than go by car and keep the air-conditioning to a minimum.

B Antoine

If I see litter anywhere, I have to pick it up and dispose of it in an environmentally friendly way. Metal cans, bottles, cartons and plastic bags sometimes get washed up on the banks of our local river. These cause environmental damage to the plants growing in the water and are dangerous to the birds, animals and fish. When I walk past the river on my way to school, I feel an overwhelming urge to get rid of any horrible rubbish. I can't just stand by and see our beautiful environment being destroyed. Once, I took off my shoes and socks and waded into the middle of the river to pull out a supermarket trolley. I wheeled it all the way back to the shop. Even though I could feel the customers looking and secretly laughing at me in my wet and muddy school uniform as I walked in, I knew it was the right thing to do. While I am here on this earth, together with the birds and the trees, the sun and sky, I feel part of it and want to love and cherish it.

C Mia

On our last school trip, we stayed on a remote island where we could study wildlife and nature. I fell in love with the wild, unspoilt landscape which is an amazing habitat for plants and animals. All you could hear was birdsong and the wind rustling through the trees. I was heartbroken when we had to return home. I could not bear to think of going back to the bleak reality of waking up and looking out on congested streets, or breathing in carbon emissions from filthy polluting factories on my way to college. I longed to be like the animals who can find new homes when their old homes are destroyed by modern roads and buildings. The strange thing is though, since having that magical experience on the island, I can now see the wonders of nature surrounding me in the city: there is life, colour and greenery everywhere – wild flowers bloom in little bits of soil and the trees are full of nesting birds. Whatever we do to harm nature, I sense it will still be with us, renewing and regenerating the world.

D Mohamed

Some people say it is down to government to stop global environmental catastrophes, such as flooding, desertification and drought. Undoubtedly, international governments should meet to stop climate change, but why wait for them? Carbon emissions from human activities have already done a huge amount of damage to animals and humans, and, if the warnings about global warming come true and we destroy the planet, none of us will have anywhere else we can go. Each individual can help save the planet by recycling rubbish and using less water. These actions could have enormous benefits. We can choose renewable sources of energy, too, like wave and wind power. I nagged my family into putting in solar panels so we can use energy from the sun for our showers. It is great for the planet and mum and dad could not help smiling when they got the electricity bill.

Writing

Reading & Writing, Exercise 6

1 There are plans to build an airport near your town. Here are some comments from local newspaper readers on the topic:

'There will be many benefits for our economy.'

'A new airport will be disastrous for the environment.'

Write a report for your local newspaper outlining your views on the proposal. The comments may give you some ideas, but you should try to use some ideas of your own. You should write 150–200 words.

Extended [16 marks]

Reading & Writing, Exercise 6

2   Your class has been involved in a nature project. The students helped to create a garden in the school grounds, which included an area for growing vegetables. Your head teacher would like you to write a report explaining the success of the project and suggesting ideas for future projects. Here are some comments from students in your class:

'We learnt so much about nature.'

'It was an interesting project, but it wasn't much fun being out in the cold and rain all day.'

'It gave us all a better understanding of where our food actually comes from.'

'It was hard physical work and we disagreed about the right way to do things.'

Write the report for the head teacher. The comments above may give you some ideas, and you can also use some ideas of your own. Your article should be 100–150 words long.

Core [12 marks]

Reading & Writing, Exercise 6

3   An article on the following topic appeared in your school magazine recently:

> Why should teenagers try to reduce their carbon footprint when new factories and roads cause so much pollution?

You have decided to write an article for the magazine outlining your views. Here are some comments from readers:

'Making a few personal changes in lifestyle now will make a big change in the long term.'

'I don't think teenagers should try to reduce their carbon footprint – it's the responsibility of the government.'

'We can't stop the building of factories and roads, but we can make changes to our own lives.'

'The future of our country depends on new developments.'

Write the article for the school magazine. The comments above may give you some ideas, and you can also use some ideas of your own. Your article should be 100–150 words long.

Core [12 marks]

Reading & Writing, Exercise 6

4   There is a proposal in your country to raise the legal age for learning to drive a car by three years. The editor of your school magazine has asked you to write an article explaining your views. Here are some comments from your friends:

'Most car accidents are caused by young people.'

'This is a sensible idea. People shouldn't be able to drive a car until they are in their twenties.'

'Learning to drive early is essential for independence.'

'You can't blame road accidents on young people – look at the way many adults drive!'

Write the article for the school magazine. The comments above may give you some ideas, and you can also use some ideas of your own. Your article should be 100–150 words long.

Core [12 marks]

Reading & Writing, Exercise 6

5   You are the organiser of a school club, 'Save the World'. The school recently paid for the club to visit an environmental centre and the headteacher has asked you to write a report saying

whether you think the visit was worthwhile. Here are some comments from students:

'*Seeing old car tyres made into shoes was fascinating.*'

'*The introductory talk was too long, and difficult to follow.*'

Write a report for the headteacher giving your views. The comments may give you some ideas, but you should try to use some ideas of your own. Your report should be 150–200 words long.

Extended [16 marks]

ADVICE FOR SUCCESS

1 *Putting forward a clear argument in a report or essay* requires the ability to think of relevant points in the first place. You can improve your understanding of controversial subjects by listening to or watching a current affairs programme once a week. Discuss matters of concern with your family or friends.

2 Take an active part in class discussions and school debates to practise thinking logically and giving your opinions orally. Offer to research a mini topic for your class and present your findings to everyone.

3 Improve your ability to write about controversial topics by reading newspaper and magazine articles that are opinion-based. Examine them carefully to see how the ideas are linked and expanded.

4 Have patience with your writing skills and be prepared to practise them. Show your written work to someone you trust and listen to their comments.

Exam techniques

5 Use a composition stimulus wisely. It is there to help you understand the rubric and to stimulate your own thoughts. Choose a few points and expand them–don't just copy them out. Give reasons of your own to support your views.

6 Express your ideas clearly and link them coherently with appropriate linking words. Remember to show some audience awareness if you can.

7 *Multiple-matching reading* exercises require careful attention to detail. Students are sometimes tempted to rush these exercises, but it's important to be patient and careful as this is where many marks can be gained.

- Read the information about where the extract comes from and what it is about before starting to match the answers.
- Read the text through, paying close attention to detail.
- Take care when selecting the answer. It may appear at first that more than one answer is possible.

Don't rush your choices. An answer can seem correct, but, although it is close to the answer required, it may not be close enough.

Exam focus

This unit has helped to prepare you for exams which test your reading, writing, listening and speaking skills. The unit has helped to develop those skills in the following ways:

- You have learnt to **give reasons and opinions in more formal articles, emails and reports**.
- You have learnt to **structure arguments** so you can write **for or against,** or **present both sides** of controversial topics.
- You have **listened** to a conversation and **taken notes** on **specific items** of information.

- You have also **listened** to **announcements** and **answered questions**.
- You have used a **range of techniques** to **answer** questions on **detailed reading texts**.
- You have also **taken notes on texts** and used them to write **connected paragraphs**.
- You have learnt how to **ask for a favour** and have taken part in **more formal discussions**.

Unit 5
Entertainment

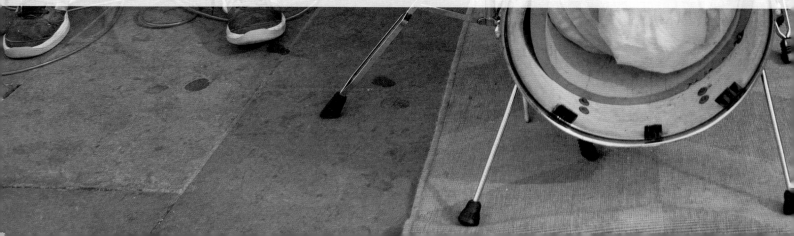

In this unit you will:

- read film and book reviews and a text about an Oscar-winning film-maker
- write a review of a film and book
- listen to discussions about films and TV violence
- practise asking for and giving information in a friendly way
- focus on the following assessment objectives: R1, R2, W3, L1, L2, S4, S5

A Talking about entertainment

1 Introduction and discussion

A What kinds of entertainment do you like? Using the list, tell your partner about the kinds of entertainment you most enjoy and why:

- listening to music – pop, rap, rock, jazz, R and B, classical, etc.
- going to the cinema
- watching films online
- accessing video-sharing sites, such as YouTube, or elsewhere on the internet
- reading a novel for pleasure
- playing computer games
- going to a concert, gig or other live performance
- going to the theatre
- listening to the radio
- watching TV or a film at home.

B Have you ever been involved in entertaining people? For example, have you ever performed on stage or helped produce a play? Explain how you felt about it. If you've never done this, would you like to? Why/Why not?

C Have you ever uploaded a video to a video-sharing site? Tell your partner about it.

D Would you like a job in the 'entertainment business'? Explain what sort of work, if any, you would like to do. Why would you like to do that kind of work?

2 Film vocabulary

As some exercises in this unit will require a working knowledge of film vocabulary, this exercise will help you be better prepared.

Complete the film review by choosing from the words and phrases in the box to fill each space.

VOCABULARY		
box office	scene	performance
cast	plot	genre
played by	characters	film
heroine	directed by	
Oscar	role	

Mission in Space

'Mission in Space' won a film award, but Selina Summers didn't win a(n) _____ for Best Actress despite her superb _____ as Helena Page, the brave and intriguing _____ who undertakes her first mission on board the space ship *Mission*. Still grieving for the loss of her husband in a car crash, Helena needs to prove to herself that life has a meaning and purpose. Her partner in outer space is Hudson Carr, _____ Jasper Hunt, who is entirely convincing in the _____ of the experienced older astronaut. The tense _____ becomes more frightening when Hudson has a heart attack and Ryan is left to cope entirely alone in a dark and mysterious universe. The final _____, however, leaves no one doubting Helena's courage or will to live. The other members of the _____ include Carolos Martinez as the voice of Mission Control, and Farley Harrison as the voice of the captain of *Mission*. They are both perfect as the calm but rather cold _____ typical of space missions. The film is _____ Hugo Bandera, who may be remembered for other _____ hits such as 'North Star'. The _____ is a welcome addition to the growing science fiction fantasy _____.

Make a note of unfamiliar words on your phone, on your computer or in your vocabulary book, with a translation if necessary.

3 Film quiz

What we look for when we watch a film is very personal. To help you understand more about your preferences and attitudes to films, complete this quiz:

What I want from a film

1 How do you choose a film to watch?
   a recommendation from friends
   b by looking at film reviews
   c I choose when I get to the cinema
   d I've got my favourite actors – I'm prepared to see any film they are acting in.

2 The following comments are often made about what makes a good film. How far do you agree with them? Mark each comment like this:

   Agree strongly ✓✓   Agree ✓   Don't agree ✗

   a A lot of suspense should be an important ingredient.
   b Fast-moving action is essential.
   c The plot should contain many surprising twists.
   d It should be acted by big Hollywood stars.
   e It should have been made recently.
   f It should contain many emotional scenes.
   g It should make a serious point.
   h It should make you laugh.
   i It should contain many special effects.

3 Select the statements you agree with:
   a There is too much violence in films today.
   b I prefer films which seem realistic and true to life rather than science fiction or horror movies.
   c My favourite films are based on true stories.
   d Seeing the film after you've read the book is usually disappointing.
   e Too many films come from Hollywood. We should be watching films that are made in our own country.
   f I'm sick of hearing about films in which evil people commit terrible crimes.

4 Pairwork: Asking for information

When you've finished the quiz, swap answers with a partner. Read your partner's answers carefully and pick out a few responses that interest you. Ask for more information in a friendly way, to show you're genuinely interested.

Examples:

May I ask why you think fast-moving action is essential / the plot should contain many surprising twists?

Would you mind telling me about your favourite actors / films that have made you laugh / films you've seen that are based on true stories?

What I'd like to know is why you prefer films that seem realistic and true to life / you don't like films about evil people.

Could you explain in more detail why you think suspense is an important ingredient / films should contain emotional scenes / films should make a serious point / more films should be made in your country?

Here are some more useful phrases for following up your partner's answers:

Something else I'd like to know is …

Can you give me an example?

What exactly do you mean by …?

Sorry, I don't quite understand why …

5 Following a model discussion about films 🔊 CD 1, Track 13

You are going to hear a model conversation in which two students tell their teacher about two films they have enjoyed.

You can follow the conversation while you listen. You will find the audioscript towards the end of the book, after Unit 10. Notice how the teacher asks for information and follows up the students' answers.

Later, when you want to write or talk about a film, you can look again at the conversation for examples of what you can say about a film.

6 Aspects of films

Which of these aspects of the films were mentioned by Marta and Navid? Scan the conversation again if you need to.

- [ ] characters
- [ ] genre
- [ ] hero
- [ ] message of the film
- [ ] plot
- [ ] reasons for recommending
- [ ] setting
- [ ] special effects
- [ ] suspense
- [ ] soundtrack.

You will need to include some of these aspects of films when speaking or writing about films later in the unit.

7 Tenses

The main tense used by Navid and Marta is the present simple.

Examples:
George finds a poisonous snake in the grass.

Betty steals a phone from a classmate and hides it in Ama's bag, so Ama gets into trouble.

Why is this tense used, do you think?

8 Comprehension

Read the following statements. Select the points which reflect Navid's view of 'The Way to the Sea':

a He thought the main character was very convincing.

b It contained some spectacular special effects.

c It was interesting but taught him nothing memorable about life.

d He found the bleak city settings very atmospheric.

Select the points which reflect Marta's view of 'You After Me':

e She identified with the setting.

f She found one particular scene very amusing.

g She thought the ending was very emotional.

i It made her realise how trust can be betrayed.

Do you feel that Navid and Marta's analyses give you an understanding of the background to each film? Why do their reasons and examples manage to convey the qualities of each film?

9 Language study: *So … that* and *such … that*

These forms are often used to give emphasis when we say how we feel.

So … that … can be used with an adjective without a noun.

Example:
The film was so scary that I was on the edge of my seat.

Such … that … is used with an adjective and a noun.

Example:
It's such an escapist film that I forgot all about my exams.

In both cases you can leave out *that* if you wish to.

Practice

Join these pairs of sentences using *so … (that).*

1 I was keen to see the concert. I was prepared to pay a lot for a ticket.

2 She was disappointed not to get the role of princess. She cried all day.

Join these pairs of sentences with *such … (that).*

3 The film took a long time to make. The director ran out of money.

4 The story was fascinating. The film company wanted to make a film about it. (Begin: *It was …*)

10 Involving your listener

People can read film reviews for themselves, but when you talk about a film your listener is interested in **your** particular responses to a film.

The following sentences make your responses sound more personal, and will engage your listener more effectively. Working with a partner, discuss how each of the sentences could end. Complete them appropriately, using a past tense.

Example:
The scene where the monster appears is so frightening that I jumped off my seat.

1 The scene where the heroine dies is so sad that _____

2 It's such an intriguing plot that _____

3 The scene was so funny that _____

4 The scene where we find out the true identity of the murderer is so compelling that _____

5 The hero gives such a convincing performance as a blind man that _____

6 The gangster scenes are so violent that _____

B Recommendations and reviews

1 Discussion

Using electronic devices and the internet to provide entertainment is such a normal part of many people's lives that it seems strange to remember that at one time all entertainment was live.

As technology progresses, it becomes less and less necessary for people to go out to places of entertainment and enjoy a production or performance in the company of others. We can create playlists of our favourite music and listen at any time. Streaming means that we can enjoy films and music concerts whenever we wish. As a result, cinema, theatre and concert audiences in some countries have fallen.

It has been claimed that these developments in entertainment have 'gone too far'. Some people think, for instance, that streaming is a poor substitute for the excitement of going out to the cinema or concert with friends and having fun together. They say we are creating a lonely and passive society. What do you think?

With a partner, try to think of the advantages, disadvantages and dangers of accessing entertainment through personal electronic devices and the internet. Add your ideas to those given.

Advantages

It's convenient.

Disadvantages

Films are less powerful watched on tablet computers.

Dangers

People can become more cut off and isolated.

2 Choosing a film

In pairs, read aloud this short dialogue between two friends, Raj and Cara. Raj wants information which will help him decide which film he should watch with his little brother.

Raj: I'd like to watch a film with Anil tonight. Have you seen any good ones lately?

Cara: What about a historical romance, like 'The Golden Ring? I saw it last week. It's set in nice countryside. It's got a really nice heroine and the historical costumes are really nice.

Raj: Mmm, maybe ... What else is worth watching at the moment?

Cara: 'Lost in Time' is a nice children's movie. The animation is very nice.

Cara: Uh huh. Can you recommend a thriller?

Cara: 'Shadow of the Wolf' is good. The acting is good too.

Raj: I'm not sure. It might be too frightening for Anil. Maybe a comedy might be more fun.

Cara: 'Crazy Arnie' is a nice comedy. It's got some good dialogue.

Raj: Well ... Anil and I like science fiction films because of the special effects. Any ideas?

Cara: 'Planet Zero' is a good science fiction film with good special effects.

Raj: Well, I'll think it over. Thanks for the help.

3 A wider vocabulary

Can you replace *nice* and *good* with more precise, revealing adjectives from the box? Make an intelligent guess about the most likely adjective for that kind of plot and character. There are more adjectives than you need, so think carefully before making a choice, consulting a dictionary if necessary.

Can you think of any adjectives to add to the groups in the box?

VOCABULARY		
impressive	amusing	thought-provoking
magnificent	hilarious	engaging
stunning	witty	mesmerising
superb	stylish	convincing
	quirky	
powerful		appealing
enjoyable	sad	likeable
satisfying	poignant	attractive
well-made	memorable	
tough	dramatic	
ruthless	gripping	
violent	breathtaking	
	mysterious	
	disturbing	

4 Collocations

A **collocation** is a combination of words which sound natural when used together. For example, the performance of an actor can be described as *convincing*, but we would not describe the setting of a film in this way. Work in small groups, look again at the adjectives in the box, and decide which can be used with the following nouns. Remember that some adjectives can go with more than one noun.

Now compare your lists with those of another group.

5 Understanding the style of short reviews

VOCABULARY		
plot	characters	costumes
setting	special effects	performance

Short reviews are designed to be read quickly. They outline the plot, mention the people involved, often include a key fact about the production, and try to give the reader a sense of the style and themes of the work.

Matching short texts to statements

Scan these eight short reviews and match them with statements 1–7. There is one more review than you need.

A

Man of Tai Chi

Tiger Chen is the sole student of the elderly Master Yang. While Tiger does well with the physical aspects of his Tai Chi training, Master Yang struggles to teach him the more philosophical side of the discipline. The Master worries about his student, but the ambitious Tiger doesn't listen, becoming determined to demonstrate the effectiveness of his personal style. Trapped by an organised crime gang, Tiger ends up taking part in a fight to the death. 'Man of Tai Chi' is a multilingual narrative and is partly inspired by the life of the well-known stuntman, Tiger Chen.

B

Maleficent

Maleficent is a beautiful young creature with stunning black wings. She has a perfect life growing up in a forest kingdom, until the day an army of humans threatens her land. Maleficent becomes the protector of her people, but is betrayed. Desperate for revenge, Maleficent places a curse on Aurora, the infant daughter of the new king of the humans. However, Maleficent comes to realise that Aurora holds the key to peace in the kingdom.

C

Never Let Me Go

In the remote countryside, innocent children seem to be enjoying their education at a traditional boarding school, but there is a dark secret: when the children grow up, they will all be forced to donate their organs.

Inspired by Kazuo Ishiguro's award-winning novel of the same name, the film 'Never Let Me Go' is not only a thriller but also a philosophical work about the choice we face between challenging our destinies or accepting them.

D

Keeping Rosy

Steve Reeves's low-budget thriller stars Maxine Peake as Charlotte, a bright girl from an ordinary background who does well in a London media agency. But a bad day gets much worse as an extraordinary chain of events leads to her losing her job and taking care of a baby girl, whom she names Rosy.

E

Ghosts

It is the eve of the 10th anniversary of her distinguished husband's death, and Helene Alving is about to open an orphanage as a memorial to his life and work. To mark this occasion, her son Oswald has returned from Paris. Helene plans to take the opportunity to reveal the truth to Oswald about his father. Richard Eyre's production of Henrik Ibsen's masterpiece is acclaimed by the critics. The play is running for a strictly limited season at Trafalgar Studios. It has also been nominated for five Olivier Awards.

F

Beyond the Edge

In 1953 Edmund Hillary and Tenzing Norgay conquered Mount Everest. This 3D documentary tells one of the world's greatest adventure stories. Colour footage and photographs taken during the climb help tell the tale of the historic triumph of the modest mountaineer from New Zealand and his expert Nepalese Sherpa. This account conveys both the climbers' heroic trials and the ambition and hope the wider world invested in their mission, at a time when people were starting to believe in a brighter new age.

G

22 Jump Street

Two police officers go undercover at a college. But instead of chasing real criminals, their task is to look for key words spoken during lectures that might suggest illegal activities. They persevere, however, and uncover information about a criminal gang. Following on from the box office hit '21 Jump Street', this new comedy is a lot more fun than you might have expected.

H

Police Story 4: First Strike

In the latest film in the popular 'Police Story' series, Jackie Chan portrays a Hong Kong police officer who is contracted by the CIA and a Russian intelligence organisation to retrieve a stolen nuclear warhead. From the snow-capped mountains of eastern Europe to a shark-infested water park in Australia, Chan pursues a dishonest CIA agent. Along the way he is attacked, assaulted, framed for murder and forced to defend himself any way he can. Everything within arm's reach becomes a weapon: ladders, brooms, tables, cars, stilts – even sharks!

1 This review indicates that the film includes original material from true life events.

2 This review tells the reader this is a live performance.

3 This review says that the film was inexpensively made.

4 This review suggests the film will make you think about the meaning of life and death.

5 This review says that the film has many different settings.

6 This review explains that several languages are spoken in the film.

7 This review indicates that this film is the sequel to an earlier film.

6 Choosing the right word

Film reviews are designed to give readers a general impression of a particular film. For that reason, it is important that a reviewer choose his or her words carefully in order to convey the most important information as effectively as possible.

1 Look at the first part of the review of 'Never Let Me Go'. In your opinion, which are the key words?

In the remote countryside, children seem to be enjoying their education at a traditional boarding school, but there is a dark secret: when the children grow up, they will all be forced to donate their organs.

Highlight the adjective that tells us the school is cut off from the outside world. Circle the adjective that suggests the children do not have experience of life or the terrible things that can happen in the world. Underline the adjective and noun that suggest that the film might be frightening. Circle the verb which lets us know that the children will have no choice about what happens to them.

2 Examine this extract from the review of 'First Strike':

From the snow-capped mountains of eastern Europe to a shark-infested water park in Australia, Chan pursues a dishonest CIA agent. Along the way he is attacked, assaulted, framed for murder and forced to defend himself any way he can.

Identify the information that tells us:

a the film has very different settings

b the CIA agent is not to be trusted

c Chan himself isn't responsible for the violence in the film.

7 Presenting a film or play to the class

Choose a film or play you enjoyed and give a short talk about it to your class.

Refer back to exercises 5 and 6 to help structure your talk.

Before you begin, make a plan.

Introduction
Mention the title and genre (and the director and stars if you wish to).

Say why you have chosen to talk about this film or play.

Plot, characters and setting
Give a brief outline of what happens, who takes part in the action and where it takes place.

Tenses
Remember that the plot and characters should be described in the present tense.

Clarity
Plots can be complicated, so keep your description short, giving most attention to the beginning of the plot.

Conveying the quality of the film or play
Say why you thought the film or play was powerful. Aim to involve your listeners when you describe your reactions (exercise 10). Remember the importance of key words in signalling information (exercise 6).

Some points you may want to consider are:

- the performance of the actors and their suitability for the roles they play
- the use of humour, suspense or special effects (provide examples of scenes)
- the underlying 'message' of the film or play.

Recommending the film or play
Say why you recommend the film or play. Link your recommendations to your knowledge of your audience. Are they very interested in a particular genre such as science fiction, horror or romance? Does the film or play raise topics that you have discussed in class (jobs, social problems, life in the future)?

Active listening
Listen attentively to the speaker. After he or she has finished, make one positive comment about what you have heard and then ask at least one question seeking further information.

Recording your talks
You may like to give your talks in small groups, record them and analyse the results. Check the clarity of each talk. Listen for accuracy in the language – tenses, articles and collocations. How would you correct any mistakes?

C Working in the film industry or theatre

1 Pre-reading discussion

A Would you like to work in the film industry or theatre? What sort of work would you find most attractive: acting, designing sets or costumes, writing scripts or directing? Why?

VOCABULARY

1 eccentric:

2 villain:

3 Plasticine:

4 models:

5 wire:

6 phonemes:

A objects or figures made out of clay or another material

B a brand of modelling clay

C thin metal that can be bent

D the smallest units of sound in speech

E a bad or evil person

F showing unusual behavior

B You are going to read about a man who has built up a successful career as an animator. Looking at the pictures, what would you expect the films to be like? Would you like to watch one? Or have you already seen one?

C What do you think are the challenges presented in making an animated film using puppets or models?

D What kind of personal attributes do you think an animator needs? Select from the list below.

- good at making things
- imagination
- good at 3D design
- ability to pay attention to detail
- determination
- a sense of humour
- enjoys working with technical equipment.

Does the job of an animator appeal to you? Why/Why not?

2 Vocabulary check

Before you read, match the vocabulary in the box with the definitions:

3 Reading for gist

Now read the article for general meaning. What did Nick study at the National Film and Television School? How many of the possible attributes listed in D above are mentioned or suggested by the text?

4 True/false comprehension

Decide whether the following statements are true or false:

1 Nick's father played a large part in helping him develop film-making skills.

2 Nick decided early on in his school career that he would take a degree in film-making.

3 A teacher at school gave him the confidence to aim for professional film-making.

4 The animated film 'A Grand Day Out' took a year to make.

5 'The Wrong Trousers' was his first film.

6 Matching his characters' speech to their body language takes less time than you would expect.

7 Nick talks freely to the interviewer about his next projects.

8 If you want to learn this work, you have to be prepared to invest in an expensive camera.

9 He has no difficulty limiting the length of his working week.

Interview with Nick Park

Philip Gray talks to Oscar-winning film-maker and animator, Nick Park, about his career and his amazing animations: Wallace, an eccentric

inventor, and Gromit, his loyal dog.

5 **'Your work is seen by audiences around the world, but what was it that first started off your interest in film-making?'**

'It all started when my parents bought a simple home movie camera, and I discovered that it had an
10 *animation button to build up films one frame at a time. As a keen photographer, my father was able to help me with the technical side of camera work, and I worked with Plasticine models right from the start.'*

'At what stage did you realise that your hobby
15 **would turn into a full-time career?'**

'I don't remember a great deal of careers advice about the film industry while I was at school. There seemed to be very little information available, and the fact that I didn't tell people about my interest in animation
20 *probably explains why I didn't have much advice. I certainly didn't find out that it was possible to take a degree in film-making until much later.*

'But one of my teachers did find out about my films – my English teacher, Mr Kelly. By watching my films,
25 *and encouraging me to show them to the school, he was one of the important influences on my early career. By the time I was 17, one of my earliest films, "Archie's Concrete Nightmare", had been shown on the BBC.'*

'What happened after school?' 30

'After completing a BA degree in communication arts at Sheffield Art School, I went on to study animation at the National Film and Television School, where I started work on the first Wallace and Gromit adventure, "A Grand Day Out". Then I joined the 35 *Aardman Animations studio. After four years, "A Grand Day Out" was completed, followed by "Creature Comforts" and "The Wrong Trousers".'*

Nick Park's art of animation

Nick's characters have been described as having 40
too-close-together eyes and mouths as wide as bananas. Created from a recipe of ordinary materials, such as Plasticine, plus modelling clay, and dental wax, they are formed around a wire frame to give them flexibility. 45

Actors' voices are used for the characters. The sets are accurately modeled on actual locations, and the remarkable attention to detail extends down to the pattern of the wallpaper in Gromit's living room.

The speech patterns of each character have to be 50
broken down into phonemes, with each frame matched to a part of a particular word and animated with appropriate body, face and lip movements. No wonder one 30-minute film takes so long to make. 55

'With a production team of nearly 30 people in "The Wrong Trousers", the list of credits reads like any feature film. I have heard you have more exciting films planned, though you may not want to give too much away about them. 60
You are obviously extremely successful. What advice can you offer to our next generation of

105

film-makers as they start out on their film-making careers?'

65 *'Firstly, I think commitment is essential in this work. Any film-maker must learn to be single-minded for those times when it is all too tempting to do other things. Setting up with expensive equipment doesn't need to be a major problem. I started with a cheap 8 mm cine-*
70 *camera and one problem to overcome – the price of film.*

'Secondly, without good powers of observation, it is difficult to find sufficient inspiration. Study examples of animation frame by frame to see exactly how they have been created.'

75 **'Working hours must be very long during production. Can you find time to relax?'**

'It's all too easy to spend very long hours on this type of work, as it certainly isn't a nine-to-five job.

Filming sessions are hectic, but I do find the time to relax occasionally, and have even managed to keep a few weekends clear just to get out into the countryside.' 80

5 Vocabulary

Match the words in the list with their definitions:

1 frame (line 10)
2 influences (line 26)
3 wire frame (line 43)
4 on location (line 45)
5 list of credits (line 55)

a in a real place
b names of the people who were involved with a film
c basic structure made of wire
d individual picture which is part of a film
e people who gave him ideas or encouraged him

Guessing meaning from context

Now try to guess the meanings of these words and phrases from the article:

6 powers of observation (line 69)
7 a nine-to-five job (line 76)
8 hectic (line 77)

Find two other places in the article where the word *frame* is used. Which of the above meanings (1 or 3) does the word have each time?

6 Spelling and pronunciation: The letter *c*

A Have you noticed that **c** is pronounced in different ways? Say these words from the text aloud to show the different ways **c** can be pronounced.

camera   advice   sufficient

Can you think of the reason for these differences?

B Study the following rules, underlining the letter(s) according to the rule.

c is pronounced /k/ before the vowels *a, o,* and *u.* This is called 'hard c'.

Examples: camera   discovered   difficult   account

c is also pronounced /k/ before most consonants.

Examples: actors   crackers   clues

c is pronounced /s/ before the vowels *e, i,* or *y.* This is called 'soft c'.

Examples: receive   cinema   exciting   icy

Before the letters *ea, ia, ie, ien* or *iou,* c is usually pronounced 'sh'. The phonetic symbol is /ʃ/.

Examples: *ocean* *conscious*

When double *c* comes before *e* or *i*, the first *c* is hard and the second is soft; so the pronunciation is /ks/.

Examples: *accept* *accident*

Practice 🔊 CD 1, Track 14

You are going to listen to a recording of someone saying the following words. Put each of the words into the correct group, according to its sound. Most of the words come from the text.

Hard *c* /k/
(as in camera)

Soft *c* /s/
(as in cinema)

Double *c*
pronounced /ks/
(as in accent)

'*Sh*' sound
pronounced /ʃ/
(as in ocean)

1	Oscar	**13**	certainly
2	career	**14**	influence
3	eccentric	**15**	communication
4	Wallace	**16**	recipe
5	scene	**17**	accurately
6	centimetre	**18**	accident
7	Plasticine	**19**	particular
8	action	**20**	face
9	comedy	**21**	credits
10	discovered	**22**	delicious
11	efficient	**23**	cine
12	advice	**24**	sufficient

With a partner, listen to each other saying the words aloud. Do you both agree that your pronunciation is correct?

7 Using words in context

Make up five sentences using words from the list. Write them down and check your spelling. Then swap sentences with a partner. Read your partner's sentences aloud.

Examples:

Yasmin built up a successful career as a make-up artist.

English shows the influence of other languages.

The telephone is an efficient means of communication.

8 Spelling and pronunciation: The letters *ch* 🔊 CD 1, Track 15

Ch has three main sounds.

In some words, *ch* is pronounced /k/.

Examples: *chemist* *technical* *school* *Christmas*

In some words, *ch* is pronounced /tʃ/.

Examples: *cheese* *check* *teacher* *rich*

In a few words, *ch* is pronounced /ʃ/.

Examples: *chef* *machine*

Practice: odd word out

You are going to listen to a recording of someone saying the following words. Listen to the three groups of words and cross out the odd one out in each group, according to the pronunciation of ***ch***. Rewrite the word in the correct sound group.

Group A	**Group B**	**Group C**
chemist	church	chauffeur
architect	watch	chute
mechanic	search	champagne
headache	scheme	sachet
chef	match	chocolate
technology	butcher	brochure

With a partner, practise saying each group of words. Do you know the meaning of each word?

9 More practice of *c* and *ch* sounds

Read this dialogue with a partner. Check each other's pronunciation.

Marc: Our drama club is putting on a production of 'Charlie and the Chocolate Factory' for the end of term.

Clare: That sounds exciting.

Marc: It is! The club is in charge of everything. We've chosen the actors, written the script, created the costumes, painted the scenery and even designed the brochure advertising it. The teachers weren't involved at all.

Clare: Sounds like a recipe for chaos to me!

Marc:	Well, we've had one or two headaches but we've concentrated very hard on getting it right. There was one little slip, though. I play an eccentric character and I have to wear a big moustache. In our dress rehearsal the moustache fell off just as I was about to speak!
Clare:	Never mind. I'm certain the audience will appreciate all the effort you've put in. How much are the tickets?
Marc:	Actually, it's free but there's a collection at the end. Half the proceeds will go to the school fund and the other half will go to *Children in Crisis,* the school's charity.
Clare:	Well, I really hope it's a big success.

10 Look, say, cover, write, check

Here are some words that often present spelling problems. Do you know what they mean? Can you say them properly? Use the 'look, say, cover, write, check' method to learn them.

VOCABULARY		
delicious	bicycle	receive
succeed	chauffeur	except
special	conscious	confidence
success	technology	
influence	conscience	

D Reading for pleasure

1 Pre-listening discussion

It is often claimed that reading for pleasure is now taking second place to entertainment that is presented in a visual form. What do you think? Would you rather watch a film than read a novel? What can you get out of reading novels that films can't provide?

In small groups, make notes of the unique pleasures that reading offers.

Examples:
You can take it at your own pace.

2 Listening for gist CD 1, Track 16

You are going to listen to a radio interview. Jonathan, a librarian, is concerned that young people are giving up reading because of television and videos.

Listen first for the general meaning and try to decide why Jonathan thinks videos are intellectually less stimulating than reading.

Strategies for interrupting
The interviewer has some difficulty interrupting Jonathan. Select the phrases he uses to try to interrupt:

- Just a minute …
- With respect …
- If I could just butt in here, …
- Excuse me, I'd like to say that …
- Hang on!
- But surely …
- If you don't mind my interrupting …
- If I could get a word in here …

3 Detailed listening CD 1, Track 16

Listen again and answer the questions:

1 What are children not getting when they watch TV and films rather than read? Give **two** examples.

2 What is the difference, according to Jonathan, between reading a novel and watching a film?

3 How, according to Jonathan, are children affected by watching violence on screen?

4 How can parents help their children to understand what they read? Give **two** examples.

Which best summarises the attitude of the interviewer to Jonathan:

a angry and sarcastic?

b bored and impatient?

c interested and concerned?

4 Post-listening discussion

A Do you feel reading quality fiction helps intellectual development more than watching films?

B Do you agree with Jonathan that violence in films and on TV influences behaviour more than violence in respected novels? Try to explain your point-of-view to your group.

5 Dialogue: Interrupting each other

Lee and Michelle are having a discussion about violence on television. They keep interrupting each other.

Read the dialogue aloud with a partner. Use a suitable phrase for interrupting each time you see the word *interrupting*:

Michelle: I agree with Jonathan that people are copying the violence they see on TV and it's time something was done about it. TV programmes are much more violent than they used to be. The crime rate is getting worse, too. Children are being influenced to think that violence is all right and …

Lee: *(interrupting)* … Children are very sensible. They can tell the difference between what happens on TV and what goes on in real life. It's rubbish to suggest that people watch a programme and suddenly become more violent. I don't think

violent scenes in books are better or worse than violence on TV. There isn't that much violence on TV anyway.

Michelle: *(interrupting)* … Some of the cartoons they are putting on even for very young children are very violent. They don't help children understand the terrible effects real violence has, or how it can destroy lives. TV makes violence seem exciting and …

Lee: *(interrupting)* … Violent behaviour comes from your background and the way you're brought up. It has nothing to do with television. TV doesn't make people behave violently. If you see violence in your home or around you in your real life, that's the example you copy.

Michelle: *(interrupting)* … Violent TV programmes will make children who are growing up in bad homes even worse. They're even more likely to commit aggressive acts. Jonathan said parents should help children read more, and I think they should say what their children are allowed to watch, too. They'll know if their children will be affected.

Lee: *(interrupting)* … That would be a complete waste of time. In the first place, children don't want their parents interfering. Surely kids have the right to some privacy about what they choose to read or watch on TV?

Michelle: *(interrupting)* … It's not only children who are influenced. Mentally unstable people, for instance, might not be able to discriminate about what they watch. They might think violence is fun, or even learn how to commit a crime. They find TV incredibly powerful and …

Lee: *(interrupting)* … Most TV programmes are really boring! I lose interest after five minutes. Not that I want to start reading so-called 'good books' instead. I get enough mental stimulation at school. What I want is more exciting TV and less boring programmes!

109

Internet use, TV and cinema across the world

A In which one of these countries do more than 90% of people use the internet?

Australia Brazil China

Norway   Japan USA

B People in these five countries watch, on average, more TV than anywhere else in the world (more than 4 hours per day). In which one of the five do you think people watch the least?

Italy Poland Spain

UK   USA

C Which of the following countries has the most cinema attendances per head of population per year?

Iceland   Singapore   USA

New Zealand   Ireland   Australia

D These are the three countries that produce the most films per year. Can you put them in order?

USA India Nigeria

E Book and film reviews

1 Pre-reading tasks

A Do you enjoy reading novels? Do you prefer murder mysteries, romances, historical fiction or some other genre? Do you have a favourite author? What do you like about his/her books? Discuss your ideas with a partner.

B Write down the title of a novel you've enjoyed. Imagine you've been asked to write a review of it for your school magazine. You've already learnt a lot about the skills of reviewing from your work on films earlier in the unit. You now need to build on those skills and extend them into book reviewing.

C The following questions may help you work out what made the novel memorable. Note down your answers.

Plot
Was the plot unusual at all? Was it gripping? Was it interesting but less important than the characters?

Setting
What did you like about the setting – historical details, fascinating details of fast-paced city life? How was the atmosphere conveyed through the setting?

Character(s)
Did the characters feel 'real'? Did they change during the book and cope with new challenges? Did you identify with any of them? Why? Think of one or more examples in the novel which show this.

Style
Did you like the style of the novel? Why?

Audience
Remember to think about your target audience. Why would these people enjoy reading the novel?

Keep your notes safely as you will use them later.

2 Reading a book review

This book review, and the film review in exercise 3, were written by students for the school magazine. Notice how the writers try to slant the reviews to their audience.

VOCABULARY

aspirations: hopes

shortcomings: personal failings

compassionate: feeling pity for others

corrupting: causing to become dishonest or immoral

integrity: honesty

Great Expectations

Reviewed by Gilang Cheung

Have you ever liked the hero in a novel so much that you wanted everything to turn out all right for him? I felt like this when I read 'Great Expectations', by Charles Dickens. I'd like to recommend it for the
5 school library because I'm sure other students will identify with the main character, too.

Set in 19th-century England, the novel tells the story of a poor orphan called Pip, who secretly helps an escaped prisoner. His good turn has unexpected
10 consequences and he becomes rich beyond his wildest dreams. I won't spoil the story by telling you how the plot twists and turns, but I can guarantee surprises!

In a style I found painfully direct, Pip shares his innermost thoughts and aspirations – even ideas he later becomes ashamed of. During the course of 15 the novel, Pip changes a lot. He becomes more aware of his shortcomings and more compassionate. He pays a high price for self-knowledge and, like me, I think you'll be moved to tears at the end.

One of the things I learnt from reading the novel is 20 how corrupting money is. Pip, for example, no longer cares about keeping promises he made when he was poor. The novel made me think about how loyalty and integrity are more important than wealth.

The novel provides a vivid and rewarding insight into 25 19th-century Britain. Students of English language and literature will find it particularly fascinating.

Comprehension check

1 What is the title of the novel and who is the author?

2 When and where is the story set?

3 Why does Pip become rich?

4 How does Pip change during the novel?

5 How do we know Gilang identifies emotionally with Pip's suffering?

3 Reading a film review

As you read this film review, try to work out the meaning of any unfamiliar words from the context.

How to Train Your Dragon

Reviewed by Lotta Svein

Do you love laughing so much you almost fall off your seat? If so, put the 'How to Train Your Dragon' films at the top of your must-see list.

The first film in this series is set on the Viking island of Berk, and centres around a misfit teenager called Hiccup. 5 Dragons regularly try to attack the island and everyone has to fight them to survive. Hiccup feels ridiculed by others as he is hopeless at fighting, but he wants to be valued by his community and to help. He decides to astonish everyone with his talent for overcoming the 10 worst kind of beast, a Night Fury. However, instead of killing the Night Fury, he feels sorry for the dragon and a gentle friendship begins between Hiccup and the beast, who he names Toothless.

The film combines lots of suspense with fun and 15 humour, and the opening scene of the attack by the dragons is truly exhilarating. The friendship scenes between Hiccup and Toothless are so touching that I didn't know whether to laugh or cry!

20 The film has a serious message, too. It showed me how, by bonding with the dragon instead of fighting, Hiccup finds happiness and peace of mind. His actions demonstrate that real peace lies not in fighting and killing, but in finding a way to live
25 with the things we used to fear.

Try not to miss 'How to Train Your Dragon'. It's one of the funniest films I've ever seen, and it really makes you think. It is suitable for the whole family, too. Younger brothers and sisters will enjoy the hilarious twists and turns, while older viewers
30 will be fascinated by the film's deeper themes.

Comprehension check

1 Why is the environment in which Hiccup is growing up in violent?

2 Why is Hiccup unhappy?

3 How does Hiccup hope to impress the people of Berk?

4 What does Hiccup learn from befriending Toothless?

5 Why is the film recommended for everyone?

6 The film shows Hiccup becoming open-minded. Do you have any experience of a time when you had to become more open-minded? Have you ever noticed this change happening in other people? Try to give an example.

4 Analysing example reviews

A The opening of each review begins with a question. Do you find this effective?

B Compare the way the story of the book/film is described in the second paragraph of each review. Underline the phrases which are used to introduce the description. How does Gilang deal briefly with a complicated plot?

C What reasons do the reviewers give for finding the book or film enjoyable?

D The fourth paragraphs explain what Gilang and Lotta gained from reading the book/watching the film. Underline the phrases they use. Contrast what each student learnt.

E Gilang and Lotta recommend 'Great Expectations' and 'How to Train Your Dragon' for different reasons. What are they? How do we know they are aware of their audience?

F Which review interested you more? Why?

5 Useful language for reviews

Here is some typical language used by reviewers of novels. Decide which of the expressions are suitable for reviewing films or live performances. Select those you would like to use in your own reviews.

Style

It's beautifully written.

It's got a style of its own.

A poetic style that …

It's an elegant style, which …

It flows beautifully.

Its light, chatty style …

Setting

It's set in …

It's set against the powerful background of …

The historical details are superb.

It's a wonderful re-creation of …

It has a marvellous sense of time and place.

Recommending

It's worth reading because …

You'll be delighted by …

It's hard to put down.

It's a real page-turner.

It's a masterpiece.

It's the best book I've (ever) read.

It's not to be missed.

It's a classic.

You'll be moved to tears.

6 Criticising a film, book or live performance

If you are writing a review under exam conditions, try to choose a film, book or live performance you found powerful. However, you might still want to mention what you didn't like.

Examples:

The performances were excellent, but the ending was very depressing.

The main character looked too old/young for the part.

I liked the jokes but they wouldn't be to everyone's taste.

The characters were engaging but the plot was too far-fetched* at times.

The violent ending spoilt the musical for me.

The plot was intriguing, but the characters were not really believable.

* *far-fetched* = unbelievable

7 Effective openings for book reviews

When writing an opening paragraph, remember that you should:

- immediately involve the reader
- make the reader want to read on
- convey the novel's special qualities
- use a concise style.

In small groups, with these points in mind, read the following opening paragraphs, A–F, of book reviews written by students. Try to rank them from most to least effective. Correct any structural errors as you work. Discuss the reasons for your choices.

A *I want to try to explain to you about a very good novel which is also very long and which I recently read called 'In Our Stars'. Extremely, the writer did his best for this book and I couldn't leave any single moment in the book without reading it.*

B *I cannot always write to the school magazine but as I have been the one in my class that my teacher has asked me to do this as I have not done it before, I decided to write you about a book I read on holiday in France last week and I think you will really get surprised. I was I nearly fainted. I read a very long book called something like 'Twisters' or something, by Harry and whose other name I forget. It is about a band but then the band gets famous and it is going on for a very long time.*

C *Last week I read one of the most powerful and moving books ever, 'The Bellmaker' by Brian Jacques. In the novel, animals are given human personalities*

and motives. However hard-hearted you are, this compelling tale of how a courageous group of animals band together to defend their kingdom against, Foxwolf, will bring a tear to your eye.

D *If you've been recently bored and willing to read a long book that I read about in someone's blog, I thought it was a true story but when I nearly finished it, I knew it was all made up and it was not true and I was disappointed. I recommend you read this book about Anna. It's a book about how a girl who lives in Alaska runs away from her boarding school into a worst place that she had never thought of before and she is trying not to stay there longer. But it is not a true story. When you finally get to finish this endless book, you will be sad about the people in it.*

E *Have you ever wanted to be the hero in a novel? No matter how you reply you'll love reading 'Dark Eye'. The hero is a likeable but naive trainee police cop who is on a hunt for a gang of criminals in New York. The suspense is great and the writing is just perfect.*

F *The book I thought was very long and want to explain you for my school website is 'Staying Alive' by Li Chang. I could read it more times too if I had time. I think the book has already sold a billion of them which is very scarce. I want to tell you about Jon (the detective in the book) who is very nice and the strange and unusual things that happened to him after gangsters put him in a cellar and are cruel to him but he is escaping. Jon is very funny and being surprising even when he is nearly dead but at the end he is alive.*

8 Writing an opening paragraph

Write the opening paragraph for your own review of a novel you have enjoyed. You may find it helpful to refer to the notes you made for exercise 1.

Remember: Aim to convey the 'flavour' of the novel and to make the reader want to find out more. Try to be concise, choose revealing adjectives and avoid unnecessary words.

9 Writing a review of a thriller from prompts

Do you enjoy reading novels with exciting plots? If so, then you might enjoy 'The Kidnapping of Suzy Q', by Catherine Sefton.

Try to build up a complete review of it from the following prompts.

113

The Kidnapping of Suzy Q

'The Kidnapping of Suzy Q' / Catherine Sefton / be / most thought-provoking / atmospheric novel / have read. It be / set / modern urban Britain / it tell / story / through eyes / courageous heroine Suzy. One day / she be making / ordinary trip / supermarket / buy groceries / when supermarket be / raided. In the confusion / criminals / kidnap Suzy / she be standing in / checkout queue.

The criminals / keep Suzy / captivity. Suzy recount / ordeal / graphic / painful detail. I be / impress / Suzy's courage / determination / refusal / panic / give up. Several incidents / novel / reveal Suzy's ability / cope / when she be threatened / them.

The story make / think / ordinary life / be changed / one incident. It be also / inspiring / make me realise / inner strength / ordinary people can have / cope with / disaster.

The novel be / skilfully written. Catherine Sefton's style be / direct / witty / characters be / strong / convincing. The plot be / intriguing / never predictable. If you like / tense novels / you find this hard / put down.

10 Writing a review of a play based on a dialogue

Here is a conversation between two friends about a play called 'Every Move You Make.' Why not read it aloud with a partner? Then try to write a review of the play for your school magazine. Before you begin writing, make a plan of the points you want to include and their order.

Fatima: I saw 'Every Move You Make' at the Red Door Theatre last night. I'd definitely recommend it. I was on the edge of my seat for the whole performance.

Josef: Is that the one based on a true story?

Fatima: Yes. It's on for another three weeks and it's really exciting.

Josef: Remind me what it's about.

Fatima: Well, Matt, the main character, is this quiet boy with a secret ability. He can unlock any password or security code, however difficult. He wouldn't dream of doing anything wrong himself, but he's kidnapped by a gang who want to use his talent to rob an international bank.

Josef: Martin Inez plays Matt, doesn't he? I thought his performance in 'Never Look Down' was really powerful.

Fatima: He's great in this, too. His character really wants to be popular and hides his talent because he

doesn't want to seem different. From the first scene, the film is full of suspense because we know the gang is monitoring Matt with hidden electronic devices– his every move is being watched by them.

Josef: Sounds like the kind of tense, disturbing drama I like.

Fatima: It also makes you realise that even the most ordinary places in the world can be dangerous. We think our passwords are secure but they might not be.

Josef: So what happens in the end?

Fatima: Matt's character changes during the play. He shows the strength to stand up to the gang. Even though his own life is at risk, he finds a way to outwit the gangsters and save the bank. Finally, the police arrest the gang and Matt is offered a top job with the police to help stop crime.

Josef: Maybe our school Theatre Club would enjoy it. I'll mention it and see what the members think.

Fatima: Good idea. By the way, there are half price tickets for student groups on Tuesday evening.

GRAMMAR SPOTLIGHT

Will for prediction

We use **will + the infinitive** of a verb (without 'to') to predict responses. This is a useful structure to use in a review:

This compelling tale … **will bring** *a tear to your eye* **(section E7)**.

Younger brothers and sisters **will enjoy** *the hilarious twists and turns* **(section E3)**.

Can you find another example like this in the final paragraph of the text in **section E2?**

Passive forms with *will* are also useful in reviews:

You'll be delighted by …

Older viewers **will be fascinated by** *the film's deeper themes* **(section E3)**.

Can you find another example like this in the third paragraph of the text in **section E2?**

The superlative

The **superlative + present perfect** is often used in recommendations and reviews:

It's the best book I've ever read.

Can you find another example in the final paragraph of the text in **section E3?**

Exam-style questions

Speaking

1 A film or play I have enjoyed

Tell the assessor about any film or play you have enjoyed recently. Explain what it was about and say why you particularly enjoyed it.

Points to consider are:

- the influence and importance of the main character(s)
- the setting and atmosphere
- why you enjoyed it (e.g. special effects, performance of characters)
- what you learnt from watching the film or play (its 'message').

You are, of course, free to consider any other related ideas of your own. You are not allowed to make any written notes.

2 Live performances

Accessing music on the internet may be cheaper than paying to hear a concert performance. However, many people think going to a live performance is money well spent. Do you agree? Discuss this topic with the assessor.

In your discussion, you could consider such things as:

- the fact that live performances enable you to see a famous performer 'in person'
- the unique atmosphere of some live performances
- the opportunity to see the details of a performance (costumes, setting, etc.) exactly as they really are
- the fact that you can listen to a song or album on a streaming service many times but a live performance is a one-off event
- the fact that some live performances can be disappointing.

You are free to consider any other related ideas of your own. You are not allowed to make any written notes.

3 Entertainment through the internet

Enjoying entertainment through the internet is incredibly popular, but some people are concerned about the lack of regulation controlling the use of the internet.

Discuss this topic with the assessor.

You may wish to use the following ideas to help develop the conversation:

- whether you use the internet for entertainment
- the benefits and drawbacks of video-sharing sites
- the suggestion that confidential data on the internet are not secure
- the idea that some people get addicted to internet entertainment and become cut off from others as a result
- whether you think governments should have stronger controls over access to the internet.

You are free to consider any other related ideas of your own. You are not allowed to make any written notes.

Writing

Reading & Writing, Exercise 5

1   Your class is starting a film club for all students. Your Head of English would like students to submit letters about films they would recommend for the club. Letters will be published in the school newsletter. Write a letter about a film you would recommend for the school film club in which you:

- say what the film is about
- describe the film's qualities
- explain why it is suitable for the film club.

The letter should be about 100–150 words long.

Core [12 marks]

Reading & Writing, Exercise 5

2   You and a friend recently made a video and uploaded it to a video-sharing site on the internet.

Write an email to your cousin in which you:

- explain what the video was about
- describe why you decided to upload it
- say how you felt about the experience.

The email should be 150–200 words long.

Extended [16 marks]

Reading & Writing, Exercise 6

3   Your school librarian has asked your class to write reviews of novels for the library blog. Write a review of a novel you have read for the blog. Here are some comments from your friends about novels they have read:

'The characters were believable and interesting'

'The setting was difficult to imagine.'

'The plot was exciting.'

'The ending was a disappointment.'

Write the review for the website. The comments above may give you some ideas, and you can also use some ideas of your own. Your review should be 100–150 words long.

Core [12 marks]

Reading & Writing, Exercise 6

4   You recently went to see a concert or other live performance with some friends from your school. Here are some of your friends' comments about the performance:

'It was magnificent.'

'It was rather slow at times.'

Write a review for your school magazine giving your views. The comments may give you some ideas, but you should try to use some ideas of your own. Your review should be about 150–200 words.

Extended [16 marks]

Reading

Reading & Writing, Exercise 2

1 You are going to read an article in which four teenagers share their views on reading in the digital age.

Extended [10 marks]

For questions a-j, choose from the people A-D. The people may be chosen more than once.

Who ...

a has been resisting the demand that they read ebooks?

b says that we don't have to choose between ebooks and books?

c tries to put the technology of the book into an historical context?

d says their approach to reading has changed?

e was given an ereader as a gift?

f appreciates the fact that books provide an escape from modern technology?

g grades the author's writing?

h writes in books?

i finds ebooks more affordable?

j is especially interested in a certain type of non-fiction?

Person A   Noah

Books and I have a long history together. Ever since I can remember I've had a book with me. I read anything and everything, but my favourite things are novels – I read one a week, at least. But I'll admit that these days the *way* I read is different. Now I do almost all my reading on my tablet, and I tend to read often and for short periods. What I like about ebooks is that they are so convenient. You can carry hundreds around with you at once in the ereader. When I go on holiday however, I always buy a paperback guidebook. I like to turn down the pages of places I want to go to. I can also make my own notes on places I visit. Some people say that reading on the screen is not the same experience and the internet is a distraction. Well, the internet can be a distraction whether you're reading an ebook or a printed book. People resist change. But we must accept that the ebook is not only the present, but the future

---

Person B   Francis

I think my experience with all of this is a bit different to the norm. You see, it's supposed to be the younger generation that's into everything new, and the older one that thinks that life was better in the past. Whoever thinks that is true hasn't met my family! My mum and dad start using new technology as soon as they can get their hands on it. Long before ebooks became popular, my parents were reading them, ignoring the old books on the shelves. They've downloaded thousands of titles on to their tablets, and sit on the sofa, gazing at their screens, faces lit by the bright light of the display. They keep telling me I have to get one. I still haven't given in. I prefer physical books. I like the colours and the feel of them. The only time I read an ebook is when I download one for the reading discussion group I go to after school sometimes. My friends and I like to read the latest bestseller, share our views and give the novelist a mark out of ten. But otherwise, I am a fan of the real book!

Person C   Liam

Although I like reading, particularly books about history, I'm a very active person. If I sit around for too long with a book in my hand, I have a sudden urge to go for a swim, or play a quick game of football in the park with my mates, anything to burn off some energy. I'm probably not the best person to write about all of this, then, but my take on reading in the digital age is this – what's all the fuss about? We haven't always had the bound book. A long time ago, for example, people used clay tablets, scrolls and parchment. The ebook is just the next stage in the evolution of the technology. It won't end here, there'll be more changes in the future: who knows how we'll be reading in 2050? Personally, I prefer physical books. Not so much because of how it feels to hold one, or anything romantic like that, but just because it's good to pick up a book now and again and get away from apps, social media updates and the blinking lights on my smartphone notifying me of another message.

Person D   Marta

You can't move for blog posts entitled 'Young People and the Crisis of Reading', and that sort of thing. OK, I know lots of people who don't enjoy reading, but that's got nothing to do with the internet or digital technology. There have always been people who don't like reading. My point is simple – you can like ebooks and books, just as you can enjoy talking to your friends face to face or only on something like WhatsApp. We don't have to decide if we want one but not the other. Ebooks are great for travelling because you can take hundreds of them at once. There is nothing better than reading a printed book in bed – it's a quieter and more relaxing experience than reading on a screen. My parents bought me an ereader a few years ago, as a birthday present. The next day, when they saw me sitting in the garden reading a printed book, they were a bit disappointed. I had to explain to them that the ereader was great, but that I would stop reading physical books just because I had one.

Listening   🔊 CD 2, Track 1

Listening, Exercise 3

You will hear six people talking about film making. For each of Speakers 1–6, choose (from the list A–G) which idea each speaker expresses. Write the letter in the box. Use each letter only once. There is one extra letter, which you do not need to use.

Core [6 marks], Extended [6 marks].

You will hear the full recording twice.

☐ Speaker 1   ☐ Speaker 2

☐ Speaker 3   ☐ Speaker 4

☐ Speaker 5   ☐ Speaker 6

A   I sometimes change my views during the film's development.

B   Disagreements make the atmosphere during filming unpleasant.

C   Things have to be returned to normal after filming.

D   I like to seem confident.

E   I protect my public image.

F   Lack of time for the job puts pressure on me.

G   The audience should believe in the character.

ADVICE FOR SUCCESS

The Advice for Success is for **you** to **help yourself**. Everyone is different. Decide which suggestions you like best and mark them. You can adapt an idea in Advice for Success to make it fun for you. Keeping track with a notebook is a good idea.

1   Practise your **reviewing skills** by exchanging views about TV programmes, books and films with your friends. Try to use some of the language you have been learning in this unit and avoid the adjectives *nice* and *good*.

2   Read book and film reviews in your own language and English to become more familiar with the language of reviewing.

3   Try to **read for pleasure** in English. Keep a book in your bag or pocket or download one onto your tablet. Allow a couple of hours occasionally to really get into a book.

   Find authors you enjoy. Book reviews are a useful source of information, and so is exchanging views with friends. Browsing on an online bookstore or in a bookshop which sells English books can give inspiration too.

4   Look for magazines in English that reflect your own hobbies and interests.

5   Try to **enlarge your range of interest**. Read about different themes (astronomy, transport, inventions) that you usually pass over. Some libraries carry a wide range of journals and newspapers. Pick up one or two about topics that are new for you.

   Try some poetry if you usually ignore it.

6   Watch again a film you have really enjoyed. Analyse why and how it appeals to you. Do this with books, too.

Exam techniques

7   If you write a **review** in an exam, choose a novel or film you know well and enjoyed. Don't write about books or films you found disappointing, as it is more difficult to write in enough detail about something which did not engage your interest in the first place. This doesn't mean the book or film has to be perfect. You can pick out its weak points as well as highlight what was powerful.

8   Use a broad vocabulary and appropriate structures to express your reactions to a book or film. Give specific details about characters, performance, special effects, etc. Avoid writing very generally: it is much better to use specific examples.

9   Don't get too caught up with **describing the plot**. Plots can be very complicated and it is not necessary to retell the story. Just give an idea of what it is about. Describing the beginning can be enough.

10 If you have to review a **live performance** (e.g. a play, dance or music concert), use the skills you have learnt in this unit to:

   • describe the costumes and special effects if appropriate
   • convey the quality of the performance
   • describe your reactions to the performance
   • describe the atmosphere in the audience
   • say why you would recommend the performance to other people.

Exam focus

This unit has helped to prepare you for exams which test your reading, writing, listening and speaking skills. The unit has helped to develop those skills in the following ways:

- You have used a range of **reading techniques** to **answer questions** on **complex and less complex texts**.

- You have learnt to **present a talk** about a **film, play or live performance** and answer questions.

- You have developed a **range of skills** for **writing a review** of a **novel, film, play or other live performance**.

- You have **listened** to a **radio interview** and **answered comprehension questions**.

- You have **listened** to **several speakers** and **matched statements to a speaker**.

- You have learnt **conversation strategies**, and taken part in **structured dialogues** and **discussions**.

Unit 6
Travel and the outdoor life

In this unit you will:

- read about a summer camp and two Italian islands
- write a description of an outdoor activities and holiday destinations
- listen to a conversation about a camping holiday
- practise expressing blame and guilt clearly and effectively
- focus on the following assessment objectives: R1, R2, W3, S1

A Holiday time

1 Holiday quiz

What do you really like doing on holiday? With a partner, rate the following points on a scale of 1 (unimportant) to 4 (very important). Add anything else you or your partner like doing.

		MYSELF	MY PARTNER
1	Staying in a comfortable, well-equipped hotel / holiday home	☐	☐
2	Seeing beautiful scenery and new places	☐	☐
3	Making new friends	☐	☐
4	Doing outdoor activities, e.g. hiking, climbing, swimming	☐	☐
5	Learning a new skill, e.g. sailing, cooking, windsurfing	☐	☐
6	Going to theme parks	☐	☐
7	Having time for reading and quiet thought	☐	☐
8	Exploring city attractions, e.g. art galleries, museums	☐	☐
9	Learning more about local culture and customs	☐	☐
10	Lazing on a sunny beach listening to favourite music	☐	☐

Share your ideas in your group. What are the most popular things to do on holiday? What are the least popular?

2 Pre-reading discussion

The brochure describes summer camps aimed at students who want to learn English.

Look carefully at the pictures without reading the text. Who can you see? Where are they? What are they doing? How do you think they are feeling? What is the atmosphere like?

English in Action

Kingswood Camps has a superb reputation for leading the way in integrated language and activity camps. Set in holiday locations that are popular with UK youngsters, all our camps combine quality English teaching with an action-packed programme of sports and activities.

Through mini projects using research and thinking skills, we focus on building confidence and developing the language skills needed in real-life situations.

The programme is filled with fun, excitement and activities. You never have time to be bored at Kingswood Camps!

Our range of daytime and evening activities provide a terrific opportunity for international students to make new friends from Britain and around the world. You can speak English all day while you swim, surf, go climbing or horse riding, try archery, enjoy discos and campfires, and much more …

Our teachers are hand-picked for their teaching ability and friendly, outgoing personalities. They always take the time to explain things carefully and to bring the language to life. Whether you are at beginner level or already quite fluent, the daily English lessons help you to understand the kind of practical language that is used in everyday situations.

Experience even more by upgrading your stay with a Specialist Holiday. Pick a favourite hobby or try something completely new and, for a supplementary cost, spend a minimum of 15 hours a week focusing on your chosen activity, sharing your passion with like-minded friends. Choose from Stable Club, Surf School, Watersports, Football Academy, Bushcraft and Dance.

From scenic river cruises, trips to historic cities and the bright lights of London, to theme park rollercoasters, famous museums and a spot of shopping, we have exciting excursions covered. One full day and one half day excursion are included in your programme.

All our residential centres offer excellent accommodation and three hot meals per day, including vegetarian options.

Whether you are travelling alone or in a group, you can choose to be met on arrival in the UK. Our special transfer service will then transport you safely to your camp.

Contact

Visit our website at www.kingswood.co.uk/international to download our brochure and to find out more.
To book, call us on +44 (0)1273 648212 or make a booking online.

Parents and legal guardians

It is important to complete and return the Pre-visit Pack as soon as a booking has been made. A booking is *not* confirmed until a completed form is received. If any information changes prior to arrival, please notify us immediately via email or phone.

Brainstorming

What do you think might be the good points and bad points, in general, of this kind of holiday? In pairs, write down any ideas at all that you can think of. Try to add at least another two or three good and bad points.

Good points

- *Trying new skills*
- *Experiencing independence away from home*

Bad points

- *Not enough time to learn a new skill properly*
- *A busy schedule which leaves little time for yourself*

When you've finished, share your ideas in your group. Add to your list any new ideas mentioned by your classmates.

3 Reading for gist

Read the brochure quickly for general meaning. Don't worry about understanding every word. As you read, underline anything that is factual about Kingswood Camps and circle anything that is opinion.

4 Comprehension: Scanning the text

Scan the text to find answers to these questions:

1   What is Kingswood Camps well known for?
2   How often can campers attend English lessons?
3   What can you suggest to a camper who likes horse riding?
4   What opportunities are there for visiting other places in the UK?
5   How is the safe transfer of campers ensured when they arrive in the UK?
6   What should you do if you would like a brochure for Kingswood Camps?
7   What do parents need to do to get a confirmed place for their child?

5 An eye-catching advert?

Who are the two main target groups this brochure is aimed at? What persuasive techniques are used to influence the target groups?

Consider:

- ☐ opinion language
- ☐ the choice of photographs (who is in them and what they are doing)
- ☐ the layout.

6 The best way to learn?

Do you think learning English through the medium of other activities is a good idea? If you are learning a new skill (e.g. water skiing or horse riding), what language would you expect to acquire?

Has this advert convinced you that learning English at a holiday camp is worth doing? Why/Why not?

7 *Quite*

The brochure says that all levels of English are catered for, whether students are *'at beginner level or already **quite** fluent'.*

Quite is a modifier often used before adjectives. It usually means 'moderately' (more than 'a little' but less than 'very'). But it can also mean 'completely', when used with certain adjectives. Which do you think it means in the following sentence?

*'Don't worry, Mrs Chavez. Your daughter will be **quite safe** at Kingswood Camps.'*

8 Shifting stress

The pattern of stress in some words alters when they are used as different parts of speech. For example, the words 'progress' and 'escort' can have different stress depending on whether they are used as nouns or verbs:

*You'll make good **pro**gress on the course.* (noun)

*You can pro**gress** to a higher level.* (verb)

*An **es**cort will meet you at the airport.* (noun)

*We es**cort** students to the camp.* (verb)

Marking the stress 🔊 CD 2, Track 2

Mark the stress in the words in italics in the following sentences as you listen:

1   The farmers sell their *produce* in the market.
2   The factories *produce* spare parts for cars.

124

3 Please *record* all accidents in the accident book.

4 His ambition is to break the world *record* for athletics.

5 I *object* to people smoking in public places.

6 She brought many strange *objects* back from her travels.

7 Black and red make a striking *contrast*.

8 If you *contrast* his early work with his later work, you will see how much it has changed.

9 I can't get a work *permit*.

10 The teacher does not *permit* talking in class.

11 I bought Dad a birthday *present* yesterday.

12 The artist will *present* his work at the next exhibition.

Now practise saying the sentences aloud to a partner. Do you both agree about the stress?

Where does the stress fall when the word is a noun and when it is a verb? Can you work out the rule?

B Outdoor activities

1 Pairwork

What is your favourite outdoor activity? Work in pairs to ask and answer these questions. If you prefer, one of your group can go to the front of the class to reply to the questions.

What / you like / do / your free time?

Where / you do it?

What / you feel like / when you do it?

What special equipment / you use?

How good / you be / at it?

How / you feel / after / activity?

Why / you recommend it?

2 Reading: Identifying leisure activities

A Read the following descriptions. What leisure activities are being described? What key phrases help you to decide? Find at least four in each extract.

Match the photographs with the descriptions.

125

126

1   *I like going to quiet places that are uncrowded. Last week, I chose a route where the rough path made it hard to keep the frame straight. I got stuck in a lot of muddy holes, which were almost impossible to pedal my way out of. On the way down, I felt like I was flying. I reached the foot of the mountain in about half an hour. I was exhausted but delighted that I had done it. To enjoy this activity, you need a good, all-round level of fitness before you start.*

2   *Each time I set myself a goal, which might be to get to the railway station or all around the park without stopping once. All the equipment you need is a good pair of trainers. While I'm doing it, my mind's blank. On the way home, I slow down gradually. I feel satisfied because I've achieved what I set out to do. This is a good activity for someone who enjoys being alone.*

3   *I often practise in a large sports field near my home. I fit an arrow to the crossbow, pull the string back with all my strength and wait for the 'thunk'! I get another arrow ready without pausing to check the target. My fingers and upper body have become very strong since I took up this activity. If you don't have the speed for ball games, this could be an ideal sport for you.*

4   *We've got a large outdoor court where you can hire a racket. I sometimes play friendly games with a partner who, like me, likes to play with someone but is not very competitive. I enjoy concentrating on the ball and I like running, so I usually get to most of the shots. I don't feel I am very skilled but I can perform the basic strokes adequately.*

5   *I always go early in the morning when everything is peaceful. I love listening to the birds and breathing the fresh, clear air. I put on the saddle and bridle and mount by putting my left foot in the stirrup. When I trot, I rise up and down in the stirrups to avoid the 'bumps'. It's an ideal activity if you prefer something non-competitive.*

6   *I've never felt scared or worried doing this. Even at the age of two or three, I loved going underwater. I also like floating on my back. I feel as though I'm weightless. It's very soothing for the nerves, it is pleasant and it's cheap. Everyone can enjoy this, however unfit or badly coordinated they think they are.*

B   Scan the text to answer these questions. Which activity:

a   is very sociable?

b   enables someone to stop thinking?

c   is suitable for someone who likes to appreciate nature?

d   develops strength in the hands?

e   is good for stress?

f   would appeal to someone who finds speed thrilling?

3 Developing your writing style

Most IGCSE students can write a simple description of an outdoor activity they enjoy. However, writing in a way that engages your listener as well as giving facts demands more skill.

Certain language structures can help you.

The **-ing form (gerund)** is often used when describing how much you like something. Remember that *love, like, enjoy, prefer, hate,* etc. are followed by *-ing* forms.

> *Examples: I like being in the open air.*
>
> *I enjoy testing my own limits.*

Clauses (beginning *which, where,* etc.) can link two ideas and provide extra information.

> *Example: There's a large outdoor court where you can hire rackets.*

Since can be used to indicate the point in time something began.

> *Example: I have been skiing since I was tiny.*

Like, as, as though, as if are used to compare one thing to another.

> *Examples: After waterskiing my legs feel like jelly.*
>
> *I felt as if I was flying.*

Using **precise adjectives and adverbs** gives your writing more clarity.

> *Examples: I felt scared.*
>
> *I can perform the basic strokes adequately.*

4 Analysing language structures

Study the extracts in exercise 2. Underline any structures or expressions you would like to use in writing about your own favourite outdoor activity.

5 Describing a favourite activity

Write a description of an outdoor activity you enjoy. Use a wide vocabulary and a range of structures.

You need to mention:

- why you like the activity
- the skills and equipment you need (check any technical words)
- when and where you can do it
- any other personal responses to it
- why other people might enjoy it, too.

Write at least 100 words.

6 Reading aloud

When you've finished, read out your description to your group. If you like, you can substitute the word *'blank'* instead of naming the activity. Let them guess what you are describing.

7 Pre-listening discussion

A Have you ever been camping? Talk to your partner about what it was like. If you have never been, look at the picture and tell your partner what you think it would be like.

B What qualities do you need to be a good camper? Do you think you have them?

C Camping holidays are good fun, but can sometimes be stressful. What might people find stressful or argue with each other about on a camping trip?

8 Listening for gist 🔊 CD 2, Track 3

Paul and Marcus have just come back from their first camping holiday with the youth club. What did they find difficult about the holiday? Note three things.

Overall, do you think they enjoyed the trip despite the difficulties?

9 Listening for detail

Now listen for detail and choose the best ending for each statement.

1 The boys had difficulty getting the tent up because:

a it started to rain when the tent was halfway up

b they were in a hurry to go swimming

c the instruction leaflet had been forgotten.

2 As a result of going on the walk, the boys:

a missed the chance of visiting an aircraft museum

b missed the chance of visiting a war museum

c missed the chance of visiting a historic village

3 The boys think Mr Barker was funny because:

a he was at least 40-years-old

b he wore a woollen hat and specs

c he didn't listen to what they wanted to do.

4 The boys blame the girls for:

a not buying bread for breakfast

b not putting food into airtight containers

c not taking their turn to put food away.

5 The boys' attitude to going on a camping trip in future is:

a negative – there are too many discomforts and problems

b cautious – OK, but there are risks involved in this kind of trip

c enthusiastic – they would look forward to going camping again.

10 Post-listening discussion

A Paul and Marcus mention the uncomfortable aspects of camping, like *stone-cold showers*. What do you think they might have enjoyed about their trip which they did not mention? Try to think of three things.

B If you went camping, where would you prefer to go? In your own country or abroad? Try to explain why.

11 Blame

Paul blames himself for forgetting the instruction leaflet. Paul and Marcus blame the girls for some of the things they didn't enjoy on holiday.

Here are some expressions people use to blame each other, admit guilt or tell each other they are not to blame. Pick the ones the boys use. Which expressions sound most critical? When would it be acceptable to use them? When would it be inappropriate?

Blaming

- *It's your fault.*
- *You're responsible.*
- *I blame you for it.*
- *It was down to you.*

Admitting guilt/responsibility

- *It's my fault.*
- *I do feel guilty.*
- *I feel bad about it.*
- *I'm responsible.*
- *I should have been more careful.*

Telling someone they are not to blame

- *Don't blame yourself.*
- *It wasn't your fault.*
- *It was just one of those things.*
- *You shouldn't feel bad about it.*

12 Comparing cultures

What do you say in your language when you want to blame someone, admit guilt or tell someone they are not to blame for something? How does it compare with what is acceptable in English?

13 Functional language: Writing a dialogue

Imagine you have gone on a picnic and find that one of you forgot to pack the cold drinks. What would you say to each other?

Write out this or a similar dialogue. Remember to refer back to exercise 11 for suitable expressions. Practise the dialogue in pairs. Finally, exchange dialogues with another pair in your group.

14 Colloquial expressions: Adjective collocations

On the recording you heard showers described as *'stone cold'*, bread described as *'rock hard'*, the night as *'pitch dark'* and boots as *'brand new'*.

In colloquial language, the meaning of an adjective is often emphasised by the addition of a noun or another adjective before it.

Examples: stone cold (noun + adjective)

icy cold (adjective + adjective)

Complete the gaps in the following sentences with an adjective or noun from the box. You will need to use one word twice.

VOCABULARY		
crystal	freezing	wide
dirt	sky	
fast	stiff	

1 Wasn't Jeremy's talk fascinating?
  I'm afraid I don't agree. In fact, I was bored _____.

2 The resort was idyllic – a beautiful sandy beach and _____ clear water.

3 I was scared _____ when the plane began to shake.

4 No wonder it's _____ cold in here. You've left the window _____ open.

5 Chantal looked so pretty in her _____-blue outfit.

6 I was exhausted after our long trek back to the campsite. As soon as my head hit the pillow, I was _____ asleep.

7 Why did you buy so many bananas?
  I couldn't resist it. They were _____ cheap.

15 More colloquial expressions

Instead of 'getting up very early', you heard Marcus talk about *'getting up at the crack of dawn'*.

Complete the following sentences with these colloquial phrases:

VOCABULARY	
a bite to eat	a drop of rain
at the last minute	hear a pin drop
a hair out of place	

1 We stopped at a café on the way home to have _____, as we hadn't had anything all day.

2 The farmers are very worried about their crops. There hasn't been _____ for months.

3 The library was so quiet that you could _____.

4 Her appearance is immaculate. She never has _____

5 Dan never plans ahead and made all the arrangements for his holiday _____.

Now work in pairs to create some sentences of your own with these expressions. You need to use the whole expression – you can't use just part of it.

16 Word building: Adjective suffixes

Many adjectives are formed by adding suffixes to nouns, etc. Below are some examples from the recording. Notice the way the spelling changes in some words.

waterproof (water + proof)

fortyish (forty + ish)

historic (histor\y\ + ic)

In groups of two or three, discuss how you could form adjectives from the following words by adding suitable suffixes. In some cases, more than one suffix is possible.

Check your ideas in a dictionary. Then try to create sentences of your own.

VOCABULARY		
bullet	Arab	scene
twenty	Islam	sound
child	boy	pink
irony	panorama	

17 Punctuating direct speech

In written English, inverted commas (also called quotation marks) must be put around all the words someone actually says. You open inverted commas at the beginning of the speech and close them at the end.

Study the following examples of the way direct speech is punctuated. Focus in particular on:

- the use of capital letters
- the position of other punctuation marks (commas, question marks, etc.)
- the correct way to punctuate quoted words within direct speech.

1   Melissa said, 'I don't have any money, do you?'

2   Mum paused and reached into her bag for her phone. 'Do you want to see our holiday photos? I took some on my phone,' she said.

3   'Have another piece of cake,' urged Mum. 'I baked it specially.'

4   Costas shouted, 'You tell me, "Don't worry about it," but I can't help worrying.'

5   'Look out!' screamed Uju. 'Can't you see that lorry?!'

Practice

Complete the punctuation in the following conversation. You need to add inverted commas and commas.

What was the best part of your holiday in America? Naomi asked when she saw Kevin again.

Going along Highway One from Los Angeles to San Francisco said Kevin without hesitation. I wouldn't have missed it for the world.

What's so special about Highway One? Naomi asked. Isn't it just another dead straight American highway?

Well replied Kevin. The road runs between mountains on one side and the Pacific on the other. The views are beautiful. Seagulls fly over the waves. There are great cliffs full of redwood trees. Yes he paused for a moment it's truly magnificent.

What was the weather like? Naomi asked. Every time I checked the international weather forecast there was one word hot.

In fact Kevin laughed we had stormy weather but when the sun broke through it created fantastic rainbows. We visited a cove where you can hunt for jade. Anything you find is yours and I'd almost given up looking when I found this. He reached into his pocket and pulled out a tiny green fragment. Here he said it's for you.

C Tourism: The pros and cons

1 Brainstorming

Tourism is now probably the world's biggest single industry.

Work in groups of three or four and jot down anything you can think of under the following headings. Pool your ideas with other groups and add any new ones.

A   What are some of the pleasures and drawbacks of being a tourist?

Pleasures

- *You can see a different way of life.*
- _____
- _____
- _____

Drawbacks

- *Your holiday is too short to get a real understanding of the country.*
- _____
- _____
- _____

B   What are the advantages and disadvantages to the host country of a rise in tourism?

Advantages

- *It creates jobs.*
- _____
- _____
- _____
- _____

Disadvantages

- *Pollution increases.*
- *Foreign companies take the profits from tourism back to their own countries.*

- _____
- _____
- _____
- _____

C How can tourists behave responsibly when they go abroad?

- *They can buy from local traders.*

- _____
- _____
- _____
- _____

2 Tourism with a difference

Tourism Concern is an agency that wants to develop 'sustainable tourism'. This means that tourists try to make sure that tourism benefits the local community. For example, they fly with a local airline and use local accommodation rather than international hotels. What do you think of this idea?

3 Pre-reading discussion

A You are going to read an article about tourism in Sicily and Sardinia, two islands off the Italian coast. First, describe what you can see in the pictures.

B What do you think a holiday on these islands would be like? What do you think you would enjoy? Would you find anything difficult to get used to? Would you like the opportunity to go? Why/Why not?

C What do you think foreign visitors expect your own country to be like? Are their perceptions correct, do you think? How do foreign visitors to your country usually behave? If you get a lot of visitors, does the atmosphere in your area change? How? Try to explain your views.

4 Vocabulary check

Can you match the following words from the article with their definitions?

1	whiff	**A**	to shine with a warm, bright light
2	gilded	**B**	growing thickly and strongly
3	glow incandescently	**C**	strong
4	pastures	**D**	to fly high
5	enigmatic	**E**	covered or decorated with gold
6	soar	**F**	grassy fields
7	gorges	**G**	a picture made by arranging small coloured pieces of glass or stone
8	lush	**H**	a brief smell
9	secluded	**I**	private, hidden away
10	robust	**J**	mysterious
11	mosaic	**K**	steep, narrow valleys

5 Reading and underlining

Read the article carefully, underlining the descriptive language as you read.

6 Comprehension check

Now try to answer the following questions:

1 What, according to the writer, is the main reason that Sicily and Sardinia have remained unspoilt?

2 Why is the writer reminded of North Africa? Give **two** examples.

3 What has been the result of the combination of Arabic and Italian influences on the architecture?

4 Which activities does the writer suggest Sardinia is well-suited to? Give **two** examples.

5 Which island, according to the article, would be:

a a good destination for a keen birdwatcher?

b attractive to someone who likes mountain views?

c a good choice for a tourist who prefers traditional, rural accommodation?

d appealing to a tourist who admires ancient Greek architecture?

e of interest to someone who is curious about volcanoes?

f a good destination for someone who enjoys evidence of prehistory?

g suitable for a family who want to stay in modern accommodation with childcare facilities?

6 Which statement best summarises the author's view? Select the correct statement.

a Overall, Sicily is a higher quality destination for tourists.

b Sardinia has the most to offer tourists choosing a holiday.

c Each island is unique with different benefits for tourists.

Offshore Italy

Unspoilt, even wild, the Italian islands of Sicily and Sardinia give an unexpected flavour to holidays in the Mediterranean.

Sicily – mosaics, ruins and churches

What most of us want is to visit a 'real' country. We want unspoilt landscapes, markets, traditions, cuisine and distinctive architecture. We want people who are welcoming yet different from us.

5 Historically, there are two ways in which local character is preserved. The first is a poor economy; the second is physical separation from the mainland – the key reason why Sicily and Sardinia have stayed unspoilt.

10 I recently went to Taormina, Sicily's best-known seaside resort. Located on Monte Tauro, Taormina can be reached via funicular* from its two bays below. Although its streets are traffic-free, they become crowded with holidaymakers in high summer. Even

15 with so many people, nothing can take away the magic of this medieval town. After all, what other major holiday resort has a backdrop that includes a world-class Graeco-Roman amphitheatre, wonderful hills and a 3 323-metre volcano, Mount Etna?

Here, in the east of Sicily, there's a link with 20 southern Italy, but move further west and the influence is decidedly more Arabic. By the time you enter the Sicilian capital, Palermo, with its street market similar to a souk and couscous cafés, there's an exciting whiff of North Africa. 25

In Palermo, this mix of the two traditions has produced some of the most beautifully decorated buildings in this part of the world. There's the Cappella Reale, the chapel that King Roger II built for himself in the 12th century. Entering from the central 30 courtyard, it takes a while for your eyes to adjust to the darkness. But gradually the gilded mosaics which line the walls come alive; while overhead, wonderfully carved ceiling paintings of exotic gardens and hunting scenes glow incandescently against a deep blue sky. 35 The chapel is the supreme jewel of the city, yet a few kilometres away, on the hilltop at Monreale, is a cathedral where the mosaics are equally beautiful.

Sicily may not have as much mountain wildness as Sardinia, but it is a lovely broad landscape with 40 rolling plains and corn-coloured hills. Life is taken at a relatively slow pace and sleepy hilltop towns come to life only for a festival or wedding. In some of this lovely country, farmers are waking up to the possibilities of *agriturismo*, boosting an income 45 by offering hospitality (converted cottages and, sometimes, country food) to enthusiastic tourists.

Visiting Sicily now, it is easy to forget that for nearly 3000 years it was the most fought-over island in

50 the Mediterranean. The ancient Greeks loved it
as one of their richest colonies and left behind a
marvellous collection of temples to prove it.

Sardinia has some of the most astonishing
countryside in Europe. Much of the population is
55 concentrated in its two main towns, Cagliari in the
south and Sassari in the north, so in the centre of
the island shepherds still herd sheep and goats to
remote valleys, visiting pastures used in Roman
times. The land is dotted with mysterious stone
60 buildings called *nuraghi*, which were left behind by
the Sardinians' prehistoric ancestors.

Eagles and black vultures soar over the mountains,
pink flamingos flash their wings by the coast –
everywhere you look there are gorges, caves, wild
65 boar, deer and flowers. All this makes Sardinia a
terrific destination for fishing, cycling, walking
and riding.

Yet, despite extensive areas of wilderness,
the island has some of the best resort hotels in
70 all Italy.

One of the most successful of the tourist developments
is Forte Village. Set in 55 acres of lush garden with a
wide range of sports on offer, there are three hotels
to choose from, plus a selection of secluded cottages,
entertainment and childminding services. It may   75
not be the 'real' Sardinia, but it's hard to find a better
quality holiday resort.

* funicular = a mountain railway where the cars are operated
  by cable

Sardinia – wild at heart, with glamorous resorts

133

7 Post-reading discussion

The writer says that when tourists go on holiday they want
to visit a 'real' country. They:

*'want unspoilt landscapes … traditions … [and] people who
are welcoming yet different'.*

However, she also mentions the popularity of specially
built 'tourist villages' which offer entertainment and
childminding services.

Do you think meeting the needs of tourists for comfort can ever
be in conflict with protecting a beautiful landscape and ancient
traditions? Do tourists expect too much? What are your views?

8 Adverbs as intensifiers

We can use adverbs before adjectives to intensify the meaning
of the adjective. There are several examples in the text:

beautifully decorated (line 32)

wonderfully carved (line 39)

relatively slow (line 48)

Combining adverbs appropriately with adjectives is a
matter of practice. There are no hard and fast rules.

Choose adverbs from the box to complete the sentences
below. After you have finished, compare your answers
with a partner's. Sometimes more than one answer is
possible.

VOCABULARY		
alarmingly	fully	strikingly
badly	painstakingly	surprisingly
dazzlingly	seriously	utterly
faintly	strangely	

1 I found the standard of service in the hotel
_____ bad.

2 He has _____ recovered from his accident.

3 The temple is a(n) _____ attractive building.

4 The buildings were _____ bombed in
the war.

5 I was _____ ill in hospital.

6 The beggar was _____ destitute.

7 You'll need sunglasses as the midday sun is
_____ bright.

8 They expected prices to be high on holiday, but everything was _____ cheap.

9 The ancient relics in the museum had been _____ restored.

10 Even after washing, the coffee stain on that white tablecloth is still _____ visible.

11 We held our breath as the coach went _____ fast around steep mountain bends.

12 The disco, which was usually very noisy, was _____ quiet.

9 Imagery in descriptions

Striking images convey a lot of information in a few words.

The writer describes Sicily as *'a lovely, broad landscape with rolling plains and corn-coloured hills'.*

Does she describe everything about the Sicilian countryside, or select a few key features? What kind of image does the phrase *'rolling plains and corn-coloured hills'* convey?

What kind of images of Sardinia come to your mind when you read that *'shepherds still herd sheep and goats to remote valleys, visiting pastures used in Roman times'*?

or

'Eagles and black vultures soar over the mountains, pink flamingos flash their wings by the coast'?

Study the examples carefully and underline key adjectives or images that suggest the area is still wild and untouched by modern life.

10 Adjectives: Quality not quantity

It's far better to be selective. How many adjectives have been used before the nouns in the following examples? How successfully do they evoke a particular atmosphere?

exotic gardens (line 40)
sleepy hilltop towns (line 48)

Choose an example of descriptive writing from the text, which you think contains pleasing images. Comment on it in the same way.

11 Comparing two styles

Compare the following two descriptions of the same place. How do the styles of the extracts differ? Which do you prefer? Why?

Style one

The village is very, very nice. Tourists like going there but there is not a lot of new development, crowds or traffic or things like that. There are stone houses near the harbour. The buildings are not painted in dark colours. They are painted white or cream. The buildings have blue, grey or brown shutters. There are hills around the village. There are many pine trees on the hills. The view from the top of the hills is very good. You can see the whole area.

Style two

The village is strikingly pretty and unspoilt. The houses, rising up from the harbour, are pale-coloured with painted shutters and made of stone. The village is surrounded by hills covered with pine trees, which provide panoramic views of the area.

12 Developing your writing style

There are a number of ways you can improve your writing style:

- Choose your adjectives with care and use them **precisely**.
- Remember that you can create adjectives by adding **suffixes** to nouns or adjectives, e.g. *panoramic, colourful.* (See exercise 16.)
- You can make adjectives more emphatic by using adverbs as **intensifiers**, e.g. *staggeringly, exceptionally.* (See exercise 8.)

- Adjective **collocations,** such as *crystal clear,* are another way of adding impact to your descriptions. (See exercise 14.)
- Use **clauses** to link ideas beginning with *which, where, when* and **phrases** beginning with *made of, with,* etc.
- Use **comparisons**: *like, as, as though, as if.*
- All the above techniques will help you to write more **concisely** – using fewer words to greater effect.

Practice

Now use the ideas in exercise 12 to help you rewrite the following description.

The town developed around a marketplace. The marketplace is very, very old. It is in the shape of a rectangle. In the town the people live in the way that they used to live hundreds of years ago. They like visitors. They will always help you. You do not need to be afraid of them. They wear clothes that are very simple. They wear long, loose, white cotton robes. The town has many very, very old buildings. The buildings were built in the 13th century. It also has many restaurants. There are many different kinds of restaurants. You can eat nice food. The food is from different cultures.

13 Writing your own description

Think about your last holiday or day out. Try to recall what was distinctive about the experience. Was it the people's way of life? The landscape? The food? The places of interest? Where you stayed? Or a combination of all of these?

What particular images come to your mind? When you are ready, write them down. Don't worry about trying to write neatly or accurately. Just let the words flow out onto the page.

Re-read what you have written and select the best images. Concentrate on those that convey the flavour of the experience. Don't try to describe everything.

Now try to write a description. Use the techniques you have learnt in the unit so far. Write about 100 words.

International tourism around the world is growing steadily.

1. From the countries on this list, try to guess the top four international tourist destinations in order of popularity.

Australia	Brazil	China
Egypt	France	India
South Africa	Spain	UK
USA		

2. Which country on the list would you most like to visit?
3. Which country would you most like to visit if you could choose anywhere in the world? Why?
4. Which holiday destinations abroad are popular with people from your country?

Share your ideas with a partner.

14 Giving a short talk

'More tourists = more economic and social benefits'

Prepare a talk of about five minutes on the above topic for your group.

Planning the talk

Use the notes you made earlier to help you produce a list of key points under main headings.

Give your talk depth by adding examples of your own. Try to think of specific ways tourism affects your country. What have you noticed yourself about the behaviour of tourists, the effect they have on the environment / local atmosphere?

If you have travelled, you could compare tourism in your country with tourism abroad. What was your own experience of being a tourist in a foreign country like? How were you treated? What did you learn about the treatment of tourists in your own country?

Presentation

Use your notes to help you give your presentation, but don't just read them out, it will not engage your listeners. Make eye contact, speak clearly, and be prepared to answer questions.

Being a good listener

Remember, it's polite to show an interest in the speaker. Listen attentively and have at least one question or comment ready to put to the speaker at the end.

15 Words from names

The island of Sardinia gave its name to *sardines*. Many words in English are derived from the names of people or places.

Try to match these names to the people in the sentences below. Check the meaning of any unfamiliar words.

VOCABULARY		
Morse	**Fahrenheit**	**Diesel**
Volta	**Marx**	**Sandwich**
Cardigan	**Pasteur**	

1 Lord _____ didn't have time for a proper meal so he devised a way of eating meat between two slices of bread.

2 Lord _____ was the first person to wear a long-sleeved jacket made of wool.

3 Louis _____ invented a method of making milk safe to drink.

4 Gabriel _____ developed a thermometer which showed boiling and freezing points.

5 Samuel _____ invented a secret code to be used for sending messages.

6 Alessandro _____ invented the electric battery.

7 Karl _____ developed the idea of communism.

8 Rudolf _____ devised a special type of oil-burning engine.

Can suffixes be added to any of the names? Which ones?

Are any words in your own language derived from these names? Compare ideas with your classmates.

16 More homophones

Problems with homophones are the root of many spelling errors. Remember that homophones have the same sound but different spellings. (Look back at exercises 9 and 10 in Unit 1.)

Work with a partner to try to find a homophone for each of these words. The words have come from the texts you have read in the unit so far.

VOCABULARY			
real	**flower**	**soar**	**sail**
scene	**sea**	**blue**	**herd**
boar	**right**	**two**	**deer**

Finally, put each homophone into a sentence.

D Personal challenges

1 Reading an example email

Read the email which describes an activity holiday. How good a description do you think it is?

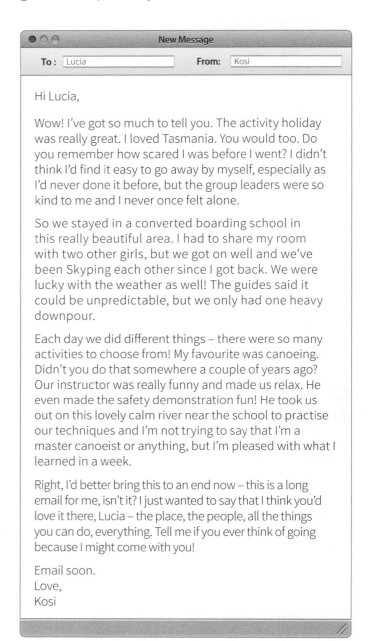

New Message

To: Lucia   From: Kosi

Hi Lucia,

Wow! I've got so much to tell you. The activity holiday was really great. I loved Tasmania. You would too. Do you remember how scared I was before I went? I didn't think I'd find it easy to go away by myself, especially as I'd never done it before, but the group leaders were so kind to me and I never once felt alone.

So we stayed in a converted boarding school in this really beautiful area. I had to share my room with two other girls, but we got on well and we've been Skyping each other since I got back. We were lucky with the weather as well! The guides said it could be unpredictable, but we only had one heavy downpour.

Each day we did different things – there were so many activities to choose from! My favourite was canoeing. Didn't you do that somewhere a couple of years ago? Our instructor was really funny and made us relax. He even made the safety demonstration fun! He took us out on this lovely calm river near the school to practise our techniques and I'm not trying to say that I'm a master canoeist or anything, but I'm pleased with what I learned in a week.

Right, I'd better bring this to an end now – this is a long email for me, isn't it? I just wanted to say that I think you'd love it there, Lucia – the place, the people, all the things you can do, everything. Tell me if you ever think of going because I might come with you!

Email soon.
Love,
Kosi

2 Comprehension

1 Where did Kosi go on holiday?

2 How did she feel before she went? Were her feelings justified?

3 What was her favourite activity? Why?

4 Why does she think Lucia would like the same type of holiday?

5 How does she feel overall about the trip?

3 Analysing the email

1 What is the main topic of each paragraph?

2 Analyse the language Kosi uses to describe:
- the place
- the activities
- the instructor
- her feelings.

3 How does she close the email? Consider the last sentence of the final paragraph, and the closing phrase.

4 Vocabulary: The weather

The weather, particularly on holiday, is a popular topic of conversation among British people. Decide whether the following statements about the weather are likely to be true or false. Use a dictionary if necessary.

1 The weather was showery so we had to water the garden every day.

2 The blizzard made driving home easy.

3 Early in the morning the grass is wet with dew.

4 At home, we switch on the lights at dusk.

5 I needed to put on my sunglasses because the sky was overcast.

6 The weather was so mild last winter that we hardly wore our coats.

7 It's not worth hanging out the washing to dry as it has begun to drizzle.

8 The gale blew several trees over.

9 Constant low temperatures and hard frosts meant there was no chance of a thaw.

10 Farmers are very pleased to have a long period of drought.

5 Spelling revision

Some adjectives are formed from nouns by adding *-y*. You need to remember the rules for adding suffixes.

A final -e in a word is usually dropped when adding -y: ice icy

The rule for one-syllable words is that we double the final consonant if the word ends in one vowel and one consonant.

Examples: sun sunny BUT cloud cloudy

6 Writing about the weather

Choose an appropriate noun from the box and change it into an adjective to fill each gap in the postcard. Take care with your spelling.

VOCABULARY		
storm	frost	chill
mud	mist	fog
haze	rain	

137

Hi everyone,

We're having a good time here but the weather isn't great. Every day starts _____ or even _____. This clears up by midday and as you can see, we do get a little _____ sunshine. We had a _____ day yesterday and the ground was too _____ for walking. It's generally _____ and I'm glad we brought warm clothes. Our boat trip was cancelled because it was _____. We're hoping for calmer weather tomorrow.

Love,
Ashwin

7 Discussion: Voluntary work abroad

Spending time in a developing country as a volunteer in a school, hospital or a charity project is very popular with young people. However, it is sometimes claimed that young, inexperienced students from affluent nations have little to offer the world's poorer countries. They enter a difficult situation with little training or worldly knowledge. They might have ideas that are inappropriate for the country. In addition, they might be very homesick – almost an extra burden on the charity.

How far do you agree with these ideas? Is there any way problems like these could be overcome? Discuss your views with your partner.

8 Building a blog from notes

Basima is working in a nursery school in Ecuador. She has started a blog so she can tell her friends back home about her new life. Use the notes to build up a complete blog entry.

At first / be very busy / but now / have time / update my blog/. I / enjoy myself here. The weather be warm / sunny / except for / last night / there be / big storm / which turn / paths / into rivers.

The family / I stay with / be very kind. The house be / three-bedroomed / and be quite comfortable. I be very close / my 'sisters' / who tell me off / if I do anything wrong! Each morning I wake up / sound / exotic birds / dart / among trees.

Yesterday I take / bus / through breathtaking countryside / to local city. I go / bustling market. Everywhere / people sell things / but I be not sure / what buy!

I help / look after / young children / nursery school. The children be delightful / and be very polite. The work be demanding / rewarding.

I miss everyone / home / but I feel / grow up quickly / and I be / more confident now.

I going to / upload / photos tomorrow and would love/read your comments.

9 Look, say, cover, write, check

The following words are problematic to spell. Most of them come from various exercises in the unit. Use the 'look, say, cover, write, check' method to help you learn them.

VOCABULARY		
Mediterranean	confidence	jewellery
separate	restaurant	accommodation
glamour	separation	jewel

138

10 Discussion: Working as a tour guide

A Talk to your partner about what you can see in the photograph.

B Study these comments made by tour guides working in the tourist industry. Discuss each of them with your partner and decide if this work attracts either of you.

1 *It's essential that you like travel and, above all, have a lot of patience with people.*

2 *Although the clients are on holiday, you've got to remember you're not on holiday and you must always be prepared to be responsible.*

3 *Touring a country with a group makes it hard to keep up friendships at home.*

4 *You have to be able to live for two weeks out of a suitcase or rucksack.*

5 *You're with the group 24 hours a day on a tour. There's not much privacy.*

6 *You've got to be well organised and methodical at all times. The arrangements you are in charge of can be very complicated.*

11 Reordering a magazine article

The following article was uploaded onto a school website. Reorder the sentences logically and divide the article into three paragraphs. Underline the words and phrases which help you to link the text.

Life as a resort rep in Rhodes, by a former pupil

a Initially, they relied a lot on me to explain about the banks and shops and to recommend local restaurants and the best sightseeing trips.

b Finally, I hope this has given you some idea of what life as a resort rep is all about.

c The work itself is very varied and I have the opportunity to meet new people and see interesting places.

d I have groups of all ages.

e In addition, there are many stunning, unspoilt beaches and peaceful villages.

f It is the first time they have been abroad.

g Although it gives you the chance to have lots of fun, it's not all glamour.

h Now, however, they are much more relaxed.

i However, if any of you are keen to get involved, I would definitely recommend it!

j It's got an impressive old town and a new town with graceful, modern buildings.

k In fact, they are more independent than many much younger tourists.

l First of all, let me give you an idea of what Rhodes is like.

m Next, I'd like to tell you a bit about my job.

n At the moment, for example, I'm looking after a group of elderly people.

139

GRAMMAR SPOTLIGHT

Adverbs of frequency

A   The adverbs of frequency *always, usually, often, seldom, rarely, hardly ever* and *never* show how often something happens.

They usually go immediately **before the main verb:**

*I **always take** too many clothes on holiday.*

*You **never have** time to be bored at Kingswood Camps.*

So if the verb has two parts, the adverb goes **before the second verb:**

*She had **never enjoyed** camping.*

B   The word *sometimes,* another common adverb of frequency, is different because it can go in three positions:

***Sometimes** I eat toast for breakfast.*

*I **sometimes** eat toast for breakfast.*

*I eat toast for breakfast **sometimes**.*

C   With the verb **'be'**, adverbs of frequency go **after** the verb:

*I **am usually** hungry after school.*

*Joel **was sometimes** late for class.*

*Students **are always** met and escorted by holiday camp staff.*

1   Look at extracts 3, 4, 5 and 6 in exercise B. Notice the frequency adverbs and underline them.

2   Correct the mistakes in these sentences by putting the adverb in the correct position. **One** sentence is already correct!

a   I ride always my bike to school.

b   Angela often goes swimming with her friends.

c   He prefers usually the buffet-style breakfast.

d   Visitors to the Taj Mahal seldom are disappointed.

e   We play sometimes tennis after college.

f   Lewis hardly ever is on time – it's so annoying!

g   The children go rarely to the cinema.

h   She never has been on holiday abroad.

Exam-style questions

Writing

Reading & Writing, Exercise 5

1 A travel company called 'Explore' awarded you first prize in a recent competition. You were given the chance to travel to any of the destinations mentioned in this advertisement. You have just arrived home from your holiday. Write an email to a friend in which you:

- explain why you chose that particular holiday
- tell your friend about special places of interest you visited
- say why you would recommend this place to other people.

Your email should be 100–150 words.

Core [12 marks]

EXPLORE

TRAVEL TO NEW AND UNUSUAL DESTINATIONS!

Wildlife and Natural History

We visit many of the world's greatest game parks – tracking mountain gorillas in **Uganda** or bushwalking with guides in **Kenya**.

Wilderness Experience

Discover the haunting beauty of the living rainforest in **Borneo** or **Costa Rica**, or experience the powerful mystique of deserts like the Namib, Gobi or Sahara.

Raft and River Journeys

River journeys can last from a few hours to several days, and range from two-person inflatables on the Dordogne River in **France** to the excitement of an Amazon riverboat in **Brazil**.

Reading & Writing, Exercise 5

2 You have just returned from a week's activity holiday. Write an account of the holiday for your friend in which you:

- describe the place
- say what activity/activities you enjoyed
- explain why you think other people would enjoy such a holiday.

The pictures may give you some ideas, and you should try to use some ideas of your own.

Write 150–200 words.

Extended [16 marks]

Reading & Writing, Exercise 5

3   A friend has emailed you complaining that he/she is bored and asking you to recommend a new leisure activity.

Write an email to your friend in which you:

- suggest an interesting leisure activity
- explain why you think he/she would enjoy it
- say if any special equipment or training are required.

Your email should be 150–200 words.

Extended [16 marks]

Speaking

1   Tourism

Imagine that an area near where you live is being developed in order to attract tourists. The new developments may bring benefits, but some disadvantages, too. Discuss this topic with the assessor.

You may wish to use the following ideas to help develop the conversation:

- how tourists might behave and the expectations they might have
- the kind of new jobs that might be created
- other ways tourism could be good for the local economy
- whether new buildings would be put up and the impact this would have
- ways to protect areas of special beauty or fragility.

You are free to consider any other related ideas of your own. Do not make any written notes.

2   Travel at home and abroad

Nowadays, many people expect to travel, either for holidays, business or for some other reason. Discuss this topic with the assessor.

Here are some possible ideas for developing the conversation:

- places you have particularly enjoyed visiting in your own country
- the suggestion that foreign travel is better than travelling in one's own country
- the idea that air travel enables family members living abroad to see each other easily
- whether you would find the idea of studying abroad attractive
- the advantages and possible drawbacks of working for a large international company.

You are not allowed to make any written notes.

3   Spare-time activities

Hobbies and leisure activities are very important to some people, whereas others have few hobbies or none at all. Discuss this topic with the assessor.

You may wish to talk about:

- the activities you enjoy in your spare time
- an activity that you would like to learn, if you had the chance
- the advantages and drawbacks of hobbies people enjoy outdoors
- the idea that everyone should have a hobby of some kind
- the view that modern teenagers do not persevere with hobbies.

You are, of course, free to use any other related ideas of your own. Do not make any written notes.

Listening 🔊 CD 2, Tracks 4 and 5

Listening, Exercise 5

Part A 🔊 CD 2, Track 4

You are going to listen to a museum tour guide talk about 'Viking history and culture'. Listen to the talk and complete the notes in Part A. Write one or two words in each gap. You will hear the talk twice.

Extended [10 marks]

The Vikings

Longships

Between the 8th and 11th centuries, the Vikings travelled to many regions of the world in wooden longships. Some longships have been dug up from rivers in one piece, as the _____ at the bottom of the river bed preserved the wood in good condition.

Description of a longship

The longships were light and narrow. The red sail of a warrior longship scared away enemies. The rack along the length of the ship held _____.

Viking weapons

Viking warriors used iron axes, spears, swords, arrows and crossbows. Children were taught _____, as these skills were needed for hunting and fighting.

Before going into battle, warriors put on cloaks and helmets made from bearskins and worked themselves into a _____. The word 'berserk' is from an early Norse word meaning bearskin.

The swords were decorated with delicate silver patterns. The warrior valued his sword highly, and it had a special _____ written on it. The weapons were buried with warriors when they died. (5 marks)

Part B 🔊 CD 2, Track 5

Now listen to a conversation between two students about Viking settlers in Iceland and complete the sentences in Part B. Write one or two words only in each gap. You will hear the conversation twice.

Pause 00'30"

Now you will hear the talk again.

Iceland in the Viking Age

Between 870 and 930, 1000 Vikings left Norway because they needed _____.

The first settler built a farm in an area which became the site of Iceland's _____.

The settlers used iron and _____ make weapons and cooking pots.

Exports: natural resources, linen and _____.

In 930, the settlers set up a yearly _____ called the Althing, which discussed the best ways to rule the island. (5 marks)

Now you will hear the talk again.

ADVICE FOR SUCCESS

The Advice for Success is for **you** to **help yourself.** Everyone is different. Decide which suggestions you like best and mark them. You can adapt an idea in Advice for Success to make it fun for you. Keeping track with a notebook is a good idea.

1   Many students have difficulty concentrating on a topic for very long. In the modern world of the internet, smartphones and tablets, sustaining attention on a topic for a long time can be quite hard.

Try to **strengthen your powers of concentration.** Time your ability to concentrate on a topic without getting distracted or having a break. Gradually try to extend the length of time you can do this. If distracting thoughts come, try to bring your mind back to what you are doing. Slowly, you will build up the length of time you can concentrate.

Exam techniques

2   Read a composition question carefully and underline what you have to do. If you are given a detailed stimulus, such as a printed text from a magazine, be extra careful. Make sure you only write what is expected of you.

3   Make a very brief **plan** before you begin. Students sometimes panic at the thought of planning because they think it will use up valuable time. However, it is essential if you are to have a clear structure for your writing. If there is no time to write a complete essay, a clear plan should gain some marks.

4   Try to **draw on personal experience** in developing ideas for a description. This will make writing come more easily.

Aim to produce a **mature style** by using some of the techniques you've developed in this unit. Avoid lots of plain, short sentences with the words 'nice' or 'good'. Use clauses, comparisons, unusual adjectives and images to make your descriptions interesting and distinctive.

5   Description alone is not enough. You will have to **explain your reasons** for liking something. You usually have to say why you think other people would enjoy whatever it is, too. Try to give clear, interesting reasons that relate sensibly to your topic.

6   As always, check through your work for mistakes in spelling, grammar and punctuation.

Make sure you have written in paragraphs. If you haven't, the next best thing is to indicate where they should be. Aim to leave enough time to do this.

7   In an exam, you may be required to scan a **sign, notice, leaflet, article or webpage** for factual detail. Look first for clues to meaning from pictures, headings, etc. Then read the information quickly to get the sense before you try to answer the questions. It's usually possible to 'spot' the information in the text.

Remember - even if a text gives information about prices, etc,. what you will be tested on is your ability to read that information carefully, not your mathematical skills.

Exam focus

This unit has helped to prepare you for exams which test your reading, writing, listening and speaking skills. The unit has helped to develop those skills in the following ways:

- You have developed skills for **describing places and activities in a more mature style, suitable for emails and articles.**
- You have **written connected paragraphs** based on **texts.**
- You have used a range of **reading techniques** to **answer questions** on **complex** and **less complex** texts.

- You have **listened** to an **informal conversation** and answered **multiple-choice questions.**
- You have **listened** to a **formal talk** and taken **notes.**
- You have **listened** to an **informal conversation** and taken **notes.**
- You have developed **conversational strategies** and developed skills for more **formal discussions.**
- You have **presented** a **short talk** on a **topical issue.**

Unit 7
Student life

In this unit you will:

- read about exam nerves and an exchange of emails about a problem
- give advice in an email, using the appropriate tone and register
- listen to a conversation about college fears and a counsellor talking about her work
- understand a speaker's opinions and attitudes in a listening exercise
- examine ways of talking about problems and giving someone advice
- focus on the following assessment objectives: R3, R4, W5, S4

A Challenges of student life

1 Completing a checklist

In Britain and some other countries it is traditional for students to leave home and attend a college or university in another city. This is usually an exciting and challenging time. If you left home to study, what do you think you would look forward to? What do you think you might find difficult?

Work by yourself. To help focus your thoughts, copy and complete the checklist. Mark the ideas like this:

✓✓ *I'd really look forward to this.*

✓ *I wouldn't mind this.*

? *I'm not sure how I'd feel about this.*

✗ *This would definitely worry me. I don't know how I'd cope.*

- ☐ having my own place
- ☐ shopping for food and other essentials
- ☐ making sure I eat regularly and sensibly
- ☐ cooking for myself
- ☐ finding new friends
- ☐ organising myself and working alone
- ☐ managing on a budget
- ☐ being more responsible for my own studies
- ☐ deciding how to spend my free time
- ☐ doing my own laundry
- ☐ keeping where I live clean and tidy
- ☐ being more responsible for my own health
- ☐ keeping in touch with my family and friends.

If you have already left home to study, mark the checklist according to what you know about your ability to cope from your actual experience:

✓✓ *I've really enjoyed this.*

✓ *This has been demanding but I've managed.*

? *I'm still learning to cope with this.*

✗ *This is a problem for me.*

2 Before you listen: Interactive skills

You are going to analyse the way two teenagers talking about starting university interact with each other.

Before you listen, answer these questions:

- What do you think makes a good listener?
- What makes a conversation lively and interesting?
- What makes it dull or boring?
- A good conversation may be likened to a game of table tennis. Why?

Improving communication

Here are some strategies people use to improve communication. Can you extend the list?

Using good body language
Looking and sounding interested. Making eye contact. Smiling and nodding.

Asking open questions
How/What do you feel/think about …?
Why …?
Where …?
Is there anything else …?

Encouragement
That's interesting. Tell me more.

That surprises me. I've always thought you were a capable student / a confident cook.

Paraphrasing
You mean …?
What you're trying to say is …?
In other words you feel …?

Asking for more information / clarification

Why do you feel like that? Can you explain a bit more?

I'm not sure I follow you. Can you give me an example?

Reflecting the speaker's feelings / state of mind

I can see you're excited / anxious at the thought of starting university / your new independence / developing a new social life.

Making suggestions / offering advice

Maybe you could …
If I were you I'd …
Your best idea would be to …
Have you considered …?
Why don't you …?

3 Reading and listening at the same time 🔊 CD 2, Track 6

Now follow the conversation. As you listen, underline examples of interactive techniques.

Dora: I'm really looking forward to having my own room when I start college.

Peter: Why do you feel like that?

Dora: Well, I've always had to share with my younger sister and she keeps bursting in when I'm trying to have a few moments to myself. She's got another annoying habit, too. She's always borrowing my clothes without asking.

Peter: I can see you'll be glad to get some privacy. But won't it be a bore keeping your own place clean and tidy?

Dora: No, because I like to keep things in order. How do *you* feel about going to college?

Peter: Actually, I'm a bit nervous about leaving home and coping alone.

Dora: That surprises me. You always seem so confident.

Peter: People think I am, but I don't think I'll be very good at looking after myself. To be honest, I've never even made myself beans on toast. Mum always does the washing and ironing so I've no experience of that either.

Dora: So, what you're really saying is that it's the chores that are bothering you rather than your social life?

Peter: Yes, you could say that.

Dora: Well, how about learning now? Get your mum to teach you a few easy recipes. You could even have a go at ironing a shirt! Why not do it while you've still got someone around to show you?

Peter: Now, that's a good idea. Perhaps I will. Is there anything else about leaving home that you're worried about?

Dora: Yes. I'm really hoping to have a good social life. I think I'm good at making friends, and I like parties and going to clubs. But I'm sure money will be a big issue.

Peter: I'm not sure I follow you. What do you mean?

Dora: I mean I'll have to be careful that I don't spend all my money at once. I'm really impulsive in shops. I don't know what I'm going to do about it.

Peter: Maybe you could work out a budget, so you know how much you'll need each week for things like rent and food. It's the opposite for me. My family can't afford to give me a lot of money, so I'll need a part-time job to get through college. There's no way I want to get into debt.

Dora: I've heard they need helpers in the college social centre. It might be a good idea to contact them. There are usually some part-time jobs in the restaurant or the office. You get paid and you can get into all the events for nothing. What do you think?

Peter: Thanks for the tip. I'll think it over.

4 Conversation study

Do you feel the conversation between Peter and Dora sounds friendly? With a partner, try to work out the tone of the conversation. To help you do this, circle an example in the dialogue that illustrates each of these points.

a The speaker shows a desire to understand.

b The speaker offers advice in a friendly way.

c The speaker feels warm and positive towards the other person.

d The speaker is using a chatty, informal register.

147

5 Developing your own conversation

Look back at the list you marked in exercise 1 about the challenges of going to college. Think about the reasons you had for your answers. When you're ready, work in pairs to develop a conversation like the one above.

You can base the conversation on starting college, or any other situation you find challenging, such as going away to stay with friends, starting a new school, or going on a group holiday without your family.

Remember:

- Explain your ideas clearly. Give reasons and examples.
- Say things that are true about yourself.
- Be good listeners to each other – interact well.
- Try to offer appropriate advice.
- Don't forget your body language.

6 Recording your conversation

Why not record your conversation and listen to it carefully? How well did you interact? Does it sound friendly and supportive? Have you helped each other explain your ideas?

7 Comparing languages

You might like to record an informal discussion in your first language and compare the similarities and differences in interactive patterns with those of English. How do these affect the tone of the conversation?

8 Reading and discussing a problem email

Read this extract from an email written by Sheryl, a young university student, to a friend. What does she enjoy about university? What is she finding difficult? Did you note any of these points yourself in your own discussion?

What advice would you give in reply? Share your ideas with your partner. Use suitable advice phrases, such as:

She should …
She could consider …
If I were her I'd …

New Message	
To : Bianca	From: Sheryl

Hi Bianca,

I can't believe I'm already in my sixth week of uni*. It took me a while to settle in, but now I'm starting to feel quite at home here. I'm attaching a photo of myself outside the university.

I meant to write earlier but there's so much going on all the time – lectures to go to, interesting people to meet, clubs to join – that I seem to be in a permanent state of confusion! I know organisation has always been my weak point, but it's getting ridiculous. I keep forgetting or losing things, or being late for lectures and tutorials*. I'm behind with my assignments as well. Sometimes I think I'll never learn to cope with it all!

Is there any way I can get my act together? What do you think?

uni = university

tutorial = class where students are taught in a very small group

9 Reading an example reply email

With a partner, read Bianca's email of reply. What do you think of the advice offered? How does it compare with your own ideas? Underline the advice phrases as you read.

New Message

To: Sheryl   From: Bianca

Hi Sheryl,

It was great to hear from you. We miss you here – you're such a special person. Thanks also for the photo – what an impressive building!

I'm not surprised you feel chaotic and a bit overwhelmed. After all, only a few weeks ago you were had your parents' routine and expectations, and a strict school timetable as well. Now you're suddenly expected to be completely responsible for yourself. When I started university I remember things were a bit scary, but I found planning ahead was the key to getting organised.

One thing you might find helpful is to make a list each morning of things you have to do that day. Try to include everything on your list, from attending a lecture to returning your books to the library. Keeping on top of the assignments is challenging, too, but all you really have to do is draw up your own study timetable and stick to it. I know you're a 'morning' person, so why not schedule demanding intellectual tasks then? When you've got a minute during the day, don't forget to tick off things you've done.

The uni social scene sounds brilliant. You seem to be having a cool time. I remember how popular and outgoing you were at school, so it must be tempting to say 'yes' to every social invitation. It's not a good idea to go out every night, though! You won't forget to pace yourself and save some time for recharging your batteries*, will you?

I'll definitely be able to make the weekend of the 22nd. I'm really looking forward to seeing the college and meeting some of your new friends. I'm sure by the time we meet you'll be super-organised and my advice will be irrelevant!

Love,
Bianca

*recharging your batteries = resting after effort

10 Analysing the example email

A How does Bianca achieve an appropriate tone in the opening of the email? Which details are included to develop the opening more fully?

B Paragraph 2 shows that the writer understands why Sheryl feels confused. How does she define the problem for Sheryl? What link does she make with her own experience? How does this affect the tone?

C Paragraph 3 offers Sheryl advice on being organised. Bianca doesn't sound bossy or superior – how does she achieve this? How is the advice linked to the writer's knowledge of Sheryl? How does this affect the tone of the email?

D Paragraph 4 shows Bianca's attitude to Sheryl's social life. Her recognition of Sheryl's enthusiasm for parties is balanced by a note of caution. How is this expressed? Do you think Sheryl is going to be annoyed when she reads this, or is she likely to accept the advice?

E The last paragraph confirms an invitation. How? Does Bianca manage to round off the email appropriately? How?

F Circle the words and phrases in the email that create a warm and informal tone and register.

11 Advice phrases

Here are some typical advice phrases. Which phrases are stronger (**S**)? Which are more low-key (**LK**)? Select the phrases which appeal to you.

- *You need to …*
- *You'd better …*
- *You really should …*
- *If I were you I'd …*
- *Why not …?*
- *Remember …*
- *You could always …*
- *You could consider …*
- *Maybe you could …*
- *All you have to do is …*
- *Try to …*
- *You may like to try …*
- *How about …?*
- *You really ought to …*
- *You absolutely must …*

- *Have you ever thought of …?*
- *Perhaps you need to …*
- *You know best, but perhaps you could …*
- *It's a good idea / not a good idea to …*
- *One thing you might find helpful is …*

12 Expressing problems

The way people express their problems or ask for advice in English varies according to the seriousness of the situation and the formality of the context. Discuss the following statements and questions with a partner and suggest a context in which you might use each one:

a *I'm frantic.*

b *I hope an acceptable solution can be found.*

c *I'm not sure what to do.*

d *I don't know what to do.*

e *What do you think would be best?*

f *I'd like some advice about this, please.*

g *I'm out of my mind with worry.*

h *What on earth should I do?*

i *I would be grateful for any suggestions you can make.*

J *Do you have any ideas about this?*

Comparing languages and cultures

How do you express problems in your own language and culture? What might be a problem in your country that isn't one in this country?

13 Tone and register in students' emails

A Oliver has just moved to a new town and started going to college. Working in groups of three or four, select one of you to read aloud this extract from an email he wrote to a friend at his old school:

The tutors are very helpful at my new college but it's hard to make friends. I spend all my spare time watching TV. How can I meet some friendly people?

If you were in Oliver's shoes, how would you be feeling? What would you hope to hear in a reply? Share your ideas in the group.

B The following are openings to emails that students wrote in reply. Take turns in your group in reading them aloud. Decide whether the tone and register sound right or not, and why.

1 *I received your email of 1st December explaining that you are not satisfied with your new life. If people don't like you, you must face the situation and solve it. There are many suitable activities you should take up, which would help you overcome this feeling.*

2 *It was great to hear from you – knowing you had problems really made my day. The way I see it is that you are glued to the TV. All I can say is you should join a sports club and get some of your weight off as well. It will be useful for your health and good exercise for your legs.*

3 *You might want to know why I haven't written. I have been working in my grandfather's shop. I get paid even though I'm working for my family. I meet lots of new people and the work is interesting too. What is your ideal career?*

4 *I hope you are now happy since writing me that awful email. Why do you feel lonely? Don't you have friends there? You said how boring you are at your new college. I think there are many places of entertainment in that area which you have not looked for. Don't always be sorry for yourself. You ought to adapt yourself to your new world.*

5 *I was sorry to hear that you are not enjoying your new college as much as you deserve to. I know how you must be feeling because we had to move a lot with Dad's job. However, have you considered joining the college drama club? You used to give some brilliant performances in the school theatre society. With your acting talent and sociable personality, I'm sure it won't be long before you are striking up new friendships.*

14 Rewriting a paragraph

Choose one of the paragraphs you didn't like and rewrite it. When you are ready, read out your new version to the group, explaining the reasons for any alterations you have made.

B The pressure of exams

1 Pre-reading task

Studying for exams can be stressful. You are going to read interviews with three students, their mothers and an education expert, about exam tension.

Here are some of the problems students say they have with exams. Read them through in twos or threes. Can you or your partner(s) suggest any solutions? Finally, share your ideas with other groups.

A *Getting bad marks in the mocks* makes me nervous about the real exams.*

B *I don't have time to watch my favourite TV programmes.*

C *My parents still expect me to help in the house even though I've got to study.*

D *I'm worried about turning up late for exams or getting the day wrong.*

E *I hate having to give up sport and seeing my friends.*

F *I've fallen behind with my coursework* and I haven't got time to catch up.*

G *There are so many websites I could use for my research, I don't know where to begin.*

H *I hate listening to other students comparing answers after a test.*

*mocks = tests which are set by teachers in preparation for the real exams

*coursework = work such as projects, assignments and classwork done during the school year; coursework is marked by the teacher but the grades go towards the final exam mark

2 Reading for gist

Skim-read the following magazine article. Does the advice given include any of the ideas you thought of? Try to work out the meaning of any unfamiliar words from the context.

3 Comprehension check

1 Select any statements that are true for Clare:
   a She works best in her bedroom.
   b She leaves the work she is doing for her exams in different rooms.
   c Her mother has tried different approaches to encourage her to study.
   d The expert thinks Clare has found the right balance between studies, her part-time job and her social life.

2 Select any statements which are true for Khalid:
   a He doesn't get anxious about exams.
   b He likes listening to music while studying.
   c His mother gave him practical help with his maths.
   d The expert thinks it is wrong for Khalid to give up sport and a social life during his exams.

3 Select any statements which are true for Felix:
   a He finds it hard to do homework unless he is very interested in the subject.
   b He was disappointed with his grades for his mocks.
   c His father was happy with his progress until a short time ago.
   d The expert thinks Felix needs to be much more motivated, and to use his parents' help to plan his study programme.

4 Which student:
   a seems the least interested in doing homework?
   b mentions being compared to another family member?
   c regrets a late night just before an exam?
   d reduced the time spent on a paid job?
   e only mentions positive influences from parent(s)?
   f seems the least stressed about taking exams?

Find keywords or phrases to justify your choices.

151

EXAM TENSION: What can you do?

Pupils of equal ability can end up with vastly differing grades. To find out why, Jay Petersen talked to three teenagers, and asked a behaviour specialist how parents can help.

5

Clare Parry, 16, is taking nine GCSEs.

What homework did you do last night?
'English and Geography essays, though they should have been in three days ago. I was tired at first but I worked until 2 a.m., mostly on my
10　laptop. I can't work in my bedroom. I like to be with others, so I work in the dining room or on the floor.'

What do you give up during exams?
'I've been working in a newsagent's every day after
15　school and on Saturdays, and going out every night.

Now I've cut my hours down at work and I only see my friends at weekends.'

Are exams stressful?
'Yes! There's so much pressure to revise and then there are exam nerves. It's stressful hearing other 　20
people saying what they've done when you haven't learnt it.'

What's the most helpful/irritating thing your parents do?
'Mum says, "I must have the cleverest daughter 　25
in the school, because she never needs to do her homework." And it can be noisy because Dad goes out to work at nights. The most helpful thing is they don't moan about the paper all over the house.'

Is there anything you'd do differently? 　30
'Although I didn't work for my mocks, I did all right. For GCSEs, I'll make a study timetable and really stick to it.'

Ann Parry says: 'I've tried nagging and I've tried not. I warn her that unless she gets on with it, she's 　35
going to panic. I've put my foot down about her going out during the week – I'm not popular! But she has only one chance and if she doesn't get the right grades, she can't go to sixth-form college.'

Expert advice: '*It does sound as though Clare is* 　40
trying to do too much. While her newsagent's job is bringing in money short-term, her long-term prospects for earning are more important. GCSEs require three–four hours' homework daily, and three nights out a week seems quite enough without a job 　45
after school (the best time for getting down to study). Rather than laying down the law, Ann should try to get Clare to see this for herself and take more responsibility for her own work patterns. Where Clare does need support and encouragement is in 　50
planning what needs to be done by when, and plenty of praise for 'getting on' and completing tasks. I felt that wanting to work in the middle of the family, rather than working in her bedroom, was Clare's way of asking for this kind of constructive 　55
daily input.'

Khalid Helal, 17, has seven B- and C-grade GCSEs. He is taking Photography GCSE this summer and Photography, Design and Theatre Studies at A level next year.

What homework did you do last night?
'None – but I did loads the night before, finishing a design assignment. It took till one o'clock in the morning.'

What do you give up during exams?
'I gave up going out at weekends and stopped my sport – mountain-biking, circuit-training and rowing – so I have put on weight. I did go to a concert the day before my Geography exam – a big mistake! I didn't get back until early the following morning.'

Are exams stressful?
'There's pressure from other students as well as the school. If they say they've finished revising, and you haven't started, you don't show you're worried about it, but you are. Music helps – our teachers say it's okay to have it on while you work as long as it's not too loud.'

What's the most helpful/irritating thing your parents do?
'Maths was a problem. I'd got a really bad mark in the mocks, so my mum gave me extra work and marked it – she's a science graduate. She bought me loads of revision books too.'

Is there anything you'd do differently?
'I should have revised more. My mum didn't push me because she was worried about my dad. He was very ill in hospital the term before the exams and she moved to London to be with him.'

Krysia Helal says: 'I had so much on my mind, the exam period just went by, but I did help with his maths. He gets exam nerves, which is a worry, and always panics afterwards when they compare answers.'

Expert advice: '*Khalid did remarkably well in his GCSEs considering the emotional pressure he must have been under with his father so ill. Krysia did an excellent job of supporting him with his maths by taking a positive interest and being prepared to be involved. She needs to encourage Khalid to keep up with his sport – sport is an excellent way to calm nerves, and a balance of work, exercise and fun is essential. Khalid should be encouraged not to compare himself with other people – he's obviously trying to do his best.*'

Felix Hall, 15, is taking nine GCSEs. He passed Italian with an A star last year.

What homework did you do last night?
'None. I don't do much unless I'm interested in it, like technology, which I do at lunchtime.'

What do you give up during exams?
'I'm out at weekends, either working in a hotel, or at football or enjoying myself. Mum and Dad want me to give up my job and they say they'll make up the money.'

Are exams stressful?
'The coursework is worrying me. It should be in by now, but I've got lots to do. Exams aren't so bad. I didn't revise for my mocks, but I got good grades. Listening to music and working out help.'

153

What's the most helpful/irritating thing your
120 **parents do?**

'I hate it when they compare me with my brother or discuss me with friends.'

Is there anything you'd do differently?

'I'd look at the exam timetable! I missed one of my
125 mocks and had to do it later.'

Fred Hall says: 'Until recently Felix was okay, now I have to nag. I don't like him going to the gym so often – he's too tired to work.'

Expert advice: 'Felix is a bright boy but he has lost his motivation. The job and the exercise have become 130 ways of distracting himself. Felix' parents need to sit down with him and his teachers to find out exactly where he is up to with his revision. Rather than comparing him with others, they should address his particular worries. Their offer of making up his 135 money is generous but must be linked to Felix using his time more constructively. As he loves music, maybe Fred could offer him a ticket to a concert of his choice for every completed set of subject coursework.' 140

4 Post-reading discussion

1 Who do you think is the most hardworking of the students? Try to say why.

2 Do you sympathise with Clare, Khalid and Felix in any way? Try to explain why or why not.

3 Do you agree with the expert's advice for each student? Do you think the expert was generally helpful or too critical?

4 What do you think, in general, of the attitudes of the parents?

5 Are there any other ways Clare, Khalid and Felix could help themselves? What do you think?

6 What are the methods you feel work best for you when you are studying for exams? Share your thoughts in your group.

7 Clare says she is going to make a revision timetable. How useful are timetables?

8 Students at Lake View School were asked where they preferred to do their homework. The results are shown in the pie chart.

   a Where do most students prefer to do their homework?

   b Which is the least popular place?

   c Which two places are equal in popularity?

   d Where do you usually do your homework? Do you feel it is a good place for you to study and concentrate?

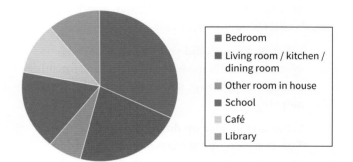

- Bedroom
- Living room / kitchen / dining room
- Other room in house
- School
- Café
- Library

5 Vocabulary: Colloquial words and phrases

A The following colloquial words and phrases were used in the text. Use them to replace the words in italics in the sentences below. There is one more than you need.

VOCABULARY		
exam nerves	loads	working out
moan	put your foot	nagging
stick to	down	

1 You *complain* about your daughter coming in late. It's time you *insisted it stopped and told her to come home earlier*.

2 Luckily, we don't suffer from *stress about exams*.

3 I have a study timetable and I am determined to *persevere with* it.

4 He enjoys *taking exercise in a gym*.

5 She does *a great deal* of work for her favourite charity.

B Do you know any other meanings of *moan, loads, working out* and *stick to?* Try to think of some examples.

6 Word building

Building nouns from verbs

Clare's mother was advised to give her '*support and encouragement*'. The suffix *-ment* can be added to some verbs to make nouns.

Add *-ment* to each of the following verbs to make a noun. Then use each one in a sentence to show its meaning.

appoint	*advertise*
astonish	*improve*
arrange	*manage*
entertain	*disagree*

Building adjectives from nouns

Khalid was described as having been under '*emotional pressure*'. The suffix *-al* can be added to some nouns to make adjectives.

Add *-al* to each of the following nouns to make an adjective. Then use each one in a sentence to show its meaning. Be careful, as the spelling sometimes changes, too.

magic	*culture*
music	*function*
classic	*mathematics*
person	*nature*

7 Language study: Giving advice

Here are some expressions the expert used in the text to give advice:

a *Khalid should be encouraged not to compare himself with other people.*

b Khalid's mother needs to encourage him *to keep up with his sport.*

c Felix's parents' *offer of making up his money is generous but must be linked to Felix using his time more constructively.*

d Felix's *parents need to sit down with him and his teachers to find out exactly where he is up to with his revision.*

1 Which advice sounds most direct? Which least direct?

2 Which advice verb is followed by *to plus infinitive*? Which verbs are followed by the infinitive without *to*?

3 How would you change statements **a**, **b** and **d** into questions?

4 How would you make **b**, **c** and **d** into negative statements?

5 Can you replace *should, need(s) to* and *must* with any other expressions of similar meaning? What are they?

8 *Should/shouldn't have*

Should/shouldn't + *have* + past participle have a different meaning from giving advice. With a partner try to work out the meaning from these examples.

1 She should have taken an umbrella with her – I told her it was going to rain!

2 You shouldn't have bought her a box of chocolates when you knew she was trying to lose weight.

3 He should have checked the exam timetable before he took the day off to play football.

4 I shouldn't have lost my temper about something so unimportant.

5 You should have telephoned to cancel your appointment if you couldn't come.

Practice

Join each pair of sentences to make one sentence containing *should have* or *shouldn't have* and a suitable linking word:

1   Joseph took a part-time job. He had exams coming up.

2   Indira went to the concert. She had an exam the next day.

3   He didn't check his bank balance. He spent a lot of money.

4   I shouted at my brother. He was trying to be helpful.

5   I borrowed my sister's jacket. I didn't ask her first.

6   Why didn't you buy some extra bread? You knew we needed to make sandwiches.

9 Using a more informal tone

Rewrite these sentences to make them sound more informal. Use the verbs *should*, *ought*, *need*, *must* or *had better*.

1   It isn't necessary for me to cook. Bruno is taking us out for a meal.

2   It is necessary to do your homework at a regular time each evening.

3   It was unwise to make a promise you can't keep.

4   It was wrong to leave all my revision to the last minute.

5   It's vital that Abdul gets more rest or he will fail his exams.

6   I regret not having listened to her advice.

7   It was wrong of him to play computer games instead of revising for the exam.

10 Spelling and pronunciation: Silent letters

Many English words contain silent letters. They can be at the beginning of words, as in:

wrinkle   **k**nitting

psychology   **h**onour

in the middle, as in:

sal**m**on   forei**g**ner

cu**p**board   lis**t**ener

or at the end, as in:

com**b**   autum**n**

Sometimes a pair of letters is silent, as in:

ri**gh**t   dau**gh**ter

Practise saying the words above with a partner. Check each other's pronunciation.

11 Crossing out silent letters

These words, taken from the text 'Exam Tension', contain silent letters. Work with a partner to cross out the letters which are not pronounced.

1   design   7   should
2   answers   8   calm
3   what   9   circuit
4   law   10 assignment
5   night   11 weight
6   science   12 hours

Now practise saying the words correctly with your partner. Do you both agree your pronunciation is correct?

12 Adding silent letters

Complete these sentences with the missing silent letters. Choose from the letters in the box.

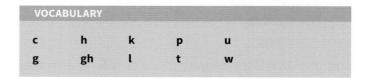

VOCABULARY				
c	h	k	p	u
g	gh	l	t	w

1   Lena must be the bri__test toddler in the nursery because she already _nows how to ta_k and say the alphabet.

2   He wou_dn't lis_en to the expert's advice.

3   He goes to the gym to do circ_it-training after college.

4   W_ereabouts do you go to college?

5   Do you want a ha_f or a _hole bag of sweets?

6   Can you _rite your ans_ers here?

7   We turn on the li__ts when it gets dark.

8   He hurt his _rist and his _nee when he fell over.

9   Snow is always w_ite.

10 _onesty is the best policy.

11 These flowers have a lovely s_ent.

12 The referee blows the w_is_le if something is _rong.

13 She _rote under a _seudonym as she wanted to keep her identity secret.

14 Their queen rei_ned for over 30 years.

15 She is _sychic and can tell the future.

156

13 Detecting patterns

A   Can you see a regular pattern for any of the silent letters? Discuss your ideas with a partner and note any patterns you can detect.

B   Are there any silent letters in your own language? Share some examples in your group.

14 Idiomatic expressions

Can you work out the meaning of these idiomatic expressions from the context? (They each contain silent letters.)

1   I find the countryside too quiet and prefer the *hustle and bustle* of city life.

2   I thought the suitcase would be very heavy, but when I picked it up it was *as light as a feather.*

3   He *risked life and limb* to save the baby from the burning car.

15 Look, say, cover, write, check

Silent letters often cause spelling mistakes. Students say they sometimes forget to include them in a word. Here is a list of words with silent letters that often cause spelling problems. First check the meaning and then try to identify the silent letter(s) in each word. Finally, use the 'look, say, cover, write, check' method to learn each word correctly.

VOCABULARY		
sign	height	calf
yacht	listener	knock
scene	yolk	daughter
rhyme	honour	drought
rhythm	doubt	government
lightning	psychiatrist	

C   Studying effectively
1   Punctuation reminders

Correct punctuation is important because it helps make meaning clear.

Full stops and capital letters

Remember, full stops are used to end a sentence. Capital letters are needed after a full stop. Capital letters are also used for proper names (*Ayesha*, *Pepe*), place names (*Cairo*, *the Amazon*) and acronyms (*BBC*, *DNA*).

Here is a description of how one student does homework. Punctuate it correctly. Remember to read it first to get the correct sense.

I need a few quiet moments to myself when i get in from school i have a drink and relax for a while then i get out my homework i work at a desk in the corner of the living room it is peaceful but not silent i like French and maths homework the best

Apostrophes

Remember, apostrophes are used to indicate possession (*Zina's pen*, *the girls' coats*) and to show that a letter is missing. (*It's hot.*)

Punctuate the next part of the description.

ive got a few reference books which i keep on a shelf above my desk i borrow my brothers paints for artwork and i use my sister's laptop for igcse essays ive used my dad's tools for some technology projects too they dont mind me borrowing their things as long as i look after them

Commas

Commas are used in the following ways.

a   To separate things in a list:
I need pens, pencils, rulers and a rubber.

b   To separate a non-defining clause or an extra phrase from the main sentence:
Mr Rivers, our geography teacher, comes from Nigeria.

c   To separate a participle phrase from the main clause:
Having run all the way to the station, we were disappointed to find the train had just left.

d   After certain linking words and phrases:
On the other hand, Nevertheless, However,

These are just some of the uses of commas. Remember – we generally put commas where we would pause in speech.

Now punctuate the rest of the extract correctly.

our school has a homework link on the school website this means that you can use the homework page to check the homework youve been set it also prevents students getting too many subjects for homework at once about two years ago i had english history german physics biology maths and technology homework on the same night it was a nightmare the homework page prevents these problems however it also means teachers refuse to accept silly excuses for not handing in homework

2 Rewriting an email

Read the following email, which was written to a student who is not able to join his friends on holiday as he needs to retake an examination.

First read it carefully to get the sense. Then discuss it with a partner and rewrite it as necessary. Expect to make at least two drafts.

You should consider:

a   the paragraphing

Remember – a new paragraph is usually needed for a change of topic.

b   the tone and register

Are they right for this situation? If not, think of alternative expressions you could use.

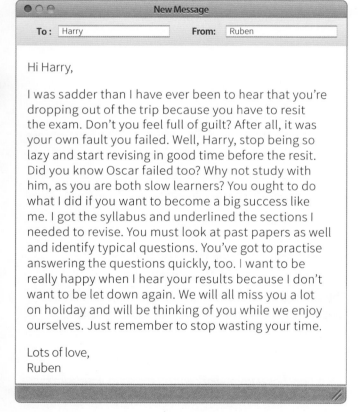

Hi Harry,

I was sadder than I have ever been to hear that you're dropping out of the trip because you have to resit the exam. Don't you feel full of guilt? After all, it was your own fault you failed. Well, Harry, stop being so lazy and start revising in good time before the resit. Did you know Oscar failed too? Why not study with him, as you are both slow learners? You ought to do what I did if you want to become a big success like me. I got the syllabus and underlined the sections I needed to revise. You must look at past papers as well and identify typical questions. You've got to practise answering the questions quickly, too. I want to be really happy when I hear your results because I don't want to be let down again. We will all miss you a lot on holiday and will be thinking of you while we enjoy ourselves. Just remember to stop wasting your time.

Lots of love,
Ruben

3 Reading aloud

Read your new version to your group.

4 More idiomatic expressions

The idioms in italics in the following sentences express feelings and attitudes. Discuss each with a partner and choose the definition you feel is correct:

1   At the party the other students *gave her the cold shoulder.*

    a   They ignored her.

    b   They offered her cold meat.

    c   They told her they disliked her.

    d   They made her promise to keep a secret.

2   When I read the exam paper I *couldn't make head or tail of it.*

    a   I realised I could not finish in the time.

    b   I could not understand any of the questions.

    c   I found the second part of the paper very difficult.

    d   I could do only half the total number of questions.

3   He's *set his heart on* becoming a doctor.

    a   He's sure he'll be a successful doctor.

    b   He's very emotional about becoming a doctor.

    c   He's very realistic about his prospects.

    d   He really wants to qualify as a doctor.

4   I've never failed an exam, *touch wood.*

    a   It's due to my careful preparation.

    b   I really hope my good luck continues.

    c   I always expect to do well in exams.

    d   I believe I'll fail the next one.

5   When I told her she'd won the scholarship, she thought I was *pulling her leg.*

    a   She didn't like the way I explained it.

    b   She was convinced I was joking.

    c   She thought I wanted something from her.

    d   She was angry and walked away.

6   I thought this training programme would be right for me, but now I feel that I'm *out of my depth.*

    a   The programme is generally too difficult for me.

    b   The programme is working out more expensive than I expected.

    c   The other trainees dominate the discussions.

    d   The instructor gave me the wrong idea about the course.

5 Increasing your stock of idioms

Select the idiomatic expressions you would like to remember from exercise 4. Use each in a sentence of your own to show its meaning.

6 Sentence correction

The following sentences from students' emails contain mistakes of grammar and vocabulary. Try to rewrite them correctly.

1 If you be wisdom one you follow your professor advice.

2 You should build up a correct concept of mind to your work.

3 The qualities of good friend is invisible but uncountable.

4 You should never smoke the cigarettes they give much trouble more than they bring the pleasure.

5 Your email talking ideas many people thinking too.

INTERNATIONAL OVERVIEW

Most popular countries for international students

1 How many countries are being compared?

2 Which is the third most popular country for international students?

3 Which country has just under half the number of international students as Australia?

4 If you were choosing to study abroad, where would you like to go? Share your ideas with a partner, explaining why that country would appeal to you.

Destination country	Total number of overseas students
1 USA	740 482
2 UK	427 686
3 France	271 399
4 Australia	249 588
5 Germany	206 986
6 Russia	173 627
7 Japan	150 617
8 Canada	120 960
9 China	88 979
10 Italy	77 732

D A range of advice

1 Pre-listening tasks

A Some people turn to professional counsellors if they have problems. The following points are sometimes made in favour of counsellors. In groups of three or four, discuss how far you agree with them.

1 Counselling is a real skill and the counsellors are properly trained and qualified.

2 Their advice is objective.

3 It's not embarrassing to see them because you won't have to deal with them in any other role (e.g. employer, friend).

B Can you see any disadvantages in going to a counsellor? Would you consult one? Why/Why not?

C You are going to listen to a college counsellor talking about her job. Her talk will cover the following topics:

- students' problems
- approaches to counselling
- her feelings about being a counsellor.

What would you like to find out about each of these? Write a question of your own on each topic. Compare your questions with those of a partner.

159

2 Listening for gist: A college counsellor 🔊 CD 2, Track 7

Listen to the interview. Which of your questions are answered?

3 Detailed listening 🔊 CD 2, Track 7

Now listen again and complete the notes:

Typical student problem

Lacking sufficient money to get through college and getting (a) _____ .

Possible solutions:

> Save money on travel and rent by moving to a cheaper flat near the college.
>
> Write to outside agencies for financial help.
>
> Apply to the (b) _____ fund at the college.

Dealing with exam stress

Apply study techniques.

Summarise notes into (c) _____ .

Quality time spent studying is better than quantity time.

As well as studying, it is important to have time for (d) _____ and (e) _____ .

Students also explore underlying worries that may be causing stress.

Personal and family problems

Ask family members to visit her too. Help students to express their feelings to their (f) _____ .

She suggests ways that a student might get more space and privacy at home.

Approaches to counselling

Everything is confidential. Students' problems never discussed with others unless something (g) _____ is involved.

Good quality counselling needs (h) _____ .

Counselling is mainly concerned with supporting people who are confused or (i) _____ to explore issues.

Problems being experienced now might be linked back to bad (j) _____ experiences.

Counsellor's attitude to the job

She remembers she is not responsible for others' problems. Only they can make (k) _____ in their lives.

Inference

What can you infer from the interview about the benefits to the counsellor herself of the work she does? Try to think of one or two things. (Remember – inference means drawing reasonable conclusions from information given when the information is not explicitly stated.)

4 Rewriting an email giving advice

A You know that a friend of yours, Roberto, has difficulty getting on with his younger brother. He says that his brother scribbles on his posters, plays with his phone and starts arguments with him. What kind of advice would you give? Note your ideas.

B **Tone and register**

Now read the advice that was written to Roberto by a fellow student. Do you think the tone and register sound right for the situation? Try to work out why or why not.

Rewrite the email, making any changes you think are appropriate.

New Message	
To : Roberto	**From:** Daniel

Hi Roberto,

I was devastated to hear of this tragic problem. It seems as if your brother has ruined your life. I know that you have always been untidy and careless. The result of this behaviour is that your little brother can find your things and spoil them. It seems as if you are bad-tempered and impatient with him too. Of course he will not like you if you are unkind to him. You must learn to put away your things and control your moods. I also have a younger brother so I am very careful to put my things away in a place where he cannot reach them. My younger brother and I have a close relationship. We play football together and I help him with his homework. We no longer quarrel because I am not selfish and have tried to understand him. We discussed the problem calmly with my parents. I did not shout or get angry which, as I see it, would be your reaction. It is a pity you cannot do the same.

Please write to me telling me that you have resolved your horrible problem. I hope to hear that there is a better atmosphere in your home.

All the best,

Daniel

5 Building a letter from a list of points

You read about this problem in your school newsletter:

'I never seem to be in the right mood for homework or have the right stuff with me. I end up on websites that have nothing to do with anything! I am always getting distracted by my phone, too. My parents are fed up with me. Any ideas? Polly.'

Discuss this problem with a partner and write down your thoughts about what could help Polly.

Now read the following list of helpful homework tips.

1 Have something special to look forward to when you finish your homework.

2 Don't leave it too late in the evening to start.

3 Make sure you understand what homework you have to do before you leave school.

4 Put your phone on silent or put it away in a drawer.

5 Keep the equipment you need for your homework (pens, reference and books) where you can find it at home.

6 On the internet, be selective and avoid clicking on links that are not relevant.

7 Plan your time: short, concentrated sessions are better than one long session.

8 Save useful website addresses for research topics in your 'favourites' list.

9 Use a clear surface to work on.

10 Keep a homework diary to help you keep a check on the homework you have done.

Add any ideas of your own to the list.

Writing

Write a reply to Polly that will be published in the newsletter. Offer her some advice about doing homework. Choose ideas from the list of tips given. Develop the points into three paragraphs. Use a friendly tone and register. Remember to add an opening and closing sentence.

6 Pre-writing discussion

Do you think bullying is a common problem? Why do you think some people become bullies? Why do some people become the victims of bullies, but others don't?

A younger friend of yours emails you saying:

A boy in my class is bullying me. When I arrive at school he calls me names, and he threatens to push me off my bike and take it for himself. He says he will hurt me if I report him to a teacher.

What advice would you give to help your friend? Write down a few ideas.

7 Email completion

Now try to complete this email of advice about bullying.

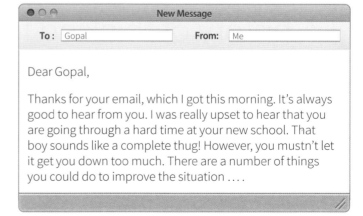

To: Gopal   From: Me

Dear Gopal,

Thanks for your email, which I got this morning. It's always good to hear from you. I was really upset to hear that you are going through a hard time at your new school. That boy sounds like a complete thug! However, you mustn't let it get you down too much. There are a number of things you could do to improve the situation . . . .

GRAMMAR SPOTLIGHT

'Text speak'

A text message is a concise form of writing. It is usually very informal and written in 'text speak' instead of proper sentences. As you already know, 'text speak' is not appropriate for formal situations.

Typical features of text messages are:

a Missing pronouns, e.g. *Will try to call* = I will try to call.

b Missing articles, e.g. *Bus is late* = The bus is late.

c Missing capital letters, e.g. *saw maya at meeting in dubai* = I saw Maya at the meeting in Dubai.

d Missing prepositions, e.g. *Train arrives madrid 8 p.m.* = The train arrives in Madrid at 8 p.m.

e Very little or no punctuation, e.g. *cant talk now will call later* = I can't talk now. I'll call later.

f Special 'text speak' abbreviations and unusual spellings, e.g. *b4* = before, *2day* = today, *l8r* = later,

c u soon = (I'll) see you soon, *yr* = your, *y'day* = yesterday, *2moro* = tomorrow.

All these features are used in order to save time when texting.

Some people use a lot of these features when they are texting, while others don't. You can, of course, make up your own 'text speak', if you think the other person will understand what you mean. There are no rules – it's up to you!

Study these extracts from text messages and then try to rewrite them in full sentences, with correct grammar, spelling and punctuation. You also need to make the style of one of them more appropriate to the situation.

1 hi libby! hope yr w/end in dublin went well

2 sorry but cant come 2nite. will fone u when i get home.

3 on way but gonna b 20 min late lotta traffic plse w8 4 me

4 hiya mr poulos! yeah gr8! i definitely want 2 take the job. thanks!

5 wl txt b4 i come round 2 make sure u r in

Exam-style questions

Reading

Reading & Writing, Exercise 1

Read the following information from the University of Sydney website and answer the questions that follow.

The University of Sydney

A history of thinking forward

Since 1852, when the doors of Sydney University opened for the first time, our founding principle as Australia's first university was that we would be a progressive institution. The first degrees were given in 1856, and, in 1881, we became one of the first universities in the world to admit female students. Our university has produced pioneers in medicine, sport, the arts, politics and science. In recent times, we are proud of famous former students who have made extraordinary contributions to the world, including advances in heart surgery, ear implants to overcome deafness and the fight against the Ebola virus.

From the start, we believed that financial issues should not stop students from learning. Students of all backgrounds, including those from lower income families, have been given the chance to access further education through grants and scholarships, enabling them to benefit from the excellent educational opportunities we offer.

Study in our famous city

As a student at Sydney University, you're never far from Sydney's famous harbour, the Opera House or its beaches. The city abounds in culture and café life. If you head to the eastern suburbs, you're near the sea and parks where you can spend a lazy Sunday afternoon, and it won't cost you anything at all.

To get the most out of your time at university, you should also explore the clubs and societies on offer. The University of Sydney Union (USU) runs more than 200 clubs and societies in which you can make new friends. The clubs and societies are student-run, which means that you can get leadership experience if you help organise a club.

Keeping active

We offer a huge range of facilities to keep you healthy. Sports membership gives you access to cardio equipment, weights, tennis courts, swimming pools, yoga classes and plenty more. Exercise can help manage stress levels, regulate sleeping patterns and boost your mood, so be sure to make time for it.

A place to live

We offer accommodation in college environments on-campus and we also have self-catering accommodation off-campus. College accommodation on-campus is a great way to make the transition to independence. You get three meals a day and laundry services. Accommodation on-campus also provides a great social support network. If your preference is for living in off-campus, we offer affordable self-catered accommodation – and you will still be close to everything you need.

Applications for a place at a self-catered residence are considered all year round, but be aware that demand often exceeds supply – many places are full before the academic year begins. If you need a place to live, why not use our accommodation database, where you can post adverts requesting accommodation?

Most students settle down quickly and easily to university life, but we do provide a one-on-one counselling service to support students who may be struggling to learn effectively due to psychological or emotional factors that affect their wellbeing. The service is completely confidential and staffed by trained personnel.

Our student card

The student card provides many benefits. As well as being proof of identity, it allows you to borrow from the library, and gives you access to a wide range of travel and student discounts. To access our 24-hour Study Centre after hours, tap your student card on the reader by the door.

Study abroad and exchange programs

If you're already enrolled at Sydney, you can take advantage of the Study Abroad Program to study at one of our 300 partner institutions. Every year, we welcome hundreds of students from around the world through our exchange programs. The Sydney Abroad Program allows you to enrol and pay your semester's fees to us. If you come to us as an exchange student, your fees are paid to your usual university while you study at Sydney.

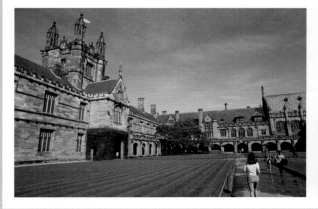

163

SCHOLARSHIPS AVAILABLE FOR YEAR 12

Scholarships are awarded to students completing Year 12 at high school, and are based on examination results and evidence of self-motivation and communication skills.

The first semester

Use the first week of semester to get organised. While most students adapt to independent learning readily, others can find it problematic. If you are confused or worried because you do not know how to organise your study time effectively, do seek advice from our student mentors who can help you structure your schedule and give you study tips.

1   When did students first graduate from Sydney University? (1)

2   How has global health benefited from the work done by graduates? Give **one** detail (1)

3   Which area of Sydney offers leisure opportunities free of charge? (1)

4   What skill can you gain by helping to organise the University's clubs and societies? (1)

5   Why is sports membership recommended? Give **two** details.(1)

6   Apart from accommodation, what other benefits does living on campus provide? Give **two** details. (2)

7   When can you apply for off-campus college accommodation? (1)

8   How can you get into the Study Centre at midnight? (1)

9   How does the University help students overcome potential barriers to learning? Make four points. (4) [Extended]

Core [9 marks], Extended [13 marks]

Writing

Reading & Writing, Exercise 5

1   You have a friend who was hoping to learn your language. However, in his last email he sounded discouraged about his progress and is thinking of giving up.

Write him an email in which you:

- say why he should continue to learn
- suggest some techniques that would help him to learn
- explain the future benefits to him of being able to speak your language fluently.

Your email should be 100–150 words long.

Core [12 marks]

Reading & Writing, Exercise 5

2 You have a friend who, although a competent student, becomes very nervous before exams and doesn't always do well in them. You know she has some important exams coming up and you would like to see her be successful.

	SAT	SUN	MON	TUES	WEDS	THURS	FRI
10.30–12.00	STUDY						
12.00–12.30	BREAK	BREAK	BREAK	BREAK	BREAK	BREAK	BREAK
12.30–2.00	STUDY						
2.00–3.00	BREAK	BREAK	BREAK	BREAK	BREAK	BREAK	BREAK
3.00–4.30	STUDY						
4.30–5.00	BREAK	BREAK	BREAK	BREAK	BREAK	BREAK	BREAK
5.00–6.30	STUDY						
6.30–7.30	BREAK	BREAK	BREAK	BREAK	BREAK	BREAK	BREAK
7.30–8.30	STUDY						

Write her an email in which you:

- describe some ways she could revise effectively
- suggest some things that would help her relax
- explain the importance of following the examination instructions.

The pictures may give you some ideas, and you should try to use some ideas of your own.

Your email should be 150–200 words long.

Extended [16 marks]

Reading & Writing, Exercise 5

3 Your grandparents, who are both quite elderly, live in another town and would like to visit you at your school or college. They would like to stay in a modestly priced guest house. They can stay for only three days and are anxious to see as much as possible. Your grandfather has some difficulty walking long distances and uses a stick.

Write them a letter in which you:

- welcome them
- offer advice about accommodation and travel
- suggest ways to make the most of their trip.

Your letter should be 150–200 words long.

Extended [16 marks]

Speaking

1 Living more independently

Many young people look forward to the day when they can leave their parents' home and live a more independent life. What problems and challenges might leaving home bring? Discuss this topic with the assessor. You may wish to use the following ideas to help develop the conversation:

- balancing a budget
- cooking, cleaning and generally looking after yourself
- coping with feeling lonely
- learning to be responsible for your own health
- coping with the possible dangers that you might meet.

You are free to consider any other related ideas of your own. You are not allowed to make any written notes.

2 The internet

The internet is popular with many students at school or college who believe it is a useful learning tool. Discuss this topic with the assessor. You may wish to use the following ideas to help develop the conversation:

- the extent to which you use the internet for your studies
- the idea that doing research on the internet can be frustrating and waste time
- the view that, in the future, the internet may make libraries unnecessary
- the problems that could arise if people copy material from the internet and pretend it is their original work
- whether 'virtual universities' should be encouraged by governments.

You are free to consider any other related ideas of your own. You are not allowed to make any written notes.

ADVICE FOR SUCCESS

The Advice for Success is for **you** to **help yourself**. Decide which suggestions you like best and mark them. You can adapt an idea in Advice for Success to make it fun for you. Keeping track with a notebook is a good idea.

1 Listening to English radio, watching TV and reading printed and online magazines, newspapers and books can help you understand more about the way people adapt their language to different occasions, and for different target groups. For example, an article for adults about ways of studying will be written in a different tone and register from an article on the same topic for 12-year-olds.

2 Speaking or writing on the same topic in a variety of tones and registers will also develop your ability.

3 Students often say they would like to improve their grammar. Here are some suggestions:

- Study the errors you frequently make. Use your knowledge of regular grammar patterns and the exceptions to try to work out the differences between your version and the correct version.
- Use a good grammar book or website to check explanations of points you usually make mistakes with. You need one which gives lots of examples, not just the rules and their exceptions.

- Work with a friend who speaks your first language. Work together to analyse your mistakes. As always, investigate the grammar pattern and think about exceptions, too. See if you can work out a rule for that particular grammar point before looking it up online or in your grammar book.

- Apply your new knowledge of grammar in different situations. This will help you remember the point, and help you understand when it is correct and when grammar has to change to fit new situations.

- Exploring meaningful patterns and their exceptions will help your spelling and vocabulary work, too. In fact, you can detect patterns in all the subjects you're learning (maths, science, art, etc.) if you look for them.

Exam techniques: speaking test

4 Usually the first part of a speaking test is an unmarked warm-up phase in which you will be asked a few questions about yourself.

5 You should aim to make the most of your ability with spoken English. Try to answer questions as fully as possible. Avoid 'Yes/No' replies or 'I don't know'. Don't be afraid to take a little extra time to think of replies that will be helpful in keeping an interesting conversation going.

Remember, communicating effectively in a natural and lively way is much more important than having perfect grammar or pronunciation.

6 Ask for clarification, if necessary, with questions such as 'Do you mean …?', 'Could you repeat that? I didn't quite understand.'

7 Aim to show that you are capable of abstract thought. Try to think around a topic from many different angles. Be prepared for a wide range of questions.

Exam focus

This unit has helped to prepare you for exams which test your reading, writing, listening and speaking skills. The unit has helped to develop those skills in the following ways:

- You have studied **tone and register** and developed skills for **expressing problems** and giving **advice** in **emails and letters**.

- You have **written connected paragraphs** based on **notes**.

- You have learnt to use a **range** of **conversational techniques** giving **encouragement**.

- You have taken part in a **structured dialogue** and **discussions**.

- You have used a range of **reading techniques** to **answer questions** on **complex** and **less complex texts**.

- You have listened to a **formal interview** and completed a **set of notes**.

Unit 8
The search for adventure

In this unit you will:

- read a version of Robinson Crusoe and a text about the rescue of a dog
- listen to an interview with two people who were lost at sea
- practise expressing surprise, consoling someone and commiserating someone
- focus on the following assessment objectives: R2, W2, W3, S5

A The call of the sea

1 Visualisation

Close your eyes and think of the sea. What sights and sounds come to your mind? What do you feel when you think about the sea? Now open your eyes and spend a few minutes writing down whatever came into your mind, in your own language or English.

2 Discussion

Discuss these remarks about the sea with a partner. Grade them as:

A *I identify strongly with this idea.*

B *This idea is interesting but I don't identify closely with it.*

C *I don't identify in any way with this idea.*

☐ 'The sea is a place of great adventure. When you set sail in a boat, you never know what you are going to find.'

☐ 'I love swimming. Being in water, especially the sea, is one of life's great pleasures.'

☐ 'I live by the sea and love the way it changes. On hot days, it's cool and restful. On winter days, there are dramatic storms.'

☐ 'When I go out in my boat, I feel free. I leave all my worries behind.'

☐ 'Below its surface, the sea is full of life. I'd love to explore its depths and see the underwater world for myself.'

☐ 'I think the sea is mysterious. Huge ships have disappeared in it, never to be seen again.'

☐ 'I live far away from the sea. My dream is to see the ocean and hear its wonderful sounds.'

☐ 'I admire anyone whose employment is connected with the sea. There are so many dangers involved.'

☐ 'Sailing presents a great spiritual challenge. In a storm or crisis, I discover unknown aspects of myself.'

3 Sea vocabulary

In pairs or small groups, circle the word that does not belong in each of the following groups. Use a dictionary to help you. You'll need many of the words later in the unit, so make a note in your vocabulary book of any that are unfamiliar.

169

Sea associations

Which word is not associated with the sea?

*spray   tides   waves   ocean   cliffs   bay   shore
rocks   hive   current   port   horizon   channel
shipwreck   voyage   cargo   dock   jetty   surf*

On the beach

Which item would you not expect to find on the beach?

*pebbles   shells   rocks   starfish   sand   spanner
sand dunes   seaweed   driftwood   turtle*

Sea creatures

Which creature is not associated with the sea?

*porpoise   turtle   lobster   whale   shark   seal
dolphin   puffin   penguin   crab   squirrel*

Words for boats

Which of the following is not a word for a kind of boat?

*yacht   dinghy   raft   tram   speedboat   liner
vessel   canoe   barge   car ferry   catamaran
oil tanker   trawler*

Occupations connected with the sea

Which is the odd one out in this group of occupations?

*captain   coastguard   solicitor   sailor   pirate   fisherman
skipper   lighthouse   keeper   mariner   smuggler*

Watersports

Which of these sports is not connected with water?

*scuba diving   surfing   rowing   canoeing
swimming   diving   sailing   windsurfing
jet skiing   abseiling   snorkelling*

Now match the four photographs with four of these words.

4 Writing a descriptive paragraph

Yesterday, you made a trip to the coast. Write a paragraph describing what you saw, the sounds you heard and the way you felt.

Write about 80 words.

5 Reading aloud

In small groups, read your paragraphs aloud to each other. Listen well and make comments on what you hear.

6 Pre-reading discussion

A   For countries with a coastline, the sea may provide useful defence in war, a source of wealth from trade or fishing and a way of maintaining separation from other countries. The sea is usually an important part of such nations' national identity. What part, if any, has the sea played in the history of your country?

B   There are many stories about the excitement and drama of the sea. Do you have any favourites?

C   Daniel Defoe's novel *Robinson Crusoe* is one of the most famous of these stories. What, if anything, do you know about it?

7 Reading and sequencing

Read the following version of the story of Robinson Crusoe. Try to guess the meaning of unfamiliar words.

As you read, number these events in the order in which they happened:

a   crusoe is shipwrecked

b   he meets Friday

c   he is made a slave

d   he returns to England

e   he manages a plantation

f   he sees an English ship on the horizon

g   he rescues the ship's captain

h   he builds a home on the island

i   he runs away to sea

j   he accepts his life on the island

k   he salvages things from the shipwreck.

8 Comprehension check

1   What future did Crusoe's father want for his son?

2   Even before the shipwreck, Crusoe had many adventures. What were they?

3   How did Crusoe feel when he realised he was all alone on the island?

4   What did he manage to do before the wrecked ship sank?

Never have any adventurer's misfortunes, I believe, begun earlier or continued longer than mine. I am Robinson Crusoe and this is my story …

I was born in the year 1632 in the city of York. I had always wanted to go to sea but my father wanted me to enter the law. Against the wishes of my parents, I joined a big trading ship when it was in the port at Hull. I knew I was breaking my father's heart but the call of the sea was too strong.   5

At first I was terribly seasick but I gradually learned to adapt and weather the great storms which blew up. On one occasion, to my misfortune, I was taken as a slave but I escaped. For some time I even ran a plantation in Brazil but I could not resist returning to the sea. This time, however, the ship was wrecked and I was the only survivor.   10   15

The sea had washed me up onto a deserted tropical island. 'Am I all alone?' I called, and my despair knew no depths as I realised I was condemned to live in a silent world, forever an outcast in this horrid place.   20

I knew I had to swim back to the ship before it sank completely and save everything of value. The task was urgent as my survival depended on it. On the boat I found the ship's dog and two cats. These creatures, with a parrot I taught to speak, and a goat, were for many years my only companions on the island.   25

For a home, I built a strong shelter close to fresh water. I explored the island and found fruit trees and a herd of goats. I sowed barley I had taken from the ship, and made a calendar to mark the passing of the days. I resolved to look on the bright side rather than the dark side of my condition.
The doings of the greedy, material world and my own past wickedness became more and more remote. I spent many hours in hard labour. I made baskets, pots, a boat and other necessities, but I always found time for spiritual contemplation.   30   35

Each year the crops increased, my 'family' was contented and I learned to love the beauty of the island. Yet I longed to see a human face and hear a human voice.   40

171

My solitude ended when, walking towards my
45   boat, I stopped, thunderstruck, at the sight of a
strange footprint in the sand. This incident was the
beginning of my friendship with a man who lived
on a distant island. He was escaping the anger of
his countrymen and I gave him refuge*. 'Friday', as
50   I called him, wanted to learn English and gradually
we learned to understand one another and
appreciate each other's way of life.

My luck changed when an English ship appeared on
the horizon. Friday and I observed a rowing boat
55   coming ashore. My guess was right. The crew of
the ship had mutinied* and the captain and some
of his loyal men had been overpowered and were
being taken shore by the mutineers. Friday and I
worked out a way to capture the mutineers and set
60   the captain free.

The captain of the ship took me back to England.
Friday, who had been as true and good a friend as a
man could ever wish for, came with me.

So, on 19th December 1686, after 28 years on the
65   island, one of the strangest stories ever told ended
as I, Robinson Crusoe, sailed away from the island,
never to return.

refuge = protection and a safe place to live

mutinied = refused to obey the captain

5 How do we know Crusoe had good practical skills that helped him survive?

6 What was the first sign that another human being had visited the island?

7 How did Crusoe finally manage to escape from the island?

8 Explain the meaning of the word *mutineer*.

9 Overall, what was Crusoe's attitude to his situation?

   a self-pitying   **b** desperate   **c** accepting

9 Language study: Narrative tenses

To help the reader follow a story and understand how the events are connected, we use narrative tenses. Useful narrative tenses are:

- the past simple (*I swam*)
- the past continuous (*I was swimming*)
- the past perfect (*I had swum*).

Study the tenses in the story of Robinson Crusoe with a partner. Underline each verb and decide which tense it is. Add * if the verb is in the passive.

Ask each other why each tense is used.

With your partner, make notes for each narrative tense, like this:

The past simple
- Typical examples in text
- Formed by
- Used in text because
- Finally, check your notes with a grammar book.

10 Beginnings and endings

Beginnings and endings are important in a story. How interesting did you find the beginning of Robinson Crusoe? How satisfying did you find the ending?

What tenses are used at the beginning and end of the story? Why?

11 Discussion: Heroism

A What do we mean when we say someone is a 'hero' or 'heroine'? In what way do you think Robinson Crusoe could be described as a heroic figure?

B Can ordinary people living uneventful lives ever be called 'heroic'? Why/Why not?

C Who are your personal heroes or heroines? Share your ideas in your group.

D Crusoe changes the negative experience of being shipwrecked into a positive one. What can we learn from our own negative experiences?

E Crusoe says he learnt a lot from Friday, who came from a much simpler society. Give some examples of what he might have learnt. Think about both survival skills and human values.

12 Continuing a story creatively

Try to imagine you are Robinson Crusoe, on your way back to England. Use these questions to help you continue his story:

- What will you most miss about your island life?
- What did you choose to take with you from the island?
- What have you learnt from your experiences? Do you feel the hardships of life on the island have made you a better and more understanding person?
- Who will remember you at home? Who will you want to see?
- How will you make your living?
- What might be the difficulties of fitting into a normal life again?

Share your ideas with your classmates.

13 Writing from notes

Most narratives use a variety of past tenses. The following paragraph describes Crusoe's return to England. Complete the paragraph in full using the past simple, past continuous and past perfect tenses:

We were standing on the deck of the ship when the captain shouted that …

We be / stand / deck / ship / when captain shout /

English coast be / sight. I feel / very strange.

After so many years /

solitude / noise / bustle / crowds / dock / almost

overwhelm me. I be / walk / towards town / when I

hear / voice / call my name. I turn / and see / sister. She

embrace me / warmly. I know / from tears / her eyes /

she forgive me / for hurt / our parents. She tell me / almost

give up hope / when she get / message / I be alive.

14 Comparing cultures

What stories in your culture have a sea theme? Think carefully about a story you know well and like. Then retell it to your group.

15 Showing surprise: Stress and intonation CD 2, Track 8

Listen to the intonation patterns in these *wh-* questions and answers. When does the intonation rise? When does it fall?

1 Who arrived on the island in a rowing boat? Some mutineers. **Who** arrived?

2 What did Crusoe use to make a calendar? A wooden post. **What** did he use?

3   How long was he on the island?
Twenty-eight years.
How long was he there?

4   Why did Crusoe call the man 'Friday'?
Because that was the day he saved his life.
Why did he call him Friday?

Listen again and repeat the pattern.

Practice

Work in pairs. Ask each question with the falling tone. Then repeat the question showing surprise.

Try to continue with some questions and answers of your own.

B   Adrift on the Pacific

1   Pre-listening tasks

You are going to hear a story about a couple, Maurice and Vita, who were attempting to sail across the world when their boat sank. They survived on a life raft for four months before they were rescued.

Narrative questions

A narrative should answer these questions:

Who…?   Why …?
What …?   How …?
Where …?   When …?

Write a question about the story beginning with each word.

Example: *Where did the boat sink?*

Try to make your questions grammatically correct.

Vocabulary check

Match these words that you are going to hear with their definitions.

1	emigrate	**A**	extremely thin
2	adrift	**B**	floating without purpose
3	counter-current	**C**	to make something using whatever materials are available
4	improvise	**D**	unaware of, not noticing
5	emaciated	**E**	a sea current running in the opposite direction
6	malnourished	**F**	to go to another country to live there permanently
7	oblivious to	**G**	unwell from lack of food

2   Detailed listening 🔊 CD 2, Track 9

Listen to an interview with the couple who survived. Try to note down answers to the questions you wrote.

3   Checking your answers

Did you find answers to your questions?

4 Listening and note-making

🔊 CD 2, Track 9

Listen again and complete the notes:

a Reason for the trip:

b Where and why the boat sank:

c Immediate reaction to the accident:

d Rowing towards the Galapagos Islands was a mistake because:

e Conditions on the raft:

f What they ate:

g Length of time adrift on raft:

h How they attracted the attention of their rescuers:

i Length of time to recover:

j How they coped emotionally during their experience:

5 Discussion: Motivation and adventure

A What makes people want to become involved in risky projects, such as sailing across the world in a very small boat, climbing a dangerous mountain, trekking in polar regions, or going into outer space? Discuss these ideas in your group:

- Are adventurers and explorers motivated by fame and money? Or a desire for risk and adventure? Or the competitive spirit?

- Is it a need to discover their potential and find out what they are capable of in the most challenging circumstances – a kind of 'spiritual quest'?

Do you think people who undertake this kind of thing have greater 'inner strength' than others?

B Is it right that each year large sums of money are spent rescuing people whose expeditions have gone wrong?

Could the desire for adventure be directed more constructively into doing voluntary work on projects, such as helping refugees?

When conditions on a dangerous expedition become very difficult, is it braver to accept defeat than to risk everything for success?

6 Ordering events

Put these statements about the couple on the life raft into the correct order by numbering them. Then link them using time expressions and conjunctions where appropriate. Choose from:

first, then, when, eventually, finally, before, until, next, after that, after many days

and conjunctions like *and, but,* etc.

For example: First, they left England for New Zealand, but the *Sandpiper* was .... .

- [ ] The *Sandpiper* was damaged by a sperm whale.
- [ ] They rowed towards the Galapagos Islands.
- [ ] They attempted to get to the Central American coast.
- [ ] The boat sank.
- [ ] A hostile current dragged them back out to sea.
- [ ] They tried to attract the attention of passing ships.
- [ ] They were rescued by South Korean fishermen.
- [ ] They returned to Britain.
- [ ] They sailed by unaware of the couple's situation.
- [ ] They escaped onto a life raft.
- [ ] They left England for New Zealand.

Check whether the order of events is correct by listening to the recording again.

7 Expressing emotions

In the interview, Vita says, 'We continued towards that coast for three weeks. Then, to our horror, a hostile current dragged us back out to the middle of the ocean.'

'To our horror' expresses the drama and emotion of the situation. Look at these similar expressions:

VOCABULARY	
to our amazement	to her disappointment
to our (great) relief	to their alarm
to my astonishment	to her concern
to their joy	to our horror
to his annoyance	to our delight

These expressions highlight the responses of the people involved in the events.

Study the following situations. Use a suitable emotional phrase to add to each description.

Example:
We were waiting outside the operating theatre when, **to our great relief**, *the surgeon came out and told us the operation had been a success.*

1   I was kayaking down the river when lightning ripped across the sky and heavy rain began to fall.

2   We feared the worst when our son disappeared driving in the desert but yesterday he sent a text to say he was safe.

3   The racing driver was driving at top speed when he noticed his brakes were not working.

4   I was making dinner when the telephone rang and I learnt I had won first prize in a competition.

5   Joe was enjoying fishing for salmon when he saw a grizzly bear emerging from the forest.

6   We were waiting to go into the aquarium when we saw a large turtle crawling through the reception area.

Tenses

Examine the uses of tenses in the sentences. What tenses are used and why? Some sentences use more than one tense. Why, do you think?

8 Dictionary work: Prefixes

The prefix *mal-*

Maurice says that during their ordeal on the raft they became *malnourished*. The prefix *mal-* means 'badly' or 'wrongly'.

Replace the word(s) in italics in the sentences below with one of these words beginning with *mal-*. Work with a partner and use a dictionary to help you.

VOCABULARY		
malfunctioning	malevolent	malpractice
malignant	malicious	malnutrition

1   The high-energy biscuits saved thousands of refugees who were suffering from *lack of food*.

2   The surgeon said the growth would have to be removed as it was *cancerous*.

3   To his horror, the pilot realised that one of the engines was *not working properly*.

4   The doctor was taken to court for *failing to care properly for his patients*.

5   Children's fairy stories often contain a character who is *very evil*.

6   This little boy is *deliberately hurtful* towards other children.

The prefix *counter-*

In the interview you heard that Vita and Maurice had hoped to get to the equatorial *counter-current*. The prefix *counter-* means 'opposite' or 'reverse'.

Complete each of the following sentences with one of these words beginning with *counter-*. Continue using your dictionary if you need to.

VOCABULARY	
counterbalance	counterpart
counteract	counterargument
counterproductive	counterattack

1   Weights of the same size on this machine should be used to _____ each other.

2 If our aim is to make the workers do a good job, paying them less would surely be _____ .

3 In spite of heavy casualties, the soldiers launched a determined _____ against the enemy forces.

4 The doctor gave the child some medicine to _____ the poison she had swallowed.

5 The Danish Prime Minister met his Swedish _____ in Stockholm today for urgent talks on the fishing crisis.

6 The accountant came up with good reasons for selling the company, but the clients put forward equally strong _____ for keeping it.

9 Revision of reported speech

When we tell a story, we may change someone's actual words to reported speech.

For example, Maurice might have said to Vita, 'It's absolutely silent here. You can't have heard the engine of a boat. No one is coming to rescue us. You must be going mad.'

If this speech were reported it would change to:

Maurice told Vita it was absolutely silent there and she couldn't have heard the engine of a boat. No one was coming to rescue them. She must be going mad.

Study the example carefully.

What has happened to the verbs? What is the rule for **tenses** when direct speech is reported?

What has happened to *must?* Do other **modals** (*would, could, should, might, need, had better* and *ought to*) stay the same when speech is reported?

How have the **pronouns** changed? What usually happens to pronouns in reported speech?

What has happened to the **infinitive**? Do infinitives in direct speech change when the speech is reported?

10 Reporting verbs

Verbs such as *admit, promise, declare, invite, ask, explain, reflect, remind, mention, suggest, insist* and *refuse* are often used when we change direct speech into reported speech. Using them is a good idea because it brings breadth and variety into your writing.

Example:

'Remember to send your aunt a good luck message,' said their mother.

Their mother reminded them to send their aunt a good luck message.

What other reporting verbs do you know?

The following comments were made by a young woman, Silvia, who is planning to sail around the world single-handedly.

Change her actual words to reported speech, using suitable reporting verbs from the box. Some of the verbs are similar in meaning, so decide which you prefer.

VOCABULARY		
acknowledge	declare	reveal
add	explain	say
admit	insist	confess
mention		

Example:

'I'm a yachtswoman and a loner. I would rather go sailing alone than in a group.'

She declared (that) she was a yachtswoman and a loner. She insisted (that) she would rather go sailing alone than in a group.

1 'I'm attempting to break the world record for sailing non-stop around the world.'

2 'I'm being sponsored by several businesses.'

3 'I suppose my worst fear is personal failure.'

4 'I'm doing it because I'm hoping to beat the present world record of 161 days.'

5 'I'm taking food and drink to last me up to 200 days.'

6 'The food includes 500 dried meals, 150 apples, 144 bars of chocolate, 36 jars of jam and marmalade and 14 tubs of dried fruit and nuts.'

7 'When I'm thousands of miles from shore, and if I'm injured, then I'll be scared.'

8 'I've been taught to stitch my own flesh in an emergency.'

9 'If there's a crisis, I think the answer is not instant action, but to think about it.'

10 'I know I can handle the boat and I'll find out whether I have the strength to beat the world record.'

11 Writing a report of an interview

Imagine that you are a journalist. You have been asked to interview the yachtswoman. Write a report of the interview for your newspaper.

First make a plan.

- Select those sentences in exercise 8 you would like to include in your report.
- Try to use a balance of reported speech and direct speech to make the report convincing.
- Invent other details readers might like to know. For example:
  - the place where you interviewed Silvia – on her yacht or in her house?
  - personal details about Silvia (e.g. her age, her appearance).
  - Give your opinions of Silvia. Do you think she is brave? What do you think about her desire to test herself?
  - Finally, decide on the correct order for the information in the report.

C A remarkable rescue

1 Pre-reading tasks

Have you ever lost anything that was important to you? In pairs, ask each other questions using these prompts:

Where / be you?

Be you / alone?

What / be you / do / when you realise / it be lost?

What / you do / when you realise / what happen?

How / you react?

How / other people react?

What / happen / in the end?

An ocean of facts! Test your knowledge

1 The largest of the world's oceans covers more than a third of the Earth's surface. Which is it?

   a   the Atlantic Ocean

   b   the Pacific Ocean

   c   the Arctic Ocean

   d   the Indian Ocean.

2 The Arctic Ocean is the world's smallest ocean. True or false?

3 The world's largest inland sea has an area of 371 000 square kilometres. Which is it?

   a   the Baltic Sea

   b   the Black Sea

   c   the Caspian Sea.

4 Which country of the world has the longest continuous coastline (37 653 km)? Choose from:

   a   Australia

   b   Canada

   c   Russia.

5 One country in the following list is the world's largest archipelago, with over 13 500 islands, of which about 6 000 are inhabited. Which is it?

   a   Indonesia

   b   the Philippines

   c   the Seychelles.

6 The world's oceans contain about ten billion tons of a precious metal, but nobody has worked out how to collect it. Which metal is it?

   a   silver

   b   gold.

Predicting

You are going to read a newspaper article about an Irish farmer who lost his sheepdog while out walking on the cliffs near his home. Look carefully at the headlines and picture. What do they tell you about the story you are going to read?

Do you think the story will have a happy ending? Why/Why not?

Language and audience

Do you expect the language to be chatty and colloquial? Or formal and serious? Why?

Who do you think would enjoy reading this story?

2 Reading for gist

Read the newspaper article carefully, trying to guess any unknown words from the context. Most of the story is told using past tenses. As you read, underline examples of the past simple, past continuous and past perfect tenses.

3 Vocabulary check

Find words in the article and headlines to match these definitions. To help you, the definitions are in the same order as the words.

1   unable to get back
2   a sudden fall
3   noticed
4   fell quickly and suddenly
5   accepting the situation
6   looking lost and sad
7   a breed of dog
8   extremely upset
9   sharp
10   very steep, almost vertical.

A remarkable rescue

Stranded sheepdog reunited with owner after 30-metre cliff plunge

WHEN Shadow the trainee sheepdog spotted a stray sheep, he did what comes naturally. The one-year-
5   old set off in pursuit across several fields and, being a young, inexperienced animal, somehow lost his

sense of direction. He came to the edge of a cliff and plummeted 30 metres, bouncing off a rock into the sea.

His owner, farmer Aidan McCarry, was very upset and immediately called the coastguard. Six   10
volunteers abseiled down the cliff but gave up all hope of finding him alive after a 90-minute search.

Three days later, a hurricane hit the coast near Ballybunion, in south-west Ireland, and a resigned Mr McCarry was convinced he would never see or   15
hear of Shadow again.

Then, two weeks later, the phone rang and a man asked him if he would like his dog back.

The area is famous for birdlife, including falcons and ravens, which can be seen on the cliff's narrow   20
ledges. Two days earlier, a birdwatcher, armed with a telescope, had been watching some rock doves when he spotted the dog sitting forlornly on a rock. While he raised the alarm, a young student,

25 Brendan O'Connor, climbed down the cliff to collect Shadow.

The black and white collie had initially been knocked unconscious but had survived by drinking water from a fresh stream at the base of the cliff. It was, as Mr 30 McCarry admitted yesterday, 'a minor miracle'.

He recalled how he had left his farmhouse with his 16-year-old niece Keira, and set off on a coast walk.

'It was a beautiful day, with just a light breeze. Keira had got her camera with her because she 35 wanted to take photographs of the seals which come close to the shore. Shadow, who was a little in front of us, was running in a field full of wildflowers. Then he spotted a sheep and began chasing after it. To my dismay, he forgot all the training I'd been 40 giving him and completely ignored my whistles ordering him to come back to us. We tried to run after him but he was too fast for us.

'They thought he ran for about half a kilometre and fell head first down the cliffs and bounced off jagged rocks into the sea. We just stood there in stunned silence. 45

'I was distraught. I had no idea how I would manage on the farm without him. We couldn't get down the cliffs because they were so sheer. I ran back to the village to get help, while Keira phoned the coastguard. 50 They turned up in seconds and a rescue party abseiled down the cliff, but they could not find him.'

Paddy Quin, who was in charge of the rescue, said the dog was emaciated, a bit scratched and bruised, but otherwise healthy. He said: 'It was an extremely 55 lucky dog.'

Vet Teresa Kelly, who was looking after Shadow yesterday, said he had survived because of a plentiful supply of fresh water.

'He was also a well-fed dog before and still had his 60 puppy fat – it was probably those few extra pounds that saved him,' she added. 'He is very thin and hungry. But considering he had been there two weeks, he seems very well.'

4 True/false comprehension

Decide whether the following statements about the story are true or false.

1 Shadow was used to working with sheep.

2 He followed a sheep over a cliff.

3 He lost consciousness when he fell.

4 His owner climbed down the cliff to find him.

5 The rescue party arrived very quickly.

6 His owner continued looking for him.

7 Shadow was identified by a birdwatcher.

8 He was a little overweight before his fall.

9 He was in poor health when he was rescued.

10 He had survived because of access to fresh water.

5 Narrative structure

Like many newspaper accounts, the story is not reported in chronological order. It begins by explaining how Shadow got lost and the failed rescue attempt. We are then told that a second rescue attempt was successful. Halfway through the report the events of his fall and safe return are repeated, with more detail.

Why do you think the story is told like this? Consider the following:

- to provide a dramatic opening which is not slowed down by too much detail
- to enable us to hear actual spoken comments from the people who were involved
- to make the narrative as varied, moving and personal as possible.

6 Writing a summary from notes

Write a summary of the story describing how the dog got lost, what the owner did and felt, and how they were reunited. Use these notes to help you:

Farmer Aidan McCarry walk / with his sheepdog Shadow near Ballybunion / Shadow start / chase sheep. Unfortunately he fall over / cliff / towards the sea. His owner contact / coastguard / and rescue team / abseil down the cliff. However, Shadow cannot / found / and owner return home / feel / distressed. Two weeks later / man / ring. He say / birdwatcher / notice Shadow / on a rock. Student / rescue him. The dog / be thin / but well. Vet say / Shadow probably survive / by drink / fresh water.

7 Vocabulary: Adjectives

Shadow is described as a *well-fed* dog who becomes *emaciated*. His owner is *distraught* when he loses him.

The following adjectives describe emotion and appearance. With a partner, try to rank them in order. Use a dictionary as necessary.

Start: 1 ecstatic, 2 happy, ...

1 obese, 2 fat ....

Emotion

*heartbroken   indifferent   distraught   happy
irritated   pleased   satisfied   ecstatic   miserable*

Appearance

*slim   emaciated   skinny   plump   scrawny
thin   fat   obese   overweight*

8 Homonyms

Homonyms are words that have the same sound and spelling but different meanings. There are a number of examples in the article 'A Remarkable Rescue':

1 'Two days earlier, a birdwatcher, armed with a telescope, had been watching some rock doves when he had *spotted* the dog sitting forlornly on a rock' (line 25).

   Spotted in this sentence is a verb that means 'noticed'.

   What does *spotted* mean in the following sentence? What part of speech is it?

   'He had a green and white *spotted* scarf around his neck.'

2 'We couldn't get down the cliffs because they were so *sheer*' (line 51).

   In this sentence *sheer* means 'extremely steep'.

   What does *sheer* mean in the following sentence? What part of speech is it?

   'Staying up all night to revise for an exam is *sheer* madness.'

Practice

Work with a partner to check the meanings of the following homonyms. Use a dictionary if you need to. Then write example sentences to show the different meanings each word can have. Indicate whether the word is being used as a noun, verb or adjective.

1 mine
2 sound
3 stamp
4 dash
5 file
6 book
7 light
8 match.

What other homonyms do you know? Share your ideas in your group.

9 Revision of defining relative clauses

Study this sentence from the text:

'Keira had got her camera with her because she wanted to take photographs of the seals *which come close to the shore*.'

The clause in italics is important to the meaning of the sentence. It is called a defining clause, because it defines or makes clear which person or thing is being talked about. Here are some more examples:

1 *The vet who treated Shadow* was very efficient.
2 They interviewed the man *whose dog had been rescued.*
3 Have you read the leaflet *which/that explains what to do if you have an accident?*
4 This is the house *where they live.*

A defining clause is essential to the meaning of the sentence. If it is left out, the sentence does not make complete sense or the meaning changes. No commas are used before defining clauses. Remember that the pronoun **that** can be used instead of **which** to refer to things in defining clauses.

Practice

Complete these sentences with suitable defining clauses.

1 They prefer stories _____ endings.
2 The man _____ has donated a lot of money to charity.

3 The student _____ received an award for bravery.
4 The shoes _____ last month have already fallen apart.
5 The factory _____ is now a tourist hotel.
6 The doctor _____ comes from Guatemala.

10 Revision of non-defining relative clauses

Non-defining relative clauses give extra information about something. They can be in the middle or at the end of a sentence. Commas are used to separate them from the rest of the sentence.

Study these examples:

1 Paddy Quin, *who was in charge of the rescue,* said the dog was emaciated.
2 Pablo, *whose father is an ambulance driver,* is learning what to do in an emergency.
3 Forecasting the eruptions of volcanoes, *which can let off steam lightly for years,* is very difficult.
4 He gave the dog some water, *which she obviously needed.*

The pronoun **that** cannot be used in non-defining clauses.

Non-defining clauses 'round out' your sentences. Try to use them, as they make your writing more interesting and complex.

Practice

Add suitable non-defining clauses to these sentences. You should use *whose* in at least one of the clauses.

1 Rahmia Altat, _____, now does voluntary work.
2 We heard about the heroic acts of the rescue workers, _____.
3 Nurse Mara, _____, demonstrated the life-saving techniques.
4 Drowning, _____, can usually be prevented.
5 Smoke alarms, _____, should be fitted in every home.
6 My cousin Gina, _____, is being brought up by her grandparents.

Try to expand these simple sentences into more complex ones, using non-defining clauses to add extra information.

7 Mrs Nazir won a trip to the Caribbean.

8 The new hospital is the biggest in the country.

9 Our sailing teacher took us to an island.

Write some sentences of your own using non-defining clauses.

11 Functions quiz: Consoling and sympathising

Working in pairs, decide which is the most appropriate way to respond to the following statements giving bad news. Select as many of the answers as you think are suitable.

1 I've just failed my driving test.
  a What a shame.
  b How horrific!
  c That's a tragedy.
  d You should have done better.
  e Better luck next time.

2 My grandma died recently.
  a Oh, I am sorry. Is there anything I can do to help?
  b You must be really fed up.
  c How sad. Was it sudden?
  d Don't get too worried about it.
  e What bad luck!

3 I forgot my door key and had to wait outside for two hours until my father got back from work.
  a How annoying!
  b That was forgetful of you.
  c My heart goes out to you.
  d I'd just like to say how sad I am for you.
  e You must remember to put it in your bag in future.

4 I thought I'd recorded 'Ocean of Adventure,' but when I sat down to watch it, I discovered I'd recorded the wrong programme!
  a Never mind. I can lend you the DVD.
  b I bet you were furious.
  c I'd have been really annoyed.

  d You've got all my sympathy for what you're going through.
  e Remember to follow the instructions next time.

Study the following comments. Write down some appropriate responses and then try them out on your partner.

5 I didn't get the job I applied for.

6 I'm really disappointed with my new haircut.

7 I broke my ankle on holiday.

12 Spelling and pronunciation: The suffix *-tion* or *-ion* 🔊 CD 2, Track 10

The suffix *-tion* or *-ion* is quite common in English. Examples in the text were *direction* and *condition*. How is the final syllable pronounced in these words?

Other examples are:

1	exhibition	**2**	fashion
3	occupation	**4**	demonstration
5	passion	**6**	invention
7	qualification	**8**	definition
9	recognition	**10**	ignition
11	promotion.		

Listen carefully and try to mark the main stress in each of the words. Then practise saying them.

Question and opinion are exceptions to the rule. How are they pronounced?

Now match ten of the words from the list to these definitions:

A will improve your chances of getting a job

B another word for work

C a machine or gadget that is original

D strong emotion

E a display of books or pictures

F the dictionary will give you this information about a word

G a better job with more money

H if this is turned off, the car will not start

I artists can work for 20 years without getting this

J the latest styles in clothes and shoes.

13 Language study: Adverbs

Adverbs have a large number of different uses.

They can tell us more about a verb.

Example: *She walked slowly.*

They can be used before an adjective.

Example: *It was fairly difficult.*

They can be used before another adverb.

Example: *He drove terribly slowly.*

They can tell us when or how often something happens.

Examples: *occasionally, regularly, never*

They can give information about how certain we are of something.

Examples: *definitely, probably, perhaps*

They can connect ideas.

Examples: *firstly, however, lastly*

Formation of adverbs

Many adverbs are formed by adding **-ly** to adjectives. *Naturally, forlornly* and *initially* are examples from the text 'A Remarkable Rescue'.

Other examples are:

quick ~ quickly, cheap ~ cheaply

If the adjective ends in *-y*, you change the *-y* to *-i* before adding *-ly*.

Example: *angry ~ angrily*

If the adjective ends in *-ic*, you add *-ally*.

Example: *heroic ~ heroically*

If the adjective ends in *-le*, you drop the *-e* and add *-y*.

Example: *reasonable ~ reasonably*

Remember that some adjectives look like adverbs.

Examples: *lovely, elderly, friendly*

Notice also: *early ~ early, fast ~ fast, good ~ well*

Practice

Correct the following report on jobs at sea, which is from a careers website for young people. Change the words in italics to adverbs. Ask your partner to mark it when you have finished to check that your spelling is correct.

184

CAREERS AT SEA

Working at sea sounds romantic but it can also be *surprising* hard work! Voyages on commercial merchant ships transporting cargo and passengers last at least a week. Supersized cruise ships, which enable tourists to visit multiple holiday destinations during the voyage, can be at sea much longer. As you will see, it is *definite* not for those who like an easy life.

Here are some of the main jobs at sea.

The Captain
The captain is in overall control of the vessel. He or she (modern captains are not *necessary* male) is *direct* responsible for the vessel, crew, cargo and passengers. It is essential that the captain

| CAREERS IN THE POLICE FORCE |
| CAREERS IN EDUCATION |
| CAREERS IN ENTERTAINMENT |

can think *quick* in an emergency. The captain *normal* takes the vessel in and out of port.

Engineering Officer

Engineering officers are responsible for the ship's engines and all the equipment that is *electronic* operated. The equipment is checked *day* and any faults must be corrected *immediate*. Officers are *able* assisted by ratings – workers who maintain equipment in the engine room and elsewhere.

The Purser

The purser is responsible for buying and storing food and making sure it is prepared and served *hygienic*. Pursers must make sure that all those on the vessel are fed *healthy* and *economic*. They are also in charge of the cooks and stewards, who are *usual full* trained chefs and waiters.

Navigating Officer

The navigating officers are responsible for navigating the ship *proper* and for making sure the loading and unloading of cargo is *total* safe. They respond *appropriate* to any changes in weather (in some areas the climate can change *dramatic* in seconds) and adjust the ship's speed *according*. In difficult conditions, when it's snowing very *heavy* for example, they may take over *temporary* from the helmsman*.

Skills and qualities needed for work at sea

You must be:

- [ ] *technical* minded (for most jobs)
- [ ] *suitable* qualified
- [ ] able to work *capable* and *efficient* for long periods
- [ ] able to get on *happy* with others as part of a team
- [ ] able to react *responsible* in times of crisis
- [ ] able to stay calm even when *frantic* busy.

* *helmsman* = person who steers a ship or boat

CAREERS IN HEALTHCARE

CAREERS IN TECHNOLOGY

14 Look, say, cover, write, check

In the text 'A Remarkable Rescue' you saw the word *distraught*. The letters *aught* are a common combination in many words. The phonetic spelling is /ɔːt/.

Use the 'look, say, cover, write, check' method to learn these words. Make sure you understand the meaning of each one.

VOCABULARY			
distraught	caught	naughty	taught

Ought is also pronounced /ɔːt/. Use the same method to learn to spell these words correctly:

VOCABULARY		
thought	fought	
bought	sought	brought

D Reacting to the unexpected

1 Pre-reading task: Making notes

Read about these unexpected events that happened to various people.

I was walking home when a passer-by collapsed in the street

We had just gone to bed when the smoke alarms went of

My neighbour knocked on the door. She was sure her little girl had swallowed some poisonous berries.

I was doing my homework when water started pouring through the ceiling.

I was chatting to my best friend when one of the party guests insisted I tried the dancing competition and I won first prize!

Have you ever had to cope with something, pleasant or unpleasant, that was completely unexpected? Think carefully about the event and then make notes under these headings.

The background to the event

- Where were you?
- What were you doing?
- Who was with you and what were they doing?

The event itself

- What happened?
- How did you react?
- What did other people do?
- What happened then?

The outcome

- What happened in the end?
- What do you feel you have learnt from the experience?
- How has the experience affected other people?
- Has the event had any other effects?

Compare your notes with your partner's. Look after them as you'll need them later.

2 Reading an example narrative

Naila Khan Afza is a journalist. This summer an extraordinary thing happened to her while she was on holiday. She posted the following story to her newspaper's blog. Do you think you would have reacted in the same way she did?

As you read, underline the tenses and the examples of non-defining relative clauses.

Comprehension check

1   What was Naila doing when the incident happened?

2   Did she have time to tell anyone else what was happening?

3   What helped the boy regain consciousness?

4   What suggests that Naila is fully concentrating on mouth-to-mouth resuscitation?

5   How do we know that Dale's parents want him to be safe in the water?

3 Analysing the narrative

A   Openings are important in narratives. Does the story interest you immediately? Why/Why not?

B   In the first paragraph, a number of different tenses are used. What are they, how are they formed and what are their functions?

C   '*To my horror*', '*Without stopping to think*' and '*To my great relief*' are used for effect. What other phrases could be used?

D   Endings are important in a narrative. The reader should not feel there are unanswered questions. Do you think the story is brought to a satisfactory conclusion? Why/Why not?

E   Remember, a narrative should answer these questions:

Who …?   *Why …?*

What …?   *How …?*

Where …?   *When …?*

How does Naila's narrative do this?

For example:

Who is involved in Naila's story?

What happened?

Where did the event take place?

The Online Journal

The biggest event of my summer

Nalia Khan Afza, blogging since 2012

By Naila Khan Afza, *The Online Journal*

It seemed like another ordinary day. My family and I had decided to spend the day on the beach. I sat in the sun watching the children throwing pebbles into the sea or paddling. I was thinking about having a swim when I noticed a strange object bobbing about in the sea. To my horror, I realised the 'object' was a child drowning. Without stopping to think, I plunged into the water and grabbed the child. With my free arm I swam back to the shore. The child, who was a boy of about five, was like a dead weight but I felt powered by a superhuman strength.

I laid the boy, who appeared to be unconscious, gently on the ground and gave him mouth-to-mouth resuscitation which revived him immediately. I was dimly aware that a large crowd had gathered and someone was telling me an ambulance was on its way. By the time the ambulance arrived, to my great relief, the boy was sitting up and talking.

Dale's parents were delighted with his quick recovery. They rang me later to thank me and we had a long discussion about the dangers of playing near water. They have arranged for him to have swimming lessons, which I think is a very good idea. I would definitely recommend that everyone learn to swim - young or old. I'd also like to remind everyone to take care near the sea, rivers or swimming pools. You can drown much more easily than you think!

4 Dramatic expressions

My hair stood on end …

My heart missed a beat …

Your sentences can be made more dramatic by starting them with this kind of expression. Make complete sentences by matching the following openings 1–6 with the endings A–F. More than one option may be possible, so decide which you prefer.

1 With my heart in my mouth …

2 A piercing scream cut through the air …

3 I froze to the spot …

4 Panic mounted …

5 With trembling fingers …

6 Sweat poured from us …

A … as we fought to rescue the children trapped by the earthquake.

B … when flames appeared at the side of the plane.

C … as the hijacker produced a gun!

D … when the hooded figure appeared in the graveyard.

E … I tiptoed past the sleeping kidnappers.

F … he struggled to open his parachute.

Now write four sentences of your own using dramatic expressions.

5 Pre-writing discussion

1 What does windsurfing involve?

2 What do you think is exciting about this sport?

3 Could it ever be dangerous? Why/Why not?

4 Does this hobby appeal to you? Why/Why not?

6 Ways of developing an outline

The following list of sentences is an outline of a story. It describes how a windsurfer was swept out to sea and what happened in the end. Read the sentences carefully. Make sure you understand all the points clearly.

I Fought To Stay Alive

I was windsurfing off the Pacific coast.
It was a calm sunny day.
I'm a very experienced windsurfer.
Everything was going well.
The wind turned, forcing me offshore.
I tried for an hour to get back to the shore.
I began to feel weaker.
The wind started coming in gusts.
The sea was rough.
I clung to the board.
A helicopter flew over.
I thought it was coming to rescue me.
I waved and shouted.
It flew over me to the other side of the bay.
I was wearing a dark wetsuit on a blue and white board.
I was part of the sea and no one could see me.
When night fell, I lay down on the board, wrapped in my sail.
I was in my own little world.
Then I heard a helicopter.
I waved.
They saw me.
They rescued me.

Obviously, a list of events does not make a complete narrative. In fact, the pleasure of reading a good story often lies not in the plot, but in the details.

What details could you add to the outline above to produce an exciting, well-written story? With your partner, select the points that could make your story come alive.

a Beginning the story with some interesting details that set the scene (e.g. *It was a beautiful, sunny day and I was doing what I like best – windsurfing.*)

b Describing the weather and the sea in a vivid way (e.g. *The wind was howling / The waves were crashing.*)

c Using dramatic expressions (e.g. *My heart sank as the board was carried far out to sea.*)

d Using emotional expressions to add drama (e.g. *to my horror / to my intense relief* (See exercise 8.2.7.))

e Writing a clear conclusion to the story that expresses the feelings of the writer about the experience (e.g. *I am so grateful to the people who rescued me. I was not ready to die at sea!*)

Don't forget!

Time expressions make the sequence of events clear (e.g. *Many hours passed, some time later, until, when, then, while, next, finally.*)

Conjunctions connect clauses or show connections between sentences (e.g. *however, although.*)

Non-defining relative clauses round out sentences and make them more interesting to read.

7 Building a story from a dialogue

In pairs, read this conversation about what happened during a school trip to the seaside:

Aisha: Where did you go for your school trip this year?

Firuza: We went to the coast. It was so hot that we all wanted to get out of the city.

Aisha: How did it go?

Firuza: Well, we had a great day, apart from one incident.

Aisha: Oh, what was that?

Firuza: Well, we all got to the beach without any trouble. We'd finished putting on sun cream and were just going for a swim when Mrs Kazan noticed that her purse, which had all our return train tickets in it, was missing.

Aisha: Oh no!

Firuza: Yes, she was really upset. She decided that the purse must have dropped out of her bag on the walk to the beach from the station. You see, Ethan had offered to carry the bag for her and she thought maybe it had fallen out then – but she wasn't really sure.

Aisha: So, did you all go back to look for it or what?

Firuza: Well, I offered to go with her, but in the end she said she'd retrace her steps with Ethan and see if they could see any sign of it.

Aisha: Poor Ethan. He must have felt awful.

Firuza: I think he did. I mean, he was just about to have a swim when he had to put his clothes back on and go back to the station with Mrs Kazan.

Aisha: And did they find it?

Firuza: Well, they walked right back to the station without seeing it. At the station they asked at the information desk but it hadn't been handed in.

Aisha: Oh dear.

Firuza: On the way back to the beach they stopped at a café for a drink. They were talking about the purse and wondering what to do next when the owner came over. He asked if they'd lost anything. They mentioned her purse and the man produced it from under the counter. A passer-by had spotted it on the pavement outside and had handed it in at the café.

Aisha: Well that was lucky! And was everything still inside?

Firuza: Yes, it was, thank goodness.

Writing the story

You are Ethan. Write an account of the incident for the class newsletter. Before you begin writing, plan what you will say. Use these notes to help you.

- Give the story a clear **shape**: background details, main events and the outcome should be clear.
- **Tenses** and **pronouns** should be appropriate.
- Try to write **vividly**, using a range of vocabulary and expressions.
- Use clearly defined **paragraphs**.

8 Post discussion task: correcting and writing a report

Each year Cheng's school raises funds for worthwhile projects. This year the headteacher is thinking about giving the funds to help an expedition of young explorers going to Antarctica. The headteacher has asked Cheng, who is a student representative, to write a report saying whether he thinks this would be the best way to use the funds.

In Cheng's report, there is one extra word in each sentence that should not be there. First, read the report to get the sense. Then read it again and delete the extra word in each sentence. The extra word in the first sentence has been done for you. Finally, show where the missing sentence should go.

Missing sentence:

In fact, a some member of the expedition previously attended our school.

Report for the headteacher

This report will consider **at** the pros and cons of supporting the young explorers going to Antarctica. I have spoken to other students in my year to find out of their views and these are given in the report.

5 The positive points of supporting to the expedition are that, firstly, the people taking part are from our town, so we would be helping local people. In addition, many of us admire the explorers because they are prepared to take risks and are testing in 10 themselves to the limits Their courage is a shining example and for encourages us to think about the importance of having challenging projects ourselves.

On the other hand, a few students have said it would 15 be better to give the money to the Town Emergency Services rather than a group of teenagers who they want to have fun. Also, the trip might it end in disaster. While it is true that exploring the coast of Antarctica is dangerous, in my view, the people going on if the expedition are taking the project 20 seriously and are well-prepared. They have spent a long time learning how survival skills. They are also going to do some research there in Antarctica, which will increase scientists' knowledge of climate change. 25

To sum up, I believe that we should support our the expedition. The explorers who deserve our help. The project is a worthwhile and inspiring one challenge. At school, we are all looking forward to reading on the Antarctica Expedition blog. 30

Cheng Fu
Student Representative

GRAMMAR SPOTLIGHT

The interrupted past continuous

The interrupted past continuous is used to show that an action stopped at a specific point, when something else happened:

I was packing for my trip when the police knocked at the door.

We use *when* to link the two tenses. If we want to emphasise two things happening at just the same-time, we can also choose as:

It was snowing as/when he climbed higher up the mountain.

The interrupted past continuous is often used to set the scene and to make the beginning of a story more dramatic or interesting.

In the text in **section D2**, you have seen:

I was thinking about having a swim when I noticed a strange object bobbing about in the sea.

Look back at the speech bubbles in **section D1** and underline any examples of the interrupted past continuous. Which actions were interrupted, and by what event?

Now complete these sentences that set the scene for exciting stories.

1 Tomaz was _____ on his life raft _____ hungry and scared, when, to his relief, a rescue ship _____ on the horizon.

2 The shipwrecked couple were_____ a conversation about what to do next, when they _____ a rowing boat _____ towards them.

3 Alan was alone on the desert island _____ to make a fire without matches, when, to his amazement, he _____ some children _____ along the beach.

4 Lorna was desperately _____ for her mobile phone when, to her horror, she felt a large hand _____ her mouth.

5 The class were _____ quietly to Mr Hamsun's science lecture and _____ notes when the teacher suddenly _____ his hand in his pocket and _____ a fistful of fabulous diamonds onto the desk.

6 Anton was walking with his children in the woods when, to his amazement, he _____ a mysterious, veiled woman dressed in golden robes.

Exam-style questions

Reading

Reading & Writing, Exercise 2

1 You are going to read an article in which four record-breaking young explorers share their views on adventure. For questions a–j, choose from the people A–D. The people may be chosen more than once.

Extended [10 marks]

Which person:

a received public recognition for achievement?

- Person A
- Person B
- Person C
- Person D

b takes preparing for an expedition to an extreme?

- Person A
- Person B
- Person C
- Person D

c prefers not to talk about future plans?

- Person A
- Person B
- Person C
- Person D

d learnt survival skills while working?

- Person A
- Person B
- Person C
- Person D

e made a mistake?

- Person A
- Person B
- Person C
- Person D

f suggests a change in routine is helpful?

- Person A
- Person B
- Person C
- Person D

g believes in determination above all?

- Person A
- Person B
- Person C
- Person D

h was surprised by the kindness of strangers?

- Person A
- Person B
- Person C
- Person D

i asked for advice?

- Person A
- Person B
- Person C
- Person D

j assisted scientific research?

- Person A
- Person B
- Person C
- Person D

A Carl

People I meet are curious about whether you need to have adventurous parents in order to be adventurous yourself. I don't know the answer as I have no idea where my interest in breaking records for kayaking comes from. As a teenager, I wasn't inspired by school, but I loved the freedom of the outdoors and I volunteered to help at an adventure club in the holidays where I learnt survival techniques, such as rope tying, which I still use all the time on expeditions. Amazingly, the club asked me to accompany a group kayaking on Lake Malawi. Undoubtedly, it was there that my desire to prove myself and take part in challenging projects really started. People ask me what special quality I, personally, have that makes my achievements possible. But I think everyone can do something amazing. You just have to keep trying to make your dreams a reality no matter what the effort. At the moment, I have all sorts of ideas about my next expedition, although I never like saying too much in advance.

B Grace

As a child, I was fascinated by explorers who had been to the North Pole. They were my heroes and I wanted to do what they had done so I wrote to them asking how they had accomplished their goals. They always wrote back, telling me how they had coped in freezing temperatures and explaining survival skills, and how they had reacted to the unexpected. I learnt so much from them but getting experience is essential. On my first solo expedition, I spent hours frantically searching for matches. For some reason, they weren't in the food storage box where they belonged. Without matches, I couldn't cook or melt ice for drinking. I was about to collapse from cold and exhaustion when I found the matches inside my sleeping bag of all places! Now, when I'm on an expedition, I store all my equipment in its proper place and pull it along on a sled, so I have to be careful about the weight of everything I take with me. In my blog, I write about how I cut off clothing labels and the metal tags from zips. I even cut the handle off my toothbrush. My team laugh at my obsessions and they gave me a prize on the last trip for always being the team member with the lightest equipment.

C Adam

From an early age, I hated walking, so when I got my first bicycle, a whole new world opened up for me. My bike gave me freedom and I loved exploring the beaches and forests around my home. I got the idea of cycling across continents from a blog by an explorer who had cycled from Dublin to Islamabad. I set off when I left school, determined to explore the world. As regards the costs of the trip, I was incredibly lucky, as, by chance, a health organisation had heard of my expedition. They were studying the physiological effects of activity and diet and, to my astonishment, they offered to pay for my trip if I agreed to eat over 5 000 calories per day, twice the average intake. Despite consuming so much, I didn't put on weight, I lost it! Overall, I think my most memorable journey was cycling alone through Asia. In contrast to what I had heard, I felt safe and the hospitality was like no other. I would love to go back there.

D   Zuleeka

When I was growing up, we spent family holidays exploring the Greek Islands. I think that's where my interest in exploring came from. My parents always involved us in the preparation for the trips, including how to pack lightly and how to read a compass. But I never considered myself adventurous. I certainly never thought I would sail solo around the world when I was 17! Although I have travelled the world, I think there are lots of adventures, big and small, waiting to happen on our own doorstep. You don't have to go to the other side of the globe to find them. In my work as an ambassador for a young people's organisation, (which I was given for breaking a world record), I encourage curiosity. To be an explorer, you need an open mind and an urge to find things out. Everyone can try out new things, even just getting off the bus earlier than usual and walking a different route home can be exciting.

Writing

Reading & Writing, Exercise 6

1   Your school plans to organise an adventure holiday for next summer. Your teacher has asked you to write a report on possible destinations. In your report, suggest places to go and say which one might be best for your age group and why. Here are two comments from your classmates:

   'I think we should go sailing. Imagine learning how to sail on the Atlantic!'

   'Could we go as far as South America? It would be great to travel into the Amazon Rainforest.'

   Write the report for your teacher. The comments above may give you some ideas, and you can also use some ideas of your own. Your report should be 150–200 words long.

   Extended [16 marks]

Reading & Writing, Exercise 5

2   You and your family were on a ship when you were hit by a storm. Fortunately, you were able to return to the coast unhurt. Write an email to your cousin, describing what happened.

   In your email you should:

   - explain what you were doing when the storm blew up
   - describe how people reacted
   - explain how you felt afterwards.

   Write 150–200 words.

   Extended [16 marks]

Reading & Writing, Exercise 5

3   You were on a school outing when one of the younger children got lost. You helped your teacher find him or her. Write an account of the incident for the school newsletter. In the account you should:

   - explain how the child got lost
   - explain how you managed to find him or her
   - say what you learnt from the incident.

   Write about 100–150 words.

   Core [12 marks]

193

Reading & Writing, Exercise 6

4 Your class recently attended a special course in survival skills. Your head teacher asked you to write a report about the course. In your report say what you thought of the course and suggest ways it could be improved. Here are some comments from students:

'We learnt useful skills such as how to build shelters and catch fish.'

'The course was quite interesting, but it was a bit too long.'

'The survival skills were difficult to learn.'

'The course taught us all a lot about how to survive to do in really difficult situations.'

Write a report for the head teacher. These comments above may give you some ideas, and you can also use some ideas of your own. Your report should be 100–150 words long.

Core [12 marks]

Reading & Writing, Exercise 6

5 Your school recently went on a visit to explore some underground caves. Here are some comments from students about the trip:

'We loved exploring a place that so few people had seen before.'

'The caves were too dark and silent.'

Write a report for the headteacher giving your views on the visit. These comments may give you some ideas but you should try to use some ideas of your own. Write 150–200 words.

Extended [16 marks]

Speaking

1 Coping with setbacks

Some people are able to overcome difficult situations more easily than others. Discuss this topic with the assessor. In your conversation, you may like to discuss ideas such as:

- the kind of situations that cause us to feel disappointed or upset
- a time in your life when something went wrong for you
- what you learnt from this difficult situation
- the view that modern teenagers are less capable of solving their own problems than previous generations
- the idea that coping with setbacks and disappointments helps us grow into stronger people.

You are free to use any other related ideas of your own. You are not allowed to make any written notes.

2 A job aboard ship

There are many different kinds of job opportunities at sea. Discuss the idea of a career aboard ship with the assessor. In your conversation, you may like to discuss ideas such as:

- whether a job at sea appeals to you
- the benefits and disadvantages of working on a large cruise liner

- the challenge of working on a small boat
- whether a job with the merchant navy* is more attractive than being part of the military navy
- whether you would ever like to have a boat of your own, and why/why not.

merchant navy = commercial navy

You are free to use any other related ideas of your own. You are not allowed to make any written notes.

ADVICE FOR SUCCESS

The Advice for Success is for **you** to **help yourself**. Decide which suggestions you like best and mark them. You can adapt an idea in Advice for Success to make it fun for you. Keeping track with a notebook is a good idea.

1 When asked to write a **narrative**, students sometimes say they don't know what to write about. The ingredients for stories are all around us: in the incidents that happen in everyday life; in the stories your friends tell you about things that have happened to them; in news articles; in the letters read out on radio talk shows, and so on. With a little creativity, you can rework ideas into your own writing.

2 The plot isn't everything. Many wonderful stories do not have particularly original plots. The main interest in a story often lies in the beauty of the writing. Giving **attention to detail** in your writing is as important as having an original plot.

3 **Planning** your composition before you start writing will help you structure it. Narratives usually start with background information. The story then develops and you explain what happened. Finally there should be a definite conclusion so the reader isn't left wondering what happened in the end.

4 Aim to **make your writing interesting** so the reader really wants to read on and find out what happened next. Here are some ways you can do this:

- Use a mixture of short sentences and longer, more complex sentences.
- Use vivid language and a range of emotional and dramatic expressions.
- Try to set the scene at the beginning in a powerful, unusual way if you can.
- Endings are important, too. Try to make the ending satisfying and logical.

5 If you enjoy reading and have any favourite authors, try to work out what you particularly like about their books. Study their style. What techniques do they use to help you 'picture' the story in your mind? Could you adopt any of these techniques in your own work?

Remember, regular readers usually do much better in exams than those who don't read very often.

6 Try to get into the habit of punctuating as you go along, by 'hearing' the prose in your mind.

Exam techniques

7 Where you are completing sets of notes in listening examinations you may be able to use the words exactly as you heard them, but at other times you might need to change the word order or use words and phrases of your own to complete the gaps.

In listening exams you usually hear each exercise twice. Use the second listening to check your answers for complete sense.

Exam focus

This unit has helped to prepare you for exams which test your reading, writing, listening and speaking skills. The unit has helped to develop those skills in the following ways:

- You have learnt to write a **narrative composition** based on **notes.** You have studied **narrative tenses,** and how to write **strong openings and endings.**

- You have learnt to add interest to your writing by using **relative clauses,** and **emotional and dramatic expressions.** You have practised building **paragraphs** from **notes and** writing **emails.**

- You have also practised **expressing views** in **formal reports.**

- You have **read** a variety of **complex** and **less complex texts** and answered a **range** of **comprehension** questions. You have written a **summary** based on a **text.**

- You have practised **techniques** for **consoling** and **sympathising** and for more **formal discussions.**

- You have listened to an interview and **made notes.**

Unit 9
Animals and our world

In this unit you will:

- read a text about zoos and medical experiments on animals
- write a blog post about animal experimentation
- listen to an interview about an 'electronic' zoo
- practise expressing disappointment
- focus on the following assessment objectives: R1, W1, W2, W3, L4, S1, S4

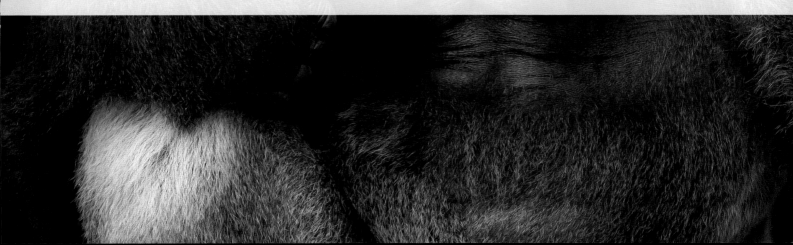

A A fresh look at zoos

1 Animal vocabulary

Working with a partner, match six of these words with the pictures. Make sure you know the meaning of all of them. Then decide whether each creature is a *mammal*, *reptile*, *fish* or *bird*.

VOCABULARY		
bear	lion	parrot
rhino	snake	camel
crocodile	elephant	salmon
lizard	penguin	dolphin
vulture	leopard	monkey
gorilla	shark	wolf
cheetah	eagle	kangaroo

2 Definitions

Choose the correct word or phrase to match these definitions. Work with a partner and consult a dictionary if necessary.

1   A person in a zoo who looks after animals is known as:

   a a carer   **c** a warder

   b a keeper   **d** a poacher.

2   The natural surroundings of an animal are called its:

   a habitat   **c** home

   b location   **d** enclosure.

3   Animals that hunt and kill other animals for food are known as:

   a scavengers   **c** predators

   b beasts   **d** prey.

4   Animals that may die out altogether are known as:

   a endangered species

   c indigenous wildlife

   b animals in captivity

   d migrating herds.

5   Animals that once lived but have now died out are known as:

   a domesticated   **c** fossils

   b extinct   **d** amphibians.

3 Pre-reading discussion

A   How do you feel about zoos? Talk to your partner about a zoo you have visited. Which aspects did you find particularly interesting?

Think about:

- the range of animals and birds
- the conditions under which they were kept
- whether they seemed contented
- the atmosphere of the zoo in general.

B   Was there anything about the zoo that you did not enjoy?

C   If you have never been to a zoo, would you like to visit one? Why?

Keep a record of your views to use later in the unit.

About   Curriculum   News   **Student articles**   Contact

Can zoos ever be animal-friendly?

The theme of our last class discussion was 'How can zoos provide animals with a decent life?' Everyone except me (I just wasn't sure) believed it was impossible for zoos to give animals the environment they need. Mr Hennessy suggested that, now the exams are over, actually visiting a modern zoo might give us a wider perspective.

I went to the zoo with an open mind and was pleasantly surprised by what I found. In our debate, many people had said that zoos are full of smelly cages containing animals with miserable, hunted-looking expressions. Metro Park Zoo, however, was set in an attractive, open environment. Trees and bushes had been planted around the enclosures. Small ponds had been dug out so the animals had access to water. In my opinion, the animals were peaceful rather than depressed.

As we entered, we were given information packs about the origins and habits of the animals. The zoo takes a lot of trouble to keep the animals' diet, living quarters and social groupings as natural as possible. Vets are on hand if they become ill.

At school, some people had accused zoos of exploiting animals for profit but at Metro Park, as I see it, nothing could be further from the truth. Most of the profits are used to improve conditions at the zoo or donated to charities for endangered species.

Before I visited Metro Park Zoo, I wasn't sure about the rights and wrongs of zoos. I couldn't deny that zoos take

By Michael Foley

the freedom of animals away. On balance, I feel that, although zoos can't provide the freedom of the wild, they can give animals a safe, secure environment where they are well-fed and protected from predators. As long as they do this well, to my mind they make a positive contribution to animal welfare. They also play an important part in educating us about wildlife. I think lots of my friends changed their minds, too.

On the bus back to school we all agreed that what we liked most was the zoo's atmosphere and we would definitely recommend it for next year's trip.

199

4 Reading an article for the school website

Hammerton High School paid a visit to a zoo. After the visit, Michael wrote about the trip for his school website. Read his article above. How does his impression of the zoo compare with your own experiences?

As you read, underline the opinion words and phrases he uses.

5 Comprehension check

1   Why did Michael's class visit the zoo?

2   What was his first impression of the zoo?

3   What did he find out from the zoo's publicity?

4   What kind of role does he think zoos have in modern society?

5   What do you think are the bad points about zoos that Michael has not mentioned?

6 Analysing the article

A   Does the first paragraph form a good opening to the article? Do you feel you want to read on? Why/Why not? How do we know that it is intended for an audience of students?

B   Paragraph 2 questions the attitudes many people have to zoos by contrasting their opinion with the reality (as Michael sees it) of Metro Park Zoo. Find the words and phrases that do this.

C Paragraphs 3 and 4 continue the theme of disagreeing with other people's opinions about zoos. Underline the phrase that expresses disagreement.

D Paragraph 5 sums up Michael's view of zoos. Which phrase tells us that he has thought about both sides of the argument before coming to a decision? Which connector is used to develop his argument and link his ideas together?

E Does the final paragraph round off the article effectively? How do we know that the writer is aware of his audience?

7 Typical opinion language

In paragraph 2, Michael introduces an opinion with *In my opinion*. What other opinion words and phrases does he use? Make a list.

What other opinion words and phrases do you know? Add them to your list.

Disagreeing with other people's views

In explaining his views, Michael thinks about and rejects the ideas other people have about zoos. Study the list and select the phrases Michael used. Can you add any phrases?

Contrary to popular belief, …
It is believed that …, yet …
People think … but …
Some people accuse them of … but nothing could be further from the truth.
Many people say that …. However, …
It's unfair for people to say that …
People make the absurd/ridiculous claim that …
Despite claims that …,

8 Making your mind up

You can show that you have considered different ideas before making up your mind by using one of the following phrases. Which do you prefer? Do you recognise the one Michael used?

Now that I have considered both sides, I feel …
After weighing up the pros and cons, I would say that …
On balance, I feel that …

There are points in favour of each argument but overall I believe …
I tend to come down on the side of …

9 Writing a paragraph

Choose one of the following topics and write a short paragraph giving your own opinions on the subject. Don't forget that you need reasons to back up your views. Use appropriate phrases from exercise 7.

Animals – better living in the wild or in the zoo?

Pets – perfect companions or dirty nuisances?

Eating meat: vital for health or unnecessary and unfair to animals?

10 Reading aloud

When you are ready, take turns reading your paragraphs aloud. This will give you a chance to get an overview of your classmates' opinions. Does hearing other students' paragraphs make a difference to your own views? If so, you may like to choose a 'making your mind up' phrase to express your feelings.

11 Expressions of contrasting meaning

In his article, Michael says that the animals in the zoo he visited were kept in 'an attractive, open environment', which was very different from the 'smelly cages' people might have expected to find animals living in.

For each of the following ideas, try to develop an expression that conveys a contrasting meaning.

Example: a bare, cramped room
a comfortably furnished, spacious room

Work in pairs or small groups, and take time to check words in a dictionary when you need to.

1   a dull lesson

2   a worn-out pair of shoes

3   a poorly child

4   a tasteless meal

5   an awkward dance

6 an untidy, neglected garden

7 ugly, illegible handwriting

8 a rusty, bent bicycle

9 a loud, aggressive person

10 a hard, lumpy bed.

When you have finished, compare your answers with the other groups. Which expressions do you think were most effective?

12 Before you listen

You are going to listen to a radio talk about the concept of an electronic zoo. Modern technology is used to show the animals in natural settings.

Write down three things you would like to find out about this type of zoo.

13 Vocabulary check

Make sure you know the meaning of these words and phrases:

> **VOCABULARY**
>
> **audio-visual**   **live exhibits**
>
> **filmed on location**   **natural history**

14 Listening for gist 🔊 CD 2, Track 11

Now listen to the radio talk. Does the speaker answer your questions about electronic zoos?

15 True/false comprehension

Decide whether the following statements about the electronic zoo are true or false.

1 Visitors to the electronic zoo will gain a greater insight into animal behaviour.

2 The large animals will be allowed to wander freely, watched by cameras.

3 The technology at the zoo will help people feel they are watching a particularly good film show.

4 95% of the world's species will be represented.

5 The pre-recorded film of live exhibits will be produced by staff at the electronic zoo itself.

6 Visitors will be disappointed if animals at the electronic zoo are asleep.

16 Post-listening discussion

A If you could choose between a visit to a 'real zoo' and an electronic zoo, which would you prefer? Try to explain your reasons.

B Do you think the electronic zoo will become popular with the public? Would it appeal more to one target group than another? Discuss your views in groups.

17 Functions 🔊 CD 2, Track 12

Have you ever been to a circus? Tell your partner what you thought of it.

Now listen to the dialogue. Silvia is expressing disappointment. Does her voice go up or down?

Malik: What did you think of the circus?

Silvia: Well, to be honest, I was just a bit disappointed.

Malik: Why was that?

Silvia: The trapeze artists weren't very exciting and I didn't like seeing large animals performing tricks.

Malik: Surely the jugglers were good fun to watch?

Silvia: As a matter of fact, they weren't as skilful as I thought they'd be.

Malik: But wasn't seeing a real live fire-eater amazing?

Silvia: To be frank, I've seen better things on television.

Malik: Sounds like a waste of money, then.

Silvia: It was! In fact, we left before the end.

Expressing disappointment

I was just a bit disappointed.

It didn't come up to my expectations.

It wasn't as interesting / enjoyable / well done / polished as I thought it would be.

I've seen better things on television.

It was a let-down.

201

Expressing disagreement informally

Surely the clowns / costumes / performances / songs were amusing/spectacular?

But wasn't a real live fire-eater / film star / pop singer / famous athlete amazing/superb/unforgettable to watch?

Wasn't it wonderful to see the real thing?

Introducing personal opinion

As a matter of fact, / In fact,

To be honest, / If you want my honest opinion,

To be frank, / Frankly,

Actually,

Commenting

It sounds like a waste of money, then.

It sounds as if it wasn't worth going to.

It sounds as if you'd have been better off at home.

18 Practice dialogues

Try to make a complete dialogue from the prompts. Make sure the person expressing disappointment sounds disappointed!

A: What / you think / electronic zoo?

B: Frank / just bit / disappointed.

A: Why / that?

B: Most exhibits / asleep / interactive video / not work.

A: Surely / sounds / elephants / African waterhole / fascinating?

B: Actually / not be / realistic / thought / it be.

A: But / not be / Magic Windows / fantastic?

B: Matter / fact / be / let-down.

A: You / be / better off / home.

B: That's right! And saved my money, too.

Try to create similar dialogues around the following situations:

- A disappointing visit to an animal sanctuary where injured animals are cared for before being returned to the wild.
- A disappointing visit to a theatre or concert to see well-known performers.
- Some other disappointing event you have personally experienced.

B Animal experimentation

1 Pre-reading discussion

Experiments on animals play a large part in medical research. Scientists say they hope to find cures for many human diseases by finding out how animals react to being given drugs or having operations.

Animals are living beings. Experimenting on them raises ethical questions. Ethical questions ask if something is right or wrong.

Ethical questions

Here are some ethical questions to discuss with your partner. Use a dictionary to check unfamiliar language.

Try to back up your answers with reasons and opinions.

1   Is it ethical to experiment on animals without painkillers or anaesthetics?

2   Is it acceptable to give a laboratory animal a human ear or heart?

3   Minor illnesses like colds and sore throats usually get better by themselves. Should animals be subjected to experiments to find cures for unimportant illnesses like these?

4   Genetic engineering can mean that laboratory animals are given genes that cause birth defects. When they reproduce, their young will be born with genetic problems. How justifiable is this?

5   Some serious illnesses are caused by overeating or smoking. Should animals suffer because of our bad habits?

6   Laboratory animals are used for non-medical experiments, too. Is it fair to use animals to test the safety of luxury products, such as perfume and aftershave?

Overall, what is your view of animal experimentation?

- *It doesn't trouble me at all.*
- *It's cruel and unjustifiable. I am totally opposed to it.*
- *It's a necessary evil – all right so long as animals are not exposed to unnecessary suffering.*

It has been said that the average pet has more stress from living with its owner than the laboratory animal ever suffers.

Do you think that's a reasonable view? Why/Why not?

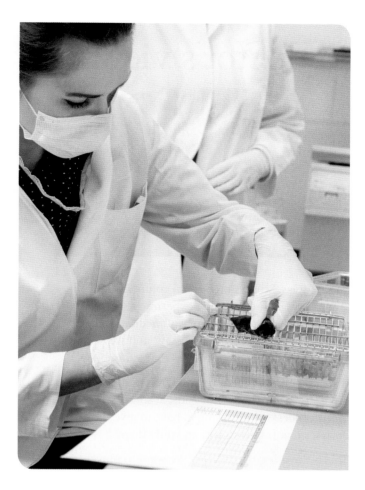

1   What does finding a cure for cystic fibrosis depend upon, according to the writer?

2   List the advances in medical understanding which have come as a result of animal research.

3   Why are particular diseases given to laboratory animals?

4   What dilemma is faced by researchers?

5   How might medical experiments on animals help animals?

5 Vocabulary

Try to match these words and phrases from the text with their definitions:

1	cornerstones (*line 26*)	A	worthwhile in terms of science
2	crucial (*line 42*)	B	reduce to the smallest amount
3	humane (*line 54*)	C	showing kindness
4	minimise (*line 61*)	D	improve
5	scientifically valid (*line 64*)	E	extremely important, vital
6	refine (*line 68*)	F	the most important elements of something

6 Post-reading discussion

The writer believes that medical experiments on animals are both humane and necessary. What do you think of this point of view? Explain your opinions to your classmates.

7 Note-making and summary

Make notes from the text about:

- the reason for carrying out medical experiments on animals
- the achievements that have come about through animal research
- the steps that are taken to make medical experimentation as humane as possible.
  (Try to find at least six points.)

Write up your notes into a connected paragraph using complete sentences. Try to use some of your own words.

2 Predicting content

You are going to read an article written by a doctor who is a campaigner for medical experiments on animals. Would you expect the opinions expressed in the article to be:

a   balanced?

b   a bit extreme?

c   undecided?

3 Vocabulary check

Make sure you understand the meanings of these phrases:

> **VOCABULARY**
>
> an *emotive* issue
> a *controversial* issue

4 Reading for detail

Read the article carefully and try to find answers to these questions. The questions reflect the opinions of the writer and not everyone would agree with them.

Laboratory animals: a doctor's view

Each year, millions of animals are used in laboratory experiments. Can their suffering be justified? Dr Mark Matfield, Director of the Research Defence Society, defends testing.

5 The use of animals for research is an emotive, controversial issue – many people oppose it on the grounds that the experiments are cruel and unnecessary.

Sixteen-year-old Laura thinks differently. Although
10 she appears healthy, she has to take 30 different drugs each day to stay alive. Every year, hundreds of children are born, like her, with cystic fibrosis. There is no cure – at least not yet.

Laura may, just may, be one of the first cystic
15 fibrosis children to be saved. A few years ago, scientists developed a new mouse – the cystic fibrosis mouse – with the same genetic defect as Laura. This made it much easier to develop new treatments. There may soon be ways of curing Laura, as long as
20 that research, using those animals, continues.

There are plenty of emotional arguments, both for and against animal testing, but let's start with the most obvious facts. If you examine the history of medicine, you find that experiments on animals
25 have been an important part of almost every major medical advance. Many cornerstones of medical science – the discovery that blood circulates through our veins, understanding the way lungs work, the discovery of vitamins and hormones – were made
30 this way.

Most of the main advances in medicine itself also depended on animal experiments. In 1988 there were an estimated 350 000 cases of polio in the world, causing paralysis or death but, thanks to the polio
35 vaccine, the disease has been eradicated in most countries. Modern surgery would be impossible without today's anaesthetics. The list goes on: organ transplants, heart surgery, hip replacements, drugs for cancer and asthma – animals played an
40 important part in these medical advances.

Animal experimentation wasn't the only type of research crucial to the medical advances that save human lives. Studies on human volunteers were also essential, and test-tube experiments were vital in many cases. But the history of medicine tells us 45 that animal experiments are essential if we want to tackle the diseases and illnesses that afflict people.

If we are going to carry out research into serious diseases, such as cancer or Aids, at some point in the process we are going to have to give those 50 diseases to animals so we can study them.

This is the dilemma we face. We want to prevent suffering. The crucial issue is how we use animals in research. Modern science has developed humane experimental techniques. It is possible to do animal 55 experiments using methods that the animals don't even notice. The worst these animals have to put up with is living in a cage with regular food and water, with animal handlers and vets looking after them.

The golden rule of laboratory animal welfare is to 60 minimise any distress involved using the principle of the three Rs. First you *reduce* the number of animals used in each experiment to the minimum that will give a scientifically valid result. Then, whenever possible, you *replace* animal experiments 65 with alternatives – experiments that don't use animals but will give equally valid results. Finally, you *refine* the animal experiments that you do, so they cause the least possible harm to the animals. If an experiment involves surgery on the animal, 70 give it an anaesthetic. When it comes round, give it pain killers and antibiotics to prevent infection.

The principle of the three Rs has been the basis for animal experimentation in many countries for the

75 past ten years or more. It has been written into the law and is enforced by strict codes of practice, government guidelines and inspections. As a result, the number of animal experiments in the UK was reduced from more than 5.2 million in 1978 to 2.7 million in 2002.

80 People who experiment on animals are just the same as the rest of us – they know it's wrong to cause suffering if it can be avoided. But just because we like animals, we can't avoid the difficult decisions that have to be made in medicine and science. Sometimes, however, those decisions 85 actually benefit animals. Distemper used to kill 500 000 puppies every year. Scientists believed they could find a vaccine but to succeed they would have to experiment on several hundred dogs, killing almost all of them. Not an easy decision. It took 90 years to produce a vaccine that worked but now, every single year, 500 000 dogs are saved as a result.

8 How the writer achieves his effects

A   The writer achieves a calm, objective-sounding tone and style. How do you think he achieves this? Write down your ideas.

Compare your ideas in your groups.

B   The following list shows techniques the writer uses to help him achieve the impression of being fair. How do the points compare with your list?

One of these points is incorrect. Try to find it and cross it out.

- He says the animals are well cared for.
- He uses a lot of statistics.
- He gives a lot of facts.
- He says researchers care about animals.
- He makes us laugh at people who campaign against animal experiments.
- He seems to try to understand the point-of-view of his opponents.

Try to find examples of these points in the text and circle them.

Compare your findings with the other groups. Is there anything you disagree about?

9 Finding the right angle

The writer suggests that the real issue is not whether you should be for or against animal experiments but HOW animal research can be as kind as possible to animals, so as to minimise any suffering to them. This is an important change in the angle of the usual argument. Why?

10 Understanding bias in an argument

A   Not everyone would say that the writer is completely fair or unbiased. What points against animal experiments did the writer, as you see it, choose not to include? Write down some ideas.

B   Study these opinions, which view animal experiments from a different perspective. Make sure you understand each one. Compare them with your own ideas and select any points that appeared on your list. Are there any ideas that you did not note but which you think are important points to consider? Select them too.

1   *'Animals are physically different from people so they react differently to drugs and medical experiments. You can't always extrapolate* from animals to people. As a result, many animal experiments are a waste of time.'*

2   *'Many members of the public think of medical research scientists as torturers and murderers.'*

3   *'Not all laboratories are wonderful. An American laboratory was taken to court recently for its disgraceful treatment of animals.'*

4   *'It's difficult for the public to see behind the closed doors of a laboratory. So scientists have a lot of freedom in the way they work and what they say they do.'*

5   *'Great improvements in health and life expectancy have come since the development of clean water systems and sanitation. This had nothing to do with laboratory animals.'*

6 *'Health education has helped people avoid disease. People have learnt about a good diet, not smoking, being hygienic and taking exercise. We don't need to experiment on animals.'*

7 *'Research studies using human volunteers have been responsible for major advances in medical understanding. For example, the link between cancer and smoking came from studying people's behaviour and their reactions.'*

8 *'Advanced technology, such as lasers and ultrasound, is improving our understanding of the causes of disease. We could make more use of advanced technology and less use of living creatures in research.'*

*extrapolate = to make predictions based on what you know

11 Writing an article for the school blog

'Is animal experimentation really worth it?'

Your class has been discussing the rights and wrongs of animal experimentation. You feel that medical experiments on animals are useful and necessary but it is important to consider alternative techniques, too.

Write an article to post on your school blog explaining:

- how animal experimentation has contributed to medical understanding
- why animal experiments do not always give useful results
- the alternatives to medical experiments on animals.

The angle of the argument

Get the angle clear. You are not writing a composition that is totally against animal experimentation, because you accept the need for it. Your aim is to show that medical experiments on animals, while sometimes helpful, do not always produce useful results. You want to explain how our health can be improved using alternative methods.

Planning the content

What points do you want to include? Can you give any explanations or examples to develop your points? How can you relate your content to the interests of the readers of the newsletter?

Structure and language

Use a strong opening for your article: get the reader's attention and keep it. Finish the article with a paragraph that leaves your reader in no doubt about what you really believe.

Structure your composition so the argument you are presenting is clear and easy to follow. Using opinion language and linking words will help you do this. Some of the expressions in exercise 7 will be helpful.

12 Prepositions after verbs

There are many examples of prepositions following verbs in the article about animal experiments.

Examples:

Hundreds of children are *born with* cystic fibrosis.

Let's *start with* the most obvious facts.

Blood *circulates through* our veins.

You *replace* animal experiments *with* alternatives.

People who *experiment on* animals are just the same as the rest of us.

Practice

Try to fill the gaps in the following sentences. Choose from these prepositions.

about   at   from   of   on   to   with

1 Is it right to experiment _____ animals?

2 Why bother _____ animal suffering when children are dying _____ incurable diseases?

3 I am surprised _____ you.

4 I object _____ all this animal rights propaganda.

5 Alan decided to contribute _____ an animal charity.

6 I won't quarrel _____ them.

7 Elephants depend _____ their keepers.

8 He died _____ a broken heart, so they say.

9 Can you provide him _____ an information pack?

10 Baby rhinos respond well _____ human contact.

What other verbs do you know followed by these prepositions? Discuss with a partner and try to make a list.

13 Spelling and pronunciation: Regular plurals 🔊 CD 2, Track 13

Most regular plurals in English simply add **-s**.

Look at this list of regular plurals. Check the meaning of each word and write a translation if necessary.

1	cats	9	horses
2	hens	10	goats
3	insects	11	birds
4	cages	12	cows
5	wasps	13	houses
6	dogs	14	monkeys
7	spiders	15	bees
8	faces	16	roses

The **-s** at the end of the noun plural can be pronounced /s/ or /z/ or /ɪz/. Listen to the list of words and write each word in the correct box, according to the sound of its ending.

```
/s/
cats



```

```
/z/
hens



```

```
/ɪz/
faces



```

Now say the words aloud to your partner. Does he/she agree the sound of each ending is clear?

14 Spelling and pronunciation: Irregular plurals

The following rules show how irregular plurals are formed. Say the examples aloud clearly, checking your pronunciation with a partner.

1 Nouns which end in -ch, -s, -sh, -ss or -x add **-es** to form the plural. The -es ending is pronounced /ɪz/.

   Examples: bench ~ benches   bus ~ buses
   rash ~ rashes   pass ~ passes   box ~ boxes

2 Nouns ending in -f or -fe replace the ending with **-ves** to form the plural. The -s is pronounced /z/.

   Examples: calf ~ calves   leaf ~ leaves   wife ~ wives

3 Some nouns form the plural simply by changing the vowel. The pronunciation changes, too.

   Examples: goose ~ geese   mouse ~ mice
   tooth ~ teeth   man ~ men

4 Nouns which end in -o usually form the plural by adding **-es**, which is pronounced /z/.

   Example: tomato ~ tomatoes

   Common exceptions: photos   pianos   rhinos

5 Nouns ending in a consonant and -y form the plural by changing the -y to **-ies**. The -s is pronounced /z/.

   Examples: fly ~ flies   lady ~ ladies

   Nouns ending in a vowel and -y just add **-s**, which is pronounced /z/.

   Example: donkey ~ donkeys

6 Some nouns are always plural.

   Examples: trousers   scissors   spectacles

7 Some nouns are the same in the singular and the plural.

   Examples: sheep   deer   fish   salmon   bison

15 Vocabulary

Work with a partner to fill the gaps with the plural forms of the nouns in brackets. Make sure you understand the meaning of each sentence. Check your pronunciation, too!

1 The _____ have just given birth to several _____ . (*sheep, lamb*)

2 Watch out for _____ , _____ and _____ if you go camping in the wild. (*bear, wolf, wildcat*)

3 If you're lucky you'll be able to see _____ , _____ and _____ in the park. (*deer, goose, fox*)

4 A pet mouse needs a friend. The problem is you might soon have lots of baby _____ . (*mouse*)

5 _____ and _____ have the most amazing _____ . (*crocodile, rhino, tooth*)

6 Tropical _____ need special care but make interesting pets. (*fish*)

7 It's strange to think that ugly _____ can turn into lovely _____ . (*caterpillar, butterfly*)

16 Look, say, cover, write, check

Are you confident you know the meaning of these words? You have already met some in the unit; you will come across others in later exercises.

Check any meanings you are unsure of in a dictionary. Then use the 'look, say, cover, write, check' method to memorise the words.

Finally, why not ask your partner to test you?

VOCABULARY	
potato	anaesthetic
potatoes	elephant
clothes	leopard
calf	laboratory
calves	innocent
leaf	benefit
leaves	terrible
vaccine	veterinary
scissors	rhino

C Animals in sport and entertainment

1 Discussion

A Horse racing, camel racing and dog racing are popular sports for many people. In addition, circuses that use performing animals draw large crowds. Do you feel it's fair to animals to involve them in human leisure activities in this way?

B How are animals used for sport or entertainment in your country?

C Sports in which animals are hunted are called *field sports*. Are these sports popular in your country? Have you ever seen or taken part in this form of sport? How did you feel about it?

2 People's opinions

Here are some reasons why people say they like animals to be involved in human activities. Discuss them with your partner and give them a ✓ or ✗, depending on whether they reflect your own views.

'I admire the skills and bravery of performers at the circus who ride on horses or control wild animals.'

'What I find so impressive about bullfighting is the total concentration needed by the matador – without it he'd be dead or injured.'

'Shooting birds demands a steady aim and perfect hand-eye coordination. What makes me cross is people who criticise me for shooting but think nothing of eating meat.'

'What I love about horse racing is the thrilling atmosphere as the horses approach the finishing line.'

3 Letter completion: My views on animal charities

The following text is a letter written by a student to a newspaper giving the reasons why she is against giving money to an animal charity. The blanks need to be filled with words and phrases that link her ideas and show her opinions and attitudes.

Working in pairs or groups of three, choose the most appropriate suggestions from the ones given. Then compare your answers to those of other groups.

Dear Editor,

I read in your newspaper that there are plans to give a large amount of money raised through our town's annual charity appeal to the Green Pastures Horses' Home. The home is a place where racehorses can live in comfort when they retire from racing. I am writing to say that (1) _____ this is a very (2) _____ idea.

I am not against spending on animal welfare, but what makes me really angry is the thought of money being spent on giving animals a happy retirement when many old people in our country are neglected and live in poverty.

It is (3) _____ that racehorses have provided people with sport and entertainment, (4) _____ I can't see how this justifies spending so much on them. After all, they are only animals and humans should come first.

People (5) _____ that animal cruelty is wrong, (6) _____ they ignore the cruel treatment the elderly receive. I think money raised through charity should benefit human beings. The care of aged animals is the responsibility of those who own them, and it is (7) _____ to expect us to support them. (8) _____, people who own racehorses are rich and have the resources to fund a good retirement for their animals. Wouldn't it be more sensible for the owners to save a percentage of the big profits they have made (9) _____ use that for their animals' welfare in old age?

Our senior citizens have worked hard in their lives. People say their pensions* are adequate but (10) _____. In fact, many old people have hardly enough money for food and bills, let alone luxuries such as horseracing.

At my school, I am starting a campaign to increase young people's awareness of the purpose of charity fundraising. I know we will not be in time to stop the funds going to the horses' home this year. (11) _____, we shall do all we can to ensure charitable funds are not wasted on useless projects in future.

Yours faithfully,
Bella Balkano

*pensions = money paid to elderly people who have retired from work

1	**a** for instance	**b** naturally	**c** I think
2	**a** unhealthy	**b** cruel	**c** foolish
3	**a** argued	**b** denied	**c** appealed
4	**a** definitely	**b** but	**c** of course
5	**a** shout	**b** demand	**c** insist
6	**a** on balance	**b** in other words	**c** yet
7	**a** unfair	**b** confusing	**c** depressing
8	**a** It's all very well	**b** As I see it	**c** Nevertheless
9	**a** also	**b** and	**c** as well
10	**a** nothing could be further from the truth	**b** on the contrary	**c** nonsense
11	**a** Despite	**b** In addition	**c** Nevertheless

When you have filled the gaps correctly, re-read the letter to get a sense of the flow of the argument.

Do you agree that the opening gets straight to the point? What do you think of the end of the letter?

209

4 Vocabulary: Words for feelings

Bella expresses her feelings and attitudes in a forceful, impassioned way. The following exercise shows how adjectives of similar meaning can be used to describe feelings and attitudes. Can you complete each group of synonyms with an appropriate word chosen from the box?

1 I am disgusted / _____ by your actions.

2 He is worried / _____ about the lack of clean water for the farm animals.

3 It is wrong / _____ to use animals in medical experiments.

4 He is sorry / _____ about the trouble he has caused.

5 It is ridiculous / _____ to say animal are as important as people.

6 I feel distressed / _____ when I hear about children being unable to get proper medical care.

VOCABULARY	
absurd	uneasy
horrified	apologetic
saddened	immoral

5 Language study: Adding emphasis

What ... clauses

We can use a clause beginning with *what* to sound more emphatic. For example, Bella says:

What makes me really angry is the thought of money being spent on giving animals a happy retirement.

This is another way of saying:

The thought of money being spent on giving animals a happy retirement makes me really angry.

Restructuring the sentence, using *what*, makes Bella sound more emphatic.

Contrast the structure of these pairs of sentences. Which one is more emphatic? Why? How has the structure been changed to achieve this?

She loves the idea that the safari park will provide jobs for people.

***What** she loves is the idea that the safari park will provide jobs for people.*

We doubted that the water was clean enough to drink.

***What** we doubted was that the water was clean enough to drink.*

I respect organisations that campaign to raise awareness of animal welfare.

***What** I respect are campaigns that raise awareness of animal welfare.*

The person who ... , the place where ...

Consider these two similar constructions for adding emphasis.

The keeper understands the animals best.

***The person who** understands the animals best is the keeper.*

Polar bears thrive best in their natural habitat.

***The place where** polar bears thrive best is (in) their natural habitat.*

So + adjective

Consider the use of *so* before an adjective:

Their attitudes were caring.

*Their attitudes were **so** caring.*

He was thoughtful.

*He was **so** thoughtful.*

Do + main verb

Consider the use of *do* before a main verb. Are any other changes necessary?

I like your project work.

*I **do** like your project work.*

We're late. Hurry up!

*We're late. **Do** hurry up!*

Take a seat.

***Do** take a seat.*

He enjoys his work with orphaned elephants.

*He **does** enjoy his work with orphaned elephants.*

Look back at the comments in exercise 2 and underline any examples of emphatic forms. Why are they effective in that context?

6 Practice

Rewrite these sentences beginning with the words in brackets, to make them more emphatic:

1   She admires attempts to reduce human suffering. (*What ...*)

2   We need better fences to stop animals wandering onto the road. (*What ...*)

3   The safari park wardens worry about animals escaping. (*What ...*)

4   You can see owls, eagles and hawks in a falconry centre. (*The place where ...*)

5   We didn't understand that animals have adapted to live in certain habitats. (*What ...*)

6   I didn't realise how people depend on each other. (*What ...*)

7 Hunters are responsible for the reduction in rhino numbers. (*The people who ...*)

8 The golden eagle prefers to nest in treeless, mountainous country. (*The place where ...*)

9 Endangered species in our own country ought to concern us. (*What ...*)

10 I want the right to object to things I think are wrong. (*What ...*)

7 More practice

Add *so* or *do* to these sentences for greater emphasis. Make any changes to the sentences that you need to.

1 *Having a purpose in life has made her happy.*

2 We all shouted, 'Tell us more about your adventures.'

3 Take lots of photos when you visit the wildlife park.

4 I never realised that baby rhinos were affectionate.

5 Raising funds for charity is worthwhile.

6 Your granny enjoys her garden, doesn't she?

7 You look tired today.

8 Thirsty animals are miserable.

9 Gordon felt sorry for the animals he saw at the circus.

10 I worry about you, you know.

11 Turn off the tap properly when you have finished washing.

12 Come in, Sophie. I'm pleased to see you.

8 Comparing languages

How do you add emphasis in your own language? Share words or structures you use with your group.

9 Writing sentences

Make up some sentences of your own using emphatic forms.

D Animals at work

1 Thinking about working animals

A In what ways do animals 'work' in your country? For example:

☐ on farms producing milk

☐ being raised for meat

☐ being raised to provide skins, leather and wool

☐ as guard dogs, customs dogs or police dogs

☐ as rescue dogs

211

☐ being used for transport

☐ as blind dogs or hearing dogs.

Are animals used for work in any other ways?

B People who keep animals have a responsibility to feed them. What other responsibilities do they have?

2 Discussing ethical issues

A Generally speaking, do you feel working animals in your country have a decent life? Try to explain your opinions to your friends.

B People who are cruel to their animals may be prevented by law from keeping them. This might mean the loss of a business or family income. Do you think this is right? Why/Why not?

3 Building an email from prompts

Using the following prompts, try to build up a complete email to the editor of a national newspaper.

New Message

To : _____ From : _____

Why it is wrong to accuse farmers of cruelty

Dear Sir,

I write / response / recent articles / say / people / keep / animals for profit / be 'cruel and heartless'. My family make / living from / keep / sheep. In my view / our life / be harder / the animals'!

In lambing time / example / there be / no day off / no rest. My father get up / as soon as it / be light / and hurry out / to first task / of day / without even bothering / to have / drink. He work / for several hours / without break. He check / lambs that / be born / in night / or attend / ewes that have difficulty / give birth. He bring / poorly lambs indoors / be bottle-fed.

He try / get round the flock / four or five times / day / often in snow / cruel winds. If there be / specific problem / he have to / go out several times / night / with flashlight. Although / expensive / vet / always call / when he be / needed.

It be / true that every ewe or lamb that / die / be a financial loss / us / so it be / in own interest / care for / sheep. Sheep / eventually be sold / at market. How / we can live / any other way? But we be / certainly not / 'ruthless exploiters' / of your article. In fact, nothing be / further from truth.

Yours faithfully,
Orla O'Connor

4 Assessing the argument

When you have written the complete email, re-read it to get a better sense of the argument. Has Orla convinced you that her family provides a high standard of care for animals?

5 The closing paragraph

Study the closing paragraph carefully. Closing paragraphs should bring an argument to a conclusion. The language you use to end the email or letter depends on what you said before.

Do you think Orla's final paragraph is effective?

6 Vocabulary: Young animals

Humans have children; sheep have lambs. Choose a word from the box to match with each animal/bird. You will need to use some words more than once.

VOCABULARY

calf	foal	pup/puppy
kitten	kid	cygnet
cub	chick/chicken	duckling

1	bear	7	goat
2	duck	8	horse
3	hen	9	elephant
4	cow	10	whale
5	cat	11	swan
6	dog	12	lion

7 Comparing languages

Does your language have special words for young animals? Discuss the words or expressions you use.

8 Vocabulary: Collective nouns

Decide which of the words in the box can follow these collective nouns. Sometimes more than one answer is possible.

VOCABULARY

bees	elephants	ants
dogs	wolves	goats
fish	sheep	deer
cows	locusts	

1 A herd of _____
2 A flock of _____
3 A shoal of _____
4 A pack of _____
5 A swarm of _____

9 Discussion: Intensive farming

Consider these issues related to food production:

Many farmers use modern technology to rear their animals intensively. Some kinds of animals and birds (calves and hens, for example) can be reared inside, in very small spaces. Feeding can be controlled very carefully. Some animals are given hormones to increase their growth. This is sometimes called 'factory farming'.

Pesticides are widely used by farmers to keep crops free of disease.

Why people object

Some people object to modern farming methods because they think they are cruel to animals. Also, they are increasingly worried about the effect of hormones and pesticides in the food chain.

Because intensive farming relies on machines, not people, this has resulted in fewer jobs for agricultural workers.

What the farmers think

Farmers using intensive systems argue that they are an efficient method of producing food cheaply.

Some farmers are reluctant to change to 'organic' farming because they have invested a lot in new technology. Also, they feel organic methods will be less reliable, will involve higher costs, and might lead to higher food prices for the consumer.

In some countries, farmers receive a subsidy (money from the government) for using intensive methods.

What are your views? How do you think food should be produced? Work in groups and note down your ideas.

10 Punctuation

The following letter was written to a farming magazine. When you feel you have understood it, rewrite it with punctuation and paragraphs.

Remember to use a comma after an introductory linking word or phrase such as *Nevertheless, …, In fact, …, Despite claims to the contrary, …*.

Fair methods of food production

Dear sir like many of your readers i want to buy healthy food which is produced in a way which is fair to farm workers and animals furthermore i don't believe food production should damage the environment many farmers in our area say that it is cheaper to rear animals under intensive conditions than it is to give them a decent life however if farmers were given subsidies they would be able to afford more space and comfort for animals farmers get subsidies for intensive methods so why not pay them for a kinder approach similarly many of the farms around here use harmful pesticides which can get into the food chain farmers say it is less expensive to use pesticides than to use more natural or 'organic' methods that require a bigger labour force and so would be more expensive what is more expensive in the end subsidies to the farmers for organic farming or a damaged environment in my view we have a right to know what is in our food tins packets and fresh food should be labelled by food companies as free-range* or factory farmed or if pesticides were used so that we know exactly what we are eating i realise my ideas might lead to higher food prices but i have no doubt at all it would be worth it

Yours faithfully
Shahar Rishani

*free-range = eggs and meat come from animals which live in natural conditions

11 Checking the text flow

When you have punctuated the letter correctly, read it through to get a sense of the way the text flows. Is the letter clear? Does it begin and end well?

12 Further thoughts

How far do you agree with Shahar's view that it's worth paying more for food that is produced ethically?

In what ways do you think intensive methods of food production could be unfair to farm workers? Try to give some specific examples.

Here are some helpful expressions similar to those you have seen earlier in the unit:

Shahar says …. and in my view

Shahar thinks … but …

Now that I have considered Shahar's opinions, I feel …

After weighing up the pros and cons of paying more for food, I would say that …

13 Rhetorical questions

A rhetorical question is a question to which you do not expect an answer. It's a device to get more attention for your opinions when presenting an argument.

Study the following rhetorical questions. What is the opinion of each speaker?

1 'Don't you think it's about time people showed more sympathy to farmers?'

2 'Who can honestly say they would enjoy eating a battery hen?'

3 'Which is worse: to pay a little bit more for food produced ethically or to make animals suffer terribly in factory farm conditions just so we can get cheaper prices in the supermarket?'

4 'Wouldn't we all be happier knowing our food was ethically produced?'

5 'Do we really need all this food from thousands of miles away?'

6 'Who can worry about animals when little children are starving?'

7 'The theory is that pets are safe and happy with their owners, but is it the whole truth?'

8 'How can you put a price on a child's life?'

14 Turning statements into rhetorical questions

Try to rewrite these statements in the form of rhetorical questions:

1 A vegetarian meal is not always healthy.
Is _____?

2 No one can say the farmers are wrong.
Who _____?

3 We can save an animal or save someone's life.
Which is _____?

4 No one knows the extent of the problem.
Who _____?

5 I think we would all be happier knowing that our food was free of chemicals.
Wouldn't _____?

6   I think it's about time we remembered endangered species at home.

Isn't _____?

7   I think we should consider farm workers before worrying about animals.

Shouldn't _____?

Look back at the email in exercise 3 and the letter in 10 and underline the examples of rhetorical questions.

You may like to use the rhetorical question device in your own arguments. One or two are usually enough.

E   Helping animals in danger

1   Discussion: Could you help animals?

Many species are being endangered by human activity. Hunting, overfishing and poaching, for example, reduce animal numbers. In addition, forests are cut down for agricultural or commercial purposes and wildlife loses its habitat as a result. Similarly, when cities expand, new roads and buildings mean wild animals and birds lose their homes and sources of food.

Do you know of any examples in your own country of wildlife being affected in this way?

Which endangered species in the world do you know about? Which do you care most about? How could you help endangered species in your own country or overseas? Write down your ideas.

The chart below shows the approximate numbers of selected big cats still in existence in the wild. Which three species on the chart are the most endangered?

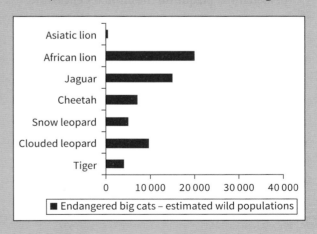

Endangered big cats – estimated wild populations

2   Reading for gist

Skim-read the following leaflet which gives information about two ways of helping to protect endangered animals. A lot of the vocabulary should be familiar from previous exercises. Try to work out the meaning of unfamiliar words from the context.

Wild action appeal

The adoption scheme

Woodland Zoo, as well as being a very special place to visit, plays an important part in protecting endangered species. The Zoo is often the last breeding ground for these animals. We have 160 different species of animals, birds and reptiles, many of which are endangered in the wild. We need your support to help these animals win their battle against possible extinction with breeding programmes funded by the adoption scheme.

Most animals in the zoo are available for adoption. Many individuals and families, as well as groups, take great pleasure in adopting their favourite animal. Companies, too, can benefit from the scheme. Our website has thousands of weekly visitors, so it is a worthwhile and cost-effective form of advertising.

What adopters receive

All adopters will receive an adoption certificate and regular copies of 'Zoo Update', the Zoo's exciting newsletter. For a donation of $50 you will receive four free entry tickets; for a donation of $100 or more you will receive eight free entry tickets and a personalised plaque on the animal's enclosure.

Our **Wild Action** appeal was launched in 2016 to support work with endangered species in their threatened natural habitats. Donations to the appeal will go directly towards the following conservation projects:

Rainforest Action Costa Rica

Costa Rica's tropical forests contain a wealth of wildlife – 200 species of mammals, 850 species of birds, 220 species of reptiles and 160 species of amphibians. All these are at risk, including the

jaguar, ocelot, margay and jaguarundi. **Rainforest Action Costa Rica** is securing an area of rainforest that is intended to stretch throughout Central America, providing a sanctuary for indigenous wildlife. Just $30 will save half an acre of Costa Rican rainforest.

The Tiger Trust

The Tiger Trust is creating two natural habitat sanctuaries in Thailand for the Indo-Chinese tiger, which is facing the threat of extinction. Tiger Mountains I and II provide a near-natural existence for tigers orphaned by poaching.

Only around 3000 tigers remain in the wild and hundreds are being trapped and shot by poachers for an appalling trade in tiger bones and body parts. A donation of $40 will go towards looking after Sheba, a two-year-old Indo-Chinese tiger, who was found next to the body of her mother. She now lives with other rescued tigers on Tiger Mountain II in Thailand. You will receive a colour photo of Sheba and a tiger T-shirt.

3 Reading comprehension

Now answer these questions:

1 Which animals are available for adoption?

2 How does the zoo use the adoption money it raises?

3 What does a $50 donation to the adoption scheme give you?

4 What is the aim of Rainforest Action Costa Rica?

5 Where are Tiger Mountains I and II, and what is special about them?

4 Writing a report for the headteacher from notes

Each year, Ken's school raises funds for charity. This year, the headteacher is considering using the funds raised to adopt a zoo animal. Ken is a student organiser of the wildlife club and the headteacher has asked him to write a report saying whether adopting a zoo animal is the best way for the school to help wildlife.

Try to rewrite Ken's rough draft of main points in the form of a finished report.

Points in favour of using our funds to adopt a zoo animal

- Queen's Zoo is our local zoo – has an adoption scheme
- opportunity to adopt from a wide range of animals
- get plaque at the zoo with the school's name on it
- get discounts on zoo entrance tickets
- gift shop – discounts
- invitations to special events (e.g. see newborn animals)
- zoo uses our money to support breeding programmes for endangered species – returned to wild when ready.

Points against

Adopting a zoo animal means we cannot help other conservation projects:

- destruction of the rainforest – projects create a safe haven for wildfe
- projects to care for animals threatened by poaching / poachers / kill / sell skins / organs / bones / for commercial products. (e.g. tiger sanctuaries in Thailand.)

Conclusion

Wildlife club – special meeting. Result: in favour of adopting a zoo animal, possibly a tiger or a tamarin monkey. Younger children love seeing/learning about a real live wild animal. Older students – more information science projects / benefit those wanting careers in science /with animals. Breeding in captivity scheme – long term benefits.

Structure

Structure the report into paragraphs. Use strong opening and final paragraphs. Use clauses to make sentences more complex.

Link ideas with linking words and expressions.

Tone and Register

Your report is for the headteacher. It should sound calm and fair. You should use opinion language to introduce your views, but be careful to provide clear evidence for your opinions.

Content

Ken makes several very interesting points. Try to provide a few details, facts, statistics and examples. Look back at previous exercises for information if you need to.

Making the report suitable for the audience

The headteacher is the audience for this report, so try to link the report to the headteacher's concerns and priorities. If money is to be given to a zoo, she will want it to be worthwhile for the animals and educational for the students. It should be of interest to everyone, not just a few students. How might adopting a zoo animal educate younger pupils about endangered species? Why might a zoo visit be better for younger students than reading about a conservation project or watching a wildlife film?

Making the report sound like it comes from the organiser of the Wildlife club

Ken is the Wildlife club organiser, so think about how you can link his comments to his role at the club. Would he discuss the idea and report their views?

Proofreading

Proofread your work for punctuation and spelling errors.

Feedback

When you feel you have produced a reasonable draft, show your work to a friend and listen carefully to his/her comments. Would you like to add anything or change anything?

217

5 Improving paragraphing and punctuation in a report for the headteacher

Put the capital letters and full stops into this report for the headteacher about a school trip to meet a wildlife expert. Finally decide where the paragraphs should go.

mr bavsar's talk about his work in southern india was so inspirational mr bavsar explained why he started his special project, the elephant information service one night a child woke up to see a small
5 elephant calf standing by his bed somehow, the elephant had got into the house and gone into the bedroom without disturbing the boy's parents the elephant made a strange noise and then turned around and left the way he had come, without
10 causing trouble as chief wildlife officer, mr bavsar was asked to investigate the incident when he visited the family, they said they were not worried but they were shocked they said that if they had known wild elephants were so near, they would
15 have been better prepared for potentially dangerous situations this made mr bavsar realise that animal and humans could co-exist peacefully, as long as they took sensible precautions to avoid conflict mr bavsar set up the elephant information service and
20 now there are early warning systems in the area the service alerts families when animals are nearby by sending texts, flashing warning lights and making phone calls the whole class loved mr bavsar's talk he was so knowledgeable and showed us his
25 personal photo collection of the rare and beautiful animals he has cared for including elephants, these sadly, are often orphaned when their parents are killed by hunters and have to be cared for in an elephant sanctuary before being returned to the
30 wild mr bavsar even brought in a large toy elephant, a blanket, and feeding bottle and encouraged the little children to practise the right way of feeding a baby elephant who has lost its mother as a result they understood as much as the older ones about
35 the needs of infant elephants overall, we felt extremely lucky that we had been given the chance to meet a true wildlife pioneer and we all learnt so much i would certainly recommend it for next year's group, if the opportunity is still available

GRAMMAR SPOTLIGHT

The past perfect passive

The passive form of the past perfect is used to describe something that was completed in an earlier past, when the action is more important than who or what did it:

Trees and bushes had been planted around the enclosures **(section A4, paragraph 2).**

(We do not need to know who had planted the trees and bushes.)

Underline another example of the past perfect passive in the same paragraph of **section A4**.

The past perfect passive is formed with *had* + *been* + **past participle**.

The negative is *had not been* (or *hadn't been* in informal English):

*In spite of the methods the farmers had introduced, the wolves **had not been driven** away.*

Write the following sentences out in full:

a   *If the Siberian tiger cub not / be / find in time, it would have died in the snow outside its den.*

b   *The tiger cub's tail be / badly / damage by severe frost.*

c   *A leg / be / bit / badly.*

d   *The wildlife officials who found the cub said they / be / shock by the cub's condition. 'We believe the poor little thing be / attack by a predator and the severe temperatures made everything worse.'*

e   *After a year, the tiger cub had made a full recovery and be / return **to the wild.***

Exam-style questions

Reading

Reading & Writing, Exercise 2

You are going to read a magazine article about four people who are interested in wild birds. For questions a–j, choose from the people A–D. The people may be chosen more than once.

Extended [10 marks]

Which person:

a has the most knowledge about birds?

- Person A
- Person B
- Person C
- Person D

b enjoys sharing their knowledge with other people?

- Person A
- Person B
- Person C
- Person D

c explains how their interest in birds began?

- Person A
- Person B
- Person C
- Person D

d describes the personal benefit they get from being outside in nature?

- Person A
- Person B
- Person C
- Person D

e seems to have the closest relationship with birds?

- Person A
- Person B
- Person C
- Person D

f expresses the most appreciation of common birds?

- Person A
- Person B
- Person C
- Person D

g is trying to improve their knowledge of bird song?

- Person A
- Person B
- Person C
- Person D

h does the hardest physical work to help birds?

- Person A
- Person B
- Person C
- Person D

i seems to be interested in birds only sometimes?

- Person A
- Person B
- Person C
- Person D

j mentions the equipment they use for watching birds?

- Person A
- Person B
- Person C
- Person D

A Yasmin

My fascination with birds began when my uncle, who is passionate about nature, came to stay and told me the names of the birds in our garden. He then sent me a bird book with beautiful illustrations. It's full of information about the habits of birds – like what they eat, which birds live here all year round and which ones only visit in the summer. I now love putting food out for birds, and, when I get up in the morning, I'm thrilled to see them waiting for me to give them breakfast! They are almost like members of my family. Of course, I never forget they are wild and can choose whether they want to visit me and how long they'll stay. I'm proud to say I can recognise some of their different songs and I've discovered a fun website with recordings of bird song. But what I like best is just watching the birds being themselves. Their comings and goings are so fascinating that technical facts about them seem less important.

B Ricky

I've always loved wild birds, and nature in general, and I'm lucky enough to live near a bird reserve. I started working there as a volunteer two years ago. You don't need to be a bird expert, but the volunteers are keen birdwatchers like me and want to keep learning. I take a special pride in doing conservation work, and I enjoy cutting back overgrown vegetation or repairing the reserve's paths. There are several large hides – wooden shelters with benches where visitors can sit and watch birds through big windows. It allows them to be near the birds without disturbing them. Another part of my work is welcoming visitors to the Information Centre and telling them about the reserve and what they should look out for. I think I enjoy this the most, especially when school groups come. They're so observant and I love seeing the students' faces light up when they see an unusual bird. There is also a café, so you can have fun watching birds on the webcam and enjoy a coffee at the same time!

C Eleanor

I've enjoyed watching birds for as long as I can remember. But since I started studying biology and zoology at university, I have become fascinated by the scientific study of bird behaviour. I've also been incredibly fortunate to have visited Borneo, Rwanda and the Galapagos Islands, to observe birds in their natural habitat. In the future, I'd love to do research into bird migration. It will be hard work but it is so worthwhile. It is extraordinary that migrating birds, like swallows, for example, can travel thousands of kilometres across continents or oceans in order to return to exactly the same place where they reared their young the year before. Experts still don't really understand how they do it. Of course, some birds don't migrate at all – they stay in one place all the year round. Perhaps that's why I find the birds we can see in our neighbourhood all the time a bit less intriguing, even though they're still lovely in their own way.

D Pablo

I love walking in the woods near my home. It's so peaceful among the trees, away from all the hustle and bustle of family life. Walking alone clears my head and I get solutions to problems while I'm just going along on my own. Sometimes, I practise my English out loud, where nobody can hear me! If I am in the right mood, I like to watch the birds that I see in the woods. My father's binoculars are very useful for this – when I remember to take them with me! The early spring, before the trees have all their leaves, is the best time to see birds as they are very active then, choosing their territories and singing to attract a mate. Woodland birds are cute but hard to spot, as they keep moving around. I am captivated when I hear a bird sing, but I never know what kind of bird it is.

Writing

Reading & Writing, Exercise 6

The comments in *italics* may give you some ideas, but you should also try to use some ideas of your own.

1   There are plans to build a small safari park close to your town. Visitors will be able to see animals from all over the world. Here are some comments in newspapers on the topic:

'I would love to see how animals look and behave in real life.'

'Animals will be unhappy and stressed.'

'It will be so exciting and attract tourists, too.'

'Wild animals should stay in their natural habitat.'

'Write an article to your local newspaper giving your views.'

Write 100–150 words.

Core [12 marks]

Reading & Writing, Exercise 6

2   Your school ecology club is trying to persuade people not to use products that have been tested on animals. Here are some comments made by your friends:

'Locally produced food is much tastier.'

'Farmers' markets are dull and old-fashioned'

Write an article for your school magazine giving your views.

Extended [16 marks]

Reading & Writing, Exercise 6

3   Local farmers are trying to persuade people to buy food in their local farmers' markets, and not in modern supermarkets. Here are some online comments from readers to newspapers:

'Our local farmers work so hard and produce lovely food.'

'I want the freedom to shop wherever I like.'

'Locally produced food is much tastier.'

'Farmers' markets are dull and old-fashioned'

Write an article to your local newspaper giving your views.

Write 100–150 words.

Core [12 marks]

Reading & Writing, Exercise 6

4   Your class recently visited an electronic zoo. Your headteacher has asked you to write a report on the visit.

Here are some comments made by students who went on the trip:

'It was so exciting. Just like a real zoo – only better!'

'It was crowded and some of the equipment was broken.'

Write a report for the headteacher giving your views and saying whether you would recommend the trip for next year's group.

Extended [16 marks]

Reading & Writing, Exercise 6

5   Your headteacher has asked for students' responses to the following idea:

The school would like to start supporting a charity. We are considering a charity that does research into animal diseases.

Here are some comments made by your friends:

'How wonderful! Animals deserve to be healthy and happy.'

'I would prefer to support a charity that helps poor people.'

Write an article to your school magazine giving your views.

Extended [16 marks]

Reading & Writing, Exercise 6

6   Your school has raised money for charity. The headteacher has decided that the money should be donated either to a tiger sanctuary **or** to a bird reserve that looks after birds and offers birdwatching facilities.

Here are some comments from the two charities:

'The bird reserve provides a wonderful, natural habitat for birds and educates the public, too.'

'Tigers are threatened by extinction. We must protect them from hunters and poachers.'

Write a report for the headteacher saying which charity should, in your view, receive the funds.

Extended [16 marks]

Speaking

1 The role of science in modern life

Scientific research has brought many benefits, but also causes controversy. Discuss this topic with the assessor.

You may wish to use the following ideas to help develop the conversation:

- what you have enjoyed, and found challenging, about studying science subjects
- whether you would choose science as a career
- how life has changed for good or bad, as a result of scientific and technological discoveries and developments
- whether it is right to use animals and human volunteers in medical research
- the idea that some scientific research is a waste of money or has caused harm to people.

You are free to consider any other related ideas of your own. Remember, you are not allowed to make any written notes.

2 Animals in a human world

Animals share the planet with us, and are often used by us for our convenience, business or pleasure. Sometimes conflicts arise because we disagree about the rights of animals. Discuss this topic with the assessor.

You may wish to use the following ideas to help develop the conversation:

- animals you find interesting or exotic
- animals that are in danger of becoming extinct
- whether or not working animals are properly treated
- the view that hunting wild animals should be banned
- the suggestion that using animals in sport and entertainment is unfair
- the idea that the plans or desires of human beings are always more important than the needs of animals.

You are free to consider any other related ideas of your own. Remember, you are not allowed to make any written notes.

3 Pets

Pets are very important in some people's lives, whereas for others, pets are of no interest at all.

Discuss this topic with the assessor.

Here are some possible ideas for developing the conversation:

- why people enjoy having a pet
- animals which make good pets
- the responsibilities people have towards their pets
- whether everyone has the right to keep a pet
- why a pet may not be suitable for every home.

You are, of course, free to use any other related ideas of your own. You are not allowed to make any written notes.

Listening 🔊 CD 2, Track 14

Listening, Exercise 4

You will hear six people talking about wildlife. For each of Speakers 1–6, choose from the list A–G which idea each speaker expresses. Write the letter in the box. Use each letter once only. There is one extra letter which you do not need to use.

Core [6 marks], Extended [6 marks].

You will hear the full recording twice.

☐ Speaker 1	☐ Speaker 2
☐ Speaker 3	☐ Speaker 4
☐ Speaker 5	☐ Speaker 6

A	I am keen to help people in my area live with wildlife.
B	We no longer worry about having dangerous wildlife nearby.
C	When I was camping, I met a grizzly bear near the campsite.
D	Human food attracts wild animals.
E	Wild animals can give people financial problems.
F	Safe crossings to protect wildlife from traffic are unlikely to be a success.
G	Human activities have had a negative impact on wildlife.

ADVICE FOR SUCCESS

The Advice for Success is for **you** to **help yourself**. Decide which suggestions you like best and mark them. You can adapt an idea in Advice for Success to make it fun for you. Keeping track with a notebook is a good idea.

1   Plan your **opinion essay or report** carefully. Think about content. Try to have enough interesting ideas to expand fully: don't run out of ideas halfway through. Engage with the subject and try to make the argument sound serious and important. Come across as convincing and you will convince other people.

2   Structure your essay so that it is clear and logical. Use paragraphs and linking words.

3   Use an appropriate tone. Opinions should sound reasonable and be supported with examples where appropriate. If you are writing a report for the headteacher you should sound polite, objective and avoid bias.

4   Devices such as rhetorical questions or restructuring sentences for greater emphasis will make your writing stronger and more persuasive, but don't overdo it.

5   Try to use a mature and varied vocabulary that is appropriate to the topic.

6   Punctuate carefully, using commas, full stops, question marks and so on. Proofread your work for punctuation errors.

7   Check your spelling carefully, especially words you know you usually misspell or words that present special problems, such as plural forms, silent letters and suffixes.

8   Try to give attention to your **handwriting**. If your composition is interesting and well-structured, and your handwriting is attractive, your work will be a pleasure to read. If you feel you have particular difficulty forming certain letters or keeping handwriting on the line, try practising using special handwriting worksheets.

9   Try experimenting with different kinds of pens in order to find one that helps you write better. A good quality pen is a good investment if you can find one that is not too expensive.

Exam techniques

10   In an exam, many students stop while writing a composition or report to count the number of words they have produced so far. This is a waste of time. Get used to seeing what 150 words, for example, look like in your handwriting. You will then be able to see whether you are writing to the right length. The lines on an exam paper are also there to help you.

The **word limit** given is a guide to the required length. Don't worry if you write a few words more or less than this.

Exam focus

This unit has helped to prepare you for exams which test your reading, writing, listening and speaking skills. The unit has helped to develop those skills in the following ways:

- You have practised giving **reasons** and **opinions about controversial topics.**

- You have written **paragraphs** based on **notes** and **emails, an article, letters and reports.**

- You have **listened** to a **formal radio interview** and **answered questions.** You have listened to **several speakers** give their **views** and **matched statements to a speaker.**

- You have practised a range of **conversational strategies** to express **opinions, disagreement** and **disappointment.** You have taken part in **discussions** and **presented a talk** to the class.

- You have practised **reading techniques** on a variety of **complex** and **less complex texts.** You have written **notes** and a **summary** based on a **complex text.**

Unit 10
The world of work

In this unit you will:

- read about the development of a chocolate bar and the opening of a fast-food restaurant
- rewrite a text to improve its style
- listen to a Human Resources Officer talk about her work
- role-play a product development meeting
- focus on the following assessment objectives: R3, R4, W5, L1, L2, S4, S5

A The rewards of work

1 Discussion

Why do people work? Earning money is one reason. What other reasons are there? With a partner, try to add four or five more ideas to the list.

Reasons why people work

They get a sense of achievement.

They feel good about themselves.

2 Skills and qualities for work

Match the following skills and qualities to the occupations you think they are essential for:

1	patience	A	software engineer
2	good communication skills	B	dentist
3	artistic flair	C	nursery teacher
4	an ear for languages	D	firefighter
5	business acumen*	E	interior designer
6	physical stamina	F	cellist
7	courage	G	labourer
8	musical talent	H	company director
9	dexterity	I	linguist
10	coding skills	J	journalist

* *acumen = ability to make good decisions quickly*

3 Pre-reading tasks

A   Think of any new products you have tried in the last year. Why did you try them? If you saw them advertised, did they live up to the advertiser's promise? How was the product advertised? How were the new products you tried different from similar products already available?

B   You are going to read about how a totally new chocolate bar is produced. What challenges do you think are involved in this process?

Examples:
You have to make it taste delicious.
You have to have the right equipment to make it.

4 Predicting

Look at the pictures in the text 'A bar is born'. What do you think the pictures show?

5 Reading for gist

Now read the text for general meaning. Try to work out the meanings of any unfamiliar words from the context. Decide if the unfamiliar word is a noun, verb or adjective. What words do you already know that might be similar to the difficult word? Sometimes the general meaning becomes clearer as you read further through the text.

Remember, you do not have to understand every word to understand a text well.

INSIDE CHOCOLATE ■ ■ ■ ■ ■ ■ ■ ■ ■

A bar is born

Despite trends towards healthy eating, many people still love eating chocolate. The Swiss consume the most (almost 12 kilos per person per year) followed by the Irish, with the British not far behind. An average chocolate bar weighs about 40–45 grams, which means that the average Swiss person eats about 240 bars in one year. The demand for chocolate in other parts of the world, including China and India, is growing, creating exciting new markets for the manufacturers of chocolate.

INSIDE CHOCOLATE ■ ■ ■ ■ ■ ■ ■ ■

Many of the mass-produced chocolate products on sale are variations of the basic ingredients of chocolate, caramel, nuts, raisins and biscuit. With popular new ingredients so hard to find, [20] manufacturers are forced to look for new ways of combining the old favourites into new products.

1 Opportunity

All chocolate manufacturers have marketing departments to think up ideas for new products. These departments analyse consumer fashions and lifestyles and try to identify opportunities for new products. One major chocolate company introduced mini-bars when they discovered that many parents cut up a full-size bar into smaller portions for their children.

Some new products come about through new technology rather than marketing. In these cases, scientists or engineers will have invented a machine that can do something new to chocolate which is noticeably different from anything that has been produced before.

It might take anything from six months to a number of years to conduct all the necessary research to assess whether the proposed new product is likely to succeed.

In the UK alone, each research exercise may cost more than £100000. For every ten ideas for new products, only one will get beyond research assessment, so the real cost of getting a new product to the development stage is approximately £1 million.

2 Product development

One of the key criteria for producing a new chocolate bar is that it should be difficult for rival companies to reproduce. No manufacturer wants to spend a great deal of money developing a brand that will quickly attract stiff competition.

Creating a new bar may involve making minor adjustments to existing machinery, or it can mean investment in a whole new factory costing millions of pounds. So it is vital that the new bar can be produced economically.

Chocolate is a price-sensitive product. Even though a manufacturer might come up with a delicious formula for a new bar, it would not go ahead with production unless it could be made for the right price.

Sometimes new products cannot be made at all. One manufacturer found that, in one bar it was developing, it was unable to stop the biscuit becoming wet and soft, and another found that the raisins always sank to the bottom of the bar. Both these projects were abandoned.

The chocolate bar must also be consistent; even the smallest change in the balance of ingredients can affect the taste significantly. Teams of expert tasters are used to identify any changes in the taste. Manufacturers want consumers to buy the same brand over and over again, and if a bar cannot meet the requirement for tasting exactly the same each time, it will not go into mass-production.

The process of development is one of constant refinement. Manufacturers rarely make their ideal product first time round, and it is not unusual for them to have up to 30 attempts at getting it right.

3 Packaging

Care is taken to ensure that the packaging is consistent with the type of bar produced. A bar aimed at teenagers may well be packaged in a red and yellow packet to appear cheap and cheerful. Blue is considered to be a sophisticated colour and is often used to package top-of-the-range brands. Whatever the design, manufacturers will make sure that it stands out enough to be noticed on the sweet counter, where it will have to compete with around 50 other brands.

The name of the bar must also reflect the right image.

4 Advertising

Most new chocolate bars are launched with a press, internet and TV advertising campaign. Advertising companies begin planning their campaigns by deciding what message they want to convey about the product. For example, is it a luxury or is it a snack? They then work on a number of advertisements before deciding which one is likely to work best.

INSIDE CHOCOLATE ■ ■ ■ ■ ■ ■ ■ ■

This process may take between 3 and 18 months. Filming the advert may cost over £250 000, and buying the television airtime to screen it may cost over £3 million.

5   Testing

Manufacturers and advertisers conduct extensive testing at all stages in the development and launch of a new product. Groups from different parts of the country are asked to give their opinions on either the taste of the chocolate or the impact that an advert has had on them. These comments then form the basis for future refinements.

6   The launch

Many new brands do quite well initially, as it is comparatively easy to get people to try a new chocolate bar once. However, for a launch to be successful, sales must be kept at a certain level over a long period of time. Achieving this is extremely difficult. Nine out of every ten new products launched fail to reach full production.

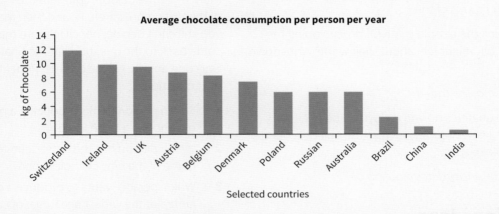

Average chocolate consumption per person per year

kg of chocolate — Selected countries: Switzerland, Ireland, UK, Austria, Belgium, Denmark, Poland, Russian, Australia, Brazil, China, India

6   Reading comprehension

1   Explain why marketing departments study people's behaviour, habits and way of life.

2   Why is it important that a new chocolate bar should be difficult for other companies to copy?

3   What kinds of information does a company want to find at the testing stage? Name two things.

4   According to the chart, which countries consumed about half the amount of chocolate consumed by Switzerland?

5   How do you think the writer wants the reader to feel about information in the article?

   a impressed (there are so many obstacles to overcome) or **b** disapproving (so much time and money goes to waste).

6   Write a paragraph of about 75 words explaining why many new chocolate bars made in the factory never reach the stage of being packaged, advertised or sold.

7   Post-reading discussion

Has the article surprised you in any way? Why/ Why not?

Do you think the way new chocolate is launched could apply to other products? Try to explain your ideas.

Some people say we should avoid chocolate, because it is too rich or too sweet. At the same time, chocolate companies provide jobs, which is good for the economy. Do you think chocolate should be advertised? What is your view?

8   Vocabulary

Look back at Section 2 of the article, *Product development*. Make a list of all the words in this section that are connected with making and selling a product.

Examples: *companies, manufacturer*

Put a **?** against words you don't understand. Look these up in a dictionary.

Collocations

Find these collocations in Section 2 of the article:

stiff competition

price-sensitive product

delicious formula

What other collocations could be made with the adjectives *stiff*, *sensitive* and *delicious*? Make a list with a partner.

Examples: *a delicious cake, a sensitive child, frozen stiff*

9 A rewarding job?

Work in pairs or groups of three.

How do you think the people involved in developing the new chocolate bar might feel about their work? Write down your ideas.

Examples: *excited, frustrated*

What skills and qualities do you feel would be necessary for working on a new product, such as the one described in the article? Make a list.

Examples: *enthusiasm, determination*

10 Sharing ideas

In exercise 2 you looked at the skills and qualities needed for different jobs. Can any of them be added to the list you came up with in exercise 9?

Share your ideas with the other groups. Listen carefully and add any other interesting ideas.

11 Understanding visual data

Visual data, graphs and charts are often included in newspaper and magazine articles and webpages, especially those of a factual type. The information in the chart often mirrors information in the text and can sometimes be quicker to process than text.

Re-read the opening paragraph of 'A bar is born'. Then study the chart in the article. How does the chart:

a reflect information in the first paragraph?

b give extra information?

12 Product development meeting and role play

Four executives of the New Planet chocolate company are meeting to discuss the production of a new chocolate bar.

Read the questions about each person at the meeting and then find answers in the following texts. This is a multiple-matching exercise. First, scan the questions to get an idea of what the texts will be about. Then read each text carefully. Answer the first question by re-reading it carefully and then re-read the text(s) to find evidence to support your answer. If the question seems to apply to more than one person, compare the information in each of the texts more carefully, and then make your choice. If you still can't decide, pencil in more than one answer, and come back to the question later to finalise your selection. Only one answer will be correct. Repeat the process for the next question.

1 Which person thinks producing a new chocolate bar may not be a good idea?

2 Which person has the most definite ideas for the name of the new chocolate bar?

3 Which person wants to produce a chocolate bar aimed at the widest age range of customers?

4 Which person seems the most interested in the appearance of the product?

5 Which person is waiting for more information from customers before deciding what kind of chocolate bar to produce?

6 Which person has an idea for saving money on advertising?

DESIGNER

You think there is a need for a new chocolate bar. It should be aimed at young children as this is where the market is strongest.

You specialise in the design of the wrappers. You prefer a bright red, green or yellow wrapper, something which will stand out and catch children's attention – definitely not anything that looks grown-up. You would also like images of animals and their young put on the wrappers. This will encourage parents to buy the chocolate for toddlers.

You want the name 'Choccie' or 'Chic-Choc'. You think this will encourage parents to buy it for their children's lunchboxes or as a treat after school. You think the taste should be very sweet and milky.

You are rather forceful in meetings. Give your opinions firmly and clearly. (You may want to look back at the opinion language in Unit 9.) You also hate to be interrupted.

MARKETING EXECUTIVE

You expect that the market research you are carrying out with customers will show there is a need for chocolate that will appeal to older teenagers and adults. In your opinion, people are rather bored with the taste of the chocolate bars you already produce and want something that tastes more of chocolate and less of sugar and milk.

You have been thinking about the 'look' of the product. The colour of the wrapper should be black, blue or gold. The advertising should suggest the chocolate is a luxury. Eating it is a pleasure and makes an occasion special. It is not a quick snack or an item for children's lunchboxes.

You are not happy with any of the names suggested for the product. You think consumers will confuse these names with other brands.

The chocolate market is extremely competitive so the advertising budget needs to be high enough to cover the cost of advertising on TV.

SALES EXECUTIVE

You are convinced there is a need for a new chocolate bar aimed at families, to include adults and children of various ages. You have some ideas for names for the product: 'Golden Bar', 'Delight' and 'Soft-Centred'. You dislike childish-sounding names, which suggest the chocolate is for young children.

The advertising should suggest the chocolate is for all members of the family. The advert could show people eating it at work, on trains, or just enjoying it on holidays and family outings.

You are going to suggest that the product is advertised in magazines and on the internet rather than on television. TV advertising is too expensive and will not necessarily increase sales.

You are a good listener. You do your best to get on with everyone.

HEAD ENGINEER

You are very unhappy with the plans to produce a new chocolate bar. You have been working on many different kinds of formulas and each time the product is unsatisfactory. Feedback from the company's expert tasters is that the chocolate goes soft too easily, that it's too sweet or isn't sweet enough. Some tasters have thought it's too dry, or it crumbles very easily. More feedback is to come.

The most satisfactory result so far was a bar that seemed very similar to one you already make. You think that if the factory invested in a new machine that could produce the chocolate in a different shape and size from the original, then the new product would seem different enough to be successful.

One possibility would be to cut the chocolate into small circles and sell it in large, family-size bags.

7   Which person might be difficult to exchange ideas with in the meeting?

You could now have a role play of the meeting. Form groups of four and choose from the roles. You need to decide:

- who the chocolate bar will be aimed at
- the name and the packaging
- your advertising strategies.

B   Facts and figures

1   Approximations

Study the following exact amounts. Say them aloud carefully, checking the pronunciation with a partner. Where does the stress fall in *per cent?*

1   4.9%
2   10.4%
3   52.3%
4   74.7%
5   98.8%
6   19.2%
7   23.8%
8   32.9%

Now match the exact amounts to these approximations:

A   getting on for three-quarters
B   a good half
C   over one in ten
D   under one in five
E   almost a quarter
F   practically all
G   nearly a third
H   about one in twenty

When facts and figures are presented, both exact amounts and approximations might be used. For example, you may hear '*19.8% of the town's population, that's getting on for one in five men and women of working age are unemployed.*'

What are the advantages of using approximations to present information? Are there any disadvantages?

2   Questioning statistics

A   Statistical information looks authoritative but you need to treat it with caution. Pressure groups, for example, may use statistics to influence public opinion.

What has the following survey found out? How does it compare with your own experience?

A recent survey found that children who come from homes where the mother works have half as many absences from school as the children of non-working mothers. Working mothers seem quite prepared to send their children to school when they are unwell.

B   Before deciding whether the above conclusion is valid, you need to ask more questions. For example:

- Who asked for the survey to be carried out?
- Why was it carried out?
- Who took part in the survey?
- What was the size of the sample?
- Exactly what kind of questions were asked?
- Were the groups of children closely matched, in terms of age, background and social class?

Why are these questions important? What kind of answers do you think you might get?

C   With your partner, make notes on the questions you would want to ask before accepting the validity of the following 'facts and figures':

The majority of the population thought that young people under the age of 18 should not be allowed out after 9 p.m.

_____

_____

A survey found that the Rio School was much better than the other schools. It had by far the best exam results.

_____

_____

3   Criticising statistics

Study the following statement and then read the reactions to it. Make sure you understand the expressions in **bold** type.

A survey of young people found the majority were not going to bother to get a decent job when they left school or college.

> It's **a total distortion of the truth**. The teenagers I know would do anything to get on a good training scheme.

> They're **fudging the facts**. We all want a good job.

> I can't stand surveys that **bend the truth**. I'd like to know exactly who they asked and the questions they used.

> **Who dreamt that up?** It's rubbish!

Look back at the statistical information given in exercise 2. Practise criticising the statements with your partner. Do you both sound annoyed enough?

4 Young lives: Good or bad?

A survey of young people produced the following results. Read each statement carefully and decide with a partner whether it gives a good or bad impression of teenagers. Mark each statement **P** if a positive impression is being given, and **N** if the impression given is negative. Underline the words that help you decide.

1   23% valued spare-time jobs more highly than their school studies.

2   Over three-quarters were concerned the schools did not arrange work experience.

3   Over a fifth said that having part-time jobs was the only way they could pay for ordinary things they needed, or buy treats such as sweets.

4   18% objected to the amount of pocket money* they received but were not prepared to work to earn extra spending money.

5   Over a quarter of teenagers were dissatisfied with the amount of freedom their parents allowed.

6   74% were happy with the amount of freedom they were allowed.

7   Reading was a popular activity for two out of three of those interviewed.

8   A third never pick up a book outside school.

9   The majority do nothing to help their community.

10   One in three teenagers do voluntary work for their community.

* *pocket money* = a small amount of money given by parents to children

Decide which statistics you would choose to present if you were:

a   an employer who feels teenagers are a bad employment risk

b   a youth leader encouraging firms to develop training schemes for young people.

5 Rewriting in a more formal style

The following letter was written to a newspaper by a teenager who disagreed with a report it had published. Discuss the letter with your partner and try to decide whether it is written in an appropriate tone and register for its target audience.

Consider the use of:

- slang
- colloquialisms
- contractions
- rhetorical questions, question forms, and question tags.

Underline those aspects of the letter both you and your partner are unhappy with.

Hi you guys at the newspaper,

Hi! It's me again! Ollie Debeer from your go-ahead high school just outside town. Your report 'Young Lives Shock!' just got me mad! I mean, the report says 'We are unconcerned about employment'. Talk about fudging the facts, eh? All my mates are dead worried about getting a decent job. I also read 'teenagers value their spare-time jobs more than their studies'. Who dreamt that up? There's no way my parents can afford to buy me the trainers or the kind of phone I want. No way! So I work for them, right? I work in a café twice a week after school and, yeah, I do find it hard to concentrate the next day, but I do extra homework to catch up. That stuff about teenage entertainment was kind of distorted too, wasn't it? 'The youth of today show a strong preference for the company of their peer group over spending time with their parents.' I mean, who wouldn't rather be out with their mates than stuck at home watching the old man snore? But it didn't say we dislike our parents, did it? Anyway, write me back, will you? It's gonna be great hearing your views!

Bye for now,
Ollie

When you are ready, try to rewrite the letter in a more formal style, and divide it into suitable paragraphs. Remember: a letter to a newspaper can include some aspects of informal style, such as the occasional idiom or colloquialism. However, the general impression should be formal.

Show your finished letter to your partner. Does he/she agree that the 'balance' of your style (neither too formal nor too informal) is about right?

C Job stereotypes

1 Pre-listening discussion

What kinds of shops do you usually like visiting? Which shops do you enjoy the least?

How would you rate the service in most shops?

If you could improve shops in one way, what would you do?

The graph shows the average worldwide take-up of tertiary education by young people within five years of leaving secondary school, as a percentage of the relevant age group. (*Tertiary* means college- or university-level.)

1　What percentage of young people worldwide were enrolled in tertiary education in 2006, 2008 and 2012?

2　Is the trend up or down?

Why do you think this change may have happened? Discuss your ideas in your group.

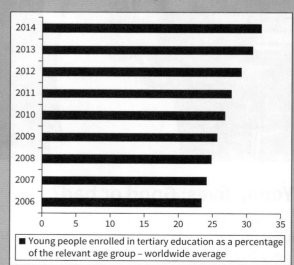

Young people enrolled in tertiary education as a percentage of the relevant age group – worldwide average

2 Predicting content

You are going to listen to Zoe, a human resources officer who works for a chain of electrical stores, talking in an informal way about her job. She aims to help the stores run more efficiently and profitably.

What aspects of her job do you think Zoe might be going to mention? Select the points on this list.

- [ ] making suggestions about new products the stores could sell
- [ ] helping managers decide whether they need full-time or part-time members of staff
- [ ] suggesting that shop staff have extra training to improve their skills
- [ ] encouraging managers to go for promotion
- [ ] disciplining staff who are performing badly
- [ ] advising sales managers if their sales are falling.

3 Vocabulary check

Before you listen, make sure you understand the meaning of these words and phrases:

VOCABULARY		
personal sales targets	influential	wide spectrum

4 Listening for gist 🔊 CD 2, Track 15

Listen to the recording. Which of the points that you selected are mentioned?

5 Detailed listening 🔊 CD 2, Track 15

Now listen for detail and try to complete each statement correctly:

1 Zoe visits stores in:
   a shopping malls
   b out-of-town centres
   c high streets.

2 A common problem is that sales staff:
   a do not look professional
   b fail to reach sales targets
   c lack interest in working hard.

3 Zoe suggests that staff should have:
   a more training and development
   b more training and better pay
   c more training and longer hours.

4 Staff may be given a camera to take home:
   a as a reward for doing a good job
   b so they can learn how it works
   c to practise selling it.

5 Staff often lack the ability to:
   a display goods effectively
   b relate to the customers
   c find goods in the store.

6 Zoe feels that:
   a a wide variety of people can do well as sales assistants
   b only people of a certain type will succeed
   c sales staff should have a similar background to their manager.

7 Zoe:
   a tries to make the managers work harder
   b lets managers blame her when things go wrong
   c is sympathetic and helpful to the managers.

6 Post-listening discussion

A Zoe says she finds managers want to recruit people who are '*just like themselves*'. What kind of people do you think she has in mind? How do you think they would look and behave, and what way of life would they have?

B Stereotypes often form around particular occupations. What would you expect a 'typical' person doing each of the following jobs to be like?
   - labourer
   - pop star
   - prison governor
   - scientist.

C Do you think the stereotype of an occupation helps you when you are choosing which career to follow? Why/Why not?

D Can you think of someone who doesn't fit the norm for their job? Try to explain your views.

235

7 Common work-related expressions

Zoe describes store managers as being on 'a bit of a treadmill'. What do you think she means?

Can you work out the meaning of the following expressions from the context?

1 I meet friends from work socially but we always relax completely and no one *talks shop*.

2 The new assistant is hard-working and enthusiastic – *a real go-getter*.

3 He got *a golden handshake* worth $20 000 when he retired from his job.

4 Although the policeman was *off-duty*, he arrested the thief.

5 I'm called an 'office assistant' but really I'm just a general *dogsbody*.

6 Not liking the structure of big companies, I got work where I could *be my own boss*.

7 He's not *a high-flyer*; he doesn't have any brilliant ideas, but you can depend on him.

8 Because of their working conditions, *blue-collar workers* are more likely to have accidents at work than *white-collar workers*.

8 Pronunciation: Linking sounds

Practise reading this advert aloud, checking your pronunciation with a partner. Does he or she feel you are reading naturally? Notice that if a word ends with a consonant and the next word begins with a vowel, the sounds are linked.

> **BRIGHTEN UP YOUR SUMMER – GET A JOB WITH US!**
>
> If you need extra cash and are 16+
> WE NEED YOU!
>
> There are lots of vacancies in our seafront restaurant.
>
> It's fun, it's easy and hours to suit!
>
> Apply to:
>
> Ian.okoro@mymail.com

Now mark the linked sounds in this advert and practise reading it aloud to your partner:

> **HEADLIGHTS HAIRDRESSING**
>
> *Career opportunities for school leavers*
> Trainees needed.
> - Learn in a leading salon.
> - If you've got energy and enthusiasm, we can take you to the top.
>
> Contact Elma – Telephone 01223 569432

9 Writing a job advert

You work in a laboratory. One morning you find this email from your boss:

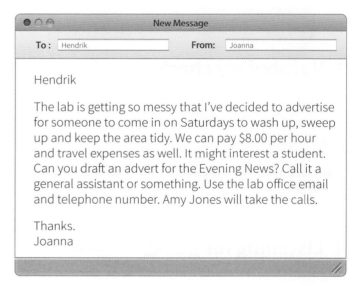

> **New Message**
>
> To: Hendrik   From: Joanna
>
> Hendrik
>
> The lab is getting so messy that I've decided to advertise for someone to come in on Saturdays to wash up, sweep up and keep the area tidy. We can pay $8.00 per hour and travel expenses as well. It might interest a student. Can you draft an advert for the Evening News? Call it a general assistant or something. Use the lab office email and telephone number. Amy Jones will take the calls.
>
> Thanks.
> Joanna

Write a suitable advert based on the note. Then mark the linking sounds and show it to a partner. Does he/she agree with the word linking?

Ask your partner to read it aloud. Correct the pronunciation if necessary (tactfully, of course!).

D Recruitment with a difference

1 Pre-reading task

A Do you enjoy 'fast food'? When (if ever) do you visit fast-food restaurants?

What do you think are the strong points of these restaurants?

236

B You are going to read an article about a fast-food restaurant, which is run by deaf staff. Write down four questions you would like to see answered in the article.

Example: *How do customers communicate with the staff?*

2 Vocabulary check

Make sure you understand the meaning of these words and phrases, which you will meet in the article.

3 Reading for gist

Now read the article. Are any of the questions you wrote down in exercise 1 answered?

Work without limits

When Aly Sarhan, 28, was asked to head a new branch of the Kentucky Fried Chicken restaurant chain in Egypt, run by deaf people, he didn't know what to expect.

'Working with 30 deaf young people is like working
5 in a foreign land,' says Sarhan, who took a crash course in Arabic sign language.

For Sarhan, however, the experience has been an eye-opening one, and has changed his attitudes towards people with disabilities. 'My staff's hearing
10 impairment does not stop them from doing anything a hearing person can do. They certainly have a whole load of determination in them,' he says.

The idea for a deaf-run KFC — the first in the Middle East — was born when KFC's top management decided to 'fulfill their obligations 15 towards society,' according to Sarhan. 'We found that deaf people existed in large numbers in Egypt, so we decided to do something for them,' he explains.

The obvious place to start recruiting from was the Deaf Society in Heliopolis. The KFC board used 20 the same criteria they apply when choosing hearing applicants. Successful candidates had to be tactful, presentable, agile, and no older than 25 years of age. 'It was very difficult turning people down, so we decided to pick the most eligible applicants, in 25 addition to drawing up a long waiting list,' Sarhan says. For KFC, this was groundbreaking work.

Sarhan, one of the youngest store managers working at KFC worldwide, says his biggest concern in the beginning was how to communicate with his 30 employees. 'I did not know a single sign, so I had to use an interpreter. Whether the kids got to like or dislike me depended on the interpreter. I was determined, however, to learn the language and remove any barriers between us,' he says. 35

That was easier said than done, he remembers. 'Arabic sign language is one of the most difficult languages you can learn, because it is mainly composed of gentle hand movements rather than distinct signs,' Sarhan explains. Having worked with 40 his staff for only 11 months, he is still a weak signer, but he knows enough to help him get by and gain the trust and acceptance of his employees.

So far, the restaurant has been a big success and
45   has helped create a supportive environment for the
employees. 'What made the kids so enthusiastic
about our new project was the fact that they get to
be in a place where being deaf is the norm. Most
of them have been through bad work experiences
50   in which they were the only person with hearing
impairment in the place, which made them feel
lonely and left out.'

This supportive environment, Sarhan says, has made
55   many of the deaf employees depend on themselves
more. 'Many of the employees had been spoilt and
pampered all their lives by their parents, out of pity,
which made them rather bad-tempered and lazy.
Once they began to like us, it was as if we found
60   previously undiscovered energy.'

At the branch in Dokki, pictures on the menu
and light signals compensate for the lack of verbal

communication. Customers simply have to point
to the picture of the food item they want on the
picture-menu. 'Despite that, lots of people come in   65
with the feeling of not knowing what to do written
all over their faces. They start making signs, and are
relieved to find out I can talk. I start carrying out the
customer's role without signing, to show them how
easy it all is,' Sarhan says.   70

The newly married Sarhan says that he considers
his staff part of his family now. He has become
something of a mentor for them and has helped
to create a friendly environment. 'This place has
helped the deaf employees psychologically,   75
not just financially. I hope more companies
will think of embarking on similar adventures.
It's great to help make a difference to people's lives,'
he says.

by Manal el-Jesri   80

4 Comprehension check

1   Why did the restaurant choose to employ deaf people?

2   How did the management decide what would be the right criteria for selecting applicants?

3   Contrast the way employees felt about work before they began their jobs at the restaurant with their feelings about work now.

4   Describe the personality changes the employees undergo.

5   What does Sarhan feel he has gained from this work? Name two things.

5 Post-reading discussion

A   Aly hopes other companies will follow the example of his restaurant and employ staff with disabilities. How can companies be encouraged to recruit a wider range of types of people? Share your ideas.

B   Aly says, 'It's great to help make a difference to people's lives.'

Jobs that are 'people-orientated', such as nursing, teaching, human resources, or the hotel trade, bring different rewards and stresses from 'product-

orientated jobs', such as those in engineering, carpentry or design.

Which kind of work would you find rewarding, and why?

C   Aly is described as being a 'mentor'. He supports and inspires his employees.

Many schools and colleges have 'mentoring schemes,' whereby students are matched with successful adults of a similar background. The mentors give encouragement and practical advice to their students. Sometimes students spend time at the mentor's workplace, 'shadowing' him or her, or doing some work experience. Do you think this is a good idea? Why/Why not?

Who would you choose for your mentor and why?

6 Vocabulary study

A   Try to put these adjectives into order, from most active to least active. Use a dictionary to check unfamiliar words.

VOCABULARY	
lazy	hyperactive
energetic	indolent

B Now put these adjectives into order, from most positive to most negative:

VOCABULARY		
friendly	affectionate	indifferent
loving	supportive	critical
cold		

C Which word is the odd one out?

VOCABULARY		
bad-tempered	cross	irritable
moody	placid	irate
grumpy		

7 Similes

Similes are descriptive forms of comparison that enrich your writing. Study these examples:

'(It) is **like** working in a foreign land.'

Notice that *like* is followed by a noun or gerund:

It's **like a fridge** in here – let's turn the heating on.

It was **like being** on holiday.

As if/as though are followed by a verb clause:

He felt **as though** his heart would burst.

Similes include traditional expressions, such as: *as good as gold, as thin as a rake, as flat as a pancake, as white as snow, like talking to a brick wall* and many more.

Complete the following sentences with suitable similes:

1 The room was so hot. It felt like _____.

2 Her hands were as cold as _____.

3 The house was so dirty. It was as if _____.

4 Samira was thrilled with the news. She reacted as though _____.

5 We're not allowed any freedom. It's like _____.

6 I was so depressed when I couldn't get a job. It was as if _____.

8 Spelling: *-able* or *-ible*?

A In the article you met the adjectives *presentable* (line 18) and *eligible* (line 20). The adjective endings *-able* and *-ible* are often confused. From the word *depend* we get *dependable*, but *convert* gives us *convertible*.

Complete the adjectives in these sentences, using a dictionary if necessary. Then learn by heart the spellings you find most difficult.

1 I'm afraid I won't be avail_____ until after the 13th.

2 The house was almost invis_____ in the fog.

3 Fortunately, the disease was cur_____.

4 I'm sure she'll make a respons_____ parent.

5 I found Ken's story absolutely incred_____.

6 That is a sens_____ idea.

7 Let's take your car – it's more reli_____ than mine.

8 Cheating in exams is not advis_____.

9 Heavy snow made the house inaccess_____.

10 Tiredness tends to make him irrit_____.

B Now complete these adjectives with the endings *-able* or *-ible* and then use each one in a sentence of your own:

1 wash_____

2 ined_____

3 digest_____

4 desir_____

5 approach_____

6 excit_____

7 bear_____

8 incomprehens_____

9 Phrasal verbs

Notice how these phrasal verbs are used in the article in exercise 3. Then use them in a suitable form in sentences 1–5.

239

turn down (line 19)
leave out (line 47)
draw up (line 21)
carry out (line 63)
get by (line 37)

1   Gavin earns so little money, I don't know how he
    _____ .

2   She was careful to _____ all the instructions
    exactly.

3   We're going on holiday next week, so I'm afraid I shall
    have to _____ your invitation.

4   All the children in my son's class were invited to the
    party as we did not want to _____ anyone
    _____ .

5   The management have _____ new
    guidelines for staff interviews.

10 'Eye' idioms

Aly says the experience of working with people with
disabilities has been '*an eye-opening one*' (line 8). What do
you think he means by this?

Match the first parts of these sentences (1–8) with their
endings (a–h).

1   Jim wanted to paint the room green, but Vera
    wanted blue,

2   As she had to do the ironing,

4   When I first saw the Pyramids, I thought they were so
    amazing that

5   Although it was very late, we walked home,

6   The children weren't supposed to be eating sweets

7   Visiting a foreign country for the first time

8   The new manager was so much more astute than the
    old one that it was impossible

A   I couldn't keep my eyes off them.

B   is quite an eye-opener.

C   keeping an eye out for a taxi all the way.

D   to pull the wool over his eyes.

E   but I decided to turn a blind eye to it.

F   was a sight for sore eyes.

G   I kept an eye on the baby.

H   so I'm afraid they didn't see eye to eye.

E   Preparing for work

1 How well does school prepare you for work?

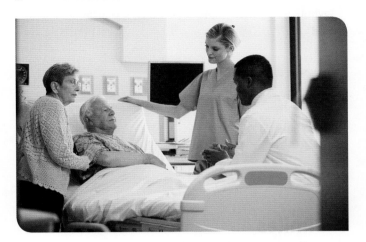

A   What kind of career would you like to have when you
    leave school or college? What general things do you
    feel you have learnt at school that will help you?

    Write down any ideas that seem relevant, even if you
    don't have a clear picture in your mind of the exact
    career you want to follow.

Examples:

I've learnt how to use my initiative when I do projects.

*I've learnt foreign languages, which will give me
international opportunities.*

*I've learnt to be more punctual, which is essential in
most jobs.*

*I want to be an engineer and my school arranged some
work experience for me.*

B Have you held any positions of responsibility at school (e.g. helped run a club or society) that might be useful when you apply for college or work? What have you learnt from 'working' at school? Note down your ideas.

Examples:

I've learnt how to get on with different kinds of people.

I've become more mature.

Keep your notes, as you'll need them later.

2 Before you read

Many schools have a prefect system. Students who are prefects help the school run smoothly by keeping a check on other students' behaviour, doing litter patrols, helping in the dining room, etc.

Do you think this is a good idea? Could there possibly be any drawbacks?

Students who show special abilities are chosen as Head Boy or Girl. In many schools, one of their main tasks is to represent the opinions of the students to the teachers.

Do you have a Head Boy or Girl in your school? What are his/her duties? How is he/she chosen?

3 Reading, analysing and writing

Read this article from a school newsletter. What is its purpose?

> ### HEAD BOY ELECTIONS
> ### by Luke Adams
>
> I know you all have your own ideas about the best candidate for Head Boy, but if you can spare a minute to read this, I'll explain why Matthew Okoro is the strongest and most experienced candidate.
>
> Matthew, who is the youngest senior prefect in his year, has shown the most fantastic negotiating skills. Do you remember when we were banned from the swimming pool at lunchtime? Matthew was the one who persuaded the teachers to let us use it by offering to supervise it himself. The fact that we can go on school trips is due to Matthew's hard work, too. He worked round the clock to raise funds for a reliable minibus to take us on trips. He might not be as keen as

> some of us on playing team sports, but he is a regular supporter at all our matches.
>
> Outside school, Matthew helps at a home for disabled teenagers. His experience has made him much more understanding of people's problems, which makes all the difference in a large, mixed school like ours.

Read the article again and underline examples of:

- complex sentence constructions, including defining and non-defining relative clauses (revised in Unit 8, exercises 9 and 10)
- comparisons, including comparative/superlative constructions
- collocations describing qualities and skills
- idioms
- audience awareness.

Now write the closing paragraph to Luke's article, trying to use the same style:

Matthew is _____

_____ .

4 Comparing two styles

Now read this second newsletter article. What are the main differences between this article and Luke's? Make a list.

Example: There are no paragraphs.

> ### HEAD GIRL ELECTIONS
> ### by Leila Masoon
>
> You've got to vote for Nicola Wilson. It's not fair if she isn't made Head Girl. She set up a social club. She worked after school every day. She worked on Saturdays as well. Before that we didn't have a club. Now we have a club. Everyone goes to the club. It is good. She has stopped the bullying. The bullying was happening a lot. She spoke to the bullies. She made them stop. Now everyone is nice to each other. She started a 'Welcome Day' for new students. Now new students are happy. They are not lonely. We had to wear skirts in winter. It was horrible. We were cold. Nicola explained we wanted to wear trousers. Now we

241

can. That was because of Nicola. The other prefects talk about themselves. They say how good they are. But Nicola doesn't. She works in a hospital on Saturdays. She visits patients. They are patients who have no visitors. She knows more about people now. You must vote for Nicola.

5 Developing your writing style

Rewrite Leila's article so that it includes a wider range of structures and uses a more formal style. Use Luke's article to help you.

When you've finished, show your article to a partner. Listen carefully to his or her comments. How far do you agree with them? Will you change anything?

6 Brainstorming

Work in small groups. Make notes about unemployment under the headings below, using the prompts to give you ideas. Remember: brainstorming allows you to write down anything you think of at the time. Don't worry about relevance at this stage.

Try to think about your own country. Note examples of problems and remedies that are relevant to your own situation.

Why are people unemployed?

- *Industries such as … have closed down because … and so ….*
- *We import goods such as … and people prefer to buy these rather than the similar products we make at home, because …. This results in … in our own industries.*
- *Modern technology has ….*
- *The level of education and training is ….*
- *Industries have moved out of city centres because … and now city centres are ….*
- *People are leaving their farms in the countryside, which means … and going to the towns, which results in ….*

What would help people get jobs?

- *Government money could be given to ….*
- *Industries such as … could be encouraged to set up in our area.*
- *Training schemes such as … could be organised.*
- *Industries which use old, out-of-date equipment could ….*

Other ideas

- *The school-leaving age is now … and it could be changed to … which might help ….*
- *Colleges should offer more courses in … because ….*
- *Unemployed people could visit advice centres to find out ….*
- *Schools should arrange work experience in ….*
- *Careers guidance at school could ….*

When you have finished, compare your notes with those of other groups and add any useful ideas. Keep your notes carefully, as you will use them later.

7 Reading an example email

Study this email which was written to a local newspaper. The writer makes four separate points. What are they?

Unhappy to be jobless

Dear Editor,

I do not usually write to newspapers but when I read your report, which suggested that young people were happy to be unemployed, I felt I had to respond.

I am a school leaver, and in my opinion school leavers need much more detailed careers guidance. Moreover, I think schools should start a 'mentoring scheme' that would match pupils with successful career people. Spending one day a week with a mentor would be a real eye-opener and provide us with the work experience companies say they want but which students find so hard to get!

Furthermore, the majority of the firms in our area are 'hi-tech', whereas some school leavers around here are not computer-literate. Firms should form a partnership with schools to develop training schemes that would enable us to learn relevant skills.

I would also like to add that the statistic in your report '85% of pupils had no idea what life without a job is like' is a complete distortion of the truth. Many of us have parents who are out of work and we definitely do not want to be in that position.

When you are at school, getting a good job is like a high wall you have to climb. Young people need all the help they can get, not criticism.

Yours faithfully,
Jennifer Aziz

8 Analysing the email

When you write formally, you should aim to use certain structures and phrases. The following list shows what you might include in a formal email. Re-read Jennifer's email and find examples for each item on the list.

- **Defining clauses**
- **Comparative structures**
- **Idioms**
- **Similes**
- **Linking devices**
- **Opening sentence**
- **Conclusion**
- **Style and register**

9 Writing an email of reply

Write an email to Jennifer describing the employment situation in your country and explaining what you think would help people in your country get jobs.

Remember to:

- keep to the topic.
- start a new paragraph for each new topic.
- begin and end the email with an appropriate phrase.

10 Correcting a report for the headteacher

Peter's class recently attended a careers talk given by a business owner about the skills he looks for in recruiting new employees. Peter is head boy and the headteacher asked him to write a report saying whether the talk was worthwhile or not.

Each sentence in the report has an extra word which should not be there. Read the report carefully, deleting the unnecessary words. The first one has been done for you.

Mr Chen's talk was the most interesting careers the event we have attended. He began by explaining how he had built up with his factory, 'Chen's Engineering,' from a small company to a large business. He explained that when he was growing up, he helped them in the family engineering business. Mr Chen most enjoyed it repairing motorcycle engines. At a young age, he realised he liked working with machines, and got a lot of satisfaction from making a damaged engine to work well again. Most of all though, he learnt him about giving good customer service. His saw that his parents they were always patient and pleasant to customers, no matter what the effort. His father he would say, 'A man without a smiling face should not open a shop.' Mr Chen says he has never forgotten of those words, as they have been essential to the success of his business.

Mr Chen then told us what he looks for in when he recruits new employees. He said that job applicants think high exam grades are everything, but they are in wrong. He chooses people, including school leavers, because they are polite, enthusiastic and willing them to learn. He expects it employees to speak in a professional way to customers, and not to say, for instance, 'Hi you guys, wanna have a coffee?' He said everyone can you learn to be respectful, talk confidently on the phone, take notes and ask for help when necessary.

We appreciated and Mr Chen's careers talk very much, especially the emphasis on good communication skills at work. As a result of the talk, some of us now want to get wider our experience. We are thinking of doing voluntary work or getting us a part time job in the holidays.

Peter Lee
Head Boy

11 Choosing appropriate vocabulary

When you read an exam question, you need to identify the topic and think of language connected to it.

This also helps you avoid 'rubric error'. This means answering the question in a way that is not relevant to the topic. For example, a question about medical experiments on animals should not produce a composition about taking your pet on holiday!

Read the following exam-style questions and the vocabulary that follows. Working in small groups and using dictionaries, decide what vocabulary is unlikely to be connected to the topic. Make sure you all agree.

Question 1

You had an important test and left home in very good time. However, something extremely unexpected happened on your journey. You arrived at the test only just before it was due to begin. Write an account of what happened for your school newsletter.

What language is unlikely to be connected to this topic? Delete it from the following list.

decide my future	*emergency services*
with seconds to spare	*not a moment to lose*
panicked	*indifferent*
yelled	*alarmed*
shoved	*strolled*
anxious	*broke out in a sweat*
grabbed	*announcements*
absolutely desperate	*share prices*
snatched	*despair*
sales figures	

Question 2

You have been selected for a special training scheme that will help you get the job of your dreams. Explain the way you felt when you heard the news and how this training scheme will help bring you closer to your chosen career.

Delete the inappropriate language.

disappointed	*over the moon*
relieved	*challenge*
thrilled	*develop new skills*
practical experience	*isolated*
delighted	*saddened*
amazed	*worthwhile*
many benefits	*colleagues*
breathed a sigh of relief	*golden opportunity*
irritated	

12 Timed writing

Choose one of the topics that you find appealing from the previous exercise. Write about 150–200 words.

Allow yourself 15–20 minutes, maximum, to write the composition.

Reading aloud

Read your composition aloud to your group and pay close attention to the feedback. How far do you agree with the comments, and what would you change?

13 Listening: Four work scenarios CD 2, Track 16

You will hear four short recordings. Answer each question using no more than **three** words for each detail. You will hear each recording twice.

1 a Maria is ringing up to change the time and date of a job interview. What alternative is she offered?

b What is Maria doing on Tuesday?

2 a According to the careers talk, what special qualifications are needed to enter training schemes for the police force?

b What two personal qualities are needed?

3 a What did the headteacher think about your friend's idea of helping at the children's clinic?

b When does your friend want to visit the clinic?

4 a Has the speaker received good news or bad news?

b What job does he want to train to do?

GRAMMAR SPOTLIGHT

1 Superlatives of long and short adjectives

Superlatives of short adjectives are made by adding *-(e)st*:

the oldest   the cleverest   the largest

With some words there are also spelling changes:

lazy ~ laziest   big ~ biggest

*She had **the happiest** smile of anyone I had ever met.*

For superlatives of longer adjectives, we use *the most* before the adjective:

*I thought Mel's presentation was **the most interesting**.*

Note these irregular superlatives: *the best, the worst, the furthest.*

The article in **section E3** contained this example:

Matthew Okoro is the strongest and most experienced candidate.

Skim-read the article and underline other examples of superlatives.

2 Adverbs of degree

We can use adverbs of degree to modify or intensify an adjective. In **section A12** the Head Engineer's opinion of the different kinds of new chocolate is:

… it's too sweet or isn't sweet enough.

Notice that *too* goes before the adjective but *enough* goes after it.

Other adverbs of degree include *very, extremely, rather, quite, a little, a bit* (informal). These all go before the adjective:

*Don't you think it's **a bit late** to start watching a film?*

Skim-read the roles of the Sales Executive and the Marketing Executive in **section A12** and underline examples of adverbs of degree.

245

Exam-style questions

Writing

Reading & Writing, Exercise 6

1 There is a proposal at your school to offer students two weeks of work experience locally after they finish their exams. Here are some comments from students about the idea:

'We will learn skills that will help us understand the working world.'

'We would not benefit because work experience is not like doing a real job.'

Write an article for the school magazine giving your views. These comments may give you some ideas but you should try to use some ideas of your own.

Write 150–200 words.

Extended [16 marks]

Reading & Writing, Exercise 5

2 You recently spent the holidays working at an international holiday camp for children aged 11–12 years.

Write an email to a friend about the experience.

In the email you should:

- describe the kind of work you did
- explain what you learnt from doing it
- say whether you think your friend would also enjoy an experience like this.

The images may give you some ideas but you are free to make up ideas of your own.

Write 100–150 words.

Core [12 marks]

Reading & Writing, Exercise 6

3   Your class recently went on a trip to a careers event. The headteacher has asked you to write about what you learnt from the event and to suggest how it could be improved for next year's group, if the trip is repeated.

Here are some comments from your classmates about the trip:

'We were given helpful information about the skills employers look for.'

'We did not find out what training courses are available in our area.'

Write the report for the headteacher.

The comments above may give you some ideas but you should try to use some ideas of your own. Write 150–200 words.

Extended [16 marks]

Reading & Writing, Exercise 6

4   Your headteacher is considering two possibilities for students in your class. They could log onto an online international careers event OR the class could go out to a local careers event. As class representative, the headteacher wants to know your views before making her decision.

Here are some comments from students on the proposal:

'We will learn more from the online event as many of us want to have a career abroad.'

'We would prefer to go to the local event as we would have the chance to make a good impression on employers.'

Write a report for the head teacher giving your views. These comments may give you some ideas but you should try to use some ideas of your own.

Write 150–200 words.

Extended [16 marks]

Speaking

1 Worthwhile work

What do you think is the most important and worthwhile work in the world today? Choose one or two jobs you think are particularly important. Say why you think these jobs are important and how society benefits from them.

In your discussion with the assessor, you could consider such things as:

- the particular qualities and skills needed for such jobs
- how more people could be encouraged to do this kind of important and worthwhile work
- whether the pay received by people who do these jobs reflects the value of the work
- whether you, yourself, would like to do this work
- the sort of job you would ideally like for yourself in the future.

247

2 The shopping experience

Some people enjoy spending time in shops and exploring different stores. They spend a long time looking for just the right products. Discuss this topic with the assessor.

You may wish to use the following ideas to help develop the conversation:

- the kind of shops you enjoy visiting and why
- ways in which shops could be improved
- whether doing some work experience in a store interests you
- the advantages and disadvantages of internet shopping
- the view that we are too concerned with luxury designer products and brand names.

ADVICE FOR SUCCESS

The Advice for Success is for **you** to **help yourself**. Decide which suggestions you like best and mark them. You can adapt an idea in Advice for Success to make it fun for you. Keeping track with a notebook is a good idea.

Revision and practice

1   Refresh your memory by studying your vocabulary records, reading through good examples of your own work and looking at the examples in your book. Take regular, short breaks and do something relaxing. You probably can't concentrate effectively for more than 20 or 30 minutes at a time.

2   Ask your teacher for exam practice papers. Time yourself answering the questions. Why not practise with a good friend?

Before your exam

3   Concentrate on staying relaxed and calm. Visualise yourself completing the paper well and in good time, and imagine the good results you will receive. Relax the night before the exam by doing something enjoyable such as watching a film.

Exam techniques

4   The order in which you tackle reading and writing papers is a matter of personal preference, but it's generally a good idea to answer those questions you feel most confident about first. Aim to complete the paper; gaining just a few extra marks on a question makes a difference to the overall score.

5   Make sure you don't run out of time because you have spent too long on answering one section of the paper. The number of marks for each individual question is shown at the end of the question.

6   Always read the questions very carefully. Don't be tempted to answer comprehension questions without reading the passage first. You will probably miss important links in the text. For summaries and compositions, make sure you understand the 'angle' of the question.

7   Never try to twist a pre-prepared essay to fit the topic of the composition. It's far better to tackle the question confidently and write something fresh that answers the question set.

8   Try to stay calm and relaxed during your exam. Flex your fingers so they do not become stiff, and stretch from time to time. Make sure you are sitting comfortably and with the correct posture.

9   If you get really stuck on a question, leave it, move on to another, and go back to the question later.

Exam focus

This unit has helped to prepare you for exams which test your reading, writing, listening and speaking skills. The unit has helped to develop those skills in the following ways:

- You have used **reading techniques** to **answer questions** on **complex** and **less complex texts**. You have written a **summary** based on a **complex text**.

- You have **listened** to a **detailed talk** and answered **multiple-choice questions**. You have listened to **short recordings** and **answered questions**.

- You have practised writing **structured paragraphs** based on **notes** and **letters, reports and emails** giving your **opinions** and **views**.

- You have **taken part** in a **role play, discussions** and **informal conversations**.

Audioscript for Unit 5, Exercise A.5

Teacher: Navid and Marta, you've each chosen to talk about quite different films. Navid, you've chosen 'The Way to the Sea' and Marta, you've selected 'You after Me'. May I ask why you chose these particular films?

Marta: I wanted to talk about a high school drama because that's my favourite genre.

Navid: I wanted to say why I enjoyed a thriller.

Teacher: They sound very interesting! Could you both tell me a bit about the plots?

Navid: 'The Way to the Sea' is set in the future. It's about George, a 16-year-old boy, who survives a massive global explosion. His family have disappeared and population are dead. He believes his family are still alive and living by the coast. He sets out to find them, but law and order have broken down and he often has to hide from bloodthirsty gangs.

Marta: In 'You after Me', Ama, a ten-year-old girl makes friends with Betty, a sophisticated teenage girl who comes to Ama's school. Ama admires Betty and is happy when Betty chooses her to be her best friend. Ama doesn't realise that secretly Betty wants to harm her. Betty steals a phone from a classmate, for example, and hides it in Ama's bag so Ama gets into trouble. Betty also encourages Ama to do things Ama knows are wrong.

Teacher: Characters are extremely important in films. Marta, would you mind telling me about how Ama and Betty are portrayed?

Marta: Betty seems sweet and kind, but actually she is very deceitful and is jealous of Ama because she's kind and has a loving family. We see Ama as a trusting child who wants to grow up too quickly.

Teacher: Well, that is very interesting. What's the hero of 'The Way to the Sea' like?

Navid: George is strong and brave. His situation is scary and unpredictable but he never panics. The character is played Julius Mani. He's ideal for the part, because he's a similar age to the character he plays, and his face is very expressive.

Teacher: Can you give me an example of how his character's personal qualities are shown in the film?

Navid: In one scene, he's threatened by a boy who tries to steal his food. I was on the edge of my seat but George keeps calm in the face of danger, and persuades the boy to lay down his knife.

Teacher: 'You after Me' is set in a Canadian town. Could you explain why you think the setting is effective, Marta?

Marta: Well, the small town setting is very ordinary. I live in a place like that myself so it felt familiar. Its cosy ordinary setting is a real contrast to Betty's bad intentions and adds to the tense atmosphere of the film.

Teacher: Navid, you've said that 'The Way to the Sea' is set in the future after a major catastrophe. Can you describe the setting?

Navid: It's sinister and shows a world that's desperate. There are burnt out buildings and dark, scary woods where gangs could be hiding.

Teacher: Something else I'd like to know is whether there are any special effects?

Navid: Yes, quite a lot actually. A powerful special effect is when George finds a poisonous snake in the grass and is able to control it by singing to it.

Teacher: Marta, dramas can have some light-hearted moments. Can you give me an example of humour in 'You after Me?'

Marta: There is a hilarious scene when Betty and Ama visit the circus and the clowns play a joke on them. I laughed so much I nearly choked on my popcorn

Teacher: I'm glad it was so entertaining. Overall however, it sounds as if the film has a serious theme. Do you think it's right that the film shows Betty setting a bad example?

Marta: Yes, because the underlying message is that evil is overcome by the forces of good. The real interest is waiting to find out how that happens.

Teacher: Navid, did 'The Way to the Sea' have a message?

Navid: I think the message is that courage is essential to achieve a goal.

Teacher: Finally, why do you think other people would enjoy 'The Way to the Sea,' Navid?

Navid: It's so full of suspense. I've been working for my exams, and it made a great break from studying.

Acknowledgements

The authors and publishers acknowledge the following sources of copyright material and are grateful for the permissions granted. While every effort has been made, it has not always been possible to identify the sources of all the material used, or to trace all copyright holders. If any omissions are brought to our notice, we will be happy to include the appropriate acknowledgements on reprinting.

Unit 1 quiz adapted from 'Are you living the life you want?' from *Women's Realm* magazine © www.timeinukcontent. com; Unit 1 adapted from article 'Happy not to be a high flyer' in *Options* magazine © www.timeinukcontent.com; Unit 1 adapted from article 'Facing the fear' by Ewan MacNaugton © Telegraph Media Group Limited; Unit 2 adapted from article 'The woman who put the word hospitable into hospital' by Jo Fairley in *YOU* magazine; Unit 3 adapted from article 'Game for a laugh' by Sally Smith published in the TES; Unit 3 adapted form article 'Sporting chance' by Sarah Farely published in the TES; Unit 3 excerpt from *NURTURESHOCK: New thinking about children* by Po Bronson and Ashley Merryman, published by Ebury Press, reprinted by permission of The Random House Group Limited, and © by Po Bronson, used by permission of Twelve, an imprint of Grand Central Publishing, all rights reserved. Unit 3 adapted from article 'Fear of swimming' by Beverley Davies in *The Lady*, © and used by kind permission of The Lady; Unit 4 adapted from article 'Mike to the future' from *Earth Matters*, published by Friends of the Earth; Unit 5 interview with Nick Park by Philip Gray from Springboard Magazine; Unit 6 adapted information from Kingswood Camps; Unit 6 adapted from article 'Offshore Italy' from *Good Housekeeping* magazine © Good Housekeeping/Hearst Magazines UK; Unit 7 adapted from article 'Exam tension: what can you do?' from *Good Housekeeping* magazine © Good Housekeeping/Hearst Magazines UK; Unit 7 material is adapted from information from the website of the University of Sydney Sydney.edu.au; Unit 8 adapted from article 'Back from the dead' by Luke Harding in the Daily Mail, used by permission of Solo Syndication; Unit 9 adapted from article 'To test or not to test' from *Zest* magazine © Zest UK/Hearst Magazines UK; Unit 10 article adapted from 'A bar is born' by John Crace in *The Guardian*, © copyright Guardian News & Media Ltd; Unit 10 adapted from article 'Faces – signs of concern' by Manal el-Jesri in *Egypt Today*

Thanks to the following for permission to reproduce images:

Cover image: Nikada/Getty Images; Unit 1 Tom Merton/ Getty Images; JGI/Jamie Grill/Getty Images; PeopleImages/ Getty Images; Liam Norris/Getty Images; AfriPics.com/ Alamy Stock Photo; Mint Images RF/Shutterstock; Caiaimage/Sam Edwards/Getty Images; Ghislain & Marie David de Lossy/Getty Images; Jack Hollingsworth/Getty Images; Hill Street Studios/Eric Raptosh/Getty Images; GUSTOIMAGES/Getty Images; Panoramic Images/Getty Images; Ascent/PKS Media Inc./Getty Images; Christy Thompson/Shutterstock; Hero Images/Getty Images; arabianEye arabianEye/Getty Images; Ridofranz/Getty Images; Unit 3 Cindy Prins/Getty Images; Monkey Business Images/Shutterstock; Niedring/Drentwett/Getty Images; Maxisport/Shutterstock; ajaykampani/Getty Images; W2 Photography/Getty Images; John Blanton/Shutterstock; Chris Ryan/Getty Images; Unit 4 Kai Tirkkonen/Getty Images; RooM the Agency/Alamy Stock Photo; Asanka Brendon Ratnayake/Getty Images; Lisa Peardon/Getty Images; RosaIreneBetancourt 4/Alamy Stock Photo; Luis Davilla/Getty Images; rep0rter/Getty Images; TomasSereda/Getty Images; Seqoya/Shutterstock; Mint Images/Getty Images; Monty Rakusen/Getty Images; Claver Carroll/Getty Images; anweber/Shutterstock; Christopher Furlong/Getty Images; FloridaStock/ Shutterstock; Craig Lovell/Eagle Visions Photography/ Alamy Stock Photo; Doug McKinlay/Getty Images; Hill Street Studios/Eric Raptosh/Getty images; Colin Anderson/ Getty Images; Franek Strzeszewski/Getty Images; AF archive/Alamy stock Photo; bjones27/Getty Images; Nicky J. Sims/Getty Images; AF archive/Alamy Stock Photo; Karina Mansfield/Getty Images; Dragon Images/ Shutterstock; AF archive/Alamy Stock Photo; Unit 6 Nick Brundle Photography/Getty Images; Kingwood Camps; Yellow Dog Productions/Getty Images; Tetra Images - Erik Isakson/Getty Images; Kingwood Camps; Scott E Barbour/ Getty Images; Kuzmichstudio/Getty Images; Wig Worland/ Alamy Stock Photo; Image Source Plus/Alamy Stock Photo; JGI/Tom Grill/Getty Images; oonger/Getty Images; BJI/ Blue Jean Images/Getty Images; Cultura Exclusive/SuHP/ Getty Images; Hero Images Inc./Alamy Stock Photo; Stuart

Forster/Alamy Stock Photo; K. Roy Zerloch/Shutterstock; Angelo Giampiccolo/Shutterstock; Anna Serrano/SOPA RF/SOPA/Corbis; Adrian Sherratt/Alamy Stock Photo; Susan Law Cain/Shutterstock; Tim Graham/Getty Images; Education Images/UIG via Getty Images; Unit 7 Anthony-Masterson/Getty Images; Wavebreakmedia Ltd/Getty Images; David Schaffer/Getty Images; Simon Grosset/ Alamy Stock Photo; Blend Images/Alamy Stock Photo; altrendo images/Getty Images; MarianVejcik/Getty Images; Hero Images Inc./Alamy Stock Photo; Hero Images/Getty Images; Brendon Thorne/Getty Images; seng chye teo/ Getty Images; Education Images/UIG via Getty Images; Unit 8 Georgette Douwma/Getty Images; Eye Ubiquitous/ Alamy Stock Photo; alybaba/Shutterstock; hpbdesign/ Shutterstock; Paulo Resende/Shutterstock; Pete Turner/ Getty Images; John Lawlor/Getty Images; Taras Kushnir/ Shutterstock; Roger Bamber/Alamy Stock Photo; Ksenia Raykova/Shutterstock; The Photolibrary Wales/Alamy Stock Photo; XiXinXing/Getty Images; Ezra Bailey/Getty Images; WILLIAM WEST/AFP/GettyImages; Unit 9 Haydn Bartlett Photography/Getty Images; Phillip Rubino/ Shutterstock; FlavoredPixels/Shutterstock; Waddell Images/Shutterstock; Erik Zandboer/Shutterstock; Albie Venter/Shutterstock; Sue Green/Shutterstock; rivendels/ Getty Images; anyaivanova/Shutterstock; Caiaimage/Chris Ryan/Getty Images; dbimages/Alamy Stock Photo; by ana gassent/Getty Images; Peter Cade/Getty Images; Sirko Hartmann/iStock/Getty Images; Ian Forsyth/Getty Images; old apple/Shutterstock; Ricardo Beliel/Brazil Photos/ LightRocket via Getty Images; davemhuntphotography/ Shutterstock; DeLoyd Huenink/Shutterstock; Jetta Productions/Getty Images; Sebastian Radu/Shutterstock; Monty Rakusen/Getty Images; Thomas Barwick/Getty Images; Juice Images/Alamy Stock Photo; Image Source/ Alamy Stock Photo; White Packert/Getty Images; Monkey Business Images/Shutterstock; Blend Images - DreamPictures/Getty Images; Peter Dazeley/Getty Images; kali9/Getty Images; Jutta Klee/Getty Images

253

SPINDLE MOULDER HANDBOOK

Eric Stephenson

M.I.M. Wood T.

STOBART DAVIES

BOOKS BY THE SAME AUTHOR

Circular Saws (with Dave Plank)
The Auto Lathe

in preparation:
Woodworking Machines: Techniques and practice

Published November 1986, reprinted 1988, 1991, 1999.

British Library Cataloguing in Publication Data
Stephenson, Eric
Spindle moulder handbook.
1. Woodworking tools   2. Spindles (Machine-tools)
I. Title
621.9'02TT186

ISBN 0-85442-031-2

Stobart Davies Ltd., Priory House, Priory Street, Hertford SG14 1RN

Printed and bound in Great Britain by BPCC Wheatons Ltd, Exeter

To my Wife and Family who afforded me the time and opportunity to devote to writing.

PREFACE

Although technologies for other woodworking machines have changed a great deal over the past few years, in the smaller workshop the role of the spindle moulder (shaper in The United States) has changed very little, but even so, change it has. This book has been prepared as a practical guide to all users and students of these machines, to update well-established practices covered in earlier and quite excellent books on this subject and to cover changes that have affected the spindle moulder. The techniques described apply both to small home-use machines and the larger production types. They are described in a way which hopefully is both informative and easily readable.

ACKNOWLEDGEMENTS
Preparation of this book has only been made possible with the help, encouragement and guidance of my many friends and colleagues, together with numerous manufacturers and establishments who have willingly provided data, technical assistance and photographs. A full list is given in alphabetical order.

I would, in particular, like to thank Mr. Malcolm Crank M.I.M. Wood T. who checked my original script and suggested numerous improvements and additional material. These are based on his own wide experience of machine woodworking, and, in particular, of the spindle moulder. I am also very grateful to Mr. C. Horsefield, H.M. Inspector, Woodworking National Industry Group of the Health and Safety Executive. He advised on those aspects relating to safety and the interpretation of the present U.K. legislation, and also suggested the inclusion of some additional material. Finally I would like to thank Mr. Henry Clayton, President of the Institute of Machine Woodworking Technology, for his introduction.

To each one I express my sincere gratitude for the help given. I would emphasize, though, that the views expressed are those of the writer alone. Great care has been taken to give unbiased viewpoints and to lay great emphasis on the safety aspects of the spindle moulder, in particular those relating to UK regulations.

It should be noted that in some cases photographs from manufacturers show guarding which in the author's opinion is inadequate, often because the manufacturers remove essential guards so that the operation illustrated is more clearly shown. However, the safety aspects are fully amplified within the text.

ERIC STEPHENSON 1986

Acknowledgements

Autool Grinders, Sabden, Blackburn, Lancs.
De Beers Ind. Diamond Division (Pty) Ltd, Johannesburg, S.A.
Delta International Machinery Corp., Pittsburg, PA, U.S.A.
Dominion Machinery Co Ltd, Halifax, W Yorks.
Elsworth Ltd, Sheffield, S Yorks.
Equipment Ltd, Hickory, NC U.S.A.
ETP Hydro-grip, FFV transmission AB, Linkoping, Sweden
W. Fearnehough Ltd, Bakewell, Derbyshire.
FIRA, Stevenage, Hertforshire.
Forest City Tool Company, Hickory, NC, U.S.A.
General Electric Company, Worthington, Ohio, U.S.A.
Graycon Tools, Wabash, Indiana, U.S.A.
Hammer Machinery Co Inc, Santa Rosa, California, U.S.A.
Holz-Her, Nuertingen, W Germany.
Inca Maschinen und Apparate AG, Teufenthal, Switzerland.
Interwood Ltd, Hornchurch, Essex.
JKO Cutters Ltd, High Wycombe, Bucks,
Gebr. Leitz GmbH & Co, Oberkochen, W Germany.
Leuco International, Horb am Neckar, W Germany.
C.D. Monninger Ltd, London.
Newman Whitney, Greensboro, NC U.S.A.
Northfield Foundry & Machine Co, Northfield, MN U.S.A.
August Oppold, Oberkochen, W Germany.
Pacific Grinding Wheel Co Inc, Marysville, Washington, U.S.A.
Powermatic Houndaille, McMinnville, TN U.S.A.
Thomas Robinson & Son Ltd, Rochdale, GM.
Rye Machinery Sales, High Wycombe, Bucks.
SCM International Spa, Rimini, Italy.
Sedgwick Woodworking Machinery, Leeds, N Yorks.
Joseph Scheppach GmbH & Co., Inchenhausen, W Germany
Sicar Spa, Carpi, Italy.
Sigrist & Muller, Rafz, Switzerland (Saturn).
Spear & Jackson (Industrial) Ltd, Sheffield, S Yorks.
Startrite Machine Tool Co Ltd, Gillingham, Kent.
Stehle GmbH & Co Memmingen, W Germany
Deloro Stellite, Belleville, Ontario, Canada
TRADA, High Wycombe, Bucks.
Universal Grinding Wheel Co Ltd, Stafford.
Wadkin PLC, Leicester.
V.R. Wesson, Waukegan, Ill, U.S.A. (Tantung)
Whitehill Spindle Tools, Luton, Beds.
WMSA, Loughton, Essex.

ROCHDALE,
LANCS.

SPINDLE MOULDER HANDBOOK.

I am very pleased to have been invited to introduce this book
written by Eric Stephenson which I am certain readers
acquainted with this type of machine will relish.

Only someone with the confidence born of wide experience
allied to a finely tuned analytical capability, and a flair for
illustration, would dare to tackle such a subject in so
comprehensive a manner. The simple title gives no indication
of the breadth of cover given by the author to the essential
preparation and back-up procedures supporting the actual
cutting process.

The manufacture and use of templates, jigs, fences and guards,
so essential to safe and efficient operation, are profusely
illustrated and described. Not only are the many optional
cutters, cutterblocks and cutter steels comprehensively
covered, along with their maintenance, but the selection, use
and dressing of the various abrasive wheels for this purpose
are similarly treated. Cutter profile development includes the
method of making useful development scales. Full coverage is
also given to optional equipment and its use for dovetailing,
stair housing, routing and even tenoning.

The book is so comprehensive, it must be put on record, not
only for the present but probably more so for future
generations the scope and versatility of this basically simple
machine. In the hands of a craftsman it is probably the most
versatile of woodcutting machines, but we must also remember
- potentially the most dangerous. Eric Stephenson, to his
credit, has treated both properties with equal respect.

H. CLAYTON F.I.M.Wood.T.
PRESIDENT
INSTITUTE OF MACHINE WOODWORKING TECHNOLOGY

CONTENTS

CHAPTER 1

INTRODUCTION

The earliest woodworking machines were pole lathes, foot-powered in a very simple way by a band or cord wrapped around the piece being turned and connected one end to a foot pedal and the opposite end to a supple tree branch overhead acting like a leaf spring.

As with many early machines the cutting tool was stationary or moved only under hand control. The workpiece revolved as with a lathe, or moved in a straight line when planing and moulding with what was then the machine equivalent of smoothing and moulding hand planes.

Rotating cutterheads originated around the time mass-produced parts were needed for a rapidly expanding navy, the wooden walls of England, and amongst the first applications was in making ships' blocks at Chatham Dockyard.

The spindle moulder in its present form is a fairly recent innovation dating from an 1853 patent by a Mr. Andrew Gear of Jamesville, Ohio, U.S.A. The machine had a vertical spindle through the centre of a horizontal wooden table very much in the present style. From this machine evolved the present spindle moulders, also power-feed shapers in their various forms with sprocket-fed jig, rotary table, linear table or powered horizontal roller feed.

Fig. 1 Typical spindle moulder shown using a straight fence (Wadkin Bursgreen).

Another version had an overhead spindle for recessing and panel raising on the surface of large pieces which were manually moved around whilst flat on the table. This variant evolved into the high-speed router, originally with hand feed and later with mechanical feed and now with a powered table and fully automatic computor numerical control.

The type of work the spindle moulder was originally intended for was then called irregular moulding, that is the shaping and square-edging or edge-profiling of table tops, chair arms and legs, etc. Straight mouldings were invariably produced on early versions of the four-sided planer and moulder (roller-fed machines which plane and mould on four sides at a single pass through, rather than a single face at a time as on the spindle moulder).

The spindle moulder was also made in two-spindle form. The spindles carried identical but opposite-hand heads and the two heads rotated in opposite directions, the work being interchanged between them so that the cut was always with the grain.

Most spindle moulders now have only a single spindle as modern high-speed tools allow slow-speed cutting with or against the grain with little tear-out.

There are some variations: for example, a tilting spindle type to reduce cutter overhang on deep moulding, multiple quick-change spindle machines for repeated, short-run work, and traversing table machines.

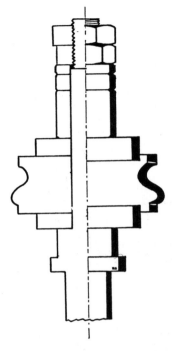

Fig. 2 Sectional elevation through a typical spindle arbor fitted with slotted collars.

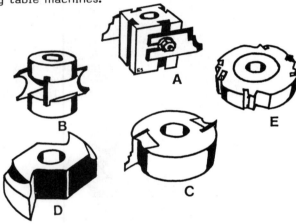

Fig. 3 Various cutterheads used on a spindle moulder
A - square cutterblock:
B - slotted collars:
C - Whitehill type (circular moulding) cutterblock:
D - solid profiled cutterhead:
E - disposable-cutter type cutterhead.

The basic machine

The main spindle is usually a plain, parallel arbor and the cutterheads have a matching plain bore. They are held between a shoulder on the spindle arbor and a top locknut (or locknuts) with spacing collars between. Cutterblocks commonly used on this plain spindle include slotted collars, square and circular heads, profiled heads and disposable-cutter heads.

Fig. 4 Alternative spindle arbors:
Left: French head:
Centre: plain arbor:
Right: collet arbor for router and similar cutters.

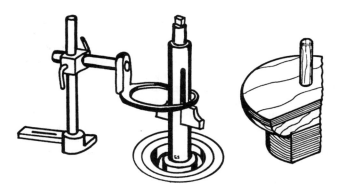

Fig. 5 Ring fence for shaping with a French head. The workpiece is sandwiched between the template and a base. Although not shown a cage or bonnet guard is essential.

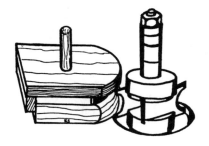

Fig. 6 Ball-bearing follower shown with slotted collars and the template directly on the workpiece. Again, a cage guard is needed.

On the more sophisticated machines the spindle arbor removes and can be replaced by other types, allowing a wider variety of tools to be fitted. These include a slotted or French spindle and a collet head for router, dovetail and similar shanked tools.

Regular equipment with the spindle moulder usually includes a one or two-piece fence for straight moulding, a ring fence or ball-bearing collar for internal or external shaping, together with the necessary guards, dust hoods and pressures. Additional equipment available for some machines includes attachments for stair stringing, dovetailing and corner-locking, etc.

Fig. 7 Chart showing maximum spindle speeds for different cutterhead diameters and types.

The sloping lines represent different cutterhead types:
S – solid profiled and disposable-cutter types.
P – planing heads.
K – keyed moulding heads with loose cutters.
F – friction-held, loose-cutter moulding heads.

Where vertical lines from the cutterhead diameter scale cross the sloping cutterhead-type lines, follow horizontally to the left to find the highest recommended speed.

The example shows in dotted outline a 150mm diameter planing head with a top recommended speed of 7 000 revs/min.

TOOL SPEED CHART

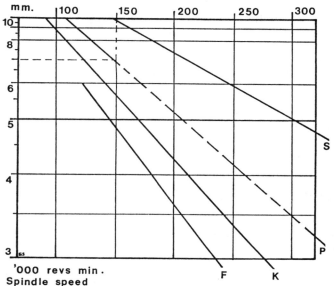

3

SPINDLE SPEEDS

Spindle speed variation is essential where tooling of different cutting diameters is used. A speed range of between 3,000 and 9,000 revs/min is fairly normal. If provided with a single speed only this must not excede the top speed for the largest diameter cutterhead used, otherwise there will be a problem with balance, and heads are unsafe when run at higher speeds than those stated. In the same way heads should not be run at too low a speed or they tend to snatch.

A speed/tool diameter chart shows the recommended combinations. Note that different types of heads have different maximum spindle speeds. Some European cutterheads have the maximum stated speed stamped on them, check against this or with the maker, taking the speeds given in the Chart as a guide only.

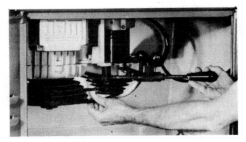

Plate 4 5-step vee-belt drive on a Delta RS-15, showing ease of speed change

Spindle drive types

For the bigger machines run off industrial power supplies the normal drive arrangement is via a flat or vee-belt from the drive motor. Multi-speed drive is often provided via stepped pulleys on the motor and a single flat, parallel pulley on the spindle arbor, with speed changed by moving the belt onto another step on the motor pulley and re-tensioning.

The golden rule with belt drives is that the belt should run with the least tension needed to transmit the power required. Too little tension and the belts wear out fast, too much and long-term damage is done to the bearings, belt life is shortened and excessive power is wastefully absorbed. There are two pointers to correct tension. A belt that squeals is usually under-tensioned and a belt that runs hot or absorbs an undue amount of power is usually over-tensioned.

When changing vee-belts it is essential to completely release tension so that the belts can be positioned whilst slack. Do not force vee belts into position under tension as this will damage the load-bearing cords.

The ideal solution is infinately-variable speed drive as this allows the speed to be matched precisely to the cutterhead type and diameter and nature of the work, but this is rarely provided. With it the belt tension is automatic via an internal spring so tensioning in the normal way is not necessary.

Some spindle moulders have a direct-drive from a motor mounted on an extension of the spindle arbor. When this is an industrial mains motor powered from a three-phase electrical supply the frequency of the supply governs the speed of the motor. Direct connection from the mains supply gives too low a spindle speed for regular spindle moulder work, so motors of this type are powered via a frequency changer to run faster.

The frequency changer is actually a rotating transformer driven by a normal mains motor either directly-coupled or with a short-centre-belt drive. In the former case it is possible to change the spindle speed by simple electrical switching, but speeds are restricted.

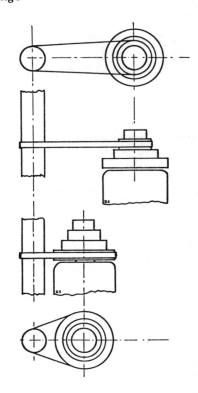

Fig. 8 Flat-belt drive from a stepped pulley on the motor (right) to a single parallel pulley on the spindle arbor.
Showing a four-speed drive from a 50 Hz motor giving 4,500 revs/min. spindle speed (above) and 9,000 revs/min. (below).

4

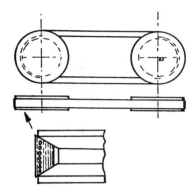

Fig. 9 Above: Vee pulley drive showing the load-bearing chords (inset) in the vee-belt. The drive is 1:1 giving 3,000 revs/min spindle speed.
Below: Infinately-variable drive. As the motor pulley halves (left) are forced together the belt contacts the sides of the vee pulley further out towards the rim to raise the speed.

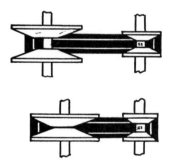

Fig. 10 The quality of the surface finish produced by a rotating cutterhead can be measured as the pitch of the cuttermark 'K'.
The cuttermark depth 'L' is more when using a cutterhead with a smaller diameter so the surface appears worse for the same pitch.

On U.K. machines with electrical switching for speed change, control should be such that the machine always starts at the lowest speed before switching to a higher speed. This is an essential safety feature. Control of this sort is possible with newer electrical gear which can also give infinately variable speeds on direct drive.

With a belt-driven frequency changer it is possible to change speeds by electrical switching, or by a stepped pulley drive and manually changing belts.

THE CUTTING ACTION

Certain factors affect the cutting action of all rotary cutterheads and it is important to know what these are and what restrictions they place on the user. They affect the life of the cutters, their efficiency, the choice of cutterhead and the operating speed, but most importantly they affect the surface finish.

Surface finish

A rotary cutterhead does not produce a perfectly flat surface but a series of scallop-like cuttermarks, each mark produced by a single cutter at each rotation. Although the surface is not flat technically it is commercially acceptable provided the cuttermarks are close and evenly-spaced. The spindle speed and the feed speed together determine the cuttermark pitch which is used to measure the quality of the surface finish. (The number of finishing cutters also affects the surface finish, but as only single cutter finish is normal on a spindle moulder this factor is ignored.)

Poorer surface quality is produced when the cuttermark pitch is large, i.e., when the feed speed is fast and/or the spindle speed is slow. In addition to the prominent cuttermark pattern formed the chips are thicker so tear-out and other machining defects increase.

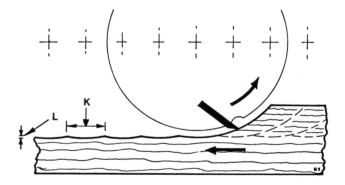

Better quality results when the cuttermark pitch is small, i.e., when the feed speed is slow and/or the spindle speed fast. Too fine a pitch, however, produces more dust, and there is a greater tendency to burn.

To a lesser extent the surface quality is affected by the size of the cutterblock. Small cutterblocks give a deeper and more prominant cuttermark for the same pitch, so a smaller pitch is needed to give the same quality of surface finish. This is shown in the feed speed chart, Fig. 11.

As a manual feed is normally used on a spindle moulder, feed speed is difficult to judge accurately except from the appearance of the finished workpiece. This shows the defects described if wrong, but only after the event. A smooth, steady feed without hesitation gives the best results. What should be avoided is a series of fast movements interspaced by a stoppage whilst the operator changes hand grip.

Obviously a mechanical feed gives the best results as the feed is continuous and can be set to a precise speed. Use a mechanical feed instead of hand feed wherever possible on straight mouldings. A guide to maximum feed speeds relative to cutterblock diameter and spindle speed is given below.

FEED SPEED CHART

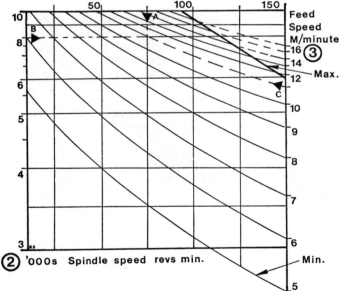

Fig. 11 Chart showing maximum feed speeds for mechanical feeds on straight moulding which give an acceptable finish.

Trace horizontally along the spindle speed line to the cutterhead diameter, then follow the curved line to show the maximum recommended speed.

Example shows: A maximum feed speed of 11 m/min. 'C' is possible for a 75 mm. diameter cutterhead 'A' running at 8,000 revs/min. 'B'. The feed speeds are correct for shallow moulding on good quality timber. For deeper cuts or with more difficult timber much lower speeds are needed. When the finish is not exposed the feed rate could be increased to double the figures given.

Hand-fed machines, such as the spindle moulder, are invariably fed with rotation of the cutter against the direction of feed. This is conventional or resistance cutting.

The timber tends to split and rive ahead of the cut and bunches of slivers often tear-out below the finished surface when cutting against the grain, that is when the grain of the timber slopes towards the cutting head in the feed direction. This can occur when straight moulding, but always when when shaping. It also happens around knots and with curly-grained timber, sycamore for example, and with interlocked-grain timber which grows with alternating growth-slope angles in narrow bands.

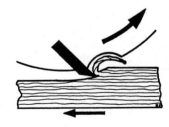

Fig. 12 Conventional or resistance cutting, cutters rotate against the feed.

Fig. 13 With large cutting angles the grain rives to split ahead of the cut. Bunches of fibres often tear out below the finished surface to spoil it when cutting against the grain.

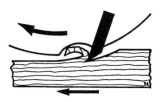

Fig. 14 Climb cutting, cutters rotate with the feed. This is never used except with a mechanical feed and secure clamping of the timber, or with a very light cut and a holding jig.

Fig. 17 Right: cutting angle of collar cutters 'E' - usually 30 degrees.

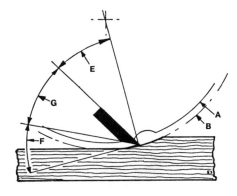

Fig. 15 Various cutting angles, etc:
A - cutterhead.
B - planing circle.
E - cutting angle.
F - clearance angle.
G - bevel angle.

Grain tear-out spoils the finished surface which then needs a lot of extra finishing. Even when correction is carefully carried out the surface never looks uniform and, unfortunately, the process is always time consumming and costly. Tear-out can usually be reduced by reducing the feed speed and/or the cutting angle.

Very occasionally the cutter rotates with the feed, which is known as back or climb cutting. The advantage of climb cutting is that the cutters cut into the timber and there is virtually no tear-out, even when cutting against the grain.

It is used only on machines with a strictly controlled mechanical feed and a clamped workpiece. Whilst climb cutting is possible with a hand-feed machine it should be undertaken only with the greatest of care as the cutters could grab the timber and throw it violently in the direction of cutter rotation. Only the lightest of cuts should be taken and the timber must be securely held and very carefully controlled using some form of holding jig.

CUTTING ANGLE

This is measured between the leading face of the cutter and a line drawn from the cutting point to the centre of the spindle arbor. Measure it with a protractor after sketching the precise shape of the cutterblock used. The way to measure it is shown in the sketches. The cutting angle is very important as it determines the aggressiveness of the cut and the quality of finish it gives.

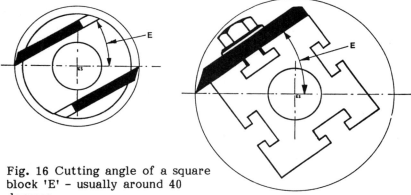

Fig. 16 Cutting angle of a square block 'E' - usually around 40 degrees.

Large cutting angles of from 30 to 45 degrees are aggressive and are used mainly for mellow softwoods. They are free-cutting, have low feed resistance, low power consumption and low noise level. However, they also tend to rive ahead much more readily that smaller angles. This can be controlled to a certain extent by slowing down the feed or setting the fences close to the cutting circle, or better still breaking-through a wooden fence to give support right up to the point of cut. The real cure is to use a smaller cutting angle or front bevel, but both have drawbacks.

Some timbers are prone to chip bruising, that is hooking of severed chips by the cutting edge to be carried round and indent on the finished surface. Chip bruising is common with larger cutting angles, on heavy cuts, with wet timber and when cutters are dull. The affect is worsened where the exhaust system is inefficient - often a spindle moulder dust hood is full of air leaks. If no air connection is fitted check that the chip path is clear at the back. Adding extra non-cutting cutters can sometimes reduce chip bruising by creating extra draft.

Small cutting angles, 5 - 10 degrees, prevent riving ahead and tear-out even on interlocked grain timbers, but take more power, give more feed resistance and are noisier. Smaller angles also reduce chip bruising.

Medium cutting angles, 20 - 35 degrees, are the most commonly used as they allow cutting of most commercial timbers without serious down-grading or having to restrict feed speed.

Cutting angle change

With most cutterheads it is not possible to change the cutting angle. It might seem simple enough to alter a profiled head cutting angle but this is not practicable as it also alters the profile slightly. The normal practice is to choose a cutterhead with the most suitable cutting angle for the work intended.

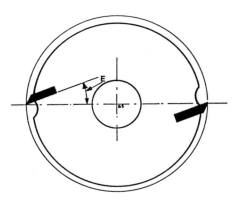

Fig. 18 Cutting angle of a circular moulding block 'E' - usually around 27 degrees,

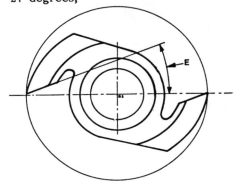

Fig. 19 Cutting angle of a solid profiled head 'E' - usually around 20 degrees.

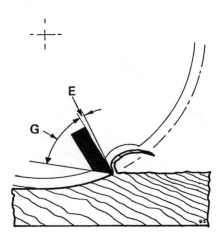

Fig. 21 A small cutting angle 'E' allows cutting against the grain with little tear-out.

With planing heads is it possible to reduce the cutting angle by adding a front bevel to the cutters but this is only necessary with the worst interlocked-grain timbers. It is rarely practiced on a spindle moulder as difficult timbers can be worked satisfactorily using regular cutting angles simply by slowing the feed rate. It is not practical to increase the cutting angle.

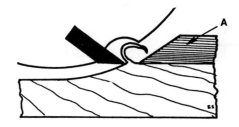

Fig. 20 A close-set fence 'A' helps to prevent riving ahead.

8

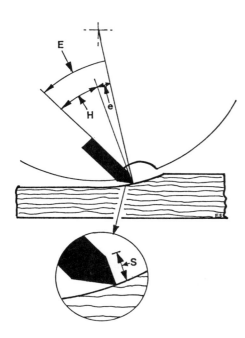

Fig. 22 A front bevel 'H' can reduce the cutting angle 'E' to a smaller one 'e' to give the same effect as a reduction in seating angle of the cutter. The depth of bevel 'S' should be at least 1.5 mm.

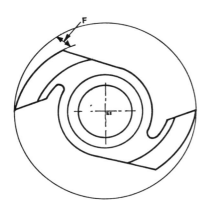

Fig. 23 Radial relief 'F' on a solid profiled head.

SPECIES	GREEN	DRIED
Basswood, Cedar, Chestnut, Cypress	25	20 - 25
Soft Elm, Hemlock, White Pine, Redwood, Spruce, Ash, Beech, Plain Birch, Hard Elm	25	15-20
Fir, Gum, Mahogany, Plain Maple, Plain Oak, Yellow Pine, Poplar, Walnut, Curly Birch, Hickory, Quartered Oak	20	10-15
Bird's eye Maple	5	5-10

Source - Graycon Tools.

Clearance angle

This is measured between the trailing face of the cutter and a line tangential to the cutting circle at the cutting point.

Too small a clearance angle allows rubbing and in extreme cases burning. It does not allow subsequent honing to re-sharpen the edge, and natural wear produces a dulled condition much more quickly. Too large a clearance angle leaves a weak cutting edge. The clearance angle is normally between 15 and 30 degrees.

True clearance is a snail-shell curve with the gap between trailing face and cutting circle increasing pro-rata the distance behind the cutting edge. This is called radial relief and is normal on solid profiled heads, router cutters and similar. This face is not touched in re-grinding as this would spoil it. Regrinding takes place only on the leading flat face.

With square and circular heads, slotted collars and French heads the bevel angle formed when profiling and re-sharpening them affects the clearance angle.

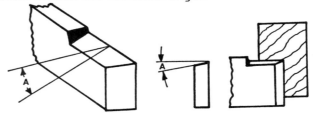

Fig. 24 Side clearance 'A' is needed when, for example, rebating.

Side clearance angle

Most cutters also have side clearance. This avoids burning where the cutting edge is almost square to the cut - the edges of rebate cutters for example. Normally 5 degrees is enough.

9

Bevel angle

This is the ground angle of the cutter measured between the leading and trailing faces. When using too small a bevel angle the cutting edge is weak, breaks down quickly and is prone to damage. If the bevel angle is too big the cutter dulls more quickly and the clearance angle is less.

The recommended minimum bevel angle is 35 degrees for HSS and similar cutters, and 45 degrees for tungsten carbide types. Maximum bevel angle in both cases is 60 degrees.

BEVEL ANGLE CHART

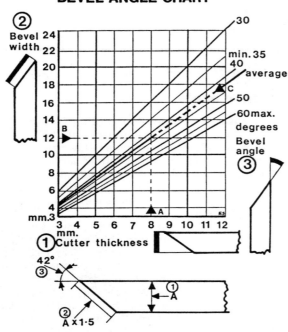

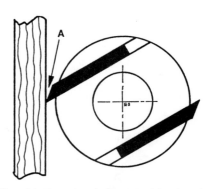

Fig. 25 Rotate the cutterblock with the cutters in contact with a sample piece to check for clearance at 'A'.

Fig. 26 Left: Chart showing relationship of bevel angle to cutter thickness and bevel width.

Example shows:
A – cutter thickness of 8mm.
B – bevel width of 12mm.
C – bevel angle of 42 degrees.

The sketch, lower left, shows the rule of thumb used to measure an average bevel angle of 42 degrees.

Fixed angles cannot be stated either for the bevel angle or the clearance angle as both vary according to the cutting angle and the cutting diameter of the cutterhead. It is possible to relate them to tables, but the simplest and most direct way to check if they are correct is to set the cutters to a sample piece of timber and rotate the cutterhead. There should be visible clearance between the fixed timber and the trailing heel of the ground face. If no gap can be seen, increase the clearance angle by reducing the bevel angle. If the gap is wide the bevel angle can be increased to give a stronger cutting edge. A rule of thumb is to make the bevel width 1.5 times cutter thickness to give a bevel angle of 42 degrees, which is a good average for many cutterheads.

A secondary clearance angle is commonly formed on cutters when honing, to give a stronger tip. This is also used for tungsten carbide cutters. The smallest practical clearance angle in this case is 5 degrees.

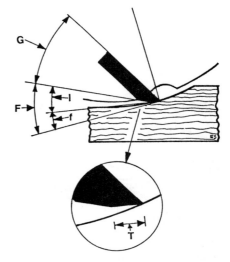

Fig. 27 A secondary clearance angle 'I' reduces a large clearance angle 'F' to a smaller one 'f'.
'T' is the width of the land, usually not more than 1.5 mm.

Plate 5 Top left: This Dominion BCB spindle moulder has infinitely variable spindle speeds between 3 000 and 9 000 revs/min.

Plate 6 Lower left: Showing easy removal of the spindle arbor on a Delta RS–15 spindle moulder. It is secured by a locknut with differential threads.

Plate 7 Lower right: This Powermatic Model 26 spindle moulder has four spindle speeds.

Operational Safety

The spindle moulder is a versatile machine capable of a wide variety of work in joinery and furniture production. The tools it uses operate at higher speeds than on most other industrial machinery and certain basic safety precautions are essential.

Specific safety points are detailed for the different cutterhead types and machine operations. Other safety points are more general in nature and apply to all types. Both should be observed in preparation and operation and a check list run through immediately before start-up.

Machine setting

Isolate the machine electrically before setting-up or making alterations.

Use the cutter equipment recommended for the job. Ensure that arbor mounting, cutterblock and cutters are clean and free from grease, rust-preventative, rust, wood residue and metallic burrs, etc. Check thoroughly for soundness, freedom from cracks and signs of overstrain on cutters and cutterheads. Replace suspect parts immediately and dispose of them.

Only use cutters in dimensionally-alike pairs formed to the same profile, and balance cutters in matched pairs after grinding. Mount them directly opposite on the cutterblock and both 'to cut' to ensure they balance dynamically. Make sure that cutter projection and retention of the cutter in the cutterblock are as recommended. Cutters wear down in use and are advanced to compensate, make sure they are still safely retained when worn.

Use only the correct spanners when tightening cutters. Never add extra leverage as this strains the bolts, causes excessive strain and leads to undue wear. Some manufacturers recommend the use of a pre-set torque spanner, but not all makers agree on this point.

Discard spanners when they wear. Tighten cutters progressively, rotating the cutterblock in the process, never fully tighten one cutter with the other still loose. When the cutterblock has several bolts or screws cross over to tighten each a little in turn until all have equal tightness. Never exceed the recommended maximum spindle speeds given in the Chart (Fig. 11). Lower speeds can be used but keep the difference as small as practicable.

Make sure that all parts are secure, the loose arbor, cutterblock and cutters. Use table rings to give support right up to the cutterhead or use a wooden false table. Guard the cutterhead as well as practicable and fit a through-fence to give the narrowest practicable fence gap, allowing ample clearance of the steel fence plates before fitting the fence. Cover the top, sides and rear of the cutterhead.

Plate 8 Speed change lever on a Wadkin Bursgreen BEL spindle moulder, showing safety interlock covering the stop push button.

Plate 9 Plug-in voltage-change feature on the electronic brake offered by Delta for their machines. The torque and brake time controls are variable, and the arbor is free to rotate when the braking cycle is completed.

12

Plate 10 Straight moulding on a Scheppach HF33, using roller hold-downs.

Use top and side Shaw guard pressures to hold the workpiece down on the table and control it sideways when straight moulding. This steadies it and prevents vibration which could cause a kick-back. Hand-fed pieces can never be properly controlled unless some form of mechanical pressure is used. This also guards the cutterhead when timber is not in position.

Check that fences and pressures are correctly positioned and properly secured. Rotate the cutterhead manually to make sure that no part fouls the machine, with extra clearance allowed for subsequent adjustment should it be necessary.

When handling small parts, when dropping-on and when shaping, use a jig with handles to control the operation.

Remove all loose items from the machine. Fit all guards and connect the dust hood to the exhaust system or make sure that the chip exit is clear before starting the machine even if only making a pre-run trial cut.

Finally check that the direction of rotation and spindle speed are correct before starting up.

Operation

Hand-feed timber past the cutterhead in as smooth and continuous movement as possible. Hold it firmly down on the table and against the fence. The operator's hands should not pass immediately across the cutters whenever practical as slippage or kickback could have serious consequences. If possible alternate the feed between both hands so that one hand maintains momentum whilst grip is changed with the other.

When straight-moulding a series of short sections, push the piece in the cut through with the following piece rather than feeding them individually. Push the last one through with a push-stick. Stand at the side rather than in line with the feed, just in case of kick-back. Spikes and push-sticks should always be used to avoid close contact with the cutters. Before starting make sure that these are close at hand. Use a jig where recommended.

Certain operations are inherently dangerous, for example stop moulding, shaping, etc. Make sure that proper precautions are taken.

Do not wear clothing that could be caught up in the machine or the cutterblock, avoid loose ties and unbuttoned cuffs, etc.

Do not overfeed. If the cutterhead slows down immediately slow down the feed. Use the brake to slow down the spindle, never run timber into the cutter to slow it. Make sure the spindle is stationary before leaving it, then isolate the machine electrically.

Plate 11 A power feed, such as this Holz-Her, is faster, safer and better for straight moulding.

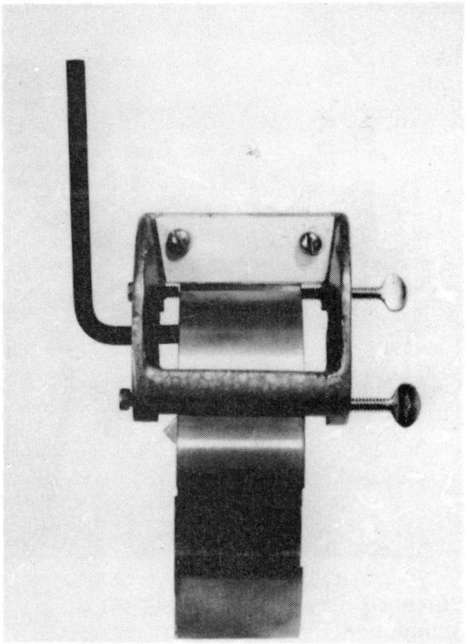

Plate 14 Top right: This Dominion cutterblock has facility to allow a cutter setting template to be fitted.

Plate 12 Top left: The Northfield spindle moulder is a heavily built machine with up to a 10 hp motor drive. It has rear-mounted Shaw-type guards.

Plate 13 Lower left: Some machines, such as this Wadkin Bursgreen BEM, can have a tenoning table fitted.

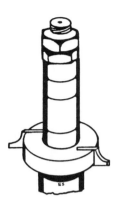

Fig. 28 A cutterhead mounted correctly near the top bearing.

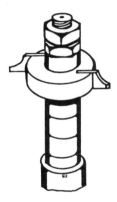

Fig. 29 Avoid this by raising the arbor.

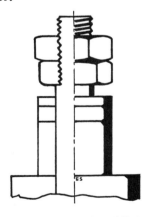

Fig. 30 By having insufficient spacing washers the nuts can lock on the arbor without gripping the cutterhead.

CHAPTER 2

MACHINE OPERATION

This chapter outlines the general principles of setting and operating the spindle moulder on two of its most common operations, straight moulding and shaping. Later chapters fully detail the techniques briefly mentioned here, along with other operations.

Preparation

All spindle moulders have an overhung spindle arbor with bearings below the arbor only; this should be borne in mind when setting-up. Very heavy spindle moulders with a removable top bearing were once used for shaping curved parts of wooden-bodied vehicles but are rarely used now.

As a general guide set the cutterblock directly on the machined collar of the spindle arbor rather than on spacing collars. Use cutterblocks which have a suitable depth for the mould wanted and use the arbor vertical adjustment to position the cutters rather than altering the height of the cutter or the block. This is not always possible, but in all cases the point of cut should preferably be close to the top bearing.

Before fitting the cutterblock make sure that the arbor is secure and that the arbor and the cutterblock are free from grit, grease, wood residue and metallic burrs. On machines with a removable key for the loose arbor make sure the retaining collar is properly fitted to secure the key in position. After fitting the cutterblock add the necessary spacing collars above it so that the top face of the top collar is a few millimetres above the thread shoulder. (Failing this, the nut may lock on the arbor itself without actually securing the cutterblock). The cutterblock must be on the plain part of the arbor - never on the threaded part.

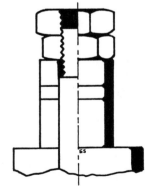

Fig. 31 Do not have the top nut barely gripping as shown here.

Don't have the top collar too far above the thread shoulder as this reduces the grip of the nut. Part of the thread should be above the nut when secured.

Add the top nut (or nuts) to fasten the assembly.

Spindle moulder arbors rarely have keys so the cutterhead is held only by friction - make sure it is properly secured. Use the arbor lock when doing this, or use a second spanner on flats on the top or the base of the arbor itself. (The spindle arbor securing nut or ring should not be used). Don't use inertia tightening, e.g.- swinging the spanner against something solid or hitting the end with a mallet.

When no key is provided the nut must tighten with rotation of the spindle, i.e, with normal counterclockwise rotation the nut should tighten in a clockwise direction. When the spindle can run in either direction it is essential to use double locknuts or an intermediate keyed washer. In this way no mistake is made when reversing the spindle direction.

The following sections: cutter selection, grinding and setting, refer mainly to user-profiled type loose cutters, used on French heads, slotted collars, square and circular heads, etc.

CUTTER SELECTION

Spindle moulder cutters normally shape the under corner rather than the top corner when moulding as the operator is less exposed. In such operations the Shaw guard can be used without hinderance and kick-back is much less likely.

A common practice with deep cutterblocks is to share a complex cut between more than one pair of cutters. This simplifies cutter selection and may allow cutters from an earlier obsolete set to be used. The cut is also broken up into smaller, safer bites.

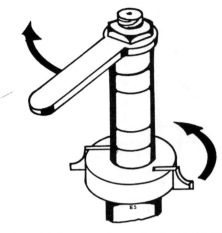

Fig. 32 When only a single locknut is used, rotation of the nut when tightening should be opposite to spindle rotation when running.

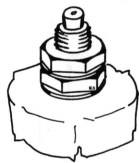

Fig. 33 Double locknuts are essential when the arbor rotates in either direction.

Fig. 34 Sometimes an intermediate, keyed washer can be used, then a single locknut is suitable.

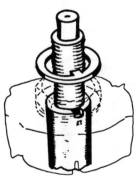

Fig. 35 Cutters normally undercut as shown here. This small section is controlled by two Shaw guards. The gap between the Shaw guard pads is closed-in so that only a spike can pass between. The cutterhead cannot be seen when timber is in place.

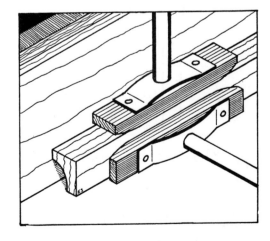

Large cutter projections should be avoided as these put extra strain on the cutters and increase the chance of breakage. It also makes the cutting circle larger and more dangerous and gives more problems in balancing. In all cases the cutting circle should be as small as possible so that the cutterhead gives maximum support to the cutters. If possible 'sink' the cutterhead. A tilting arbor is also useful in reducing cutter overhang.

16

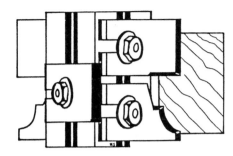

Fig. 36 Dividing the cut between three pairs of cutters on a square block.

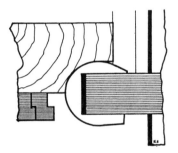

Fig. 37 'Sinking' a Whitehill head into a large ovolo.

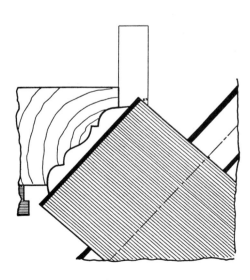

Make cutters deeper than the mould depth by perhaps 5mm. at each side if practicable. If the cutters have a narrow cutting face make them wider and stronger where clear of the through-fence.

CUTTER DEVELOPMENT

The cutter profile normally differs from the mould it produces due to the angle at which it meets the cut, the cutting angle. Only when the cutter meets the cut square-on, as with a French head, is the cutter profile exactly the reverse of the mould it produces. In all other cases the cutter needs to be slightly deeper than the mould, although width-on-cut remains the same.

When the user profile-grinds his own cutters the correct cutter shape must be developed-out. This can be done geometrically, or by using a development rule or a cutter projection template. These give much more accurate results than merely guestimating the cutter shape.

CUTTER GRINDING

With the exception of disposable types, cutters are removed when dull and ground to restore the cutting edge. Many are also hand-honed 'in situ' during a run.

Cutters used on French heads, slotted collars, square and circular heads can be ground off-hand using a twin or multiple-wheel grinder. For better control of cutter profile and ground angles a copy grinder can be used to form the cutter profile to exactly the same shape as a metal template. A profile grinder uses the same basic principle but automatically allows for the difference between the cutter profile and the mould it produces. Cutters must be hand-honed to remove the grinding burr after grinding, otherwise they quickly dull.

Except for the French head, a pair of cutters is used for each mould or section of mould. Normally both cutters are ground to the same profile and should be dimensionally alike, especially when using heavier cutters as on square blocks. After grinding, cutters must be carefully balanced and any inbalance made good by grinding off the heavier cutter. Use a cutter balance or scales to check this. Set both cutters 'to cut'.

If cutters are not properly balanced, or if they are balanced but not both set to cut, the vibration caused will give a poor finish and may damage the machine.

Fig. 38 A tilting spindle reduces cutter projection on some moulds.

Solid and tipped profile heads are ground straight across their face using a universal tool room grinder. Disposable cutters are not re-ground (normally not, they can be but there are practical difficulties) they are simply replaced so grinding and setting does not apply in their case.

17

CUTTER SETTING

The normal way of setting cutters is 'in situ' on the machine using a sample mould. Place this against the through fence and down on the table. Make sure it is properly seated, particularly if the mould is large and the sample small. It is an advantage to clamp the sample in position, otherwise you may find you need three hands.

Adjust the spindle vertically to give maximum support to the cut. Make sure the bearing housing does not foul the workpiece or filling-in rings fitted later. Make sure the cutterhead and any cutterbolts or lips clear the sample by fitting cutters and rotating the cutterblock. Adjust the fence as needed.

Set both cutters to 'cut', to just scrape the sample mould, and lock them securely in place. It isn't easy to know when cutters are correctly set because contact is difficult to see. Sometimes contact can be seen when viewing along the fences from the infeed, but it is near impossible then to reach the cutters to make adjustment.

Do not simply move the cutter against the sample whilst holding the cutterblock stationary because setting will be wrong, the cutterblock must be rotated.

After cutter setting check and correct depth and height using a straight-edge with short rules fitted. Finally, add the guards, pressures and exhaust hood, then run through a check list before starting-up.

Template setting

Setting is made easier if using a template of some sort. The template can be a simple rectangular piece of plywood, aluminium, plastic-faced hardboard or similar, anything that can be pencilled on and the pencil lines later erased for re-use.

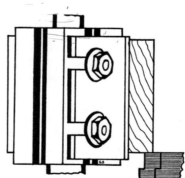

The template should be straight on the underside. It normally rests edge-on the table, up to the cutterblock and with its face against the cutter face. In its simplest form the template merely needs just one basic line permanantly marked on it, the planing line. This can be marked after setting planing cutters to the minimum cutting or planing circle, as follows:-

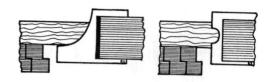

Fig. 39 Cutters should be wider than the mould they produce.

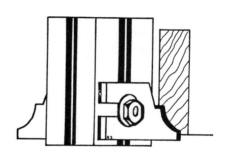

Fig. 40 Cutter setting 'in situ' on the machine.

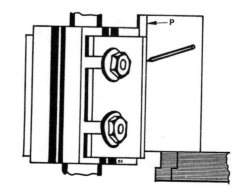

Fig. 41 Left: Set planing cutters to a piece of hardwood clamped across the fences and adjusted to just clear the bolts.
Below: Mark along the cutting edge to show the planing line 'P'.

18

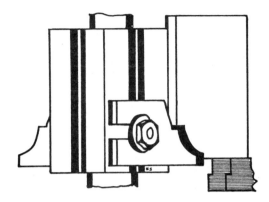

Fig. 42 The template can rest on the table and the underedge taken as the table line.

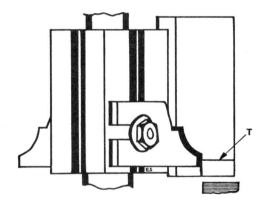

Fig. 43 Alternatively, the template can be notched out to rest on the cutterblock. In this case a table line is added 'T'.

Clamp a piece of straight, flat hardwood across the spindle fences. Mount the cutterblock in the usual way and with the regular thickness of cutters in position. Set the fence so that the inside face of the hardwood clears the cutterblock body, lips, cutterbolts, etc., by 1.5mm.

Set planing cutters so that their cutting edges just scrape the face of the hardwood piece, i.e. to the minimum cutting or planing circle. Place the template in position and carefully mark along the cutting edge of the planing cutter. This is then the line to which planing cutters should be set and beyond which all mould cutters must project to clear the cutterblock.

A second line can be added square to the planing line to show the table line, perhaps 12mm. above the bottom edge to allow cutters to be more easily seen when setting. Using this requires the spindle initially set high, then lowered before use.

It is possible to use the underedge of the template as the table line. As the template rests on the table when setting, the spindle is initially set to the correct height so re-setting is not necessary.

An alternative is to notch-out the template so that a small projection locates on the top of the cutterblock. This type is popular because it is more convenient and can be used off the machine.

The planing and table lines should be permanently marked on the template. The method varies according to the type of template used:

PLYWOOD TEMPLATES - Use birch or some other light-faced plywood about 3mm. thick and mark the lines in HB pencil. Lacquer over the complete template (back and front to prevent warping) using a matt finish lacquer. Finally scrub with wire wool to give a suitable surface to accept pencil marks.

FACED-HARDBOARD TEMPLATES - Scribe the lines with a sharp point then carefully sand level and finally scrub with wire wool.

ALUMINIUM TEMPLATES - Scribe the lines with a sharp point then carefully emery-cloth level, finally use a wet and dry emery cloth, wet, to give a suitable matt surface.

In all cases cutter-profile lines are made in pencil and deleted with a hard eraser. Mark the template for the precise position of the cutters using the planing and table lines as the starting points. The vertical (height) setting is marked-off using a regular rule.

Horizontal setting (depth-on-cut) is marked-off using a projection rule, or by rule-of-thumb adding 2.5-3.0mm. for every 10mm. depth for square cutterblocks and 1.5-2.0mm. for every 10mm. depth for other cutterblocks. This rule-of-thumb is not accurate but good enough in many instances. (See also development templates). The template fits to the cutterblock itself and if there is any damage to the lip accurate setting is not possible.

Pre-setting

Pre-setting in a tool room on a setting stand is easier and simpler that setting on the machine because the cutters and sample or template are clearly visible. A setting stand has a dummy arbor carrying the square or circular cutterhead, setting rollers for planing cutters, clamps for short sample mouldings and usually a template holder for either plain or development templates.

NOTE: Pre-setting is not practicable with conventional slotted collars because cutters slip on transfer to the machine.

Straight moulding

This is used when forming house trim, architraves, door and window sections, etc., when a mould shape, rebate, groove or similar is formed along the full length of timber.

The straight fence should be used with a through-fence for additional support and safe operation. Normally, the fences are in line when face-moulding only part of the depth but can be off-set for edging, to form a bullnose, for example. Timber is usually held down and against the fence with pressures which can be individual spring leaves or finger-like guides. In this case a front guard is essential above the timber, plus other guards to enclose the cutterblock when timber is not in place. Preferably use Shaw guard pressures which also form an enclosing box guarding the cutterblock.

Table rings fill in the table gap so both this and the fence gap are the smallest practicable. Shaw guards are fitted to hold the timber and to enclose the cutterblock when timber is not in position. Guards then complete the enclosure of the cutterblock, one above the timber spanning the gap, and a cover over the back often formed as an exhaust hood.

With deep moulds it is normal to 'sink' the cutterblock to form complex moulds as a series of steps. With deep moulds or small sections the timber may be unstable after leaving the infeed fence, so add a spacer guide at the outfeed fence to support the newly formed mould. Even so, pieces tend to snipe (vibrate to form an unacceptable surface) and it is usual to allow extra length so that these end defects can be cut off.

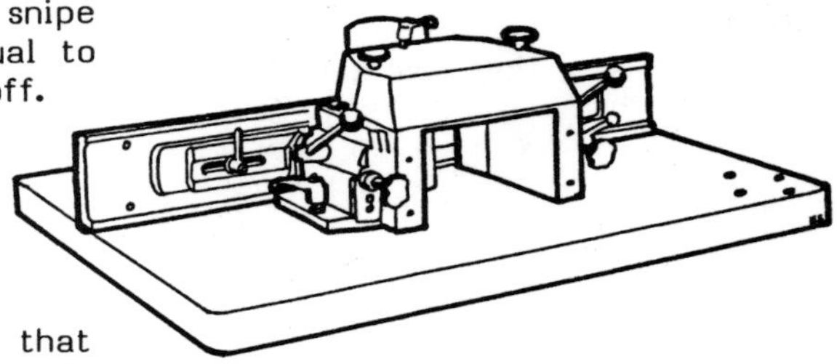

Support long pieces at the infeed and outfeed so that their weight does not lever them off the table. Use a spike in the left hand to avoid close contact with the cutterhead and always use a push-stick or a push-block to follow through. When handling small pieces use some form of jig with secure handholds which afford the operator a firm grip. If stop-moulding, that is forming the mould only part-way along the timber, end-stops must be used. Follow the recommended methods. Never stand directly in line with the timber.

Fig. 44 This shows a straight fence from the rear, complete with a guard fitted but without exhaust hood (Dominion).

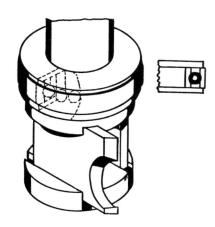

Fig. 45 Slotted collars with a ball-bearing follower.

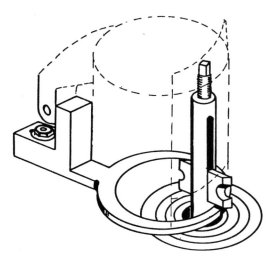

Fig. 46 A ring fence used with a French head. The dotted line shows the cage or bonnet guard.

MECHANICAL FEED

Many users find that a mechanical feed on the spindle moulder not only produces work faster, but also provides a better quality finish, greater safety and makes cutters last longer. The speed can be regulated to give the correct and consistant surface finish on the moulds, whereas hand-feeding gives an irregular finish. It is safer because it guards the cutterhead very effectively and does not need close contact of the user's hands with the cutters.

For feed speeds see Chart 11, Chapter 1.

Shaping

Shaping is forming the outline shape of table tops, chair parts and similar work, either square-edge shaping only, or simultaneously shaping and edge-moulding.

The size and outline of the piece being shaped is controlled by a template made from plywood or similar material. The roughly sized workpiece is fastened to the template so the assembly handles as a single unit. Usually the template is fastened on top of the workpiece, but the template could be underneath. All templates need secure handholds so that the operator can control the work safely, also finger guards where possible. A supporting saddle can be used for compound curves.

SHAPING TEMPLATE

The template edge contacts the pattern follower. This is a ball-bearing mounted on the spindle arbor, a circular 'ring' fence fastened to the table, or a table ring. A cage (bonnet) guard, or similar, protects the spindle above the workpiece, at the rear and around the sides down to table level - leaving the smallest practical gap for the workpiece. Some form of pressure/guard is needed to keep the assembly flat on the table. In shaping, move the assembly around to keep the template in contact with the follower so that the cutterhead simultaneously edge-profiles and shapes the workpiece to the same overall outline.

Ring fence

The ring fence is a static guide having point contact with the template. The ball-bearing type spins with the arbor when running free, but slows down to roll with the template immediately contact is made. This eliminates friction between template and follower and allows that light touch essential to fine detail work. A plain follower can be used, but this rotates with the arbor to create friction and cause wear on the template. It should be used with caution and only when no ball-bearing follower is available.

The template is usually the same size and profile as the finished part to correspond with the planed edge or the highest point of the edge-mould, so template manufacture is relatively straight forward. It is also simple to check the blank against it for size and shape.

Often the blank is first bandsawn to rough shape so that only a light finishing cut is needed. With gentle shapes the spindle moulder can shape and edge-mould simultaneously without pre-cutting. Alternatively, the shape can be formed initially by using planing cutters, and the mould added as a second operation working off the previously formed square-edged shape. In this case the shaped part needs fastening to a jig with secure handholds.

The template can form the edge profile completely around a single piece, for example, a table top. In this case it is essential to ease-in the cut when starting. With a ring fence this is done by starting at any point other than the centre mark on the ring. When using a ball-bearing follower the cut is started against a starting block or by using a lead-in on the template.

Alternatively a template can form only a part of the edge profile, say the inside or outside edge of a chair leg. When handling narrow or small pieces which are only part-profiled use a jigged template which both locates and secures the part in position and has secure handles. The template forms part of that jig.

Often a multi-station jig is used to form part-profiled workpieces, or small and narrow parts in two or more steps. Each part is transferred from one station to another in sequence and several cuts made at a single pass. This is also used to handle full-outline pieces too small to work safely as individual parts.

Plate 15 Above: Setting planing cutters to rollers on an Autool profile grinder.

Plate 16 Below: Setting moulding cutters to a sample on an Autool profile grinder.

CUTTER SETTING

Cutter setting is critical. When a ball-bearing follower is used set the cutters so that the highest point of the mould is directly in line with the contact face of the follower so that the planing diameter is exactly the same as the follower diameter.

When using a ring fence the planed surface or shallowest part of the mould is aligned with the centre mark on the ring. Using a ring fence allows independent adjustment to make small corrections or to suit different diameters of cutterhead.

Cutter pre-setting is as described previously, but the cutting diameter has to be precise when using a ball-bearing follower. This is possible in a number of ways, perhaps using a knife-edge setting roller on fixed centres, or using the Q3S system.

Setting on the machine to a sample part is not easy as cutter contact is difficult to see. Setting, in fact, has to be made both by sight and feel.

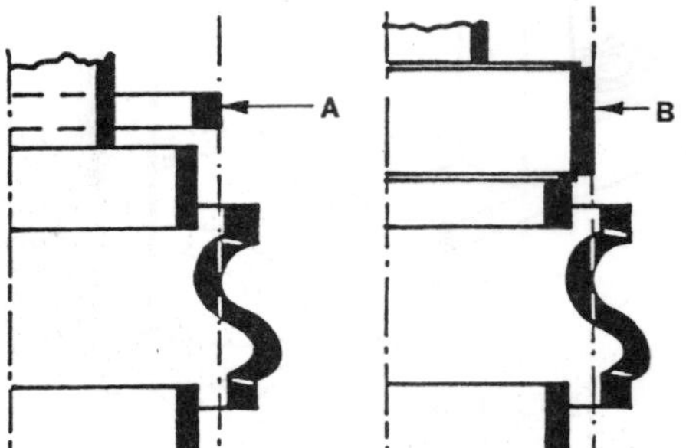

Fig. 47 The highest point of the mould (deepest point on the cutter) should align with the centre mark of the ring fence 'A' or the ball-bearing follower 'B'.

22

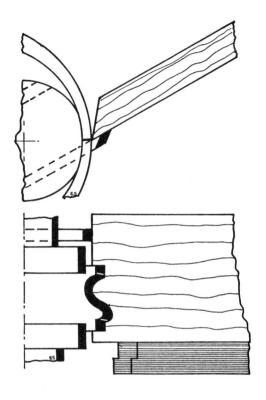

Fig. 48 Cutters can be set with a bevelled–off straight-edge, shown with a ring fence.

Plate 17 Setting moulding cutters to a template on an Autool profile grinder.

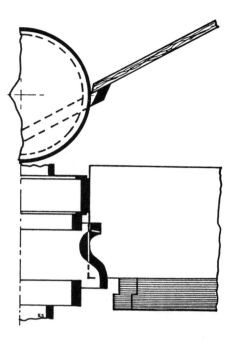

Fig. 49 Alternatively a template can be used, shown with a ball bearing follower.

It is possible to use a wooden straight-edge, moving the cutter forward until its deepest point is in line with the bevelled edge set against the follower. Then adjust the spindle vertically until the point corresponding with the underface is in line with the underside of the straight-edge, or at the same height as a jig base if used.

The template is used generally as described previously, but is cut along the planing line and bevelled clear on the reverse side. The planing line then abuts either the ball-bearing follower or the central point on the ring fence to set cutters as with the straight-edge.

In the case of collars the straight-edge or template is used to actually set the cutters. With a ring fence it is used to set the fence to the cutters which are initially set to project in the normal way.

Plate 18. One of several SCM spindle moulders, the T160 features five speeds and a tilting spindle.

CHAPTER 3
CUTTERHEAD TYPES

All cutterheads used on the spindle moulder have one or several cutting edges and rotate at high speed whilst the timber feeds past. Heads vary in size, type and design according to the work for which they are intended.

French head

The single, simply-prepared cutter is inserted through a slot in the arbor (different arbor diameters are available) and is locked by a single vertical screw. The cutter has a slightly negative cutting angle and a poor scraping cut even when properly burred-over.

The steel from which these cutters are made is often unhardened gauge steel, unhardened because it needs to be relatively soft and malleable for burnishing - to bend under pressure rather than fracture. The hardness is much lower than with other cutting tools used in woodworking and as wear resistance is almost directly related to hardness French head cutters dull much more quickly than other types.

Some makers supply a high speed steel type of cutter, tempered-back to be more malleable. This has better wearing characteristics but poorer burring-over capability.

APPLICATION

The French head is small in diameter and for this reason safer than many other common heads, and the slightly negative cutting action gives less tear-out when cutting against the grain. Even after burnishing, the cut is only a little better than a scraping action and nothing like as free as, for example, slotted collar cutters. This can be an advantage when working interlocked grain or when cutting against the grain inside tight corners, but is a disadvantage for other work.

The cutting rate is slow, only light cuts are possible and cutters quickly dull. The tool is best suited for short, non-repeating runs where the low-cost and easy preparation of cutters is an advantage and their short machine life is of little consequence.

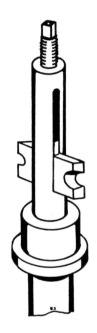

Fig. 50 A slotted arbor or French head.

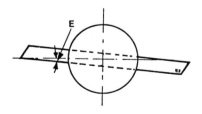

Fig. 51 The cutter has a slightly negative cutting angle E,

The French head was popular for shaping in furniture making for many years as it is suitable for both inside and outside curves down to very small radii. When this type of work grew less the tool was already in decline and with the return of more complex work the router will almost certainly take over.

French head cutters are amongst the simplest to grind as the cutter shape is exactly the reverse of the mould wanted (on most other cutters it is not). It can be checked for shape by holding it square onto a sample mould or flat on a drawing.

Grind the cutter to a bevel angle of 35 - 40 degrees, to give a clearance angle of 50 - 55 degrees. After honing to remove any grinding burr, forcibly burr over the edge using a burnishing tool at two angles against the ground face. Apply relatively heavy pressure and travere along the cutting edge and slightly towards it. A grinding burr is brittle and breaks-off in use, but this cold-formed burr is stronger and does not. Some users also burnish the front face at about 2-5 degrees prior to the burring-over.

The burnishing tool is held at two angles to the ground face to form what is in effect a hook to increase the cutting angle. Some form of lubricant is necessary when burnishing, perhaps a light oil. Traditionally spit is used and old hands claim better results from this, and seem to be right! When the tool becomes dull re-burnishing will partially restore the cutting edge, otherwise repeat the grind-hone-burnish sequence.

Burnishing tools are not easy to come by, most users make their own from a discarded triangular file with the teeth ground-off and the corners rounded-over. Any similar hardened tool will do as only the corners are actually used.

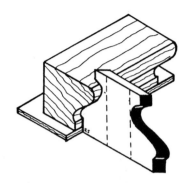

Fig. 53 Cutters should be ground to fit the mould when square-on to it.

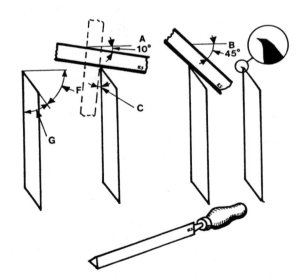

Fig. 53 Bevel angle G should be 35-40 degrees giving a clearance angle F of 50-55 degrees. A shows the first burnish and B the second to give the effect shown. Sometimes the front is also burnished as C. The other sketches show an enlarged view of the burred edge and a typical burnishing tool.

Straight moulding

As with other spindle cutters setting is not critical - the fence can easily be adjusted for cut depth. Cutter projection with a new cutter should include due allowance for subsequent grinding, but must not be excessive.

It is quite common practice for the cutter to cut on one end only with the opposite edge shaped to roughly the same profile and set barely clear of the cut to give reasonable balance. As the cutter is ground down, keep it central on the arbor by reducing diameter to maintain balance.

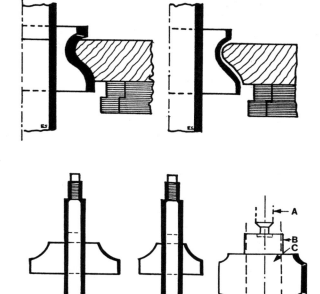

Fig. 54 Left: the cutting end forms the moulding whilst, right: the opposite end is ground to barely clear.

Fig. 55 Left - New cutters.

Centre - The same cutter when worn should still be in balance.

Right - A notched French head cutter C, showing a clamping piece B and the securing screw A.

Shaping

Cutter projection is much more critical if the spindle itself or a plain ring on it is used as a guide. In this case cutter projection beyond the contact face must match the cut depth needed. It is essential to measure this before starting so that the cutter is made to the correct length.

The French head itself can be used as a guide when shaping, but this is not recommended as contact is 'live' against a rotating spindle. At best this gives a 'rough' feel to the feed and at worst could grab and kick-back. Preferably fit a ball-bearing follower to give rolling contact, or use a ring fence.

As wear takes place the tool shortens and has to be advanced to keep the same projection and cutting diameter. The cutter is then no longer central and progressively becomes more and more out-of-balance. Because the tool is physically small in diameter the effect is also small, but the vibration it causes can be transmitted directly to the workpiece via contact of the template with the spindle or follower.

27

This tool is reasonably safe to use and no special points need making except to ensure that the cutter is safely secured. Some operators notch-out the cutter to engage with a collar underneath to prevent the cutter flying, or notch-out to straddle the arbor seating itself - but this must be accurately milled to give proper seating. Use a top clamp piece so that the cutter top edge is not damaged with the securing screw. Possibly, also, notch the clamp piece to prevent this flying. Never stack French head cutters for multiple cuts; it can be dangerous. For safe cutter projections, see Fig. 56.

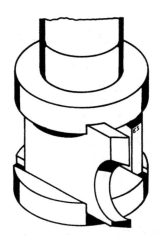

Fig. 56 Maximum cutter projection B should never excede either the retained cutter length C (French-head diameter) or three times cutter thickness A.

Slotted collars

This consists of a pair of slotted collars between which a pair of square or bevelled-edge cutters are clamped. In their original form they were held by friction only between cutter edges and slot seatings and were prone to flying.

Some makers incorporate a safety pin in each slot to engage with a corresponding edge notch in both cutters. These are essential with high spindle speeds and heavy cuts,

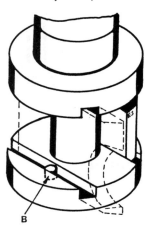

Fig. 58 Right - Slotted collars with a safety pin B and a matching notched cutter A.
Notched cutters, either of this type or the American pattern, are much safer than regular plain-edge cutters.

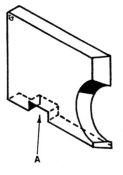

Fig. 57 Typical slotted collar.

The notches must be ground to keep precisely in step with the cutting edges as wear takes place - so that notch and pin are in contact when the cutter is in position. Failing this, the cutter can creep forward in use until they are in contact - but will never 'fly', of course. Creep can pass unnoticed in a production run spoiling many pieces before it is noticed.

American shaper heads have adjusting screws in the top collar to engage with the notched top edge of the cutters to combine fine adjustment with safe cutter retention. Normally these cutters have a bevelled top edge and collar slots, which allow different thicknesses of cutters to be fitted. A new U.K. cutter system uses the pin as a means of precise cutter setting, the Autool Q3S. See later description.

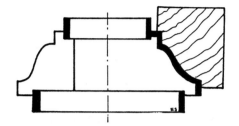

Fig. 59 Unequal collar diameters give more support with this sort of mould.

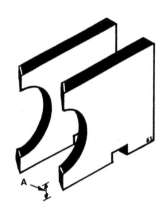

Fig. 60 With collar cutters the edge-to-profile distance A must be identical on both cutters.

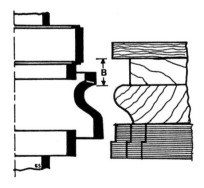

Fig. 61 Distance B should be as small as practicable.

Normally, collars of a matching pair are exactly the same diameter. For the heavier industrial machines they are 75 - 100mm. diameter, and for lighter work 50 - 75mm. diameter. Cutting angle is usually 30 degrees; a good average for most commercial timbers. However, because the cutting angle quickly reduces as the depth of cut increases, the average cutting angle is actually much less.

There have been odd pairs of slotted collar types made in the past; for example, pairs of collars of unequal diameter but equal slot spacing. They are intended for use with large coves and scotias (and other similar assymmetrical, or one-way, moulds) to give more support to the longer cutting edge.

The cutters used can be solid HSS, HCHC, or HSS brazed or welded onto a low carbon steel back. The latter are the most popular, and this type is known as plated bar when sold in the length. Individual pairs of cutters are also available with tungsten carbide, Tantung or Stellite facing.

Collar cutters are normally 6mm. thick and in widths-on-cut from 12 - 75 (or 100)mm. Length is determined by collar diameter and depth of cut. When ordered as pairs, slotted collar cutters are normally supplied 75mm. long - unless otherwise stated, or if supplied by the maker for his own slotted collars. Larger users buy plated bar and cut this off to whatever length is needed. This is more economic and the length can be varied. American shaper cutters can be of different thicknesses to give much more flexibility.

PREPARATION

Slotted collar cutters normally have a bevel angle of 35-40 degrees giving a clearance angle of 20-25 degrees.

Because the cutters are edge-clamped between the collars they cannot be tilted to correct a wrong profile nor can the cutters be adjusted up or down relative to each other. This means that two points must be carefully controlled in cutter grinding.

1 - The distance from the under-edge to the mould must be absolutely the same for both cutters, especially when forming a complex profile using both cutters each to form one part only. When profile-grinding cutters loose, use a side fence to maintain the correct edge-to-profile distance. With hand-ground cutters formed to the same profile the non-finishing cutter is usually deliberately ground to clear the mould. When shaping, the distance of the mould from the upper edge is critical when template dimensions are tight.

2 - The cutter profiles must match the mould precisely when held level with the latter and at the correct cutting angle. The cutter length must be correct to give safe retention when set. The length of a new cutter should be such that the tail end (opposite to the cutter edge) barely clears the cutting circle. The cutters then have the longest possible life and maximum retention in the collars.

29

Always use the largest diameter collars practical as this allows longer cutters to be fitted and these have a proportionately longer life. With larger collars, the longer grip also allows longer, safe cutter projections, and the cutting angle does not change so much in deep moulding. Use small diameter slotted collars only for internal shaping which includes tight curves.

CUTTER SETTING

Straight moulding

Slotted collars are often used for straight moulding. The through fence needs a cut-out for the collars so that the cutters project only enough to give a 1.5mm. working clearance between the collars and the closest part of the piece being moulded. It is also possible to use collars without a fence cut out; but cutter projection beyond the collars then becomes 1.5mm. plus the through-fence thickness. In both cases the top edge of each cutter needs forming with a 5 degree side clearance bevel.

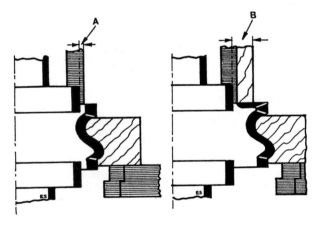

An exception to the general rule is when forming a bull-nose or similar moulding when the full edge is being machined. In this case the deepest point of the cutting edge can be inside the collar diameter to give more support to shorter cutters.

Shaping

Slotted collars are ideal for shaping. With a relatively small cutting diameter they are easier to guard, are capable of shaping relatively small internal diameters and are better to work with than other larger cutterheads. Normally they are used with a ball-bearing follower, but can be used with a ring fence. The deepest point on the cutter should line up with the ball-bearing follower or ring fence.

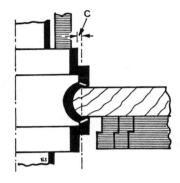

Fig. 62 Normally the cutter should project a minimum of 1.5mm beyond the collars C, but can be inside when bull-nosing or similar. In this case a cut-out in the through fence is essential for the collars. The collars can be edge-bevelled to allow more clearance when inside the planing line. (See Fig. 66.)

Fig. 63 Collar-to-fence-line gap should be 1.5mm. A, left, or 1.5mm. plus through-fence thickness B, right. Alternatively, hollow-out the rear of the through fence so that the top collar needs less cutter projection. It is possible to cut through or into the fence for collar clearance by breaking-through initially at a higher setting and to a smaller cut-depth.

Plate 19 Startrite ring fence and guard, with fine screw adjustments for setting height and position.

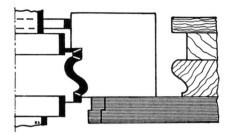

Fig. 64 A setting template can rest edge-on the table or on the jigged template base when setting cutters. (Shown with a ring fence.)

Template setting

The template normally rests on the machine table when straight moulding and on either the table or the jig when shaping. Bevel it away to contact the collar when straight moulding or to contact the follower when shaping.

Pre-setting in a tool room is not practical with conventional slotted collars because the cutters shift once the lock-nut is released. The spindle arbor could be removed completely for setting in the tool room, but this is not practical.

The only types of slotted collar which can be pre-set have separate screws to lock collars and cutters together after setting. This allows pre-setting and transfer back to the machine as a single unit.

Special, simple setting stands using setting fingers or setting wheels can be used in pre-setting and are ideal for shaping applications. Q3S cutters allow precise cutter setting by re-grinding the location notch after profile grinding. See later notes.

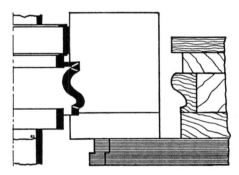

Fig. 65 Alternatively, the template can be marked with the jig base line. (Shown with a ball-bearing follower.)

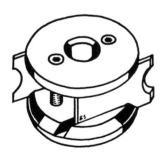

Fig. 66 These Rye collars can be pre-set in a tool room.

OPERATIONAL SAFETY

Pairs of cutters have to be precisely the same width, parallel and with perfectly square (or bevelled) edges. Makers supply cutters in matched pairs and it is essential to keep them this way; never use odd pairs of cutters, even if of the same nominal width, because different makers, and even the same maker in different cutter batches, cannot guarantee absolutely equal width.

With long bars always make cutter pairs out of the same bar; never one out of one bar and another out of a second. It is also important to make sure that the cutter edges and slots are free from burrs and lumps, etc. and that both are free from dirt, grease, chips, etc., before fitting cutters. Any of the above, singly or in combination, could give incorrect seating and unequal grip, with the loose cutter possibly flying out or slipping on start-up.

31

There are no specific regulations concerning safe cutter projection. The only guide that remotely applies gives a 20mm. projection as the maximum for a cutter thickness of 6mm. Likewise their are no international regulations concerning the shortest retained cutter length. There is, however, a universally-accepted guide that cutters should be discarded when their retained length is equal too or less than half the slot length plus their projection beyond the collars. As cutters wear their safe limits of projection also reduce; take care to watch this point. Small diameter collars obviously allow less cutter projection.

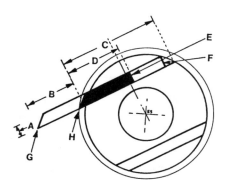

Fig. 67 Cutter retained length D must be greater than half the slot length C plus the distance from the collars to the maximum point of the cutters B.
Cutter projection B must not excede three times cutter thickness A.
Other points are:
G - maximum projection.
H - minimum projection (planing circle).
F - new cutter-tail position.
E - maximum forward position of the cutter tail for planing only - for moulding the tail must be further to the right.

Plate 20 These Forest City slotted collars feature bevelled seatings so that different cutter thicknesses can be fitted, lockscrews to allow pre-setting, and fine screw adjustment via a notched edge to provide precise setting and secure holding of the cutters.

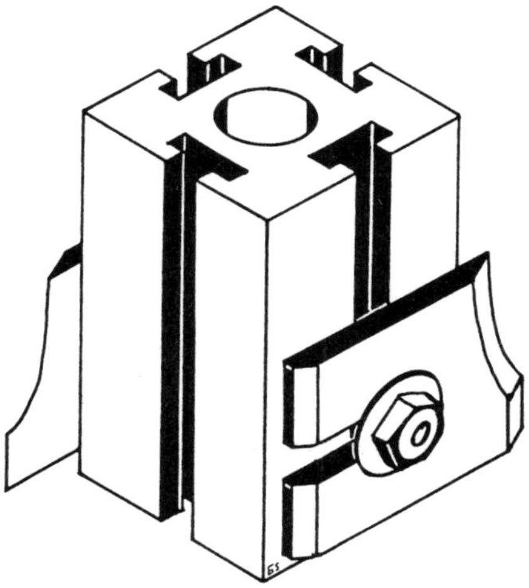

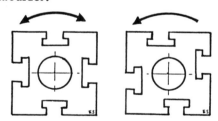

Fig. 68 A typical square, unlipped cutterblock as used on a spindle moulder.

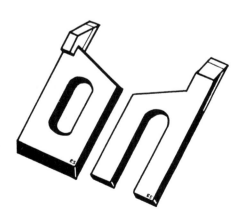

Fig. 69 Left: a centre slot cutterblock can rotate in either direction. Right: an off-centre slot cutterblock must rotate as shown.

CHAPTER 4

Square blocks

These are square in section and cutters can be bolted to all four slotted faces using nuts and bolts: Cutters of a wide variety of width, length and slot configuration can be fitted. The blocks can be provided with or without lips - but usually for spindle moulder work the unlipped type is used.

The cutterbolt slot can be central in the cutterblock face or off-set. Unlipped cutterblocks with central slots can rotate in either direction. Cutterblocks with off-centre slots must have the slot always closest to the cutting edge of the cutter it secures.

Bolts should be high tensile steel type; use no other type than those supplied by the makers. The correct washers are fully machined, bevelled-off to avoid damage (to be fitted bevel outwards), and are large in outer diameter to give full support to the cutter.

Cutters

Cutters are flat, with open or closed slots and usually 9 to 13mm. thick. Thicker cutters are used for heavier cuts, but where a narrow cutter is used for deep grooving it is common to reinforce the back. (There are larger moulding cutters having reinforcement ribs welded to the back, but these are for heavy guttering or cill work on four-sided moulders, not spindle moulders.)

Most cutters are faced, usually with HSS or HCHC for regular work and sometimes with Tantung, Stellite or tungsten carbide for abrasive timbers. The backing material is stiff enough to withstand normal cutting pressures but is intended to bend back rather than break in a smash.

Cutters can have closed slots which are retained by the bolts if slippage takes place, or open-slots which fly completely off the cutterblock if they loosen whilst in use.

Fig. 70 Left: A closed slot type with a reinforced grooving cutter.
Right: An open slot rebating cutter.

APPLICATION

The cutting angle is around 40 degrees and tends to be vicious and with a big 'bite'. It is fine for heavy work on free-cutting softwoods and straight moulding such as large window sections, doors and frames. It is not really suited to light spindle moulder work, is of little use with furniture parts and unsuitable for shaping unless of very heavy section. 'Bite' is the theoretical amount a single cutter can remove with an uncontrolled feed. It can be anything from 12 to 40mm.

Cutters can be set anywhere in the depth of the cutter-block, varied in projection and mounted either square-on or slewed at an angle. (Slewing cutters is poor but common practice which allows a cutter to form a slightly different bevel or profile than that for which it was originally made.) Cutters must be used in pairs; this is absolutely vital, but more than one cutter can be secured to a single face of the cutterblock provided there is room.

All this adds up to a cutterblock which is versatile and low in cost. These are the two main attractions of square blocks which have kept them popular for over a hundred years. However, their very versatility makes re-setting difficult and with their safety now being questioned it seems that other types will replace them.

PREPARATION

Cutter selection

Narrow cutters up to about 80mm. wide have a single centre slot and are fixed with a single bolt. Wider cutters have two slots and need two bolts. Cutters are available in a wide range of sizes and it is important to choose the correct one when initially setting.

Most larger square blocks are fitted with 15mm. bolts, and a few smaller ones with 12mm. bolts or their imperial equivalents, and cutters are slotted accordingly. It is important to use the correct bolt for the slot-width and cutter thickness, so check with the makers.

The slot length is correct if the slot end barely clears the cutterbolt when the legs or cutter tail just clear the planing circle. This is also the correct new cutter position. Cutters for some small square cutterblocks are chamfered at the tail to give extra clearance and the greatest possible contact with the cutterblock. (The planing circle is described by planing cutters set to clear the cutterbolts and cutter lips by 1.5mm.)

Cutter width-on-cut is dictated by the work required. For small moulds a single pair of cutters is used. For intricate moulds it is usual to divide the mould into individual parts and use separate pairs of cutters for each part. This allows cutters to be used for more than one application. For example, different sizes of rebate cutter can be combined with different mould cutters to give a wide range of window-section profiles from relatively few cutters.

Cutter length (cutting edge-to-tail) is dictated by the size of the cutterblock and the mould depth. Planing cutters should be such that when their tail just clears the planing circle the cutting edge just reaches it. Longer cutters can be used, but this increases the planing circle which should be kept as small as possible. Shorter cutters can be set forward to reach the planing circle but this reduces cutter life.

Moulding cutters should reach the full mould depth when their tail just clears the planing circle. Longer cutters can be ground down, or the cutting circle increased. Shorter cutters can be moved forward, but cutter life is lost and shorter cutters are less safe.

34

It will be appreciated that cost savings are possible when a range of cutters are stocked. A useful aid is to make a full-size drawing of the cutterblock complete with cutting circle. Add extra circles at pre-set distances, say every 10mm. from the planing line, to represent depths-on-cut. It is possible then to actually measure lengths of cutters needed for both planing and moulding.

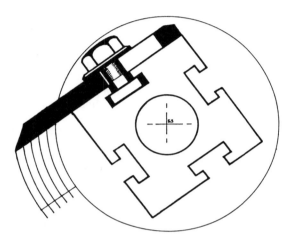

Fig. 71 Draw out a cutterblock full size and add depth-on-cut lines at 10mm. spacings. Use a pair of compasses to draw cutting circles to shown cutter lengths needed for different depths-on-cut.

Whilst cutters are rarely the precise cutter length needed, because of standard sizing, the nearest standard length is readily identified. If a choice of wrong cutter length has to be made, a rule of thumb is that a cutter can be longer by up to 7mm. and shorter by 3mm. As wear takes place with longer cutters the cutting circle will gradually reduce until the cutters are the correct length, after which they are gradually advanced on re-setting.

Grinding

Normally square-block cutters have a bevel angle of about 35 degrees which usually gives enough clearance, but check this at the minimum cutting circle.

A larger bevel angle is essential with tungsten carbide tipped types, but as there is barely enough clearance on square blocks for a larger main bevel angle, a secondary clearance angle is necessary.

Make sure that cutter pairs are dimensionally alike and balance them before using. Square block cutters are larger and heavier than other types and correct balancing is very important.

Setting

Cutters must be used in balanced pairs and mounted diametrically opposite on the cutterblock with both set to cut. Whilst this is also true of other types, square-block cutters must be given special attention because of their weight.

35

Cutters can be set to a sample or to a template. The template for square blocks is usually notched-out to rest on the top edge of the cutterblock and contacts the cutterblock lip or body. The normal unlipped type of cutterblock gives reasonably accurate registration for the template, but the cutterblock must be cleaned first and be damage-free.

OPERATIONAL SAFETY

Square block cutters sometimes fly out on starting or during use. The weight of these cutters and the speed at which they travel can cause considerable damage and injury.

A simple human error which can cause accidents is to start the machine with the cutters only partially tightened, but other factors which can cause accidents are; The use of dangerous cutters; cutterblocks or cutterbolts; insufficient friction between cutter and block; and chip wedging.

Each cutter must be in full and proper contact with the cutterblock when tightened. Both need absolutely flat faces (some blocks are purposely hollowed to ensure better contact at heel and toe) and both surfaces must be burr and dirt-free. Regularly inspect the cutterblock for damage and deformation. Badly deformed blocks should be returned to the makers.

Old and incorrect cutterbolts can be dangerous, cutterbolts for the square block are of a special high-tensile type. Cutterbolt threads which are stretched or deformed are dangerous. They appear different when compared to new threads.

Thread deformation often causes stiffness when tightening, but this is difficult to distinguish from normal tightening resistance. Check resistance with the cutterbolt and nut removed. Both faults result from persistant over-straining and/or over-long usage.

For safe operation use cutterbolts in rotation and examine each before fitting. Immediately discard any showing wear or deformation of the thread, cracks, rounding of the corners of the nut, etc. Never use a non-matching cutterbolt and nut.

Sometimes a cutter can bend or twist and then shift on tightening. This is not merely a nuisance when setting, it shows incorrect seating and the chance that cutters could shift again in use. Check cutters for bend and twist on a flat plate. Do not just use a thin straightedge as this only shows bend, not twist.

Some users flatten bent and twisted cutters by controlled bending in the opposite direction, but this could well lead to fatigue failure, or to invisible and dangerous cracks forming. Bent cutters should really be discarded.

The use of packing between cutter and cutterblock is widespread as a means of increasing frictional resistance to prevent cutter creep. The thickest packing recommended is thin brown wrapping paper. Cutter slippage on tightening when using only this is a sure sign of something else wrong which wants making right, not thicker packing adding.

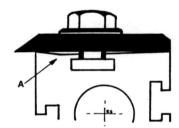

Fig. 72 Some cutterblocks are hollowed, as at A, to ensure better cutter seating.

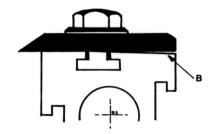

Fig. 73 If used, thin paper packing is inserted at B.

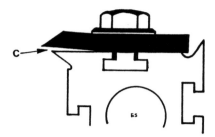

Fig. 74 Chip packing starts at C – particularly on a lipped block as shown here.

Fig. 76 Maximum cutter projection C should not be more than 3 times cutter thickness A, dimension F should never be less than 8mm. and washer G should cover the cutter tail at H.
Other points are:
J – New cutter tail position
H – Worn cutter tail position
E – Minimum projection (planing circle)
D – Maximum projection.

Chip packing or wedging results from dust being forced between cutterblock and cutter, forming a thickening wedge of hard, resinous material. Packing starts when the cutter seats badly, or because of damage to the lip or corner. Check all these points regularly.

The spanner used to tighten the nuts should be the one supplied by the makers. Never add pipes or other extensions and use only normal hand pressure. Some makers quote a specific torque and can supply a pre-set torque spanner, but not all makers agree with this practice.

The maximum cutter projection is about 3 times their thickness beyond the cutterblock. (There are no specific guidelines, but the figure given is widely accepted.)

Cutters wear down through re-grinding and have to be advanced to compensate. Cutters have a limited life, and this is reached when the washer no longer covers the legs or when there is less than 8mm. purchase behind the slot, whichever occurs first.

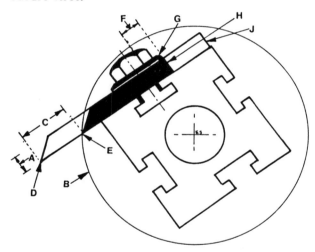

The closed-slot type of cutter can only be moved forward until the slot-end contacts the bolt. The slot on cutters from reputable makers is dimensioned so that enough grip remains when in this position. Other closed-slot cutters have a shorter distance slot-end to tail, so with these the 8mm. minimum purchase behind the slot applies.

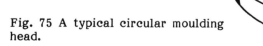

Fig. 75 A typical circular moulding head.

Circular cutterblocks

These are basically circular in section and usually have two cutters when made for the spindle moulder. Three-cutter heads are sometimes used, also four-cutter heads which are suitable for complex moulds.

Cutters are usually solid HCHC, HSS, or with a low-carbon steel back and facing of HSS, Tantung, Stellite or tungsten carbide. Thickness varies from 3mm. for planing only, to about 8mm. for deep moulding. Cutter width is normally the same as the cutterblock itself, or the wedge length if two or three wedges are used, but wider than the cutterhead when narrow moulding heads are used.

Circular moulding heads are infinitely safer than square heads. The cutting action is much less vicious and the cutters are smaller, lighter and cause less damage if 'thrown', something which is less likely to happen anyway. The 'bite' is also much less and the cutting diameter smaller.

The first circular moulding cutterhead was the Whitehill type and this has been copied around the world. Whitehill cutters are thin and are normally profiled all-round for use on any one of their four cutting edges. A regular range of shapes made by Whitehill (and others) make up into a surprisingly large variety of compound shapes. Whitehill cutterblocks are used widely for moulding, planing and rebating. They are extremely versatile as the cutter can be turned to any angle. The cutterhead can be readily sunk to give maximum support to the cutter on deep and stepped cuts. They are very popular with spindle hands.

Whitehill heads normally have two cutter seatings for 4mm. thick cutters. Other versions may accept a different cutter thickness, or a range of cutter thicknesses. It is important to find out from the makers just what can be fitted as fitting a wrong cutter could be dangerous. Don't use cut-up planer cutters, for example, they are too thin for moulding.

The normal cutting angle is around 25 degrees, a good average for most commercial timbers. One cutterhead, the Monninger Diangle, gives a choice of two angles, one for softwood and general use and the other for interlocked-grain timber.

Fig. 77 Some of the Whitehill range of cutters.

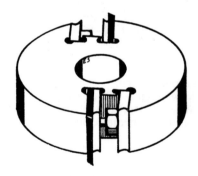

Fig. 78 A Monninger Diangle cutterhead having two cutting angles.

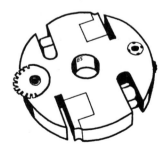

Fig. 80 Whitehill cutterhead with spur cutters for rebating.

Some cutterheads are formed to angles other than 25 degrees, and some makers will produce them to any required angle, but on a spindle moulder this really isn't justified.

Fig. 79 Whitehill cutterhead with backing support.

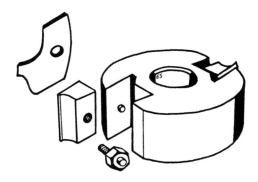

Fig. 81 A pin-type safety head.

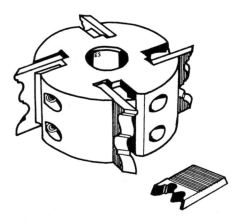

Fig. 82 A serrated-back cutterhead

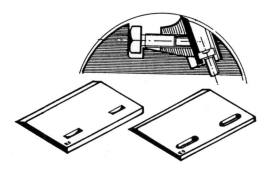

Fig. 83 A Rye screw-adjusted planing head.
Below: two types of cutter slots.
Left: recessed slots.
Right: through slots.

Circular moulding cutterheads range in diameter from 100mm. to 250mm., and in width on cut from 25 to 100mm. or more. Some types have an edge-chamfer to give more support on deep scotias and similar. Special versions are available with spur cutters for rebating and with back supports for excessive cutter projections.

Most circular cutterblocks use a form of internal wedge in front of the cutter to force this back against its seating on tightening. There are various forms but they all work on the same basic principle with either a nut tightened by a spanner or a socket screw tightened by an allen key.

Cutters were originally held only by friction between their faces and the wedge and slot seating. They are still produced and used in this way and remain the most popular type for spindle moulders with an excellent safety record. The remote possibility of cutters flying during use has recently led to a profusion of keyed-cutter type circular moulding heads for spindle moulder work. Examples are: cutters with a large through-hole or face counterbore to engage with a pin or screw, serrated-back cutters which engage in matching serrations milled in the cutter seating, or with one or more notches and some form of fixed key or keys.

Pin type

This usually has a central pin fitted either to the wedge (always key-locked with this type) or through the cutterblock body. Retained cutter types always need more assembly than friction-only types as in fitting the pin must engage in the hole or recess. The pin positively retains the cutter if normal grip is lost and restricts cutter adjustment to within safe working limits. It does not, however, prevent cutter creep nor twist until pin and cutter are in positive contact, by which time spoilage and damage may have taken place. Some newer types have an adjustable key, or two or more pins for better stability.

Serrated-back type

The cutters have serrations at 1/16 in. spacings to engage with matching serrations in the cutterblock. When the cutters are secured the serrations positively prevent outward cutter movement. Various wedging actions are used similar to the friction-held types. These heads are extremely safe in use.

Blanks are available for profiling by the user - but this sets a problem. The serrations which hold the cutter so securely also prevent adjustment outwards except in 1/16in. increments, and they cannot be tilted. For this reason cutters need grinding with precision, to be absolutely correct when fitted in mould depth, slew and alignment. Hand-grinding is impracticable, they are intended for grinding with the cutters mounted in the head using a profile grinder. A drawback is that the planing circle varies as wear takes place, so they are not ideal for shaping using a ball-bearing follower.

Slotted types

Some cutterheads incorporate an adjusting screw with a cap head that engages in a slot in the cutter. These offer fine adjustment of the cutter and safe retention. Another type, the Q3S, has two pins formed on the wedge engage in precision edge notches in the cutter which pre-determine cutter projection.

APPLICATION

Circular moulding heads are used for virtually every spindle moulding application. The Whitehill types are extremely versatile as the cutter can be seated at virtually any angle to produce a wide variety of shapes from only a few basic cutters. For example, a single, straight cutter will form any angle of bevel or chamfer simply by altering its setting.

Unlike most other cutterheads, Whitehill cutters are intended to project both above and below the cutterhead for 'sinking' the head into the cut. In this way the head gives maximum support to the cutter on deep cuts, so both cutting circle and bite are appreciably reduced when compared to other heads. The heads with top and bottom chamfer give better support on certain profiles and are, perhaps, the most universal type.

It is possible to run Whitehill heads in tandem and span a long cutter between the two, but it is important to use only a matched pair for this work. Never attempt to use two non-matched heads as the cutter slots may not align. Tandem heads are manufactured as a pair for perfect slot matching.

Continental versions of the Whitehill head are much less versatile as the cutters supplied are profiled or intended to be profiled only on one edge and the degree of tilt is more limited. Deep circular heads are also intended for single-edge cutters but not for 'sinking' - except for rebate cutterheads with spur cutters fitted. Conventional serrated-back heads are excellent from a safety standpoint but need profile-grinding and are primarily intended for heavier work on a four-sider.

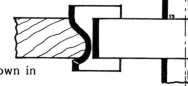

Fig. 87 The moulding cutter shown in position.

PREPARATION

The bevel angle on all circular cutters is normally between 35 and 45 degrees, but this depends on the cutting angle. Check for clearance as previously described and record the bevel angle for future use. Cutters are ground on an open, copy or profile grinder and are then balanced before fitting.

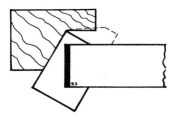

Fig. 84 A Whitehill planing cutter tilted to form a bevelled rebate. Normally the top edge is formed at a slight angle to give a clean under-face (as shown in dotted outline).

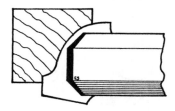

Fig. 85 A Whitehill chamfered cutterhead gives more support for moulds of this type.

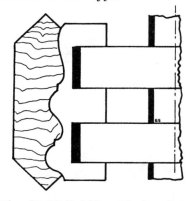

Fig. 86 Whitehill cutterheads used in tandem. They must be bought as a matching pair.

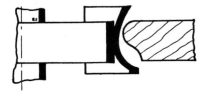

Fig. 88 The same head as Fig. 87 showing a balancing cutter set close to the profile. Both cutters must weigh the same.

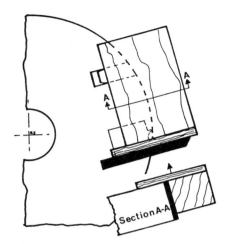

Fig. 89 Above: A Whitehill template can be fixed to a shaped block to register better.
Below: Mark on it:
D - Planing line.
E - Maximum depth of cut (12mm.).
B - Block clearance line (allow 2mm.).
C - Maximum projection above and below (12mm.).
A - Minimum cutter retention line (18mm. into the slot).

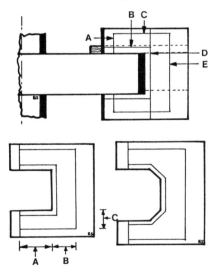

Fig. 90 Setting out a template for any circular moulding head
A - Cutter retention,
B - Maximum cutter projection in depth-on-cut,
C - Maximum cutter projection above and below.

Cutter setting

Cutters are easy to set with all circular heads. The cutters are usually tightened enough to snug only whilst checking them against the pattern, and they can then can be gently tapped into correct position. Use a soft mallet for this - but remember to fully tighten when set.

The Wadkin type with a spring-loaded ball-bearing in the wedge for steadying the cutter is ideal when setting in this way.

Cutters are normally used in matching pairs, but for the smaller heads it is permissible for one cutter to form the mould, balanced by a second cutter of equal weight but with a non-matching profile. The balancing cutter should be set as close as possible to the cut, but without actually touching, to keep the running balance true. Template setting makes this easier.

Wide circular heads have cutters of the same width as the head and often have no means of drawing-out a cutter if wrongly set. Take care with this type not to set the cutters in too far, otherwise they have to be released and re-set, which is something of a nuisance.

The cutterhead types with screw adjustment are more convenient. There are two versions: One has recessed or slotted cutters into which the screw heads lock to move the cutter 'in' or 'out'.

The other has plain cutters to seat on the screws which can only move them 'out'. With these the normal practice is initially to set each cutter slightly too far 'in', then screw out to the correct setting. If initially set too far out, the cutters could be tapped back a precise amount after setting-back the screw, but they are easier to adjust as described.

Standard serrated-back cutters are set in the head prior to profile grinding, not after, usually on a setting stand using a sample. Insert spacing pieces under the cutters so that they engage into corresponding serrations. It is practical to re-set previously-ground serrated cutters and use them without a further re-grind, but only one cutter will finish.

Template setting

The most convenient way to set circular-head cutters (other than standard serrated-back and Q3S types) is to use some form of template.

For the continental and wider heads both the table-mounted and notched types of template are suitable and are used generally as described for square heads.

Templates for Whitehill types should be notched for about 20mm. inside the planing line to project both above and below the heads.

The template can register against the cutter clamp, but is more accurate when fastened to a hardwood block shaped to fit the outer curve of the cutterblock, and with a ledge to rest on the top face.

Mark the planing line, top and bottom block clearance lines (including bevels if any), and minimum cutter retention line. Set-out the cutter shape within these outlines so that the cutter profile just clips the planing and clearance lines for maximum support by the head.

Dominion supply a setting template which fixes to their circular moulding head for cutter setting. Tool-room setting is more convenient than setting on the machine.

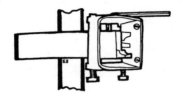

Fig. 93 Dominion provide a template which clamps to their cutterhead.

Fig. 94 Cutter projection B should not excede either cutter retention D or three times cutter thickness A. C should not normally be less than 10mm. (Manufacturers recommendations vary, check this point). Other points,
E - Tail position for a new cutter.
F - Tail position of a worn cutter.
H - Minimum projection (planing circle).
G - maximum cutting circle.

NOTE: Cutter projection is not normally more than three times thickness, but can be more at lower spindle speeds and should be less at high spindle speeds.

OPERATIONAL SAFETY

Regularly strip, clean, oil and inspect the cutterheads and the clamp assembly in particular. Replace worn, damaged or suspect parts before returning to use. Store heads in an oil bath if used infrequently. Take care to wipe oil from the cutter slots before use.

If using serrated-back cutterheads note that two different types of serrations are commonly used, both with the same pitch. Make sure the cutters used have matching serrations as otherwise the hardened cutter could damage the cutter seating when clamped. The Fearnehough universal serrated cutter is the only type, to date, which fits either type of serration.

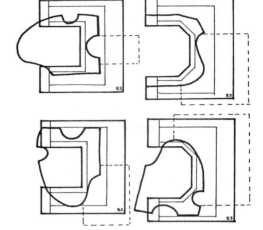

Fig. 92 Set cutter profiles just to clip the minimum projection lines and be within the retention line.

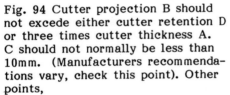

Fig. 91 Two profiles are used on serrated-back cutters;
Above: 45/45/90 degree angles.
Below: 60/60/60 degree angles.
Check that you have the correct one, or use Fearnehough cutters with universal serrations which fit either.

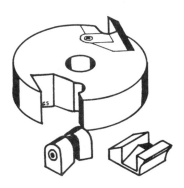

Fig. 95 A Dominion twin wedge-lock cutterhead taken apart for cleaning and to show the double-wedge clamp.

Safe cutter projections beyond the cutterblock directly relate to cutter thickness and cutter retention within the cutter slots. Ensure that cutters do not exceed the safety guides. With the original Whitehill heads the only cutter thickness used is 4mm., so maximum cutter projections can be shown quite specifically setting the template out as Fig. 89.

In all cases an overriding factor is the need of safe retention by the clamp or wedge in front of the cutter. In no circumstances should the inside edge of the cutter be closer than 10mm. to the securing screw centreline, but some manufacturers use the inside edge of the clamp as a guide beyond which the inside edges of cutters must not be set. With serrated-back types the makers usually state the maximum distance between the bottom of the cutter seating and the inside edge of the cutter.

The cutter should not normally be narrower than the cutterblock, except when two or more wedges are used in one cutter seating. In all cases the cutter must be as wide as, or wider than, the wedge. When using cutters narrower that the cutterblock, fill up to the full seating width by adding extra wedges and cutter blanks.

Plate 21 Startrite two-cutter circular moulding cutterblock with alternative moulding cutters and grooving segments.

Plate 22 Left: Forest City serrated-back circular moulding head with hydraulic fitting.

Right: Forest City shear-cut and segmented planing cutterhead.

Plate 23 Left: The Startrite T30 has a built-on sliding table and a spindle speed of 6 000 revs/min.

Plate 24 Centre: This two-part tipped profiled cutter is mounted on an ETP Hydro-Grip sleeve CXE. This provides fine screw adjustment of the two halves, plus secure hydraulic locking on the arbor.

Plate 25 Lower right: Forest City tipped profiled cutters; left, for straight-bore mounting; right, with hydraulic sleeve mounting.

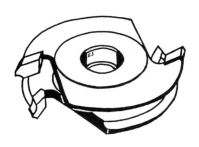

Fig. 96 Solid profile cutter.

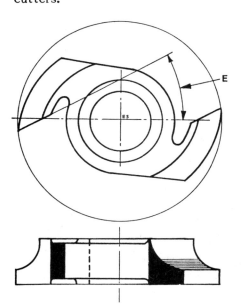

Fig. 97 Tipped combination profiled cutters.

CHAPTER 5

Profiled cutters

With these heads the profile is formed by the maker during manufacture and the user merely grinds the flat leading face when sharpening. The two basic types are: solid heads completely made from tool steel, or a non tool-steel body with HSS or tungsten carbide facings brazed-on. The second type has a common body with interchangable bits or cutters which are profile-ground by the maker. These are used commonly on four-sided moulders, but rarely on spindle moulders, mainly because their cutting diameters are too large.

The type normally used on a spindle moulder is a two-point solid or faced profiled-head, though three and four point types are also used as a one-piece or as part of an interlocking combination.

Profiled-heads can be made with a cutting angle to match the timber to be moulded. This or the class of timber being worked should be stated when ordering, or the head will be made to the manufacturer's standard angle to suit most commercial timbers. If the cutting angle is important, for example, to work interlocked-grain timber, it is essential to emphasize this when ordering because the angle cannot be altered later.

Fig. 98 Left: Cutting angle E measured at the planing circle. The cutter has no side clearance.

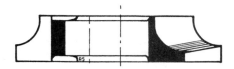

Fig. 99 Above: A one-way solid profiled cutters with side relief.

The cutting angle can be measured at the planing circle or at the deepest point of the cut. As the difference between the two can be large, clearly state both cutting angle and where measured. Previous tables state the cutting angle at the planing circle.

The outer surfaces are precision ground to profile and radial relief and are never ground or honed in use. It is usual for the makers to grind side clearance on heads where clearance is only in one direction, i.e. for quadrants and coves, etc.

This is not normal on shapes where both left- and right-hand clearance is needed, unless including cutting edges square or almost square to the arbor which otherwise burn. When left- and right-hand side clearance is formed on a one-piece head the profile alters as wear takes place. Alteration is small enough with faced types to be disregarded, but not with a solid head.

If pattern change is not acceptable when needing two-way clearance, the head can be made in two or more interlocking and overlapping parts each with clearance in one direction only. The change in profile on grinding is corrected by bringing the parts closer together or further apart using thin removable shims or screws. Take care when using shims that dirt is not trapped to tilt the head. The best adjustment is by using an ETP Hydro-grip sleeve CXE. This is a double sleeve with hydraulic grease to centre the tool, and which also incorporates fine screw adjustment.

Combination heads are now sold by some makers consisting of several cutters which combine in various ways to make up into different and often complex profiles.

Profile heads are straight-bore for mounting on a plain arbor. Cutting diameters for use on a spindle moulder are normally about 100-130mm depending on the depth of profile. These heads usually have a common outer diameter so that the planing circle varies with mould depth.

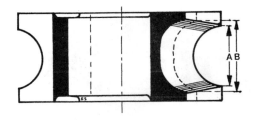

Fig. 100 Showing alteration of profile width A to B through wear on a one-piece solid profile cutter having two-way side clearance.

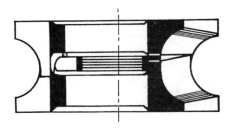

Fig. 101 Change in profile width can be avoided by making the cutter in two interlocking halves and adjusting their spacing by use of shims or screws. Alternatively, use an hydraulic sleeve with fine-screw adjustment, such as the ETP Hydro-Grip CXE. See Plate 24.

Fig. 102 A combination head with section shown

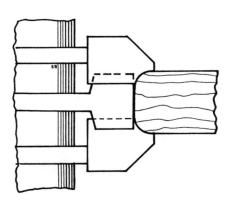

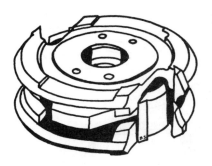

APPLICATION

The biggest advantage of profiled heads is that the maker forms the profile which then remains true for its full life. No setting is needed except for mounting the head, correcting width if two-part and setting height and depth.

It is very quickly put into production and is ideal for repeated runs of identical mouldings. The heads are used for all types of moulding including shaping, but with a ring fence rather than a ball-bearing follower because of diameter variation.

Plate 26 Leuco disposable-cutter type cutterhead fitted both with straight and moulding cutters for planing and corner rounding.

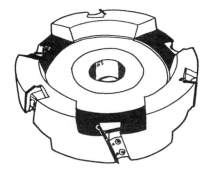

Fig. 103 A disposable-type edging head with opposite-hand shear cutters.

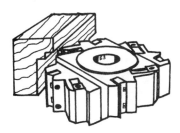

Fig. 104 A disposable-type, double-rebate head.

PREPARATION

Grind flat on the leading face only, making sure that the original cutting angle is maintained. The outer face must not be touched except to remove any slight grinding burr. The only setting required is to correct the width on multi-part heads.

OPERATIONAL SAFETY

Profile heads are exceptionally safe due to the one-piece construction. The normal safety guides apply but no special measures are needed. One point to watch when grinding worn solid-type heads is to avoid forming a sharp corner in the gullet which concentrates stress and could start a crack. Avoid this by well-rounding the grinding wheel, and discard heads when worn to the minimum tooth width.

Disposable-cutter heads

This type is a recent innovation. It uses special heads with small, solid tungsten carbide cutters which are used once only on each cutting edge and are then discarded. Most cutters of this type have two usable cutting edges, but some square ones are made with four usable edges.

The cutter seating is milled precisely in manufacture so cutters always seat in exactly the same position and are pin-retained for safety. The cutters themselves are precisely made to a uniform width and with a highly-honed cutting edge. Conventional cutter grinding and setting is not needed and the cutting circle remains exactly the same regardless of the number of replacement cutters used.

The heads are straight-bore and are available in different diameters, numbers of cutters and width-on-cut using cutters of standard size. Cutting angle is normally about 15 degrees.

Two-cutter heads are used for edge-planing solid timber. When edge-planing faced particle (chip) boards with a straight cutting action the outward pressure can edge-splinter and lift the facings. Avoid this by using a special shear-action head to enter the cut at the outer face and shear in towards the centre. On these the plastic is severed ahead of the point where splintering occurs and pressure is turned harmlessly inward. With double-faced boards opposite-hand shear cutters are used. These are fitted to cut inwards from both facings to meet and overlap in the centre.

This type of head can have tungsten carbide scribing cutters for rebating, and combinations are manufactured to use regular tungsten carbide cutters to produce any mouldings which can be formed by intersecting straight faces and a few regular curves. Cutterheads are also made for special profiles to customer's drawings with a guarantee of exactly-shaped replacement cutters to the same profile. Users are, however, begining to regrind these mould cutters themselves on a profile grinder or send them to a service centre.

APPLICATION

These heads are simple and safe. Cutters can be replaced quickly, accurately and without need of normal setting. Regrinding is not recommended as the cost of replacement cutters is less than re-grinding costs - according to the makers. If ground, most cutters can only be used in a fractionally smaller cutterhead in any event, so cutterhead costs double or treble if doing this.

The primary application is in edge-planing or edge-moulding particle boards, but increasingly this type of head is being used to form profiles in solid timber. The main attraction is simplicity of use, ease of cutter replacement and maintenance of profile and cutting diameter. A fixed cutting diameter is essential when shaping using a ball-bearing follower.

Cutter setting

Cutters locate on their inside cutting edge against the milled seating and are locked and keyed usually by a taper-locking action which pulls them firmly into the seating.

OPERATIONAL SAFETY

These heads are very safe in use with a mild cutting action and a small bite. As the cutters are retained by one or two pins they never fly out in normal use. The normal safety points apply. Any special points are given by individual makers.

Chip-limiting heads

Many cutterheads have an aggressive cutting action when the cutting angle is large and if the timber is insecurely held, knotty or badly-grained. This can cause vibration and spoilage, and in extreme cases the timber can be grabbed and thrown back at the user.

A chip-limiting head restricts the bite of individual cutters to within safe limits to steady the cut and prevent kick-back. Purpose-made shoulders or a formed chip-limiter project close to the cutting circle to actually contact timber under excessive feed conditions and prevent a dangerous bite being taken.

Special circular moulding heads are produced with profiled chip-limiters fitted at a negative angle immediately in front of the cutters. Setting of both cutter and chip-limiter has to be exacting, but control is absolute through the full mould depth.

There are other versions: for example, solid or tipped profiled cutterheads which serve the same purpose. Profiled cutters may have a negative-rake profiled chip-limiter similar to the loose-cutter type, or chip-limiting shoulders to align with flat or angled sections of the profile. The latter are more easily maintained at the proper height than the fully-profiled type.

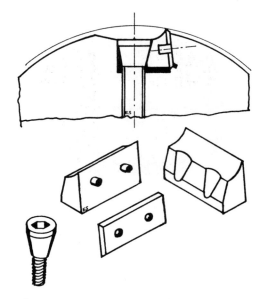

Fig. 105 One method of fitting disposable cutters, showing the wedge viewed front and rear together with one cutter and screw.

Fig. 106 A chip-limiting head with loose-type cutters and chip-limiters.

Fig. 107 A solid-profiled chip-limiting head.

48

Plate 27 Oppold circular moulding head with keyed cutters and chip-limiters.

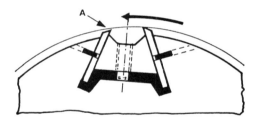

Fig. 108 The chip-limiter A is immediately in front of the cutter, facing the opposite direction and fractionally below the cutting circle.

Fig. 109 A typical collet arbor fitting for a loose-cutter head.

APPLICATION

Chip-limiting heads can replace most other comparable cutterheads for virtually any straight moulding or shaping operation on the spindle moulder. Their main advantage is that they are the safest head available with virtually no danger of kick-back.

PREPARATION

Loose-cutter type heads need both cutters and chip-limiters profile-grinding accurately in profile and overal length tip to tail because they rely on precise seating for accurate projection. The cutter must project no more than 0.75 mm. beyond the chip-limiter as otherwise it will not act as intended. If the cutters are set too high a bigger and unsafe bite will be possible. If the cutters are set too low the cutterhead will simply not cut at all.

Profiled head types are reground as regular profiled heads, but as the cutting tip is worn down the chip-limiter must also be ground down in step to maintain the original height difference.

With the negative-angle profiled type, the chip-limiter face is ground-off by the same amount as the cutter face to do this. With the simple, flat-shoulder type the shoulders are ground down as needed, but when new tips are fitted their projection must correspond with the height of the worn chip-limiting shoulders. Cutting tip to chipbreaker height should be as the loose-cutter type.

OPERATIONAL SAFETY

These heads are extremely safe to use provided normal safety guides are followed, the cutters correctly secured when of the loose-cutter head type, and the chip-limiter height maintained.

Chip-limiting heads are for hand-feed only. Never use them with a mechanical feed unless the feed is very slow. A mechanical feed usually makes chip-limiting unnecessary in any event, and over-feeding could actually cause a jam or run-off.

Router cutters

These are usually shanked tools for mounting in a collet-type arbor. The common type has a parallel shank, the diameter of which may vary according to tool diameter. A few router cutters have a form of morse taper and/or screw fitting.

There are two basic router cutter types: the single flute (or spoon bit) and the twin flute.

One type of single flute cutter is ground concentrically on the outer surface and is fitted in an eccentric chuck to give the necessary clearance; it is then mounted in the collet and carefully balanced by adding, removing or switching small screws.

It has a clean and free cutting action and allows a small amount of adjustment either to maintain a constant cutting diameter or to give slight cutting diameter variation. Several eccentric chucks are needed when a range of single-flute cutters are in use. The advantages of these cutters are more important on a router, they are not commonly-used on a spindle moulder. Other single-flute router cutters are ground eccentrically for mounting concentrically in the collet.

Twin-flute cutters have two cutting edges and, as their outer surfaces are radial-relief ground, they lose diameter as wear takes place. Straight router cutters can be solid HSS, tipped with tungsten carbide, solid tungsten carbide, or have disposable tungsten carbide tips. Profiled router cutters are usually solid HSS or tipped with tungsten carbide and often have a shear-cutting action when the profile is deep.

Fig. 110 Loose-cutter shank-type tool.

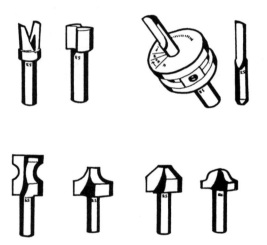

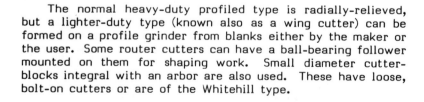

Fig. 111 Typical straight router cutters:
Left, twin-flute.
Right, single–flute router cutters loose and mounted in an eccentric chuck.

Fig. 112 Profiled router cutters.

The normal heavy-duty profiled type is radially-relieved, but a lighter-duty type (known also as a wing cutter) can be formed on a profile grinder from blanks either by the maker or the user. Some router cutters can have a ball-bearing follower mounted on them for shaping work. Small diameter cutter-blocks integral with an arbor are also used. These have loose, bolt-on cutters or are of the Whitehill type.

APPLICATION

Router cutters are used for relatively shallow profiles and light cuts only where regular heads are too large in diameter or are unsuitable. Examples are in shaping twisted handrails, spade-handle grips and tracery. They are also used for cutting grooves along or across the grain and with attachments for stair trenching or drawer dovetailing. The cutting angle is small but the finish produced is good whether cutting with or against the grain provided a high spindle speed and a slow and steady feed are used.

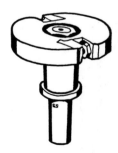

Fig. 113 Whitehill shank-type cutter-head with a taper/screwed shank.

PREPARATION

Solid and tipped cutters are ground in the flutes only using a tool and cutter grinder with some form of dividing head. The wing type can either be flute or profile-ground. Loose-cutter types are prepared in the same way as small flat cutters.

No setting is needed except to secure the shank in a self-centring collet (except the loose-cutter type which needs cutters setting first). Make sure that the shank corresponds in size to the collet used and is of the same measure (either imperial or metric). Collets can squeeze onto a smaller shank than that for which they were made, but will not grip the cutter correctly or safely.

Problems may arise with routing on a spindle moulder because the cut is underneath the workpiece and cannot be seen until complete. For this reason the spindle moulder is not a substitute for the router.

OPERATIONAL SAFETY

Router cutters, being one-piece, are a reasonably safe tool to use and no special precautions are necessary. Make sure proper tools are used for routing, though; the wrong type can be dangerous. Never use twist drills or other non-routing tools when routing, they have insufficient strength and could snap in use.

Plate 29 Above: Flute grinding a router cutter on a Sigrist and Muller (Saturn) universal tool grinder.

Plate 28 Lower left: Various Forest City tools tipped with PCD for machining the most difficult materials.

Plate 30 Below: Oppold carbide inserts for disposable-cutter tools.

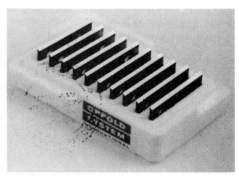

51

Plate 31 The Sicar S1000M features a sliding table and extended rear fence for tenoning and similar work.

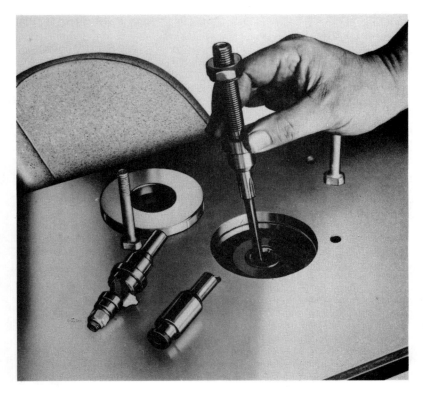

Plate 32 Interchangeable arbors on a Delta two-speed spindle moulder. Note the router cutter with a ball-bearing follower on the left.

52

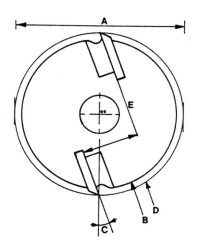

Fig. 114 Typical circular cutterhead showing:
A – planing diameter.
B – cutterhead outline.
C – cutting angle.
D – planing circle.
E – cutter spacing.

Fig. 115 Check the cutter profile against a sample mould at the correct cutting angle C. For accuracy support the cutter with a plywood triangular-shape piece. E is the reciprical of the cutting angle (90 degrees - cutting angle).

CHAPTER 6

CUTTER PREPARATION

The cutter profile normally differs slightly from the mould it produces due to the angle at which it meets the timber - the cutting angle. If it cuts square-on, i.e, with zero cutting angle as a French head, the cutter and mould profile fit one another precisely when the cutter is held square to the mould. With all other cutterheads the cutter profile must be deeper than the mould profile to compensate for the cutting angle.

The amount of 'throw' - the difference between the cutter profile and the mould it produces - is greater with large cutting angles and less with small cutting angles. When checking the cutter profile allow for 'throw' by holding it against the mould at the proper 'cutting angle'. Alternatively, develop-out the profile using geometry, a development rule, a development template, or a profile grinder.

CHECKING TO A SAMPLE

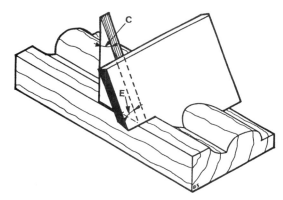

The most ready and practical way of checking the ground cutter profile is to hold the cutter at the same angle to the mould as when cutting - the cutting angle of the cutterhead. Obviously the angle has to be accurate, but most experienced grinders simply estimate this, relying on the skills developed over the years.

For the less experienced some form of guide is needed. Draw out the cutterhead full size and measure the cutting angle with a protractor. Make a triangular piece of plywood to the cutting and reciprical angles, and use this to support the cutter when checking it's profile. The reciprical or support angle is 90 degrees minus the cutting angle, e.g.; cutting angle 30 degrees, support angle 60 degrees, third angle 90 degrees.

Another way is to saw-off the moulding at the 'support' angle and check the cutter against this. Alternatively, place the moulding angled-face down on a piece of paper, plywood or a template and scribe or draw around the profile.

There is an error in all these methods because they are based on a single cutting angle but, in cutting, this continuously changes. For greater accuracy the 'cutting angle' used should be that measured at mid depth-on-cut - so a different support is theoretically needed for each mould. Unless the mould profile is exceptionally deep, the cutting angle large or the cutter small there is little angle change, so only two or three supports are needed for each cutterblock catering for cut depths of, perhaps, 10, 20 and 30mm.

Fig. 116 Another way to check cutter profile. Cut-off the sample mould at the reciprical angle E. C is the cutting angle.

The error can best be seen in checking the cutter shape needed for a 45 degree bevel, which has to be be slightly rounded to produce a perfectly flat surface. By using these methods the cutter profile has the correct slope but a perfectly straight cutting edge and produces a slightly rounded surface on the timber. A similar distortion applies to all moulds, so slightly deformed profiles are always produced. This is usually acceptable for most applications, but not where a precise matching profile is needed.

When a mould profile is critical a better method is needed. Either geometrically develop the cutter profile, or use a development rule or template.

Two basic cutterblock dimensions are needed, the cutter spacing and the planing (or minimum cutting) circle. The shape, type and size of cutterblock does not affect cutter development, two different types with the same basic dimensions need exactly the same cutter profile.

The cutter spacing is the shortest distance between the leading face lines of cutters fixed on opposite sides of the head. With a three-cutterblock the cutter spacing is double the distance between one face line and the cutterblock centreline. The planing circle is the diameter as measured from the cutting point of one cutter to the cutting point of the opposing cutter when both are set to the minimum cutting circle. See Fig. 114.

54

GEOMETRIC DEVELOPMENT

With this a section is taken geometrically through the mould and projected against a radial line drawn from the centre of the cutterblock, around the centre of the cutterblock then square-off the cutter face line.

Draw out the cutterhead full size complete with cutters, bolts, etc. Draw a radial line from its centre parallel to any cutter-face line (the leading face of the cutter). Add the planing circle (the smallest circle which clears the cutterblock body, bolts, etc.) and draw a line square to the radial line from where it crosses the planing circle. This is the planing line. Draw out the mould full size with the fence face on this line and with the mould on the opposite side to the cutterblock.

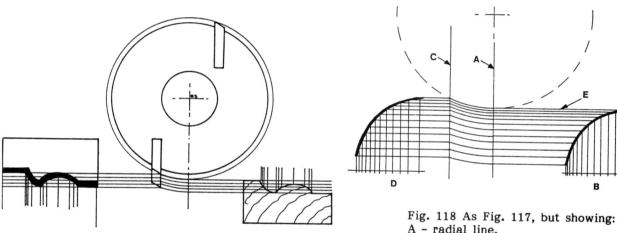

Fig. 117 This shows the general lay-out for development with the sample mould shape on the right and the developed cutter profile on the left.

Fig. 118 As Fig. 117, but showing:
A – radial line.
B – mould profile.
C – cutter-face line.
D – cutter profile.
E – planing or fence line.

Draw several lines square to the planing line to divide up the mould profile. Draw parallel lines at the same spacings at the far side of the cutter-face line and clear of the cutterblock. The number of lines and their spacing is not critical, but for the best results divide along the profile itself at even spacings. The more lines and the greater the accuracy - but development then becomes complex. To make development easier number or letter each corresponding line.

From the intersection of each dividing line and the mould profile draw a line parallel to the planing line and up to the radial line. Using a pair of compasses continue the lines concentric to the cutterblock centre to meet the cutter-face line. Finally draw lines parallel to the face line from all these points to intersect with corresponding dividing lines already drawn. Join the intersections to outline the true cutter profile. This is the profile to which the cutters must be made.

Cutter profile developer

The Robinson cutter profile developer is a device which duplicates the movements of any cutter to mechanically develop out the correct cutter profile from a true section of the required mould. It adjusts to any cutterblock size.

Cutter projection rule

This is a simple rule divided on one edge into regular spacings and on the opposite edge into the equivalent projected dimensions. Make one as follows:

   Draw out the cutterblock full size, and add the radial and cutter-face lines. Divide up the radial line into regular divisions from the planing circle outwards. Draw concentric lines from each point up to and square from the cutter face line to form the projected scale. Also mark on this the cutterblock lip or body line. Mark the projection rule on opposing edges with these two scales. Label the radial scale-edge as the 'measure mould' scale, and the cutter-face scale-edge as the 'mark cutter profile' scale. Cut the rule off along the 'lip' line.

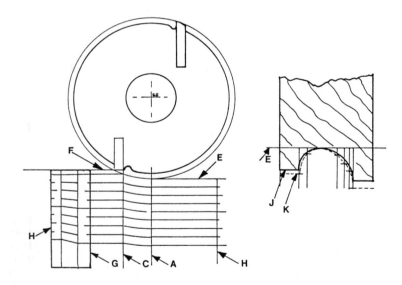

Fig. 119 The basis of a cutter projection rule showing:
A - radial line.
C - cutter face line.
E - fence line.
F - 'lip' line.
G - mark cutter profile scale.
H - measure mould scale.

A typical use is shown with the mould profile in solid outline J and the cutter profile in dotted outline K. Fence line E is added together with several lines at right angles to this. The mould is measured from the fence line using rule H and the same measurements set out with rule G and seen as short lines. The profile is finally developed out by joining these points.

   In use draw out the mould profile full size and add lines square to the face (fence) line at any suitable spacings. Measure along each dividing line from the face line to the mould profile using the 'measure mould' scale. Mark corresponding points on the same lines also measured from the face line, but this time using the 'mark cutter profile' scale. Join the developed points to outline the true cutter profile. Draw the cutterblock 'lip' line square across to show cutter projection needed beyond the cutterblock.) If using with a template the cutterblock 'lip' line should also be the template cut-out.

Cutter projection template

This is a board of plywood, faced hardboard or aluminium marked out as previously described (Chapter 2), but with additional permanent lines marked as a graph in depth and width-on-cut.

The width-on-cut lines are marked out with the 'measure mould' scale of the development rule and are square to the planing line. When the template is marked with the table line or cutterblock clearance lines, as in the case of a Whitehill block, start the scale at these lines.

The depth-on-cut lines are marked out with the 'mark cutter profile' scale of the development rule and are parallel to the planing line. When making a projection rule for a Whitehill block the template is divided up for depth-on-cut both inside and outside the planing line and all are projected as lines onto the template.

The required mould is measured at several points in width from the table line and in depth from the fence line. Corresponding points are marked on the template using the graph as the measure. The cutter profile is developed out by joining these points.

Each different size of cutterblock needs its own projection template, and each template is suitable only for the cutterblock for which it was made.

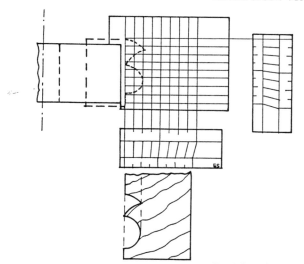

Fig. 120 Use a projection rule to make a projection template as shown here. Measure the mould with a regular scale but set it out on the template using these lines as the measures.

Robinson Estephagraph

This is a commercially-produced template system designed by the writer for use with most common types of moulding head. It comprises a gauge for measuring the mould profile and a series of templates for different cutterheads. The gauge has a graph with an inverse-development scale in mould depth and a regular scale in mould width. Each template has a graph to regular scales in both width and depth, with the planing and table lines also marked.

The mould required is traced onto a plastic sheet and placed on the gauge, face uppermost. Development of the cutter profile is by draft projection, i.e., marking corresponding points on the template to those on the gauge where the mould profile intersects them.

The difference between mould and cutter profile, the 'throw', is determined by the spacing of the depth-on-cut gauge lines and is varied by placing the mould profile at different positions on the gauge. The position for any size of cutterblock is found simply by moving a sliding scale until the cutter spacing and planing circle measurements align with one another. The section needed is shown by an arrow and by numbered lines which correspond to those on the template.

The templates themselves are individually fitted to the cutterblock by cutting them away until the planing (adze) line corresponds with the edge of a planing cutter set to the planing circle.

The gauge and graph lines are permanently sealed-in under plastic so that guide lines can be pencilled-in and erased. A single gauge can be used with any number of templates used 'in situ' or on a setting stand.

Plate 33 Sedgwick medium-duty spindle moulder GW.

Plate 34 The Northfield double spindle moulder cuts with the grain regardless of outline shape by passing the assembly between the two spindles. These rotate in opposite directions. Note the rear-mounted Shaw-guard pressures.

CHAPTER 7

CUTTER GRINDING

Free-hand grinding is the conventional and accepted method for spindle moulder cutters. The old-fashioned multiple wheel grinder, probably the best type for this operation, allows several grinding wheels of different thickness and profile to be mounted at the same time on the same arbor - but used independently. The conventional practice is to form one wide and one narrow wheel to a square section, and the remainder to half-round sections of different radii.

Flat sections of cutters and external curved profiles of large radius are formed on the widest of the square wheels. Small external curves are formed on the largest diameter half-round wheel. Internal curves are formed on the half-round wheel nearest too, but smaller than, the curve needed. The narrow square wheel is used only to form grooves and similar. By using these different combinations reasonably smooth control is possible for all profiles.

A smoother internal curve is formed if the shape of the wheel closely fits that wanted on the cutter. The profiles of many cutters combine curves of different radii, and cutters are freely transferred from one wheel to another in grinding. This is the great advantage of the multiple wheel grinder, rapid interchange between wheels without having to change them.

Many popular grinders, though, are now either the single wheel section of a plane and mould cutter grinder, or a double-wheel grinder. Multiple-wheel techniques are impracticable on these machines as constant wheel changing would be needed to match the wheel profile to that of the cutter. This slows down the process and is also bad practice. Grinding wheels should be changed as little as possible to avoid damaging them and to reduce the wasteful re-shaping always necessary after fitting.

The usual compromise is to use one flat wide wheel and one narrow half-round wheel. However, smooth movement is difficult on the larger internal curves - more skill is needed in grinding and the result is never as good. The alternative is to re-shape a commonly-used wheel each time a different curvature is to be ground. This gives better grinding conditions but plays absolute havoc with grinding wheel usage.

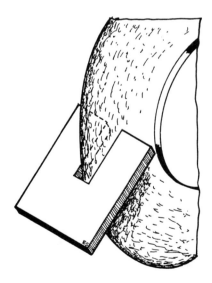

Fig. 121 The best cutter grinding support, or rest, extends on both sides of the grinding wheel. Keep the wheel-to-support gap small.

GRINDING WITHOUT A REST

Mould-cutter grinding wheels all grind peripherally (on their rim) and usually grind into the cutter, from cutting point to heel.

Grinding on an open grinding wheel without a rest is difficult but not impossible - as experienced grinders prove every day. The skill is to hold the cutter securely, at the correct swivel and tilt angle to the wheel, whilst moving it around to form the correct profile.

With an open wheel there is always the chance of the wheel snatching and damaging the cutter. The danger time is on first contact with the grinding wheel. Preferably lightly contact first with the cutter heel, then carefully tilt downwards until the full grinding face makes contact. If contact is made first with the cutting edge the chance of damage is greater.

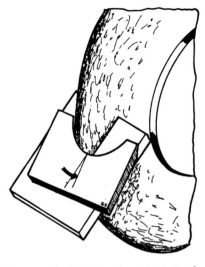

Fig. 122 Swivel to the right to form side clearance on the left-hand side.

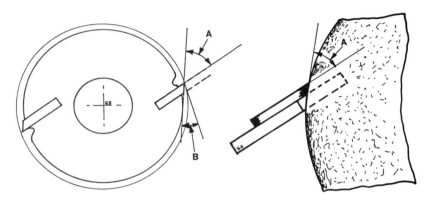

Fig. 123 Above: Set the support to form the correct bevel angle A to give a clearance angle B of between 15 and 30 degrees.

Fig. 124 Right: A typical completed cutter with main and both side clearance angles ground-in.

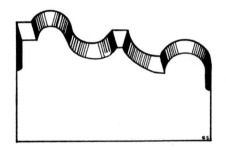

Fig. 125 Below right: Swivel to the left to form side clearance on the right-hand side.

GRINDING WITH A REST

The cutter rest should be slotted to support deep-profiled cutters at both sides of the grinding wheel. The wheel-to-rest gap at sides and front should be the absolute minimum, and give support right up to the wheel to reduce the levering effect of the down-cutting wheel. This makes the cutters easier to control and the operation a great deal safer. Maintain a gap of not more than 3mm. by adjusting the rest as the wheel wears - and after changing grinding wheels.

Set the rest to the correct bevel angle - to suit the worst conditions at the planing circle. Check the setting using a cutter ground to the correct angle. When forming side clearance angles keep the cutter flat on the rest but swivel it between 5 and 15 degrees to form a 5 degree side clearance angle. It is not possible to precisely control side clearance, but with practice a reasonable degree of repetition is possible.

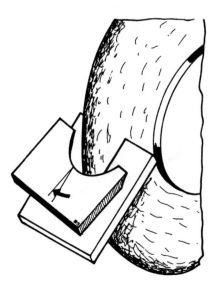

60

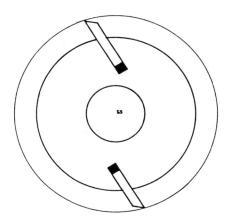

Fig. 127 Use cutters in pairs and of the same profile and weight.

Above: When both project alike the cutterhead balances.

Below: With unequal projection the cutterhead will be dynamically out of balance.

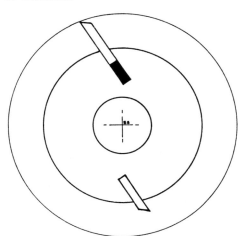

GRINDING TECHNIQUES

When forming the profile, move the cutter around flat on the rest whilst maintaining it at the correct swivel angle. Grind slowly, removing weight in two or more light grinds rather than in a single heavy grind, and keep the cutter well quenched by frequent dipping in water. (Some early machines had a drip feed which proved so messy that the type was abandoned; most grinders are now dry.) Keep the cutter moving continuously and smoothly, and use wheel profiles which closely fit the internal curves needed. Check the final shape against the sample or a template. Finished cutters should be dimensionally alike to aid balancing. When heavy cutters are used always grind both cutters of a pair to the same profile, don't use one finishing and one balancing cutter.

Blanking cutters

It is normal when blanking-out cutters (forming a profile from a square blank) to initially grind with the cutter rest set to form a square edge instead of a cutting edge. By doing this the profile is easier to see and the cutter is less likely to burn. When the profile is fully formed re-set the rest to the correct grinding angle and finish-grind to a cutting edge.

Fig. 126 Relieve the cut by cutting-out vee-sections, shown in black, leaving only the shaded portions to profile-grind.

Where excessive grinding is needed it is quicker and easier to first cut-out sections. Mark the cutter face with the developed profile, then add vee cut-outs from the edge to skirt the profile and show where cuts can be made. Fit a special, reinforced, cut-off grinding wheel. Set the cutter rest square to the wheel and feed the cutter slowly into the grinding wheel following the marked lines. Use it like a circular saw by feeding straight onto the periphery, take care to avoid side movement. Keep the cutter well quenched.

BALANCING CUTTERS

It is essential that the cutterhead is in perfect balance; if not it will vibrate to deflect the arbor and produce an erratic cuttermark pitch and a poor finish on the surface of the timber. Excessive vibration eventually ruins the arbor bearings and could cause an accident.

All cutterheads must have a true running balance, large ones especially because, as cutting diameter increases, so does the affect of imbalance. Even a small imbalance creates problems at high spindle speeds.

Because the effect of centrifugal force increases by the square of the increase in speed, the greatest care has to be taken when balancing heads for high arbor speeds. The correct method is to use cutters in perfectly matching pairs, balance them, then finally set both 'to cut'.

Cutters need balancing after grinding to correct any imbalance that grinding may have produced. Use a pair of sensitive scales or a cutter balance. Some check the balance of a complete head using a balancing stand. This is necessary with heavy cutterblocks, but rarely necessary with small spindle moulder heads unless very complex set-ups or high spindle speeds are used. (It is also essential that all cutterheads and other fast-running parts are accurately balanced on a dynamic balancer. Usually the makers see to this.)

Balancing stand

The simplest has two level knife-edged bars fitted knife-edge up. Mount the head on an arbor and gently place it so that the arbor rests on the knife edges with the head between them.

To check balance roll the arbor along the knife edges and mark the head at the top when it comes to rest. This is the lightest point. If it comes to rest very quickly and quite positively the head is badly out of balance. If this happens slowly and indecisively then it is almost in perfect balance. Final balance is correct when the assembly does not stop at any particular position. To balance, remove and grind the heavier cutter on the tail, then re-set and re-check.

Most modern balancing stands now have two pairs of knife-edge rollers in place of the knife-edge bars and are much easier to use.

Balance can only be checked statically, i.e. when stationary, not dynamically as when running. There is an important difference which must be appreciated. Take an example of a cutterblock with cutters which have the same weight and projection and are also diametrically opposite. The cutterhead would show as being in balance on balancing rollers - and would also be in true dynamic balance.

If the cutters are shifted sideways, one to one end of the cutterblock and the other to the opposite end, the cutterblock would still be in static balance, and seem correct when on the balancing stand. It would, however, be dynamically unbalanced because the pull from the cutters is not directly opposite - so the head would vibrate badly when run.

Put in a nutshell, each pair of cutters should be dimensionally alike, balanced as a pair, set diametrically opposite and to exactly the same projection, and both set 'to cut'. If this is carefully carried out the cutterhead will be in true dynamic balance.

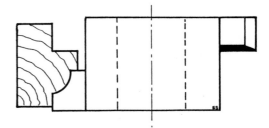

Fig. 128 Above: This head is dynamically out of balance because cutters are not set directly opposite - even though it might be in perfect balance and appear correct when checked on a balancing stand.

Below: This head is in perfect dynamic balance with pairs of identical cutters mounted directly opposite one another.

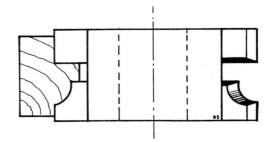

CHAPTER 8

PROFILE GRINDING

When moulds are regularly repeated it is quicker and better to grind cutters using some form of copy or profile grinder. Both machines use a metal template to control the cutter profile in grinding. The cutter and template are normally fixed to a horizontally-floating carriage. The cutter is opposite to the fixed grinding wheel and the template moves with it to contact a fixed copy pin or stylus.

The grinding wheel grinds down, and the cutter is commonly held face-down to grind from the heel to the cutting edge. This seems wrong but isn't. The excessive wire edge initially formed when rough grinding almost disappears when finish-grinding.

The metal template is formed to the reverse of the mould profile required. It can be cut-out on a fine bandsaw or jigsaw, then the edge ground, filed, and finally highly polished using fine emery cloth - wet. For the best finish finally burnish the edge (follow the profile with a hardened tool whilst applying relatively heavy pressure).

Most users make templates from sheet iron. Normally this wears well enough, but some makers recommend that templates are hardened after manufacture. It is also possible to make templates from plastic sheeting which is much easier to work - but these wear badly.

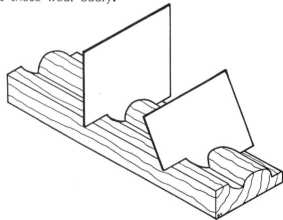

Fig. 129 A template for a copy grinder must be developed out to compensate for cutting angle, so tilt it when checking against a sample, right, or develop the shape geometrically. With a profile grinder the template fits square-on, left.

In grinding, the carriage is moved around so that the profile on the template follows against the stylus, whilst the the cutter profile is formed simultaneously by the grinding wheel. This type of machine normally has a coolant system using an oil and water mix to allow rapid cutter grinding without burning.

Copy and profile grinders vary in design and operation but are basically similar. The following describes specific machines but which are fairly representative of their types.

63

Copy grinder

On copy grinders the cutter is ground to precisely the same shape as the template, so the template profile first needs developing-out using any of the methods previously described. If the same shape has to be formed by two different cutter-heads, then two similar but slightly different templates are needed. This is necessary, for example in window work, when using a square cutterblock for moulding straight stiles and slotted collars to form the curved rail above the top light, both of which must have matching mould profiles.

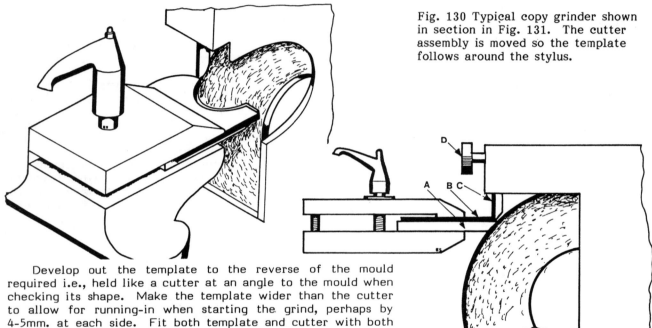

Fig. 130 Typical copy grinder shown in section in Fig. 131. The cutter assembly is moved so the template follows around the stylus.

Develop out the template to the reverse of the mould required i.e., held like a cutter at an angle to the mould when checking its shape. Make the template wider than the cutter to allow for running-in when starting the grind, perhaps by 4-5mm. at each side. Fit both template and cutter with both in approximate alignment, then use the stylus adjustments for fine setting. Setting is correct when, as the stylus is traced around the template profile, the grinding wheel precisely follows around the cutter profile. Cutters should be roughly ground to shape before copy grinding.

The grinding wheel normally forms a grinding angle of around 40 degrees regardless of wear. Dress the grinding wheel, whilst running, by adjusting it outwards towards a diamond dresser operating through a slot in the clamp-on guide. Finally adjust the stylus to contact the template all the way along whilst the cutter barely clears the grinding wheel.

Start the grinding wheel and the coolant, and trace around the stylus keeping the template in light contact. Adjust the stylus so grinding takes place, and continue grinding and adjusting until the full cutting width is ground.

As with all grinding operations allow the grinding wheel to grind freely, don't crowd it, and regularly dress it. Add side clearance by swivelling the cutter holder.

Fig. 131 Section through a copy grinder showing:
A - Cutter.
B - Template.
C - Stylus.
D - Adjustment for the stylus.

Profile grinder

With a profile grinder the cutters are usually fastened to a block on a rotating arbor and are supported on a rest directly in front of the grinding wheel. Cutters can be ground in the head or on a dummy block (which must match the parent cutterblock in cutter spacing and diameter).

When grinding, the template remains level and the cutter rocks on the rest to repeat the same cutting angles as when moulding, so the true cutter profile is developed-out automatically by the grinder. As development is therefore not needed, the templates for profile grinders are simpler to make as the exact reverse of the mould required. Make each to match the full-size drawing of the mould, or to fit a sample mould square-on. Allow overlaps of both cutter beyond the mould and template beyond the cutter.

Plate 35 Profile grinding on an Autool PR230H. The template and stylus can be seen at the front left-hand side.

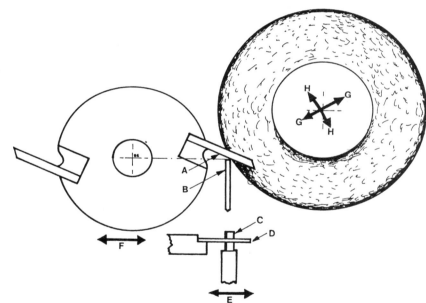

Fig. 132 Section through a profile grinder showing:
A - Cutter ground in the head.
B - Cutter support.
C - Stylus.
D - Template.

The template mounting moves with the carriage as F.
The stylus can be adjusted for grinding cut as E.
The grinding wheel adjusts to compensate for wear G, and for clearance angle H.

Fit the template, then set the closest point of the cutterblock to clear the cutter rest by 3mm. Holding the carriage in this position, adjust the stylus to contact the deepest point of the template profile (usually the planing line). Set cutter blanks far enough forward for the edge to contact the grinding wheel when the carriage is reset so that the stylus touches the shallowest point of the template profile. Cutters can project slightly more if necessary. It is also possible to draw cutters out to touch the grinding wheel if short, but grinding life is then lost and cutters are less safely held. With previous-formed cutters fit them and set the machine as described under 'Re-grinding'.

There are three main movements in addition to the two-way free movement of the table or carriage. One is a screw-adjusted forward movement of the grinding wheel during or after dressing. This adjustment is normally on an angle so that clearance-angle setting remains the same regardless of grinding wheel wear.

The second grinding wheel movement alters its vertical position to vary the clearance angle between about 15 and 40 degrees. As the profile grinder maintains a fixed clearance angle, the grinding angle on the cutter varies in step with changes in cutting angle. This ensures that clearance is never less than the minimum set, and that the cutter is given the maximum possible cutting-edge strength.

(In grinding tungsten carbide tipped cutters it is normal to alter the clearance angle setting between facing and backing to grind them independently and with different types of grinding wheels. With HSS and similar cutters a single clearance angle setting is used and is commonly the same for all heads).

The third movement on some machines allows the grinding wheel to be tilted to 5 or 10 degrees either side of vertical to add side clearance. On other machines the grinding wheel remains vertical and the carriage is slewed to add side clearance.

GRINDING WHEEL DRESSING

A built-in diamond dresser keeps the grinding wheel true. Regular dressing is essential to maintain grinding wheel profile and cutting ability. Always dress the grinding wheel prior to finish grinding.

In dressing, the grinding wheel and dresser are brought into contact, whilst rotating or traversing the diamond, until the grinding wheel is fully formed. When the dresser is fixed at the point of grind the grinding wheel adjusts and aligns automatically with the stylus on dressing - making operation simple and error-free. When the dresser adjusts in dressing, it is necessary afterwards to manually re-align the dressed grinding wheel with the stylus. This takes longer and is prone to error.

The grinding wheel is dressed to a half-round section by rotating the diamond dresser on its axis. For square and angular dressing, the dresser is moved across the wheel usually in a swivelling action. The dresser is only used for conventional grit grinding wheels. Diamond and CBN grinding wheels are already formed to profile and should not be dressed.

Grinding wheel profiles

The regular grinding wheel shape for rough grinding, and for finish-grinding all profiles other than internal squares and angles, is half-round. The grinding wheel thickness is usually between 4 and 6mm. This allows fairly small radii to be formed, yet is of reasonable width so that the grinding wheel does not wear excessively.

Plate 36 Above: The grinding head tilts to give side clearance on this Autool PR grinder.

Plate 37 Below: The Autool PR grinders feature point-of-grind dressing, in this case dual-radius.

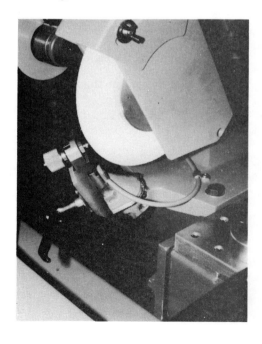

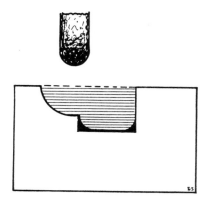

Fig. 133 Above: Finish-grind as much as possible using the half-round grinding wheel.

Below: Grind-out remaining corners only using a square wheel.

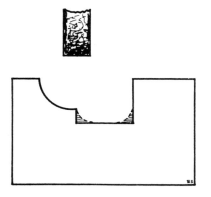

Thinner grinding wheels are used, but normally only for the small internal corners that the regular half-round grinding wheels cannot form. It is possible to use thin, regular-grit grinding wheels, but they are fragile and damage too easily; preferably use a thick, tapered grinding wheel.

Regular grit grinding wheels with small radii and sharp corners should be fine-grit types, but these are not suitable for fast grinding. It is possible to form small internal radii grinding slowly using the corners of a square grinding wheel, but the finish is poor and corner-wear rapid. Keeping regular-grit grinding wheels to a sharp profile is a problem on profile grinders - a better solution is to use a formed CBN grinding wheel instead, or a dual template.

GRINDING TECHNIQUES

The best technique is to finish the cutter profile as completely as practical with a half-round grinding wheel, then merely clean out the internal square or angular corners and small radii using a grinding wheel of different profile. When changing the grinding wheel it is essential also to change the stylus as the two must always match. The stylus must also accurately align with the grinding wheel. After replacing both grinding wheel and stylus, check both for alignment by traversing along the fully finished section of the profile, then correct any mis-alignment by adjusting the stylus.

In grinding, the carriage is moved to make the stylus follow the template so that the grinding wheel forms the cutter to the correct profile. The cutter must maintain contact with cutter-rest immediately in front of the grinding wheel, so exert pressure via a handwheel on the cutterblock arbor. With a profile grinder the cutting edge cannot easily be seen because of the angle and the coolant, so watch the template and stylus to anticipate the movements needed. This is contrary to hand-grinding practice and, perhaps, the most difficult thing to become accustomed to.

Grinding should be light enough to not crowd the grinding wheel. Allow it to cut freely, if necessary riding on the grinding wheel to leave a gap between template and stylus until the cutter is ground away. Keep the cutter moving and in the smoothest possible way. Grinding is complete when the full cutter width can be traversed with the stylus in full contact with the template.

Direct the coolant to the point of grind to allow fast, burn-free grinding. If anything, coolant should flood from above and below, and at the cutter rather than the grinding wheel, to avoid splashing.

Grinding from a blank

When first using a profile grinder it is an advantage to set the stylus to give a shallow grind of only 2-3mm. at the deepest point. When this has been fully formed step-back the stylus by stages of 2-3mm. to allow further grinding until the cutter is fully profiled.

Mark the stylus position before grinding the second cutter so that this exact setting can repeated. With this method much less can be ground-off the cutter and a new operator feels he has more control - so confidence is built up quickly.

Invariably, though, most operators eventually grind the full depth at a single setting, allowing the cutter to initially ride lightly on the grinding wheel, progressively grinding down to the full depth.

When profiling cutters from a blank the recommended method is to make a series of parallel plunging cuts directly into the grinding wheel to form a series of close slots, finally traversing across to remove the scallops remaining. However, I prefer to traverse across in small, deepening arcs applying pressure only from the furthest point to the deepest point until the full profile has been formed.

Always have the grinding wheel vertical or the carriage square-on when grinding from a blank, adding side clearance later. If the grinding wheel is tilted or the carriage slewed when plunged in, it could apply side pressure to possibly shatter the grinding wheel. Pressure must only be applied to the periphery of these grinding wheels.

Profile grinding is exceptionally fast when compared to other methods as coolant makes continuous grinding possible and template control prevents errors. A Whitehill cutter, for example, can be formed along one edge from blank to finished cutter in just three or four minutes.

Grinding side clearance

As a last operation, side clearance is added. On some machines the grinding wheel is tilted to one side and the cutter reground, then tilted to the opposite side and ground a second time. Side clearance angles are controlled mechanically and repeat precisely.

On some machines additional adjustment is necessary during this operation to grind to a feather edge where side clearance is added, and to avoid spoiling the cutting edge elsewhere. Autool profile grinders and a few others require no additional adjustment when adding side clearance, so machine setting is simple and error-free - and the two grinds blend perfectly.

With swivelling-table machines the table is swivelled in the appropriate direction individually for each section, but grinding is a continuous sequence. On some machines the swivel angle has to be estimated. This needs greater skill and is complicated because different swivel angle settings are needed when the machine setting is changed. In swivelling the table, because the grinding wheel presents a slightly different profile to the cutter, only half-round and knife-edge grinding wheels can actually be used in the way described. With other wheel shapes a different grinding wheel and stylus profile are needed for grinding square-on, also for left- and right-hand side clearance.

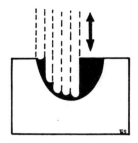

Fig. 134 Above: Plunge-grinding to remove weight.

Below: Part-circular roughing is a better alternative.

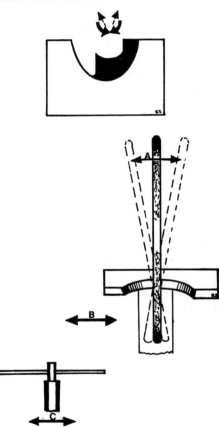

Fig. 135 Adding side clearance on a tilting-head profile grinder as viewed from the rear. The movements are:
A - side clearance tilt.
B - carriage sideways movement.
C - stylus sideways adjustment.

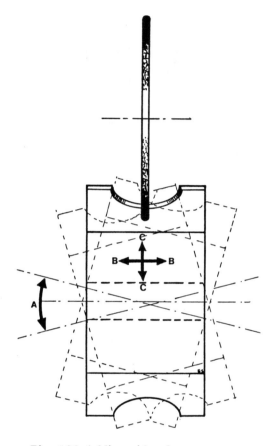

Fig. 136 Adding side clearance on a swivelling-carriage profile grinder as viewed from above.
The swivel movement A varies with changes in cutting and clearance angles.
The two arrows B and C are the operating movements of the carriage.

Finish grinding

Because the cutter profile is mechanically controlled it is practical to 'spark-out' the grind by making repeated passes without adjustment to the stylus. For absolute accuracy the process should be repeated two or three times, dressing the wheel between operations. This is normally necessary only when blanking cutters or when grinding-out excessive cutting-edge damage.

The surface finish is greatly improved by sparking-out even when using a relatively coarse grinding wheel, so that the cutter then produces a better surface and lasts longer. The more the process is repeated, the better the finish. Sparking-out should always be part of normal grinding practice.

When the first cutter is completed grind the second. If grinding in the head simply rotate for the next cutter. If grinding on a dummy block replace the first cutter with the second making sure both seat against the side guide and back fence so they finish exactly the same size.

Because they are dimensionally alike, of the same profile and with the same grinding and clearance angles, the cutters remain in balance, so balancing after grinding is not needed.

Re-grinding

Re-grinding is similar to grinding from a blank, except that roughing-out is usually unnecessary. First, accurately align cutters with the grinding wheel using the side and front-to-back adjustments of the stylus. Once alignment is correct the only adjustment needed is depth-on-cut to progressively increase the grind until the cutting-edge is fully restored.

Slotted collar cutters are best ground individually on a dummy block. Whitehill and other circular and square-head cutters can be ground in the cutterblock or on a dummy block as preferred.

Grinding in the head

The correct technique is to first balance the blank cutters in pairs, then pre-set both equally so they project enough to be fully profiled without resetting. Check that the cutterblock does not foul either the grinding wheel or the cutter support when at the deepest point of the grind.

Use a setting stand in pre-setting. Notch-out the end of a sample mould square to the face and to a parallel depth just beyond the deepest point of the mould. Position it so that the top surface of the notch is in line with the centre-line of the arbor. Set to give normal clearance between mould and cutter-head, plus allowance for regrinding. Set cutters so that the blank cutting edge sits in the corner of the notch to project the correct amount.

69

By grinding in the head cutters are ground to the same profile, the same radial height and in perfect side-ways alignment. Balancing is simpler, and cutterheads have a better running balance than when prepared in the conventional manner. When cutters remain in the head, regrinding is faster and simpler as there is no need to remove and re-set the cutters each time.

Profiled cutterheads can be re-profiled on a profile grinder after re-tipping in exactly the same way as a conventional cutter. Use a regular grit or CBN wheel for H.S.S tips, and a diamond wheel for tungsten carbide tips.

Tipped router cutters can be ground in the same way, but with a router chuck fitted in place of the regular arbor. In this case the arbor is locked by a dividing mechanism as cutting-edge projections are too small for the cutter support to be used.

Plate 38 Grinding a profiled cutter on an Autool profile grinder.

CHAPTER 9

PROFILED CUTTERS

Profiled-heads and bits are are formed to pattern on their outer surface. They are face-ground only, using some form of dividing head or finger register, on a machine with either a traversing table or a traversing grinding wheel.

Fix the cutter directly onto the grinder arbor, or on a self-centring bush and finger tighten. Cutters can face either direction - unless clearance is restricted. Fit the saucer grinding wheel with its concave face against the ground face of the cutter.

SETTING THE CUTTING ANGLE

Most operators set by trial and error. To do this cross-adjust the grinding wheel whilst turning the cutter loose on the arbor until the two fit snugly, then lock the cutter to the arbor.

Plate 39 A JKO four-wing solid profiled cutter.

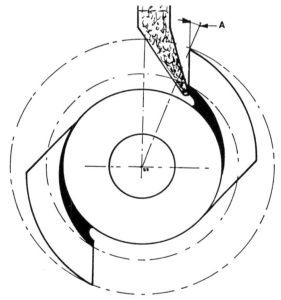

Fig. 137 Grinding a solid profiled cutter using a saucer grinding wheel. Although only touching on the rim, the grinding wheel grinds the full vertical face. The cutting angle is shown at A.

It is difficult to tell when setting is correct as contact is between a flat face on the cutter and the relatively narrow grinding surface of the saucer grinding wheel. Some makers provide a flat dummy metal wheel to fit in place of the grinding wheel for setting purposes. After using this, and replacing it with the grinding wheel, simply cross-adjust as needed to bring the ground face of the cutter and the grinding wheel into contact.

Setting the grinding wheel and cutter face in true contact is technically wrong; it should actually bear harder against the tip to maintain a constant cutting angle (see later note).

INDEXING THE CUTTER

All grinders have some form of indexing to accurately position each face in turn. If indexing is not accurate cutting-edge heights will vary, so take great care in this. Three types are used; dividing head, face registration and peripheral registration.

A dividing head positively locates the arbor at pre-set angular positions by means of plunger to engage in holes or slots. The dividing head is the most convenient type and the most positive.

Having set for cutting angle, set the dividing head for the correct number of points on the cutter and engage the plunger at any position. Index to check that the cutter locates at the required angles. Finally, release the cutter and turn on the arbor to set any face against the grinding wheel, then re-secure. Some dividing heads have fine rotary adjustment to correct a wrong angle setting. Use the cross adjustment of the grinding wheel in setting the cut-depth.

With face registration a fixed finger locates each ground face in turn before locking the arbor. The line of the grinding wheel is off-set from this finger by the depth of grind needed (this setting is also used as cut control). Usually each face is ground once only, regrinding the complete cutter a second or third time if much wants grinding off. Because register is against a previously-ground face, grinding errors can and do build up.

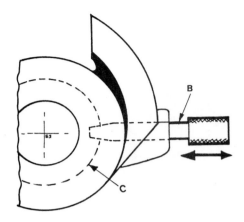

Fig. 138 The cutter can be indexed for position by plunger B and dividing disc C.

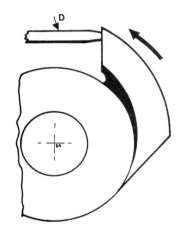

Fig. 139 Indexing the ground face against a fixed finger D.

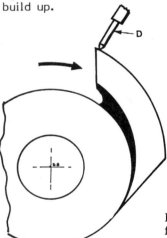

Fig. 140 Peripheral indexing using a fixed finger D or a dial indicator.

With peripheral registration the cutter is turned against normal rotation to bring the outer face of the cutter just short of the cutting face into contact with a fixed finger-stop. The modern version uses a dial indicator instead of a stop, and has fine screw-adjusted rotary movement and a positive arbor lock. Adjustment is made until the dial indicator shows the same reading each time before locking the arbor. This takes more skill as each face needs individual setting, but gives excellent results.

Machine setting

Tool-room types with a table-mounted cutter arbor and a horizontal grinding wheel arbor:

Set the grinding wheel height so that its lower edge just clears the inside edge of the ground face. Set the table traverse limits so that the cutter clears the grinding wheel at the operator's end for safe indexing without danger of fouling the wheel, and at the opposite end for working clearance between wheel and cutter.

Radial feed types:
Position the wheel at the deepest point of the cut to project beyond both extreme points by an equal amount. With symmetrical profiles the grinding wheel should be central to the cutter.

With assymmetrical profiles the grinding wheel and cutter need off-setting. This adjustment is possible either by adjusting the wheel or the cutter - which depends on the machine type. Such adjustment may not be necessary with a large diameter grinding wheel, but may be with a small diameter grinding wheel, a wide cutter, or a shallow gullet. Set the forward movement so that the wheel stops just short of the bottom of the gullet.

GRINDING TECHNIQUES

When the cutting edge is badly worn or chipped so that an excessive amount wants grinding off, two different techniques can be used: continuous adjustment, or grinding to a zero.

With continuous adjustment each face is ground in sequence, adjusting the feed after each complete rotation of the cutter until all cutting points are restored.

When grinding to a zero several passes are made on the worst cutting edge, progressively adjusting the grinding wheel feed until the edge is fully restored. All subsequent faces are then ground to exactly the same grinding wheel feed-setting.

Where the grinding wheel feed-adjustment has a scale and pointer, note or temporarily mark the position after grinding the most worn or chipped cutting face. Index the next face, shift the wheel clear, then progressively feed in until the original scale setting is again reached. Repeat with the remaining faces.

On machines with a loose graduated collar and a click-stop, set this to zero after grinding the worst face, then simply grind the remaining faces to zero.

Zero-grinding gives much the same result as continuous-adjustment but does not take grinding wheel wear into account. To do this finally regrind each face at the same machine setting. (If CBN grinding wheels are used the wear factor can be ignored). Whatever method is used grind until no more sparks are produced to give a good ground surface and accurate cutting point height.

Plate 40 Accurate centering on the grinding machine arbor is guaranteed by using an hydraulic sleeve such as this ETP Hydro-Grip.

Plate 41 Grinding a tipped profile cutter on a Stehle universal grinder. This machine features automatic positioning using a sensor.

73

Grinding faults

By setting to the previously-ground face this is progressively ground-back in a series of parallel steps. This seems correct because the original setting is apparently repeated, but it is not, the cutting angle and mould depth both slightly increase.

The correct way is to measure the cutting angle on a new cutter and always set to this, ignoring the actual fit of the grinding wheel to the cutter. The simplest way is to shape a metal plate with a vee cut-out to fit the extreme cutting points when new, then check before and after grinding.

Because the grinding wheel normally adjusts in parallel steps, the angle also changes but to a lesser degree when grinding an excessively dull or chipped cutter. In practical terms angle change is very slight and can be ignored - provided setting is made each time to the correct angle and not to the previously-ground face.

Users often think that accuracy is inherent in profiled cutters, it is not; it depends on the accuracy of the cutter mounting and the care taken in the grinding operation. The grinding machine bearings and dividing head mechanism must also be absolutely true - otherwise good results are never possible.

The accuracy of the dividing head is easily checked. Fit and carefully grind any suitable cutter, allowing the grinding wheel to fully spark-out. Re-set the cutter loose on the arbor by one spacing and lightly re-grind the complete cutter. If the grinding wheel contacts the faces unevenly the dividing head is suspect.

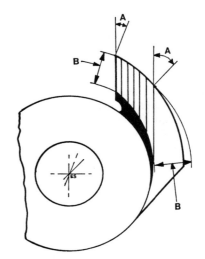

Fig. 141 Above: Wrong method of grinding in parallel steps - this practice increases both cutting angle A and mould depth B.

Below: Correct method of grinding keeps a constant cutting angle A and mould depth B.

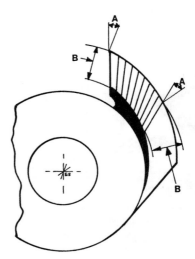

Correcting inaccuracies

If the dividing head is not correct, grind the cutter using a dial indicator mounted on the grinder or, less conveniently, one mounted on the spindle moulder itself. First mark the cutter and the spindle arbor so that the two can be replaced in exactly the same position. Check each cutting point in turn by rotating the cutter past the dial indicator finger - to first contact the heel. Mark the measured height on each point, then grind the faces until the higher points are reduced by the difference between the these and the lowest point.

74

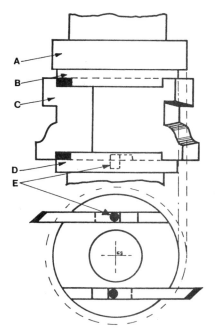

Fig. 142 Q3S slotted collar assembly:
A – ball-bearing follower.
B – top collar.
C – cutter.
D – bottom collar.
E – pins.

To set the cutter, simply move it forward until against the pin – then secure.

Fig. 143 Make a master template for each collar diameter:
H is the distance from the back of the pin to the cutting circle A.
Measurements are:
B – 20mm.
C – 5mm.
D – 15mm.

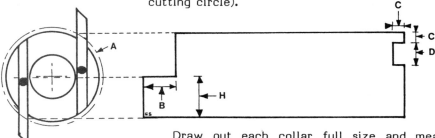

The slot aligns with the cutter edge, allowing the template profile to project beyond.

Q3S SYSTEM

This is a keyed, quick-set tooling system designed by the writer for slotted collars and circular heads. The cutterheads have pins fitted to engage in slots in the sides of the cutters. Slotted collars have pins in the bottom slot and circular heads have pins each side of the cutter clamps. Cutters are set so that the slots engage with their pins. This locks them in place to set the cutters quickly, accurately and automatically. Cutter creep is impossible and cutters cannot fly out of the cutterblock.

The same basic attachment and technique are used for both heads. It fits on Autool profile grinders and incorporates an independent dummy block, notch template and separate notch stylus.

SLOTTED COLLARS

Profile-grind both cutters generally as described earlier but using the dummy block section of the attachment. This is fixed at the same diameter and cutter spacing as slotted collars and has a fixed side guide and adjustable rear fence. Cutters are ground individually whilst clamped in place against these so that they finish dimensionally alike.

When a new profile is formed for the first time the opposite end of the template is made as a gauge to set the machine for notch grinding. First make a master gauge for each size of slotted collars to the precise pin-to-planing-circle distance. The planing circle is a maximum of 3mm. beyond the collars when shaping using a ring fence, and corresponds with the follower diameter when shaping using a ball-bearing collar. When straight moulding the planing circle is the collar diameter plus clearance of 3mm., plus double the through-fence thickness. This allows the cutters to cut through the fence without the collars fouling. (It is possible to cut-out the fence for the collars to give less cutter projection. This is more trouble, but gives a smaller and safer cutting circle).

Draw out each collar full size and measure along the cutter face from the planing circle to the back of the pin (H). Notch out the master template by 20mm. deep to leave this width out from the back edge. For new templates use the master template to mark distance H, then add the mould depth of the profiled cutter, and cut out to form the notch setting gauge.

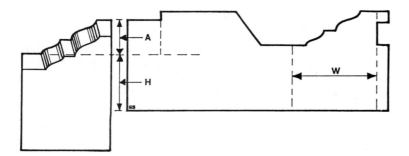

Fig. 144 The cutter width is shown as W.
Add the mould cutter depth A to H to give the correct gauge width.

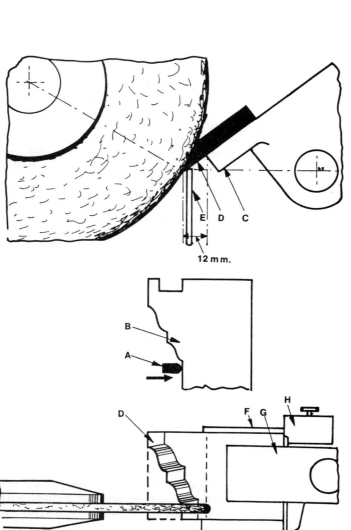

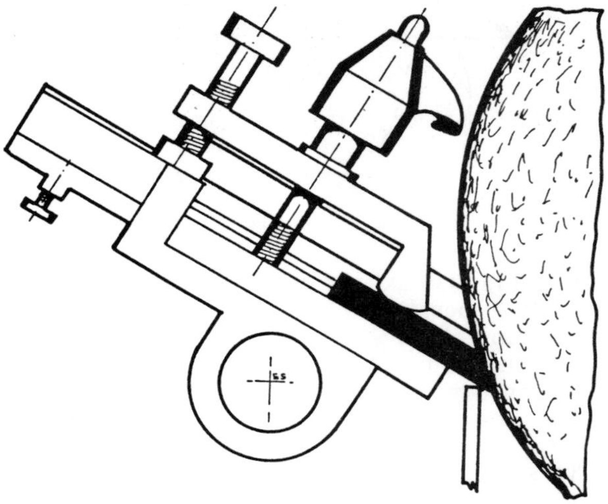

Fig. 145 Section through the Q3S dummy block showing the cutter clamped in position and resting on the cutter support. The dummy block caters for all collars between 65 and 300mm diameter.

Fig. 146 When setting shaped cutters, adjust stylus A when against the planing section of the template B to give a 12mm gap between dummy block C and cutter support E. Cutter D should rest on the cutter support.
The grinding wheel contacts the planing section of the cutter when ground.
The cutter is set against side guide F, back against rear fence H and is held by clamp G.

Plate 42 Grinding Q3S cutters loose
on an Autool PR230.

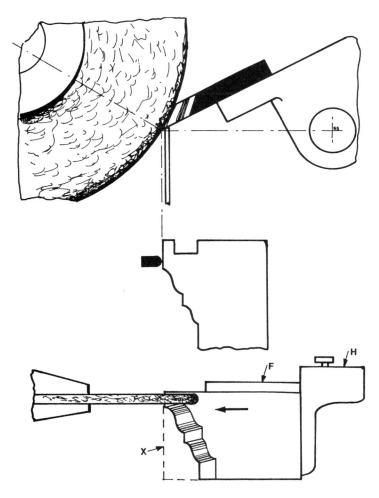

Fig. 147 When grinding from a blank
move the carriage so the stylus
contacts the furthest point of the
template profile, then move the
blank cutter forward to contact the
dressed grinding wheel. Clamp the
cutter in this position against side
guide F, and fit rear fence H against
its tail. X shows the outline of a
blank cutter.

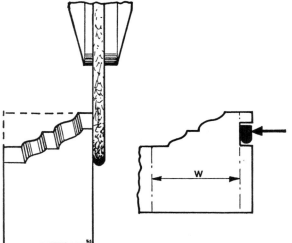

Fig. 148 For sideways alignment butt
the cutter against the vertical
grinding wheel, and adjust the stylus
until against the slot end (this
corresponds to the cutter edge).
W is the cutter width.

To use the gauge, fit the setting pin in the attachment and place the template end-against the angled guide with the gauge cut-out against the pin. Move the fence tight against the back edge of the template and lock in position, then remove template and pin. Clamp each cutter in turn side-against the angled guide and cutting-edge against the fence. To grind the notch, rotate the attachment on it's arbor so that the cutter rides on the regular cutter support.

To grind, move the carriage so that the notch stylus engages in and follows the slot in the notch template. The notch is then formed automatically in the edge of the cutter at the correct pre-set distance from the cutting edge.

Plate 43 Above, and Fig. 149, left: Fit setting pin A and trap the gauge section of template B between this and fence C. Side guides are at D.

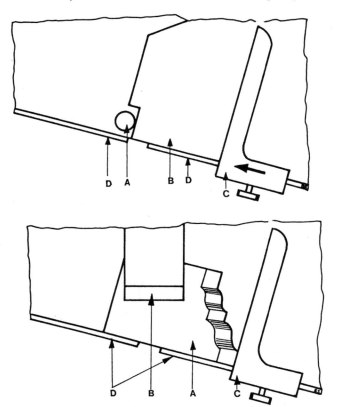

Plate 44 Below, and Fig. 150, left: Remove the pin and template, then butt the cutting edge of profile cutter A against fence C and secure by clamp B.

Cutters are then ready for use. Set them in their slot so the notch contacts the pin, and secure. This precisely aligns the planing line of both cutters with the follower, or sets for normal cutting projection beyond the collar.

When cutters are re-ground they are also re-notched, each time locating the newly-ground cutting edge against the fence pre-set by the gauge. In this way the distance between cutting edge and notch remains fixed throughout the life of the cutter, giving automatic compensation for grinding loss. When setting cutters they repeat precisely their original projection, so cutter alignment remains absolute regardless of cutter wear.

Plate 45 Above, and Fig. 151,
Flip-over the table so notch
template D contacts fixed notch
stylus E. Notch cutter A whilst
resting on the regular cutter
support. The notch template adjusts
for depth after releasing screw F.

The cutters used are regular collar cutters with plain,
squared-edge or bevelled sides. Slots are ground-in on the
grinder. The slot grows longer as cutters are worn down. When
only 3mm. remains behind the slot the cutters are discarded,
so it is impossible to use them when dangerously short. (In
some cases a bigger distance should remain; see safety notes
for slotted collars).

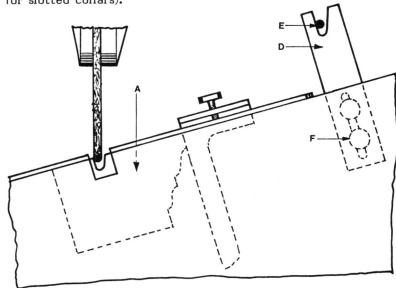

CIRCULAR CUTTERHEAD

These have the same basic concept as Q3S slotted collars but
each cutter has two opposing notches and each clamp has two
pins formed on it. The regular cutterhead has four cutter slots
and normally has a constant planing circle when used as
described for slotted collars.

Q3S circular heads have a different cutting angle to
slotted collar cutters, so pre-set the back fence to the setting
pin and fit the cutters tail-against this. Set and use the
grinder as for slotted collar cutters. To fit cutters remove the
clamps and the wedges, locate clamp pins in the cutter
notches and insert in the cutter slot. Add wedges and secure.
Springs push the cutters out so the notches always contact the
clamp pins.

The basic technique is to grind cutters to a constant
planing circle, but this is not absolutely necessary. The
regular cutter length allows for a 17mm. deep profile. With
shallower profiles, cutters can be left their original length to
initially have greater projection and a longer overall life. The
notches are re-ground only when the cutters wear down to
normal projection - and then retain the regular planing circle.
The template is not used to initially notch the cutter. Instead,
fit the setting pin to locate the tail fence. Place cutters
tail-against this to slot for maximum seating conditions.

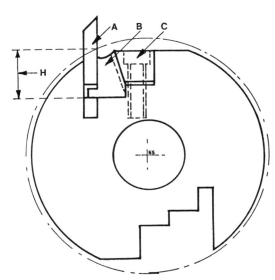

Fig. 152 Above: Section through a
Q3S circular moulding head showing:
A - one cutter.
B - clamp with locating pins.
C - wedge lock.
H - is the minimum pin-to-planing
circle distance.

Plate 46 This SCM spindle
moulder/tenoner combination
features stacked cutterheads to
give rapid programme change-over
from one section to another.

CHAPTER 10

CUTTER GRINDING

Cutters perform best when newly sharpened but, during use, a point is reached when they no longer cut cleanly and the surface produced is not acceptable. Dull cutters take more power, sound noisier, resist the feed more and have a greater tendency to kick back.

Steel-based cutters tend to wear more or less evenly to a rounded point, but sintered cutters begin to break-down rapidly when initial sharpness is lost, so sharpen them before this point is reached.

Grinding to restore sharpness leaves a scratch pattern on the surface. When the ground surface is rough a jagged cutting edge is formed which can break down quickly. To give the best edge and the longest cutter life use a fine grinding wheel with coolant and a relatively slow grinding movement. Finally hone to make the surface as smooth as practicable and to completely remove the burr which grinding forms.

It is important to know when the cutting edge is restored to sharpness because further grinding wastes time and money without improving cutter performance. With HSS and similar cutters a fine grinding burr is formed, so stop when this point is reached. With sintered materials no burr is formed so frequently examine the edge under a good light using a magnifying glass and grind only until the wear pattern is completely removed.

Plate 47 Grinding planing cutters in the head on a Saturn universal grinder.

GRINDING WHEELS

Grinding wheels consist of fine abrasive grains bonded together in a matrix. The grains have naturally sharp edges which cut fine, thin slivers from the tool in grinding. The matrix holds the grains in position whilst they remain sharp, but releases them to expose fresh grains when they loose sharpness. Grain loss or 'shed' results from the extra pressure and heat generated when the grains no longer cut effectively.

Few types of abrasives are used in grinding wheels for woodworking tools. The main type is bauxite (aluminium oxide) which can be natural or manufactured. Natural abrasives vary considerably in performance and have largely been replaced by manufactured abrasives which can be closely controlled for quality and crystal size. Most abrasives are now made by refining and fusing either bauxite ore (clay), or residue from smelting aluminium. Electric furnaces are used for this, and afterwards the end product is crushed, seived and graded to the various grain sizes.

The least pure form, commercially used, is made from the clay and varies in colour from a light or dark grey to brown or blue, according to the origin of the clay and the processing temperature. This type is used for manufacturing general-purpose grinding wheels.

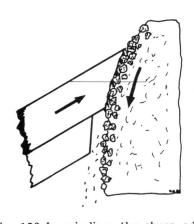

Fig. 153 In grinding, the sharp edges of the abrasive protrudes from the surface of the wheel to pare or abrade-away the metal as thin slivers rather like very fine wire wool.

The purest form, made from the residue of aluminium smelting, is almost white and is known as white bauxilite. This generally is the best type for HSS cutters as it grinds exceptionally fast with minimal heat generation. Chromium oxide is added to white bauxilite by some makers, which makes the grinding wheel pink and the grains slightly tougher and less likely to crumble under pressure. This type also has some application in woodworking, but it is used mainly for tool steels of higher alloy.

The other abrasive in regular use is silicon carbide. It is harder and more brittle than bauxite and varies in colour from black to dark and light green. The different coloured abrasives have similar physical properties, although the light green is the purest form. Light green (or green grit) wheels are used in woodworking for rough grinding tungsten carbide. Silicon carbide is also used in a mixture with bauxite to produce grinding wheels for special applications.

The way a grinding wheel performs is due to the grain material, grain size of the abrasive particles, the type and amount of bond used and the closeness of the abrasives. With many combinations used, widely differing performances are possible.

Specifications

The specification of each grinding wheel is printed on its compressive washer (or blotter) usually in six groups of letter and number combinations, but not all makers conform.

ONE: This is the abrasive size. Identification letters vary, but 'A' usually indicates aluminium oxide, and 'C' silicon carbide. Numbers indicate either a specifix mix of abrasive, or a mixture of more than one type.

Fig. 154 Fine (small) grains give a good finish but grind slowly.

TWO: Abrasive grain size, ranging from 8 (large) to 1200 (very small). Grinding is basically an abrading operation with small particles close together each cutting a narrow track across the part being ground. When grains are large (low numbers) heavy cuts are possible so grinding is fast but the surface finish is poor. When grains are small (high numbers) the surface finish is good but grinding is a slow process.

THREE: Grade or bond strength, ranging usually from E - soft to Z - hard. This is governed by the proportion of bond to abrasive and determines the grip the bond has on the grains. When the bond has a strong grip the grains are retained longer and the wheel is termed as hard. Hard grinding wheels wear slowly but tend to glaze and fill-in readily so needing frequent dressing. A soft wheel has a weaker bond and loses grains more quickly to expose fresh grains beneath. These grinding wheels wear relatively quickly but perform well and consistantly. The bond is stated as a letter, or as soft, medium or hard. Hard cutters need a soft wheel, and soft cutters need a hard wheel.

Fig. 155 Coarse (large) grains grind fast but give a poor finish.

Fig. 156 Close-structured vitrified wheels give more support when grinding thin edges.

Fig. 157 Open-structured vitrified wheels have numerous voids and grind cool on large areas.

Fig. 158 Grinding wheel types:
A - plain.
B - cup.
C & D - saucer or dish.

Arrows show the grinding surfaces.

FOUR: Structure, ranging from 1 - close to 15 - open. This indicates how closely the grains are packed. A close-grade wheel gives a steadier and more controlled grind. An open-structured wheel is freer-cutting and less easy to control.

FIVE: Bond type. Four bond types are used in woodworking - vitrified, resinoid, shellac and rubber.

Vitrified wheels are by far the most predominant type in woodworking. They have a porous structure with the grains held together by bridges of glass or similar vitreous material giving a rigid grinding wheel suitable for most operations, and they are used either wet or dry.

Resinoid wheels have a bond usually of phenol formaldehyde, sometimes with fillers to form a more flexible grinding wheel which gives a better finish on flat grinding. Often this type of grinding wheel is used dry as the heat of grinding is the means of breaking-down the bond.

Resinoid, shellac and rubber-bond, sometimes with reinforcements, are used for cut-off applications when parting cutters or relief-cutting.

Types

Plain or peripheral grinding wheels are flat and from 3-36mm wide by up to 300mm in diameter. They mount on an arbor between flanges and are intended for grinding only on their periphery. Often the periphery is formed to a half-round or square section when used for grinding flat cutters to a profile. Never grind on the side of a plain wheel as this thins and weakens it, also the grinding wheel lacks the necessary support for side grinding and could shatter under side pressure.

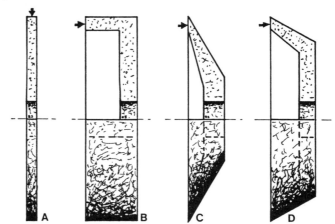

Cup and dish wheels are shaped, as their names suggest, with parallel sides in cup form and with angled, tapering sides in dish form. They mount to overhang the arbor with the securing nut or ring below the abrasive level. They are for flat grinding only on their radial faces.

Cup wheels are used when grinding planing cutters either flat or with a slightly hollow grind. Dish wheels are used for face-grinding profiled-cutters, router cutter flutes, etc., and are tapered back for the necessary clearance.

SAFE USE OF GRINDING WHEELS

There are many safety regulations for grinding wheels. Make sure that these are understood and observed, and that only qualified operators are allowed change the grinding wheels.

Storage

All grinding wheels are brittle and can easily be damaged through mis-use. Take care to handle and store them carefully. Grinding wheels should be stored in medium temperatures away from strong sunlight and high humidity, and where they are unlikely to be damaged.

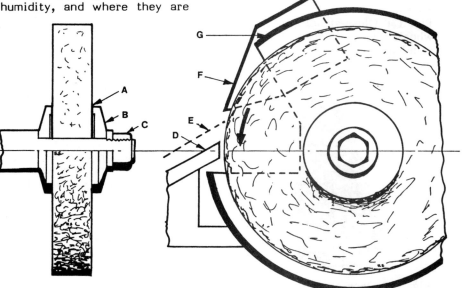

Some grinding wheels deteriorate with age, so do not store them for long periods. Keep only a small stock and replenish this regularly. Handle grinding wheels from storage with care. When moving them around support and protect them from damage. Never use a wheel that has been dropped and never roll wheels along the floor.

Fitting

Before fitting a grinding wheel carefully check it to make sure there are no visible cracks. With vitrified wheel types tap the wheel sharply with a piece of wood (never metal). A crack-free grinding wheel will 'ring' quite clearly.

Fig. 159 A plain grinding wheel for rim grinding showing:
A – compression washers fitted both sides of the wheel.
B – relieved flange.
C – securing nut.
D – cutter rest.
E – cutter shown in dotted outline.
F – nosing which should be set close to the wheel to reduce sparking and to complete the enclosure of the wheel.
G – grinding wheel guard.

Wear eye protectors when grinding, also others in the vicinity.

Plate 48 Grinding the flute of a router cutter on a Saturn universal grinder, using a dividing head for location.

A cracked wheel does not ring and actually sounds cracked. Never fit a cracked or suspect grinding wheel. Resinoid and rubber wheels do not 'ring', so only visual inspection is possible.

Each grinding wheel should have the maximum running speed printed on the blotter. Check that this exceeds the speed of the arbor on which it is to be used, and never use a grinding wheel which is marked with a lower maximum speed.

Before mounting the grinding wheel clean all parts. Check that the mounting flanges are true, also damage and warp-free. They should be equal in diameter and bearing surfaces, and their diameter should be at least one third that of the grinding wheel. Flanges should be recessed to contact only with their rim and the inner flange should be fixed to the arbor.

Ensure that the grinding wheel is a good push-on fit to the arbor. Never force a grinding wheel onto its arbor and do not use a grinding wheel that is a sloppy fit.

Always fit compressive carboard rings (blotters) on both sides of the grinding wheel to cover the entire contact area These cushion the clamping action, give a better grip and lessen the chance of the wheel cracking on tightening. Tighten up the securing nut evenly and progressively, but not excessively.

Before switching-on the grinding wheel replace the guards. Check that all parts are secure and that the grinding wheel is free to rotate. Make sure that anyone around is wearing goggles or a suitable visor, and that no one is standing in line with the grinding wheel - just in case. Allow a newly-fitted grinding wheel to run free for one minute before attempting to use it.

It is possible that the grinding wheel is out-of-balance when initially started up. This is not acceptable and must be corrected before using it. Sometimes dressing will reduce the out-of-balance effect or, failing this, improvement can sometimes be made by turning the grinding wheel on its arbor and again dressing. If the imbalance still persists the grinding wheel should be returned to the maker.

Speed

All grinding wheels are intended to run at a stated maximum speed relating to the peripheral speed when new, a factor determined by the makers. It is this speed, which is usually printed on the blotter, that should not be exceded.

With plain grinding wheels the peripheral speed reduces as they wear down in use and they then grind as a softer wheel. To avoid this raise the running speed when worn, but always keep below the maximum recommended speed. The effective hardness of a grinding wheel can be changed by altering the running speed; running faster makes it harder, running slower makes it softer.

Peripheral speeds of vitrified-bonded grinding wheels are normally between 25 and 30M/sec., but resinoid-bonded grinding wheels can operate at speeds in excess of 33M/sec.

Plate 49 Profile grinders, such as this Autool PR230H, grind on the rim of thin, plain grinding wheels.

Truing and dressing

Truing is the operation of making a grinding wheel run true (concentric with its arbor) or restoring its profile to the shape required by mechanically removing uneven abrasive. Dressing restores the cutting action of the grinding wheel by dressing-out metal deposits filling-in the pores, and by eroding away high bonding to expose the sharp grains. Theoretically, no sharp grains are dislodged in dressing, but a few usually are. The two processes are often combined as part of the same operation. Normally a rotary mechanical dresser is used, or a single diamond.

The rotary dresser is a either series of star-shaped, corrugated or twisted discs alternating with plain discs on a ball-bearing spindle at the end of a handle. This dresser is used dry and is manually held to lightly traverse across the grinding wheel whilst resting firmly on the cutter support. Star-shaped cutters leave the wheel open and fast-cutting, other types leave a smoother surface which is slower-cutting but gives a better finish.

The diamond type is usually a single diamond. This can be used in the same way, by hand, but preferably it should be machine traversed. Traverse slowly, with a only small feed and repeat several times to give the finest surface to the grinding wheel and the best finish to the ground face. A single-point diamond is commonly fitted to profile-grinding machines. Preferably use coolant when dressing with a diamond.

Grinding fluid

Grinding wheels intended for wet grinding should be used with suitable grinding fluid, normally an oil and water mix. This cools the cutter and assists the grinding action by lubricating the cutting points of the abrasive. It also flushes away the grinding chips and helps to prevent wheel loading. Preferably the jet of fluid should be directed at the work rather than the grinding wheel. The fluid is more effective by doing this and there is less spray from the grinding wheel. The supply should be ample and continuous, an inconsistant supply is more harmful than none.

Vitrified wheels are porous and absorb a great deal of coolant which gravitates to the lower half of the wheel when stopped. The grinding wheel then is unbalanced and vibrates on starting. To avoid this start the grinding wheel before switching the coolant on, and switch-off coolant well before stopping the grinding wheel.

The grinding fluid improves the surface finish, allows a faster, burn-free grind and makes grinding wheels last longer. Choose the coolant carefully as it can also cause problems - so get expert advice from the coolant manufacturers.

Defects

Glazing occurs with a grinding wheel which is too hard. The grains are retained long after they loose sharpness and take on a glazed appearance. A glazed wheel does not grind effectively because the particles are rounded-over to rub and burn the ground surface.

Loading occurs when material which has been abraded away from the cutter lodges and fills the pores of the grinding wheel instead of being thrown clear. This physically prevents the grains cutting: an effect similar to glazing but with a different cause. Loading can be reduced by using a wax-added grinding wheel when dry grinding, or by using a grinding fluid. (Some grinding fluids are more effective than others, check with your supplier.)

A grinding wheel which is glazed and/or loaded can be made good simply by dressing, but this does not cure the problem if the grinding wheel application or coolant is wrong. One possible solution for both is to is to use a softer-bonded grinding wheel.

SUPERABRASIVES

Two extremely hard abrasives are now being widely used: natural or synthetic diamonds for grinding tungsten carbide, and CBN (cubic boron nitride) for grinding HSS and similar tool steels. The latter is sold as Borazon by The General Electric Company (U.S.A.), and as ABN (Amber Boron Nitride) by De Beers Co., of Johannesburg, S.A.

Superabrasive wheels are available in a wide range of sizes, sections and profiles. The least costly wheels have only a single layer of diamond or CBN crystals electrostatically-plated on a formed wheel. Both abrasives can also be formed in thicker layers with a metal, vitrified or resinoid bond, but mostly the latter for woodworking. They have only a relatively thin layer of diamond or CBN bonded to a metal or phenolic-resin body.

It is possible to vary grit size and bond strength, and both effect the grinding action as with grit wheels. An added factor is the concentration, the ratio of crystals-to-bond. The balanced concentration is 100, but this ranges from 50 to 150.

Diamond and CBN wheels interchange with regular grit wheels on suitable grinders. CBN wears much slower than grit wheels and, whilst costing more, can show an overal saving when grinding HSS and tool steels, and give a higher quality and more consistant finish.

Mounting

Superabrasive wheels for woodworking are pre-shaped and trued by the maker, not on the machine, so it is necessary to mount them with considerably more care than regular grinding wheels.

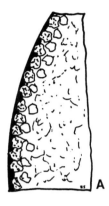
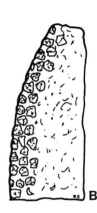

Fig. 160 A - loaded grinding wheel filled-in with grinding debris. B - glazed wheel with grains rounded-over but not dislodged. C - dressed wheel with fresh grains exposed after removing dulled grains, debris and high bond.

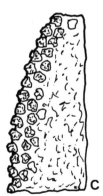

Take care that all mating surfaces are clean and true before mounting, and do not use blotters. After mounting, check and correct each wheel for roundness and truth using a dial indicator against the register groove (if provided). Preferably these wheels should have individual arbors for morse-taper mounting to maintain accuracy.

If the wheel runs out radially when mounted on a plain arbor, this can sometimes be corrected by turning it independent of the arbor to a different position. When the best position has been determined mark both arbor and wheel at the top as fitted. When re-mounting re-align these marks to give better repetition.

Dress all wheels regularly using an abrasive stick, commonly a fine-grit medium-bond aluminium oxide type, by pressing this lightly onto the running abrasive. With dressing the colour of the wheel surface changes. Rapidly increasing dressing-stick wear shows that dressing is complete. Dressing erodes away high bond left by fragmenting crystals and any grinding debris.

Superabrasives are manufactured for either dry or wet grinding and should be used accordingly - or efficiency suffers. Grinding fluid is usually a soluable oil and water mix, although a neat oil can be used.

Pure diamond is for grinding tungsten carbide only, so separately grind tungsten carbide tips by using different wheels with angles for body and tip which differ by about 5 degrees. Some modern grinding wheels will grind both tip and body of cutters simultaneously. These can be used with a single bevel.

CBN wheels are best for highly-alloyed tool steels, HSS and similar. Do not use them on tungsten carbide and avoid low-alloy steels.

Properly used, superabrasives produce good finishes efficiently and economically. Badly used, they can prove a very expensive mistake. They will not upgrade an old and worn grinding machine to produce better work; the grinding machine should be new, in the best condition and with bearings and arbors which are accurate and true. The machine must also be heavy, rigid and vibration-free, coolant systems ample and dependable and the grinding machine-controlled.

HONING

Natural hones are the Washita which is a coarse and fast-cutting type used for initial sharpening, and the Arkansas, a harder and denser type more suitable for fine finishing. Artificial hones have a grit either of aluminium oxide or silicon carbide. The bond is normally vitrified and hones are available in different grits similar to those in grinding wheels.

Silicon carbide, usually a light green in colour, cuts faster than aluminium oxide and grain sharpness is retained longer. It gives fast results but is less than ideal for finishing. Aluminium oxide is best for finishing as the grit more readily levels-off and evens-out when lightly honing. Colour varies from brown to blue-grey.

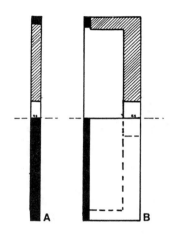

Fig. 161 Typical diamond and CBN grinding wheels.
A - plain.
B - cup.
C & D - saucer or dish.

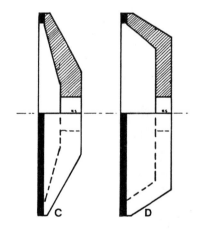

88

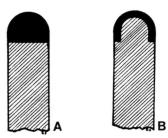

Fig. 162 Shaped superabrasive wheels can have a solid tip on a square body A or a shaped body B. Electrostatically deposited wheels C have only a thin layer of metal-bonded crystals. They cost less but have a short life.

The normal practice is to use coarse or medium-grit for initial work, then finish-off with a fine grit. Flat hones are used for straight cutters and external curves, and shaped hones for internal shapes.

Hones should be used with a light oil or oil and paraffin-oil mix to give a fine finish and save wear on the hone. Use a circular movement where possible as this evens-out flaws and is quicker. When finishing-off, if possible move more along than across the cutting edge to remove any peak and valley effect.

Hones wear hollow and occasionally need dressing level using a grinding wheel. They also may glaze or load. Soaking in paraffin oil or cleaning with petrol and a wire brush helps to clear loaded hones, but glazed hones need dressing.

Completely remove the grinding burr on newly-ground cutters using a hone, or the burr breaks-off in use to leave a jagged edge. Dull cutters can be honed, often without removing them from the machine. In sharpening hold the hone flat on the ground face of the cutter until a honing burr is formed, then alternate between front and ground faces to remove this burr. Honing is quicker on very dull cutters by holding the hone at an angle to the ground face rather than flat, but take care not to round the edge over or the cutter will rub on the heel.

TOOL STEELS

Most tools used in woodworking are made from, or contain, alloys of steel, and are hardened and tempered to give a hard, tough cutting edge. The most commonly-used type is HSS (high-speed steel). One of the most important alloys is tungsten, the content of which varies from 3 to 22 percent. In general, cutters with high tungsten content last slightly longer on harder timbers.

Another steel used is HCHC - high carbon, high chrome, a lower-cost steel which gives reasonable results on softer timbers. Some cutters are now made from a very low-alloy steel which is carburised and heat-treated. This gives a very hard but shallow skin which compares favourable with through-hardened steels on softer timbers. Carburised cutters are particularly susceptable to hardness loss even with modest grinding temperatures and must be ground wet and with care.

NON-STEEL TOOLS

Three non-steel cutting materials are used in woodworking tooling: Tantung, Stellite, tungsten carbide and PCD (poly-crystalline diamond).

Stellite is a cobalt-based metal which is most commonly-used in rod form for weld-depositing, either in making a new tool or in building-up a worn one. The cutting edge outlasts HSS by a factor of about 10 when cutting slightly abrasive materials. Tantung is a similar solid cobalt-based metal brazed onto softer-backed cutters. These metals can be ground with regular grit or CBN grinding wheels.

Tungsten carbide is a sintered metal brazed or mechanically clamped to a cutter or solid head. The cutting edge outlasts HSS by a factor of about 100 on highly abrasive materials and is essential for such as chipboard edging and plastic trimming.

Tungsten carbide cutters need special treatment. Small bevel angles must be avoided, make them not less than 45 degrees and grind slowly and without excessive pressure. Tungsten carbide is susceptible to cracking, so make sure the coolant is ample and dependable if used. Re-sharpen tools before becoming dull, otherwise the edge rapidly breaks-down and needs excessive re-sharpening.

A perfectly sharp edge is needed to clean-cut softwoods and give long life. Sharpening takes much longer than for conventional tools and is often wrongly skimped by some users in the name of expediency.

Tungsten carbide is ideal for factory-produced throw-away cutters for use on planing, edging and certain moulding heads, router cutters and drill bits.

Polycrystalline diamond comprises of a polycrystalline aggregate of artificial diamonds of about 0.5mm thick bonded together and to a tungsten carbide substrate from 1.5 - 3mm thick. This is then clamped to a steel body or brazed on at low temperature. The highly specialised material is made under the name Compax by The General Electric Company (U.S.A.) and under the name Syndite by De Beers Co.(S.A.).

This tooling is as yet in its infancy, but already has proved greatly superior to tungsten carbide. Because of its high cost and limited shapes and sizes, applications so far have only been with difficult materials in mass-production lines.

Small cutters for circular heads and slotted collars are made from solid tool steel or a composite with a thin (2-3mm) brazed-on facing of tool steel on a softer steel back. Router cutters are solid HSS, tungsten carbide or a composite. Profiled cutterheads can be solid steel, usually some form of cobalt-chrome, or with a softer body and HSS, tungsten carbide, Tantung or Stellite facing. The HSS types are much less costly to produce than solid profiled heads, but have a limited life compared with them.

Plate 51 Above: Wadkin PCD router cutter.

Plate 50 Below left: Solid profile cutters normally are of a cobalt-based steel. This shows a Saturn cutter.

Plate 52 Below right: This Leuco panel-raising cutterhead has carbide disposable cutters fitted.

90

CHAPTER 11

GENERAL MOULDING
Straight moulding

Straight moulding is undertaken by feeding the workpiece on the table and edge or face-against a straight fence. The workpiece is controlled by pressures and guides to keep it running true, and is manually fed by hand or using spikes, push-sticks and follow-up blocks. To make the operation safer a through fence and table rings or bed must be used to close up the cutter gap. A feed unit can be set to press timber down on the table or against the fence.

Plate 53 When edge moulding long, thin pieces use an outrigger support as on this Scheppach spindle moulder.

Fig. 163 Using a feed unit A is safer and better even with short runs.

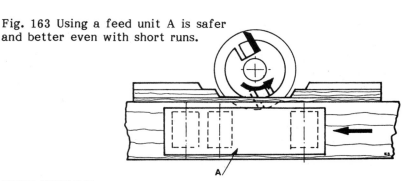

THE FENCE

The fence can be a U type, which can be moved as a unit but with independent adjustment of the two fences, or two separate halves operating in some form of slide or with a keyway to keep them parallel. Most fences allow lever springs or a Shaw guard to be fitted, also a front guard to bridge the fence gap and an exhaust hood.

The fence is first set as a unit to give correct cutter projection for the mould depth wanted, with fence plates adjusted laterally to keep the fence gap small for safety and to give solid support right up to the point of cut. A through-fence should be added, making sure that there is enough clearance between fence plates and cutterhead to allow for the wooden fence to be subsequently broken through safely, also to allow for minor fence adjustments after initial setting.

Fence plates can be steel or wood. The steel type are durable and virtually wear-free but obviously damage the cutterhead if the two come in contact. They usually have counter-sunk holes to screw on wooden through-fences. Hardwood fence plates have some advantages. They need replacing periodically because they wear and are not quite as precise as steel fences, but temporary stops are easily fixed using screws or nails, and because they do not damage the tools it is practicable to cut into them with the cutterhead to close the fence gap.

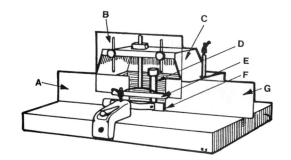

Fig. 164 Typical fence unit:
A - outfeed fence.
B - transparent front guard.
C - rear cover and exhaust hood.
D - spindle arbor.
E - top Shaw guard.
F - side Shaw guard.
G - infeed fence.

Setting aids

Settings for cut depth (beyond the fence face) and height (above table) need to be accurate so that repeated re-settings and test runs are kept to a minimum.

Often a test cut is wrongly (and in the U.K. illegally) made without guards or pressures to save the trouble of later removal for adjustment. Unfortunately, test cuts are often the time when accidents occur which proper guarding would prevent or make less serious. To avoid the problem use precise setting devices.

Plate 54 Micro adjustable controls to a two-part fence on a Wadkin Bursgreen BEL spindle moulder.

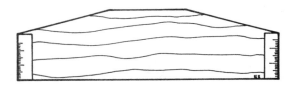

Fig. 165 Hardwood straight edge with inset rules for setting cutter height and depth.
Note end bevels for clearance.

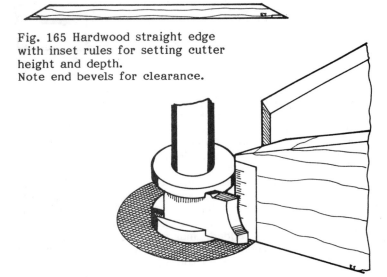
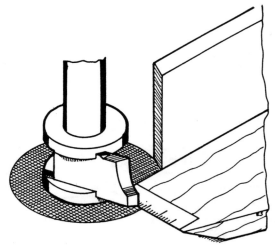

Fig. 166 Left: Checking cut height.
Right: Checking cut depth.

Make a seasoned hardwood straight-edge with vertical short rules inset at both ends on the same face. Sand or plane the ends to leave the rules as pointed edges with a 60 or 45 degree bevel. Use the straight edge vertically edge-on the table to set height, and horizontally against the fence to set depth. Some shapes are difficult to measure like this, for example chamfers, bevels and nosings. Use the method later described under 'breaking through a fence' to aid accurate setting.

THROUGH-FENCES

These are an essential safety feature. They leave a gap-free surface round the projecting cutters to prevent small sections and flexible timber dipping into the fence gap. A softwood through-fence fastens to the normal fence plates or replaces them. (Plywood could be used but it abrades and prematurely dulls cutters. Hardwood fences tend to warp and twist).

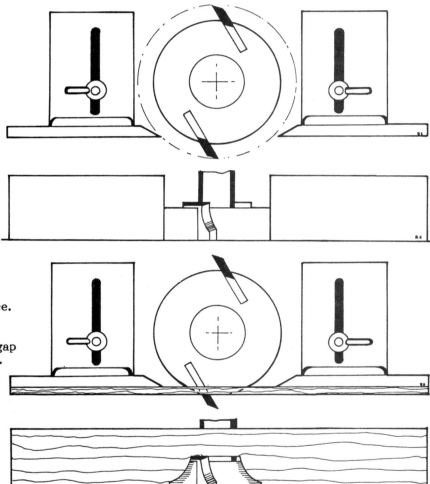

Fig. 167 Above: Fences as the makers supply them, note the wide open gap for cutter clearance.

Below: The same set-up with a through-fence fitted. The cutter gap is closed to the absolute minimum.

Normally the through-fence is the same overall length and depth as the regular fence, but may be longer if using end-stops, or shorter if moulding bent timber. (When feeding large section and rigid parts such as door casings and window frames hollow-side against the fence, long fences prevent face contact at the cutters - so the mould or rebate is formed shallow. With a short fence the cutting depth remains consistant but the part is less stable in feeding).

When replacing regular steel fence plates the through-fence must be thick and stiff enough not too deflect in use. Fasten it either through the fence plate slots by studs screwed into the back, or by countersunk coach bolts, washers and wing-nuts.

When a through-fence is fitted to existing fence plates, these give extra support so a thinner piece can be used and cutter projection beyond the block can be less. Most steel fences have holes to secure wooden fences from the back - using woodscrews. If they haven't, add them. 'G' clamps could be used but may interfere with the feed. When the machine has wooden fence plates the through-fence can be nailed or screwed in position (but don't fix a back-stop to a nailed fence). Perhaps the best combination is to fix 20mm thick wooden fence plates to the steel fence plates, onto which a 10mm false fence can be nailed securely - but quickly and easily removed.

Fig. 168 Different types of false fences.
A – Thick fence fence 'A' replaces the regular fence.
B – Thin false fence 'B' screwed to the fence plates 'C'.
C – Thin false fence 'A' nailed to wooden fence plates 'D'.
D – Front view of sketch C showing nail positions at 'E'.

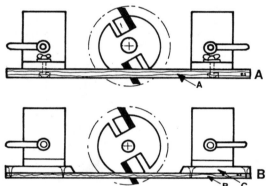

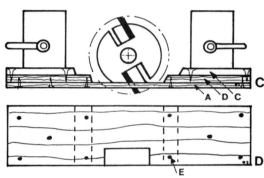

Plate 55 A through fence fitted on a Delta light duty spindle moulder. Guards other than that fitted to the arbor have been removed for clarity.

To use a through-fence properly the cutterhead should break through it when running. An irony is that the through-fence is much safer to use than a two-piece fence, but breaking through can itself be hazardous.

When breaking through follow a strict sequence in addition to taking all normal precautions. First pre-cut the gap using a bandsaw so that less needs cutting out with the head itself. Keep a stock of through-fences with different-size cut-outs already in them. Initially make the fences deeper than really necessary so the under edge can be planed off to remove an oversize cut-out for further use.

Check that the cutter is suitable for cutting through the fence by grinding a clearance bevel on the top edge, and by forming the mould shape close to the top edge of the cutter so that the least amount of fence is cut out. Bevel both edges when intended for over-cutting, as with grooves and similar, keeping the projecting cutter as narrow as practical - but within safe operating limits, of course.

Plate 56 Wooden fence plates fitted to a Delta two-speed heavy-duty spindle moulder.

PRE-SETTING

The through-fence should be temporarily attached to, or replace, the original fence plates; a gap should be left below to allow cutters to be rotated. Where practical fit cutters to project above the block to clear-cut through the fence and possibly sink into the mould. Set the head to the proper height and cut depth beyond the outer face of the through-fence using the straight-edge. Check that cutters and cutterblock amply clear all parts both when in the starting position of the fence before break through, and when in the operating position.

Whitehill type cutterheads allow cutters to project above the top face and below the under face to give ample cutterblock clearance on both sides. With heads that are not sunk check that the through-fence misses the cutterhead. If intending to chipbreak with the through-fence check that the subsequent adjustment needed for edge renewal is allowed for by leaving clearance between cutterhead and infeed fence plate, or between the through-fence securing bolts and the slot end.

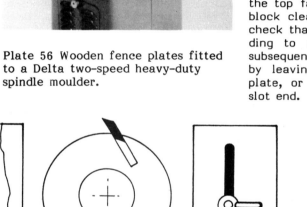

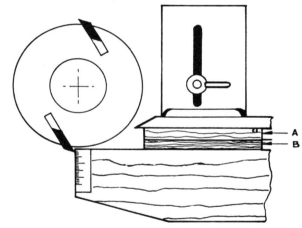

Fig. 169 Checking cutter depth before the through-fence is fitted. Sandwich the through-fence or a piece of equal thickness between the regular fence and the straight-edge as at A.

Fig. 170 Sometimes the cutterblock prevents depth measurement as shown, so sandwich a piece of hardwood of specific thickness B in addition to the through-fence A. Add thickness B to the depth measured.

BREAKING THROUGH

Most users break through by moving the fence back into the rotating cutterhead. With an undercut it may be more practical and safer to break through by raising the cutterhead under power whilst the fence remains fixed in place. Mark or note the correct vertical setting of the spindle or set a stop to give absolute repetition, then lower the spindle to clear. Finally fix the through-fence.

With the spindle running and the vertical movement lock slackened, raise the spindle slowly to cut upwards into the fence until the previous setting is reached. As a check, mark the highest point of the mould on the fence with a pencilled line parallel to the table. Note the deepening cut on breaking through and stop when at the proper height.

Raising the spindle is a safe way of breaking through on the right machine. Not all machines are suitable, only those where vertical adjustment is via an easily accessible hand-wheel, and where the machine runs steadily and vibration-free with the rise and fall lock released. The drive must also allow vertical spindle movement when running, not all do.

Moving the fence

Breaking-through a fence live must only be attempted by experienced spindle hands. Vibration is created to give an entirely different feel to normal movement and which can be dangerous. New users should first roughly shape the cut-out, then chip away the wood fence by rotating the cutterhead manually whilst easing back the fence. This is a tedious, but a safer, operation.

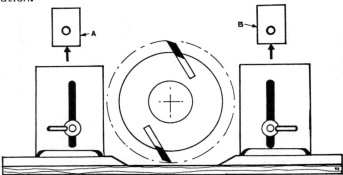

Fig. 171 After setting for cut depth fix back stops A and B against the rear of the fence to limit movement back. The fence is shown drawn clear of the cutters before breaking through.

For the experienced the method of breaking through using a live spindle is as follows:-

After setting the fence in the correct running position clamp secure back-stops to the table against the rear of the fence or the two fence halves to prevent over-run on breaking through. Move the fence clear of the rotating cutters before fixing the through-fence and rear guards in place.

Make the usual safety checks, then start up the cutterhead and slowly move the fence back into the cutters, allowing these to cut their way through until they project the amount required. Then stop the cutterhead and secure the fence. Before starting the run, rotate the cutterhead manually to make sure it still clears. If not, chip it away.

Note that if cutters run in contact with the false fence they run noisily and dull quickly. Preferably break through the fence to a depth marginally beyond that actually required, then draw the fence forward to the proper depth - at which it should also clear the fence. (This does not apply when using the fence as a chipbreaker as close fitting is essential).

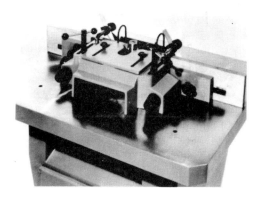

Plate 57 Rear view of this Delta RS–15 spindle moulder shows the fine adjustments and ample dust chute giving good protection from the rear.

The way in which a fence adjusts determines how safe or otherwise breaking through actually is. The worst type of fence to adjust is the one-piece fence that simply locks down but has no fine adjustment as a unit. With these, the locks need partial tightening only, to allow manual movement without excessive pressure, but provide enough friction between fence and table for the fence to remain in position when pressure is released.

Some operators lock one side as a swivel point and move back the opposite end, then reverse the movement, and so on, moving back in alternate steps. This is safer than with both locks partially released and gives surer control. In either case a back stop is absolutely essential, of course. (If the machine is fitted with this type of fence it is safer and better to raise the spindle to break through a fence already fixed in place, rather than attempt to shift the fence). With one-piece fences allow more clearance of the steel fence plates as the unit may swivel in being moved and come closer to the cutterhead than had been anticipated.

Whenever locking or releasing the fence always retain grip with one hand, and keep hold until the fence is completely locked down. This also applies when the fence is in position and the spindle is being stopped - keep one hand holding firmly onto the fence. By doing this, both hands are kept out of danger.

Some fences have screw adjustment. With single-screw adjustment the whole fence moves together, so breaking through is simple and safe. When the two halves move independently, both handwheels should be moved equally to keep the two plates precisely in line. This is not quite as easy, but break-through is a controlled operation.

Moving the table

On some machines the table adjusts on slides or swivels on a pivot. Moving the table is the safest means of fence break through and, where provided, should be used in preference to shifting the fence.

First set the fence for correct cutter projection and set the table movement back-stop to repeat this position precisely. Move the table so that the cutterblock clears, then fasten the through-fence in place. Start-up the head and break through in a controlled manner by moving the table and fence as a unit under mechanical control.

GAUGING HEIGHT AND DEPTH

The correct moulding cut height from the table, and depth from the fence, can both be accurately gauged by noting the expanding fence cut-out as this is moved back into the rotating cutters.

The height is precisely the same as the cut height on the timber and can be shown as a horizontal line on the fence face parallel to the table. When moving the fence back on a mould having a level top section, such as a rebate, start with the cutter marginally low, then raise it to the proper height when a cut is clearly visible. This is not practical with a bevelled top edge because the cut deepens as the fence is moved back, so carefully set height before breaking through.

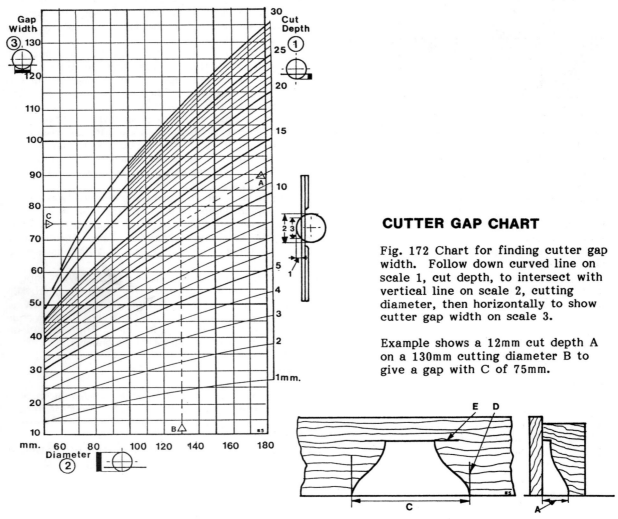

CUTTER GAP CHART

Fig. 172 Chart for finding cutter gap width. Follow down curved line on scale 1, cut depth, to intersect with vertical line on scale 2, cutting diameter, then horizontally to show cutter gap width on scale 3.

Example shows a 12mm cut depth A on a 130mm cutting diameter B to give a gap with C of 75mm.

Fig. 173 Above: Cutting depth A gives a specific width C according to cutting diameter, see chart for details. Mark the fence for cutting height E and width D and constantly check the widening cut-out against these when breaking through.

The width of the fence cut-out gives a very accurate measure of cut depth, being the cord of the cutting circle at this point. Carefully measure the cutting diameter at the furthest points of cut (in the case of a bevel, level with the table when at correct height setting) and note the cord from the chart for the cut depth needed. Using bold vertical lines mark this precise width on the fence face equally each side of the spindle.

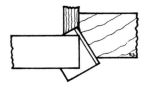

Keep moving the fence back until the cut-out equals the spacing of these lines. This method is particularlly suitable when forming bevels and similar which do not have precise points from which the cut depth or height can be set in the conventional way. With a bevel cutter set the top point just inside the false fence and finally raise it to the setting required to keep the fence gap to the minimum.

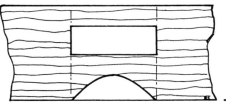
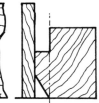
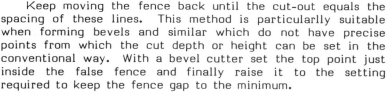
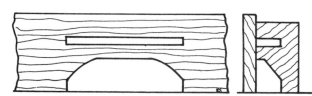

Fig. 174 Above: Cut-out shapes are not always what you expect. A bevel or chamfer produces a shape geometrically called a parabola. It may in fact be a truncated parabola with both halves separated by flat section as shown here.
When bevelling, set the bevel cutter in this way.

Right: Check the cut-out to ensure that sash cutters, for example, project evenly.

Fig. 175 Centre right: When nosing and edging, barely break through the fence, then split it at A using a fine handsaw.

Fig. 176 Lower right: After splitting the fence, screw back the infeed fence, as B, to give the depth of cut needed.

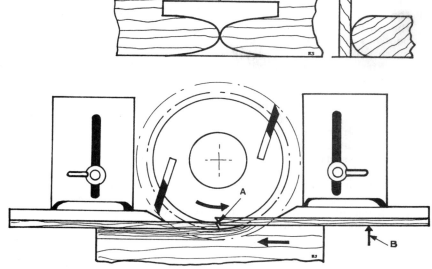

When forming nosings and other similar full-edge moulding where the edge is also to be cleaned-up, move the fence back until the smallest diameter barely breaks through to line-up precisely with the fence face. A gap of only 1 or 2mm is enough. With moulds of this type the infeed fence is normally stepped back to allow for edge clean up (see later details). This isn't possible with a one-piece through fence, so split it from the top to the cut-out using a tenon saw held at a slight angle. By doing this independent movement of the two fence halves can then be made, so finally set back the infeed fence by the cut depth needed.

Checking cutter profile

The fence cut-out clearly shows the cutter profile in deep-ended form where it cuts into the infeed fence. Examine this before moulding to make sure the profile is what you want and, if necessary, correct it before starting the run. Various cut-out profiles are shown in the sketches, check that yours complies. It may be that the balancing cutter interferes with the profile - without this being obvious. If it does interfere, this shows up on the profile cut-out of the fence and can be corrected before running the first piece.

A through-fence gives support across the gap to prevent 'dipping', guards the cutterhead very effectively and fully supports a partially-moulded workpiece so that horizontal pressures can be used across the fence. A wooden through-fence also throws fewer chips at the operator and retains broken pieces of cutter within the guard should an accident happen.

It can also act as a chipbreaker to reduce spelching on the square outer corners of rebates and ovolos, etc. To be effective in chipbreaking, timber has to be tight up against the fence, and the wooden fence must be clean and sharp at the infeed edge. After some use this wears rounded and becomes ineffective, so periodically restore the sharp corner by shifting the fence towards the cutterhead.

First make sure there is enough clearance between steel fence and cutterhead for the movement needed. If not, move the steel fence further out and re-set the through-fence to compensate. Finally, partially loosen the fence plates and, with the spindle running, tap the infeed-fence end to drive the wooden fence 2 or 3mm into the cutters to re-form the sharp corner. Secure the fence and finally check cutter clearance before re-starting.

The same chipbreaking action also reduces tear-out on difficult and interlocked-grain timber to give a better finish. As before, timber and fence must be in tight contact and a sharp corner maintained at the infeed side.

Although normally set for an undercut, the fence can be broken through well above the table line when forming a centre-groove, drip or similar. In this case make sure both top and bottom edges of the cutter have clearance ground-in to cut through the fence to the full depth needed, and use a cutterblock that will not foul in breaking through. A through-fence is useful when stop-moulding as back stops and guides, etc, can be screwed to it quite easily.

THE BED
Table rings

The table normally has removable rings of decreasing size which fit one inside the other. Use them to reduce the gap between table and cutterhead to give maximum support right

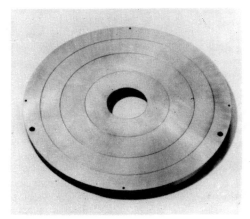

Plate 58 Removable table rings as used on a Delta RS–15 spindle moulder.

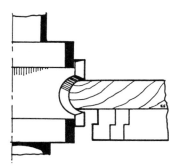

Fig. 177 Above: Fit table rings to fill the gap.

Below: Alternatively shape and fit a wooden bed.

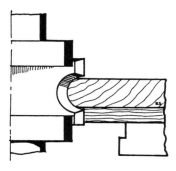

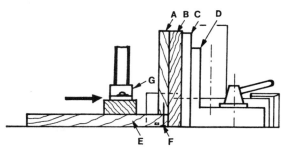

Fig. 178 Section through a wooden bed E nailed to the underside of false fence A which in turn is fixed to the wooden fence plates B. The steel fences are at C and the fence support at D.
Also shown is a Shaw guard G to control movement.

up to the cutters. Where no rings are provided the table may have a ledge to support a hardwood filling-in piece. This should be flush with the table top, have turn-buttons on the underside to hold it in position and a hole to suit the diameter of the cutterhead. Make a range of fill-in pieces with different size holes.

Wooden bed

Another form of support used with a straight fence is a wooden bed or false table.

Slotted tables

This is a piece of seasoned hardwood or laminate, fastened to strips wedged in the fence slots. Shape this to support timber right up to the cutterhead by cutting into the running head. Make the under-strips a good fit and set the bed clear of the cutters. After setting the fence for cut depth, carefully shape the bed by moving it into the running cutterhead until it meets the fence. Use a top Shaw guard to steady the bed when shaping. If an existing bed has a deeper cut-out than needed, saw off or surface this edge so that it can again be used. Make the strips short of the fence edge so that removal is not needed for edging.

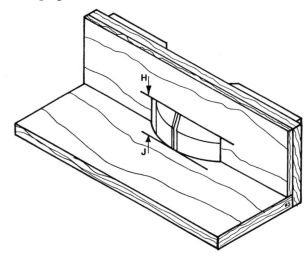

Fig. 179 Mark the fence at H for cut height and the bed at J for cut depth.

Plain tables

Slots collect chips to score the underside of workpieces and interfere with the feed movement, so modern machine tables usually have a series of tapped holes. With these, first shape the bed, then mark the hole positions from the underside and fit securing screws. The problem is in shaping the bed in the first place.

One way is to fasten the bed-piece using a single screw at one end only close to the fence. Move the bed-piece at the opposite end away from the fence to clear the cutterhead, then start this up and carefully swivel the bed until against the fence. Finally, fasten down with two or more screws. Another way is to slot the bed for the securing screws so that these can be fitted and snugged before shaping, then tap the outer edge of the bed to drive it into the cutters until fully shaped. This is an easier and safer way.

Alternatively, treat the bed as a workpiece and shape by dropping-on using a back-stop. See "Stopped moulds". If the table swivels or traverses use this movement in shaping the bed in preferance to any other way.

The simplest method is to fasten the bed to the underedge of the false fence and break through fence and bed at the same time. Use a Shaw guard on the bed to steady this and control the movement when breaking through. To gauge the height and width of cut, accurately mark both bed and fence with prominent depth and width-on-cut lines.

GUARDS

The Shaw guard - use as a pressure

The best pressure for the spindle moulder is the Shaw guard. This is a wooden pad perhaps 100 to 200mm long fastened to a leaf spring centrally held to a supporting bar. Pad width varies according to use; see later notes. The pad is often cut away for cutter clearance when used as a top pressure for over-cutting, but otherwise use a plain pad with end curves front and rear.

The Shaw guard can be used as a top or side pressure, or two can be used together, either mounted from the same support or individually fitted to the fence and bed. Most types need pre-loading manually for pressure. On some machines the contact pad is held by individual leaf springs at each end, with vertical screw adjustment from a support on the table to control both setting and applied pressure.

The Shaw type is easily the best type, having a large contact area to give even pressure yet allowing a smooth feed. Some wax the underside of the pad and the table to combine effective pressure without making the feed difficult or irregular. This adds safety, as excessive feed-resistance gives a jerky feed movement, a poor finish and more chance of kick-back or accident.

Use as a guard

As its name suggests, the Shaw guard acts both as a very good pressure and as a guard to protect the user by covering the cutters when timber is not in place.

With workpieces which are more or less square in section the top guard pad should extend from the fence to the outer edge, and the side guard pad from the bed to virtually meet

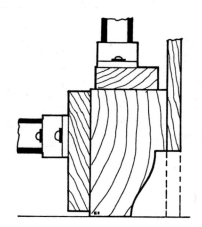

Fig. 180 Use wide Shaw guard pads to enclose the cutter when timber is not in position. Off-set the springs to apply pressure directly opposite the flat vertical or under faces.

the top pad. This boxes in the cutters, so that parts are fed end to end in a continuous stream with the last piece pushed through with a follow-up block. When feeding parts individually leave a small gap for a spike to feed between and past the pressures. Naturally the gap should be too narrow for fingers to reach the cutters.

When a single top guard only is used on wide board edging make the pad much wider than the furthest extent of the cutters. When a side guard is used on wide boards fed face-against the fence, make the pad much wider than the highest point of the cutters. Pad width and distance from pad end to the cutters at both ends relates mathematically to the gap between pad and fence or bed as given on Fig. 181. This gives pad sizes for single pads, also the distance from pad-end to cutters with all pads. Following this guide safely guards the cutterhead when timber is not in place. Pads made to these dimensions give a high degree of safety but may, however, prove unwieldy in use. If this proves impractical, size the Shaw guard to give the best possible protection in the circumstances.

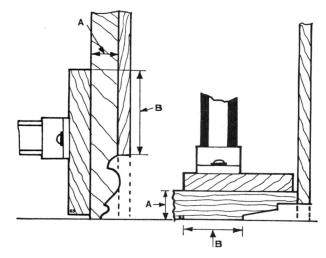

A	6	10	12	15	20	22	30	40	mm.	Max.
B	40	65	90	140	165	190	320	400	mm.	Min.

Fig. 181 When using only a single Shaw guard pressure make the pad extra wide. Dimensions A and B should correspond to the table. Distance B should also correspond to the distance of the leading and trailing pad ends from the cutterhead.

Spring pressures

Another type used either as side or top pressure is the leaf-spring. Normally fit one side or top spring before the cutter-head and a second after it. With small sections use two pairs of springs; one pair from the side and the second from the top. Leaf springs are very insensitive and give line contact only. Few operators like or actually use them, though makers persist in fitting them. They tend to resist forward movement on meeting the workpiece and lack the smooth feed possible with a Shaw guard. They do not guard the cutterhead and extra guards are always essential, so throw them away and use only the Shaw guard type.

Custom pressures

Custom pressures can be made from hardwood blocks. The concertina type has band-saw cuts alternately from each end to just short of the opposite end, with cuts close together and parallel to the contact face. With this type light pressure is applied over a large area. Make the part next to the timber thicker to round-off at infeed for easy entry and at the outfeed to avoid flicking. Make them in various lengths and thicknesses to vary spring pressure and to cover the cutters, as with a Shaw guard pad. Slot or drill for hold-down bolts.

The finger type type has several sawcuts close together but at an angle to the contact face. They form a series of close, springy fingers which press individually on the work and give flexible but light pressure. The fingers should be narrow and flexible but not so thin that they snap off. If using hardwood, make sawcuts along the grain by cross-cutting the board at an angle. Alternatively, glue together a number of thin strips and spacing pieces to make up a laminate.

Pressures of this type are fitted with the fingers trailing in the cut to act as an anti-kick-back trap, but give little resistance to forward feed. If a workpiece has to be drawn back first stop the machine, then slacken off the pressure.

Plate 59 The Shaw guard on this Inca spindle moulder is cantilevered from the rear.

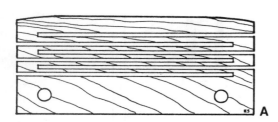

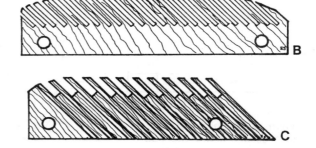

Fig. 182 Custom pressures:
A - concertina type.
B - individual finger type.
C - laminate type.

SAFETY AIDS

All these are essential with any hand-fed machine as, unlike fingers, they are easily replaced. A push-stick should be purpose-made; don't use just any old piece of scrap that happens to be lying about. Shape the contact end to a vee cut-out for end contact or fix a spike to dig in at any point. Taper both to a small section which readily passes guards and pressures. Make the opposite end comfortable to grip as an aid to safety, a push-stick is more likely to be used if it looks and feels right.

It should also be handy when needed. Permanently fasten it to the spindle moulder using a piece of cord long enough for normal use but without danger of becoming tangled (which obviously can be dangerous in a kick-back). The cord keeps the push stick where needed and prevents others borrowing and forgetting to return it. It is also practical to provide a box under the machine table to hold the push stick in readiness for use.

Follow-up blocks are sometimes better than push-sticks for feeding through the last piece of a small section.

Securely fit some form of comfortable handle, as otherwise, being flat on the table or against the fence, there is little to push against. The handle can be a rounded block, a small section of wall handrail, a large drawer handle, or a push-stick cut off at an angle. Most woodworking shops abound with ideal off-cuts. The follow-up piece proper, is best if screwed to a commonly used block so this can adapt to any section. Fix the handle so that both this and knuckles can feed clear past the guards without fouling.

Fig. 183 Above: Typical push sticks:
Notch type A pushes against the rear of the workpiece.
Spike type B digs-in at any point and is usually held in the left hand in preference to direct hand contact.

Right: Typical push-blocks showing, on the left, as used against the end of wide boards whilst, on the right, with a nailed-on section as a follow-up block. Make sure the handle clears the Shaw guard in feeding past.

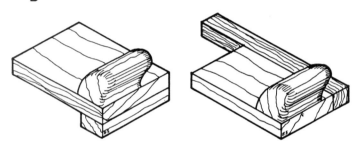

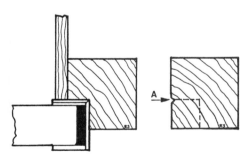

Fig. 184 Left: Rebating cutters should project above the top of the cutterblock, and need relieving along the top edge. Break through the fence to leave a clean rebate edge.

Right: Scribe along the rebate line A, before machining, to prevent spelching beyond.

REBATING

Rebating is possible on any cutterblock using a simple square cutter having a top bevelled edge. When set in the normal way for deep rebates cutters have excessive projection. To reduce projection set the top edge of the cutter slightly above the cutterblock so that rebate depth is limited by the spindle above, not the cutterblock itself. The planing circle in this case is also the rebating circle, and using a cutterblock in this way is termed "sinking" the head. It is commonly used for rebating and deep scotias, etc. A square head is not really suitable for rebating; use a Whitehill or another circular head.

The cutter has a scraping action along a top edge and tends to spelch on the outer corner. Whilst slowing down the feed rate improves this, it doesn't cure spelching on difficult timbers, but there are several techniques that do.

One is to use a through-fence to support timber where spelching occurs. This is effective only if the timber is pressed firmly against the fence and if the fence remains sharp. (See earlier notes).

The second way is to scribe the timber along the rebate line using a joiner's scribe. This severs long fibres so that they break off only up to this line when rebating. The rebate edge and scribe line must correspond absolutely to be successful, but mis-alignment is likely unless that timber is perfectly flat, square and straight. It is possible to fix a scriber to the machine infeed fence in line with the top edge of the cutter to scribe the timber immediately prior to rebating and keep perfect alignment. This needs extra pressure to keep timber and scribe in contact and may, in fact, drag in the cut to give an erratic feed movement.

The third way is to form a scribe on the top edge of the rebate cutter to scribe ahead of the main cut and prevent it spelching beyond. The vee formed in the corner slightly weakens the section remaining, but this is only a problem when double-rebating narrow glazing bars. Cutter projection can be decreased to reduce this, but then is less effective.

The fourth way is to grind the top edge of the cutter slightly over-square. This gives less of a scraping and spelching action, but obviously forms a slightly out-of-square rebate which might not be acceptable. Normally a rebate cutter is ground slightly under-square to touch only at the leading point but still form a perfectly square corner.

Scribing cutters

Scribing cutters are often fitted as separate, special-purpose cutters to the cutterhead itself. Set these slightly higher than the top edge of the rebate cutters and to project slightly more. Rebate and scribe cutters can be set on the spindle moulder, but more easily and more accurately on a setting stand. Fix a flat piece of hardwood parallel to the cutterhead arbor spaced for correct cutter projection. Grind the top edge of all cutters at a slight clearance angle tip to root and front to back. First set scribe cutters to scribe a line 15 - 20mm long when rotating the head. Set the main cutters to barely scrape the face of the timber and with the top edge mid-way in the vee-cut formed by the scribe cutters.

Purpose-made rebate cutterheads, such as some Whitehill types and special circular-heads, have scribing cutters fitted. Some have a saw-like form to give a more effective scribing action with less projection. The same setting guides apply as for single-point types.

Rebate heads are also available with throw-away tungsten carbide cutters which always align correctly, so replacing worn and damaged cutters is quick, simple and precise. With all scribed-type heads the vee shows in the corner, so use it only for hidden rebates. Where a rebate is purely decorative other methods must be used.

Rebate and plane

One way to form a spelch-free rebate is to rebate and plane simultaneously. A single cutter can be ground to both rebate and plane, but needs a square internal corner which is troublesome to grind and needs considerably more grinding from a blank than individual cutters. It is ideal for small pieces, but unusual for large rebates in door casings and similar.

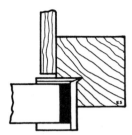

Fig. 185 Form the rebate cutter to a point to scribe whilst rebating.

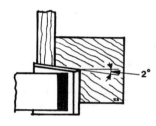

Fig. 186 Making the cutter over-square (by about 2 degrees only) reduces spelching and gives a cleaner face, but the edge is out of square, dulls more quickly and tends to burn on abrasive timber.
To prevent burning even on long runs with dulled points, some make cutters under-square so that only the point touches, see Fig. 188.

Fig. 187 Purpose-made rebating cutterblock.

Double-rebating

All regular rebating methods have a basic fault. One face has a scraping cut to give a woolly finish even with sharp cutters on good quality timber, a condition which rapidly worsens as cutters dull.

If the rebate has to be smooth for appearances sake, plane both rebate faces at separate settings. Form the rebate in the normal way then, after turning the workpiece end for end and reversing height-to-width setting of the cutterhead, plane the scraped face only at a second pass. Timber must be flat and square and cutter settings precise. If not a stepped corner forms, or the previously-planed face is scraped, or the previously scraped-face skipped. All spoil the finish and, as they are difficult to avoid, use this technique only in exceptional circumstances.

Tilted-spindle rebating

With a tilting-spindle machine set cutters to form a vee cut-out, but tilt the arbor to produce a square rebate. Feed timber in the usual way - flat against the fence or flat to the bed. This may seem an odd technique, but it planes both faces giving neither break-out nor spelching. Because of throw the edges have to be slightly curved and out-of-square, so take care in cutter development - or use a profile grinder. Setting for rebate height and depth is strange because height adjustment also alters depth; so set height first.

This method is also possible with a non-tilting spindle, but not so simply. Set the cutterhead as for a tilting spindle with an undercut rebate, but use an angled fence and bed to hold the timber at 30 degrees. With workpieces roughly square in section use a Shaw guard side pressure with a 30/60 degree vee rebate to contact the outer corner only. Oblong sections need two Shaw guards with pads having a 30 degree bevel.

To keep the wedge-bed small and the cutterhead low, this method should only be used for small rebates and relatively narrow pieces. Alternatively, use it to edge-rebate wide boards by tilting the opposite way - rebating as an overcut. This needs a bevelled support for the rebate to avoid dipping on exiting. The drawbacks are as previously detailed for over-cutting, but these are made more complex because of the angle.

GROOVING

Several different tools are used for grooving: loose cutters fitted to regular heads; a grooving, drunken or wobble saw; and specially made grooving heads.

Grooving cutters used on square blocks are normally of the reinforced or humped-back type to compensate for their narrow width and relatively big projection. Some Whitehill blocks have provision for adding cutter reinforcement when grooving, so regular-thickness grooving cutters can be used.

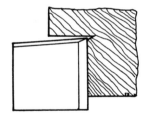

Fig. 188 Above: Form a scribe cutter to a point and with a slight angle.

Below: Set the plain rebate cutter just below the scribe mark.

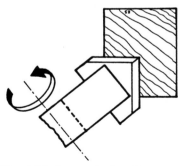

Fig. 189 An angled cutter on a tilted spindle give rebates which are both spelch and scrape-free.

107

By staggering the cutters, it is simple enough to vary the groove size from the actual width of the grooving cutter to slightly less than double this. Because they are no longer directly opposite they run slightly out of dynamic balance, so limit staggering with a single pair of cutters to narrow grooves only. With wide grooves use two pairs of identical grooving cutters and stagger in pairs to retain perfect dynamic balance.

If both grooving cutters are ground square-ended, feed has to be slow to avoid spelching on brittle timbers. To prevent this make one cutter with top and bottom scribes, also slightly wider than the matching square-ended cutter. As with scribe cutters used for rebating, setting has to be precise - but the effect is the same. The vee for the scribe cutter is easily formed on the edge of a square grinding wheel.

Alternatively, form both cutters to a flat and a scribe combination, one scribe up and the other down. Shape small bevels on both edges of a square grinding wheel in order to grind the main cutting edge and scribe bevel at the same time.

For wide grooves, a Whitehill head with scribe cutters top and bottom is probably the best tool. For grooves wider than the head make two or more passes. Scribe cutters are not needed when grooving and rebating at the same time.

Drunken saw

The traditional tool for grooves is the drunken or wobble saw; a thick, heavy saw clamped between double-wedged collars. The saw tilts so that the groove formed is wider than the saw kerf. This is controlled by the amount the adjusting section is twisted to the fixed section of the collars. Setting marks on the two show the saw tilt, not the actual groove width which varies with the diameter and kerf of the saw. Groove width setting has to be by trial and error.

The saw gives a poor finish as it cuts with a series of points; also the base of the groove is slightly curved. Both faults can be resolved by setting the saw to mid-position of tilt and dressing flat with a jointing stone. This can be done safely by barely breaking through a fence and using a fine jointing stone to dress. Fix the stone to a wooden arm pivoted on the outfeed fence and move the arm end up and down to pass the stone fully across the saw in dressing; this avoids ridging it. (A ridged stone rounds the upper and lower teeth.) Set the amount of dress by adjusting either or both fences. Keep hands well clear of the saw in dressing, and wear grinding goggles. Dress the saw until each point shows a witness mark as a filing guide.

Sharpen the teeth with a file held level but at a large side angle. File until the dressing mark disappears along the full tooth width at the same time to give a flat-cutting tooth. This is easier to form using a hook-tooth instead of the conventional peg-tooth so the front and top can be filed individually. Prior to dressing, set teeth outwards at the forward leading face.

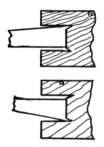

Fig. 190 Use cutters with left and right-hand scribe points for spelch-free grooving.

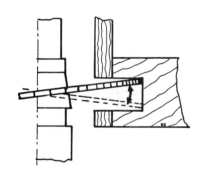

Fig. 191 A drunken saw in cross-section.

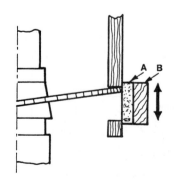

Fig. 192 Dress the saw flat by barely breaking through the fence and using a fine stone A supported on a pivoting arm B.

108

Plate 60 Leuco disposable-cutter type rebating head.

Plate 61 Above: Oppold variable angle head with disposable cutters.

Plate 62 Below: Oppold adjustable grooving head with disposable main and scribe cutters.

The problem with all these tools is dynamic imbalance when tilted because the two halves of the saw are not directly opposite. Vibration worsens with increase in tilt and/or diameter, so restrict tilt to within acceptable limits of vibration.

Fig. 193 File saws with a large front and top angle to leave a flat-topped tooth.

Other types

Solid grooving saws, or those with brazed-on tips, were commonly used, but the general trend is towards one or two-piece tungsten carbide tipped cutters - because they are dependable, easy to use, long lasting and safe. All have main cutters and scribes - which must be kept at their proper heights.

One works on the same principle as a wobble or drunken saw, but uses a twisted body with hard tips instead of a conventional saw. It is similar to , but better than, the conventional wobble saw. Others use the split-tool principle in which the two halves are spaced by removable shims. These give a solid feel to the head but are messy to adjust and their many faces trap chips and dirt. Some tools have screw adjustment for infinate width variation via a setting dial. Both types retain dynamic balance regardless of width. There are several versions of the throw-away-cutter type of head for this application, but generally for wide grooves only.

CAUTION: Grooving tools project more than others and extra care is needed in guarding them, either by a guard fastened to the through-fence or an extra wide Shaw guard pad.

BEVELLING AND CHAMFERING

These are formed using cutters mounted at an angle, and the Whitehill type is ideal for small bevels and chamfers. When forming a large angle, the cutting edge has to be slightly bowed to produce a flat face. These cuts are simpler with a tilting spindle using a simple planing block as there are no complications with cutter profile. Some throw-away heads have tilting jaws. These allow straight cutters to be tilted up to 45 degrees to form any angle whilst running timber flat against the table or fence.

MOULD PROFILES

Woodworking mouldings are traditionally based on just a few basic forms; even the most complex moulds merely combine two or more classical moulds with perhaps and extra fillet here and there. The basic shapes are ovolo, ogee, lamb's tongue (cyma recta and cyma reversa), half and quarter rounds (pencil rounds, quadrants and bull-nose) and torus, plus a few combinations of chamfers and bevels.

Moulds can be Roman type based on true quarter and semi-circles, or Grecian types based on quarter and semi-elipse, parabola or hyperbola. All these shapes can be drawn geometrically; see the examples. It is usual for all moulds combined in a single profile, part, or group, all to be either Grecian or Roman type - but rarely a mixture.

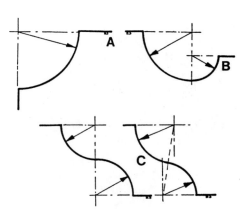

Fig. 194 Roman moulds are based on parts of circles.

Ovolos and coves at A and B are usually quarter circles. (All moulds can be viewed from either side to make two different shapes such as ovolo or cove, but geometric construction is the same).

Cyma recta and cyma reversa, lamb's tongue and ogee, are shown at C; left, as two quadrants when width is half depth or; right, as part quadrants when width is slightly less than half depth.
A bull-nose is a half-round D.

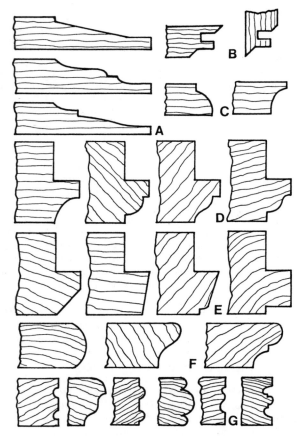

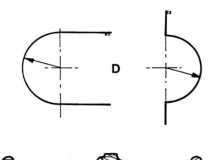

Fig. 195 A few typical moulds:
A - raised panels.
B - mitre glue joint.
C - drop table leaf moulds.
D - traditional sash sections.
E - modern sash sections.
F - edge moulds.
G - decorative moulds.
H - bolection moulds.

Fillets are an integral part of some moulds and must be in correct proportion to look right. Those who originated them had a great respect for these qualities. Cutters forming fillets parallel to the table are worked with a scraping action and may give a woolly finish or a spelched corner.

Plate 63 These Forest City tools show the many profiles available.

Fig. 196 Grecian moulds are based on quarter elipses for ovolos A and coves C, half parabolas for lamb's tongue and ogee B and bull-noses as semi-elipses D.

Proportions can be varied more than with Roman moulds and shapes are better in my opinion.

In all cases the lines are divided-up equally, then points where corresponding lines cross as shown are joined with a continuous curve.

To cure this slow down the feed or carefully break through a wooden fence to act as chipbreaker. A better cure for both is to form moulds using either a tilted spindle or an angled fence/bed. This gives a better cut and also reduces cutter projection. See section on rebates.

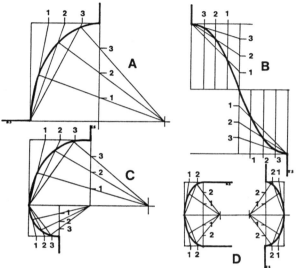

Combination moulds

With crown moulds and similar it is unusual to form the full depth with a single cutter. All combination moulds naturally divide up and can be formed by separate overlapping cutters. They could be mounted on a single cutterhead, or more conveniently fitted in sequence and the mould formed at several subsequent passes.

There are some advantages in the latter. Each cut is relatively light, and adjustment of individual cuts to match properly is a simply a matter of spindle height or fence adjustment; easier than aligning several cutters on the head itself. Combination moulds can often be formed using regular shaped Whitehill cutters, but one-piece cutters are always special. Joints between mould sections should be external corners, hard to form on a one-piece cutter, but easy by overlapping two cutters.

The disadvantages and cures of moulding as sections are: possible instability in later stages of moulding - see "deep non-symmetrical moulds"; longer running time - spindle moulder runs are short so this counts for little; and possibility of spelching on surfaces previously finished - plan so that spelching from one cut is removed by following cuts.

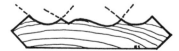

Fig. 197 Combination moulds are based on several shapes in combination and can be formed with individual cutters mounted on the same block - but more easily at separate settings.

111

Mould blending

Pencil rounds, bull-noses and similar shapes should blend perfectly into adjacent faces in theory, but this is not practical as any slight fault in flatness or squareness of the timber gives a mis-match. This looks untidy and unprofessional, especially with a high-gloss finish. Mis-matches can be sanded to blend better, but this takes time and never looks right. As a fillet-type mis-match looks very poor most operators deliberately off-set the profile, so the mis-match then forms as a wavering line which is less noticable.

These problems grow worse the nearer the cutter is to an 'ideal' shape, so don't attempt perfection. Instead, form the cutter with a lead-in angle of about 10 degrees for both face and edge. Allow 3mm projection beyond the blend line on small radii and proportionately more on large ones. The intersection lines these then form have a more acceptable appearance where planing is not perfect. When surfaces are to be face-sanded make the moulded profile slightly deeper to compensate.

If the part for pencil-rounding is relatively thin, machine the timber flat on the spindle moulder table and edge-plane and mould at the same time with a one-piece cutter. (See edge-planing). Form the edge square - a lead-in angle is not needed - and allow extra width when pre-sizing. Don't try this method with the workpiece flat against the fence to undercut the edge; it gives problems and could be dangerous.

Edge-plane whilst bull-nosing to give a clean edge. Form the cutter with a lead-in angle of between 20 and 30 degrees, or even more. A bull-nose is rarely a true 180 degree semi-circle, normally it is a smaller arc of a larger circle. The same profile is usually suitable for bull-nosing boards of slightly different thicknesses. With thick boards make the shape a semi-elipse rather than a semi-circle.

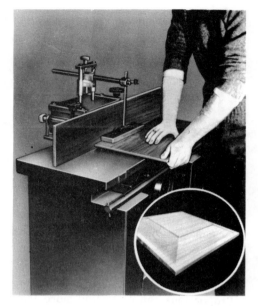

Plate 64 Under-cutting a raised panel using a through-fence and Shaw guard on a Startrite spindle moulder.

Fig. 198 Left: When corner-rounding angle the contact faces about 10 degrees from vertical and horizontal to form an acceptable mould blend.

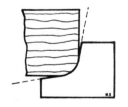 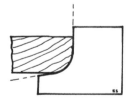 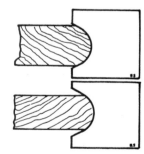

GENERAL MOULDING

There are two basic ways of forming most moulds: with the cutter above the workpiece, an overcut; or cutting below, an undercut.

An overcut is used when panel raising or when forming a deep mould on a small section of timber. A Shaw guard holds down the piece securely with its underface flat on the table so that it remains reasonably stable throughout the cut. The mould is thicknessed accurately but is prone to spoilage and violent kick-back if timber accidently lifts out of contact with the table. This is likely with a bowed piece, also with a long thin piece, if allowed to 'bounce' in feeding.

Centre: When full-depth edge moulding only angle at the under-face.

Right: Angle bull-nose cutters in a similar way. The same cutter can bull-nose boards of slightly different thickness.

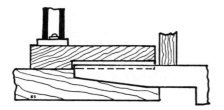

Fig. 199 Section through an overcut on a raised panel. Note the extra wide Shaw guard pad.

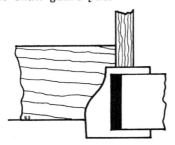

Fig. 200 Mould shallow edge cuts with the workpiece flat on the table.

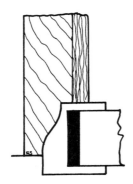

Fig. 201 Mould shallow face cuts with the workpiece flat against the fence.

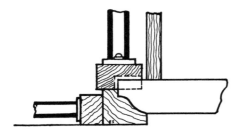

Fig. 202 Small moulds are more stable as an overcut.

Wherever practical form the mould as an undercut. This gives less risk of accident and, if the workpiece accidently lifts from the table, it simply moves clear of the cut with little danger or spoilage or kick-back. If the cut is roughly equal depth-to-width, for example, a 45 degree bevel, timber can be moulded either flat on the table or upright against the fence. Usually it doesn't matter which, although long boards are more stable if fed upright.

When depth-to-width is not equal set cutter depth (projection) to the smaller dimension and feed the workpiece either flat or upright to suit - unless there are other over-riding reasons not to. By keeping cutter projection small the fence and bed gaps are also small and the operation safer. This may involve edge-shaping long, thin boards flat on the table. The weight from the overhung parts may possibly spring it away from the table at the point of cut. To avoid this use outrigger supports at infeed and outfeed.

Setting pressures

When forming a wide mould, make sure that the Shaw guard for side pressure is longer than the gap width, otherwise parts fed singly can be forced into the fence gap when entering or leaving, to kick-back or snipe. (Some allow more length than really needed so that these defects can be trimmed off.) It is common practice and safer to fit a side pressure in line with the mould to reduce chattering at this point. Use a deep pad to cover the exposed cutter gap and apply pressure mainly opposite the solid part of the fence.

A small section may become unstable for the last few inches on leaving the infeed fence, and which normal pressures may not control. This can be lessened by pushing each piece through with the following piece rather than moulding short lengths individually.

Small sections

Avoid moulding small sections, if possible, as they smash and break too readily. If unavoidable run as an overcut with the underface flat on a support and hold down with a top pressure. Set a Shaw guard so that the cut-out just clears the cutters. This keeps full-length contact with the mould top face and avoids a possible jam.

If the workpiece is small in relation to the cut, vibration problems increase dramatically, so small pieces need pressing down on the table and against the fence by two Shaw guards. Where the section is to small to use this particular combination, rebate out the continuous edge of a Shaw guard pad, and round-in from each end for easy entry and exit. Set the rebate on the outer corner of the timber, and apply light vertical and horizontal pressure before securing. For regular use twist the pad the opposite way round so that the rebate faces out.

Leading and back up pieces

Even with all these precautions the Shaw guard may tilt and deflect timber into the fence or bed gap when entering the first section and when pulling-out the last. Keep the Shaw guard level by using scrap pieces to lead and back-up the moulds. Make them the same thickness as the mould if using only one Shaw guard, or the same section if using two.

Before starting the cut grip a scrap piece with the Shaw guard at the outfeed but clear of the cutterhead. This keeps the pad level as the timber is first fed in, and is pushed out by the first piece. The same piece can also push the last part completely through to leave a cleaner and smoother cut, or stop just short of the cutters allowing the last piece to be pulled through from the outfeed.

Make sure that the follow-up piece it is close to hand when moulding, otherwise the machine is left running with the piece in the cut as you hunt around.

Spacer guides

Where an undercut leaves little fence and undersurface on the mould it can become unstable on leaving the infeed fence. Outer guides and pressures help to control this, but for the best results use a spacer guide beyond the cutterhead to steady the deepest point of the cut. Setting and alignment has to be absolutely accurate, of course, and this isn't easy if the spacer fits directly on the fence. Instead fix the spacer guide to a wooden bed to allow fine independent setting. Use this with a through-fence, leaving a gap beneath for the bed support and spacer guide. With a spacer guide it is practical to fit a Shaw guard directly opposite the cut - but use a follow-up piece and take all precautions previously outlined.

Deep moulds

Deep mouldings need excessive cutter projection when a single cutter forms the whole mould, but cutter projection should be small. A single cutter also gives a heavy and dangerous cut for hand-fed operations and has to be specially shaped.

With deep moulds it is better to divide up the profile into individual cuts moulded at separate set-ups. This reduces weight in all cuts. It also reduces cutter projection beyond the cutterhead and by 'sinking' the head into the mould it narrows the fence gap.

Complex moulds usually combine several different shapes which can be formed as individual cuts using regular, shaped Whitehill cutters. The cut can be made as a series of deepening steps, each new cut registering against the spacer guide, but this needs many different settings. A better way is to form the deepest cut first from the opposite face as a shallow cut, then turn the moulding end for end for following passes. Run the mould section formed at the first operation against the spacer guide for all remaining cuts.

Plate 65 Over-cutting a raised panel on a Scheppach machine, with this clamped to a sliding table. The guard is raised for clarity.

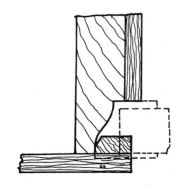

Fig. 203 Use a spacer guide on the wooden bed to support the deepest point of the cut.

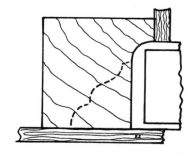

Fig. 204 The first cut on a large cove should be full depth but shallow.

114

Fig. 205 Second stage, using a spacer guide to support the mould fully across the fences.

Fig. 206 Final stage with the spacer guide in the same position.

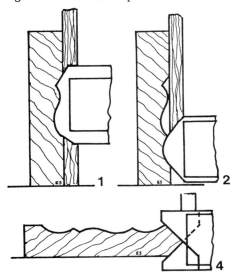
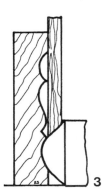

Fig. 207 Stages in forming a crown moulding from a flat section, showning sequence 1 to 4. Right: Showing in dotted outline the waste if moulded from a square.

Form each section from the nearest face so that the cutter never projects more than half mould depth. If the shape is one continuous curve there could be a problem in matching cuts where they merge, as timber rarely runs the same twice. In most cases cutters can overlap at the external corners. Because of this the two cuts can vary to one another without destroying the profile and, in addition, a perfectly sharp corner forms without need of grinding tricky internal corners in the cutter.

Tilting spindles

On machines with a tilting spindle, deep moulds can be formed without excessive projection by tilting to give roughly equal cutter projection top and bottom. Moulds can be machined from the squared-up section, or can be partially relieved by pre-bevelling or rebating. In both cases feed one flat face down and the other against the fence using regular pressures for control. If a large relief cut is made, fit a matching support on the infeed fence. Matching is easier if the pre-cut is a rebate. Use a spacer guide on the outfeed fence.

The same technique is possible, but more difficult, using a vertical spindle and angling the timber. Form a bevel on the surfacer or, for greater accuracy, by feeding on a vee-shaped bed on the thicknesser, then place this face-against the spindle moulder fence.

Crown moulds

Crown moulds are often formed from a flat, wide section rather than a square piece. This saves timber as a smaller section is needed, less is cut to waste and cutter projection is smaller to make operation safer. Mould it with the wide face to the fence which, being planed, is truer than a relief bevel. It leaves a triangular gap when in position for easier bedding.

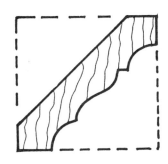

Surface and thickness the board to leave as a square-edged section. Draw out the profile on both ends to avoid error, but make sure you reverse the profile at the opposite end. If practical, first machine the centre section then work outwards to keep the mould stable against the fence. During final passes close to the edges, the remaining support may be cut away, so fit a spacer guide to keep it stable, or form high points near both edges to barely skim the face.

Finally add corner bevels, feeding mould up and back-face flat on the table. Both bevels can be formed at the same time, or individually. Always work flat-face down with an overcut for the inner bevel and an undercut for the rear bevel. Machine off the square corner to a point exactly on the edge line, or off-set the outfeed fence and plane a little off to make sure it cleans up.

When forming true rounds use a quarter-round cutter and turn at each pass so square faces go against fence and table.

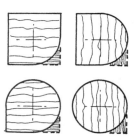

Fig. 208 Sequence in forming a round section.

EDGE MOULDING

When full-depth edge-moulding with fences aligned, the cutters may skip parts of the original planed edge if this wavers even slightly. To cure this, off-set the fences so that the spindle acts as a surfacer to fully clean up the edge and form a smoother and more consistant edge-profile. Set the infeed fence back to just clean up the edge, but leave the outfeed fence exactly in line with the deepest point of the mould.

In setting, initially have both fences in line and slightly back from the planing circle. Fit a top Shaw guard to steady the cut, then feed-in the first piece keeping it hard against the infeed fence until the leading end laps the outfeed fence by 50 - 75 mm. Stop the machine, leaving the workpiece held in place by the Shaw guard, then split the through-fence and adjust the outfeed fence until it barely buts against the moulded edge. Check the cut depth and, if wrong, adjust the infeed fence, then feed in the normal way.

The cutterblock removes timber in doing this, so allow extra width in preparation. It can also clean up sawn or rough edges and will edge-straighten bent or rough timber to a certain extent, as does a surfacer, so some preparation work can be skipped. See Figs. 175 and 176.

Plate 66 Edge-moulding on such as this sash frame is always better when using a feed unit such as this Holz-Her.

Thin beads

This technique is used for easy production of thin beads which are difficult to mould in finished size as they tend to flex, smash and jam. Instead of finish-sizing the beads, plane random width boards to a thickness equal to the bead width needed. Set the spindle to straighten, clean up and edge-mould by off-setting the infeed fence enough to remove saw marks. First mould both edges of all boards on the spindle, then saw off both beads on a clean-cutting saw and return to the spindle for further edge-moulding, sawing off, and so on, until only a thin waste piece remains from each. The beads might be acceptable if cleanly sawn, but if they are not, follow the method described under 'Thickness moulding' to plane up the sawn edge.

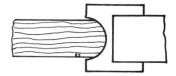

Fig. 209 Above: Set-up for edge-moulding and cleaning-up.

Below: Sawing-off the bead.

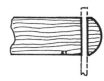

116

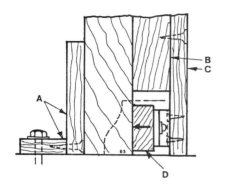

Fig. 210 Using a rigid outer guide A and spring-loaded infeed fence D. The extra-thick strip fence B is fastened to the regular fence C.

Using an outer guide

A rigid outer guide can be used to stabilise boards fed through upright. Fasten this to the table with the board a good fit between this and the fence, and use only a top Shaw guard.

Possibly fit an outward-pressing spring near the cutter-head on the infeed fence to keep timber in tight contact with the guide at this point. The spring must be recessed to project only slightly beyond the infeed fence. Projection can be altered by varying the thickness of either the spring or the wooden fence. Add a second spring at a higher point if the workpiece is deep.

With this type of set-up boards must be straight and equal in thickness, and the fences and guide accurately set. If they are not, the boards could jam or chatter.

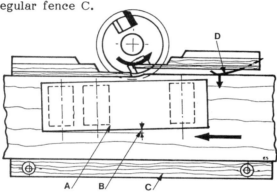

Fig. 212 When using a mechanical feed unit A for widthing, in conjunction with an outer guide C, angle this by about 6mm, B, to keep in contact with the guide. Spring D is used for initial contact only.

Widthing

Combined edging and widthing is common practice with drawer sides and similar sized parts. Prepare these by thicknessing, under-edging and sawing to width - to finally edge-mould and simultaneously width on the spindle moulder. Drawer sides could be thicknessed to width but, being thin, they tend to keel over when fed individually through a planer, or chatter when fed as a pack. Moulding to width on the spindle moulder is simple and better.

Set the outfeed fence as for edge moulding with a wood spring on the infeed fence to push the drawer side "out". A spring could be used on the outfeed fence also, but a fixed fence is more stable.

The guide should be a straight piece of hardwood fastened to the table parallel to and the correct distance from the outfeed fence. Feed the sides between the guide and the pressure, and follow up each with the next. Use a push-stick or push block for the last piece or, preferably, use a mechanical feed for this type of operation.

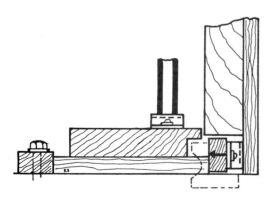

Fig. 211 Moulding drawer-sides to width using a spring-loaded infeed fence and fixed outer guide.

Thicknessing

It is feasible to 'thickness' thin sections using the same technique, either edge-planing or edge-moulding. This is the final part of the 'thin beads from wide boards' method described earlier. Planing rather than edge-moulding is the prefered last cut because this has a smaller and less-severe cutting action with less chance of breakage. With rebated beads the final cut is edge planing and rebating. Shape the fixed guide to the reverse of the mould to seat this better and give a steadier and a less vibration-prone feed action.

TYPES OF JIGS

Short pieces fed individually butted end to end tend to dip into the fence and table gap to end-snipe. Feed is intermittant and marks form where the feed stops momentarily. Preferably mould pieces as long strips and cut to length afterwards. When short lengths are unavoidable, grip and feed these in some form of holding jig.

The simplest jig is a block at least double the length of the piece, of the same thickness, and with a cut-out at mid-length to house the workpiece. This makes the mould virtually a continuation of the jig, so effectively increasing its length for safer handling. The jig needs handles both at the leading and trailing ends, for example large dowels or blocks, and must be wide enough for the handles to miss the top pressure. Only top pressure is needed, side pressure is applied via the handles. Fit the blank in position and feed the assembly through as a single piece, using a steady and continuous movement to give the best finish.

The jig can have a top piece added incorporating brads to grip the workpiece firmly. The brads are best driven in by positioning the jig on the workpiece and tapping home. Take care that it butts against the back fence and stops, or the part may slip in machining or be moulded under-size. To eject the finished timber quickly, drill a large hole through the top piece and tap through on a rounded handle on the machine.

The Shaw guard presses on the jig, not the part, but has the same effect. If the jig is made large and heavy a top pressure may not be necessary, but still use a Shaw guard for protection. With a fully-bradded jig a full-depth cut is possible on the workpiece, using the top piece as a template guide against the fence.

A variation of the above uses a bradded and jigged template to accurately size and edge-mould straight tapered pieces. The jig itself is parallel, but has an angled back fence and end stops. Use it both for edging and for taper-cutting blanks from wide boards. The boards are initially equal in width to the wide end, plus the narrow end, plus saw-cut and edge-planing allowance. Angle the back fence for the piece to feed with the grain, i.e., thick end first. Make sure the workpiece is properly seated against the trailing end-stop or it could shift and spoil.

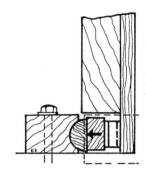

Fig. 213 Thicknessing a small bead using a spring-loaded infeed fence and shaped outer guide.

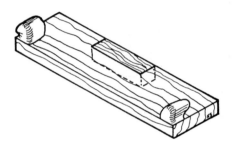

Fig. 214 Typical jig for feeding short and small parts.

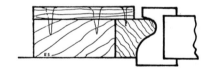

Fig. 215 Above: First cut in forming drawer pull. This could be a stop-mould if front and back-stops are fitted, or if the jig is made captive by a fixed pin through a slot in it.

Below: Second cut in forming a drawer pull with the mould seating against a rebate.

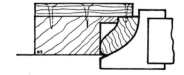

118

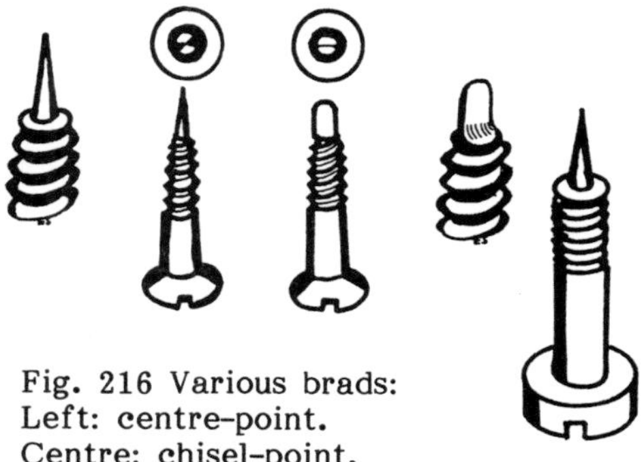

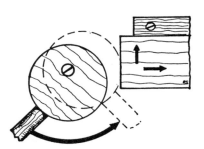

Fig. 216 Various brads:
Left: centre-point.
Centre: chisel-point.
Right: shouldered bolt.

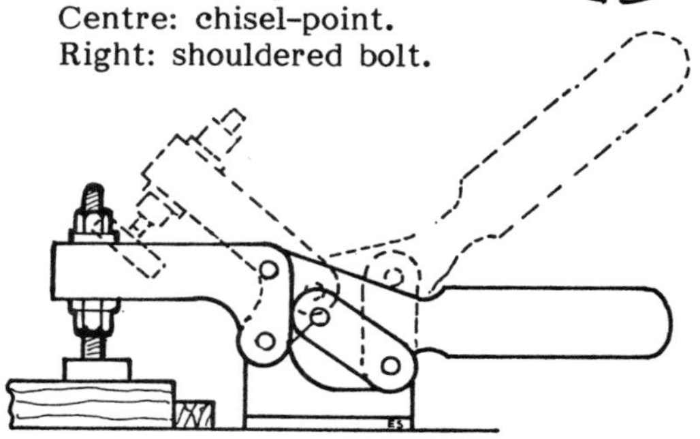

Brads and clamps

Most jigs and fixtures require brads and clamps. Brads are best made from woodscrews driven clear through the template or jig which are easily replaced when damaged or worn. For Plywood and chipboard, etc., grind or file the screw end to a centre point. For solid timber form a chisel edge to align with the grain so the brad penetrates easily but leaves little visible damage. With a box jig insert a metal or nylon screw-seating into the jig and use a screwed bolt turned to form a centre point and square shoulder. When driven in, this type both clamps and prevents sideways movement.

Toggle clamps are widely used. When released this type gives ample room for part removal and replacement, yet has a secure clamping action. Circular hardwood pieces pivoted eccentrically and with a dowel fitted for leverage provide cheap and easily-made clamps. When used alone this type moves timber in two directions, a feature used to bed timber against two stops or fences. Using a fixed section of hardwood formed to provide a slip between clamp and workpiece allows end pressure only. Single pieces shaped as a comma are also used in this way, but take care to form a true eccentric.

Fig. 217 Toggle clamp.

Fig. 220 Right: Bar-type eccentric clamp for single or multiple use.

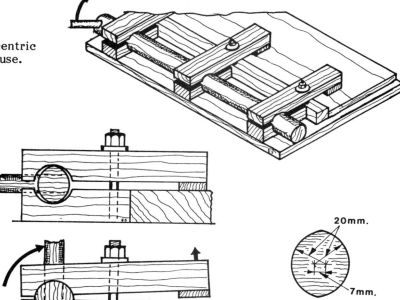

Fig. 218 Eccentric wooden clamp.

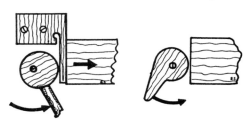

Fig. 219 Left: Eccentric clamp with a slip.
Right: One-piece 'comma' clamp.

An eccentric clamp can also be made from an egg-shaped strip using half-round cutters on a piece too narrow to form a perfect full round. Use this type with a single clamp, or to operate several in-line clamps with a single movement. Adjust individual clamp pressures by means of the hold-down screws.

20mm.

7mm.

119

General purpose clamp

It is impractical to make individual holding jigs for every new part, so make a general purpose jig suitable for small parts of different width, length and thickness. One type, based on a French idea, has a wide stable base with a substantial support fastened vertically to this and with a reinforcing bracket. A large diameter hardwood disc turns eccentrically on a horizontal pivot and is operated via a lever and handle at the outside. The disc and handle are connected by a nut, bolt and bush through a slot in the support. The clamping thickness is varied by connecting the operating lever to alternative holes drilled through the disc.

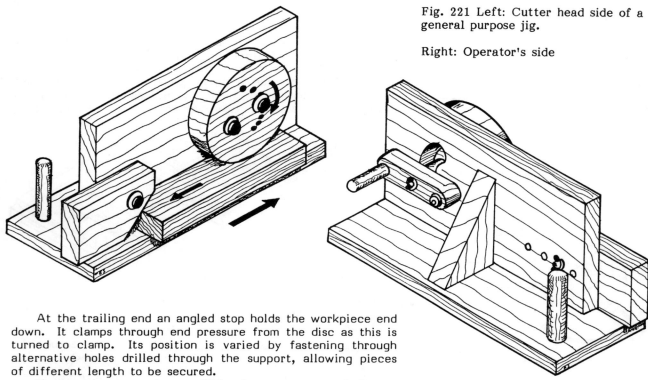

Fig. 221 Left: Cutter head side of a general purpose jig.

Right: Operator's side

At the trailing end an angled stop holds the workpiece end down. It clamps through end pressure from the disc as this is turned to clamp. Its position is varied by fastening through alternative holes drilled through the support, allowing pieces of different length to be secured.

Narrow pieces overhang. Wide pieces are supported near the cutterhead by a strip bed against the fence (of equal thickness to the base). When feeding, the lever handle is held down and the trailing handle is used to push the assembly forward.

STOP MOULDING

Stop-moulding is moulding along only part of the workpiece by running the mould in from the leading end, starting part-way along and running out to the trailing end, or starting and stopping it within its length.

120

In some cases moulding may start and stop at more than one point, or even change profile at different points. Examples are the head, sills and transoms of windows which need different sections for alternate opening and fixed lights.

Stop-moulding gives a decorative effect to priory-type furniture or similar. It also simplifies tenoning of moulded window frames with mortise and tenon joints. (The mould stops short of the mortises, allowing simply-formed square shoulders to be used which do not need complicated scribing.) The practice is common on furniture to avoid difficult scribes, and to add interest to an otherwise plain part.

Use a top Shaw guard when stop moulding to steady the cut, but do not apply excessive pressure which might prevent easy movement towards and from the fence. Wax the Shaw guard pad and the table to make starting and stopping easier and safer. The points to start and stop can be indicated by guide lines, or controlled by stops. Guide lines can be clearly marked on the fence. Stops are fitted to a through-fence or the table.

First set-up the machine, then fit and break through a wooden fence. Mark prominent vertical lines on the fence where the longest point of the cutter passes through. Mark a thick horizontal line between the vertical lines, and above workpiece level, to show the effective width of the cutter.

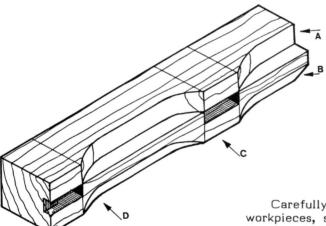

Fig. 222 In this window section the rebate and chamfer A and B are started and stopped at C and D for the mortises.

Carefully mark start and stop points on the top face of all workpieces, squaring the lines round from the mortises. Use these and the fence marks to show where to drop-on and pull-out when using a jig, or when setting the stops. With a Shaw guard fitted fence marks may be difficult to see, so repeat them on the wooden bed or table.

Running-in

Some moulds run-in from one end. These can be worked quite safely by feeding forward as normal then, after first slowing-down to a crawl so that tear-out reduces, simply stopping forward feed where needed. Without stopping the machine, lever the workpiece out of the cut simply and safely, pivotting on the remote end by pushing the trailing end outwards. Take care not to feed the workpiece forward in doing this.

If the mould has to be stopped precisely use a stop block. Fasten this to the outfeed fence or table. Position it against the end of the workpiece when the stop-line on the workpiece is opposite the right-hand vertical mark on the through-fence. Extend the through-fence if necessary.

Parts are often machined in pairs. When these have a symmetrical mould running in from one end, for example an ovolo, 45 degree bevel or quarter round, both cuts can be run-in. Feed one face down and the other face against the fence so that the mould runs-in from the leading end regardless of hand. Not all moulds are suitable as the sweep-out appears slightly different on the two pieces.

When the form is not symmetrical, for example a mould such as a lamb's tongue, both halves of a pair can still be run 'in' by using two pairs of opposite-hand cutters. Set one for an overcut and the other for an undercut. Run-in both from the leading end to give matching sweep-outs. Alternatively, both can be formed as an undercut by using cutters with the profile turned through 90 degrees.

Making opposite-hand cutters or different cutters just to do this, though, is hardly justified. The simpler alternative is to run one mould 'in' and the other 'out' after dropping-on - in both cases using the same setting.

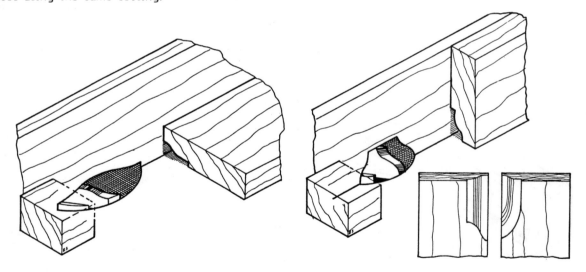

Fig. 223 Non-symmetrical moulds on pairs of parts can be stopped by running-in with an undercut from the same end (if the cutter profile is changed) - but the sweep-outs do not match.

Dropping-on

When the mould starts part way along the timber it has to be 'dropped-on', that is moved into the cut at the appropriate point before being fed forward. Moulding may run out to the trailing end, or run only part way involving dropping-on, feeding, then stopping and drawing-out. Some may require stop-moulding at more than one section.

With very small mouldings on heavy workpieces, for example, a pencil-round on a newel post, dropping-on can be safely carried out by an experienced spindle-hand using only a holding jig and a top Shaw guard. Taper the Shaw guard pad upwards away from the fence for easy entry width-ways. With larger moulds or lighter pieces take great care, and use aids such as a back stop, or cam and template.

Operation

Never drop-on by attempting to move the workpiece up to the fence in a parallel movement. Instead set the workpiece under the Shaw guard pressure so that its leading corner contacts the outfeed fence, but angled to clear the cutterhead. Securely hold the workpiece with both hands, preferably to the right of the cutterblock, and, using the opposite end as a controlling lever, carefully swing it towards the fence by pivotting on its leading corner in a gentle and controlled movement. Take care to avoid snatch, and do not to allow the piece to move back when starting the cut. Preferably feed slightly forward to make sure neither happens. Once in full contact with the fence, feed forward in the usual way.

Always use a top Shaw guard and make sure that the table surface is clean so that movement is smooth. If the table is slotted use hardwood strips to fill-in the slots level with the table top. Always start with both hands to the right-hand side of the cutterhead so that they are thrown clear should a kickback occur. By gripping at this point they also have better control in dropping-on.

The correct starting position for dropping-on is with the start mark on the timber and the left-hand mark on the fence or bed in alignment. It isn't easy to hit the correct position because the two marks are initially separated by a gap - and may not correspond when in contact. Preferably start slightly forward, but make no attempt to draw back once in the cut as this will kick-back. Instead move the timber clear of the cutters, draw back slightly, then drop-on a second time.

Back-stops

Dropping-on is dangerous because kick-back is likely, i.e., cutters can grab timber and throw it violently back at the operator. A Shaw guard helps to steady the part but preferably use a back-stop. Using a back-stop is not only safer, but quicker and more accurate. Most authorities recommend using a back-stop, even for small cuts, as does the writer.

The obvious place for a back-stop is secured to the table. It can be fastened to the infeed fence, but must extend from the fence, and both fence and back-stop must be secure. Fix the back-stop against the end of the workpiece when the start mark on it aligns with the extreme left-hand mark on the fence. The stop must be securely held, as a kick-back on dropping-on too quickly could shift both this and the workpiece.

Sometimes chips get trapped between timber and fence when dropping-on. After the first contact draw the timber clear so that chips are blown away before dropping-on a second time. Leave a small gap between back-stop and fence so that chips blow clear.

The back-stop must extend well away from the fence so that the workpiece is in full contact with it when in the drop-on position: i.e., angled to touch the outfeed fence but well clear of the cutterhead. In this way the timber is under control before the cutters start to grip. The Shaw guard pad should grip the workpiece when in the start position so that no sideways resistance is met in actually dropping-on.

A front-stop limits forward movement to prevent over-run, but need not extend much from the fence. When in contact with the front-stop draw out the trailing end of the workpiece, pivoting its leading corner on the front-stop.

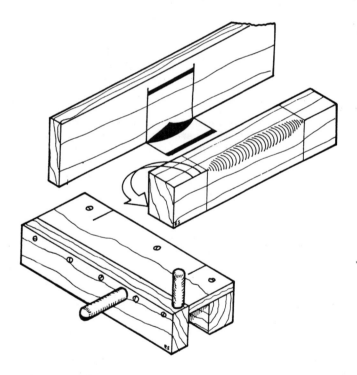

Fig. 224 Left: Mark vertical lines on the fence where the extreme points of the cutter break through. Mark the piece all round for the start and stop positions.

Below: The recommended sequence of dropping-on and stopping using front and backstops.

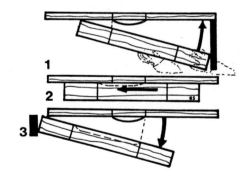

Left: Alternatively, use a holding jig and work to marked lines. Make the jig wide with an outer support and control handles.

Cam stops

With long workpieces a back-stop may not be practical, so nail or screw a 25mm thick hardwood template to the top face of the timber for use with a cam on the fence. Form a 45 degree trailing bevel where the mould begins - with the heel where the mould actually starts. Form a similar bevel at the mould stop point, but facing forward.

124

Securely fit a cam with 45 degree bevels at both ends to the fence, barely clear of the timber and to contact the template. The cam should be fractionally wider than the effective cutter width at furthest projection, just outside the vertical lines drawn on the through-fence, and project slightly more than the cutters. Thickness can be about 25mm.

The cam and template control both start and stop positions. Place the timber at an angle so the end contacts the outfeed fence, with the template edge in contact with the cam so that the cutters are clear of the timber.

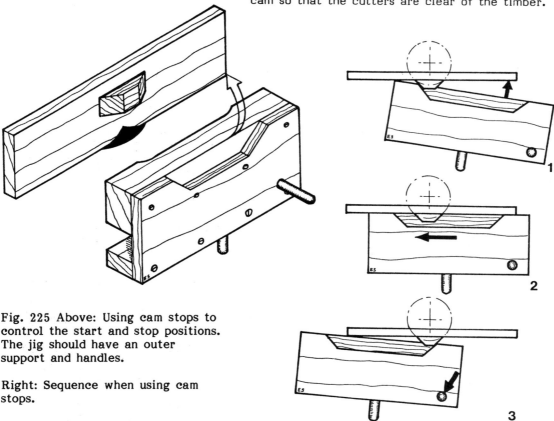

Fig. 225 Above: Using cam stops to control the start and stop positions. The jig should have an outer support and handles.

Right: Sequence when using cam stops.

Start the cutterhead and move the timber forward and in so the start bevel follows down the angled slope of the cam. This commences the cut safely and without chance of kick-back. It helps if the angled faces are smooth and polished. The stop cam feeds the piece out automatically and smoothly at the proper point. This method allows several stop moulds to be made on a single piece simply by adding start and stop bevels where needed on the template.

It is tedious to repeatedly nail the template in place if several workpieces are to be identically stop-moulded. Preferably make the template as part of an open-sided box fastening parts by a clamp at the leading end.

Moving table machines

Machines with a moving table offer a safer alternative to any of the above - and, in fact, the safest method of machining stopped moulds. One example is the Robinson spindle moulder with a swivelling table, lock and screw-adjusted movement. Set-up is made as previously described, then move the table clear of the cutterblock. Fit the workpiece against the fence and end-stop, and under the Shaw guard.

To drop-on, start the cutterhead, then release and move the table back into the operating position. Feed the workpiece forward in the usual way until against the stop block, then move the table out. The operation is under full mechanical control with the workpiece against the fences throughout.

Fig. 226 A box jig for stop-moulding with the template as part of the box top.

Plate 67 The Robinson EN/T spindle moulder table swivels, and has a screw-adjusted movement.

Most moulding is with the grain, but sometimes moulding is needed across the grain, for example, in rounding over the tops of uncapped newel posts. Cutters work reasonably well either with or across the grain, though a slower feed is needed for cross-grain moulding. Most end-grain work is on a narrow face, so certain precautions are essential as workpieces are unstable and prone to back-spelching as the cutters break through the trailing face.

Preferably use a tenoning attachment, or the spindle table itself if of the rolling type. With these the traverse is under mechanical control and one or more pieces can be clamped firmly in position to back-up one another. This gives a better cut than any other method, and much safer working conditions. To reduce break-out, use a backing piece to initially project slightly beyond the moulding line.

The full depth can be safely formed at a single pass because the clamp holds the timber firmly. Make the pieces slightly over-long for moulding and length trimming at the same time. On double-end trimming, gauge the first position from an end-stop, and the second from a sprung shoulder stop.

When moulding one end only, use a fixed stop to locate the opposite end. (See section on Tenoning.)

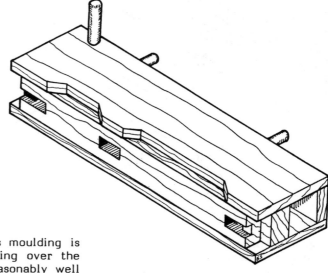

Plate 68 The table position of the Robinson EN/T is clearly seen from the front.

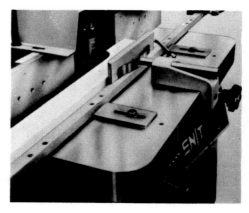

126

END GRAIN MOULDING

If the workpiece has a large cross-section it remains reasonably stable when end-wise against a through fence; examples are large newel posts or short, wide boards for pencil-rounding only. With these a large block-type back-up piece is all that is needed to keep the workpiece square and stable, provided the two are clamped together in some way and an undercut is used to mould only part of the depth. It is essential to use both a through-fence and wooden bed to give the smallest possible gap and continuous support to the parts. Grind the profile near to the top edge of the cutters, to leave the maximum amount of fence above the cutters.

Use the back-up piece to steady the cut and prevent spelching by feeding the two together underneath a top Shaw guard. Make sure the back-up piece is tightly held against the workpiece during the complete movement, perhaps 'G' clamping them together or fitting brads in the back-up piece to drive into the workpiece and lock the two together. Nail a replaceable facing to the back-up piece to allow a quick change for any profile.

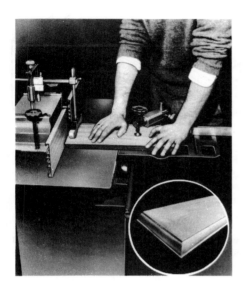

Plate 69 Using a sliding table on a Startrite spindle moulder to end-mould parts safely. In addition to a Shaw guard a through-fence is needed. Edge moulding is a following operation with timber fed in the normal way to remove any spelching.

Fig. 227 Back-up block for end-trimming large sections or wide pieces. The face provides back-up to prevent spelching, and is a loose piece which can be replaced. Hold the workpiece to the back-up block securely using a clamp or brads.

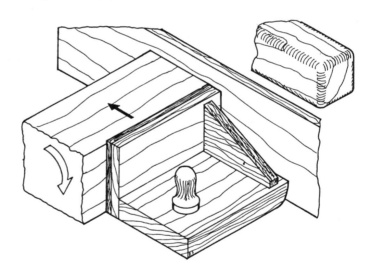

Plain table machines   Jig working

When dealing with narrower pieces that are less end-stable, make a wide jig with a large piece of plywood as a base to ride against the fence, and screw a back-up block to the right of centre. Grind the cutter narrow to cut the least amount from the jig base. Push the timber and the base against the fence to properly end-align them, then clamp firmly to the back-up block or base by any suitable means such as eccentric wooden or toggle clamps.

By using a sliding jig several pieces can be clamped horizontally and end-moulded together. This is an advantage as the set-up is more stable and each piece is firmly supported by the piece following, so there is less break-out.

It is impractical and dangerous to mould the full depth at a single pass with this set-up. Mould only a part of the depth as an undercut so that the unmoulded section remains supported by the through-fence. Mould the rest at a second set-up, preferably using a reverse-shaped support for the previously moulded profile.

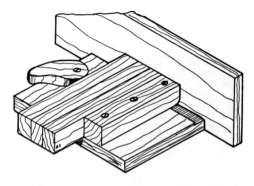

Fig. 228 Above: A sliding jig running against a through-fence and with several pieces clamped together against a square fence.

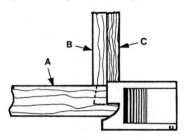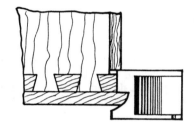

Fig. 229 Above left: Rebating and rounding drawer front A flush with side B by running against strip fence C.

Above right: Rebating and rounding the drawer front top edge by running the drawer side top edges against the strip fence. The drawer tops are usually down slightly from the frame underside.

Below: The two stages in forming a complete end-trim. The first stage is shown on the left. The second stage is on the right. In the latter, the profile previously formed, now uppermost, rides against a reverse-shaped strip fence. Use a Shaw guard.

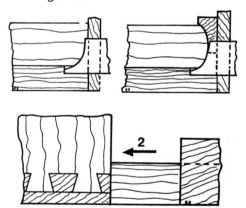

Fig. 230 When making the cut for the left-hand end, use a follow-up block against the drawer underside to prevent break-out.

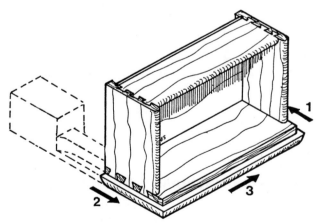

An example is when forming a full bull-nose. First form slightly more than half the bull-nose as an undercut quarter round. The second pass uses the same set-up, but with a shaped strip fence added to the through-fence to match the quarter round already formed. The pieces ride against this support for the final cut.

Fig. 231 Left: Sequence of cuts to prevent spelching.
1 - Right-hand drawer end.
2 - Left-hand drawer end using the back-up block.
3 - Drawer-front top at a separate set-up.
Arrows show the direction of feed.

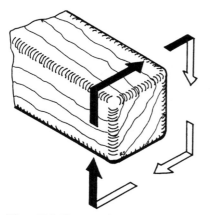

Fig. 232 Top-easing a newel post. Arrows show the sequence of cuts, so rotate the post the opposite way. Use a clamped follow-up block.

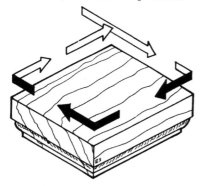

Fig. 233 Forming a newel cap. Arrows show the sequence of cuts, so rotate the cap the opposite way. With small parts it is essential to use a holding jig.

Another example is in rebating and rounding the ends and the top edge on the fronts of assembled kitchen drawers. The fronts are first sized marginally over depth and over length. The set-up has a strip fence fitted to allow the drawer front to pass underneath when face down on the table. The rebate and round are best formed at a single pass. Initially, set the rebate cutter in line with the strip fence to rebate the drawer front ends flush with the drawer sides. Use a follow-up block to back up the drawer under-edge to prevent break-out. Reset the fence to give the usual step between the top-edge rebate on the drawer front and the drawer side top edge.

Form the drawer top edge by running the drawer side top edges against the strip fence. Make sure the strip fence has a clean, flat and damage-free face, or the top edge will mould unevenly. This final cut removes any break-out at the top edge resulting from the end-moulding cut.

Operating sequence

When workpieces are moulded on three or four corners using set-ups such as this, the sequence has to be correct or spelching results. The correct sequence is to work so that any spelching is machined-out by following cuts.

When forming a bevel or quadrants around the top and long edges of a capless newel post, mould all these using an undercut head, through fence, Shaw guard and follow-up block.

First form the mould around the top with the newel post flat on the table, end against the fence and steadied by using the follow-up block. When turning for the next cut, rotate the newel post clockwise (viewed from the lower end) so that the next cut starts where the previous cut ended and might have spelched. This cleans up all corner spelching bar the last cut, which should be fed slowly to keep spelching to the absolute minimum. Finally, make cuts along the grain for the four remaining long corners using the same set-up, but feeding in the usual way. The sequence in this case is unimportant. If end-grain moulding a square or similar workpiece on all edges, turn between cuts to give the same cutting conditions as above and for the same reason.

Template sizing

The spindle moulder can be used very successfully to dress and edge-mould to size shapes having straight sides, by using a tenoning attachment, or a sliding table. A template serves the same purpose, though, and is quicker in use, keeps a constant overal size and allows all cuts to follow one another in proper order to complete sizing at a single handling.

The template should be a piece of plywood or similar, trimmed exactly to the overall size wanted, i.e., to the outside dimensions of a square-edged workpiece, or the overal size measured to the outside point of an edge-moulded part. Fasten the template to the workpiece by nails (which want extracting individually) or use brads which keep in place when the template is sprung-off.

Fasten a strip fence (which is thicker than the amount to be trimmed off) to the through-fence, positioned to allow the untrimmed workpiece to pass beneath. Set planing cutters exactly in line with the outer face of the strip fence and to project only about 2mm above the workpiece (so the least amount is pared off both strip fence and template). For the same reason grind the mould close to the top edge of the moulding cutters. Set them so that the deepest point of the mould aligns with the strip fence. Make the template thick enough to leave a deep contact face when the cutter breaks through the fence, or use a spacer between workpiece and template.

Place the workpiece flat on the table and fasten the template to it. Run each end or side in turn, with the template riding on the strip fence, to size and mould at the same time. Rotate counter-clockwise between cuts to prevent spelching. The operation is similar to shaping using a ball-bearing collar or ring fence, but a straight fence makes the operation steadier and safer.

The method is ideal for squares, oblongs and other shapes bonded by straight lines, either as individual pieces or part-assemblies. Use it, for example, in sizing and edge-moulding window sashes. These are machined and assembled with the outer face square for easier and less critical manufacture. Precise overall size is difficult to guarantee when fully machining in small lots, but no problem when sizing is the final operation.

There is an additional advantage; it gives a uniform and cleaner appearance at the corners without complicated tenoning to end-profile, which might not match in final assembly anyhow.

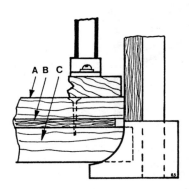

Fig. 234 Sizing-template A to form a quarter-round on the part C.
B is a sandwich piece to ensure the template fully contacts the strip fence.

Type of template

Either an over or under template can be used; there are pros and cons for both. An over-template allows guards and handles to be fixed to the top surface for safer and easier feeding. This type also protects the user better because cutters are below the template. On the other hand, when machining open frames, the assembly needs flipping-over before use then flipping back to unload and reload.

Brads aid in locking template and workpiece together, but with open frames fit location strips and inside eccentric clamps to firmly lock the assembly. These also support thin sections which might otherwise spring or vibrate.

Machines set for an overcut are more convenient and quicker for open frames. The operator can also see the cut and better judge the correct feed speed needed. The main disadvantage is that the cutterhead is more exposed and needs extra guarding which with these set-ups is always poor.

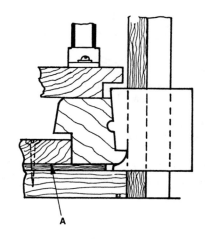

Fig. 235 Sizing a frame using an under template.
Block A locates the frame in position and makes it secure.

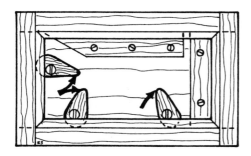

Fig. 236 Top view of a jigged-template for sizing frames. The frame is locked by eccentric clamps which in tightening pull the frame against blocks.

Reducing spelching

Regardless the type of template, correct operating sequence is essential to reduce spelching on frames. To do this rotate the assembly counter-clockwise to mill-out spelching from the previous cut. There is one additional and important factor with plywood and assemblies such as window frames. If each side is fully machined in turn, a following clean-up cut is made at each corner except the last. This can only be supported (to avoid break-out) by using a complicated, reverse-shaped back-up piece, but this is never entirely satisfactory.

To resolve this without using a back-up piece, simply start and finish the cut about half-way along one long side. Start the sequence of cuts by dropping-on, follow-up as through cuts after turning counter-clockwise, with the first and final cuts matching-up at the drop-on point. This gives better corners than the best back-up piece.

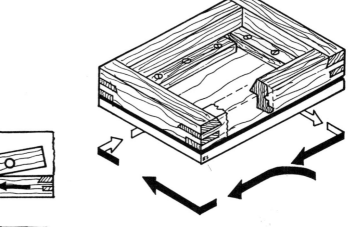

Right: Use a wide back-stop swung from the fence which pushes clear when through-feeding.

Fig. 237
Above: Sequence of cuts for the frame. Arrows show the cuts, so rotate in the opposite direction. Make the first cut part-way along one long side to avoid end spelching.

Take all the basic precautions detailed earlier for dropping-on using a back-stop. The latter must flip or swing clear after the first cut as the remaining passes are through cuts. Because the work is a series of four following cuts these can be interrupted to shift the stop, but a swing-away stop is more convenient. Starting position is not critical, but should be about mid-length of one long side to give a suitable leverage when dropping-on.

TRIMMING OPERATIONS

Box corners

Another example is trimming fingers and corner-rounding corner-locked boxes. A strip fence is again needed with an under-gap slightly more than the thickness of the box sides, and a wooden bed with a similar gap along the fence line. Align the quarter-round cutter to the faces of the strip fence and the bed. When the boxes are placed face down on the bed and end against the fence, the fingers and excess glue project into the gaps so that the cutters remove the projecting fingers and round the corner at the same time. Use a clamped follow-up block and Shaw guard.

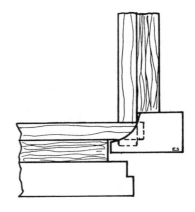

Fig. 238 Corner-rounding and trimming finger-jointed boxes using a gapped fence and bed.

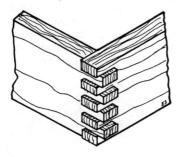

Fig. 239 Make the fingers protrude slightly on assembly.

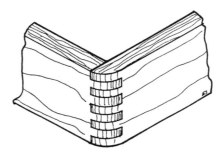

Fig. 240 The same joint after trimming and rounding.

Skins

A narrow strip fence can be used for trimming frames clad in plywood, veneer or plastic. Usually the frame is made to size, or sized after assembly, then skins are trimmed down flush with the frame after fixing. (It is impractical to pre-trim skins to a precise size and expect them to align perfectly with the frame).

Use a full-length strip fence marginally thinner than the frame, together with a double grooving head spanning the strip fence and with cutters precisely aligned to it. In use, simply feed the assembly with the frame riding on the strip fence, so that the skins are trimmed level with the frame.

If the corners need chamfering or rounding this is possible either as a following operation or at the same time. Whichever way is chosen, preferably form as an under-cut only, turning the assembly over for the second cut. A dual cut could be used to form upper and lower cuts at the same time, but the danger is that any slight springing of the frame could dig the cutter into the top surface and spoil it. To avoid spelching at the last corner when sizing all round, drop-in part way along either long side.

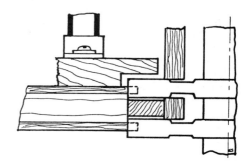

Fig. 241 Trimming skins to the frame overall size using a strip fence.

132

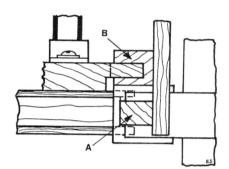

Fig. 242 Trimming skins and frame simultaneously using a strip fence on the infeed and an in-line outfeed fence. The original edge rides against strip fence A, and the finished edge on outfeed fence B.

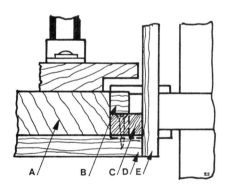

Fig. 243 Right: Using a sliding jig to trim frame ends. The frame is locked against a guide on the sliding jig in line with the planing cutters. To trim, move forward against a stop, then flip and repeat.

Above: Section through frame end trimming set-up showing:
A - door rail.
B - projecting frame end.
C - guide strip.
D - sliding base.
E - fence.

Facing

Regular edging trims down to the frame but doesn't clean-up the frame edge itself. This is possible using a planing block aligned to the outfeed fence. A strip fence is needed only at the infeed fence, and must be set-back by the cut-depth needed. The frame first rides on the infeed strip fence, then on the outfeed fence. The operation is equivalent to surfacing or mould edging.

Only a single pass is permissible; if further passes are made extra is planed-off in the same way as when surfacing. Use a back-up block, but never start the cut part way along.

It is essential to control movement firmly, particularly when machining the ends of long ,but narrow workpieces, otherwise side ways rocking is likely to form an uneven edge which takes a lot of making good. As this set-up also needs a fence gap there is always the chance of dipping when starting or finishing the cut.

These problems are best resolved by using a template as described earlier, but the strip fence is quicker to use and less troublesome. It gives acceptable results if workpieces are of about normal cupboard door size.

Ends and tenons

With mortise and tenon frames, it is difficult to machine them so precisely that, when assembled, the tenons and ends are perfectly flush with the frame. Doing this is rarely successful - tenon ends and horn invariably either sink or protrude. Preferably machine them to project slightly, then trim flush after assembly.

One set-up for frame end or horn trimming has a base sliding on the table to bear edge-against a through-fence. A narrow guide screwed to its top surface and flush with the fence edge extends fully across, but with a working gap at the cutterhead. Stops limit the movement of the base so that the guides stop short of the cutterblock in both directions. Set planing cutters to just clip the top edge of the base and to align precisely with the outside edge of the guides when the base is against the fence.

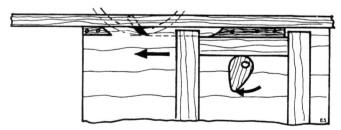

Fit the frame edge-against the guide and with the end for trimming leading and central in the working gap. To make the frame more stable fit inside eccentric clamps to lock it or fit a second close-fitting guide inside.

Draw the jig clear of the cutters before starting up, then feed forward so that the cutters merely plane off the projecting ends flush with the frame.

The position and size of the guides is governed by the size and construction of the frame. It could, in fact, simply be a series of separate blocks leaving gaps for untrimmed ends. A simpler form uses the same basic principle but with a loose spacing piece to ride against the fence and move with the frame. This is quicker to use than a sliding base, but is less stable and could allow the frame to dip into the fence gap.

For tenon trimming use upper and lower strip fences, or groove-out a wooden fence, so that the tenon projects into the gap. The cutter operates between the strips (or in the groove) and is flush with the outer face. To trim tenons flush with the frame simply feed the frames across the fence gap.

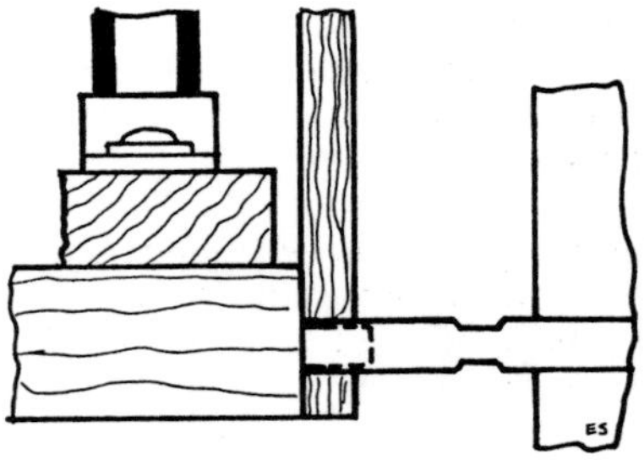

Fig. 244 Strip or slotted fence for tenon trimming.

CORNER ROUNDING

Frames can be corner-rounded by shaping with a template as described later, but if the round is a quarter of a true circle it can be formed using a pivotting jig. This is screw-pivotted to a wooden base fixed to the table, and to trim through 90 degrees. The pivot screw must be in line with the spindle arbor, and spaced from a planing block cutting circle a distance equal to the radius of curvature. The jig needs side guides to locate the workpiece at the correct distance from the pivot.

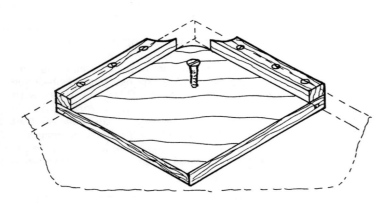

Fig. 245 This jig for corner-rounding has a wooden bed which pivots directly opposite the spindle cutterhead.

Set the spindle fences to control the 90 degree movement needed to form the quarter-round. The distance that the fence is set back from the cutting line equals the width of the side guides. To protect the cutterblock, fix a block across the fence gap immediately above the workpiece, or use a front guard.

Swing the jig against the outfeed fence. Fit the workpiece, clamping it if small or unstable, then simply rotate the two together counter-clockwise through 90 degrees to form the rounded corner.

Fig. 246
Left: Start the corner-round cut with the jig against the outfeed fence.

Right: Finish the corner-round cut with the jig against the infeed fence. The arrow shows the direction of movement.

Clamping isn't absolutely vital, and for faster operation the frame can be held up to the guides by hand pressure - but use a top Shaw guard. Make the cut with the grain by positioning the workpiece with the grain parallel to the fence when in the start position.

When the workpiece is a frame with cuts against the grain regardless of how it is machined, for the first cut rotate through only about 45 degrees before drawing clear out. Flip it over, then re-insert and finish-off the same corner to meet the first cut part-way round.

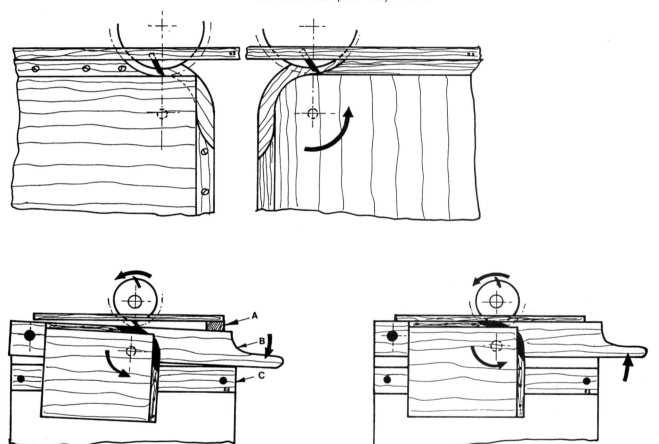

Fig. 247 If the cut is a heavy one, mount the corner-rounding jig on a pivot and swing out to insert a spacer A, then make a roughing cut. The jig is moved by handle B. Bed strip C remains fixed to give support.

Fig. 248 Final position with the spacer removed for the finishing cut.

If the radius is large and formed from a squared corner, relieve the main cut with a pre-cut. To do this pivot the jig on a base which itself pivots near the end of the outfeed fence. The technique in this case is to draw the jig away from the fence using a lever handle at the right-hand end and fit a spacing block to restrict movement towards the fence.

Fit the frame in position and make the pre-cut. Then move the assembly out, remove the spacing piece and repeat, this time machining the full depth. In addition to allowing a precut this alternative method also also allows the workpiece to be fitted and removed when well clear of the cutters, so it can be an added safety factor even when no pre-cut is needed.

EDGING CIRCLES

This uses a jig sliding between guides on a base fixed to the spindle table. The jig has a number of holes drilled in it for pivot centres to locate a turntable at various distances from the fence. Final size is controlled by the distance of the base from the fence.

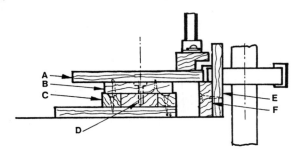

Fig. 249 Section through a sliding jig for making circular parts showing:
A – workpiece.
B – turntable.
C – fixed slide guide
D – base slide mounting the pivot.

The whole unit moves towards or away from the fence to give different diameters, and also has extra pivot holes.
The through–fence E is a necessary safety feature, and F is a support block fastened to the fence.

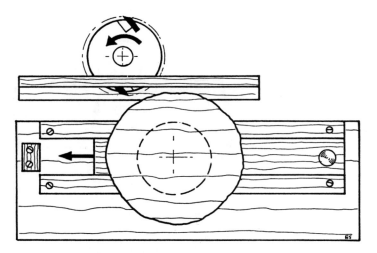

Fig. 250 Top view of the circular jig in the start position. The arrow shows the initial movement.

The turntable supports the piece being machined and holds it via several brads driven-in from the underside. A stop-block prevents further forward movement of the jig when the pivot is directly in line with the spindle. The spindle can have an edging or moulding head, and is broken through a fence in the normal way for a slightly deeper cut than the maximum amount needing trimming-off the rough parts. Use a top Shaw guard.

136

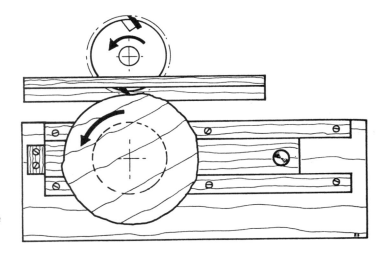

Fig. 251 Top view of the circular jig when rounding. The arrow shows the direction of movement.

Draw-back the jig so that the part can be positioned on the turntable whilst clear of the cutter. (Guide lines drawn on the base can show the proper position for the workpiece, or fix a shaped guide piece and jig stop at the infeed for more precise setting). Move the jig forward against the front-stop, holding the part steady and rotate the part counter-clockwise to trim it. Draw back before removing and reloading.

Plate 70 Profiling and sizing a sash frame on a Wadkin Bursgreen BEL/T spindle moulder provided with a rolling table and front support rail.

Plate 71 Edge moulding a sash frame on an SCM spindle moulder. It is also practical to use a template for sizing.

Plate 72 Whitney heavy-duty spindle moulder for complex shaping. Spindles run in opposite directions and the assembly is transferred between them.

Plate 73 An example of a good jigged template for edge profiling and moulding. The ring is slewed on this Startrite spindle moulder to give more support to the assembly. Note the hand-holds well clear of the cutters.

CHAPTER 12

SHAPING

Shaping is square-edging or edge-moulding solid timber, a frame, or a laminate to an outline shape. A follower, on or near the cutterhead, contacts a template fastened to the workpiece to control both shape and overal size, whilst the cutterhead edge-planes or moulds it.

Many different heads can be used for outside shaping. For inside shaping the cutterhead must be much smaller than the smallest curve to avoid snatch; also small cutterheads are easier to guard and safer to use on what is a dangerous operation.

The French Head was once popular for this, but it has a poor cutting action and is used only where no other head is suitable. Slotted collars are widely used in combination with a ball-bearing follower. Whitehill and circular planing heads are excellent, and matching ball-bearing followers are available. Solid profiled heads can be used, but there is a problem in matching them to a ball-bearing follower because their diameter grows less as they are ground down. Tipped profile heads reduce less and are better, but not ideal. Both can be used with a ring fence.

Square heads are not really suitable because they have a big bite and could snatch, particularly when cutting against the grain. Because the cutting circle is large they are difficult to guard and dangerous in use.

Disposable cutter type heads are fine for shaping as they have a small bite. Chip-limiting heads are exclusively used in Europe for all spindle moulder work and because they do not kick back they are very safe for shaping. They are rarely used in the UK as they are higher in cost and are more difficult to maintain than other types.

FEED DIRECTION

Feed must be against the rotation of the cutterhead when shaping. Never attempt climb or back cutting as a kick-back will almost certainly result. Take particular care when dropping-on or starting, as a shaped workpiece/template combination is more difficult to control than a straight mould.

It is possible with most outlines to shape and edge-mould at the same time. Alternatively the part can first be edged-planed to outline using a template, then the mould added as a second operation. (The jigs and templates all show shaping and edge-moulding at one operation, but all could be separated).

Shaping first, then edge-moulding later, divides the cut; it is a safer way of working because both cuts are lighter so there is less chance of kick-back; also the moulding cutters dull less because they remove less. Against this, of course, there are two separate operations. In moulding, it isn't essential to use the jigged template, instead the follower could contact the edge-planed section of the part. A deep enough section must remain against which the follower can run, or if not, moulding can be split into two operations. It is possible to make the second cut running the follower against the first mould; preferably a square cut such as a rebate. Where this is not practical, use the template both for initial shaping and later edge-moulding.

When edge-moulding without a template, it is essential instead to use a holding jig with secure handles. A holding jig, for example the general-purpose holding jig shown earlier, can be simpler and quicker to use than the original jigged template. Perhaps the easiest way, though, is to again use the jigged template, but not necessarily following the template outline against the follower.

TEMPLATE FOLLOWERS

The follower used in shaping, against which the template bears, can be one of three types: a table ring, a ball-bearing follower mounted on the arbor, or a ring fence.

Plate 74 Using a ring fence and cage guard on a Wadkin Bursgreen spindle moulder.

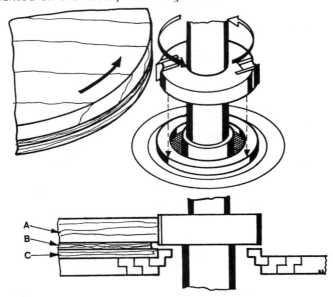

Fig. 252 Using an inverted table ring as a follower, showing:
A - the workpiece.
B - spacer.
C - template.

The upper sketch shows the cutterblock and jigged template raised so the ring is visible.

Guards are not shown but are essential for all work of this type. They are ommited from most sketches solely for clarity.
Use a bonnet or cage guard to enclose the cutterhead from table level, leaving a working gap wide and deep enough only to admit the workpiece and template.

TABLE RINGS

Most spindle moulders have table rings to fill in the gap between cutterhead and table. Some turn over so that a raised flange on them projects above table level to use as a template guide for an under-template. As the rings are absolutely concentric with the spindle, in theory, contact is possible from any side. In practice, however, there could be some slight eccentricity to produce slightly different cut depths at different points of contact. Planing cutterblock diameter must match precisely the ring diameter, and the template (or template plus spacer), must always be slightly thicker than the ring flange.

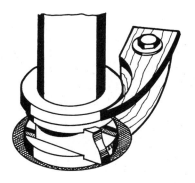

Fig. 253 Using a starting block with a slotted collar and ball-bearing follower. The block has a projecting section opposite the template, perhaps with a wear strip fitted.

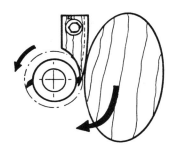

Fig. 254 Starting position when shaping using a ball-bearing follower and a starting block. Follow around the starting block to ease-in the cut.

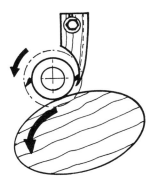

Fig. 255 Operating position, contact can be made at any point.

BALL-BEARING

Plain followers are not recommended as they give a rough feel to the work and tend to grab the template. A ball-bearing follower is commonly used and fits on the live spindle. Initially it spins with the spindle when started-up, but slows down to roll with the template when the two are in contact. This gives smooth and frictionless movement, probably the most sensitive of all the types used. The ball-bearing follower is absolutely concentric with the spindle so can be used from any direction without altering cut depth. This allows difficult shapes to be followed more easily than with a ring fence, for example, because contact does not have to be maintained at a precise point.

As with the table ring, cutterblock planing diameter must correpond with the ball-bearing diameter. This limits the heads that can be used to those with loose, adjustable cutters and disposable-cutter types. Most ball-bearing followers are used above the cutterhead with an over-template, but there is no reason why this could not be reversed.

Safe starting

Both the table ring and ball-bearing follower need a run-in to start the cut, otherwise the head snatches on first contact. With a part-outline template, a safe run-in is possible simply by extending the leading section of the template. Add pieces underneath at the leading and trailing ends and the side of the same thickness as the part to give stability. With a full-outline template, or when a part-outline template has no lead-in, use a starting block, the normal form of which is a comma-shaped piece of hardwood. This is fastened to the table to curve into the cutterhead level with and close to the follower. To fit close it may be necessary to pare the starting block away with the cutters.

The starting block should have a projecting wear strip to bear against the template. With this, rough timber makes no contact with the starting block, so movement is smooth when first starting the cut.

The block is normally fixed to the right-hand side (with counter-clockwise rotation) so that the cutterhead is accessible at the normal working position. The leading end of the template first contacts the block well clear of the cutterhead, then feeds clockwise around the curve to enter the cut in a controlled and safe manner. In a similar way, full outside shapes first contact the block and follow around the curve, without actually rotating, to enter the cut safely. Once fully in the cut the workpiece is rotated in the usual way.

An alternative is to use a loose nosing on the template to start the cut, but which easily pulls off during the shaping operation.

Inside shapes are a little more tricky. When working inside bull's eye windows and similar, the starting block must be small enough to avoid fouling the workpiece in operation. The

141

template first contacts the starting block, and is then shifted around the curve towards the head and rotated against the cut at the same time. This is not as easy as it sounds because grip on the assembly has to changed, and this could lead to a kick-back. Don't simply try to swing the assembly on the starting block, you must feed forward at the same time.

Fig. 256 Sometimes a loose nosing can be fitted to start the cut as an alternative to a starting block or ring fence. This must be secure in use, but easily pulled off during shaping.

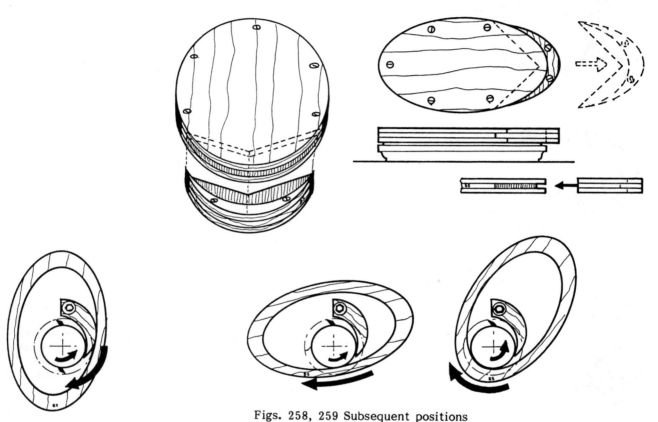

Figs. 258, 259 Subsequent positions in shaping an inside shape.

Fig. 257 Using a starting block with an inside shape.

There is a good case with inside shaping for an extra, rear starting block on almost the opposite side of the spindle, leaving working space between the two blocks. First contact the rear block at an angle to clear the cutterblock. To enter the cut, move the assembly across the cutterhead right to left, without rotating it, whilst retaining the same grip. The front block prevents the workpiece contacting the cutterhead except when intended.

An alternative method of safe starting with inside shaping is to fix a starting strip partially across across the outline which can be swung clear as the assembly is rotated.

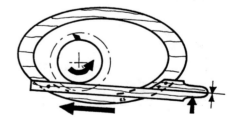

Fig. 260 Another way of starting an inside shape using a swivelling start strip. In starting the cut the strip is clamped manually against a fixed handle.

142

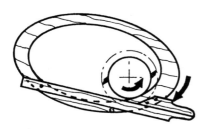

Fig. 261 Once in the cut the workpiece is rotated as normal.

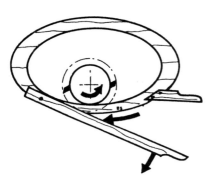

Fig. 262 The start strip is swung clear to complete shaping.

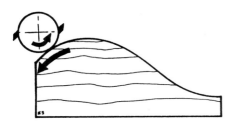

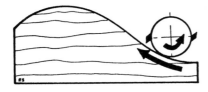

Figs. 265 In using a ball-bearing follower the point of contact doesn't matter. The template can be shaped without swinging it, so it is easier to use and there is little chance of inaccurate shaping.

RING FENCE

This is a ring surrounding the spindle and mounted on a support fastened to the table. The ring is eccentric, and with an operating point furthest from the support perhaps 5mm wide. This point is marked to show where template contact should be made. Set the ring eccentrically to the spindle so that cutters project the correct depth beyond the ring only at this point - at all other points cutter projection should be less or none at all. Because the ring is set to the cutterblock, whatever its diameter, any type of cutterblock can be used, and diameter reduction through wear is no problem.

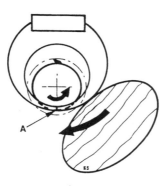

Fig. 263 Starting position with a ring fence; work around the fence without rotating the workpiece until opposite the operating point A.

The ring fence can be fitted above or below the cutterblock and is used as a ball-bearing follower combined with with gap-free starting blocks at both sides.

Start the cut by working around the infeed curve but, unlike a ball-bearing follower, once in the cut the template must contact the ring fence only at the marked point. If contact varies the outline will be wrong.

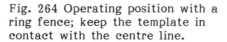

Fig. 264 Operating position with a ring fence; keep the template in contact with the centre line.

As contact must be maintained at the marked point, complex profiles are difficult to follow because the template has to be continuously swivelled. One example of a difficult shape is a serpentine or wavy-edge form. With a table ring or ball-bearing follower the assembly is fed roughly in a straight line whilst allowing the template to swing in and out to maintain contact, though at a constantly changing point.

STRAIGHT FENCE SHAPING

When forming outside curves it is practical and preferable to use a rigid hardwood strip fence across the false fence instead of using either a ball-bearing follower or a ring. Mark the fence with a clear vertical line directly opposite the spindle. Set cutters to this, and work against it, as with the centre mark on a ring fence.

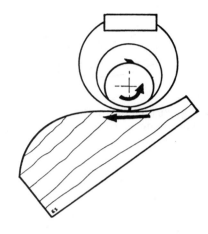

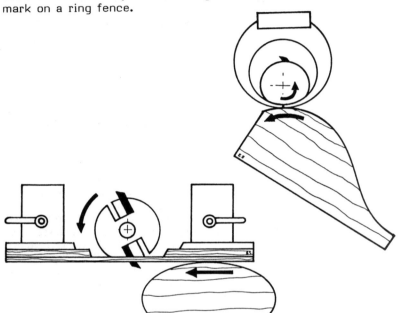

Fig. 266 In following a shape similar to this on a ring fence, swing the template around always to keep contact at the marked point - otherwise shaping will be inaccurate.

Fig. 267 Using a thick strip fence for outside shaping.

Above: Start the cut by feeding the assembly parallel to the fence without rotating it.

Below: Rotate when opposite the centre mark shape - as with a ring fence.

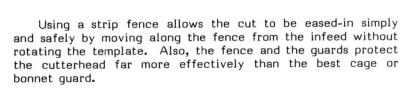

Using a strip fence allows the cut to be eased-in simply and safely by moving along the fence from the infeed without rotating the template. Also, the fence and the guards protect the cutterhead far more effectively than the best cage or bonnet guard.

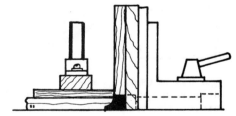

Fig. 268 Section through strip fence for shaping.

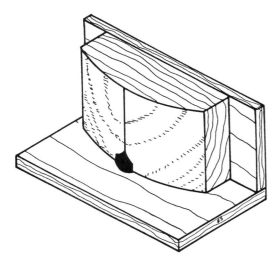

Fig. 269 Fence saddle and bed for true-circle inside curved work.

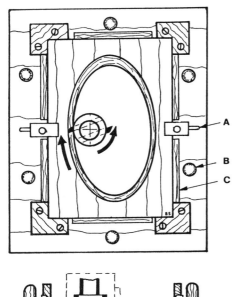

Fig. 271 A jigged template for an inside shape can be made large. This shows an under-template with clamps to hold down the workpiece A, push handles B, and finger guards C.

For the same reasons a fence saddle is better on shallow internal curves which form part of a true circle. Make the template to exactly the same curve. In this way both keep in full and stable contact as the template follows round, giving the same control as when straight moulding.

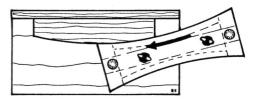

Fig. 270 The saddle should match the template to give stability in feeding.

TEMPLATE TYPES

There are two basic types of template; full-outline templates used to form the complete outer edge of a table top or an opening in a panel, for example, and part-outline templates used where only part of the outline is formed, examples are shaped chair legs and arms. Sometimes a full outline is formed at two separate set-ups using two templates. An example of this is the outer curve of a table leaf at one set-up, with a following set-up to form the straight folding bead on the matching edge. Each template in the latter case is a part-outline template. Templates can be used either above or below the workpiece. There are pros and cons for both, as explained later.

Full outline

These, used for forming a complete outside profile, are often flat templates fastened to the workpiece by brads. The template is made exactly the same shape and overall size as the part wanted. Any moulding on the workpiece must be inside the template outline with outside shapes, and outside the template outline with an inside or negative template (as used for the inside of porthole windows or an opening in a panel). Avoid the mistake of forming the template to the outline of the mould at it s full cutting depth.

Templates can be made from plywood or durable, rigid plastic. They must be perfectly flat, and thick enough to give full contact with the ball-bearing follower or ring fence when the cut is made. Allow the minimum overlap for the cutter so that it pares away only a small portion of the template edge, or fix a spacer between template and workpiece to allow more overlap. Fit handles and finger guards to aid feeding and to protect the operator. Make templates for inside shapes well oversize for stability and ease of handling.

Template size

A large template can become unstable when used on a spindle moulder with a small table. Before starting the cut make a trial run over the full movement (with the machine stopped) to check that the template does not overhang so much that it becomes unstable and tends to overbalance at any point. A ball-bearing follower needs less swinging about, so movement can be planned to avoid this, but take care in shaping to follow the same path each time. More template movement is needed with a ring fence, so check thoroughly before use. In some cases it may be an advantage to re-position the ring fence to give better support to the template assembly.

Make the edges of all templates accurate and smooth as even the smallest lump or notch repeats prominently on the finished workpiece. Fasten the template to the workpiece by brads. Make these from screws driven through the template and ground to a point so removal for sharpening and replacing is quick and simple. With solid timber, sharpen brads like a chisel and align then with the workpiece grain for ease of driving and so that the cut they form is less noticeable.

Fasten the workpiece and template together by tapping with a mallet when positioned; i.e., with the workpiece projecting beyond the template by an equal amount all round. For accurate registration use a fixed register block to locate both template and workpiece to one another. Take note that brads are not absolutely reliable in securing the workpiece. With very heavy cuts use two part-outline templates instead which allow toggle clamps to be used.

Small and medium workpieces with a full outline should not be worked individually, it is dangerous. Preferably handle them two or more up using a much bigger template, forming only two sides at one pass on a multi-station jigged template rather than the whole outline. This makes the whole thing safer and allows easy fitting of handles and guards on both over and under templates. See multi-station jigs.

When the jigged template needs unloading and reloading on machines with small tables, move the assembly to workbench alongside and at the same height by sliding it along. Doing this is more convenient because there is more room, and safer because it is clear of the cutterhead which is usually left running. (The guards used in shaping rarely give complete protection when the template is out of position).

Guards

Set a Shaw guard at the point of cut with pressure light enough to keep control without making movement difficult. Preferably wax the the table to make movement smooth, also the underside of the template if used template-down. The Shaw guard should only make contact outside the maximum cutting circle with top templates, or it could tip the assembly during the final cut to snatch and possibly throw-back.

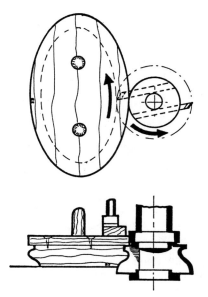

Fig. 272 Using an over-template fitted with handles.

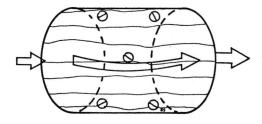

Fig. 273 For small parts use a double-size template and switch from one section to the other to complete the work.

Plate 75 Edge sanding a part on a Scheppach spindle moulder prior to adding the moulding.

Plate 76 Inside shaping on a Delta light duty spindle moulder with a Safe Guard 11 mounted directly on the spindle arbor. This gives protection together with an excellent view of the work.

With a top template fit handles to the top surface for grip, also finger guards in case of slippage, but both must clear the Shaw guard. Handles are an essential safety feature with all templates. They should afford a firm and dependable grip for the user, well clear of the cutters and guard in case of kick-back. Position them to give proper and complete control in shaping, fitting more than two on a full-outline template to allow easy grip-change during the cut. Never hold the toggle clamps to control the jig; they are uncomfortable to grip and could accidently release during the cut if the user is distracted. Fit and use control handles.

A cage guard is essential with all shaping operations. This should neatly fit around the cutterhead down to table level except for a small working gap, also above template level at this point. Make sure the cage guard gap is only wide enough to allow the assembly to be swept around comfortably without fouling. This is especially troublesome on internal work.

A cage guard restricts the cut to a small segment of the head, but this is normal practice in any case with a ring fence. A ball-bearing follower and table ring can both be used through 360 degrees in theory, but this is only theory. In practice, contact is always made roughly within the same small arc for ease of operation, so again this is not too restrictive.

Before starting the cut with any shaped work make a practice run with the machine switched-off to make sure nothing interferes with smooth movement. Take care to repeat exactly the same path in shaping.

Because guards restrict sight of the cutterhead, the spindle is sometimes worked without a guard when shaping. The reason usually given is that the cutterhead can be seen more clearly without a guard, taking the view that something dangerous has to be watched. Older guards were poor in this respect, but modern ones have clear protective panels which allow viewing but still provide good protection. Shaping is a dangerous operation, much more than straight moulding, so don't attempt to shape unless both a Shaw guard and a cage guard are fitted, even when making a trial cut in setting.

Template position

A template above the workpiece partially guards the cutterblock to make operation safer, and allows handles and finger guards to be easily fitted. When the cut is deep and the workpiece small the assembly may not be stable when fully machined, so use an under-template as this has a larger bearing area. Make sure that the template is flat on the table before contacting the follower, or it could ride over the top with disastrous results. As a protection against this it is absolutely essential to use a Shaw guard.

An under-template must be truly flat and with its top face absolutely parallel to the underside, otherwise the mould face-alignment varies. It isn't possible to use any form of handle or guard when working template down (except when shaping an open frame or a part-outline template), so grip and guarding is much more difficult. Only use these with large parts that allow hand-grip for proper control well clear of the cutterhead - in case of kick-back.

Part outline types

Part-outline templates are used to form workpieces along only part of the outline at a single pass. They can be similar to full-outline types as a simple brad-held template, but it is better to use a jigged form of template. These are much safer to use because the jig can be physically bigger than a simple outline jig and easier and safer to handle. Also finger guards and handles can be fitted with less restriction. The simplest form has an over-template with spacers underneath level with the workpiece so that the assembly lies flat and stable when starting the cut.

It is possible to fix the workpiece simply by brads - after projecting it the proper amount beyond the template. As width can vary doing this, preferably fit back and end blocks to quickly and precisely locate the part. A full-length back fence can be used, but blocks near to each end and against the ends are usually enough. If the ends of the workpiece are square it may be possible to use a toggle type end-clamp against one end with the opposite end against a block and with brads in both.

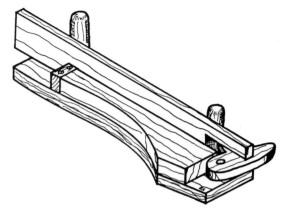

Fig. 274 General view of a typical jigged template for a part-outline shape, fitted with handles and finger guards.

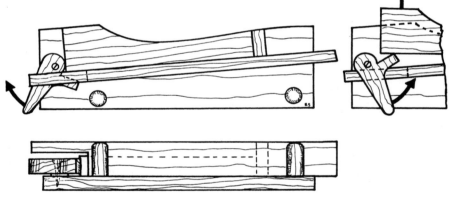

Fig. 275 Sketches of the template jig shown above. The eccentric clamp pulls the part back against the fence in fitting, then kicks it clear when shifted the opposite way. Use the handles to move the jig, never the clamp.

The assembly can be made as a jigged template on a substantial base with the workpiece sandwiched between base and template. In this form it is normal to fit toggle clamps against the ends or to act vertically through cut-outs in the template. An alternative form has the base as template with back and end blocks fitted to the topside where the workpiece sits clamped in place. This type is easy to load and can have top toggle clamps for speedy operation. Make sure any gaps at the ends of, or between, parts are filled-in, and with finger guards for protection when the jig is not fully loaded. In this way the cutterblock is never exposed when the jig is in position.

148

Allowance for lead-in

When the template is the same length of the workpiece the cut starts at the full depth, so use either a ring fence or a starting block to enter the cut. It is easier and safer to extend the template at start and finish to allow run-in and out with the template in full contact with the follower, but with cutters clear of the workpiece. Make end blocks with an over-template the same thickness as the workpiece to make the assembly stable. Project them slightly beyond the cutting line as a support to reduce break-out when cutting against the grain or working brittle timbers.

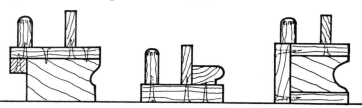

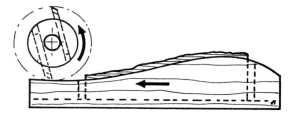

Fig. 276 Various types of jigged template to the general form shown below. The template itself is extended to lead in and out safely.

The sketches above show:
Left: Template above.
Centre: Template below.
Right: Box-type jigged template.

MULTIPLE JIGS

Part-outline jigs need not be for a single profile only. It is practical to form two or more profiles on the same jig using two or more work-stations. If a narrow workpiece needs two edges moulded it is safer and more efficient to mount both on the same jig and edge-mould both in following passes.

An example is a narrow table leg moulded both edges. A simple double-edged template could be used for this, but could be unstable. Also the leg must be carefully positioned or the shape and edge-planing many not marry.

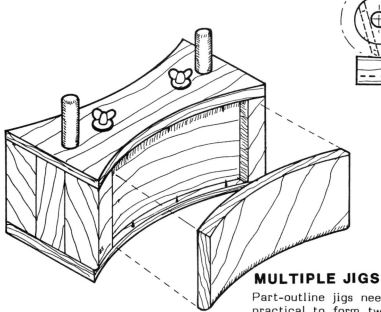

Fig. 277 Double-sided template for moulding chair rail corner-rounds using the fence saddle shown in Figs 269 and 270.

An alternative way is to form a double-width template with opposing edges formed to the two outlines wanted, which need not be the same profile. Separate back and end blocks should precisely locate both workpieces for each cut. Both legs are fitted, one in one station and the second in the other, then the two outer edges are formed at consecutive passes without stopping the machine.

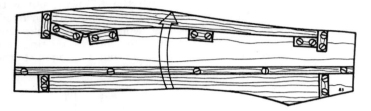

Fig. 278 Double-width jigged template for inner and outer leg profiles.

Where the edge-profile is formed along the full length, seat this against shaped blocks in the second station. In making the initial first pass fit legs at both stations, but only edge-mould that in the first station. Remove the part-finished leg and fit in the second station, fit a blank in the first station then edge-mould both. Repeat this sequence for the full run. To keep the final cut stable re-fit a finished leg in the first station but do not shape it.

Fig. 279 Double-width template for handling narrow parts safely. Both form the same shape. Shape small parts two or more up for safety; separate after shaping.

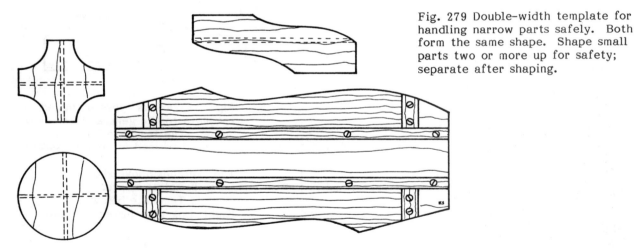

Templates of this type are stabler because they rest either on a wider base when template down, or on two parts side-by-side when template up. It is also easier to fit finger guards and handles. Because parts locate against blocks replacement is quick and alignment precise. When used for handling parts too small to fully shape individually, part form at one station, then transfer between stations to complete. Where parts are very small, shape them two or more up for safety, then separate later.

CUTTING AGAINST THE GRAIN

Shaping often involves cutting against the grain at some point because grain never follows the profile wanted. Wherever possible timber should be chosen, prepared and worked so that most of the cut is with the grain. In this case a normal hand-feed speed is used for most of the cut, slowing down only where against the grain to reduce tear-out to an acceptable level.

Fig. 280 Using separate jigged templates to cut always with the grain when forming an oval shape. Arrows show the cut directions.

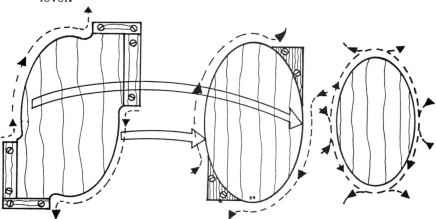

Where workpieces are moulded both edges and the finished product is wedge-shaped in overall appearance; for example, the tapering sides of a magazine rack, it makes sense to form the two edges at separate operations rather than forming both at a single handling where one cut is always against the grain. On a part-outline form for either square-planing or a symmetrical edge-moulding, such as a bull-nose, there are two choices: either use two single-edged templates arranged to cut with the grain and switch the part to complete it, or, a single jigged template switching parts edge for edge and inserting loose spacers for position.

Stacked jig

A stacked jig can be used to shape workpieces two-up and back-to-back forming opposing cuts on both pieces at the same time. A double-depth cutterhead is needed with a jigged template on a wide base. Use toggle clamps to secure the workpieces in place, with double-depth back and end blocks or fences. Make the template profile to feed mainly with the grain. Fit side and end blocks to locate for the second operation directly on the base, with blocks for first operation fixed on these.

Make two cuts at a single pass and remove both pieces. Re-fit the first cut (top) part directly on the base after flipping, fit a blank on top, then clamp and shape. Repeat as needed. The same method can be used as an alternative to the double template, but is more trouble to load and unload.

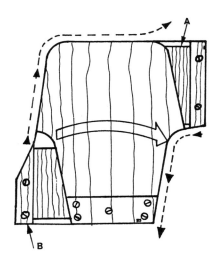

Fig. 281 Arrows show the cut directions to mould with the grain using a single jigged template. Flip the part to repeat the same cuts on sections not previously shaped. Mark the template for second-cut position, or use loose spacers A against side guides B.

151

The method is fine if the workpieces are consistant in thickness and perfectly flat. If there are any irregularities in the bottom piece, the top part miss matches even if the piece itself is perfect.

Paired shapes

A simple template with brad fittings to fit either face can produce shapes in true pairs. Use one way up for one hand and complete the initial run. Flip the template and reverse the brads to the opposite face for the opposing hand, and complete the opposite hand workpieces. By doing this, cuts are with the grain in both cases. This is no problem with brads made from end-sharpened screws, simply screw these out and insert from the reverse face after flipping. End blocks must also be fitted on the reverse face.

All the above jigs assume that most of the cut is with the grain and that slowing down the feed is enough to avoid tearing-out on those sections when feed is against the grain. On some timbers and certain outlines this method does not give acceptable results, so possibly use a sandwich template.

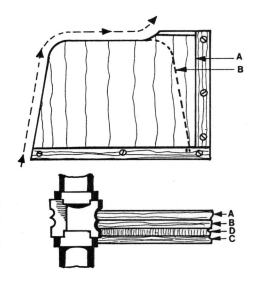

Fig. 282 Forming cuts with the grain on a stacked template. The part for the first cut is A, for the second cut B, whilst C is the template and D a spacing piece.

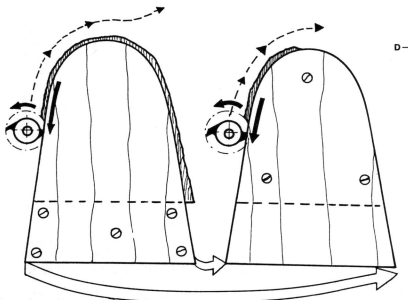

Fig. 283 Sequence of cuts on a sandwhich template showing one template A, the second C, part B and locating fence D by which the two halves are locked together.

Sandwich template

This is a double template with the part sandwiched between. First shape all sections where the cut is with the grain by dropping-in and running out, then flip the template and run in the opposite direction to complete those sections of the outline where the cut is now with the grain.

152

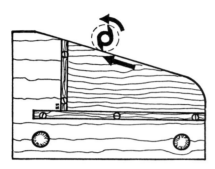

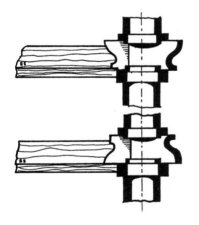

Fig. 284 Two ways of forming paired parts both to cut with the grain. The upper sketches show separate settings for each, and the lower one a double set-up with stacked parts.

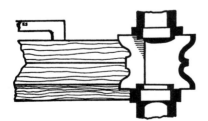

An example is when shaping an oval table leaf to a bull-nose. The first cut is made from the centre towards the trailing end. The assembly is then flipped over to repeat the cut from the centre towards what originally was the leading end but which now trails. The same applies with a part-circular cut-out on, perhaps, an inwardly-curved dressing table top. In this case, start the cut at the leading end and finish at the centre, then flip and repeat.

Absolute alignment of separate full-outline templates can be difficult in regular workshop practice because they must separate completely. One method is to use a register block fixed to a bench and shaped to the reverse of the template outlines and rough workpiece. The rough workpiece and both templates are pressed against this to align them before fastening together with brads. However, alignment can easily be out to show prominently as a mis-match. Alignment also needs repeating precisely and individually for each part. Being made-up of three separate pieces the various parts can shift in used. For safety's sake use a full-outline sandwich template only on light cuts and with any open frame through which screws can clamp both halves together.

With heavy cuts preferably use a part-outline sandwich template which can have secure toggle clamps, and form the outline at two passes. Part-outline templates align precisely because the two halves fasten together via the back fence and blocks. Regular fixed brads cannot be used, so use screw-in brads which are flush with the surface when driven in. Brads must be screwed bolts with precise, turned centre-points, otherwise they shift the workpiece on fixing. There is no need for brads at both sides, simply fit the workpiece when the brad screw heads are uppermost for fitting, then flip as needed.

The templates need not be identical, so it is practical to automatically feed in or out where cut-direction changes by slightly modifying the two outlines. This type is easy to use, simply follow the profile. Operation is quick as there is no danger of cutting against the grain accidently. Take care that the template not in use is well clear of the cutters, or other parts where it could foul, during the full shaping movement whilst using the other template.

A serious problem with sandwich templates is that control handles must be screw-in types that can be switched quickly from one face to the other when flipping the template. This adds considerably to the cost of making, and is a nuisance to the user however easy change-over might be. But handles are an essential safety feature - do not shape without them.

Single-sided types

A single-sided part-outline template can be used to form opposing cuts if the shape is symmetrical both in outline and profile. An example is a full table top moulded to a bull-nose profile. With non-symmetrical moulds use two set-ups, or stack parts and use a double-depth cutter.

TWO-SPINDLE OPERATION

The traditional way to cut with the grain regardless of outline is to use a two-spindle machine, one spindle rotating in one direction and the other in the opposite. Both spindles mount identical cutterheads when the cut is symmetrical, but need opposing profiles with non-symmetrical moulds. Both can run at the same time, though it is safer to run only one, and the workpiece is transferred between them as needed so that all cuts are made with the grain.

This technique easily gives the best results and the shortest handling times, but there are some disadvantages. Apart from the obvious one that a two-spindle machine and two sets of cutters are needed, opposing cuts are in opposite directions so extra dexterity is needed on the operator's part to work alternately right hand or left hand without error and with a smooth feed movement.

With a double spindle, the second spindle creates an extra hazard even when not operating; so take care not to swing the assembly to foul it. Regardless of profile, a one-piece template is normally used. Clearly mark this to show points between which opposing cuts are made. The operator then enters and exits the cut as needed. Some form of lead-in is essential using either an eccentric ring fence or a starting block.

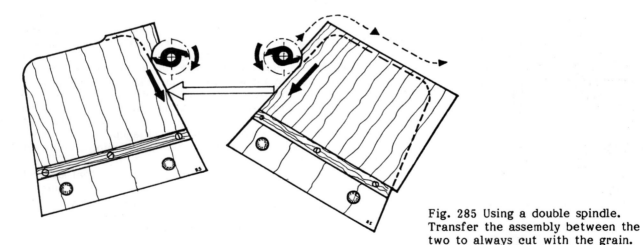

Fig. 285 Using a double spindle. Transfer the assembly between the two to always cut with the grain.

To make operation safer and error impossible set the two template followers at slightly different heights to each contact a different level of a double-stacked template. Make each template to a slightly different profile to incorporate automatic feed in and out where needed. At the change-over positions where both cuts are parallel to the grain the two templates are level, but could cross mid-way at a slight angle to merge better.

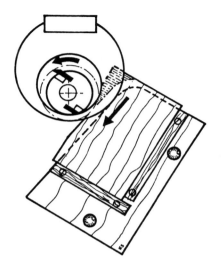

Fig. 286 Easing a heavy cut by first shaping against on off-centre section of the ring fence, above. The final cut is shown below.

CUT-RELIEVING

Where sweeps are gentle the full cut depth can be shaped at a single setting, however, a deep cut chances a kick-back and it is better to cut-relieve before the final pass, perhaps in a pre-shaping cut, using a ring fence. If making a rounded corner from a square, for example, first mill-out the weight by feeding whilst in contact with the ring well clear of the centre mark. Then move nearer to repeat, and so on, until only a light cut remains for the final cut. An alternative is to make the full cut at two passes, setting for a smaller first cut by using a larger diameter collar, or resetting the ring and handling the workpieces twice. The method is rather messy and takes much longer than normal, but it is okay for short runs.

A common way to cut-relieve prior to shaping is to band-saw into shaped blanks which previously have been outlined in pencil using the template or finished part as a guide. Cutting blanks first into regular squared shapes might seem a nice tidy way of doing things but it can be uneconomical. Complex shapes could well interlock and save timber if marked directly-on a wide board. Don't simply place the template guide always in a regular pattern; move it around or even flip it to get more pieces out; it doesn't usually matter provided the run of the grain is correct. Mark around the template or guide using a thick pencil to allow enough overlap to clean-up fully on shaping.

In bandsawing, the drawn outline is followed only roughly, taking care not to cross the line. It is also possible to first divide-up the board roughly into blanks each with a single piece, then fit to a template and use as a bandsaw guide. Fit a small pin to the guide in line with the bandsaw teeth and about 3mm to the right-hand side. Move the template around to always line-up with the next immediate section of cut and feed to keep template and pin in light contact.

Fig. 287 Left: The correct grain direction.
Centre and left: Incorrect grain direction which allows sections to readily break off.

Set-out as shown at the extreme left to bandsaw.

It is essential to get the grain direction right with solid timber, or the parts may be short-grained, i.e., with corners that easily break-off. Generally, the curve should by tangential to the grain, roughly to follow the grain at the centre point of the curve. Curved parts often interlock when cut from a board.

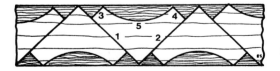

Thin plywood gives no problems in grain direction. Often several pieces can be bandsawn and shaped at the same time by nailing from one side, then nailing the template from the reverse face to make the pack secure. If curves are part of a true circle a pivotted jig can be used in bandsawing.

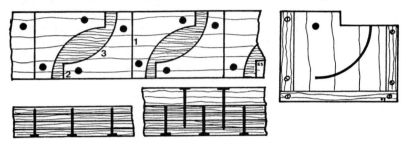

Fig. 289 Left: Jig for bandsawing curves on a pivotting jig.
Right: The initial square-in cut .

Fig. 288 There is more layout scope with plywood. Nail several sheets together for bandsawing and shaping as a single piece. Nail on the template from the opposite side.

When shaping fragile parts such as glazing beads for a decorative door opening light, use the same jig for shaping and bandsawing as following operations. Make the blanks over-long, and clamp vertically, between side guides. Use a simple gauge to project the sawn piece the proper amount to cleanup in the shaping operation. Following the sequence shown makes the beads absolutely parallel when bandsawn. Finally sand flat the seating face using a bobbin sander.

CURVE ON CURVE WORK

The most intricate and dangerous work on a spindle moulder has curves in two planes. It could be assumed that with CNC and floating head routers now used for this, hand work is no longer needed, but this is not always the case. If proper jigs and fixtures are made it is possible to operate curve on curve work in reasonable safety. The methods that are used are not always theoretically correct, but give acceptable results. Three specific points need noting:

Firstly, do not use square-in cutter profiles, such as rebates, as the cutters score the surface at other points. Always form cutter shapes at an angle to avoid fouling other parts, See Figs. 312 and 315 relative to simple sweeps.

Secondly, when forming curves to the top or under faces blend them with the same angle to level. This moulds an acceptable junction line even though a true blend isn't possible. Do not attempt a perfect blend, the result will disappoint.

Finally, to reduce errors to the minimum, use a small diameter head and a large diameter saddle, curve or ring fence.

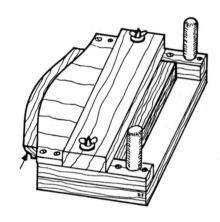

Fig. 290 Above: Jig for shaping, then bandsawing, narrow glass beads and similar. The arrow shows a moulded bead ready for bandsawing off.

Below: The upper sketch shows the moulding operation. The lower sketch shows the following bandsawing cut. Note the bandsaw guide pin at A.

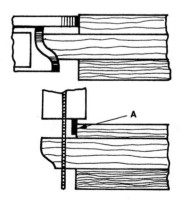

Fig. 291 The base saddle for curve on curve work fixes to the machine table with the cutterhead opposite the lowest point of the sweep.

Chair backs

Some chair back rails are typical of curve on curve work. The first process is to square-edge shape the rail, but without the mould. (To combine edge-shaping and moulding is difficult in the extreme and makes the operation unnecessarily dangerous. Whether bentwood, laminate, or shaped, the rails rarely match one another exactly, nor do they form part of a true circle. Any template would be very complicated for this reason and never satisfactory.)

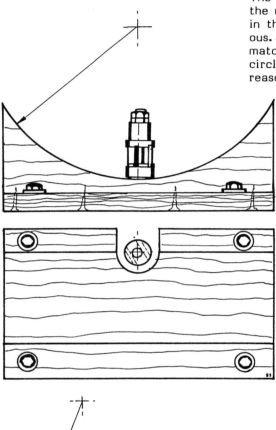

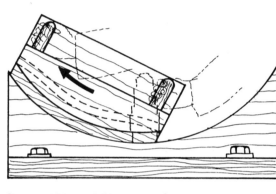

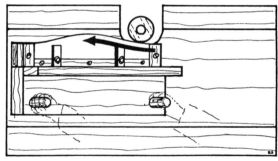

Fig. 293 In rocking the jig, keep it parallel to the base edge whilst following the ball-bearing.

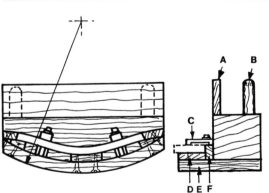

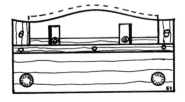

Fig. 292 The rocking carriage seats the chair rail on blocks D, held down by clamps C and back against rear fence F. The curved base E is also the template. Handles B and a finger guard A are essential.

157

To edge-shape and plane use a rocking jig which roughly follows the chair rail curve. Make the contact face of the jig a true part-circle. Support the chair rail on blocks and against end-stops so that it lies more or less evenly, then clamp in place. The underside of the jig is also the template and must be edge-shaped to the required rail profile. Fix a finger guard and handles to the outside.

The jig rocks on a shaped seating formed in a base fixed to the machine table. The base should partially wrap around the cutterhead at the deepest point of the sweep. Use a small-diameter cutterhead with the follower beneath the head and level with the template of the rocking jig.

The jig is moved around the curved seating and simultaneously in and out to keep the template against the ball-bearing follower so that the cutters edge-mill the rail to profile. Before starting the cut make a dummy run to ensure that the template can maintain full contact with the follower. The jig must not swivel in any way in rocking, it must always move in and out, parallel to the base edge. This is why a ball-bearing follower is needed; a ring fence would not give the proper outline. Cutters must be much deeper than the thickness of the chair rail and perfectly square to the table because the rail edge height varies in shaping. Wax both jig underside and base topside to keep movement smooth.

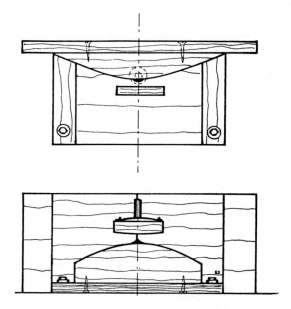

Fig. 294 Top and front views of a bed and fence saddle used for moulding chair-back rails.

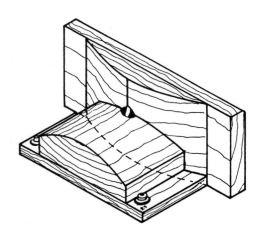

Fig. 295 General view of the fence and bed saddle set-up.

The second operation is to add the mould using a very small diameter cutter such as a router cutter. Shape a bed saddle to a curvature side to side but level front to back. The curve should be slightly less than the smallest internal face-curve in the rail. Fasten it to the table with the top dead centre of the curve directly opposite the cutterhead. Also fix a saddle to the fence to match the smallest edge-curve and with the highest point central to the cutterhead. Break through the bed and fence saddles by raising the cutter to line up as shown. Mark the contact point clearly on the fence saddle. Fit a top Shaw guard pad with a curved undersurface.

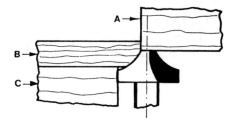

Fig. 296 The rounding cut on the rail at B is made on a bed saddle C and a fence saddle A.

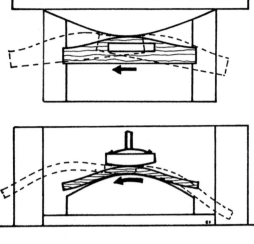

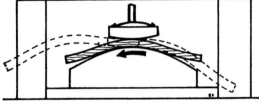

Feed the rail inside-curve down on the table saddle, always so that the section opposite the cutterblock lies level. Swivel it to keep the template in contact with the highest point of the fence saddle, as with a ring fence. It is technically wrong to swivel the rail as shown, but there is no other choice, and the distortion this gives is of little consequence.

Fig. 297 In feeding keep the rail curve-down, level with the table at the contact point and touching the contact point of the fence saddle.

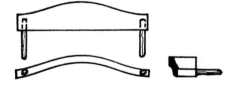

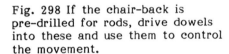

Fig. 298 If the chair-back is pre-drilled for rods, drive dowels into these and use them to control the movement.

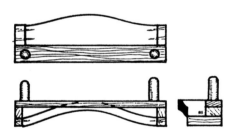

Preferably a holding jig should be used to control the chair back, having clamps or other fastening means and control handles. Allow extra length for screwing or driving-in through brads from end plates on the jig. Alternatively, if the rail is pre-drilled for chair rods, temporarily insert control handles in these holes. A holding jig should be made so as not to foul the saddle - unless under-profiled to the same shape of the chair rail, in which case it could add stability to the operation.

Fig. 299 Screw-on holding jig. Use the turned screw shown in Fig. 216 to end-clamp and pierce the part with the brad point to give extra holding power.

Stair handrails

These are amongst the most difficult parts to machine and often caused accidents when they were regularly produced on badly-guarded machines. The twisted section of handrail joining two handrails square to one another on a kite-tread turning is probably the worst type, as each is individual according to the stair layout and distance in from the fulcrum of the kite treads.

It should be a quarter turn in plan view, but from any other viewpoint the finished handrail appears twisted. Plan for a quarter turn which is not too tight, then vertically measure the height from the joint of the lower handrail to that on the upper handrail.

The first process is to bandsaw the vertical inside and outside faces to the quarter turn shape shown in plan view. Use a pivotting jig for this. Make two cuts in it as a guide to size and to position the block.

Fit a support to angle the block to the height measurement taken, allowing overhang for later trimming. It is difficult to be certain of the proper size without complex geometry, so make trial cuts in scrap pieces before cutting the piece selected.

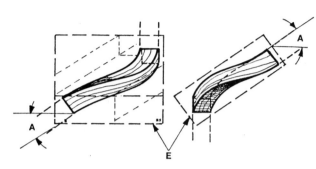

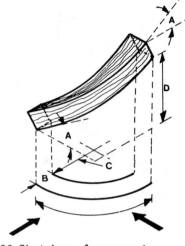

Fig. 300 Sketches of a curved handrail showing:
A - stair rake angle.
B - handrail width.
C - inside radius.
D - distance from lower to upper handrail.

The left and centre sketches are horizontal views in the direction of the arrows on the right-hand sketch.

The grain on the block should be diagonal to generally follow the handrail curve. Cross-cut the board at about 45 degrees to produce either true squares or, to use less timber, squares but with inside and outside diagonal corners missing.

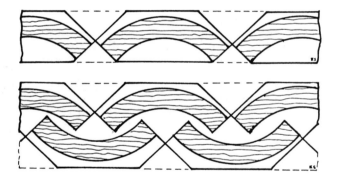

Fig. 301 Typical layouts for cutting handrails from wide and narrow boards.

For the bandsaw cuts fix a pivot square to the bandsaw but at different distances from it to produce the two radii. Do this by having two pivot seatings in a clamp-on base, or use a fixed position on the base and re-set the base sideways. Stop the first cut short of breaking through to keep the block in one piece for the second cut. Stop the bandsaw before drawing back so that the blade is not accidently pulled-off its wheels.

Separate the parts, then replace the handrail alone on the bandsaw jig in its original position and carefully mark out the angle and depth of the matching stair rail at top and bottom along the inner curve. Join the lines with fair and parallel curves to blend into the drawn angles. The curves vary considerably from one staircase to another so only general guides can be given.

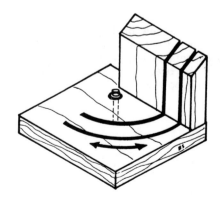

Fig. 302 Pivotting jig used in bandsawing.

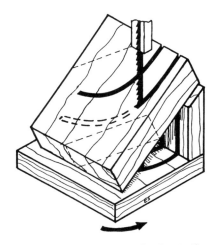

Fig. 303 Support the block at the correct angle. Follow the plan view of the curves in bandsawing by setting the pivot square to the bandsaw blade.

Fig. 304 The final top and bottom cuts are made on the bandsaw to follow the lines drawn on the inside curve. Keep the handrail flat on the table at the saw.

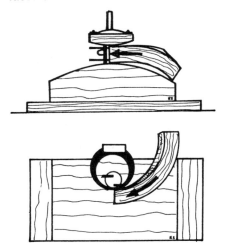

Make the final bandsaw cuts for the top and bottom faces of the handrail by following these drawn lines. Keep the section where the saw actually cuts flat on the bandsaw table by following a curved path in feeding. Finally, clean-up and size the handrail on a disc and bobbin sander using a shaped saddle similar to that shown for moulding. This is very much a hand trial and error operation. Controlling jigs and templates would be so complex as to be impractical, and would, in any event, vary from stair to stair.

The final operation is moulding the rail on a table saddle, held down by a shaped Shaw guard to run against a double ring fence. The saddle should have a single curve only side to side with the top dead-centre section opposite the cutterhead and level front to back. Some use à double-curved saddle or pudding-bowl, but this type is extremely unstable and dangerous to use.

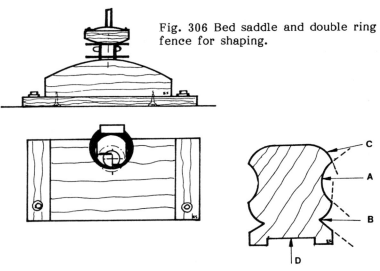

Fig. 306 Bed saddle and double ring fence for shaping.

Fig. 305 In moulding the handrail make cuts in the sequence A, B, C. The groove at 'D' is the baluster seating.

Fig. 307 Top and front views of the shaping operation showing the starting position.

Use only the type of saddle shown, together with a small-diameter cutterhead and the largest diameter rings which will follow the inner curve of the handrail. Set one ring above and the other below the cutterhead to contact the side of the handrail. Guard the cutterhead with a cage guard open only at the front between the ring fences. Form the mould one small section at a time starting from the centre and working out to retain contact with both rings for all except the final top cut.

Feed the handrail underside down. Keep it level at the point of contact and in contact with the marked point of the top ring. For the final top cut, run top surface down, and with both rings set to contact suitable points on the profile. On a fully top-rounded handrail do not attempt to meet on centre when using a saddle. This ensures that the part remains stable during moulding. Leave the overlap for hand finishing. Form the inside curve first and the outside curve as the final cut.

Bear in mind always that this is a dangerous operation, take great care to check and double-check before making any cut. If practicable fasten a rigid holding jig to the ends of the handrail and with fitted handles to give better and safer control. Similar methods can be used to those shown in making curve-on-curve rails.

Jigging for curved handrails

The type of handrail described above is only used with kite treads. The more common types, which are easier to make, are used on stairways with quarter or half-space landings at the turns. The sketch shows a U-turn on a staircase with a halfspace landing laid-out so that only a single curve is used at any point, either a level quarter turn or an up or down sweep. Usually each section is made individually for bolting together with handrail bolts.

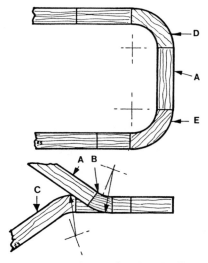

Fig. 308 Sections of a handrail:
A - straight sections.
B - short upsweep.
C - downsweep and straight section.
D & E - level quarter turns.

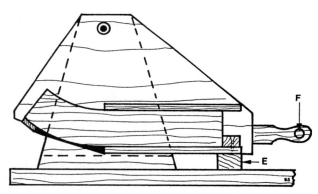

The level quarter turn inside and outside faces can be handled flat with conventional jigged templates of the types previously described. After planing and bandsawing, shape and mould them on jigged templates using a small diameter cutterhead and a ring fence. Use separate wide-based templates to form the inner and outer curves individually for safer handling.

The same machine setting is used, first completing the inside curve, then using the second jig for the outside curve. (The inner curve has more contact with the cutterhead, so the assembly needs to be as stable as possible for this first cut.) Because the jigs are used interchangeably make sure they match perfectly for height and size. Volutes and similar are formed in more or less the same way, but using router cutters and preferably a router.

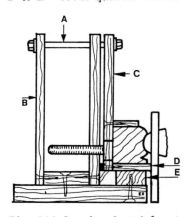

Fig. 309 Sectional and front views of a sliding base and carriage for moulding up and downsweeps, either as short curves as an extension of a straight section, showing:
A - pivot.
B - support frame.
C - swinging carriage.
D - bearing strip.
E - levelling block.
F - extended control handle for the swinging carriage.

162

The edge profile on the up and down sweeps cannot be moulded flat on a jigged template. The top and bottom curved faces can by moulded flat, after bandsawing, using two jigged templates, generally as for quarter turns. It is also possible, and very convenient at this stage, to form the centre groove for the balusters and the central section of the top curve on the handrail. Form these at a following operation to square-edge shaping, possibly using the same jigged templates.

For side or edge moulding use fixtures similar to that shown. It consists of a sliding base with two vertical supports carrying a substantial horizontal pivot. Hung from this pivot is the carriage for the handrail, with the distance from pivot to handrail correct for the curvature wanted. This can usually be made a standard dimension.

The carriage supports the handrail in a trough and against an end-stop for precise location. If several rails are being machined, end-trim them precisely to the same length relative to the curve, as they have to be re-fitted several times. Form the underside of the trough and the end support for the curved section as a rubbing strip to bear against the fence. Lock the rail in place by captive brads through the top section of the trough. Fit a block to support the carriage when the handrail is level.

Fit controlling handles both to the carriage and to the sliding jig. Fit and break through a fence for each cut, gauging the height from a section tacked or drawn onto the leading end of the handrail. Fully mould one side before forming the opposite using a separate fixture, but make sure both fixtures correspond. A fixture could be made to mould both curve-leading and curve-trailing sides, but this might be unwieldy if the level sections are long.

Work the mould in the sequences shown, matching to the previously formed central top curve at the final cut. Always work with an upward curve; top 'up' with an upsweep and top 'down' with a downsweep.

When the curve leads, first position the pivot directly opposite the cutterhead and fix a backstop behind the sliding base. Check that the proper movements are possible before making the cut, then mould as follows. Raise the carriage by its handle to clear the cutters when the sliding base is pulled back against the backstop. Holding the sliding base back and with the rubbing strip in contact with the fence, start-up the spindle and gradually lower the carriage making a sweeping cut until level, then hold the carriage handle down and feed forward against the fence until clear of the cutters.

Try to make to make the level cut a continuation of the curved sweep so that no static-cut marks are formed. It is possible to interlock the fixture so that forward movement is impossible until the handrail is level and in contact with the stop. This consists of a curved stop fastened to the infeed fence to follow the path of the extended handle of the carriage in moving. The only gap is at the level position.

When the curve trails fix a front stop for the sliding jig to locate it with the pivot directly opposite the cutterhead. This time hold the carriage handle down, starting the cut clear of the cutterhead to the right.

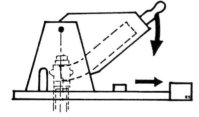

Fig. 310 Starting position for a leading curve.

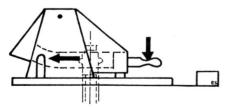

Fig. 311 Level run.

163

Feed forward until against the front stop, then, holding the sliding jig down, gradually raise the carriage handle until the rail clears the cutters. Again try to make it a continuous cut from level to curve and out. Fit a spring latch to hold the carriage when raised to allow the machine to be stopped in safety. An interlock is possible using a level rail fixed to the fence to contact the extended carriage handle and with a gap only when the sliding jig is against the stopblock.

The up and down sweeps described extend into straight sections when used for spanning short distances. The same part is also made as a curve only. In this case the same jig is used but is fixed in position opposite the cutterblock. With both types the curvature is always extended beyond the point actually needed to allow trimming on site. By doing this the precise angle of the stairway does not need to be known. The stairway angle can vary slightly yet still use a standard curve. Simply trim the handrail at the correct point of curvature to precisely match the stairway rake. Use the pitch plate as a guide to find the proper joint-line point, then draw across square to this to show the joint-line needed.

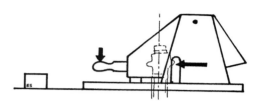

Fig. 313 Starting position for a trailing curve.

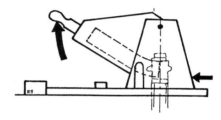

Fig. 314 Finishing position for a trailing curve.

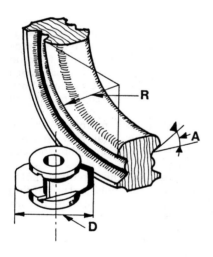

Fig. 312 Check dimensions R and D to find the smallest acceptable mould angle A on the chart.

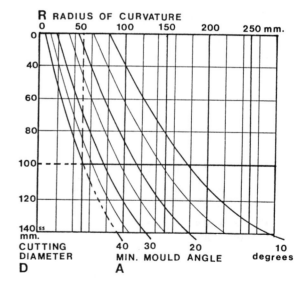

Fig. 315 Chart showing minimum mould angle on upsweeps, downsweeps and similar.
Example shows 100mm cutting diameter which allows a minimum mould angle of 40 degrees when the handrail has a curvature of 50mm at the mould.

When moulding curved handrails of this type and similar there is a chance of the cutter fouling other parts due to the complex geometry. This is governed by the angle formed on the cutterhead, its diameter at the deepest point and the radius of curvature at the point being moulded.

CHAPTER 13

ROUTING

The spindle moulder can be used for some routing, but is no real substitute for an overhead router: the spindle speed is too low for small diameter cutters, there is no convenient fast movement into a blind cut, also the cut is out of sight and is difficult to monitor. Any fault can only be seen when routing is complete which, in most cases, is then too late to correct.

Router cutters are ground in their flutes. They fit in the split collet of a stub arbor replacing the regular arbor.

Fig. 316 Below: Forming open-end grooves. The workpiece is controlled between hardwood guides and butts against an end-stop. A Shaw guard is needed on all routing operations but is ommitted on all drawings for clarity.

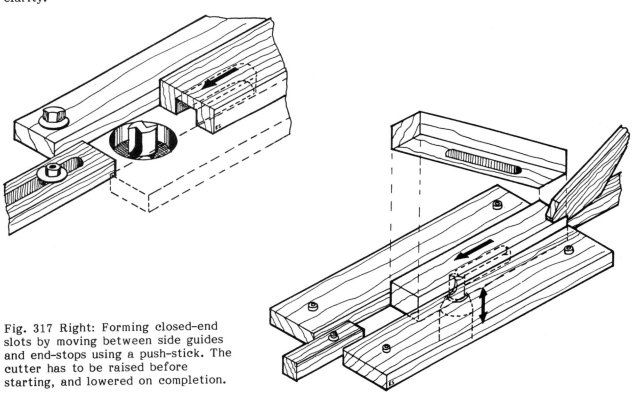

Fig. 317 Right: Forming closed-end slots by moving between side guides and end-stops using a push-stick. The cutter has to be raised before starting, and lowered on completion.

USING GUIDES AND JIGS

Where straight slots are needed parallel to the sides of a narrow workpiece, guide these by hardwood fences at each side, and hold down by a Shaw guard.

When the slot is open to one end, run-in from this end up to an end-stop set to the length needed. For closed-end slots fit stops at both ends. Wind the head up into the cut at the start position, then form the slot, using a push stick to give a smooth and even feed movement. Finally stop and lower the head before removing the finished workpiece and inserting the next. Working this way means removing and replacing the Shaw guard each time. This is tedius, but essential, as running without a top pressure is dangerous.

The spindle moulder should, preferably, have positive vertical setting via an adjustable stop on the slide. It is possible to rely on marks or a scale on the vertical movement or an angular setting of the handwheel, but these can give variation between one cut and the next and it is all too easy to overrun.

If the slot is straight but at an angle to the workpiece edge; for example, sloping shelf grooves in cupboard sides; some form of jig is needed. A simple type is a pair of guides between which a sliding piece operates and having a centre groove through which the cutter projects. The jig fastened to the slide is merely a piece of plywood, having side fences to angle the workpiece so that the required slot is parallel to the guide. Eccentric clamps hold the workpiece in place. For accuracy, first fit the router cutter, then slot through the plywood as a guide when fitting the fence. Add a hardwood block to guard the router cutter when in the rest position.

Stops are needed at front and rear to limit the slide movement, and to regulate the slot length. If open one end, set the cutter at the proper height and run into and out of the slot. Open-end slots can be handled very simply. The jig is drawn back clear of the Shaw guard so that the finished piece can be removed and the next quickly fitted. If closed both ends, the piece must be positioned at the start of the slot and the cutter raised into it as described before. Reverse the angle of the fences for opposite hand sides.

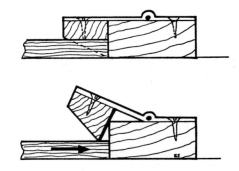

Fig. 319 An end-stop made in this way lifts automatically when the workpiece is pushed against the fence.

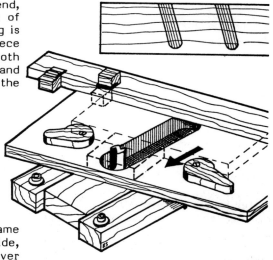

Fig. 318 Forming stopped or through angled slots or housings on a sliding jig.
Flip-over end-stops allow several housings to be cut.
Eccentric clamps hold the side in place and a block guards the cutter.

Where a number of parallel slots need cutting in the same piece, again taking the example of shelves in a cupboard side, the jig has a rear fence with front eccentric clamps. Flip-over stops on hinges provide end-wise location.

Alternatively, for easier operation, make the stops taper upwards and away from the fence. By placing the side flat or corner-on the table clear of the stops, all the stops lift automatically when the side is then pushed towards the fence. In operation; shift the workpiece sideways clear of the next stop to be used, so that this drops into place, then back against it for positioning. Repeat for all the remaining cuts.

166

Plate 76 A scale close to the rise and fall handwheel on this Delta spindle moulder shows the precise relative height.

Fig. 320 Forming a sill groove using a small-diameter flush-top circular cutterblock.

Plate 77 Height stops on this SCM spindle moulder give precise vertical setting control.

MOULDING

Being a flush-topped cutter, the router bit can be sunk into the cut to reduce projection on deep mouldings. This type is not a heavy-duty tool and is unsuitable for the heavy cuts common with larger cutterheads. There are, however, some uses that it is particularly suited for.

It is suitable, for example, for stop moulding where sweep-in and out needs to be of small radius. Fences and pressures are used in much the same way as with regular cutterheads, and with similar techniques.

Router cutters can reduce projection on what would otherwise need over-long cutters in conventional set-ups. One example is in forming the throating groove in large sills. Normally these need long cutters to reach across the long sill bevel, if worked with regular cutterheads from the side. A suitable router-type cutter for this operation forms only the groove, and can either be a solid router cutter, or a flush-topped circular cutterhead with loose cutters fitted. The sill is worked upside-down, supported on guides fastened to the table. Cutter projection is quite small, with the cutter under-cutting well inside the bevel.

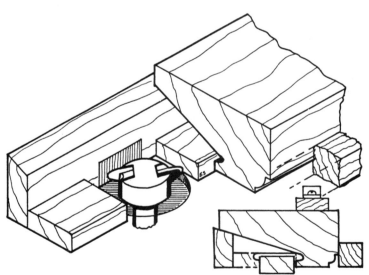

A jig is used when forming a stopped throating on windows where fixed and opening lights alternate, but in this case the jig mounts the sill supports, and has eccentric clamps to lock the jig and sill together. The cutter operates through a slot in the jig base, and the jig and sill assembly runs against a regular through-fence fitted with stops or a cam system. The same arrangement can be used to modify rebates for opening lights.

167

USING A TEMPLATE

Template routing is difficult on the spindle moulder because the cutter is not visible when working, and with inside cuts the cutter has to be wound up before the cut, and down again after. In all cases a Shaw guard is essential to steady the cut. The template can be used below or above the workpiece.

Template below

The template lies on the table and supports the workpiece, which is fastened to it. It needs to be large enough to be both stable itself and support the workpiece. This is not easy with small workpieces, which are better worked two-up on a double-size template making the cut at two passes.

The template can contact the plain shank of the stub arbor as a guide. This not really suitable because it spins with the arbor, tends to burn the template, and gives a rough 'feel' to the work. It is better to use a ball-bearing follower, but templates then have to be made even smaller and less stable. To make operation safe, use a ball-bearing follower only with large templates.

Because the shank or ball-bearing is bigger than the cutter at its planing diameter, the size and shape of the template has to be modified to take this into account, so template-making is complicated. In use, neither the template shape nor the cut can be seen clearly, so the operator works blind with inside shapes and is badly sighted with with outside shapes. In practice, this method is only suitable for the simplest of work, perhaps cutting the drain grooves in drainer boards. (It is possible to taper drain grooves on this, or other similar routing work, simply by tilting the workpiece on the template).

Template above

The template is fastened to the top of the workpiece, which then lies directly-on the table. It is sometimes possible with an over-template to use a router with a small ball-bearing fitted at the end as a follower. This can be used for a light trimming cut, when the workpiece is already virtually the right shape and overall size, or for corner trimming, either by using a template, or by running against the edge of an already trimmed workpiece.

When routing from a blank, the template follower must be separate from, and suspended above, the router cutter, but absolutely concentric to it. Some manufacturers provide a dowelled fixture for this so that alignment is guaranteed. In other cases the support adjusts, and is aligned by lowering the follower near to the chuck and setting concentric to it. This relies on the operator for accuracy of alignment, and can vary each time. The template follower is a ball-bearing on some machines intended to roll with the template and give that essential light touch, but more often is a static pin.

168

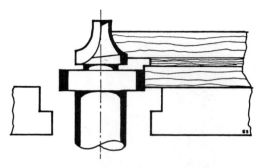

Fig. 321 Routing with the template underneath to contact either the shank or a ball-bearing.

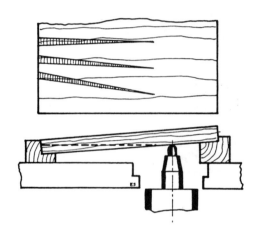

Fig. 322 Forming tapered grooves by tilting the workpiece.

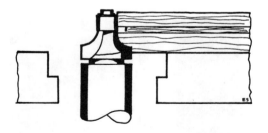

Fig. 323 Routing with the template above to contact either a plain shank, a small diameter ball-bearing or a pin suspended above the cutter.

A starter pin or block should be used where the shape is a full outline, as with regular shaping. This is not normal practice with regular routing, but spindle moulder speeds are lower, so there is a tendency to snatch on initial contact. When cutting inside shapes, the cutter needs raising when in the cut. Use a Shaw guard to hold down and steady the assembly and place the pin firmly against the template in a suitable position before switching-on.

With outside shapes, feed counter-clockwise when spindle rotation is also counter-clockwise, but with inside shapes rotate clockwise. In both case, movement is such that cutter rotation keeps the pin hard against the template. With wrong feed direction the cutter runs uncontrolled away from the template to a much greater extent than on a router because of the lower spindle speed. Preferably, take a heavy cut in two or more stages, raising the cutter between cuts so that no cut is excessive. This takes longer but makes the work easier and gives less chance of kick-back.

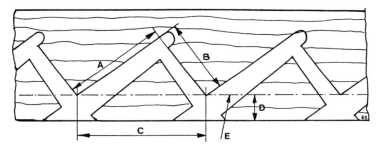

Fig. 324 Basic measurements of a string.
A - going.
B - rise.
C - pitch.
D - margin.
E - pitch line.

STAIR HOUSING

The spindle moulder is quite efficient at housing stair strings. A jig for this is available from some machine makers as a light-weight, clamp-on template, which usually has fixed tread and riser thickness and a standard tread nosing, together with an overhead guide follower.

First make a plywood pitch board to the required going, rise and pitch. The going is the distance from the face of one riser to the face of the next measured horizontally. The rise is the distance from the top of one tread to the top of the next, measured vertically. The pitch is the distance from one tread/riser intersection to the next, and the pitch line is that parallel to the string edge to join the inside corners of the tread/riser. All these dimensions must be within specified ranges or the stairs will be difficult to climb because they are too shallow, too steep or have too long or too short a tread.

169

There are somewhat involved guide lines to be followed to give the right combinations, and these vary between different countries.

In the UK domestic guides, the rise should be between 160 and 220mm, and the going between 220 and 280mm to give a pitch angle of not more than 42 degrees. The sum of twice the rise plus one going should be between 550 and 700mm.

In the USA, the rise should be between 7 and 7 5/8in, and the going between 10 and 11in to give a pitch angle of between 32 and 37 degrees. The sum of twice the rise and one going should be between 24 and 25in, and the sum of one rise and one going should be between 17 and 18in.

To find the precise dimensions, the overall height of the stairs, floor to floor, must be measured accurately, also the overall going. The calculations needed are quite simple when measured metrically, using a modern calculator with squares and square roots. (The following calculations apply to UK domestic stairs, but similar calculations are used for USA stairs).

Assume an overall height, floor to floor, of 2 340 mm. Divide this by the average rise, say 180mm, to give, in this instance, 13 treads. (If the number is not even, round this up or down to the nearest whole figure, then divide back into the overall height to find the correct rise. This may be hard to measure accurately, but necessary to get the pitch board right.)

Next find the total going which should be 13 x 220 (the average going) in this case 2 860mm. Check if this distance is acceptable and, if so, make this the total going. (Actually the overal distance is less by one going because the top tread is actually where the upper floor starts, but for calculation purposes it is easier to include an imaginary full top tread). If the distance available is a bit short, cheat by shortening the going to fit in with this, but don't overdo things. It can also be stretched, but not by very much.

In all cases, however, the final figures must comply to the guides. In the example, the total of 180 + 180 + 220 is 580mm, well within the UK recommendations, also the pitch angle is 39 degrees, again well within the UK limit of 42 degrees.

Finally, calculate the overall stair pitch, so that the total pitch line, floor to floor measured along the stair slope, can be found. Calculate the square root of the sum of the going and rise after squaring both. The rise is 180mm, squared this is 32 400. The going is 220 mm, squared this is 48 400mm. Add these together to give 80 800mm, then find the square root which in this case is 284.25mm. The pitch board must be made to these dimensions precisely. Multiply the pitch by the number of treads, 13, to give an overall pitch of 3 695mm, to which the string length is made.

The plywood is triangular in shape, with two adjacent sides square to one another. Mark in from the square corner the going on one edge and the rise on the other. Join the two marks with a straight line, the pitch line, and check that this corresponds exactly to the pitch calculated.

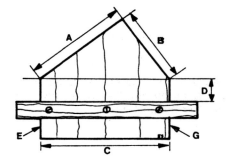

Fig. 325 A typical pitch board. Dimensions as Fig. 324, but with the two gauge lines E & G added.

Assumming that this measurement is correct, draw gauge lines about 100mm long square to the pitch line from these two points, and carefully cut along them. The dimension between the two gauge lines must correspond exactly with the calculated pitch. The two obtuse corners are where the outside faces of the next tread below and the next riser above intersect.

Draw an underedge line parallel to the pitch line and spaced between 25 and 75mm from the pitch line. Fasten fences on both faces, to this line, as a margin gauge. The margin is the distance from the pitch line to the underedge of the stair string - which is not critical unless the string itself is narrow. To maintain the correct distance from the nosing line (a line joining the nosings of the treads), the margin width can be varied, as necessary, to compensate for any width error of the string. This top edge is sometimes moulded to add interest, but then needs extra width in this case.

Preparation

Make the string to the overall pitch calculated, plus extra for trimming on site at the foot and the head of the stairs. A rule of thumb is to allow 125mm from where the bottom riser crosses the floor line to the bottom end of the string, and beyond the upper floor line. This allows enough room for a vertical mitre with a 150mm skirting board. Preferably make the string over-long to trim on site.

To make sure the string is housed correctly for the treads and risers, one string needs marking out in full using the pitch board. Mark the reverse face so that the correct positions for clamping the template are clearly visible. Use the pitch board first to mark the upper floor line on the string. With the margin fences against the under edge, mark along the tread line. Extend this line, using a straight-edge, to the upper edge of the string. With the pitch board still in place, also mark along the lower gauge line and the top rise face line.

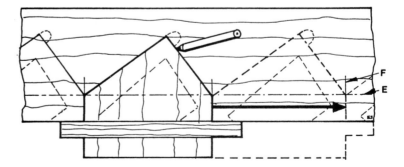

Fig. 326 Marking out a string using the pitch board. The pitch line is E and the gauge line F.

Move the pitch board along, its fence still firmly against the under edge of the string, until the top gauge edge of the pitch board corresponds with the drawn gauge line. Draw around the tread, riser and leading gauge line, then repeat,

171

moving along the string in stages, until the lower floor end is reached. The lower floor line cuts the pitch line where the lowest riser meets the floor. Check that the overall length is what was calculated in the first place.

Another way is to draw in the overall pitch line, floor to floor, and divide equally for the number of treads needed. It can be done with a rule, but is easier using a pair of joiner's dividers. Set these to the calculated pitch and step along the pitch line adjusting, as necessary, until the distance pitches-out exactly for the number of treads needed (including the top floor line). Square across from each point to the pitch line to show the gauge lines. The pitch pitched-out should also correspond with the spacing of the gauge lines on the pitch board. After pitching-out fully, mark the reverse face of the string using the pitch board.

Plate 78 Stair housing attachment on a Dominion spindle moulder.

Machine setting

Set the template follower concentric to the router bit and adjust it vertically to barely clear a single string. Set the height of the router cutter to form the full depth of stair-housing needed. (It is tempting to cut the housing in two steps when using a light spindle moulder. Preferable, though, cut the full depth at a single pass, but more slowly. Many stair-housing cutters are slightly tapered, so that the treads and risers bite-in at the string face to give a better fit. Cutting the groove at two bites reduces this effect).

Place the left-hand string inside-face down on the machine table, and set the fences on the template so that the outer edges of the tread and riser slots in the template guide correspond exactly with the lines drawn on the string for the first housing. Clamp the template in place. Position the assembly so that the template slot is directly below the follower, when the router cutter is clear of the string. Lower the follower to engage in the template, check again that the cutter is clear of the timber, then start the machine.

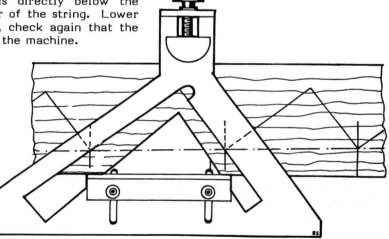

Fig. 327 Typical stair-housing template positioned via guide lines drawn on the reverse of the string.

Move the assembly so that the follower moves around the template as required, so that the router cutter mills an identical housing. Always move the assembly so that the cutter pulls against the template in feeding; otherwise it is difficult to control. If the left-hand string is being housed the

172

tread template is to the right, (assuming the nosing faces the operator - this is the normal direction when stair housing). The sequence is to cut-in and follow-round the outer face of the riser, the nosing, the top face of the tread and out.

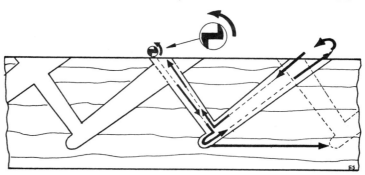

Fig. 328 Follow the sequence shown to keep the follower against the template and to avoid spelching where it shows. Note that the string is shown from above, but the housing is shown as solid lines for clarity on this and the following sketches.

Enter a second time against the under face of the tread, then back along the inside face of the riser and out. Make sure each housing is cut properly by going around a second time. Any lump formed during the first cut is easily removed at this time, but much more difficult to make good later.

Move the string well clear of the cutter and stop the machine. Raise the follower then re-set the template for the next tread and riser and mill as before, and so on until complete. Take care to set the template accurately or tread and riser width will vary.

CAUTION: If the cutter is sharp and the timber mellow little spelching will occur, but it can happen. Break-out at the unseen parts is not so important, for example the underedge, but, if excessive, cure this as follows:

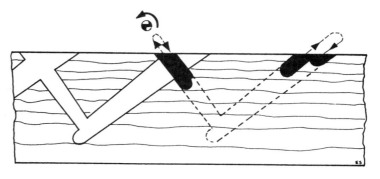

Fig. 329 To avoid under-edge spelching form initial cuts as shown in black prior to the main cut.

Before making the complete housing first notch-in about 50mm deep at the tread under face and the riser outer face, as though to start the housing, but withdraw along the same path before completion. Then cut in the same direction but just short of 50mm deep and, this time, against the opposite faces, the top edge of the tread and the inside face of the riser. The cutter will try to run, so feed slowly and carefully. Doing this forms the full width at the exit points and reduces breaking-out along the back edge.

173

The only other point that break-out is likely, and which must be avoided, is at the outer internal corner between tread and riser. When cutting the left-hand string, this only occurs when cutting top tread first and working down to the bottom tread, so always start with the bottom tread and work up. The housing for the riser cuts across the previous housing for the next tread below, but in the right direction, so that spelching doesn't occur where seen. It might spelch at the inside face of the next lower tread, but this is acceptable if crossed slowly.

Spelching is always possible if the route described is not followed exactly. See Fig. 328.

Housing the opposite string

The right-hand string can be housed by flipping-over the template and repeating the sequence described above, but with the following changes: Assuming the tread is now to the left, begin to house the outer top of the tread, then around the tread nosing, riser outer face and out. Re-enter against the inner face of the riser, then back against the under face of the tread and out. To avoid spelching make notching cuts intially against the riser inside face and tread top face, then against the opposite faces of both. Start at the top housing and work down to avoid spelching at the external corner between tread and riser.

Using a string as the template

An alternative which is faster, simpler and error-free, is to use the first string as a template for its pair. (The strings will match precisely, but any error in the first string repeats exactly in the second).

Nail the two strings back to back, taking great care where you place the nails of course, and work left-hand string up as a template. The first housing must be absolutely clean-cut, and the router cutter must be precisely the same diameter as the follower. (The cutter is the same when new, but wear reduces its diameter, so check. This is no problem when housing strings individually).

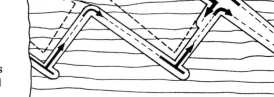

Fig. 330 House the second string as shown here when using the finished string as a template.

The second string can be worked in two stages. Start with the outer face of the top tread, around the nosing and outer face of the top riser, the top face of the second tread, around the nosing and outer face of the second riser, and so on, until the lower end is reached.

The second cut is a series of individual cuts starting this time at the bottom riser inside face, then along the under face of the bottom tread and finally out along the remaining housing for the outer face of the next riser. Re-enter to cut the remaining top face of the next tread, then along the inside face of the next riser, under face of the next tread and exit via the remaining section of the outer face of the third riser, then repeat. Sounds complicated, doesn't it? well, it isn't really, just follow the routes shown.

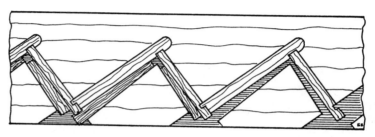

Fig. 331 The string is finally fitted with treads and risers interlocked as shown.

Variations from standard

Templates provided for housing strings on a spindle moulder have a fixed tread and riser thickness, though going, rise and pitch can be varied. Most incorporate wedge room to tighten the treads and risers after assembly. If thinner treads or risers than allowed for are to be fitted, house as before and make-up the difference with thicker wedges.

If thicker treads or risers than the template allows for are to be used, fit a router cutter which is bigger in diameter than the follower by the difference needed. For example, if the regular tread is 30mm but a thickness of 40mm is called for, use a 30mm router cutter and a 20mm follower (or 40mm and 30mm respectively) to cut the correct width. When setting the template on the string it must, of course, be off-set from the gauge marks of the tread and riser by half the difference between cutter and follower.

The most accurate way is to align the upper tread line of the template with the upper tread line drawn from the pitch board. The cut does not then precisely align, but off-sets each time by the same small amount. The riser housing is also housed wider pro-rata, so cut thicker wedges to suit. If subsequently using the first string as a template, replace the router cutter, or the follower, because the diameter of both must correspond exactly for this operation, even though, in housing the first string, using the machine template, the cutter and follower are of different diameter.

Other changes possible are: to fill in the nosing with hardwood shaped to produce an alternative nosing profile, either shorter or of a different shape; and filling in the riser slot to produce tread-only (riser-less) stairs.

After completing the strings, fit treads and risers individually to mark out, on the tread, the housing for the riser and the rebate on the back edge to tongue-into the next riser. Mark on the riser the groove to accept the tread tongue.

Plate 79 Dominion dovetailing attachment being used on the Dominion spindle moulder.

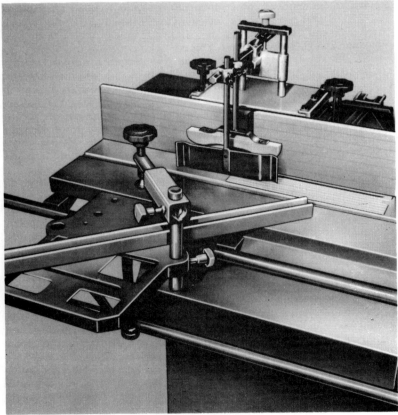

Plate 80 Startrite spindle moulder fitted with a sliding table for tenoning, end moulding and similar operations.

176

CHAPTER 14

DRAWER AND FRAME JOINTS
Dovetailing

When dovetailing was a primary method of jointing solid cabinets, some spindle moulders had attachments for dovetailing the frames - in addition to drawer dovetailing. They were versatile, but produced a square pin which did not seat properly in the rounded tail formed by the dovetailing cutter. Modern ones produce rounded pins which match the tails precisely.

Most current attachments are designed for drawer dovetailing only and, whilst very good for this, will only dovetail other sorts of frames within this capacity range. The attachment is a casting, with a finger-guide to form pins and tails at the same time, clamps for sides, fronts and backs, also left and right-hand side-stops to locate them.

OPERATION

Clamp the drawer side upright to rest end-on the finger guide with its inside-face 'out'. Clamp the front horizontally inside-face down and butt firmly against the outside face of the drawer side.

The router-type dovetail cutter fits in a collet of a stub arbor and should run at the highest speed available on the machine. Slide the attachment on the spindle moulder table, manually guiding it so that the plain shank of the dovetail cutter follows around the finger plate. By doing this, pins are cut on the drawer side and tails in the drawer front at the same time. Dry-lubricate the spindle moulder table so that movement is easy.

SETTING

To vary the pitch of the dovetails the attachment often has interchangeable finger plates with dowel-pin location. The normal pitch is 25mm (1in), but others of 20 or 40mm (1/2 or 1.1/2in) can be substituted. Fit the appropriate plate for the drawer size; small pitches for small drawers, large ones for extra large drawers, but the common 25mm (1in) pitch for most regular sizes.

Different dovetail cutters are needed for each pitch. Makers can give details, but if in doubt measure the dovetail cutter diameter about 1/3 down from the top. It should equal half the pitch for which it is intended. A cutter 10mm diameter is for a 20mm pitch finger plate and to produce dovetails pitched at 20mm.

Some dovetail cutters are plain, that is without spurs. Others have spurs, either a single spur per edge, or multiple spurs. Those with spurs are less likely to spelch at lower spindle speeds. Sharpen and fit the appropriate cutter.

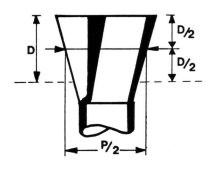

Fig. 332 The dovetail cutter diameter measured as at P/2 is half the pitch for which it is intended.

Fig. 333 All these types are used in dovetailing.

Left: without spurs.
Centre: with two spurs.
Right: with multiple spurs.

177

Dovetail cutters of different sizes usually interchange on the stub arbor, but have different shank diameters where they contact the finger plate. Set the cutter to the correct height (see notes on adjusting dovetail fit) and add fill-in rings to close the gap around the stub arbor.

Drawer side

Position the drawer side front-end down, with the groove central to one finger of the finger plate. This pin then neatly fills in the drawer groove. Set the side-stop against its under edge.

Check where the top edge of the drawer side then lies on the finger plate. Preferably it should be between fingers so a full pin is formed near the top. If a part pin is formed this looks untidy, so shift the side so that it does not - provided the groove still lies largely on a finger. If this is not possible there are two options:

a) Position the side so that a full pin forms close to the top edge ignoring the under edge, which is normally unseen, and fill the groove gap after assembly.

b) Position the side with the groove central on one finger, but do not form the part-cut at the top edge of the drawer front when dovetailing. Match this by cutting off the part pin on the top of the drawer side. See notes and Fig. 335.

Drawer front

Fit the drawer front firmly up to the drawer side with its under edge off-set inwards from the drawer side under edge by half a pitch. Set the side-stop against the drawer front under edge. Make sure this leaves the under edge of the side projecting beyond the under edge of the front for two reasons:

a) When the drawer side top pin needs cutting off, the corresponding part-cut must not be formed on the drawer front. If off-set as described it can easily be missed-out; if off-set in the wrong direction, it forms automatically when cutting part of the top pin on the side

b) Part of the side is unsupported when dovetailing because of the off-set - which may lead to spelching. This is less conspicuous if close to the under-edge.

A quick, simple and accurate way of off-setting, when positioning the drawer front stop, is to use a setting piece. Notch-out a scrap drawer front to hook onto the underedge of the drawer side and give the correct off-set for the pitch of drawer being dovetailed. Flip for the opposite hand. Keep different setting pieces for different pitches.

Tail depth

On some attachments the pin and tail depth are fixed so that no machine setting is necessary, but the joint strength remains

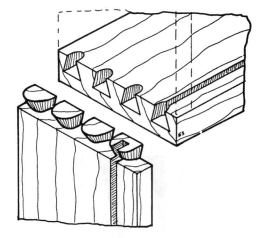

Fig. 334 Drawer fronts are preferably positioned so that the drawer side pins fills in the drawer front groove on assembly.

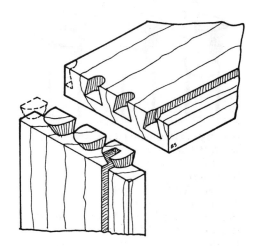

Fig. 335 Leaving part of a pin looks untidy; instead, cut it off and take care not to form the corresponding tail. Both are shown in dotted outline.

exactly the same regardless of drawer side thickness. As the tail depth suits a regular drawer side, there is no gain in joint strength by using thicker sides.

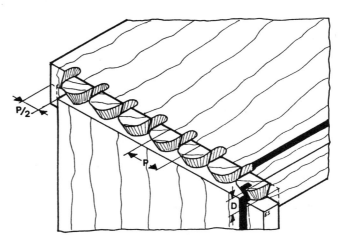

Fig. 336 Right: Off-set for dovetailing by half a pitch (P/2). D is the dovetail pin height.

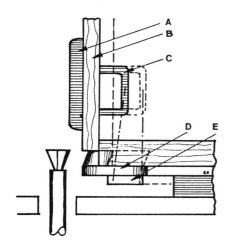

Fig. 337 Above: Section through a Robinson dovetailing attachment with automatic tail depth control:
A - fixed front plate.
B - drawer side.
C - adjustable clamp.
D - finger plate.
E - depth control bar.

Fig. 338 Right: Joints produced on drawer sides of different thicknesses as shown by the corresponding distances between arrows. The right hand sketches show an attachment with fixed depth control; and the centre sketches show an attachment with automatic depth control.

On other attachments the tail depth cut is manually pre-set to correspond with the drawer side thickness - to give the strongest possible joint. Check it by cutting a test dovetail using scrap pieces of the same size.

On the Robinson attachment the tail depth is set automatically to the thickness of the drawer side, to give the strongest possible joint. It also guarantees a flush fit without need of adjustment or trial and error machine setting.

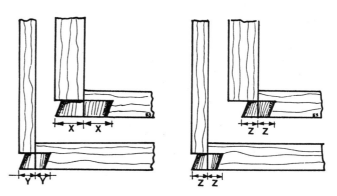

Dovetail fit

Check tightness of the assembled joint on any suitable scrap timber by dovetailing and fitting. Adjusting the dovetail cutter height varies the tightness of the joint; so if tight, lower it, and if slack raise it.

179

When correctly set, clamp a scrap drawer-front in the attachment to project just beyond the fingers and form a dovetail in it. Use this as a guide when setting height in future - but always check the fit before starting the run. The setting guide must be properly seasoned timber or it can shrink or warp to become useless. As the dovetail cutter is sharpened its diameter reduces and a lower height setting is needed, so replace the setting piece periodically to take account of this.

DOVETAILING OPERATION

Some makers show the dovetail attachment held from the rear, but this is so that the attachment shows clearly - it is not the way to use it. Most users, including the writer, work with the attachment on the far side of the dovetail cutter and span this to grip it either side. The inside of the drawer side faces the operator and the drawer front extends away from him at the rear. This gives better control and allows the cutting action to be seen clearly.

Before starting the dovetailing cut proper, form a scribing cut across the full width of the drawer side, moving the attachment so that the cutter cuts 'in'. Only a shallow scribing cut is needed, perhaps between 1 and 2mm deep. No guide is normally used so careful control of the cut is essential. A depth guide could be fitted temporarily on the finger ends, but most users find scribing in this way easy enough after little practice. If a scribing cut is not made prior to dovetailing there is a chance of spelching when using spur-less dovetail cutters.

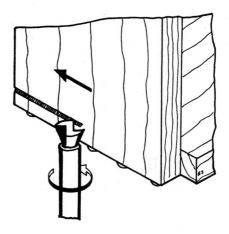

Finally, cut the pins and tails simultaneously in the drawer side and front by carefully following round the finger guides. To prevent the cut running out of control move the attachment so that cutter rotation forces it against the guide fingers (as when routing). With normal rotation, start the cut at the right to finish at the left. Take care that contact is maintained throughout the full cut otherwise the joint may not be a flush-fit on assembly.

Fig. 339
Above: Scribing movement.
Below: Dovetailing operation.

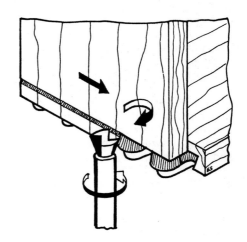

Notes

1. When cutting the pin at the groove end of the drawer side move slowly so that it does not spelch-out at the back (the outer face when assembled). If this still happens, fit a hardwood backing piece alongside the front arranged to butt against, and lap, the drawer side. If the backing piece is firmly fixed it could, in practice, replace the normal side-stop.

2. When the top part-pin on the drawer side is to be cut off, do not form the corresponding part-tail in the drawer front. Either stop at this point, or start further along - depending on the hand being cut. To cut off the pin, release the drawer side only and move it sideways so that the part pin overhangs

180

a gap between fingers, and re-clamp. Leave the drawer front in its original position for support, then cut-off the part tail by running-in the dovetail cutter.

3. It is essential that drawer parts are cross-cut square. If not, the drawer alignment wiil be incorrect on assembly. This is because the side-stops are distanced from the finger plate.

4. When fitting, press the drawer front hard against the drawer-side to prevent break-out on dovetailing.

Qpposite hand

Drawer sides are dovetailed in pairs, so, if several drawers are being dovetailed, set the machine for both left and right-hand at the same time. Take care that the methods detailed are followed exactly, including the cutting sequence which is precisely the same for both hands.

The most convenient way of dovetailing is to complete dovetails at both ends of the front and one end of both sides in a following sequence. In this way the front is handled once only, simply reversing it end for end for following cuts.

Drawer back

Drawer backs are normally flush on their underside with the top of the drawer side groove so the drawer bottom can be fitted after assembly. There are two alternative methods:

a) The drawer side can be dovetailed to a pin, and the back to a tail, as a duplicate of the drawer front fitting. In this case the drawer front and back are the same length. Use the drawer front stop settings, simply inserting a spacer between the side-stop and drawer back for the off-set needed. The spacer should equal the distance from the drawer side under-edge to the groove top. Make just one spacer and use it at both sides. When forming the pins on the drawer side do not form pins below the groove or above the back top edge, merely round them over.

b) Alternatively, form the drawer back as pins, and the drawer side with tails, to make a neater fitting. This may also allow better placing of the pins and tails. Part tails are acceptable on the under-edge, but the top pins must be whole. With this assembly the drawer front and back are different lengths, so carefully calculate this or the finished drawer will taper.

Clamp the back in position vertically, and butt the side against it. Set the stops to correctly align the drawer back under-edge with the groove top. Use a scrap drawer back which is notched for easier setting, or the spacer previously described (equal in thickness to the under-edge to groove-top distance).

Lapped and open dovetails

Most dovetails are lapped; that is the drawer sides and back

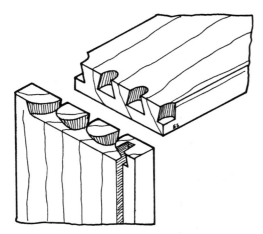

Fig. 340 One side-to-drawer back dovetail joint.

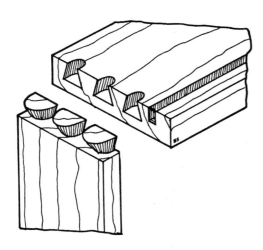

Fig. 341 An alternative side-to-drawer back joint.

181

are thicker than the pin length so the tail does not break through. This masks the assembled joint to give a neat appearance. If the sides are too thin for lapping, use a worn cutter which has less height, a stubbier cutter for the same pitch, or a smaller pitch-plate with a shorter pin.

Some users like to see the dovetail ends. They can look well in hardwood when varnished, but must be a good fit. They are easy enough to produce simply by making the drawer back thinner than normal so that the cutter breaks through on dovetailing. It is usual to make the parts thinner than the pin length so the pins project for sanding flush after assembly. Take account of this when sizing the drawer parts.

Lipped drawers

Kitchen drawers are often lipped at the top edge and both ends to disguise an otherwise poor fit. Dovetailing gives problems on some attachments, but is practical on those machines having an adjustable depth bar. Cut the drawer front to drawer width plus double the lip needed. Normally the lip is trimmed, so initially allow more than really necessary. After dovetailing and assembly, trim the projecting tails flush and round over the lips as a final operation. (See previous chapter).

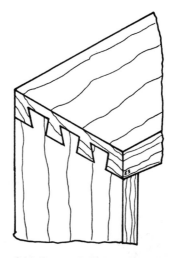

Fig. 343 Lapped dovetail assembled.

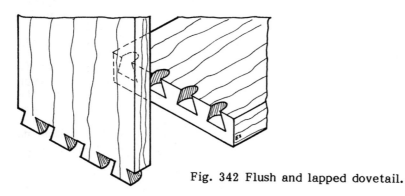

Fig. 342 Flush and lapped dovetail.

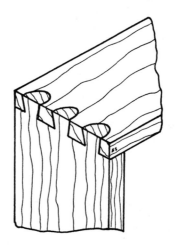

Fig. 344 Open dovetail assembled.

With attachments having a fixed tail depth, first dovetail the sides in the usual way using a scrap drawer front as back-up. Take care always to fit this in the same position, or the cut gradually widens to give inadequate support. If practical, leave the back-up piece in position and only switch the side.

When dovetailing the front, set the end forward of its normal position by the lip depth needed, and dovetail this alone. An easy way to locate the front is to rebate the end of a scrap drawer side by this amount, and clamp it at a higher position so the front butts against the rebate. The finished joint looks a bit odd, but allows the side to set-in by the lip-depth needed on assembly and gives an acceptable appearance when cleaned-up. See Fig. 349.

182

With adjustable depth-stop types, the front and side can be dovetailed at the same time by adjusting the depth bar to suit. On the Robinson attachment, the side and back are also dovetailed at the same time, simply by inserting a spacer between drawer side and clamp to automatically deepen the tails. The spacer should equal half the lip depth needed.

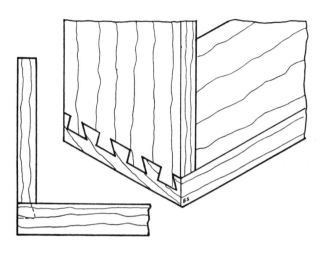

Fig. 345 Flush and lapped dovetail assembled.

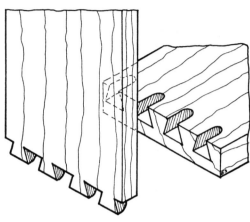

Fig. 346 Lipped and rebated drawer dovetail exploded.

Fig. 347 Lipped and rebated drawer assembled.

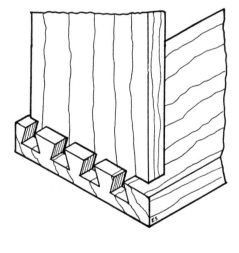

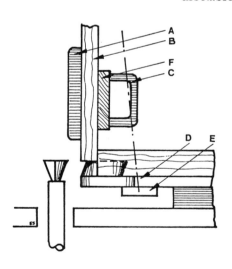

Fig. 348 Section through a Robinson dovetailing attachment set up for lipped drawers and showing the parts as under Fig. 337, plus the spacer F.

Sloping front drawers

It is possible to dovetail drawers with a sloping front by cutting off the sides at an angle and placing them so that the angled end seats properly on the fingers. The slope angle limits the width that can be dovetailed - wide pieces or large angles will not fit. The front is butted squarely against the side, off-set by half a pitch, and the dovetail formed as before. It isn't easy to position the front and side with absolute accuracy, so make the fronts a little wide, and off-set a little more than normal to allow fitting after assembly.

183

The same method can be used to make other frames with a sloping front and/or back, but the two sides must be upright. Trying to make these slope also simply is not viable.

Hidden dovetails

Most users think a machine cannot form hidden dovetails, but this is possible on some attachments if the side is double the normal thickness, or roughly equal to the pitch. The fixed-depth types cannot do this; fronts and sides need separate settings.

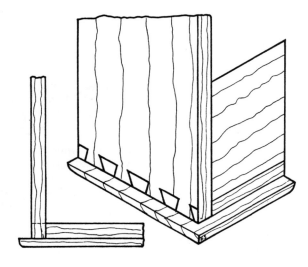

Fig. 349 Assembled drawer after rebating and nosing.

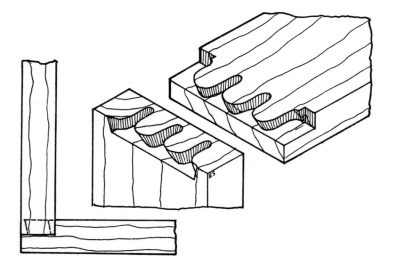

Fig. 350 The machine version of a hidden dovetail needs some hand work.

Clamp the side in position and set the depth bar accordingly to limit the cut depth so that the cutter is just

184

short of breaking through. This gives the appearance of a combination pin and tail. On the Robinson attachment wedge a spacer against the automatic depth bar (equal in thickness to the side) to give the same effect and leave the spacer in position. Raise and reclamp the drawer side to allow the front to barely slide underneath. Use the drawer side as a guide to set the drawer front end in line with the outer face of the side (and off-set as usual). Dovetail as before.

When assembled, the joint looks like a lap dovetail, but which is actually a blind dovetail. To completely baffle the curious, form the two outer edges of the side as part pins, then stop short of the edge to leave this square. Chisel-in the drawer front to form an assembled joint which gives no clue as to the way it was actually formed.

Finger jointing

Both jointing and tenoning operations are possible with make-shift set-ups on the spindle moulder, but for safe operation and dependable results use the proper attachments.

The finger-joint attachment consists of a table with a front fence and side clamp rolling on a guideway fixed to the spindle moulder table, or a sliding section of the main table. The cutters used are two-wing type, stacked between spacers of equal thickness and mounted on a special keyed spindle. Cutters have a keyway so that, when correctly assembled, the cutting edges spiral to stagger the cut. The diameter is around 150mm, and they to run at 5 000 revs/min., or thereabouts.

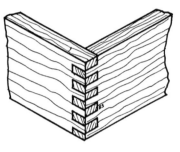

Fig. 351 Finger-jointing, showing the two settings with cutters off-set half a pitch.

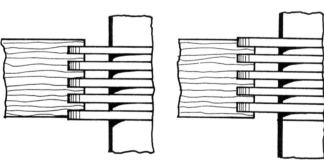

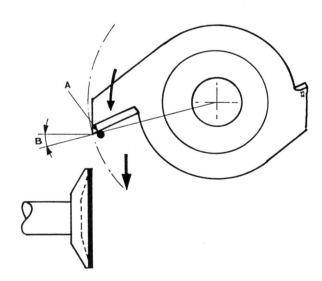

Fig. 352 Grind all finger joint cutters to the same cutting diameter by butting and clamping the cutter front-face against a fixed pin A. This is off-set from the centreline to give the required clearance B.

Set the assembly so that cutters just clear the leading fence. Set the height initially so that the underside of the lowest cutter is barely below the rolling table surface. Check the workpiece depth against the cutters, and adjust the height, if necessary, so that the bottom cutter lap equals the

185

lap of the top cutter, or the lap of the space above it. Fit the guard to protect the cutter assembly.

Use the regular steel fences to gauge the length of the fingers, but make sure they are in line and absolutely parallel to the slideway. Do this by clamping a setting block on the attachment to just touch the cutters. By moving the attachment fully across, with a spacer fitted between block and fence, the fence position can be set accurately at both ends. The spacer should equal the finger length needed.

Parts for finger jointing are cut to neat length and stacked several together all face to back. Carefully butt their ends against the infeed fence and seat them properly before clamping against the front fence. With the cutters running, pass the assembly across the cutterhead, then draw fully back before stopping the machine to unclamp and reload. Finger joint the opposite end after turning end for end, keeping the same under-edge down. Repeat as necessary.

The opposite-hand pieces are clamped the same-edge down, but move the cutterhead up by the thickness of a single cutter so that the joint matches properly when assembled. This is possible by using the vertical adjustment of the machine, but a simpler and more accurate method is to release and remove the cutter assembly complete, then insert a single spacer before replacing and relocking.

GROOVED SIDES

When finger jointing grooved sides, position two cutters in the first set-up one above and the other below the groove, and finger joint as before. For the second set-up use an extra spacer as before and replace the finger now opposite the groove by a cutter smaller in cutting radius by the groove depth. By doing this the groove is filled-in by the finger joint.

Preventing spelching

In finger-jointing as a pack the feed is steadier and the pieces each support one another, so spelching only occurs at the back of the trailing piece. To stop it altogether, sandwich a piece of hardwood between the pack and the clamp as a back-up. Take care that this seats properly, then screw it to the clamp to keep it in the position needed.

Sharpening cutters

As with all cutters, finger joint cutters should be kept sharp. Normally they are a specially-made set to correspond exactly in cutting width both with one another and with the spacers supplied with them. Sharpening is only carried out on their outer faces, and care should be taken to keep them all precisely the same diameter. Don't sharpen them on the face or edge as this reduces their thickness. Use a universal type of grinder. Position the front face firmly against a fixed pin, and clamp in place. The pin positions the cutter to form the correct clearance angle, so adjust it accordingly. Grind all at the same setting using a CBN wheel for accuracy.

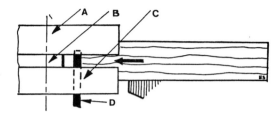

Fig. 353 First cut on square-cut tenons:
A - top tenon head.
B - spacer made-up to tenon thickness required.
C - bottom tenon head.
D - end-stop.

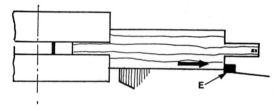

Fig. 354 Second-cut on square-cut tenons. Butt the first shoulder against the spring-loaded shoulder stop E.

Plate 81 Robinson finger-jointing attachment for their spindle moulder.

Tenoning

The attachment for this is similar to the finger-joint attachment, but with a wider table and a back fence, top clamp, an end-stop for the first cut and a spring-loaded shoulder-stop for the second. The cutterhead is a large diameter type, usually about 300mm (12 in) diameter, in two halves which are separated by spacers fitted according to the tenon thickness needed.

Each cutterblock carries two cutters. These form the shoulders with their cutting edges, and the tenon proper with the inside corners. Only a relatively short tenon can be produced - limited by the cutterblock and spacer diameters.

Fit the cutterblocks with the cutters staggered, and with spacers between the two halves. Spacers are provided in 2, 3 4, 5mm (1/16, 1/ 8, 1/4in) thicknesses, etc., so any tenon thickness can be made up using the right combination. Set the spindle speed to 3,000 revs/min for 300mm (12in) diameter heads and 4,200 revs/min., for 230mm (9in) diameter heads, then fit the cover guard. Position the slideway so that the cutters clear the edge of the attachment tenon table, then adjust the spindle arbor vertically to give the proper underface-to-tenon distance.

Place the piece for tenoning on the table and back against the rear fence, then clamp in position. Tenon a scrap piece to check alignment on assembly. To use the attachment, butt the workpiece against the end-stop to gauge the length of the first tenon. The endstop usually fits on a bar projecting from the slideway base, and first needs off-setting from the cutting line to the required tenon length. It is practical to measure this from the shoulder of the backing piece. Tenon the end by slowly feeding the piece clear past the heads, then draw back well clear of the cutters and release.

Keeping the same face down, turn end for end and set the shoulder against the spring-loaded shoulder-stop for tenoning the opposite end. The shoulder-stop is pre-set from the cutting line, again measuring from the shoulder on the backing piece.

STEPPED TENONS

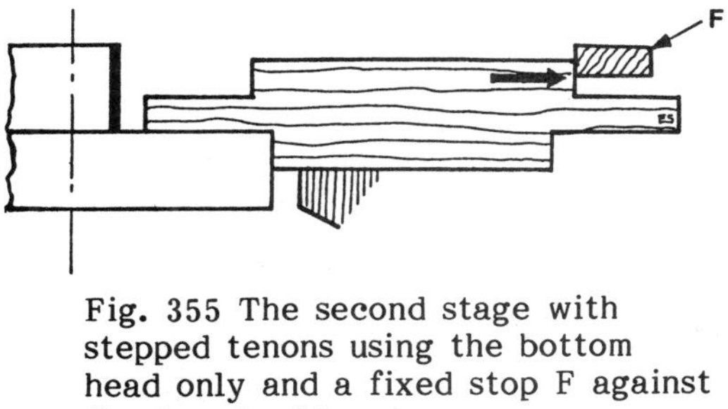

The regular cutterblocks are fitted with square-end cutters to produce square tenons which are also square across. It isn't safe to project cutters more for the stepped tenon needed to match a rebate. For these, first cut tenons square to the longest shoulder length, with the shoulders to be shortened face-down. Remove the top tenon head, then fill-up with spacers and re-lock. Do not alter the height of the spindle arbor. Fit an end-block against the back fence to butt against the top shoulder when the bottom shoulder projects beyond the cutting line by the step needed. Re-tenon all the pieces same-face down locating the top shoulder against the end-block.

Plate 82 Dominion tenoning attachment fitted on their spindle moulder.

Fig. 355 The second stage with stepped tenons using the bottom head only and a fixed stop F against the top shoulder.

187

An easy way to set the end-block is to first secure it against the top shoulder of the last piece whilst this remains in position for the initial tenon. Re-clamp the workpiece nearer the cutterhead so that a spacer equal to the rebate depth is sandwiched between shoulder and block (or measure this distance), then simply re-set the end-block against the top shoulder.

SCRIBED TENONS

When the tenon has to fit a mortised part which is moulded it needs reverse-moulding (scribing) to suit. The regular tenon cutters can be replaced by others shaped to the scribe profile, but because very precise setting is needed it isn't worth the trouble for only a few pieces. An alternative is to first tenon pieces with square shoulders, then add the scribe at a following setting. Use either a router cutter fitted in the stub arbor or Whitehill cutters ground to suit in a flush-topped block. In both cases the tenon attachment needs re-setting nearer the spindle arbor so that the tenon projects over the top. Gauge the workpiece position for both ends from the same shoulder-stop, preferably against the top shoulder.

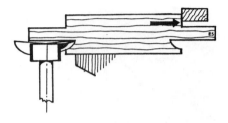

Fig. 356 Adding a scribe to square-cut shoulders using a flush-top Whitehill head or a router cutter.

FINGER JOINTING SASHES

The attachment is also suitable for finger jointing small window frames and similar using two-wing cutters of different thickness, together with matching spacers. Often these are provided in matching sets so they form scribed profiles to suit standard window sections. The most convenient method is to change one complete set for another when setting for the opposite hand. In this way no vertical spindle adjustment is needed, yet face-alignment is ensured. In some cases one or more cutters may be used in both set-ups. Grind cutters only on their outside faces as a complete set, grinding the same off each to retain correct alignment.

NOTE: The tenon attachment can be used for finger jointing thin boards, but only when clamping a single piece at a time. If a pack needs finger-jointing add a horizontal G-clamp to hold them solidly together to prevent individual pieces being pulled violently out. To do otherwise is dangerous. In preferrance, of course, use a finger-jointing attachment which has the proper front-to-back clamping action.

Plate 84 Oppold tenoning cutterheads fitted with disposable cutters and scribers.

Using a backing piece

A small fence only is provided on these attachments, but there is less spelching if a wooden backing piece is also fitted. Make this from hardwood to project beyond the table edge, and always set the slideway so that the cutters just clip this to give a clean leading edge. Feed past the rotating cutters once the machine is set, then use the shoulders formed on the backing fence to accurately set both tenon and shoulder length. If only a few pieces of different length are to be tenoned, mark these individually. There is no need to set the

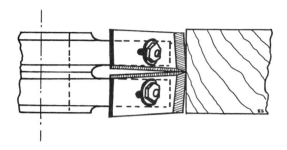

Fig. 357 Showing clearance angles on the cutters when set together and against a square-ended piece.

Plate 83 Using the tenoning table on a Wadkin Bursgreen BEL/T spindle moulder.

tenon and shoulder gauges; instead simply set the marked lines against the backing fence shoulders.

Cutter sharpening

Grind cutters slightly out-of-square so that the tenon shoulder fractionally leads the root, and so that the inside edge of the cutter only contacts at the leading corner to taper-away beyond. Set cutters to a precise tenon equal in thickness to spacers fitted between the cutterheads.

To sharpen cutters, place the heads one on the other with cutter faces in line and with a 2mm (1/16in) spacer so the inside corners do not foul. Sharpen, using a hone across both cutters as though they were a single cutter. This keeps them both precisely to the same cutting circle and prevents the hone dubbing-over the root corner.

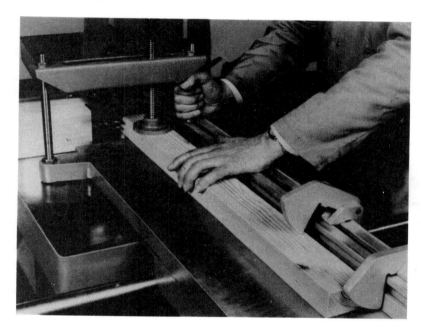

Index